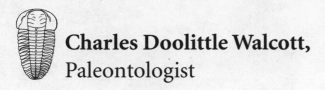

Charles Doolittle Walcott,
Paleontologist

Charles Doolittle Walcott, 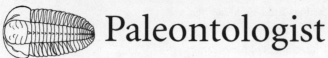 Paleontologist

Ellis L. Yochelson

The Kent State University Press

Kent, Ohio, and London, England

© 1998 by The Kent State University Press, Kent, Ohio 44242

All rights reserved

Library of Congress Catalog Card Number 97-36490

ISBN 0-87338-599-3

Manufactured in the United States of America

05 04 03 02 01 00 99 98   5 4 3 2 1

Library of Congress Cataloging-in-Publication Data

Yochelson, Ellis Leon, 1928–

    Charles Doolittle Walcott, paleontologist / Ellis L. Yochelson.

      p. cm.

    Includes bibilographical references and index.

    ISBN 0-87338-599-3 (alk. paper)

    1. Walcott, Charles D. (Charles Doolittle), 1850–1927.

    2. Paleontologists—United States—Biography.   I. Title.

    QE707.W35Y63 1998

    560'.92

    [B]—DC21   97-36490

                                                  CIP

British Library Cataloging-in-Publication data are available.

Designed and composed in Adobe Minion by Hillside Studio, Inc.

Printed on Turin Book natural stock (an acid-free, totally chlorine-free paper)

and bound by Thomson-Shore, Inc.

To my wife, Sally—

consummate cook, conscientious critic, caring companion. (Many years ago, the late J. B. Knight stated that the only intelligent thing I had ever done was to marry Sally.)

Contents

Contents

Preface and Acknowledgments

Despite the raging storm, the tall, new bridegroom struggled, with the fishermen crew by his side, to reach the elusive island, but alas in vain." It is possible to write in such a fashion and, rarely, there are even occasions for which this particular literary style is appropriate. An account of the life of Charles Doolittle Walcott is not one of them. Walcott wrote plainly and to the point, eschewed superlatives, and never used words such as *eschew.*

The opening sentence could be used to describe an 1888 incident in his career. Walcott would not have cared much for that, either, for in his view one should start at the beginning of a subject and proceed in logical order. If he were reading it, he would want to know who the man was and what brought him to that particular place.

By current standards, Walcott's story is peaceful, containing neither sex nor violence. Many of his written comments appear anachronistic in this cynical age, yet when he indulged in sentimentality, he meant it. Walcott was not a boy wonder but a late bloomer. Though he was not born poor, the first third of his life resembles a Horatio Alger story, not that anyone reads that author anymore. When Walcott became an important government official, he undertook additional administrative initiatives simply because there were things to be done that he was sure would benefit the country. Though scandal might spark greater reader interest, there was none accompanying his efforts. Walcott is almost too good to be true, but true he was. He may be viewed as the quintessential workaholic, both in administration and with his beloved fossils.

Walcott kept a diary and each day jotted a few lines; to do so requires discipline. The diary was important; it allowed him to keep thoughts in order as to what was significant that day and document his time so as to later compose monthly and annual reports. Some of his endeavors, not otherwise recognized in his many publications and official accounts, are mentioned in the diary; on the other hand, some of his actions and honors are missing. The diary was a private document, and its entries provide insight on his feelings as well as chronicle events. His punctuation and random capitalization improved a little through life, though his handwriting got a little worse; I resisted the impulse to add commas or periods, change & to "and," modify capitalization or otherwise tinker with his writing. Where the spelling is particularly worrisome, a "[*sic*]" is included; rarely, bracketed material is added for clarification.

Dates in parenthesis in the text refer to quoted diary entries. Time was important to Walcott; he frequently recorded when meetings began and ended and when he started or arrived from a trip. There was never enough time to do all he wanted to do, which may account for his preoccupation with hours and minutes. The older Walcott became, the greater his concern with time became.

Publications not directly quoted are cited by author and year; those quoted include the page numbers. Although the reference list suggests every Walcott paper is mentioned, that is not so; a more complete listing, still lacking a few items, was published (Yochelson 1967). Letters and other unpublished sources are numbered in sequence for each chapter. Repositories of that material are noted; consider the excellent biography of Walcott's friend F. C. Cottrell (Cameron 1952), which does not indicate where any material quoted was obtained.

This text more or less follows a chronology. If there is a great literary style or impressive quotes to remember, they are Walcott's words, not mine. Accordingly, an appropriate question for a reader to ask is why bother to read this work rather than just reading Walcott's publications?

Walcott's story as a scientist highlights the importance of fossils in the study of geology and in one aspect marks the high-water mark of American paleontology. His administrative efforts document development of a number of government organizations, and a few private ones. He was a dedicated federal employee and a proper family man, a role model if you will. Even now, I cannot understand how he was able to conduct so much basic research in the midst of so many other activities.

This is also a story of an era in America which has passed and will never return. Walcott went from the days of candles, through whale oil lamps, kerosene lanterns, and gaslight, to incandescent bulbs. He went from walking to work, to wagons and buggies, to steam autos, and finally, to internal combustion engines. His travels were in the heyday of trains and river boats, but he later played a role in making aviation into an industry. Throughout it all, he was a geologist and paleontologist performing fieldwork and writing descriptions in virtually the same way they are still done today.

Geologists tend to view paleontologists as a necessary evil, seldom as co-equals. I consider myself both paleontologist and geologist and hope therefore

I understand what Walcott was doing and why he was doing it. My particular interest is in long dead snails rather than in trilobites, but that is "close enough for government work." Because I was employed by the U.S. Geological Survey, with offices in the Smithsonian Institution, United States National Museum, I have some understanding of the two organizations most closely associated with Walcott's career.

Originally, Walcott was a poorly known figure to me, pictured in a textbook as a bald-headed man who had described some fossils. There are biographies of Clarence King, first director of the Geological Survey, and of John Wesley Powell, the second director. Nine decades after their deaths these men continue to provoke interest. There has not been a biography of the third director, who made the policies of both King and Powell really work. Not until Gould's (1989) *Wonderful Life* was Walcott exposed to "the intelligent layman," and that author's portrayal of him was neither complete nor, in my estimate, accurate.

I can date my interest in Walcott precisely. In 1959, my mentor, the late J. Brooks Knight, gave me five hundred dollars, an enormous sum for a government employee at GS-9 grade married with three small children, to attend the International Zoological Congress in London. It was my first time overseas and in the major leagues. To my amazement, Sir C. J. Stubblefield, director of the Geological Survey of Great Britain, invited me, Mr. Nobody, to his office for a glass of sherry. Alcohol on government property was another eye-opener for a beginning federal scientist.

Dr. Stubblefield showed me a picture of a fossil in a Walcott paper and asked my opinion of a particular morphologic feature. I knew Walcott's one-line explanation was wrong and voiced my view, even though I had not seen the specimen. Upon my return to Washington, I examined the fossil and wrote a paper. As often happens, my interpretation of it was also wrong.

Meanwhile, I became interested in a man who could make such a strange remark and illustrate a specimen from British Columbia in a publication on fossils from China. I spoke to the very few people around the National Museum who had joined the staff before Walcott's death in 1927. Among them was Alexander Wetmore, long retired as sixth secretary of the Smithsonian Institution, but then still very active in the Division of Birds.

To my surprise, six months after we spoke, Dr. Wetmore asked me to write Walcott's biographical memoir for the National Academy of Sciences. Shortly after Walcott's death in 1927, this memoir had been assigned to David White, who suffered a stroke. Then, four other academicians gathered comments about Walcott, but no one put them together; writing by committee seldom works.

Next, the Second World War came along and the memoir was pushed aside. Dr. Wetmore was home secretary of the academy from 1951–55 but could not find anyone to prepare a manuscript. He had been employed by Walcott, and having this memoir written was a matter of honor. By now as a GS-11, I was not entirely a Mr. Nobody, but even though my interpretations of dead snails were sometimes accepted, it was obvious I would never be a member of the National Academy of Sciences. Writing a biographical memoir for that group would be difficult. Three years later, I completed it, depending largely on obituaries and short biographies prepared at the time of Walcott's death. The memoir (Yochelson 1967) was judged adequate and even got a favorable nod in a review. It was clear to me, however, that more should be done to document Walcott's career.

For the next two decades, I did this and that professionally for the Geological Survey. Whenever possible, I searched for letters outside of Washington or spoke to geologists about areas where Walcott had worked. Early in this period, I visited Trenton Falls, New York; a local historian, the late Howard Thomas, gave invaluable advice that if one wants to write, one should sit down and write. Good advice is seldom taken, and for years I talked of writing a Walcott biography.

A year into retirement, it finally occurred to me that I should either write a biography or stop talking about it. After false starts, I finally settled down for five years; for three more years, the manuscript was running me. Completing it was a duty, in the Walcottian sense of duty, to bring his efforts to public attention. In so doing, I have invaded his privacy, but he was a human being, not a cardboard figure, and one has to understand a person to comprehend why they did what they did.

No one does anything alone, especially in sciences and humanities, for there is a foundation provided by the past. It is therefore incumbent upon me to acknowledge institutions which assisted me in this endeavor. Walcott was an extremely organized man in his scientific writing, but his letters are scattered over many miles. Some letters cited may be duplicated in the Smithsonian Archives, but his handwritten letters and personal notes from the field are one of a kind.

I do not know the names of all librarians and archivists who assisted. Some places I visited; others were queried by mail. All responded cordially to my requests. I collected a large number of letters and I had my perspectives broadened. Bless both librarians and archivists, persons of different temperament and outlook, but in common having a spirit of cooperation and enthusiasm for any researcher who crossed their paths.

Alphabetically below are institutions contacted; from some of the sources, unpublished material has been quoted, and these have all kindly granted permission to publish: American Museum of Natural History, New York; American Philosophical Society, Philadelphia; Amherst College, Amherst, Massachusetts; British Museum of Natural History (now Natural History Museum), London; Brown University, Providence, Rhode Island; Canadian Pacific Archives, Toronto; Case-Western Reserve University, Cleveland; Cleveland Museum of Natural History, Cleveland; Columbia University, New York: Cornell University, Ithaca; Field Museum of Natural History, Chicago; Geological Society of America, Boulder, Colorado; Geological Society of London, London; Geological Survey of Japan, Iburski; Hamilton College, Clinton, New York; Herkimer County Historical Society, Herkimer, New York; Huntington Library, Pasadena, California; George Washington University, Washington, D.C.; The Johns Hopkins University, Baltimore; Middlebury College, Middlebury, Connecticut; Munson-Williams-Proctor Institute, Utica, New York; Museum of Comparative Zoology, Cambridge, Massachusetts; McGill University, Montreal; Minnesota Historical Society, Minneapolis; National Archives of Canada, Ottawa; New Brunswick Museum of Natural History, St. John; Narodni Muzeum, Prague; New York Public Library, New York; New York State Library and State Archives, Albany; Ohio Historical Society, Columbus; Ohio State University, Columbus; Paleontologisk Museum, Oslo; Peabody Museum, Salem, Massachusetts; Provincial Archives of Newfoundland and Labrador, St. John's; Princeton University, Princeton; Royal Ontario Museum, Toronto; San Diego Society of Natural History, San Diego; Stanford University, Palo Alto, California; State Historical Society of Wisconsin, Madison; Syracuse University, Syracuse, New York; University of Alabama, Tuscaloosa; University of Adelaide, Adelaide, Australia; University of Birmingham, Birmingham, England; University of Cambridge, Cambridge, England; University of Edinburgh, Edinburgh, Scotland; University of Maryland, College Park; University of Iowa, Iowa City; University of Michigan, Ann Arbor; University of Minnesota, Minneapolis; University of Pennsylvania, Philadelphia; University of Pittsburgh, Pittsburgh; University of Rochester, Rochester; University of Wisconsin, Madison; Utica Public Library, Utica, New York; Vassar College, Poughkeepsie, New York; Wisconsin Historical Society, Madison; Yale University, New Haven.

Anyone with a modicum of geographic knowledge will note that only one place listed above is in Washington, D.C. A general rule in geologic mapping is to start farthest from camp and map toward that spot, so that as the season progresses and one tires, the distance to travel each day is shorter. It is a good rule for this kind of investigation. I made many local visits but concentrated on these during the later stages of writing.

Places consulted near the city of my birth include the National Library of Medicine, Bethesda, Maryland, and the U.S. Geological Survey Library, Reston, Virginia. An adjunct of the latter, unknown to many, is the photographic collection in Denver. Walcott was second or third only to G. K. Gilbert in the total number of pictures he took which are preserved in this library, and some are artistic gems as well as scientifically useful. Personnel in the USGS who were personal friends obtained Walcott's official Civil Service records from the National Archives and Records Service office in St. Louis; I did not ask how.

In Washington, I saw the Daughters of the American Revolution and the Sons. The National Geographic Society and the Washington Academy of Sciences produced nuggets of information. The Cosmos Club unfortunately had discarded old records, but the University Club knew of Walcott and even had his picture on the wall. The Carnegie Institution of Washington Archives are marvelous, though it better to visit after summer heat has left the city. The National Parks and Conservation Association and the National Forestry Association were friendly. The Columbia Historical Society and the Washingtoniana Collection of the Martin Luther King Jr. Library, like all other places, are staffed with helpful people. The National Academy of Sciences allowed me to examine their files with a minimum amount of fuss.

The National Archives and Records Service was just across the street. Even better, the Museum of Natural History Library was a block away, and inside the building. As an indication of how long ago I began and my snail-like pace, I may have been the first person granted permission to use a word processor in the Manuscript Division of the Library of Congress. As a former U.S. government employee, I am biased, but my judgment is that federal archivists and librarians are as skilled and helpful as those in academia, state governments, or private institutions. It is the custom nowadays to war on the Civil Service, yet the civil servants keep the country running, and in the limited part of the government I knew, I never met a federal scientist who was not busy and productive.

The main depository for Walcott's papers is the Archives of the Smithsonian Institution in the old Arts and Industries Building. I was in so often to read Walcott's diaries and Walcott's letters there was joking about providing me an office. To all of the archives staff, the only way I can repay their unremitting assistance is to do the best job of writing that I can. Without meaning to slight others, both living and dead, who aided my search, I am particularly indebted to William Cox and James Steed.

In naming people who have contributed to my understanding there will be sins of omission. If I listed all who advised or assisted, willingly or unknowingly, the list would probably be twenty pages long, even with titles and addresses eliminated. A few of the persons in Canada who helped me understand Walcott and his work: the late Thomas Bolton, Ottawa; Desmond Collins, Toronto; William Fritz, Ottawa; and Randall Miller, St. John. For decades, the late Gunnar Henningsmoen, Oslo; Adrian Rushton, Nottingham; and Harry Whittington, Cambridge answered my questions.

How to craft history has to be learned like any other craft. Methodology, outlook, and tricks of the trade were provided by many willing to guide an aficionado. Some of these people are: Michele Aldrich, Janice Goldblum, Pamala Henson, Alan Leviton, Clifford Nelson, Dove Menkes, Steven Pyne, Mary Rabbitt, Nathan Reingold, and Marc Rothenberg. The casual contact in one library who suggested I use a mirror to read through the back of an otherwise illegible letterbook copy is an example of the kind of debt that I cannot repay.

Many, many geologists and paleontologists in the United States deserve to be mentioned, but again, I must limit the list: Stanley Beus, Sedona, Arizona; William Breed, Flagstaff, Arizona; Frederick Collier, Cambridge, Massachusetts; Dr. G. A. Cooper—a role model for all paleontologists—Raleigh, North Carolina; Barry Doolan, Burlington, Vermont; Robert Dott, Madison, Wisconsin; Donald Fisher, Kinderhook, New York; Charles Hunt, Salt Lake City, Utah; Robert Milici, Reston, Virginia; Clements Nelson, Bishop, California; Allison Palmer, Boulder, Colorado; Keith Rigby, Provo, Utah; Richard Robison, Lawrence, Kansas; Reuben Ross, Wheatridge, Colorado: Thomas Whiteley, Rochester, New York; Don Winston, Missoula, Montana; and Hatten Yoder, Silver Spring, Maryland.

There are others to thank, absent for many years. These include two former secretaries of the Smithsonian, Charles Abbot and Alexander Wetmore, and Alphonzo Jones, Walcott's chauffeur. Ray Bassler, U.S. National Museum; Carl Dunbar, Yale University; Benjamin Howell, Princeton University; Waldo Schmitt, U.S. National Museum; Howard Thomas, Trenton Falls; and John

Wells, Cornell University all helped illuminate the man and his research. Preston Cloud gave me a position with the Geological Survey in 1952 which allowed me to pursue official duties and to grow as a paleontologist, but which also laid the basis for my hobby.

I never met Walcott's daughter, Helen Walcott Younger, but she kindly answered a letter shortly before her death. Her husband, the late Cole Younger, found twenty years of missing diaries and donated them to the Smithsonian Archives. Erin Younger, of Seattle, granddaughter of Helen, has been a recent correspondent. I had the opportunity to meet Sidney Walcott, his second son. For years Mr. Walcott sent me photographs, family papers, and letters crammed with information; this material, intermixed with my own, is in the Smithsonian Archives.

Sooner or later inspiration begins to flag. Fortunately, the American Philosophical Society had the faith in me to provide a travel grant in 1993. James D. Aitken, Geological Survey of Canada, retired, expanded my horizons in Alberta and British Columbia, and provided insight into pack horses, camp cooking, and a host of other practical matters, along with a running lecture on geology. This rejuvenation provided final incentive to complete the manuscript.

A manuscript is not a book. I knew too much about Walcott and wanted the world to know it all. Fortunately, John T. Hubbell, at the Kent State University Press, saw nuggets of merit amidst loads of verbiage. At a late stage, three good friends, who also are perceptive critics saved me from myself—a trite expression, but there is no better. Tom Dutro, Al Leviton, and especially Michele Aldrich (with Mark) helped provide a better biography.

To summarize, Walcott was an important unknown figure, surely an oxymoron, but to pursue the comment would involve more convolutions then are in Umberto Eco's *Foucault's Pendulum*. Charles Doolittle Walcott was good man; I hope I have provided the good account that he deserves.

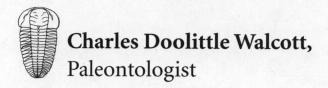

Charles Doolittle Walcott,
Paleontologist

1

The Beginning: Ancestors and Motivations in Mid-Nineteenth-Century New York (1850–1871)

> History happens after you die. It's the life lived by the dead.
>
> —Richard Cohen, 1993

THIS STORY could begin in 1850 at New York Mills, New York, the last Sunday in March, time of day no longer known. However, no one is born as a clean slate, for heredity and environment affect both newborn and growing child. One American stereotype is the WASP—white, Anglo-Saxon Protestant—noted in literature ranging from one-line bad jokes to learned treatises. New England is the natural WASP habitat, but this Empire State descendant qualified for the appellation in temperament and physical appearance. Logic dictates that Walcott's story mention the westward migration of his ancestors.

Although "Walcott" is not "Smith" or "Wright," the name is an ancient English one, combining *weald* and *cot,* a cottage in a wooded country; it may have come from *wald,* for "wood." In southern England, a dozen places are named Walcott in one form of spelling or another. Earliest family records in the New World are not clear, but about 1636 William Walcott of Devonshire came to Salem Village, Massachusetts Bay Colony, and married Alice Ingersoll (A. S. Walcott 1925). He did not fit the Puritan mold, with results that included one public whipping; authorities forced him to leave in 1647. Jonathan Walcott, probably born in 1639, was among the children left as the first generation in North America. He served in King Phillip's War against the French and Indians; a decade later, Salem Village formed its own militia troop, led by Captain Jonathan Walcott.

The captain had two wives in sequence and seven children by each. Salem Village was the site of public accusation run mad in the witch trials and executions.

Charles Doolittle Walcott, Paleontologist

A daughter of Jonathan's was an accuser, as was Ann Putnam, Jonathan's niece, who repented her part in the terrible affair. "Mary Walcott, 16 at the time, was one of the group of teen-age girls who would scream and cry and even go into convulsions claiming they were being attacked by invisible witches."[1] This hysteria may be the only public scandal that ever touched the Walcott family. However, William, born in 1691 or 1692, had a different mother than Mary; he was the fourth of seven children born by the captain's second wife.

William moved to Attleboro, Massachusetts, and thence to Cumberland, Rhode Island, to become a prosperous farmer, "trusted and respected" by neighbors. The eighth of his nine children, Benjamin, was born in 1729. Like his father, he was a good, solid farmer, of no remarkable distinction, though he may have started a foundry during the Revolutionary War. Benjamin begot ten children, the oldest Benjamin Stuart, born in 1755.

Stuart served in the Revolutionary War, of course for the Continental army. After being mustered out, he invented a nail-making machine and subsequently became involved in a fulling mill, wherein cloth is cleaned and thickened; Fuller's earth is a special clay used in fulling cloth. This activity gave rise to a cotton yarn mill in Rhode Island. Benjamin Stuart became wealthy, though late in his life business went sour. Before that, in 1785, he sired his first born, another Benjamin Stuart.

This Benjamin Stuart left New England and moved to Oneida County, New York. Utica, on the site of old Fort Schuyler in the Mohawk Valley, was growing rapidly, for the Revolutionary War brought the demise of Mohawk Indians, who had dominated the region; new settlers moved to the valley in droves. Benjamin Stuart and his father owned what was possibly the first yarn and knitting mill in New York (Wager 1896, 628–32). Cheap water power and cheap labor were available, and within a few years the Erie Canal provided excellent transportation to Albany. Benjamin was plant superintendent and very good at the business, for after some years he owned a whole series of mills at New York Mills, New York, just to the west of Utica. His first wife, Irene Doolittle, bore seven children before she died; Grandmother Judith, his second wife, had another five.

Of the seven, the second was William Dexter, the fourth was Charles Doolittle, and the seventh, another Benjamin, who moved to New York City rather than going into the family business. The daughters provided many cousins, but mostly they moved away with their husbands and do not enter the mainstream of the story. Other family members did well; Walcott, Iowa, is named after

Benjamin's brother William, who helped organize the Chicago and Rock Island Railway. Charles Doolittle Walcott, the subject of this account, had cousins scattered over the countryside; he was cordial to all but close with few.

Charles Doolittle Walcott, the father, born September 14, 1818, spent his maturity as a partner with his father and five-year-older brother, William; Charles was in charge of the upper mill. In 1840, he married Mary Lane of New York City and sired five children; she survived him by many years, dying in Utica in 1897. The oldest child, Mary Josephine, was born in 1842. She lived with her mother and, as became a spinster lady, devoted herself to charity and other good works; after her mother died, Josie moved to Washington to be near her youngest brother, dying in that city in 1908. Ellis Pitcher was born two years after Josie; following the Civil War, New York was too cramped and he moved to Minnesota, dying in Wisconsin some time during the First World War. William Lane was born in 1846; he also left New York after the war and died out of state before he was twenty-seven. Another infant died at birth in 1848.

Charles Doolittle Walcott, the son, was born March 31, 1850; apparently he was a sickly child and received considerable attention from his mother and sister Josie. Less than two and a half years after his birth, Walcott's namesake father died, on September 15, 1852. Even by the standards of that day, his life was short. He had gone to Florida to help cure his illness, probably tuberculosis. "It is supposed that two thousand persons attended the funeral of the lamented Mr. Walcott. Hundreds followed his remains to the grave" (Kirk 1852, 32).

Size of the funeral, erection of a family tomb, and printing of the sermon indicate just how prominent the Walcott family was in the community. Grandfather Benjamin was so wealthy that he retired in 1856 to travel in Europe and the Holy Land, the mills then being run by Uncle William. Benjamin contributed liberally to local charities and the Presbyterian Church, willing money for a new building; one can attend the Walcott Presbyterian Church in New York Mills. He endowed a professorship of Christian morals at Hamilton College, at that time a Congregational Presbyterian institution. The college is in Clinton, New York, a few miles south of Utica, far enough from any city that theology students would not be led into temptation. Uncle William, until his death in 1890, followed in his father's footsteps as a contributor to the church. He was also a trustee of Hamilton College and gave a further endowment.

If one draws anything from this account, it is that nowhere was there any indication of academic or scientific pursuits, even among more distant relatives.

Charles Doolittle Walcott, Paleontologist

Granted that rich families have opportunity for more cultural pursuits than poor ones, the Walcotts were of the business community, not the intelligentsia. On the maternal side, in Utica, Doolittle relatives were nearly as prominent in business. In 1866, President Johnson and General Grant visited grandfather Charles Doolittle.

Nothing is known of the early years of little Charles, but one may guess that widow Walcott and her young brood could have moved in with grandparents. Such an arrangement could be expected of Grandfather Benjamin, a pillar of the community, who had room in his Grecian revival mansion. Before Charles was eight, city directories show that the family lived in Utica, at 50 Fayette Street. It was a short distance move, and New York Mills is now a suburb of Utica.

The reason for this move given in obituaries is that Charles could attend a good school, but there might have been more to the matter. Sister Josie may not have been thought to need proper education, but the two older brothers could have profited from more cultured Utica. When Grandfather Benjamin retired and Uncle William became head of the extended family, there may have been house shuffling and no more room for widow Walcott. She had money from her husband's estate, but was definitely a poor relation. Charles apparently adored his grandfather; there is good evidence he had difficulties with Uncle William.

Under occupation, the Utica city directory lists Mary Lane Walcott as "widow." A wealth of symbolism is wrapped up in that word, as used in pre–Civil War society. Except for the fact that the family was never in want, she would have been classed as part of the genteel poor, not expected, or permitted, to do anything except exist. Widow Walcott had a growing daughter, two teenage sons, and a small child to contend with when she left New York Mills. Three moves in the first three years suggest she had difficulty adjusting to Utica. Later, she boarded at a hotel and moved several more times. When the boys left, she gave up any pretense of homemaking and lived with Josie in a hotel.

Walcott began schooling in Utica at eight and ended it at eighteen. "He was sent first to a select school at the corner of Genesee and Hopper streets kept by Miss Webb, but he disagreed with the teacher and left it three times. After that he went to the public school in Blandina Street, where he remained three years. Later he attended the Advanced School and Academy, but did not graduate."[2] The first academy building burned in 1865, and when it reopened in 1867 on Academy Street, the school had a principal and three assistants. The school year of three terms was forty weeks long. Instruction was probably adequate, rather than outstanding. Nothing is known of Walcott's grades.

When school was out, the boys of Utica lived a sort of outdoors existence. Charlie had two older brothers to tag after when they roamed. Woods and swamps were near the city, and while the Mohawk River was not the Mississippi, it was still fairly impressive for a lad. One could hunt relics of Indians driven from the Mohawk Valley not too many years earlier. If all else failed, looking at barge traffic on the Erie Canal, north of town, brought with it the notion of travel.

The great American geologist James Dwight Dana grew up in Utica before joining Yale University and was already famous from his work on the United States Exploring Expedition (1838–1842) of Lt. Charles Wilkes. Utica had a natural history tradition, and being curious about nature was a respectable pursuit for young minds. The twelve-year-old Utica boy, G. H. Williams, who later founded the geology department at Johns Hopkins University, wrote: "I am getting together a cabinet now in which I have got the minerals Uncle George had in his cabinet, a slab from Ninevah Uncle Fred sent etc. Last Saturday Willie Abbott and I went up to Sulphur Springs to dig for trilobites. I got some heads and an Athosorus we took two hammers and a small crowbar" (in T. Williams 1896, 30–31).

Walcott's interest in the natural world came early: "As a boy he took considerable interest in the study of natural history, and with David S. Foster he made a collection of birds eggs which was later destroyed. The next year he tried collecting butterflies"[3]; had butterflies or eggs been as sturdy as stones, Walcott might have ended up as a zoologist. "At 7 years of age he was already a collector of natural objects that attract the attention of the country boy, and at 13 the curiosity aroused by some fossils he found started him on the way to the study of local geology" (Smith 1927, 1).

Another obituary mentions his meeting Colonel E. Jewett, a geologist and the third curator of the New York State Cabinet, an early term for a museum. Hammer handles protruding from a basket caught the boy's eye, and from there it was an easy step for Jewett to show him fossils. In later years, Jewett lived in Utica, and Walcott often called on him.

A family story is that Walcott begged for a trilobite for his birthday and one brother bought a specimen. He received permission to clean it by soaking overnight in water, but in the morning had only a jumble of pieces which a local collector had glued together. An annual report of the United States National Museum mentions receipt of a fossil collection from the Hurlburt family. "The elder Mr. Hurlburt was a distant relative of Dr. Charles D. Walcott and encouraged his start in paleontological field work many years ago" (Bassler 1936, 48). Ed Hurlburt was a boyhood friend, but not a relative, and they were classmates at the Utica Academy.

To Charles, the Civil War must have been a terrible jolt in an otherwise tranquil life. Uncle William was too old to fight, but various cousins went off to war and one did not return. Grandfather Benjamin donated the cost of a river steamer to the Union; he died in January 1862, before serious battles began. Brother Ellis left Norwich University in 1862, just after his eighteenth birthday, and enlisted in the cavalry for four months. In 1864, he reenlisted in the artillery for a year.

The growing Charlie Walcott expanded his horizons. "During the war, a redhaired boy from Utica came to work on Rust's farm for the summer" (Thomas 1951, 127). A third-hand report from an old resident puts Walcott on the Rust farm, near Trenton Falls, at age eleven. It makes sense that the boy could help a farmer, with so many young men away fighting for the Union. It makes equally good sense that widow Walcott would take some of her brood out of Utica when local politics engendered by the Civil War boiled over; it might also have been a good idea to take young Charles away while Grandfather Benjamin was ailing.

To give the overall setting, the ancient hard rocks of the Adirondack Mountains form the principal feature of the northeastern corner of New York State, rising above the average elevation of the state. South of the massif is the Mohawk Valley, the Mohawk River running from Oneida Lake eastward to Albany. The Erie Canal parallels the Mohawk River for part of its route.

All of New York was glaciated, with resultant disruption of drainage and development of a large number of swamps along the valley floor. This aided canal diggers, for dirt is easier to move than rock, but the swamps formed outstanding homes for mosquitoes. In summer, the Mohawk Valley is hot, humid, and unpleasant.

Once spring rains are over, it is easy to go north across the Mohawk River and up the long steep slope of Deerfield Hill, on the southwestern flank of the Adirondacks. Trenton Falls, on West Canada Creek, is only fourteen miles from Utica. With the opening of the first segment of the Black River & Utica Railroad in 1855, travel to that hamlet was easy.

It is difficult to imagine that for half a century this was a stop on the Grand Tour—Saratoga Springs, Trenton Falls, Niagara Falls—having one of the nation's finest resorts. Thousands of tourists came to Trenton Falls from all over the country and Europe. In 1863, Secretary of War Stanton met diplomats of seven foreign countries at Trenton Falls and persuaded them not to recognize the rebellion in the South. The falls were minuscule compared to Niagara Falls, but engendered a fair amount of prose, poetry, and art (Schweizer 1989).

Geology in this part of New York is fairly straightforward. At the western edge of the Adirondacks and proceeding straight south, strata are nearly flat lying, the country rising to the Pennsylvania border in series of wide, low escarpments, which are progressively younger. "Oneida County affords an excellent field for the study of the Paleozoic series of rocks" (Brigham 1888, 17). It is the best place in the state to see more kinds of sedimentary rocks in the shortest distance. Along the Mohawk River and for a considerable distance to the south in the broad valley, the rocks are mostly soft shales and layering is not obvious. Close to the Adirondacks, the rocks are no longer nearly flat lying, but are inclined a few degrees toward the south.

Because of superposition, the rocks north of Deerfield Hill are older than those in the river valley. Further, they are all limestone, a harder rock than the shales of the valley. Because of glaciation few natural outcrops occur, with one notable exception. West Canada Creek, rising in the Adirondacks, cuts through the limestone layers as it travels southwest to join the Mohawk River at Herkimer, New York, fifteen miles east of Utica. West Canada Creek flows vigorously and must have carried a phenomenal amount of water when the glaciers melted. It is an ideal place to see layer piled upon layer. As a consequence of small vertical breaks, blocks of rock have moved differentially, thereby in part causing the series of falls along the stream. The scenery in the gorge is spectacular and is deserving of at least some of the elaborate nineteenth-century touristic prose.

Limestones are a characteristic deposit of warm, shallow seas, areas where marine organisms are abundant today. Living conditions were similar in the past, and the lime-depositing seas of this area swarmed with organisms. Although the physical environment was comparable, the biological material of the past was strikingly different. The organic remains in the ancient limestone strata along West Canada Creek do not resemble shells a modern-day beachcomber can collect. The fossils of the Trenton Limestone, as it is called, are somewhat different than those of the Utica Shale, partly because that interval of rock is slightly older, but mainly because the environment of deposition of a limestone is not the same as that of a shale.

By the time of the Civil War, Trenton Falls had been settled for about half a century. A veteran of the Revolutionary War, Abel Rust moved in 1818 from Kent, Connecticut, to Russia Township, on the eastern side of West Canada Creek

Charles Doolittle Walcott, Paleontologist

(Rust 1891). Early real estate developers, like their descendants, glamorized by giving exotic names to townships, areas of six square miles; Norway and Poland are near Russia. In many respects, the city of Canton, New York, on the north side of the Adirondacks, is as distant from Canton, China, as is possible, but it is an example of this use of the exotic in advertising.

Almost overnight settlers determined that dairying, not plowing, was the only way to farm in limestone country. Every gourmet is familiar with Herkimer County sharp cheese. West Canada Creek forms the boundary between Oneida and Herkimer Counties. If one is given to sociological approaches, the creek separated the tourist milieu in the Trenton Falls resorts from the life of the farmers. The Rust farm was in "Russia across the creek," but the creek was not a hard line like the wrong side of the railroad tracks in a city, for some farm families took in summer boarders to supplement their income.

Though limestone was impossible to plow, it formed a key part of the local economy as a natural building material. Every farmer had a small quarry for house and barn foundations, and occasionally for selling stone. At one time at least eight active quarries were on the eastern side of the creek. Abel Rust is remembered as the first in the area to build a lime kiln to manufacture quicklime for mortar.

Dairying is a more predictable way of farming than, say, raising vegetables, and allowed occasional moments to pursue other work. Quarrying of stone in those days was hand work and could be stopped at any point to go milk the herd. The locals moved from barnyard to stoneyard, with visits to the woodyard for firewood and logs. Within the great thickness of limestone exposed were subtle differences in the ability of various layers to break where desired. Successful farmers were able to distinguish good quarry stone from bad, but good or bad, the fossils almost fell out of the rocks. They were a phenomenon of nature that could not be ignored by men swinging sledge hammers.

Rock formation names are derived from geographic localities. The Trenton Limestone in now considered by geologists as a major division, a group, and has been subdivided into a number of formations and these into members (Kay 1943). The Coburg Formation includes two divisions, the lower being the Rust Member. It is named after Rust farm, not Abel Rust, but keeps the name of the old quarryman-farmer from being lost.

Although work was hard, some of the farmers were thrifty and lived a fairly good life. Winters were long and quite cold, giving time to read and to speculate on the differences in the rocks layers and the fossils. Everyone had a few fossil and mineral specimens in the parlor as conversation pieces. The New York farmer wanted to know about nature because of his close association with the environment and his need to understand it. Partly to satisfy this desire, in 1836, the state started a natural history survey which continues to this day.

As early as the first quarter of the nineteenth century, the fossils of Trenton Falls were well known. Descriptions of them and the excitement of fossil collecting were used as an added inducement to attract tourists. Truly, it is exciting to break open a rock and find a shell inside. Even more exciting is to find a trilobite. To the untrained eye, many fossils resemble modern sea shells, but trilobites have real character. They consist of a head, a central part of numerous segments, and a tail. The only living thing which approaches them in general shape is a sowbug or a lobster. Trilobites look like creatures from a long distant past.

Even today many people collect fossils, and during the nineteenth century such collecting had elements of a craze. In 1849, a New Yorker wrote: "The little lingula [shell] of the Potsdam would interest me more, could I but have one, than the splendid I. gigas [trilobite]—though polished by the hand of old Rust to boot!"[4] One has to know a lot about paleontology to get the full flavor of the joke, but there is no question that Trenton fossils were long known and envied by collectors throughout the state.

Abel Rust died in 1842 at the age of ninety-three. The "old Rust" reference could have been to him, or to his son Hiram, born in 1794. Like Walcott's father, Hiram was a seventh-generation immigrant. He is listed in the family genealogy as "farmer and geologist"; people had their priorities right in those days.

Hiram married Mary Taylor of Russia in 1820, and they had eight children. These are mentioned to set the scene in the Rust household. The oldest, a daughter, died when she was twenty-six. Cecelia, born in 1823, was the family old maid. The third child, a boy died at age fifteen. William Palmer Rust, born October 2, 1826, was the family mainstay and remained a bachelor. Brother Abel was killed at the battle of Petersburg; another brother died at eleven. Cynthia, born in 1837, married but returned to the family house when her husband joined the 117th Regiment of New York State Volunteers; he was killed at Richmond, Virginia, in 1864. Lura Ann Rust was born April 6, 1843. To round out the family, the children of the widow Cynthia were Clarence, born in 1857, and young Jessie, the last girl, who arrived in 1861.

Charles Doolittle Walcott, Paleontologist

Like his father, Hiram, William Rust is listed in the family genealogy as farmer and geologist. Father and son sold fossils to Michael Moore, proprietor of the most famous resort at Trenton Falls. William was known as the greatest local collector and had the finest cabinet of trilobites in the state.

William's farm was 172 acres, which meant there were always chores to be done, and even a young lad could do something useful. Family life in the Rust house seemed warm to the boarders. William was twenty-four years older than young Walcott, just about the age of the father he did not have; the word "surrogate" comes immediately to mind.

Walcott came into the limestones of Trenton Falls and fell in love with the fossils. He soaked up all that William could show and tell him about these forms and quickly learned which fossils characterized which layers. Later he recounted:

> In a small drift block of sandstone which I found in 1867 on the road between Trenton and Trenton Falls, Oneida County, New York, there is an unusual apparent association of Upper Cambrian (Hoyt limestone) and Ordovician (Aylmer sandstone, Chazy) fossils. . . . When as a boy I found the rounded block of sandstone referred to I broke out all the fossils possible, as at the time I was well acquainted with the Trenton limestone fauna, and the fossils in the block were all strangers to me, . . . The following winter I endeavored to locate the stratigraphic position of the trilobites, but could not, further than they were of pre-Trenton age. (Walcott 1916, 254)

This was an extremely sophisticated observation for a beginner.

Teenage Walcott ended schooling in 1868. The next logical step would have been college, but that never occurred. This is a lapse hard to explain, for the family could afford the cost, even if it meant borrowing from Uncle William; brother Ellis had begun advanced studies before the Civil War. As with all professions, geologists gossip. Reverend A. Brigham, for many years a distinguished geographer at Colgate University, grew up next door to the William Walcott family. He mentioned to a student, who in turn passed along the story, that the family decided early Charles Walcott should go into the ministry. The Hamilton College chair may have been set up to insure a sinecure for the sickly, fatherless youngster. One can almost picture a Victorian melodrama with Uncle William insisting on the ministry or nothing and Nephew Charles responding with geology or nothing.

There was more attraction to the Rust farm than fossils. If the seventeen-year-old Walcott was driving a wagon for William Rust in 1867, the twenty-four-year-old Lura would have been at hand every day, and, to rush ahead, they married.

She was a grown woman a year younger than his sister, but was not his sister. Ancillary to love was family life during the summers at Trenton Falls, along with the opportunity for a young man to develop his muscles. Compare this to boarding in a Utica hotel, talking day after day to Mother and Sister, and college to study for the ministry.

In March 1868, O. C. Marsh, the first professor of paleontology in America, a position his uncle bought for him in 1866 by establishing a chair at Yale University, saw the Rush collection and then visited Walcott (Schuchert and Le Vene 1940). The day before his eighteenth birthday, Walcott wrote Marsh:

> You said that you would like a specimen from the Utica Slate when you examined my collection. I enclose the Triarthrus Beckii; it is the only Trilobite found here in the slate, there are orthoceras or casts of them filled with sulfate of iron and near two shells; if you wish to exchange minerals for specimens from Trenton and Utica, you will oblige me very much.[5]

The reply is lost, but another letter was written a week later:

> I received yours of 31st and in replying cannot send you specimens as I intended. I have had a severe cold and was unable to go in search of fossils. I expect to start next week and take a trip to Trenton Middlevill[e] little Falls and around the different localities where fossils are found, if I succeed in finding any good specimens, and that are duplicates to my collection I will send them to you. The Triarthrus Beckii that I sent you I found in Deerfield at the mouth of the ravine on Buggs Creek 1½ miles south of Utica, the slate lies in the bed of the creek that the specimens ar[e] dug from, farther up in the ravine, the slate runs into a brittle brown shale in which I found no signs of fossils after digging half a day. there may be some farther up, I will try again to make sure.[6]

Walcott had problems in spelling and punctuation, but he had a grasp of local geology and collecting. Not much more is known about him from ages eighteen to twenty. At least the second of these years he worked in a hardware store. A love-struck, stubborn youth could well quit school at age eighteen before graduation, when he was a "man." He would go to work, determined to support himself and marry the love of his life. That may not be exactly the way it happened, but it is a good story and might be correct. In 1871, Walcott wrote a few figures, each accompanied by a date: 1868–790.00; 1869–765.35; 1870–513.38. If these indicate annual income, they support a view of his leaving school for an opportunity to make a lot of money quickly, followed by a year of employment, and a second incomplete year at a higher wage.

Charles Doolittle Walcott, Paleontologist

Before his twentieth birthday, Walcott began a daily diary. From 1876, until shortly before his death, he wrote a few lines each day, commonly just noting the principal events of the day, but occasionally recording his feelings; the entries help amplify him as a man, rather than as a machine which in later years ground out publication after publication. Walcott's first record is "At the store of J. C. Roberts during the day. Commenced working there April 15th 1869. Ellis at Aunt Fannie, Mother and Josie at the Clarendon. Went to Church & then to the Picture Gallery. Accompany'ed G. W. G. home. Want to be thinking of Friday evening Jan 26, '70" (March 4, 1870).

Perhaps in January Walcott and G. W. G. touched hands or he saw an ankle. As to the picture gallery, bustling Utica now had thirty-five thousand inhabitants. Whether Will and Charles were still living with Mother at the hotel is not clear, but probably at least Charles was. J. E. Roberts & Company, long since vanished, was a large hardware store located at 49 and 51 Genesee Street.

The next day, Walcott recounted he paid the astounding sum of $1.75 for the little diary which would easily slip into his pocket. He prepared a Sunday School lesson and taught for the first time, thoroughly enjoying the experience. Religion always played a role in his life. He was a staunch Presbyterian, though that may be a redundancy, but never had personal relations or scientific investigations influenced by religious beliefs. A listing of goals early in the diary gives insight, even if punctuation and capitalization were still developing:

1. Govern Temper, Tongue & Conduct.
2. Think about, Life, Death & Eternity
3. Wish for Health, friends & a cheerful spirit.
4. Pray for Faith, Peace & Purity of heart.
5. Contend for Honor, Country & friends.
6. Love. Courage & Affection.
7. Admire. Intellectual power, dignity & gracefulness.

Today these still may be values one strives for, but almost no twenty year old keeps a diary, let alone writes such remarks. It was a different time. One of the most difficult tasks for anyone interested in history is to keep from using the present day to interpret the past.

Consider the hardware business. Few places exist today where one opens a wooden nail keg to weigh out six pounds of ten-penny nails. Bridles and horse collars were common and light bulbs nonexistent. Walcott opened the store before 7:00 A.M. and faced at least a twelve-hour day. It was boredom without customers and hard manual labor when they came. There was no beginning or end, and the only tangible result was money. Even on Sundays he had to stop by to ensure that all was well at the store. For this he was receiving $41.80 per month.

"Weather very stormy. No business during the day. Closed store at ¼ of 7. P.M. After dinner called on Hattie L. Came home and wrote L. A. R.[ust] Retired at 11. P.M. All well" (March 16, 1870). "Same old story. W. L. W. came after me help him out of trouble, did so. He promised to leave town & behave himself. Hope he will" (March 19, 1870). There is much human drama in the middle brother asking his younger sibling for help, probably as a loan, and likely not the first one.

A reply from Lura Ann Rust came six days after Walcott wrote her, and he arrived for a two-day visit at the Rust farm. Back in Utica, Walcott "Opened store at 6:30 A.M. Birthday presents from Mother and Josie. Studied geology in evening" (March 31, 1870). Walcott helped organize a baseball team in April when spring finally came. "Weather pleasant. Last day of my first year in business. Have liked it very well. Have had no trouble with my employers & all seems satisfactory" (April 13, 1870).

All was not satisfactory, as three days later Walcott had a severe headache and stomach pains. He was often ill; how much was psychosomatic and how much was real is not important. Electric battery treatments were then in fashion, and Mrs. Shepard doctored Walcott with charges. She did not kill him, and he thought the treatment helped; perhaps the thought was therapeutic. Still, it was a week more before Walcott was strong enough to go out.

Two days later, young Walcott took a major step: "Told Messers J & R & Co that I could not work any longer for them. Decided to go to Trenton Falls & recouperate [sic]" (April 28, 1870). Late on Saturday afternoon, two days after his decision, Walcott was in the Rust farmhouse. Monday he took the first step in his life's work: "Practiced writing an hour in the morning. In afternoon went down to Gray's brook to dig for fossils. Found a fine specimen of Leptaena a" (May 2, 1870). Gray's Brook, unnamed on any current map, forms the eastern edge of a golf course and meanders south behind the Rust house in a steep valley.

"Went trilobiting on the brook. Found a specimen or two" (May 4, 1870). "Tried the brook again found a fine A. gigas" (May 5, 1870). In fishing terms, Walcott was hooked. He did more digging for fossils, both on the brook and at

Charles Doolittle Walcott, Paleontologist

Prospect, New York, two miles north on West Canada Creek. Walcott helped William plant corn and build a fence, and walked in the woods with L. A. R. It was not until the second week in June that Lura is mentioned by name. The urge to collect fossils was strong, but Walcott was young and had other equally strong urges.

He hoed corn, watered the garden, and drew stone for the lime kiln. The idyll was broken in mid-June when Lura became ill. It was so serious that Walcott went to Utica to bring a doctor. He took the doctor home and brought sister Josie to nurse Lura. After a week, she was seemingly on the mend, but this was only the first of many subsequent similar events.

Lura being better, Walcott could go back to picking berries, weeding, and geologizing. He returned from a quick trip to New York Mills, in time for a visit from Prof. S. G. Williams. Prof. Williams was a favorite correspondent, but none of the letters have survived. Williams moved to Cleveland and then back to New York when he joined the faculty of Cornell University. He wrote a book on geology, but made his name as a teacher of pedagogy.

Between planting and harvesting, William Rust had time for an occasional day of fossil hunting, along the brook and in Poland township. Brother Ellis came for a few days and somehow the summer flew by. "Dug on the brook all day. Found several handsome crinoids" (August 16, 1870). Crinoids are rare today but exist in tropical seas and deep water localities. These "sea lilies" consist of a long stem, a cup, and arms extending from the cup edges. They are related to starfish and like them have a fivefold symmetry.

Walcott went to Utica to see his family, but also to call on Colonel Jewett; he may have wanted to tell him of the crinoids or seek more information on the forms. "After dinner Ellis called with Patterson. J.E.R. & Co. do not wish me to work for them. Ellis said goodby as he leaves for St. Paul Wednesday" (August 27, 1870). So the hardware prospects in Utica were closed to him, and his older brother was leaving. Walcott returned, helped cut corn, fixed a gate, made a flower stand for Lura, and went off to Utica again briefly.

After another quick trip to Utica Walcott helped repair fences and corncrib; Sunday he was down at the brook collecting. He sent off a box of fossils to Professor A. H. Worthen, the state geologist of Illinois and another favorite correspondent. There is no trace of Worthen-Walcott correspondence, but a few remarks in the diary suggest that they exchanged specimens several times.

E. William Simpson, born in the area in 1864, recalled that in his boyhood days "'Charlie' Walcott the tall red-headed youth who lived with the Rusts and later rose to prominence as a geologist, was a familiar figure as he strode through the fields with a hammer, cracking rocks in an effort to uncover some rare fossil. And it was Simpson who wandered into Otis Borden's novelty shop to catch the Trenton Falls 'expert' manufacturing trilobites out of plaster of Paris" (Thomas 1951, 166). Like the cows, tourists were a valuable resource to be milked.

Fall comes early to the fringes of the Adirondacks, and tourists leave, taking the stimulation they provided. Fall is also a busy time on any farm. Walcott helped dig potatoes, husk corn, and pick apples. The first Sunday in October was the first time Walcott went to a church that season. Country folk were just as religious as city folk, but they were busier. Cows must be fed and milked every day, including Sunday.

After several days in the Rust stone quarry, he went to Utica for a family wedding. Walcott saw Colonel Jewett and R. P. Whitfield, assistant to James Hall, state paleontologist. He took a couple of field trips in the Utica area to build up his collection. October 27 he was back on the brook breaking rock, the day before the first snow. Then he was building fences and threshing oats. Farm work may slow at times, but it never stops.

Walcott's career nearly ended with an attempt to prepare fossils by softening the limestone matrix: "Worked on the fence in the morning. After dinner placed a piece of rock in oven with caustic potash on it. Took it out in about $15m$ when it exploded throwing fine rock & potash into my eyes. After suffering for an hour the rock &c was removed & am doing well. Cannot read &c" (November 4, 1870). It is a wonder that he was not blinded.

That fall, the Democrats carried the state. After the election Walcott painted the barn, dug stone, helped plow, built more fences, put down a carpet, and put up a stove. Late in November the weather turned warm and he got in a day collecting on the brook. Mother was ill, so the first week in December Walcott was in Utica; Colonel Jewett was also pleased to see him.

Walcott returned to the farm to help butcher a cow and a pig, a long way from a city lad working in a hardware store. He wrote Elkanah Billings, paleontologist of the Geological Survey of Canada, and unpacked fossils sent by Whitfield. The farm Christmas was quiet, and 1870 passed away without comment.

"Read the Bible & Survey of Illinois after dinner. Retired at 9 P.M. with a headache" (January 3, 1871). Throughout his life, Walcott kept his science and kept his religion without conflict; the headache was coincidental. Several obituaries paint a glowing picture of farm life with a few chores and the rest of the time for study, but that was not true. Walcott wrote to his cousin Asa Pettibone in Indianapolis indicating that he would like to work in a hardware store at six hundred dollars per year. Eight long years later, when he obtained a position with the federal government, that was his salary.

Next on the agenda for the new year was a raging toothache. Walcott had a session with a Utica dentist and returned to find William laid up with a bad ankle and Lura ill. Duty called, so Walcott chopped wood, sawed it up, fed cattle, milked cows, and worked around the house; so much for leisure. Then he read aloud from T. H. Huxley's *Lay Sermons* to the incapacitated.

The extreme cold sent Walcott back to the dentist to have the tooth filled. He developed a cold which Josie nursed. He played chess with friends and went to the dentist for another round. Walcott returned to the farm and examined the fossils Worthen had sent him.

It was Walcott's turn to take sick. "Lura is a kind & watchful nurse. She is hardly able to get about yet is about me most of the time" (January 23, 1871). He and Lura decided they needed a home of their own: "There is considerable feeling with the older sisters. Lura has 29 acres & a small house which if repaired is good enough for us to live in & we can live in peace & Lura will not have to overwork & I can have a chance to live & enjoy health. Shall move" (January 27, 1871). Imagine the two men with Cecelia, Cynthia, Lura, and two children snowbound for weeks. It almost made the hardware business seem good.

Walcott was realistic enough to note that nothing could be done in his personal life until next fall at the earliest. Lura fell ill again, and Walcott tried to cheer her with plans for a house they might build some day. The cold persisted and the next chore was to fill the ice house. Walcott helped draw wood to the lime kiln and cut fence posts, but he had a weak back and was not the ideal hand to assist William. From Canada, Billings wrote that the fossils "sent him were not worth the express. I think he is playing sharp" (February 12, 1871).

William bought an ax for Walcott, cost $1.50; "I shall try to learn to chop" (February 14, 1871). Walcott noted he had 325 fossil species labeled and packed away. He cut several trees along the banks of the brook to increase the spring flow and wash away dirt. There is more of a personal nature: "Wrote to mother about my future plans. Hope that mother will help me although I have said to the contrary. Pride & strong wilfulness often does more damage than good" (February 19, 1871).

Walcott was finally better and drove to Utica, in part to send fossils to Whitfield and Worthen. His last entry for a day mentions he gave Lura an engagement ring. "Lu's ring excited considerable curiosity. Fannie Millar returned me my letters & picture. Shall do the same for her. Very foolish I think" (February 22, 1871). Marriage was a big decision for a young man with no money and no prospects, but the decision had been made.

Walcott wrote Billings to return his fossils, but when books arrived from Canada, he decided Professor Billings was honorable. He finished reading Huxley, commenting that points on common sense were overdrawn, and started reading Darwin's *Descent of Man*.

The snows were melting, and he found a couple of trilobites along the brook, but with further hunting he became ill with neuralgia from standing in the cold water. William found a starfish, a rare fossil, but afterward he too became sick. Lura was ill once more, as was her older sister Cecelia. "Lura some better. W*m* ditto. I am rather blue as the pain has gone to my old spot the small of my back. Fear it will be some time before I get over it" (March 14, 1871).

Tension among the sisters was so great that Walcott repeated the thought of living apart. He fixed the fence and gate at Lura's place, but the house was a wreck. Somewhere he found the names of persons in St. Paul and Boston with whom to exchange fossils. Exchanges were like stamp collecting wherein one trades the local stamps for those from other areas. Still, spending time on fossils was an escape from reality. "Lura & I had a talk over our future. I shall want about $375 to go to housekeeping &c. Do not see where it is coming from" (March 22, 1871).

The first wildflowers bloomed, a sign that spring was not just a day on the calendar. The next day, after a fruitless day on the brook, he found two new species of trilobites—a tonic to the spirits—before he left for Utica. Mother and Josie were well, and Walcott bought his own copy of Darwin before going to see Uncle William in his lair, concerning an offer to go west. "Think the inducement offered by Uncle W*m* not sufficiently strong. I wrote up to him declining the offer" (March 30, 1871); Walcott's prospects were not improving.

2

Rust Farm: Cows and Collecting / Tilling and Trilobiting (1871–1876)

> I have secured the fine collection of Trenton fossils of Mr. E. [*sic*] Walcott of Trenton Falls. It is particularly rich in trilobites. Mr. W. called my attention to one which he was confident would settle the one only question of the presence or absence of legs in trilobites. And truly there can be no doubt left upon this point.
>
> —Louis Agassiz, 1873

IF ONE KEEPS A DIARY, twenty-one is a fine age to write noble sentiments. Unfortunately, Walcott's eyes failed him and it was two weeks before he left Utica. At the farm, Lura was better and his eyes improved, but then several family members became ill at the same time. Suddenly Lura was so sick a doctor was called, an extreme measure for country folk. "Commenced at 6 A.M. to run about waiting on the sick &c. Clarence ill from overwork. Cecelia lying quietly" (April 14, 1871). "Feel blue on account of health & dubious prospects but hope for the best" (April 15, 1871). Lura improved and moved to the couch, and Walcott prattled about future plans—anything to raise her spirits. Sick or well, farming must be done: "Out planting potatoes back of the barn. W*m* sowed oats. Measured up a load of lime. Do not like the business. Lura not very much on the gain. She is worn out. Wish I could help her" (April 18, 1871).

Walcott cut up seed potatoes; each piece had to have a sprouting eye. While William and young Clarence sowed grass and oats, he stayed with Lura. He escaped the house for fence mending at Lura's place. "Think I was never in such a fix as I am now. Do not see my way out. Hope that all will come out right. Health is the one thing to be desired" (April 21, 1871). Dr. Guiteau came again to see Lura. Walcott sat with her most nights; days he slept in nearby houses to get some rest. Though the weather was good, Lura grew steadily worse. The doctor returned, Lura sank further, but she suddenly rallied and a dark cloud lifted.

"Dug fossils on the brook all day. Found Ceraurus pleurexanthemus, A. gigas & several crinoids. Shall dig a month as mother said she would give me money to pay my board. Lura better. Set up 1½ hours in afternoon. Found that I have one rare Trilobite unnamed" (May 1, 1871). Intermixing of intimate details of life with scientific results was characteristic of Walcott's diary. He covered his better digging spots as William warned him of visitors coming to collect. In a few days, despite rain, he was back at the brook with Charles Haskell from Holland Patent, a hamlet west of Trenton Falls; Haskell will reappear.

The month moved on with collecting and packing away of specimens. In mid-May he withdrew money in Utica for a collecting trip. Walcott went south to Madison College, now Colgate University, at Hamilton, New York. He had a letter of introduction to A. S. Bickmore, who taught natural history, prior to becoming first director of the American Museum of Natural History in New York City. Years later, Bickmore wrote: "One of his first trips as a student of fossils was to Colgate University. . . . Young Walcott was such an enthusiastic lover of geology that we immediately became fast friends."[1]

The rocks around Hamilton are crowded with fossils. These Devonian-age shales are younger and differ in composition from the Trenton Falls limestones. In a quarry east of the college, Walcott collected specimens of twenty species new to him. The next day Bickmore drove him to west to Cazenovia for another orgy of collecting. He spent his third day in a quarry to the west of Hamilton and ended up with sixty-two species for his collection. Back in Utica, Walcott tried and failed to obtain a position on a surveying party; nothing was working out for him.

Mother and Josie determined that he should accompany them to Jackson Falls, New Hampshire; a reasonable surmise is that Mother wanted him off the farm and, especially, away from Lura. He went to Rust farm to leave fossils and collect his clothes: "Found Lura better than when I left. . . . Trees leaved out apple trees in blossom & everything looks bright" (May 26, 1871).

Travel in the 1870s left much to be desired, particularly if one did not follow a main route. The Walcott entourage departed Utica on the 6:15 A.M. train. Three days later they were at their destination, changing trains multiple times, taking a ferry, and, finally, a stage. After all that, the fishing was poor at Jackson Falls: "The Falls consist of a large amount of granite & a small amt of water" (June 3, 1871).

Charles Doolittle Walcott, Paleontologist

Apart from attending the Baptist church, Walcott collected a few minerals and partridge eggs. Writing letters on birch bark was the local thing to do; Walcott sent several to Lura. Mother did not like the place and moved her brood to Conway North. Walcott read, played cribbage, squired the ladies to Echo Lake, and climbed Mount Kiarsarge, the local thing to do.

Walcott missed church because of a sore foot; "Foot about as aggravating as possible" (June 19, 1871). He reread the first chapter of *Descent of Man* and noted he would have to go over it again to understand. The trout fishing was better, and he went to the other side of Mt. Kiarsarge to fish and geologize. The "intervale" provided a place to dance in the evenings, and Walcott made use of it. Lura was not there, but other young women were.

Walcott celebrated Independence Day in Boston with Ed Hurlburt. They exchanged fossils with a local enthusiast and left to see the Museum of Comparative Zoology and call on Louis Agassiz. The Boston Museum of Natural History, where Alpheus Hyatt presided, was their final stop; for these two young men, it was a most satisfying day. Walcott went west to Albany to visit R. P. Whitfield, who showed him James Hall's collection. Whatever Mother might have been trying to convey on the vacation vanished with the sight of so many museums with so many fossils.

"At 7 am started for Trenton Falls. found Lura better & also all the family. Am glad I am back. Trenton Falls is as good as place to live in as I have seen. Talked with Mother about going to school again. Dislike the idea after thinking it over" (July 8, 1871). Walcott helped with the haying; the work went so well that he and Haskell stole off to fish. Next it was time to hoe the corn. On Sunday, Walcott "Wrote to Josie about marrying Lu in the Fall &c. Hope that she will take a fair view as I dislike family fuss" (July 16, 1871).

"William & I spent most of the day on the brook. I found 6 Wm 4 Asaphas. Think we have found a school" (July 22, 1871)."Letter from Mother. Sorry that it was written. Wrote to Mother. Did not ans[wer] her letter & never shall" (July 23, 1871). This is life imitating soap opera, the concern of a doting mother for her youngest, ensnared by a sickly older woman without money.

Needed rain came, a blessing to the farmer, but the sun soon shone so that haying could continue, another blessing to farm folk. Ed Hurlburt came out for a day of collecting on the brook; Walcott vowed to his truest friend that he would wed Lura in the fall or winter. A nice farm was offered him by Mr. Traylor, but he did not even have the prospect of a down payment.

Lura was finally better; Walcott, and occasionally William, spent a few days collecting along the brook. "Went blackberrying in the morning. Clarence took berries down to Mr. Morris. Selling berries to buy clothes with is a new thing for me. But I commence to learn to live economically & earn the best way I can. Provided it is honest" (August 11, 1871). A day fossilizing and it was back to black-berries, eleven quarts. Fence posts were cut and sixteen quarts of berries picked. Attending church was a relief.

The month rushed by with more posts cut, fences repaired, and another six-teen-quart day among the blackberries. Picking berries is not so romantic after the first few are eaten. William bought thirteen sheep and took Walcott along to help move them. In a fall lull, Walcott and William geologized at Cold Brook, Poland, and Rathbun Brook. To a few paleontologists, they are the best places in the world to visit.

"Cut corn with Uncle Hiram all day" (September 11). "Very lame & sore from yesterday. About the house all day" (September 12, 1871). "Worked on the brook in the morning. . . . called on Dr. Guiteau. He advised me to go to Ann Arbor if I wished to study medicine & remain 4 months & the return & read in his office" (September 13, 1870). "Wrote to mother telling her that I should like to study medicine, and that I needed help, about paying my way" (September 17, 1871). Lura left for a few days with some friends: "Lu & I sat in the old rocking chair and bid goodby as lovers always do" (September 22, 1871). Mother's reac-tion was exactly as one would predict in a Victorian melodrama—she would support her son if he would forego marriage. Walcott declined.

Between corn husking and potato digging, William and Walcott enjoyed a day prospecting north of Cold Brook. Because of lateral changes in the strata, com-bined with minor upward or downward movement on vertical faults, a collec-tor cannot predict what fossils might be discovered at a new place. Next, it was time to bring in pumpkins and pick apples. William sold the last of the lime, which meant the kiln had to cleaned and refilled with broken rock. With Lura away, this made October dreary. Walcott collected fall leaves, dug on the brook, and, to keep historic perspective, received a letter that Chicago was burning.

As a poor but enterprising young man, Walcott traded fossils for thirty dol-lars worth of photographs and hung them in his lady love's room before going off to Utica. The main reason was the trip was several sessions with the den-tist. These were the days of nitrous oxide and drilling with a foot-powered trea-dle; slow drilling makes for heat and more pain. Walcott saw Colonel Jewett, started work on a geologic map of the Russia area, and wrote letter after letter, probably looking for work.

Over the years, the story of people's lives become blurred when an incident is reworked by several obituary writers. "In 1868 he left the Academy and dur-

Charles Doolittle Walcott, Paleontologist

ing the following two years was a clerk in shops. In 1871, at Indianapolis, he met the state geologist, Professor E. T. Cox, who restimulated him to take up the study of paleontology, which had been dear to him since his fourteenth birthday, when he found his first fossil" (Schuchert 1927, 455). Walcott was at Trenton Falls for more than a year before Indianapolis was mentioned. Further, he was stimulated toward paleontology long before meeting Cox; the presence of a skilled collector, like William, keeps one stimulated.

"Received letter from Mr. A. G. Pettibone telling me that a situation in Indianapolis was open to me. I wrote that I would come on immediately as soon as I could get things together" (October 30, 1871). Walcott hurried to Russia, packed, and said a sad farewell to Lura. At Indianapolis, Cousin Asa met him and Cousin Libbie took him to her boarding house. Obituary writers, trying to make a good man better, mention a fine business opportunity which Walcott declined to pursue his career in paleontology. A nice touch, but not true.

Monday, Walcott was in Hildebrand & Fugate's hardware store. He was no longer used to this kind of work and his feet hurt. A tooth started aching and got steadily worse. Friday night, he admitted crying himself to sleep: "Feel dubious about my success as a hardware merchant" (November 10, 1871). By the next Monday, Walcott had his own room and life was not quite so grim. He made a few sales, but more important, he met Professor Cox. "At the store 14 hours. Cannot stand to work so hard" (November 18, 1871). "At the store. Worked steadily. Feel I cannot stand it during the winter. The weather is so disagreeable" (November 21, 1871). He wrote Lura he would be returning soon. Another turning point in his life was reached.

Cox allowed Walcott to copy drawings of trilobites published in Prague by the paleontologist Joachim Barrande, and they discussed his returning next summer as a geological assistant. Cox gave him some Silurian fossils, intermediate in age between those at Trenton Falls and the Devonian at Hamilton, New York. Hildebrand & Fugate gave him half a day off for Thanksgiving.

Walcott told Cousin Asa he was leaving. "My month at the store was up today. I talked with Mr. Hildebrand, he said he wished me to remain, he was satisfied with me. I told him I must return for the present at least. Called on Cousin Asa & told him I was to be married &c. Called on Mr. Thurston to see his cabinet" (December 2, 1871).

Lura was delighted to see Walcott, and he reciprocated the sentiment. For two days the returned lover was happy, until a headache took him out of affairs for three days. William became ill, and it was midmonth before Walcott wrote Hildebrand & Fulgate declining their offer. At winter's official start, December

21, the temperature in Russia was twenty-six below zero, about as cold as it gets in the namesake country. The cows had to be taken care of, but otherwise it was too cold to be out. Fussing over the Devonian fossils kept Walcott occupied.

Christmas was quiet; Walcott made few presents and received fewer. He went to Utica to attend the wedding of Miss Campbell, daughter of Uncle William's partner. As might be expected, it was a glittering affair. He saw Colonel Jewett and went to New York Mills to discuss finances before returning. Lura and a girl-friend worked on dressmaking; Walcott worked on firewood. 1871 began and ended on a Sunday: "Attended church at Trenton with Wm & Clarence. The old year goes out with a thaw & rainstorm. Altogether it has been a year of haps & mishaps but I am better than I was Dec. 31 1870. Physically & mentally & hope morally" (December 31, 1871).

On New Year's Day, Charles visited Mother and Josie and found them well; Mother gave him a Webster's dictionary and presumably assurance that she would attend the wedding. She could not prevent it, and to refuse might have meant a break with her headstrong son. Wedding preparations went on between the chores of sawing wood and tending livestock. Walcott took time to look at his Devonian fossils, perhaps to soothe bridegroom nerves.

"Can hardly think that that which I have waited two years for is to be. I have passed through" (January 6, 1872). Sunday, Walcott was at church, and Monday was another farm work day. "It seems strange that I am to be a married man. Such is life" (January 8, 1872). "At 11. A.M. Rev. M. Millard of Hol. Patent united Miss L. A. Rust & C.D.W. At 2 P.M. Wm Ellen & co. started for Rome. Reached there at 5 P.M. Present at the wedding Mr. & Mrs. H & N Rust, Cecelia, Cynthia, Jessie, Clarence, Mother & Josie. All well" (January 9, 1872). If there were comparisons between the Campbell wedding two weeks earlier and this gathering, Mother and Josie kept them to themselves.

The newly married couple spent the evening with the Gray family near Rome, New York. The next day Walcott was out with George Gray fox hunting, but there was "nary a fox," and he stopped to see mastodon bones, a clue to Lura that her loving husband never forgot science.

The Walcotts took the train to Syracuse and the road south to Rouseville, Pennsylvania. This was in the Oil Creek Valley during the great petroleum boom. Fortunes were made and lost where the oil was produced; it was exciting, though hardly the place for a honeymoon. Walcott looked at oil wells, climbed the hill near the house, and managed to sprain his ankle, which laid him up for three days. That provided time for letters, including one to Joseph Henry, secretary of the Smithsonian Institution.

Charles Doolittle Walcott, Paleontologist

"I am desirous of obtaining the Smithsonian Reports, as far as possible. I am interested in natural science, and have a large collection of fossil from the N. Y. rocks. As there are so many valuable papers in the reports I wish to obtain as many as possible. *Col. Jewett of Utica, Prof. A. H. Worthen* Illinois, Prof. Whitfield Albany will certify to my wishing them for practical use." After a respectful close, Walcott wrote on the back of the page: "I am now in the oil regions. Is there any sound treatise upon the subject of oil wells &c. Are fossils desired in the collection (Trenton limestone mostly)."[2]

Another letter went to O. C. Marsh of Yale, who four years earlier had examined Walcott's fossils in Utica: "Jan 11 I visited a farmer who has dug a number of large bones (probably mastodon) from a muck hole of which he has cleaned one half. From his description of the bones in the position in which he found them I judge the head and other portions still remaining buried. . . . I shall return to Trenton Falls by Feb. 1*st* where a letter will reach me. Will such remains be of any value to the cabinet."[3] These two letters show that Walcott was not shy in writing to senior scientists.

He hobbled to church on Sunday and after a few more days went overnight with an acquaintance to Foxburg and Petersburg. "Spent the morning visiting oil wells & coal mines. First coal mine I was ever in. Do not think I should enjoy living in one" (January 25, 1872). Back at Rouseville, he and Lura were around the house for several days. She became ill and they missed church. Then Walcott took sick, which changed their plans to return home. After the second day, a doctor was called: "He is my idea of a stylish Doc. Sat six feet from [me] looked a minute. Wrote prescription took his pay & left. I took his medicine. Cola" (January 30, 1872).

"We are sorry that we have to remain here as our visit has been long and we are causing work" (February 2, 1872). Lura actually did receive a more traditional honeymoon of one day, for they went from Rouseville to Niagara Falls. The couple spent the night, drove across the bridge to Canada, and then caught the cars for Utica. When they finally arrived in Russia, they had been away for five weeks and three days, far longer than planned.

Walcott again wrote Marsh about the bones near Rome: "The owner is a close man and will not part with them unless paid. What would you consider a fair price for them. I have never bought anything of the kind and should like to be posted."[4] He also mentioned hearing there were no Trenton fossils in the Yale collection and offered to trade fossils for literature, especially the works of Barrande; the reply is lost.

There had been a great deal of snow, and it was followed by more. "Storm over. A light snow falling all day. We get up about 8. am, eat breakfast at 8½, do the chores, saw a little wood, read &c. until 9 or 10 P.M. & retire" (February 15, 1872). Walcott began to compile a list of fossils from the Utica Slate, as the unit was then called, and the Hudson River Group. The weather broke, which meant three days of outside chores.

At a lull in farm work, Mr. and Mrs. Walcott went to Utica and had a congenial visit, a sign that Lura was part of the family. It was back to the farm chores; on Sunday, the roads were too bad for a trip to church. Walcott wanted to pursue chess, but there was no one to play with. "Very cold. high winds. Worked at fossils. Packed up those I had out. Have 965. 417 species ready for cases. All well" (March 6, 1872). Walcott sent a collection to Ed Hurlburt and another to one of his correspondents.

In mid-March, Walcott went to Utica and saw Uncle William about buying land; he returned the next day to speak with the more sympathetic Mr. Campbell. "After dinner went up to the mills. Met messrs W. & C. Drew $800 from the estate making $1000 drawn so far" (March 25, 1872). That Sunday, Walcott recorded his birthday thoughts: "I am twenty two this day. Am living in the Town of Russia, Herk. Co., N. Y. with my wife's family. Intend to study geology and farm a little the coming year. Am in fair health Lura not very well" (March 31, 1872).

He moved the couple's bed to the cabinet room where collections were displayed, and the former bedroom became a parlor. "Painting most of the day. Find it disagreeable work" (April 2, 1872). Walcott purchased six and a half acres from William for four hundred dollars, as there was every indication that Russia township was to be his home indefinitely. He put lime on his acres and assisted William and Clarence with manuring. For those not familiar with farm work, this is exactly what it sounds like. Walcott helped draw eleven loads out of the barn to put on his newly acquired land. He doctored a sick cow and put up pantry shelves.

"Mr. Moon & son Cha's called to obtain fossils for Prof. Newberry [Columbia School of Mines and state geologist of Ohio] to describe. Rather friendly to Newberry but not to Wm & I" (April 21, 1872). Walcott was lame from shoveling manure, but farm work had to go on. In the Adirondacks, spring and summer are too short to permit any delay in preparing the fields. The fields were frozen near fence lines, so plowing began in the center. The last Sunday in April William and Walcott went to the creek for a bit of fossilizing, but snow banks blocked them; at least the wild flowers were out. With the manure moved, it was time to draw stone to the lime kiln—twenty-eight loads of stone in two days. On occasion hard work is rewarded. "Found the most perfect C. Senaria I have ever seen" (May 1, 1872). Three days later, the young couple finally had a meal alone upstairs in their own quarters, another reward for hard work.

Charles Doolittle Walcott, Paleontologist

Throughout May, Walcott farmed with only one day for collecting. It was planting potatoes, oats, and corn, and then manuring the fields and mending fences. Unexpectedly in June, brother Will visited: "He is west selling musical instruments. Never saw him looking better. He has a young boy so I am an uncle" (June 7, 1872). "Spent the day at Utica. Mother leaves for the east tomorrow morning. She needs the rest from dull boarding life" (June 13, 1872); that was worse than farm chores.

Walcott spent time breaking stone in the quarry to fill the kiln. He found a partner and decided to go into the wool buying business, but there was not enough to make it worthwhile. He decided to try it on his own. Back at the farm, dreadful heat led to a great storm which knocked down half a mile of fence. "Worked at fences until noon & then went trilobiting, had good success" (July 4, 1872). Walcott hoed corn, went in partners with William on a horse, hoed more corn, fixed fences, and milked. He did have two days to collect before it was time to start mowing. Cattle moved in and ruined five acres of his crops because of poor fences.

By now it must have become evident to Walcott that one could either farm or geologize, but a body could not do both. He wrote to Marsh asking the cost of a three-year course, though obviously he had no money.

> The mastodon bones I have not been able to obtain, as some person has told the farmer they are worth $2000 and he says he have that amount for them.
> Do you wish to make any addition to the suit [sic] of Trenton fossils if so send me a list of species wished & I will send such as I have in duplicate.[5]

This letter was hardly more than a pause in the endless chores.

"Worked at fence all day. Very tired at night. Lura is gaining flesh. Looks better that she has in two years" (July 27, 1872). Walcott was not feeling well, but knew the cure. "After dinner went down on the rocks & blasted out rock. Did not find any fossils" (July 30, 1872). Walcott finally finished his work on the fences, for the time being, but oats had to be cradled and bound. Even the short time he had for collecting on the brook yielded little. During the dog days of August, William and Walcott geologized several afternoons with indifferent results.

> General Grant & Horace Greeley have been nominated by the opposing political parties. Grant by the straight Republican & Greeley by a colalation [sic] of dissatisfied republicans, Democrats &c. Think I shall vote for grant [sic], as the party he represents is to my idea the one to which the government should be trusted and from his former course I think he will carry out the laws as a president working for the interests of the nation should. His op-

ponent in my judgement is not as well fitted for the office and his political support is not as strong on the principals of national unity, finance and true reform as that of Grant. (August 17, 1872)

"Drew a load of wood from the falls & worked in the stone quarry in the morning. Cut wood after dinner" (August 31, 1872). Corn and more corn was cut. A small dairy farm growing feed for livestock is about as close to a perpetual motion machine as has ever been developed in America.

Apart from several days collecting, in September there was another entertainment: "At 3. P.M. Cynthia, Jessie, Clarence, Lura & I went to the Methodist camp meeting. I did not like it myself. Think that religion is not helped by such ways of propagating it" (September 8, 1872). "Prof. R. P. Whitfield & son called. He was pleased with the fossils" (September 14, 1872). Walcott hauled lumber, built a potato bin, dug potatoes, churned butter, and found a new fossil snail at the brook. The family went to the Trenton fair, which Walcott characterized as more of a horse trot than a fair. "Drew in corn stalks & pumpkins and finished my fall harvesting except apples" (September 24, 1872).

Walcott took Lura to Utica, where he ended his wool-buying efforts. Early in October, Mother and Josie reciprocated and spent several days at Rust farm. They left, and apple picking season arrived, during which Walcott had a fall. "My knee still confined me to the house. Worked at fossils. I have 8 species crinoids, 4 star fish & 2 cystoids from the Trenton &c up to date" (October 11, 1872). Next it was digging a well and chopping wood for the winter. The end of October he went back to fossil collecting. In early November, the water must have been icy cold and the working conditions along the brook simply brutal. One day of that and it was time to run the thrashing machine. William ended up with 130 bushels of oats and Walcott with 36, not too bad for a beginning farmer.

"Voted for U. S. Grant for President and General Dix for gov. Went to Utica at 3 P.M. Met Ellis. He seems in better health" (November 3, 1872). Not unexpectedly, Grant won; more unexpected was a letter from Mother that Ellis was to be married. Lura and Walcott overcame headaches and went to Utica. They bid farewell to brother Ellis, who was off to St. Paul with his bride. Back at the farm, Walcott transformed himself into a carpenter and repaired cellar windows. "Thanksgiving day. Lura & I ate dinner alone" (November 28, 1872).

Walcott noted that snow had possession of Russia. Ed Hurlburt visited bringing a box of fossils, an exchange from a collector in Pennsylvania; both agreed the material was not very good. "Assisted W*m* drawing wood. We had a hard job. I hurt my knee & W*m* is about sick" (December 6, 1872). Walcott packed up fossils to sent to their correspondent, mentioned that all the snow made for fine sleighing, and got on with drawing in the wood from the wood-yard. "Sawed wood, worked at fossils &c" (December 14, 1872). Walcott returned to Utica and went south to Clinton, to see Professor Root at Hamilton College. The reason was not stated and the attempted meeting failed; a guess is that Walcott was exploring another option for higher education. "Worked at fossils until 10:20 A.M. and then outdoors all day. Shoveling snow, sawing wood &c" (December 21, 1872).

"Merry Christmas. Nice presents from Mother & Josie. Worked at odd jobs &c. All well. Cold. Cold. Cold & Happy" (December 25, 1872). A visit William and Walcott had sought for months finally transpired. "Prof. J'as Hall examined W*m*s & my collection of fossils says they are the best in the country" (December 29, 1872). Walcott took Hall to the depot the next day, buoyed by his pronouncements. "Worked on fossils all day & at chores. Am better in health & wealth & I fear not mentally or morally but not any worse" (December 31, 1872).

New Year's Day came and went. "We have been married one year today. If all years of married life pass as smoothly we cannot but be thankful. Our ties are stronger than a year ago. I hope by another year they may be stronger and that Lura may have a vigorous health. I am well but she is not. Strength seems to be lacking" (January 9, 1873).

Day in and day out, chores were a given on any farm, hot or cold. Walcott helped William draw logs to the sawmill, learned how to doctor chickens, and filled in time by extending his correspondence. "Did chores, studied a little latin &c" (January 13, 1873). "Worked at wood &c. Read a little. Unpacked English fossils" (January 14, 1873). Probably Walcott exchanged with a collector in England, for there is a London address in his diary. "Letter from Prof. Jas Hall & Mr. Hayes N. Y. C. respecting sale of fossils" (January 15, 1873).

With sleighing good, there was visiting between chores. A neighbor with a telescope showed Walcott four moons of Jupiter. Hall sent a package of books. A reform ticket won the local election, with William the new local assessor. The ice house had to be filled. Bowing to practicalities, Walcott rented the house he and Lura might have occupied to some tenants; hope for their own home receded. "Ploughed out the road. Stormy. Lura sick all day with headache. Letters from Prof. Hall & book from Prof. S. G. Williams. No decision about fossils by Prof. Hall" (February 21, 1873). Walcott tried his best to close the sale with Hall:

> In yours of the 19th you ask our plans as regards the collections. We wish to have both go to the Museum, as one collection is imperfect without the other. But if the Authorities do not see fit to purchase them, they will be devided

[*sic*]. Prof. Marsh of Yale College wishes to obtain the Trenton fossils, and parties in New York wrote for general fossils some time since. I have not seen Marsh or written to him since you were here, but the last time I saw him he said I must *write to him* if I entertained any idea of parting with the fossils. I shall not write at present. How long will it be before you will know whether the Legislature will vote the money or not. And if they refuse shall you give up obtaining them.

I am desirous of obtaining books. What are the ones you speak of and what are the prices asked.

Would there be any object in my going to Albany to see any political parties, or is it dependent upon the Action of the Board of Regents.[6]

That is a pretty fair business letter from one not yet twenty-three. Walcott knew how politics might affect science and the problems of obtaining an appropriation.

Even by local standards, this winter was harsh. "Hope for thaw soon. Woodpile low and woods inaccessible" (March 2, 1873). "Letter from Prof. Hall. He has not received any warrant to buy fossils as yet" (March 3, 1873). A cold snap was followed by more snow: "East wind, blustery. Read studied latin &c. I must have a separate room to read and study in or else give up. Application & constant interruption cannot go together" (March 15, 1873). "Nothing but snowbanks to write about" (March 25, 1873). The couple was finally driven to doing laundry, a hard task in the cold. The weather warmed, and more snow came.

"I am 23 years old this day. Am very well. Wht 160 lbs. Lura not well. I have not improved a great deal the past year in my studies, have done more outdoor work. I shall try and make the next year a better one in the book of life" (March 31, 1873). Snow finally began to melt, a good sign, but Hall still had not made a decision, not a good sign. While waiting for word from Hall, Walcott sawed wood and put new windows in the old house. It was time to unload the winter's crop in the barn—fifteen loads of manure one day, sixteen the next, and eleven on the third. He drew field stone for a fence, and received fossils from the enthusiast in Pennsylvania. Hall wrote again, still equivocating.

In mid-April Walcott finally got to the brook and had success collecting. On a Sunday shortly thereafter, Walcott wrote: "Read & talked most of the day. Wrote to Ellis. Chilly. North West wind" (April 20, 1873). Thereafter is a gap of more than a month in Walcott's diary before he records calling on Judge Johnson in Utica to see if the sale to Hall could proceed. He bought a load of corn for William the following day, and there is again nothing written until July 7. When in Utica, Walcott received a telegram from Hall that the professor could not meet him in Albany; he was still dodging the issue of purchasing the collection.

Charles Doolittle Walcott, Paleontologist

The New York State Museum was one of the few places theoretically able to expend a large sum for fossils. Hall may have wanted to buy, but the legislature had not appropriated funds. William and Walcott were left to dangle.

The lack of diary entries is difficult to explain, but the routine of never-ending farm work probably was too much even for Walcott's discipline. Combined with a sickly wife and the absence of any future prospects as Hall dragged out negotiations, such a life would discourage almost anyone.

Walcott's credit and debit accounts are kept up until September, making the lapse in diary writing even harder to understand. The figures include a ticket to Chicago and payment for an undertaker. Brother Will died in August 1873, and almost certainly Walcott went west to the funeral; it is strange he did not write of this. The only picture of Lura has on its back a date of September 13, 1873. One wonders what was the occasion to take a photograph eighteen months after marriage.

The lack of diary entries is all the more inexplicable, for sale of the fossils moved forward, though not quite as Walcott had anticipated. In early October, he wrote to Louis Agassiz, founder of the Museum of Comparative Zoology (Lurie 1960): "Prof. Hall writes that you wish to purchase the collections of fossils which he was negotiating for. He did not write any particulars, and as I shall not see him I should like to hear from you. Has he written you the price &c." Walcott's business sense was keen and he added a postscript: "Does Prof. Hall see to the packing &c. They were to be delivered at the cars here."[7] "Here" referred to Trenton Falls depot. Walcott was not negotiating price nor paying freight charges. Agassiz responded positively, and ten days later Walcott sent a letter detailing his collection. There was a scent of money in the air:

> Prof. St. John's letter is received. The collection was entirely collected by my brother-in-law Mr. Wm. P. Rust and myself, with the exception of a few western and foreign specimens which are labeled. The locality of every specimen is known, and as far as can be the names attached, except the specimens from the Trenton group, many of which are not described. Prof. Hall wished the collection to "work up" the Trenton Limestone and the specimens were not labeled, but packed with only the locality given to each lot as they were collected within an area of six miles. The original price was $4000, but as they were to be placed in the N. Y. Museum, $500 was taken off for a few coal ferns and unlabeled specimens. Prof. Hall agreed to take them delivered aboard the cars here and pay $3500. He wrote that you had taken the agreement from him and to take the specimens to Cambridge, but I wished to receive written instructions from you.

Prof. Hall and many geologists from Europe and America have pronounced the collection of trilobites and crinoids the finest known from the Trenton Group. 325 Entire Trilobites 190 crinoids 6 starfish 15 or so cystoids and of corals, brachiopods &c. many new species. 175 species from the Trenton and as Prof. Hall said, "It is the best collection I have seen and we must have it." Serious financial difficulties is the reason of his giving it up.

If you wish I will leave here Wednesday with the collection, and go with it to Cambridge. If you will send a telegraphic dispatch to Trenton N. Y. as soon as you receive this and decide as circumstances require that I should know by Wednesday.

I will write a list on the following sheet.[8]

According to some accounts, Agassiz and Hall were close colleagues. Hall may have agreed to buy the collections and when he found he could not, Agassiz came to the rescue. More likely, Hall never had the money, but felt that he could always borrow the specimens from Agassiz, particularly since he got these farmers to reduce their price. Walcott's list is given below:

	No. species		
Birdseye	12	20	
Trenton	175	1500	Russia Herkimer County N.Y.
Hudson River	37	139	Oneida Co., Deerfield
		(21 trilobites)	
Utica Slate	10	72	" "
Medina	3	7	Medina N. Y.
Clinton	16	28	New Hartford Oneida Co. N.Y.
Niagara	34	74	NY & Indiana
Lower H'lb	187	231	Lichfield, Herkimer Co&Albany Co
Oriskany	4	10	
Corniferous	14	24	Madison Co. &c.
Upper Hl'd	14	19	
Hamilton	103	294	Hamilton, Madison Co & Ithaca NY
Chemung	20	47	Ithaca
Sub Carboniferous	10	18	Illinois & Indiana
Carboniferous	34	39	" "
Cretaceous	80	184	New Jersey &c England &c
From St. Paul, Minn.			
Trenton & Niagara	30	100	

I have partial lists of the specimens but not complete as to individual specimens. Many blocks from the Trenton have from 2 to 100 individual specimens so that a true estimate cannot be made unless all are unpacked. The above list is the number of pieces of rock holding specimens. Since commencing to write I have received a letter from Prof. Hall asking me to reserve for him the privilege of using for description a portion of the Trenton fossils i.e to use them from the Cambridge collection when he reviews the Trenton group. That I will leave to your decision.

Genera of Trilobites & No of Individuals entire

Asaphus	80		species 3 Hall says 4
Calymene	46		" 2
Ceraurus	48	2	
Phacops	7	1	
Dalmanites	7	1	
Illenus	6	1	
Acidaspis	21	3	
Trinucleus	2	1	
Bathyurus	2	1	
Undescribed	3	1	
"	2	1	
Lichas	1	1	

100 entire not enumerated of the above genera. The above is made out from a list which does not mention the duplicate specimens—and there are a number of species represented by fragmentary specimens. 17 species in number belonging to the Trenton Group.[9]

The names on the first list are those of rock formations or groups, some of which are still in use. The first four represent strata in and near Trenton Falls. Most of the rest were formations either collected by Walcott or obtained through exchanges.

For many collectors, complete trilobites are the prize, and Walcott made a point of listing them. The rocks at Trenton Falls were buried under a great thickness of strata, now removed. As a result of this burial, the organic matter in the trilobite carapace was changed to a black color. When seen against the light blue-gray rock matrix, these specimens are striking.

The specimens were painstakingly prepared and identified. Considering that this was the labor of Walcott for three years, and William for somewhat longer, the price is not unreasonable, especially when Walcott was willing to clerk in a hardware store for six hundred dollars annually. Still, for farmers, who saw few dollars any year, thirty-five hundred dollars was a gift from heaven.

Walcott took the collection to Cambridge and spent a week unpacking and arranging it. Memory plays tricks, and years later Walcott recounted that in September 1873 Agassiz inspired him to study trilobite appendages. Unless Agassiz came to Trenton Falls, Walcott had the month wrong. Be that as it may, Walcott found inspiration on this short visit; only two scraps remain of the trip. First, the last published item Agassiz wrote was a short note based on a trilobite in the Rust-Walcott collections (Agassiz 1873). Second, after Walcott's death, Frank Springer, a lawyer-paleontologist, recalled a letter from Walcott about their first meeting in Agassiz's museum in 1873. What a pity Walcott did not keep his diary during the entire year. There is a postscript to the trip, for when Agassiz died December 14, Walcott wrote his widow:

> I take the liberty of writing to you as I wish to express sympathy for the loss you have met and also to ask a favor. In the short time I was at your house the uniform kindness with which I was received completely won my heart and when I returned I looked to Professor Agassiz as a guide in whom I could trust and follow. I never knew what it was to have a father; most of my friends were bitterly opposed to my geological tastes. I had always fought my way and when Prof. Agassiz received and treated me as one who was not wasting his life and was doing what was right, he instilled into me an enthusiasm and determination to follow natural history as a pursuit that can never be eradicated.
>
> I am as yet but a boy of 23 years and shall devote the remainder of my life to this one object.
>
> The news of Prof. Agassiz's illness and death came to me as none other ever before. You may wonder at this but it is a true ernest feeling that I cannot be express. I have been reading the books you gave me. Everywhere I find this tribute to the Great Mind that created the objects of his study. It is a consolation to think of his meeting the reward which the long life of devotion to truth brings. Much as he is missed we cannot but accept it, and know that the spirit freed from the bonds of the physical nature will advance as it could out here.
>
> I wrote to Prof. Agassiz respecting Prof. Hall's collection mentioning some things which if seen by others, and returned to Prof. Hall might cause ill feeling. I also wrote a few facts about the interior structure of trilobites which I do not care at present to have generally known. If you will be so kind as to have the letters destroyed you will greatly oblige me.[10]

Charles Doolittle Walcott, Paleontologist

The last paragraph shows Walcott had taken his first steps toward study of the biology of trilobites. It also hints that Hall could do Walcott harm. He was to figure prominently in Walcott's budding career. Hall's action or inaction in regard to purchase of the Rust-Walcott collection, combined with stories he had heard, cautioned Walcott not to trust that man too far.

In view of Walcott's indication of inspiration from Agassiz, it is not amiss to remark on what William Rust taught him. Before he came to the farm, Walcott was an enthusiastic collector. However, William must have shown him subtle differences in the rock layers at Trenton Falls and the changes to be seen laterally in certain beds. Far more significant, he emphasized by example the importance of steady work day after day at a locality. Like collecting, preparation of fossils requires hours of effort. Using a hammer to break rock or a needle to scrape away adhering matrix are physically different, but require the same mental toughness to keep at the task.

Collectors come in all varieties. Some pick up objects because they appear strange, some pick up items considered aesthetically beautiful, and some are intellectually challenged. The second and third categories seem to apply to William. He had choice specimens, gathered as time from farming permitted. If a tourist wanted to part with good money for one of his treasures, all to the good, but that was not the main purpose of collecting.

Walcott, being city-bred and not farm-bound, had a stronger theoretical base and a broader world view. He could make contacts and exchanges which William had neither time, knowledge, nor inclination to pursue. William had a firsthand knowledge of local geology, Walcott had a concept of zoology, and the two made a good team. As hard as Walcott worked, he still had more free time than any hired hand of the era, and this must have been thanks to William relieving him of some of the farming duties.

There is a vague line between an amateur and a professional collector. Walcott began to see that along with the intrinsic value of the Trenton fossils as mentally stimulating, they might have extrinsic value beyond casual sales to tourists. As an intellectually curious young man, Walcott probably hated to part with his fossils, but as a poverty-stricken young husband, he must have been delighted to sell. Dedicating the collection to science by placing it in a museum while receiving cash was a marvelous solution. The encouragement and money from Louis Agassiz came at precisely the time that Walcott needed both.

In 1874, Walcott was gathering more fossils. The money from Agassiz made life easier and he could devote more time to study. As a result of Agassiz's inspiration, Walcott was enthusiastic about investigating the limbs of trilobites. However, farm work still must have eaten into his time. Lura's health began to decline, but whether this was a steady weakening or a series of ups and downs, as in earlier years, is unknown.

An incomplete 1874 diary is mainly devoted to descriptions of trilobites and recording collections, quite unlike the previous documents. An 1875 notebook has more counts of trilobites collected and an inch-by-inch section of the strata up the valley wall from the level of Gray's Brook. It was the raw material for the next step of publications. In becoming an author in scientific journals, in a sense, he became a scientist. A vast gulf separates a collector of fossils, be he amateur or commercial, and a describer.

Walcott's first paper is in the *Cincinnati Quarterly Journal of Science*. The rocks on which that city are built are among the world's most fossiliferous and are renowned for the variety, beauty, and abundance of fossils. At the level of the Ohio River, the oldest rocks exposed are about the same age as the youngest rocks at Trenton Falls. Fossils in the overlying strata are similar to those from the Rust farm, but differ slightly because they are younger.

Cincinnati prospered as the Ohio developed into a major trade route, and it became an intellectual and cultural center. The fossils sparked the interest of educated men, especially the Germans who emigrated after 1848. Their influence was so strong that the first volume of Newberry's geological survey of Ohio was published in both English and German editions. The city is one of few places in North America where self-trained paleontologists played a significant role (Caster 1982). After the Civil War, members of the "Cincinnati school" formed a natural history society, and S. A. Miller, a local lawyer and paleontologist, launched a journal. Nearly one-third of its contents were from his pen, mostly describing his own fossil finds. Another third were papers from other amateur paleontologists or naturalists, and the remainder consisted of translations or articles reprinted from other journals. Miller's journal lasted for only two years, but it sparked the Cincinnati society into starting its own publication. The isolated amateur at Trenton Falls, corresponded and exchanged fossils with several Cincinnati enthusiasts during the early 1870s, and that led to his contact with Miller.

In July 1875, there appeared "Description of a new species of trilobite" by "C. D. Walcott of Trenton Falls, N. Y." (Walcott 1875). The details of *Spherocoryphe robustus* fill slightly more than one page, including a dorsal and side view of the form. For those who wonder at the name "trilobite," the fossil has three parts, head (cephalon), middle (thorax), and tail (pygidium). The pygidium is commonly a single piece, the cephalon is commonly a large region which may have a smaller portion to either side, and the thorax consists of a number of segments. Complete articulated specimens are uncommon.

"New species of trilobite from the Trenton limestone at Trenton Falls, New York" (Walcott 1875a) appeared in the October and final issue of the journal. This short paper was twice as long as his first. For practical purposes, trilobites are known from the dorsal, or top, surface. In rare instances the edges which bend over to the ventral surface are exposed. Even more infrequently, an extra plate or hypostome is on the ventral side. Walcott found this part and illustrated it. One copy of the paper bears a note in Walcott's handwriting: "Pygidium incorrectly copied by the engraver." Alongside the remark is a sketch showing how it should have been portrayed. Attention to detail is important, something Walcott had learned long before he began to publish.

Two short papers appeared in the *Annals of the New York Lyceum of Natural History* and were "read June 7th, 1875." This means that they were presented to the membership at a meeting. It is not necessary for an author to "read" his paper, so there is no reason to assume that Walcott was in New York City in June. Both are on the same trilobite, follow consecutively and fill seven pages, plus a plate of illustrations drawn by Walcott and a page of captions. "In the present article, it is proposed to consider certain facts of occurrence, which seem to bear upon the habits and mode of life of one of the principal species of the Trenton rocks, *Ceraurus pleurexanthemus*" (Walcott 1875b, 155).

Walcott described the occurrence of this trilobite found at the base of a thin limestone layer. He commented that 326 complete specimens occurred in an area of thirty by forty feet, documenting intense effort in collecting. An addition at the end of the paper reads: "To October 16, 1875, 1160 specimens of *Ceraurus pleurexanthemus* have been noted on the under surface of the thin layer ('Ceraurus layer'). Of these 1110 lay on their backs; while but fifty presented the dorsal surface up. Forty-five of these fifty were very small, the remaining five of medium size" (Walcott 1875b, 159). A reasonable surmise is the second figure was based on quarrying and collecting done in 1875. Reopening of the Rust-Walcott quarry in the early 1990s confirmed Walcott's remarks on orientation of these trilobites and other comments about the occurrence of associated fossils.

One legend about Rust is that he buried fossils for some months in manure as part of the preparation process. The *Ceraurus* at the base of the layer are often covered with a thin film of shale and ammonia, and the cow manure may have been just strong enough to weaken this layer so it could be easily removed. Walcott's nearly disastrous experiment with caustic potash and heated rocks were an attempt to speed this etching process.

Trilobites are extinct, so that all one can do in discussing their life habits is speculate. The prevailing view was that trilobites swam on their back. Walcott judged his distribution data confirmed this interpretation, though that concept did not remain many years longer in the literature. Walcott may have been incorrect, but he was providing the kind of information that no one else had gathered. The current view is that *Ceraurus* and the other fossils were probably killed where they lived by a sudden influx of sediment; most individuals were flipped over by the sediment-bearing current and smothered.

The second paper (Walcott 1875c) was a highly technical description of the interior of *C. pleurexanthemus*. Several key points are detailed as to how segments of the thorax articulated, and lateral and cross-sections are illustrated. Walcott may not have been the first to consider the mechanics of the trilobite carapace, but he was an early student of paleobiomechanics.

These works are more significant scientifically than the first two papers, and they appeared in a more respected outlet. Cincinnati is not New York, and a private journal is not the same as publication by a distinguished society. The Lyceum, organized in 1817, was the fourth oldest scientific society in the United States (Fairchild 1887). Like all aging bodies, it was experiencing difficulties, reflected in the date of publication for Walcott's *Annals* papers. Priority concerns scientists, patent applicants, and similar endeavors in which a date is critical. Some of the nastiest fights in science concern who thought of an idea first and who published it first.

The Lyceum covered the entire spectrum of natural history, but because of the limited number of pages published, a volume stretched over several years. Volume 11 began in 1874 and concluded in 1877. Numbers 7 and 8 of this volume, according to the title pages, came out in February 1876.

Printed on a page of Walcott's first article is "November, 1875." That month Walcott could have purchased preprints, technically a separate printing in advance of publication of the number or volume; Hall often did this. The key date is when the paper is available. If a paper is printed in December but distributed in January, for priority, the publication is really a year younger than the year printed on the title page. In March 1876, Walcott distributed reprints, not preprints, so it could be that these are 1876 works. On the other hand, the Lyceum secretary could have distributed preprints in 1875. Walcott and his contemporaries consistently used an 1875 date. The rule is that the date given is correct unless evidence is clear that it is wrong. The work on *Ceraurus* thus remains as Walcott 1875.

There is no direct indication of how Walcott came to publish in the *Annals,* but it does not require contorted speculation. In 1868, John Strong Newberry became Lyceum president and remained in charge until his death. If Newberry was approached by this young man who had exchanged or given him fossils, he would have approved the manuscript. If President Newberry approved, the manuscript would be published. Neither the *Annals* nor the Lyceum are to be found today, because in 1876 Newberry transformed the ailing organization into the New York Academy of Sciences, which now publishes *Proceedings.*

It takes time to write even a short manuscript, make suitable illustrations, and correspond with an editor. Probably Walcott wrote his two papers for Miller's journal in sequence; description of a new species carried him over to description of another form. The other two papers are broader in content and might have come later. Late fall of 1874 and early winter of 1875, when Lura was still more or less able to move about and farm activities had slowed, would seem when these manuscripts were prepared.

In 1875, Walcott lectured as well as wrote. The first week in December, the Central New York Farmer's Club held a discussion on geology of the area and its relation to the interests of farmers.[11] Walcott was the featured speaker and a local paper printed his remarks. He also exhibited fossils and the subject was so well received the club voted to continue the subject at its next meeting, with Walcott as one of the contributors. Personal circumstances kept him from attending that meeting.

Starting in 1876, Walcott kept his daily diary for half a century without a break. Included in it are a few newspaper clippings which help show his frame of mind. In 1876, these are "A buried love" and "A fathers advice." The only known picture of Lura is in this diary, and he lists birth and death dates of close family members.

The year 1875 was hard & disheartening one to Lura & me ["I" written over]. She lying on a bed of suffering—and I taking care of her with little hope of her recovery was a task we both endured only through our affection for each other. . . . Holiday week was one of the most trying seven days I ever passed through, thinking that it was not Lura, but an invalid rendered less sound in judgement by illness. I now try to forget. . . . The confidence so true between us has received a shock & wound that years alone can heal.

Lura very low. Dr. Guiteau thinks she cannot long survive. For nearly two years she has lain on a bed of suffering. Her system is thoroughly diseased & if the choice lies between the life she has lead the past year & death, the latter would be preferable. To give her up seems impossible but the dictates of reason urge that is for the best. In a higher world she would be free from pain & sorrow. (January 7, 1876)

For two days Lura was a little better. "At odd moments I endeavor to utilize in working on my geological collection and studying. It gives my mind & body a rest from the strain caused by having a loved one ill, so long a time. I cannot endure to remain near Lura nearly as well as the first year she was ill" (January 8, 1876).

Walcott read Sir Richard Owen's textbook on paleontology with its criticisms of the development theory, better known as Darwinian evolution. He translated Latin descriptions of trilobites and tried to describe a new species from Cold Brook. Three inches of snow fell and he wrote that it was good for neither sleighing or wagoning, the sort of state that Walcott himself was in. "Returned home and worked at Drift fossils H.[udson] R.[iver] Group, also after dinner. Studied one fragment with much interest as it proves to be a piece carrying characteristic Niagara fossils. How it came in the drift at this place is a problem" (January 14, 1876). Drift blocks are pieces transported by a glacier. This rock was younger than those in the general area and had come from far away. Walcott's science was a way of taking his mind away from his dying wife.

He papered the living room, not because he wanted to but because he had promised Lura. Walcott read Croll's *Climate and Time,* with its explanation of the cause of the glacial epoch, and glanced at fossils collected at Rathbun Brook. Mostly Walcott waited. Lura was failing rapidly. "I fear I shall give out unless the strain on nerve & muscle is not lessened. It seems Lura suffers more than she ought for one who is so delicate & pure minded" (January 20, 1876).

Lura rallied twice in two days, though she was unable to eat. Mother arrived from Utica on the last evening before Lura died. "Oh God I ask that thou will receive the soul which has gone to the unknown world" (January 23, 1876). William took his brother-in-law to the Gravesville cemetery to select a plot and obtain a coffin. "A bright beautiful day. Such a day as Lura loved. If she in the spirit could have been present all might have been satisfactory for her as far as we can see. The great mystery of the unknown world surrounds her and until that is penetrated, we cannot but wait & hope" (January 26, 1876).

Charles Doolittle Walcott, Paleontologist

There is such a condition as grief-struck, and Walcott suffered its anguish. His mother stayed, but even her presence could not help. Looking at Lura's possessions unsettled him. He wrote in his diary that he was not as certain of an afterlife as he had been eight years earlier.

The third of February Walcott took his mother back to Utica. He had a wrenching moment when Ed Hurlburt introduced his new bride. Sunday was terrible; "Lura has been gone two weeks tonight. It hardly seems so long so many things have occurred to break up the time" (February 6, 1876). Then inexplicably, Walcott plunged into science: "Busy during the morning at my lathe at Mr. Hackets" (February 7, 1876). This is something new and important and must have had an antecedent. A lathe is a machine on which a piece turns in a circular motion, at that time by a foot-powered treadle. He may have put a chunk of limestone on the lathe and held a tool or blade against it to make a cut while the chunk turned. Better cutting is to hold a wire against the stone. The wire breaks frequently, but because iron is harder than limestone, eventually a cut will be made. Walcott must have tried this earlier to have invested in the cost of his own lathe.

"Working on lathe all day. Hope to finish it tomorrow. It is the first attempt I have made to work up limestone scientifically and I hope to reap good results" (February 9, 1876). "Wrote Prof. Hall A.M. asking him about my working for him & asking if he could visit T.[renton] F[all]'s about the 15th" of March, to Mrs. Agassiz asking information in regard to labeling collection now at Cambridge etc" (February 11, 1876). Three days later, he had seven cavities filled in the midst of treatments with Mrs. Shepard's battery. It is a wonder his head stayed on his shoulders.

Walcott constructed a stand for a magnifying glass and wrote a species description. William came with a wagon and took his trunk and lathe. Walcott noted that Lura had been gone for four weeks and wondered where she had gone. He went to see Uncle William about his father's estate. Walcott left Utica and missed Lura welcoming him. "I love Mother & Josie & wish to make them happy but to live in Utica will completely use me up for practical work of which I must do a great deal if health is given me. I am inclined to be lazy now but hope to brighten up to work during the spring" (February 23, 1876). Walcott worked on his Trenton fossils. He wrote a description and almost every day complained of his head hurting. The widower was very much unsettled.

Read & destroyed a lot of letters that I wrote to Lura before we were married. The letters carried me back in remembrances of many happy days spent in writing to the one I loved. The one great wonder to me is how could Lura love such a lover. I was not worthy of such a depth of love that she gave me. She was mature & had a pure deep soul. I was young and unfit to appreciate the delicate characteristics and sensitivities of her nature. I loved her truly but did not realize the gem I had secured until it was slipping from my hands. (February 26, 1876)

Walcott wrote Hall about a possible visit to the farm in March or April and indicated in his diary hope for summer employment. Notwithstanding his gloom, Walcott got his lathe in order and plunged into research. "Cut up several C. ps. had fair success. I think I shall determine their interior structure if it can be determined" (March 1, 1876). The "Ceraurus layer" is about two inches thick and, as Walcott had written, virtually all trilobite specimens on the lower bedding plane have the dorsal surface down. On top and bottom of the layer are prize *Ceraurus* which can be cleaned and prepared.

Within the thin limestone layer are more trilobites, but they do not commonly break free. Rather, they break across so that only a cross-section is seen, and therefore they are worthless to the collector who desires a complete individual. Some of these specimens are dorsal, some are oblique to the upper surface of the bed, and some are ventral. Many are flexed, not rolled, that is curved through a few degrees of arc. They are individuals which were trapped by a sudden influx of sediment and struggled upward unsuccessfully to escape the mud (Brett et al. 1997)

During collecting, Walcott suddenly realized that these entombed individuals preserved the legs. The limbs themselves had rotted away, but the holes were filled with calcite and appear as flecks of white calcite against the gray matrix. It was not obvious how this discovery could be exploited, but Walcott figured that out. If the limestone was cut to properly orient the cross section, it then could be ground down until the calcite of the limbs was visible. With enough sections, one might determine the number of limbs, their relationship to the segments, and some details of the appendages themselves. To have recognized the merit of these useless, broken cross-sections and how to study them was genius!

Whatever the details of his preparation process, Walcott had good success. "Busy the entire morning cutting & grinding C. p's. found three sections which will be of use to me in working up C. p." (March 6, 1876). Walcott had developed research fever and spent all the next few days on his sections. He also wrote a short note of his findings regarding "Bathurus tuberculatus." "Ground sections of trilobites in the afternoon. Found the Calymene senaria has the same character of appendages that C. p. has. Wrote description of C. p. after supper" (March 10, 1876). As an analogy, this was like discovering lions and tigers had the same general leg structure, when no previous investigator was even able to prove these animals had any limbs.

After the pleasure of sending reprints of his two *Annals* papers on *Ceraurus pleurexanthemus* to friends, Walcott "Commenced to block out notes for an article on C. p. in relation to the evidence I have gained by cutting sections. I now need to be at Cambridge to study the recent crustacea. As it is, I shall try to do the best I can with the means at hand" (March 13, 1876). He read what literature on the affinity of trilobites that he could find and polished more sections. Walcott felt ill, for he had exerted himself beyond his strength.

James Hall wrote and received an immediate reply. Walcott wanted a position in Albany. There was upset in the air which might lead to an opening. A digression is needed here to mention Hall's assistants and his relationship with them. First was Fielding Bradford Meek, who came in 1852 (Nelson 1987). The papers by Hall and Meek were written mostly by Meek. In the middle of the night Hall would threaten Meek with a shotgun to encourage him to work faster. The last straw was Hall taking credit when Meek recognized a European geologic system of rocks not previously known in America. In 1858 Meek escaped to the Smithsonian Institution, where he lived for years in Joseph Henry's "Castle."

Robert Parr Whitfield was second. He began as a draftsman with a salary of $550, plus a house, the understanding being that Hall could call on his services day or night. In 1869, Hall took credit for work that was to be published as Hall and Whitfield (Cooper 1931). This particular injustice festered for years, but relationships between the two were so strained that it is hard to pinpoint any one item (Batten 1987).

To complicate matters, Hall sold his collection. In 1873 there was talk of Agassiz buying Hall's material for one hundred thousand dollars, but it was only talk. In 1874, Hall opened secret negotiations with the American Museum, and the next year they paid sixty-five thousand dollars for Hall's one hundred thousand fossils. In turn, the museum sold ten sets of duplicates, so that Hall's treasures are scattered worldwide.

During negotiations for the sale, Whitfield applied for a position at that new institution. Director A. S. Bickmore knew he was the only one who could make sense out of Hall's material and eventually hired Whitfield. Hall took umbrage at his assistant trying to leave and eventually had him fired. To further confuse the matter, Newberry attempted to have the State Museum in Albany abolished so that all collections would come to New York City. No wonder there was upset in the air in 1876.

To return to Rust farm, Walcott wrote, "I find that I have 3000 specimens in my collections & 1500 duplicates collected the first three summers" (March 15, 1876). As a act of foresight, Walcott sent a letter and a drawing of a trilobite to A. S. Packard, a specialist on crustaceans. "In the morning cut up trilobites. Found a beautiful section of the appendages. It is fascinating work. The hope of finding something new or definite keeps spurring one on" (March 17, 1876).

His terrible headaches came again. Trilobites could not hold his attention indefinitely, and he started a scrapbook with a sermon admonishing mankind to repent and believe. Despite headaches, Walcott packed up fossils for Newberry. "Working on sections of C. p. 2/3 of the day prospecting for sections about the head" (March 23, 1876). "Cut up & ground specimens of c. p. in the morning. After dinner arranged blocks of small fossils in the hall" (March 23, 1876). The headaches persisted. Walcott shoveled snow and helped break the roads, but physical activity was little help in changing his mood: "Not feeling like making any effort at anything" (March 26, 1876). Research fever waned.

Walcott made several sleigh trips to the depot, for though Hall and Bickmore promised to visit, they never arrived; the next day Hall explained in a letter. Newberry sent him a copy of *Geology of Ohio*. "Drew on section of c.p. am. Not able to work long at close work on account of weakness in my eyes" (March 29, 1876). The intense intellectual effort on the trilobites faded as abruptly as it began, and grief returned.

On his birthday Walcott was in Utica: "26 years old this day. I feel more like 36. I trust that the next 10 years may be years of improvement in health physically, mentally & morally" (March 31, 1876). His birthday was followed by a call at New York Mills: "I do not think I shall visit the Mills frequently as there is little sympathy in feeling between Uncle William's family & myself. I shall endeavor to succeed in my own work" (April 1, 1876).

Walcott went to church with the ladies in the morning, but was laid out in the afternoon by a headache. He pulled himself together and used a friend's microscope to examine his trilobite sections. He wrote that Mother and Josie were to remain in Utica for another year; Walcott hoped that something would happen to brighten their drab lives. He had a tooth pulled and another electric treatment, part of the "pleasures" of Utica.

"At 6 P.M. met Prof. Hall & returned to my Russia home. Prof. Hall mentions serious charges against Mr. Whitfield. Retired at 12 o'clock" (April 5, 1876). "Busy showing Prof. Hall my collection and of conversing with him on the subject of geology. Drove to Trenton Depot at 6 P.M. with Prof. H. Nothing decisive was arrived at respecting fossils or future work" (April 7, 1876). The next week was a lackadaisical time, for snow remained two to three feet deep and cold persisted. Headaches also persisted, and Walcott, concerned over his health, puttered around, slowly assembling a collection for A. H. Worthen. He rewrote a description of a species, but was candid enough to comment that his head was out of order.

Before the middle of April, Walcott was in Albany, as Hall had asked him to visit. Hall discussed fossils with Walcott, but mainly was interested in talking about his fight with Whitfield. Walcott remained a day or two more in Albany with Dr. Woolworth, secretary of the board of regents, who ostensibly had control over Hall. "Called and counciled with Dr. Woolworth in regard to the difficulties between Prof. Hall & Mr. Whitfield. I trust that it may be amicably settled between them as it is necessary for the interest of science in this state" (April 13, 1876).

Whitfield came and made a statement to them of his claim against Hall, and later Hall made a statement. It appears strange for young Walcott to be in the midst of this feud as a peacemaker, yet there he was: "Prof. Hall & Mr. Whitfield do not make any positive settlement" (April 15, 1876). No mere mortal could have brought peace to the dispute.

Walcott gave up on Albany and the unresolved feud. He returned to Utica, not feeling well and very much at loose ends. He had a treatment with Mrs. Shepard's battery almost every day. He visited with Ed, played backgammon with Josie, tried to learn the Greek alphabet, corresponded with Hall, and planned to visit Hamilton College but managed to miss the train. Walcott went to church, and "After dark wrote to Prof. Hall advising moderation on his part towards Mr. Whitfield" (April 23, 1876).

He visited Grandmother, and as grandmothers sometimes do, she surprised Walcott with money to attend the Philadelphia Exposition. After a battery treatment the following morning, he escorted Josie to friends in Albany and saw Hall and Bickmore, up from New York City. Like Walcott, Bickmore was trying, without success, to moderate the dispute. In Utica he had another battery treatment and was convinced this had saved him from severe illness.

Walcott went back to Russia in time for three more inches of snow. On May 2, he was on the brook and wrote the old chestnut in his diary concerning the spirit being willing but the flesh weak. He had to content himself with only a little work each day, a phrase he used several times in the ensuing months. He walked to Trenton Falls to speak to Lura's best friend. He looked at her grave, was anxious to obtain a headstone, and could not find any peace.

"Wrote a little on a preliminary note noticing the discovery of appendages in trilobites. Not feeling very well. head clear but eyes still bothersome" (May 6, 1876). "I feel Lura's loss now that I am alone at night. I long to have her with me. A home with Lura was the one bright hope of my life. Now I look every way for comfort but find very little. I wish—No! there is no use of that. I must meet the issue & do the best I can & not give up to the trial of ill health & sorrow" (May 8, 1876).

His eyes still gave trouble, and for relief, Walcott gardened and studied the appendages of *Ceraurus pleurexanthemus*. He picked a bouquet of wildflowers, the kinds Lura loved, and continued mourning. Thus far every day in May had brought rain, which did not help his spirits. Walcott decided he needed to work off his gloom and dug for fossils in the rain. Sunday, he and William walked to look at the falls and he climbed a hill near the house. There still was no peace anywhere.

Walcott helped William with corn planting before leaving for Utica and church. He ordered a headstone for Lura and the long-dead Sergeant Abel Rust, and went back to breaking up the limestones in the brook. "I am stronger, but not able to stand much work" (May 23, 1876). He was healing, though not healed.

Walcott finally had a morning of "good success" collecting in the brook and in the afternoon "finished copying article on c. p. & c.s & wrote Prof. hall respecting the publication of my descriptions of fossils etc" (May 26, 1876). "Worked out on brook A.M. & ground several c.p.'s. Found axial appendages & also brachial ditto in calymene senaria" (May 27, 1876). Sunday, Walcott was gloomy again with thoughts of Lura, made worse when the wind knocked one of her vases off a shelf. He went back to the brook but had the good sense to hire someone for the heavy work of digging and prying up slabs in the Asaphus layers.

The summer heat was on, and as the crops were sowed, William, Clarence, and Walcott went fishing. "I like a fishing excursion very well. The one drawback is the black flies & mosquitoes now & punkies later" (June 9, 1876). He still had eye trouble and sick headaches every day, and eventually went to see Dr. Guiteau: "He gave me medicine. I guess it will either kill or cure me" (June 14, 1876). By the weekend he was slightly better. Charles Moore, the owner and host of the finest resort in Trenton Falls, dickered with Walcott for some fossils, and he made a nice sale.

The summer solstice was marked by another visit to Dr. Guiteau. "I should like to work but cannot so have to be patient under the circumstances" (June 21,

1876). He drove to Jessie's school; they picked ferns and went for a ride. Walcott noted this specifically as the first time since Lura's death he had tried to enjoy himself. Near the end of the month he went to the brook for the first time since June 1; William and Clarence had pried up a large amount of rock. Walcott worked for a couple of hours and still at loose ends, decided on a trip to Utica. Fortunately, William drove to the station before the train came to tell Walcott that S. G. Williams had come for a visit.

Walcott enjoyed a few days geologizing with the professor. Independence Day was quiet, and the next day the two were in Utica. Walcott visited friends and napped, commented on the heat, and, after a week, finally collected a few Utica Shale fossils; he was healing. He saw his grandmother and made an obligatory call to Uncle William. Walcott seemed to enjoy Mrs. Shepard and her battery treatments or the dentist far more than visiting his uncle. After battery treatment, he was on the Utica and Black River Railroad to Trenton depot. This was only an overnight pause to pack some clothes before Walcott was back in Utica and then en route to the Finger Lakes of central New York. He spent the night in Geneva and took the steamboat to Glenora, where he was met by Dr. Willis and his family. The doctor is one of those shadow figures about whom virtually nothing is known, although Walcott had written him for years. Walcott had a relaxing time along the lake. He went on family walks, rowed on the lake with a Miss White (and told her about the glacial epoch), searched for fossils, and picnicked. Despite this rest, Walcott was still not feeling well when he left for Trenton Falls. For the first time that year, he wrote in his diary about the farm, commenting on the poor yield of oats and the depressed price of farm products. He packed for an extended trip to the seashore to gain more rest and heal his spirit.

The first of August, Walcott was in Albany, where he had tea with Hall. "He wishes me to work for him commencing the 1st of November. I hope to be able to work, if not for him. Took sleeper to Boston" (August 1, 1876). From Boston, Walcott went to Provincetown. He remarked about the town strung out along the shore, and after a day moved from hotel to boardinghouse. He went rowing, had several sailing excursions with fellow tourists, and swam in the ocean. The net result was another sick headache. "Feeling dumpish. Decided that Provincetown as a seaside resort is a fraud and that the sooner left the better off I should be. Mr. V & wife are of the same opinion" (August 8, 1876).

The fleeing couple and Walcott took a tedious schooner trip to Boston. He called at the Agassiz Museum to see Count Pourtales, who had assisted him with information on living crustaceans. He took his possessions to South West Harbor on Mount Desert Island, and "put up" at the Stanley House. Walcott rowed, sailed, played cards, saw old-style dancing, helped catch half a barrel of cod, watched the waves crash on the shore, and lay on the rocks. He rowed with a Miss Robinson and briefly regained some of his old spark, for she wrote out letters that he dictated to his correspondents in Cincinnati, and he played croquet with her, but to no avail. "Not feeling at all well in the morning foggy nearly all day. . . . Feel discouraged about my health as the set back I now have places me where I was in July & I fear farther" (August 25, 1876). Miss Robinson read to him, as he watched the waves, sunk in melancholy.

When Miss Robinson left the Stanley House, Miss Getchell arrived. They too went rowing, watched the waves break, and wandered the beach. Walcott found glacial markings which he explained to her. "I feel that the object I came for, health, will not be obtained so I must try for a little pleasure" (August 30, 1876). They admired the scenery as he rowed to Jamesville; she now became Belle, and they went trout fishing. He enjoyed a gale, conversation with Belle, and more trout fishing; receipt of a photograph from Miss Robinson did not affect his interest. On a visit, they agreed Bar Harbor was only suited for tourists.

He saw the sunrise and bade farewell to Belle, who reminded him of Lura. Walcott went sailing, grappled for giant seaweed, the kelp of the north Atlantic, and mounted several pieces for a herbarium. Walcott looked at the local granite for glaciation effects and collected shells from a postglacial lake clay. He did the local glacial geology of a valley and then loafed and played cards. Lura was beginning to recede into the distance.

Walcott left South West Harbor by steamer and was storm-bound for a day. Eventually the ship reached Portland, and he took the train to Boston. The first day of fall, Walcott met a Mr. Bicknell, who gave him some pointers on the sawing of limestone. He saw Count Pourtales and ventured that the Museum of Comparative Zoology would not develop along the lines Louis Agassiz had hoped, a correct prediction (Winsor 1991). Walcott paused in Albany; Hall wanted him to come to work November 1.

Walcott went on to Glenora and the Willis family, for though the seaside had helped his spirits and strength, he still felt low and weak. Miss Willis read him Huxley's evolution lecture, but otherwise he lounged about for several days, excessively tired. He got up the strength to do a little rowing and later walked along the shore collecting fossils, still healing. Another day of fossil collection and he returned to Utica.

Charles Doolittle Walcott, Paleontologist

Walcott arrived in the city in time to hear a speech for presidential candidate Tilden, a prelude to one of the fiercest of American elections. He had his eyes examined and another tooth filled; Dr. Priest must have made a small fortune from Walcott's cavities. Walcott skipped church, but it was in the cause of calling on Grandmother. He made plans with Ed Hurlburt for a little collecting, and Monday they were looking for fossils in more glacial erratics near New Hartford.

After a day of that specialized collecting, Walcott went to Rust farm, happy to return after two months away. "Am feeling tired & pretty well used up" (October 3, 1876). He walked down to "see his old friend the brook" and was impressed with the amount of excavation done by William and Ed. With Walcott back, William left for the Philadelphia Centennial Exposition.

He spent a few hours breaking rocks by the brook. "Received a letter from Count Portales [*sic*] & specimens of Branchipus. Also diamond dust from New York. Tried using it on wheel & failed—shall try again" (October 7, 1876). "Experimented in cutting stone A.M. Half a failure this time" (October 9, 1876). "Busy during the morning breaking up c. p. layer & also taking up plants for winter. After dinner Jessie assisted me in making paper trays to put in spcm. case" (October 10, 1876).

Several days later William returned from Philadelphia, ill. "After dinner went down on the brook as the day was a bright pleasant one. It seemed like old times to be on the spot where I have spent so many pleasant hours of work &, to me, play" (October 13, 1876). A second pleasant day followed, the only two good days in four weeks. Good weather and good collecting were for naught; William was so much worse that Dr. Guiteau visited.

Walcott was steadily labeling and arranging his fossils. Brother Ellis and wife Sarah invited him to come to Minnesota. "Cannot think of going. William feeling somewhat better. My work thus far does not seem to tire me as much as I had anticipated" (October 14, 1876). He spent three days on the brook, some of it in snow and strong wind, breaking up the limestone, but with limited success.

With William improving, Walcott took the train to Brooklyn, where Mother visited relatives. They went to Philadelphia and the following morning spent hours at the exposition. "Enjoyed ourselves very much. The display is extended & very fine in many respects" (October 25, 1876). After three more days of seeing the sights, Walcott took Mother back to New York City. He met several people, particularly Newberry at the School of Mines. "Talked over the H & W matter. Dr. N. thinks H. an unreasonable man" (October 30, 1876).

Walcott arrived at the farm November 1, a tired "Centennial Pilgrim." He wrote Hall, sent fossils for exchange to Cincinnati collectors, and gathered up odds and ends. "Worked out & mounted on a block an Illaenus n.[ew] sp[e]c.[ies], a rare & beautiful specimen. Cleaned up room with Jessie's assistance, or rather the other way round" (November 4, 1876).

Sunday, Walcott saw that Lura's grave was in order and commented he would sod it in the spring. "Winter from the lonely sound of the wind without is approaching, and soon 'Old Russia' will be buried in its 5½ months of snow banks & ice. I expect to be away most if not all the winter" (November 6, 1876). Walcott voted Republican, except for the office of president. The following day, he learned that Tilden was elected, though when electoral voted were counted, Mr. Hayes had won. He packed up specimens for the Museum of Comparative Zoology and prepared more trilobites for cutting.

On November 11, Walcott left Russia and the Rust farm for the position offered him by James Hall. He maintained contact with his family and visited from time to time, but this part of his life was over. As regards Lura, seemingly she never appeared again until he listed her name on a 1914 marriage certificate. She is not mentioned in biographical sketches written during his life. One surmises that his grief at her death was so great that when he finally recovered from it, this was as though a door to a room had been locked never to be reopened.

When Walcott left that Saturday for Albany, it was a major step forward to his first position in geology. To indulge in metaphor, one might liken the Trenton Falls area to an undergraduate campus and William to a favorite teacher. Walcott was leaving for a difficult graduate school where the head of the department had a reputation as a tyrannical taskmaster. Some people have fond memories of graduate school, but commonly only after they have been away for years; few ever speak of graduate school as the best years of their lives.

3

Onward to Albany: The *Palaeontology* of James Hall (1876–1879)

> With regard to the accusations and insinuations of dishonest
> purposes and practices, to which I was at first inclined to reply,
> I shall say nothing at this time.
>
> James Hall, 1872

SATURDAY AFTERNOON, November 11, 1876, Walcott arrived in Albany and spent the remainder of the day with Professor James Hall (Yochelson 1987). This may have been the best place with the best person to learn the craft of paleontology. The population of Albany was just over seventy-five thousand, still clustered around the state capitol near the top of the river bluff. Manufacturing and politics were the reasons for the city's being, with politics becoming ever more important.

James Hall spent a little of his time at the New York State Museum on State Street at Lodge, just downhill from the capitol. In 1856, this "Geological and Agricultural Hall" was dedicated with great pomp during the meeting of the American Association for the Advancement of Science meeting; Hall was president that year. The building was not new, for it was the "Old Capitol" refurbished, yet the place provided reasonably good quarters for "the state cabinet of natural history and the historical and antiquitarian collections annexed thereto." By 1870, the cabinet evolved into the State Museum of Natural History (Fakundiny 1987). As a minor consequence of the change, R. P. Whitfield was listed in the *Annual Report* as assistant in geology and palaeontology, though Walcott never was. The museum was, and still is, supervised by the board of regents of the University of the State of New York; regents are appointed by the legislature.

Mostly Hall was at his private estate on a large tract purchased in the early 1850s. Hall's buildings were uphill from the capitol building, near the headwaters of the Beaverkill, a few blocks west of State Street, less than a mile from the museum downhill:

> On this estate Hall had built a red brick retreat in which he assembled all the personnel and paraphernalia of his work. It was a spreading one story structure with one large room and galleries for his collections assembled in some thousands of drawers, with a study framed in books. Not long after he removed his family to a dwelling on the place and some twenty-five years later built another more elaborate house nearer to his brick "office" but during many years this red office was his real home. (Clarke 1921, 236)

Hall had another building for printing lithographic plates and storage. All are gone but the original building, which stands in Lincoln Park, near the present State Museum in Empire State Plaza.

"Just off his large library or 'office' was his bedroom—nothing more than a cell with an iron cot, a wash-hand stand, a looking glass, a small table with spirit-lamp and teakettle, and a shotgun on the wall; and if the night was an uneasy one he was wont to sally abroad, candle in hand, among his fossils or to sit at his desk and rid his mind of restless thought" (Clarke 1921, 411). As to conditions under which his assistants labored, Hall might be described as high-strung, though more colorful words were used by underlings and professional associates. Tradition has it that one duty assigned to an assistant in the 1890s was to visit the farmers' market every Saturday and find a woman for the professor; Mrs. Hall paid the costs.

He was born in 1811 in Hingham, Massachusetts, walked to Rensselaer Institute in Troy, New York, and graduated in 1832. In 1836, the Natural History Survey of the state started with four principal geologists; Hall was assistant to Ebenezer Emmons in the Adirondack region. In a shuffle the following year, Hall became geologist of the fourth district, essentially western New York, replacing Timothy Conrad, who became paleontologist. After the Natural History Survey was completed in 1843, its findings were published in thick quarto volumes; Conrad published annual reports, but no summary volume. The four geologists urged founding of a cabinet to preserve the natural history treasures of New York. When this was finally enacted into law, J. W. Taylor became—briefly—state curator, Emmons, state agriculturalist, and Hall, state paleontologist.

The rocks of New York are fantastically rich in fossils, and Hall became passionately interested in describing them; the adjective is not chosen lightly. Mostly through the force of his will, by the 1870s Hall had raised money from the legislature to publish four lavish volumes. He devoted his life and money to making known the extinct creatures of New York and elsewhere in the United States. Hall is justly considered a major American scientist of his century, and every foreign geologist knew of Albany and Professor Hall; he was a giant of geology.

Hall was a particularly complex man. He ran several state surveys and also contracted with the federal government while being paid to conduct paleontological research for New York, he simultaneously supported different people for the same position, he speculated in land and mining claims, and he was miserly toward his help, all to keep together his establishment for description and illustration. Along the way, he amassed a huge collection of fossils.

It was said he invited people to donate their collections to gain the honor of having them described by the great James Hall. If flattery did not work, he borrowed collections and forgot to return them. If borrowing was not feasible and the fossils were watched too closely to steal, he would hire the collector as an assistant; of course, the collection came to Albany. Between completion of the original Natural History Survey and 1865, when Hall became curator of the State Cabinet, he never wavered from the goal of describing New York fossils.

In retrospect, Hall probably violated almost every present-day propriety in his crusade to amass fossils. As discussed, in 1873, he negotiated with Louis Agassiz to sell his collection to the Museum of Comparative Zoology, the one that in 1875 was purchased by the American Museum of Natural History. At the same time, Hall urged the legislature to purchase the Rust-Walcott collection so he could describe those forms. The one saving grace is that James Hall poured his life and money into the *Palaeontology of New York,* without a penny or a moment going toward sumptuous living. In the final analysis, the winner in this ethical maelstrom was Hall's insatiable mistress, Science.

When Walcott arrived, Hall's empire was foundering, as the project to describe all the fossils of New York was far behind schedule. Volume 4 of the *Palaeontology* eventually was published in 1872, and that year Hall had a nervous collapse; he left on a European tour to recover. Meanwhile, it was not obvious to the legislature that the scientific reputation of James Hall was of any direct benefit to the state. A depression was on the land and study of fossils appeared a luxury. Hall's sale of fossils to the American Museum smacked of scandal to many in Albany, even if he plowed the proceeds into research. The regents wanted closer control, and Hall was limited to five volumes total to complete description of the New York fossils.

Hall operated by selecting specimens to be illustrated and accumulated drawings for years. In 1876, *Illustrations of Devonian Fossils* was published. Ostensibly, this book of plates was to test a new method of printing, but it was really to show restive legislators that a product resulted from the annual appropriation. Some plates in this volume never were incorporated into the *Palaeontology,* for in the end there were just too many New York fossils even for Hall to describe.

Now, finally, back to Walcott. On Sunday, he and the professor looked at fossils and literature; presumably, this was a social activity which did not violate the Sabbath. Monday he was housed with Philip Ast and Ebenezer Emmons Jr. in Hall's lithographic shop. Walcott was immediately given the task of describing trilobites from Wisconsin of about the same age as those from Trenton Falls; in a few days, as soon he completed some notes, he was given associated fossil snails to describe.

Walcott arranged to room with Hall's son, a physician and occasional paleontological assistant, Dr. James W. Hall, but it took only two days to see his error; by week's end, he was at Mrs. Brainard's on Westerlo Street. No sooner did he start looking at the snails than he was "Busy during the day at the State Museum assisting Dr. Hall at cutting sections of cephalopods. Wrote note & sent notice of trilobite remains to Profs. Dana, Packard, Newberry & Worthen" (November 16, 1876).

Walcott outlined his schedule:

At 6:30 A.M. arose and dressed. Took breakfast at 7:15 A.M. and then walked up to Prof. Hall's museum ¾ mile. Worked out fossils from Wisconsin most of the day. Ate lunch at 12:30 P.M. At 5 P.M. returned to my room. Washed emery dust for the purpose of making microscope sections. Ate tea and then wrote an hour, copying description of two n[ew]. sp[ecies]. of Asaphus for publication. Wrote in journal and then retired *tired.* (November 24, 1876)

The cut limestone was rubbed on an emery dust–covered glass plate to wear it away, but it was critical that all larger pieces of emery be removed, hence the reason for the washing. "I hope I may be able to endure the strain upon my strength, but fear that it will prove too much for me" (November 25, 1876).

Despite the depression, the regents obtained funds for museum displays. Professor Henry Ward of Rochester supplied several large African animals for exhibition. Inside a fortnight of his arrival in Albany, Walcott helped move a rhinoceros to the third floor of the museum. There were not many natural history museums, and hardly any had a stuffed rhino. Experience in organizing and labeling displays in Albany was the kind of on-the-job museum training not available in any college.

R. P. Whitfield, who followed Meek as principal assistant, had come to Hall originally to draw pictures of fossils and only later developed the facility to describe them. By this time, Ebenezer Emmons Jr., Phillip Ast, and George Simpson, Hall's nephew, were all good artists and the illustration problem was under control. Walcott had the skill to describe fossils without supervision and could replace Whitfield in that capacity.

Three weeks after arriving, Walcott ate Thanksgiving dinner alone in the basement of the museum. That evening he had a conversation with Hall and the following day noted, "About to agree with Prof. Hall about my continuing with him. He wishes me to remain & I wish to & shall if we agree & I have health" (December 1, 1876). "My work is essentially the same from day to day & probably will be during the winter if I remain here. Prof. Hall needs some [sic] to assist him and I hope to be able to do it" (December 2, 1876). Before Christmas, Walcott and Hall concluded a mutually satisfactory agreement.

At Trenton Falls, between summer farm chores and winter snows, church attendance was uncommon, but Albany provided the widower mental balm. He sought out the Presbyterian church of the Reverend Anson J. Upson, recently moved to Albany from Hamilton College, where the Walcott family had religious connections. Walcott was a faithful attender, illness being the only reason for missing a Sunday service. When in the field for Hall, if Walcott could not attend church, he at least rested on the Sabbath. Walcott had his own views on religion after one sermon: "Was not impressed as I do not feel or think that doctrinal points are what I need" (December 17, 1876).

The city provided other stimulation when he met a few kindred souls to discuss paleontology. He had access to Hall's library and fossil collection of many ages from many areas. Walcott was also pursuing his own research on the trilobites from Rust farm. He was in the museum basement on Thanksgiving to use Hall's new equipment for sawing rocks and fossils. Making a thin section is a process of polishing away material, and to remove even a small thickness of rock is exceeding laborious. If one begins with a thin slice of rock cut on either side of the critical area, the time involved in grinding the rock to translucence is considerably reduced. In 1876, Professor Hall had a small steam engine installed to provide power for a saw turning a cutting disk made of tin (Hall 1879, 8). Even better, Hall's son devised a mechanism for holding a specimen so that several parallel slices could be cut (J. W. Hall 1884). This was more efficient, easier, and faster than the laborious slicing Walcott had done with his lathe.

Walcott made good use of the saw: "After tea cut a thin section of C. senaria in two, showing the ventral membrane beneath the axial lobe & the appendages. They end on the outside of it. It furnishes strong proof & was what I had long hoped to discover" (December 5, 1876). Fifteen days later, he noted writing his report on the structure of trilobite limbs "and retired—tired—tired?—tired???" (December 20, 1876).

The prevailing view in Hall's fossil factory was that work on systematics should be published quickly to establish priority; such preliminary papers lacked illustrations. Thus Walcott's note on trilobite appendages consisted of four pages of text; it was distributed before the end of year as a preprint, in advance of the twenty-eighth *Annual Report* of the State Museum (Walcott 1876).

What is particularly insightful is that this is really two discrete short papers. The first, dated May 26, 1876, ends with the address of Trenton Falls, whereas the concluding page reporting new data is listed as New York State Museum of Natural History and dated as December. The ideas were all Walcott's, and he made absolutely sure to establish that point. The letters sent off just after he arrived were a further safeguard of his priority. Hall was known to be a sharp operator, and this two-part scheme was a logical way for Walcott to tell the world he had started his work before coming to Albany.

Walcott spent Christmas in Utica with Mother and sister Josie and then visited the farm, where Mother Rust was quite ill. He packed up his possessions to bring back to Albany, but still had Lura on his mind:

> Stormy day. Remained indoors all day with the exception of a call up to Mr. Gray's. I bid this year goodby gladly. It has been one of trial to me. It leaves me broken in health but not in spirit. Situated as I am I need health & strength & shall try to secure both. As compared with last year I am better off in many ways. Only—in the loss that I cannot—replace. (December 31, 1876)

Some knowledge of fossils Walcott learned directly from Hall, though he absorbed more by reading in Hall's library and examining the great variety of specimens gathered. However, Hall did impress, forcefully, upon Walcott the importance of study of politicians, and he taught the rudiments of the legislative process as it is practiced in real life. Walcott's pocket diary for 1877 begins with a newspaper clipping listing members of the new legislature. Near the end of the book is a quote: "Years unravel what years have spun. The web of ill shall be undone, after the shadow covers the sun."[1] Following this doggerel is a list of the finance committee members. Walcott learned the basic lesson of need for close contact with those who hold the purse strings.

In justifying his budget of twenty-five hundred dollars for the 1877 legislative session, Hall wrote: "I pay a special assistant $75.00 per month."[2] Another assistant received $65.00 and a laborer, $30.00. The remainder was for fuel, taxes, repairs and other items. In typical Hall fashion, the budget did not note that several months a year Walcott was off the payroll. "Mr. Starbuck in the Senate objected to certain moneys [*sic*] being appropriated for drawings for Palaeontology. Saw him after the session & he agreed to go with me & examine the condition of the work tomorrow at 3. P.M." (March 13, 1877). "Walked up to the capital after dinner. The $2500 stricken out of the Professor's appropriation in the Senate was restored in the conference committee" (March 21, 1877).

As regards the nearly lost appropriation, Hall construed the event, probably correctly, as an attempt by A. S. Bickmore at the American Museum to have his operations transferred to New York City and self-servingly wrote: "I know that my own objects have been the advancement of the State Museum and the scientific work connected therewith, even to the sacrifice of all leisure, of personal comfort and even of health, and I do not want to see the work of a generation rudely crushed for the advantage of few interested persons or the jealousy of others who may be willing to promise much, but who have not yet performed anything."[3]

The year 1877 was the nadir of Hall's legislative problems; the following year, after seeing the energetic Walcott in Hall's entourage, some of the concern that the work would never be completed may have softened. In January, Walcott also attended several meetings of the board of regents, and he fretted over who would fill vacancies on the board. Hall had the knack of spreading his concerns about the future to one and all and dragging one and all in to assist, thereby saving himself from the brink of disaster time after time.

With the regents, as with the legislature, Walcott learned by observing, and by 1878 he was deep into the process of influencing the selection of regents who would be favorably inclined toward Hall. Walcott occasionally visited Dr. Upson's home, and for some years the minister had been a regent. Upson probably asked Walcott about Hall's work and its importance; this contact could have affected Hall's rising fortunes.

Even with the legislative session and the occasional politician who came into the museum, Walcott was able to continue curatorial efforts several days a week. For research, Hall now had him working on sections of Devonian corals. That same busy month of January, "Descriptions of new species of fossils from the Trenton limestone" (Walcott 1877) was published; most of these fossils were in the collection Walcott sold to Louis Agassiz. Hall's publishing system assumed eventual preparation of longer works to incorporate the short notes, but it did not happen in this case or with the other short descriptive papers that Walcott (1877a, 1879a) wrote during his Albany years.

That Walcott authored papers for the *Annual Report* is, in itself, remarkable. Naturally, there were many papers in the various yearly reports by Hall. The only paleontological works which Meek or Whitfield were allowed to publish during their years in Albany carried Hall's name as senior author. Assistants who followed Walcott also almost never published alone, even if they had done all the research and writing.

> Hall had never before made such a concession as to permit an assistant to publish independently in his reports upon the geology of New York and it was an arrangement bound not to continue long, though it was kept in perfect amity and mutual helpfulness, for Mr. Walcott was a young citizen for whom a member of the legislature had no terrors and he did not refrain from personally urging among those members a sane public support of Hall's researches. (Clarke 1921, 414, 415)

The only museum publications during 1877 were those by "Mr. C. D. Walcott, special assistant" (Hall 1879, 6). Walcott wrote, "Prof. Hall thinks that the work is in better shape than it has been for years and that its future success is well assured" (January 13, 1877). What praise for a young man after only two months.

With so much going on, too much was going on: "Working on Prof. Hall's collections at his private museum. I am hardly in fit condition to work as both my nervous and physical condition is anything but good. Shall keep at it however as I may improve in a week or two" (January 29, 1877). The theme of ill-health runs throughout Walcott's stay in Albany. Usually there were several visits to the dentist each year and repeated headaches, often treated in his room by currents from an electric battery.

Despite health concerns, his work on the trilobite sections progressed. He composed a letter to an eminent British authority on these fossils and sent it off for sister Josie to copy over for him. She was equally helpful to Charles when he needed French translations of Joachim Barrande's observations on trilobites.

Mid-February took Walcott to Utica in connection with his father's estate. After a few days, he moved on to Trenton Falls. Partly the visit was to obtain more material for sectioning and partly to see his "second family," especially the ailing Mother Rust. There may have been another factor, for Walcott missed Jessie, Lura's niece. Although she was ten years younger than he, they corresponded frequently during the short time Walcott had been in Albany. He teetered on the brink of falling in love.

The pleasant trip to old haunts made winter-bound Albany all the more cheerless upon his return. Some of Walcott's health trouble was old-fashioned homesickness and loneliness. As Hall's dedicated assistant, he led essentially a monastic existence, and interesting as trilobite sections may be, they do not make good companions. Apart from church on Sundays, and making sections in the evenings, Walcott's only other activity had been a fairly voluminous correspondence. Even allowing for walking between the professor's establishment and the museum, there was limited exercise. Small wonder he was restless.

In mid-March, he moved to the Bowers residence at 184 Swan Street, which was to be his home during the remaining two years in Albany; it was midway between museum and laboratory. He shared a sitting room with Lee E. Brown, a younger assistant of Hall whom he had met his first day at the laboratory. This was an improvement, and the world was not quite so gloomy. Brown sympathized with his headaches, and on occasion they would treat each other with the battery. On Walcott's twenty-seventh birthday, he wrote, "I am quite as well as I was the 26th birthday. Am recovering from the shock of Lura's illness and death as rapidly as I can expect. Am looking forward to a better year than last as I have a stronger mind and better start" (March 31, 1877). These sentiments were followed by another bout of ill health and another quick trip to Utica.

In spite of having two papers published during his first four months in Albany, Walcott was disappointed with his disparate and disjointed activities under Hall:

At the museum until 10: 15 A.M. & then went up to the capitol and remained until 1 P.M. At the museum during the afternoon. After went down to capital and remained until 11 P.M. Have been watching a bill for Prof. H. in its passage through the senate. It is tiresome business for me, as I wish to be at work on other things. Have learned little scientific knowledge this winter. (April 11, 1877)

Walcott also wrote that he feared a breakdown and determined that work, not rest, was the only cure.

Spring finally came late to Albany. At the museum, Walcott helped make displays of Indian relics and arranged fossils from England. He tried to get some intellectual order into the place by writing to the Smithsonian Institution. "Will you be so kind as to send half a dozen copies of the circular relating to the Rules of Nomenclature to this Museum."[4]

Despite a cold, he described some fossils from Wisconsin for a contemplated revision of the paper which had been published in January. Moving from one task to another and from the hill to the museum in a helter-skelter fashion was not to Walcott's liking. By late April, he determined that he "Shall not return to the Museum unless the Professor specially requests it, as I wish to put his private collection in order, and also to prepare to go out collecting if the Professor desires" (April 20, 1877).

This resolve to focus his efforts helped, and Walcott's outlook on the world improved, along with the better weather. By now he was concentrating on a single group of fossils, the Devonian snails. Much of this work eventually appeared in volume 5, part 2, of the *Palaeontology*, published in 1879; Walcott is not mentioned in the acknowledgments. Clarke's biography of Hall states that Walcott did not work on the *Palaeontology*, but that is incorrect. Because at this time Hall was officially limited to five volumes, volume 5 was split in two, and in true Hallian fashion, part 2 was published before part 1.

With good weather in Albany, life was not all bad. "Mr. Brown & I eat our dinner in the laboratory and rather enjoy our bachelor way of living, both at our room & at the museum" (April 25, 1877). A few days later, he liked "the work of identifying & labeling fossils as it affords me an opportunity to learn their names & characters that can not be obtained in any other way" (April 28, 1877). Winter's shadows and fears lifted, but ill health caused spots before the eyes and bad digestion persisted. Social life consisted of attending evening lectures at the Albany Institute. He still scribbled an occasional diary note grieving for Lura.

That spring Walcott made one of his few comments on Darwinian evolution: "Bought Page's Where, Whence & Whither? It is a small work ably written. The

subject is of great interest & to me at the time especially, as I am on the borderland of doubt & uncertainty in regard to the great question of the day the
development theory" (May 19, 1877).

During the spring, Hall had Walcott skipping around from one group of fossils to another, with much label writing and other nonintellectual tasks. "My
journal is almost like the school boys ('got up, washed, and went to bed') in the
monotony of my daily routine of labor & exercise. Working at the Professors is
apt to be of the same character & when away from work I remain very quiet"
(June 12, 1877).

Hall arranged for fieldwork in the Saratoga Springs area north of Albany. In
the region between the Adirondack Mountains to the west and the folded
Taconic Mountains to the east, the rocks are not contorted. Most of the strata
are limestones and, though nearly flat lying, are broken by simple faults; the various blocks moved up or down, like the situation at Trenton Falls. At first glace
all limestones look similar, so geologic interpretation requires close attention to
detail. As is common in such humid limestone terrain, there are few outcrops
and one must depend on manmade exposures.

Walcott went off in high spirits with Jake Vanderloo, Hall's longtime clerk.
They broke a great deal of rock in the local quarries and found some excellent
crinoids. Walcott was sure that Hall "cannot but be pleased." Some strata in the
area were like those at Trenton Falls, but others were older. They spent one day
in scouting these "Calciferous" beds and another searching shales overlying the
main limestone sequence. It was a good trip and Walcott judged Vanderloo an
excellent man.

After several days in Albany, the two went to Clarksville in the Helderberg region, south of Albany. By walking though the plowed fields, they gathered many
fossils that had weathered free from the enclosing rock. They also examined the
stone fences piled up by the farmers; where the rocks are nearly flat lying, this
is an excellent field method. The weather was fine and collecting good, but
somehow Walcott managed to get bitten by a dog, which cut short his fieldwork.
A few days of limping around Albany brought back thoughts of Lura: "How I
miss her when I am not feeling well" (July 8, 1877).

Despite his slowly healing leg, Walcott continued with the professor's work.
In addition, he wrote more descriptions of fossils for another paper in the *Annual Report* and returned to the trilobite sections, which he had put aside for

months. "Find that they show much more than I had anticipated they would. The more I study & compare them with the recent crustacea, the more readily I can see the true relations of the various fragmentary parts" (July 12, 1877).

"Found that the branchial & axial appendages of trilobites belong to the same central system of appendages" (July 13, 1877). Some of the interpretation published last December was wrong; Walcott was learning to be an critical scientist, not just a descriptive technician. "I spent most of the day writing & studying trilobite section. Find that my knowledge is not yet equal to the work. I wish to publish a note of progress & delay final action until I obtain better material and can study it more thoroughly" (July 18, 1877).

Walcott made drawings of sections which became a plate in a September preprint (Walcott 1877b). With information on a specimen from Cincinnati and reworking, the material was republished in the thirty-first *Annual Report* (Walcott 1879). Walcott's investigation of trilobite limbs ranks as a landmark in paleontology. "The discovery of the nature of the limbs of trilobites 'adds a fresh laurel' to use a fossilized expression, to American palaeontology" (Packard 1877, 694). Notwithstanding the compliment, Walcott commented on this review: "It says very little about it" (November 15, 1877).

With study of the limbs of Trenton Fall trilobites carried as far as it could go, in mid-July Walcott embarked on vacation, train to Boston, steamer to Rockland, Maine, and a second ship to Bar Harbor and Miss Robinson again. She and her married sister, an acceptable chaperon, were most agreeable companions during a leisurely ten days. The only scientific observation was dinner comparison of lobster appendages to trilobite limbs.

A day after the ladies left, Walcott headed to St. John, New Brunswick, home of George F. Matthew, government employee at the Custom House, and another semiprofessional, self-trained paleontologist (Miller 1988; Miller and Buhay 1990). Around St. John, fossiliferous Primordial rocks—Early Cambrian in current nomenclature—were exposed and Matthew was describing them. This was Walcott's first field experience with such ancient faunas, though he had seen a few specimens in Hall's collection. An unexpected bonus was the presence of Alpheus Hyatt from Boston, a renowned specialist on cephalopods and on evolutionary matters. Walcott accompanied him in the field and mentioned work on trilobites. "He advises me to publish immediately as he thinks it worthwhile" (August 4, 1877).

Charles Doolittle Walcott, Paleontologist

Walcott was already smitten by publishing; just after arriving at St. John, Walcott wrote to J. A. Lintner, the museum assistant in charge of zoology: "You are very kind to push forward my article at the cost of delay of your own. I was not aware but that the entire amount to be printed could be set up & proofs struck within a week or two. I like to push things through & get them off my hands as soon as possible, and in this case there was a little more of an incentive so I used more persuasion than may have been needed. One reason for it was the natural tendency to delay that seems to pervade the direction of the affairs connected with the Museum."[5]

Matthew was particularly helpful to Walcott. Though he could not accompany his visitor, Matthew provided explicit directions to localities within St. John and in the surrounding areas. There were several days of rain, as might be expected in this part of the world, but Walcott had a fine time collecting. A few hours standing in a stream while breaking rock must have reminded him of Gray's Brook on the Rust farm. Despite the cost of travel to St. John, even here Walcott did not work on Sunday. In mid-August, Walcott packed his four boxes of fossils and hired a farm wagon to take him to the steamer back to Prof. Hyatt's laboratory in Eastport.

The few days with Hyatt were spent examining living crustaceans and talking to the students who had studied them, enlightening and invaluable additions to his knowledge. Whether Hall had much interest in living animals is not clear, but he certainly did not use space in his writings comparing recent and fossil forms. "Accompanied Prof. Hyatt, Mr. Murdock, Gardiner & Marshall down the river. Took quite a long sail. Returned at 10. P.M. I do not generally do such work Sunday but its being my last day here & the only pleasant day since I arrived I departed from my rule of observing Sunday at home" (August 19, 1877).

The boating excursion was a good sendoff for the long train trip back to Albany. He paused briefly in the capitol city to see the printer and confer with Lintner at the museum. The accepted manuscript routing was for Walcott to submit a draft to Lintner, who, after reading, sent it on to Hall.[6]

Finally it was to Utica and Trenton Falls, where Walcott did intensive collecting from the trilobite bed. The layers in Gray's brook were flat lying in a steep valley. Overlying rock has to be removed and shoveled away to expose more of the bed; the further one cut into the valley wall, the thicker the overburden. There is a great difference between hard work one wants to do and drudgery; one person's pain is another's pleasure. "It seems like old times to go down there and work in the mud and the water" (August 25, 1877).

The limestone bed had to be broken, for most of the trilobites Walcott sought were on the interior. There are some elements in common between fishing and fossil collecting; some days are just better than others. For example: "Spent the day working on the brook. Took up a small section on the upper part of the exposure. Found the C. p. layer to be of good thickness and quality but with few trilobites on or in it. The trilobite layer very poor. The fish layer fair but having nothing good to offer. Very tired at night" (August 29, 1877).

In early September, Walcott went out a few times with William Rust to collect at other localities, and to see Mother and Josie at Holland Patent. Strangers dropped in to admire his fossil collection. He had good days collecting in the brook and with William and Ed Hurlburt, his lawyer friend, broke a lot of limestone.

All fine things must end; mid-September found Walcott in Albany. Immediately, Hall started him examining Early Devonian bryozoans, tiny colonial animals which build a calcareous skeleton superficially like that of a coral; dried specimens are occasionally sold to tourists under the name of moss animals. "I dislike the work on account of the demand made on my eyes. Still it is instructive and good for me" (September 17, 1877).

Even with moving from one assignment to another, Walcott had made solid progress at the museum:

> The Palaeontological series, through the lower and upper Silurian and Devonian formations, has been reviewed and in part rearranged; some errors in determination have been corrected; and fifty labels changed in conformity to the present nomenclature. A few additions have been made to the collections in the cases. On the second floor the collections of British fossils, of the Silurian, Devonian, Carboniferous, Permian, Triassic, Cretaceous, and Tertiary formations have been rearranged in the table-case; and fossils of the same formations which had occupied eighteen drawers have been incorporated with them filling the entire space; while the remaining part of the Jurassic and Cretaceous fossils are arranged in drawers beneath the table-cases. (Hall 1879, 8).

No credit is given, but Walcott was the major, if not the only, force involved.

Study of bryozoans pushed relentlessly ahead, eyestrain or not, but later in the week the professor unexpectedly suggested a collecting trip to Waldron, Indiana. This is a classic locality in the United States for Late Silurian fossils and Walcott had examined some collections from there in the spring. Even nicer for the budding scientist, the preprint of the trilobite article came out. "It is not as full & complete as it should be, but still must answer as I have no more time for it now" (September 20, 1877). This publication was mentioned by the *American Naturalist,* though the journal said little about it.

As was common in Hall's operations, plans were modified as soon as they were put into operation. Bryozoans were cast aside, and the following week Walcott was at Caledonia in western New York, again with Vanderloo, and again searching the fields for corals in the Corniferous limestone. They worked over the area for nearly a week and moved on westward to Leroy. The countryside was bucolic but hot, and they were out collecting from near sunup to sundown. Still, in Leroy, members of a young ladies' academy provided Walcott a pleasant evening of conversation; his grieving days were fewer.

The collectors moved on to Akron, where they collected corals from the underlying Waterlime limestone. Walcott again found young ladies to talk to in the evening. Along the line, he damaged a foot; Walcott was accident-prone in the field, but he kept going.

> Mr. C. D. Walcott with Mr. Vanderloo were occupied for a considerable time in making Collections [*sic*] from the corniferous limestone of Western New York. The results are as follows: From Caledonia, N.Y, for [*sic*] barrels and two boxes; from Leroy, ten barrels; from Falkirk, three barrels. These collections are chiefly of fossil corals which are in a good state of preservation. (Hall 1879, 10)

Eclectic spelling and punctuation are symptomatic of Hall's reports.

From Buffalo the collectors moved to Cleveland. Jake Vanderloo went directly to Waldron, Indiana, for he was familiar with the locality and much happier with what he knew than in prospecting new territory. Walcott stopped off to see S. G. Williams and his daughter Flora, then took the train to Cincinnati and spent an afternoon meeting S. A. Miller, C. B. Dyer, and other amateur paleontologists known only through correspondence and exchange of fossils. Eventually, on October 16, he got to the diggings at Waldron.

Hired help assisted with stripping of the overburden and some of the rock breaking, but it was still exceptionally hard work. The first days were warm, but each day was chillier than the last, and the water was bitter cold. One rainy day Vanderloo went into town to buy mustard for mustard plasters put on aching muscles. The necessity of finishing persuaded Walcott to work on a Sunday, the only day he had broken the Sabbath since his boat ride with Hyatt during the summer.

On November 10 Walcott went to Indianapolis and Danville, Illinois, to see relatives and to collect. Three days later, he was back working in the creek.

E. T. Cox, state geologist of Indiana and a friend since 1871, came out to see them. Finally, on November 20, they finished washing fossils from rocks; no need to comment how cold the creek was by then. When they completed their quarrying, rock breaking, and washing, the yield was a wagon load of three and a half tons, which required three horses and two mules to pull. Even allowing for the weight of adhering rock matrix, that is a lot of fossils.

From Albany, Hall directed that they should continue to collect. The pair went south to Bedford in southern Indiana to investigate whether a sandstone lying on the Silurian beds was the same age or older than the Devonian rocks of the Helderberg region in New York. Vanderloo and Walcott became disconnected; Vanderloo rested a week at New Albany, Indiana, while Walcott collected in the rain.

As party chief, Walcott had enough trouble just keeping account of the expenses, and he certainly did not need the extra aggravation caused by Vanderloo's disappearance. Notwithstanding that and the cold, on November 30 they moved on to the Louisville area. The famous falls of the Ohio River are caused by a Devonian fossil coral reef forming a hard layer in the river bed. It was a marvelous collecting locality and they made the most of their time there. Next they traveled to Cincinnati, and Jake Vanderloo departed for home.

In Hall's yearly summary, he rationalized activity out of state.

For the purpose of comparison with the New York forms, five barrels of corals were collected from the same horizon in Southern Indiana. At Pendleton, Ind., a sandstone at the base of the corniferous limestone, bears a fauna which is characteristic of the Schoharie grit of New York; and from this formation was obtained three barrels of specimens. Besides these an extensive collection was made from the Niagara group, at Waldron, Ind. of about 7,000 thousand pounds. This will be a valuable addition to the Museum, since the beds of corresponding age at Lockport, N. Y. are now difficult of access. (Hall 1879, 10)

On this midwestern trip, Walcott picked up more than just fossils. He learned that Hall was not universally liked—and why. The professor was viewed as one who stole collections or obtained them under false pretenses; his detractors had only to tell the truth. Walcott had time to reflect on his work in Albany and was troubled by what he heard: "After tea I wrote Prof. Hall about his personal enemies & their work in defaming him. Also about work at Albany. I wish either to be his assistant at his work or else a museum assistant" (December 5, 1877).

Cincinnati was the second largest American center for paleontology, though everyone involved was an amateur. Walcott lingered to talk to the members of the Cincinnati school of hobby geologist-paleontologists, and they were more than cordial in showing him their collections. Earlier in the year, C. B. Dyer had written about a new trilobite he had obtained for Walcott.[7] S. A. Miller had a long correspondence with him, none of which seems to have survived. A key problem of the day was correlation of the Hudson River group of rocks in New York to the Cincinnati group; there was much to discuss.

Finally, on December 12, Walcott left for Columbus, calling on paleontologists there. Then it was a night in Cleveland with the Williamses, and finally to Utica and Trenton Falls after more than two months in the field. He spent a few days unpacking and fussing with his private collection. During his absence, William had planted a young orchard for Walcott. With 150 trees on a lot and a colt of his own in the pasture, the prospects were Trenton Falls might eventually become his permanent home.

After this brief respite, Walcott went to Albany to check in with the professor concerning fieldwork. That fall, Mother and Josie had decided to spend the winter in New York City, and he hastened there on December 22, just in time to attend the formal opening of the new American Museum of Natural History, where President Hayes officiated. Walcott also talked to J. J. Stevenson about Hall and his activities.

Once more he overdid and returned to Albany ill. Walcott was sick for most of the last week of the year, but had a few partial days arranging museum collections and straightening out the finances of the collecting trip. In his year-end summary, Walcott noted better health and opportunity to travel. He mentioned being out of debt; some of his expenses, particularly his trip to New Brunswick, must have come from his father's estate and not from his salary. The year 1877 had been good: "I thank the giver of all good for it and shall endeavor to deserve the favors given me" (December 31, 1877).

The first of January was cheery enough. Customarily, government officials held open house and Walcott accompanied James Hall to call on Governor Robinson. The next night he was at the Albany Institute when Hall was elected president, and later they settled accounts for 1877; in all aspects, life was better than when he left the farm. Walcott plunged into work on the Pendleton fossils from southern Indiana. "The week has passed very quickly & I am hardly aware of where the time has gone. Busy hands and brain passes time away like flying clouds which cast a shadow of light or shade at every moment and have some effect on the world no matter how slight it might be" (January 5, 1878).

The following week, he scurried between Hall's laboratory and the museum, worried that the assistant in mineralogy might leave. Next he met with the board of regents and discussed prospects for a lecture course at the museum. He did the legwork in appointment of former Governor Seymour to the board and checked into activities of the legislature. Walcott was more than just a junior paleontologist.

Withall, he still managed time in the evenings to grind sections of trilobites; the state of the art was such that he even had to have the glass slides for the sections specially cut. At the museum, he "Did no special work. The fact is that it is a great place to waste time & energy" (January 16, 1878). Regardless of that judgment, most of the next week was spent installing new drawers and labeling them. During the evenings, he unpacked fossils sent by S. A. Miller from Cincinnati.

Late in January, Ebenezer Emmons Jr. made drawings for him, probably views of trilobites which appeared in his 1881 paper. If Hall had one chief competitor and enemy before the Civil War, it had been Ebenezer Emmons, yet for decades Hall employed his son. This was both an example of Hall's quirks and his ability to surround himself with talented people.

As in 1877, January's end brought another legislative crisis with an assembly resolution to abolish the *Palaeontology*. Next day, Walcott was calling on politicians, including the assistant secretary of state, and squiring members of the assembly through the museum; he accompanied Hall when that worthy testified before the Ways and Means Committee. Walcott wrote a politician regarding the sale of Hall's fossils; one would think that Hall would defend his own action. Less than two weeks after the first scare, Hall's appropriation passed the assembly. "I am pretty glad of it as he can now go on with his work if the Senate and Governor does not interfere to stop him" (February 12, 1878). They did not, and once again the professor was safe. In fact, because annual reports of the museum had been delayed, the authorization allowed printing of three years in arrears.

Walcott had a life outside of the capitol. He continued as a faithful Presbyterian, occasionally sampling a few other sects, and near the end of January made a serious decision: "I wish again to join the church after my nine years of absence as I feel that it is better for me in every way" (January 27, 1878). Jessie continued to write affectionately, and perhaps concern as how to sever the affair without hurting his niece by marriage moved him to this step. For counterpoint, "Prof. Hall became a little angry about a vinegar barrel & gave some amusement" (January 28, 1878). A pleasant incident in February was Walcott's election to the Nature Club, at about the time Mother and Josie arrived in Albany for a long visit. Hall called on the ladies and was charming; he might have been reciprocating for the yeoman job Walcott had done with the legislators.

Walcott continued with the trilobite sections; sister Josie may have helped with the chore of grinding. "Mother has finished labeling those I have made this year, 58 in number" (February 16, 1878). If one uses a steam-powered saw to cut rocks, one works in the winter when steam is available. As perspective on this six weeks production, he made a total of 95 thin sections in 1878. During 1876 and 1877 combined, he had made 122 sections. These, with 25 opaque sections, provided data for his major study of trilobite limbs.

In mid-February a problem arose with the janitor, but like so many positions in Albany, it was a political job and one had to tread lightly. "During the winter I have at Prof. Hall's suggestion endeavored to have a new janitor appointed for the museum. Through neglect on Prof. Hall's part it has failed & I now have the enmity of Mr. Huber & a failure in management" (April 6, 1878). Walcott learned another hard lesson in Hall's school of practical experience.

In the face of all that was being done for him, both scientifically and politically, Hall still decided that it was time to replace Walcott so that he could obtain another collection in the process. The Reverend Henry Hertzer in Ohio had large collections, particularly from the Devonian-age Columbus Limestone and the overlying black shales. Hall first wrote to the Methodist bishop and then to Hertzer.

"I want a competent industrious assistant for a few years to work with me in the Palaeontology and to have charge of the Geological and Paleontological collections of the State Museum. To such a person I would pay a fair salary and his future could be assured in connection with our museum."[8] The reverend was flattered by the offer, but economics were all against it. He had six children and could make more in the ministry than as a museum worker. "The position as assistant was politely declined" (Clarke 1921, 419).

Hall would later expound, "No man should be permanently retained as an assistant in such an institution. A period then of five years is sufficient time for him to work. Discipline and study to earn a better position than the museum is able to offer [*sic*]. This the universal experience that it is not wise to retain a man in such a position more than five or six years."[9] Such was from a man who had kept R. P. Whitfield as a browbeaten helper for two decades.

Once Hall determined to hire Hertzer, justifications for the change had to be invented. Walcott and Hall talked on a Sunday; "Prof. Hall said that he was

Jr. clerk at the museum, i.e. performed the duties of, & that matters were not attended to by his assistants" (March 10, 1878). Two days after Hall gave a speech to the assembly, "Prof. Hall flew in [*sic*] a passion about a written label which I wrote in pencil to copy in ink. Sorry to see him act so foolishly over a small matter" (March 16, 1878). Ever so often Professor Hall went off the rails—there is no better term—and he was heading for yet another crisis in his self-imposed difficulties. The Reverend Hertzer sent a large collection, and Hall calmed down. As a quirk of fate, Hall had Walcott, suddenly the disposable man, spend half of April unpacking and arranging the Hertzer collection.

The incident with the label was trivial in itself; judge what Walcott had accomplished the previous year:

> The geological collections contained in the wall-cases have been rearranged, and labelled so far as the Devonian rocks. For want of other space these cases have frequently been made the receptacle for rock specimens, without due regard to their value. The removal of all specimens not important to the completeness of the series has relieved the over-crowded cases, and made room for the proper exhibition of the collections. Each specimen is now accompanied by a card-label, indicating its name, geological position and locality; and a transcript of the card is attached to the specimen. (Hall 1879, 7)

Walcott had come to Albany to aid in research but became chief shovel-wielder in Hall's Augean stables of a museum.

Having labeled the Devonian fossils on the first floor, Walcott, being also the exhibit staff of the museum, made a new display. "A colored Geological Section, exhibiting the order of succession of the New York formations, has been placed above the wall-cases, extending around the room, and so arranged that the representation of the succession of the formations corresponds with the series in the cases. The section is distinctly lettered with the names and subdivisions of each formation, and, in connection with the series immediately beneath it, affords a source of instruction to the student or amateur which has not before been presented in the Museum" (Hall 1879, 8).

More than twenty-five hundred labels were in the cases and there was no official complaint from Hall regarding the lettering on these labels or on the wall chart. Walcott also made a map of the continent as it may have appeared in the Huronian era, prior to the appearance of most fossils; that must have been a new geological idea for him to ponder.

J. W. Dawson, principal of McGill University, and the most distinguished Canadian paleontologist, had discovered what he considered to be the oldest organism on earth in the Huronian. However, the debate as to whether "Eozoon" was a former living organism or a result of metamorphic processes raged for half a century (O'Brien 1970). Walcott was now an expert on making thin sections and wrote Dawson:

> I wish to obtain fragments of rock containing Eozoon for the purpose of making sections for illustration when speaking of it. If I can obtain the material—in a rough state—from you or from someone to whom you may refer me, I will return an equivalent in fossils if desired. . . . I have cut 95 sections of trilobites the past winter, i.e. 95 successful ones who show interior structure or the parts beneath the dorsal shell. I now have 245 sections. They show that the trilobites had legs, branchiae, and mouth as I mentioned in my notice of Sept. 1877.[10]

Dawson replied promptly, and by April Walcott mailed well-preserved trilobites in exchange and wrote, "I have made seven sections from the two unetched specimens of Eozoon."[11] On the second Monday in April Walcott spoke to the Nature Club, pointing out small tubules, a larger canal system and the complex wall structure in Eozoon. However, it now almost universally agreed that this "genus" is not a fossil (Hoffman 1971).

With the Hertzer collection catalogued, Walcott examined the Trenton age fossils collected last year at Saratoga Springs, before more fieldwork with Vanderloo. They took the Unionville stage to collect Devonian fossils at the Helderberg escarpment. The first field day entailed a ten-mile hike, and the second day, Walcott hurt his knee in a rock slide. Collecting was good, and five days later they were back in Albany.

Mostly they were hunting for bryozoans. The small, commonly twiglike skeleton of these animals is best studied in thin section, as in Walcott's trilobite studies. Fortunately, Hall transferred Simpson, from scientific illustrator to bryozoan paleontologist, relieving Walcott of these eye-straining fossils. Walcott got along famously with Simpson, who had taken some of Walcott's trilobite thin sections to New York City to see if it were possible to photograph them.

Walcott unpacked and arranged the Helderberg collections before a brief visit to Utica. On May 2, he and Vanderloo took the train to Attica in western New York and began collecting in the fossil-rich shales which overly the prominent limestones of the sequence at Alden. After a week, they moved north to Batavia. The rocks in the region are virtually flat lying, so the geology is simple: the farther north, the older the rocks. Outcrops are poor, except along streams, and they combed the banks of Tonawanda Creek following the Corniferous limestone.

After that, the collectors went to the local quarries and ended up with more than two tons of fossiliferous rock. A mysterious A. L. O., from Alden, whom Walcott had seen for several evenings, came to visit, and he returned to Alden to see her. She provided a major distraction from the rocks and they met again at Geneva. It was apparently a serious romance, but another one terminated by Walcott.

Lee Brown joined them briefly before they moved a few miles east back to Leroy where they had worked last summer. They boarded with a local farmer and put a significant portion of his limestone fences into barrels. Boarding on farms was important to avoid a long walk each day. Vanderloo left and the professor came out from Albany. Walcott spent two days showing him where they had collected around Alden and Leroy.

Walcott moved to another farm and had another sick day; even so, he was still filling about a barrel a day of fossils for Hall. He met up with John Eyres, a local newspaperman and geological enthusiast. Together they "went over the Corniferous limestone & reviewed my section. Found 150 feet of rock. Prof. Hall mentions but 71ft 4in" (June 26, 1878). Hall had first worked in this region forty years ago, but even allowing for haste and primitive working conditions, that was a bad error on his part.

They drove to a salt well being drilled near Leroy, now down fifteen hundred feet after a year's effort. Eyers suggested a summary of local geology, and Walcott spent the last days of June writing for the newspaper. It is a good description of the geology in popular form, giving all the significant details, and the well drilling made the subject particularly pertinent.[12]

Walcott left Leroy for his vacation; the terms of his contract with Hall are not known, but there is indirect evidence that he received one or two months of unpaid vacation each year. He returned to Trenton Falls for several days breaking up rock excavated last fall from the trilobite layer. A hard day's work yielded six trilobites, not a particularly good haul. It seems a strange way to recuperate from strenuous fieldwork, but for Walcott this was relaxation. Each blow of the hammer on a rock brings with it the prospect of uncovering a specimen better than any collected before, or even a form never seen previously.

Vague stories persist in Trenton Falls about seances at the Rust Farm. Walcott may have been around for a few of them, but he was a nonbeliever: "After tea Cecelia got agoing on *ghosts* & told of the phenomena she had witnessed in times past. Hallucination is at the bottom of it. Ill health the cause of that" (July 5, 1878). At times Walcott may have been a romantic, but he was a scientist and had no patience for the supernatural.

Charles Doolittle Walcott, Paleontologist

The following Monday, Walcott was in Utica, asking former Governor Seymour to support Joseph Lintner for the position of State Entomologist, a long step up from zoological assistant in the museum; Walcott never forgot those who helped him. Continuing has strange vacation, he hurried to Albany, did a variety of museum chores, ran errands for the professor, and spent a day collecting Primordial fossils east of Troy, across the Hudson River from Albany.

Next Monday saw him at Saratoga Springs. The collecting he had done in 1877 with Vanderloo whetted his appetite for another look at the Calciferous limestone. These were the oldest rocks in the vicinity, though younger than those at Troy. When this fieldwork is combined with his earlier trip to New Brunswick, one senses that Walcott was systematically trying to teach himself the sequence of faunas in the older rocks. Once off the train, he got a buggy ride from Dr. Haskins, a local friend of last year, to a small quarry. The only way a geologist without a horse could go from point A to point B was hike, and this ride was a real boon. The next day he broke rocks for ten hours in Hoyt's quarry and got a fine lot of fossils out of the Calciferous. Saratoga Springs has expanded and the quarry site is now in town, across the road from a "petrified sea garden" of large algal heads.

Cracking limestone in a quarry in July is very hot work, and he recorded the temperature as ninety-eight degrees. Despite the heat, he worked another quarry in younger rocks and found some crinoids. To this day, geologists, who will not even cut a lawn at home, when in the field will do difficult physical work under terrible conditions. By Friday he was back in Albany with a barrel of fossils. Hall had left for Paris to be the honorary president of the first International Congress of Geologists. Walcott did not see Lintner, but kept him informed:

> Owing to unusual heat of last week I was obliged to cease work in Saratoga Co. . . . I was agoing [sic] to ask you to let me know if anything of importance occurred in relation to the affairs of the museum or the work on the hill. I should remain here [Rust Farm] until September collecting material with reference to working up my trilobite investigations more thoroughly.[13]

Much of early August was rainy, which inhibited digging along the brook. Instead, Walcott labeled and catalogued, for fossils with locality data are virtually useless. He recorded more than five hundred fossils from his Saratoga Springs trip. He was a methodical record keeper, and had Jessie to assist him. Walcott had Hall's accumulations of fossils in Albany as an example of problems caused by poorly organized collections.

Lintner sent a letter to which Walcott responded:

I have a few n. sp. of fossils from Saratoga. It is quite necessary that they should be described & published at once as I think parties from New York are now working there. When does the Albany Inst. have its next meeting? If within a month will you present a paper, by title, of Dsrpr.[Description] of n. sp of fossils etc? Mr. Munsell can then print copies at my expense.

I am very busy working up specimens & also collecting. I have one species of trilobite with 2, 3, 4, 5, 6,—14 segments. If I get a specimen with 1 segment & another with the head & pygidium I will have the first full series of the metamorphosis of an American trilobite. I guess I will have it by Winter.[14]

In this letter, Walcott was staking out a claim; interlopers from New York City should be warned off by public announcement that he was describing the fauna. The second part dates the beginning of a study of the metamorphosis of *Triarthrus becki*. Like other arthropods, trilobites grew by molting, and finding a growth series was one more facet of their fascination.

The weather cleared, and collecting along the brook improved with discovery of a few crinoids and cystoids, their extinct first cousins. Charlie Haskell of Holland Patent sold Walcott some trilobites from the Utica Shale. Ed Hurlburt came up from Utica for a few days of rest and relaxation breaking up rock at the brook. They visited other local collecting spots and generally enjoyed the outdoors.

Walcott remained intrigued by Saratoga Calciferous fossils: "Found that I have a number of (to me) new species" (August 19, 1878). By the following evening, Walcott completed preliminary descriptions of three new trilobites. Next, he went back to the Utica slate trilobites. Finally, he put the brook diggings in order for next year. By letting freshly quarried rock sit out over the winter, natural weathering processes weaken them, so that the following season they are more readily broken.

Near the end of August, Walcott took the morning train north to Watertown for the day. The limestones there were older than those at Trenton Falls but younger than the Calciferous at Saratoga Springs. Walcott met local collectors, but, far more significant, he looked over the geology of the town accompanied by both the secretary and deputy secretary of state of New York. Walcott had learned that the best time to lobby for legislative support is when it is not necessary to lobby. It may be coincidence, but thereafter Hall had no legislative difficulties like those of 1877, and to a lesser extent in 1878. A newspaper reporter noted, "Mr. Walcott is an enthusiast in his field of investigation, and is a rare scholar as well."[15]

Charles Doolittle Walcott, Paleontologist

He spent a few more days at the farm, packing fossils, putting in a sink, help-ing with chores, but not accomplishing much; heavy rain on Sunday prevented a visit to Lura's grave. Then in Albany: "Saw Prof. Lintner and arranged about publishing *nsp* of Calciferous fossils" (September 4, 1878). J. A. Lintner was the senior staff person and presumably Hall had left him in charge. Lintner acted on Walcott's manuscripts in 1877 and presumably could authorize space in the next annual report for this one. The following day, Walcott was in the field at Leroy.

Lintner wrote that proof would soon be ready, and Walcott provided his fu-ture movements: "I received a long letter from Prof. Hall just after I wrote you. He requests me to go to Cayuga C.[anada] U.[pper] as soon as practicable & thence to Hamilton Ont. . . . I sent in 12 barrels of fossils from here yesterday."[16]

Walcott moved west, pausing in Buffalo, both to look at collections and call on Judge Clinton, one of the regents. From Buffalo, he continued west into Canada, following along the escarpment of Devonian limestone. Near the tiny town of Cayuga, Canada, on the north shore of Lake Erie, he went out with John DeCew, a local fossil collector, to obtain more corals from the Corniferous lime-stone, the strata he had investigated at Leroy. Within a week, they shipped more than two tons of coral-bearing rock. This had to be broken in the field, moved to the house, packed in barrels, and manhandled to the railroad depot. For food, lodging, expert guidance in the field, assistance in collecting, use of horse and buggy, and other miscellaneous services, Mr. DeCew received fifty dollars; both parties were pleased.

Hall's collector moved north to Hamilton, Ontario, at the west end of Lake Ontario, and met Lieutenant Colonel Grant, another local fossil enthusiast. He spent slightly more than a week with him examining Silurian beds, underlying those collected earlier in the month. Once again, he found many fossils, though nothing like the hoards in the Devonian; one day he recorded a fifteen-mile walk to collect at a locality. The proof of his paper caught up with him. "I return it with but one or two minor changes. Your careful review and correcting left but little for me to do. The genus Conocephalites is masculine & requires calcifer*us* for the specific name. Many thanks for your kindness in attending to it."[17]

After scouting out the quarries near Buffalo, Walcott went to Cleveland, where he stayed with Prof. S. Williams. "This visit is one long looked forward to and is one of the pleasant episodes of my life during 78" (October 21, 1878). More was involved than good fossils and an older man to look up to. Miss Flora was a lovely young lady; indeed, a few weeks later, Walcott wrote her a long letter but destroyed it before mailing. He could make up his mind, but seemingly never his heart. Meanwhile, Walcott had been physically up and down all field season, but now he was really sick. After a day in bed he took a lake steamer, in a storm, from Sandusky to Kelly's Island, to pursue more Corniferous corals. For several days he persisted collecting in the rain. Then it was back to Cleveland to dry off and be soothed by Miss Flora before more collecting at Williamsville.

Hall gave a scant report on his assistant's long field season and bountiful harvest:

> In the western part of the state, during May and June, Mr. C. D. Walcott assisted by Mr. Vanderloo, made large collections of corals from the upper Helderberg limestone and the Hamilton group. At a later period Mr. Walcott continued collecting, especially fossil corals, in the limestones of Genesee and Erie counties; and also in the same limestones in Canada West and Kelly's Island in Lake Ontario. (Hall 1879a, 8)

One day back from the field and Walcott was involved in the net of intrigue which always surrounded Hall. He met friend and fellow collector Hurlburt. "Ed told me of a conversation he had with Prof. Bickmore in New York. B is again trying to undermine the Museum in the estimation of the public" (November 2, 1878). After several more days in Albany, Walcott went to Trenton Falls in time to vote the Republican ticket.

With voting over, Walcott conduced some business: "After tea talked with W*m* about his collection. Offered him $1000 for his collection. He accepted the same" (November 5, 1878). That princely sum engendered second thoughts. "Spent the day packing W.P.R.'s collection and I find he has about 2500 specimens. I think I paid quite as much as the lot is worth & will consider myself fortunate to get the money back" (November 6, 1878). Walcott gave William $150 in cash and a note for the rest.

He arranged to clear a lot and have stone walls built, more indication of plans to live on the farm. Then Walcott was off to Albany with a cold and chills; perhaps this time sickness was a premonition. On Sunday, he "Wrote a little & then called on Prof. Hall at 11. A.M. Found him feeling very tired. He goes back on his contract with me & hedges in. Will see him tomorrow" (November 10, 1878). Walcott continued work at the museum, though he told James T. Gardner and a few others in Albany of his latest problem with Hall.

It would be nice to have more details of this difficulty, but Walcott's diary is fairly clear. "Called to see Prof. Hall at 8. A.M. Had a talk with him as I felt he had not treated [me] right. He said it was his thought that our agreement expired Nov. 1st instead of Dec. 1st which explains statement of Sunday 10th. He says he will nominate me to the Regents for a position in the Museum in January" (November 14, 1878). Apparently Walcott still took the professor's word as his bond.

Walcott kept working, despite further deterioration of relations with Hall. A newspaper clipping on selfishness was put into his pocket diary. "Prof. Hall thinks I did not act rightly in collecting at Saratoga Co. N.Y. & then not giving fossils to him ['or to the museum' was added later]. Right or not, I so considered it (right) and collected them. Then described five species. I will turn all over to him mss & specimens on payment of the cost of fossils to me" (November 18, 1878). The reference is to the manuscript Walcott discussed with Lintner.

This is a murky ethical situation, but the rocks in New York were open to everyone to collect, and in the fall of 1878, Ed Hurlburt had gone fossil hunting in the same quarry, after Walcott showed him what he had obtained. Hall could argue about the propriety of Walcott's collection being at the museum, but the note on Trenton fossils Hall published in 1877 was based on specimens that had gone to the Museum of Comparative Zoology. Furthermore, one reason Hall was able to obtain the sum that he did from the American Museum of Natural History was that all the material he had illustrated in the *Palaeontology* and his earlier Fourth District Report was included in the sale. Hall was a poor one to lecture on morality and ownership of fossils.

Walcott was upset by this attack and this time Hall's irresistible force met a nearly unmovable object. "After tea took labels off Calciferous specimens. Will give Calciferous collection over to state cabinet, at cost of collecting and working. If that does not satisfy Prof. Hall of my intentions (original) I cannot do more" (November 19, 1878). They patched up this difference, and a preprint on these fossils was off the press just after the New Year (Walcott 1879a).

Walcott kept busy, but it must have been a tense time for all. "Prof. Hall talked rather severely to Mr. Lintner respecting the neglecting of certain duties by Museum assistants" (November 21, 1878). With a great deal of charity, one could argue that the strain of completing another volume of the *Palaeontology* was hard on the professor's nerves; one could argue with far more evidence that from time to time Hall was a rotten human being.

Toward the end of the month, Walcott investigated the fossils from the Utica slate, the rocks he collected from as a boy. Though many fossils had been described from the Utica, there were still undescribed forms. He also became more interested in the life history and developmental stages of *Triarthrus becki,* the trilobite which is the hallmark of that formation. Using his collections of more than a decade, Walcott sorted out the various molt stages. Between that study and cutting sections of the Trenton Falls trilobites, plus a few miscellaneous duties for Hall, he was fully occupied.

The first week of December, Walcott went to Utica to see his family for a few days; the professor accompanied him, so their problems much have been smoothed over. Ed gave him twenty-five trilobites from the Utica slate for his future research. He moved on to the farm, where he methodically removed his green labels from the Calciferous fossils; Walcott kept his part of the bargain. Then he ransacked his Utica collections for good specimens: "I am somewhat disappointed with my trilobites as I expected to find specimens completing the missing links in the chain of development of Triarthrus becki" (December 18, 1878).

Walcott returned to Albany December 20 with the Calciferous fossils, even though there was no more paid work at the State Museum or Hall's establishment. "Called to see Prof. Hall at 9.30 A.M. I think he will give me the cold shoulder & no work" (December 21, 1878). The next day being Sunday, in addition to his normal correspondence, Walcott wrote to Regent Clinton in Buffalo, "respecting Prof. Hall's action in not keeping his understanding with me" (December 22, 1878). On Monday, he "Called to see Prof. Hall A.M. He is sorry that *I misunderstood* his plan etc. I am ditto?" (December 23, 1878).

Notwithstanding Hall's shabby treatment, Walcott was loyal to Hall's grand project. He saw Secretary of the Board of Regents Woolworth, who understandably was concerned about Hall pushing the *Palaeontology* far beyond what the state had ever expected. Without any equivocation, Walcott told him that "it was necessary to complete the work!" (December 23, 1878). The scientist in Walcott respected the contribution to knowledge of fossils in this compendium, even if he had lost respect for the man in charge. Walcott always did what Hall wanted and more, yet it did not satisfy the old rascal. In the final analysis, this could have been a matter of personality; Hall wanted all around him subservient and Walcott did not kowtow to anyone.

On New Year's Day, Hall started his own letter to Judge Clinton about the museum in the coming year. After reading the draft, one understands why Vanderloo copied the letters to improve syntax and punctuation; the more excited Hall got, the worse his penmanship. As usual, the first paragraph noted the necessity for more space, a perennial topic of all museums. Then he got to the real meat of the matter; an omitted paragraph details Hall's failure to recruit Reverend Hertzer:

Charles Doolittle Walcott, Paleontologist

In the same connection comes the question of employment of assistants. The collections of the museum are now so completely labelled that there is little work to be done, and we have no room where a collection of field material could be arranged in working up or properly displayed in any way.....

If we have assistants, they should work *for the museum,* and for *its advancement,* and *not use the position for their own personal advancement.* I hope therefore that the Regents will consider this matter seriously—We cannot afford to have men in such positions whose personal objects are paramount to the interests of the museum—.[18]

This letter is James Hall at his purest. To Walcott's face, Hall offered him Whitfield's old position at the State Museum; behind his back, he condemned him by innuendo. Hall accused Walcott of working only to further his own fame. Worse still, Walcott had deliberately sabotaged the *Palaeontology* by discouraging Hertzer, even though Hertzer himself had written that he could not afford to come to Albany. When things did not go Hall's way, it was always the fault of an enemy conspiring against him. Hall's sentiments were Walcott's reward for two years of determined labor in Albany and hard work in the field.

Walcott put the job loss behind him without further comment. The drawings of most of the Utica fossils having been completed, he concentrated on growth stages of *Triarthrus becki* and tabulated measurements of specimens. In a week he finished, and for a scholar perhaps the best time is when the ideas resulting from a particular study are all in place; assembling data and dealing with actual publication are not fun. Sorting out the metamorphosis of this trilobite was a solid contribution and an excellent end to the year.

In his summary for 1878, Walcott mentioned the lifting of the financial depression which had gripped the country: "Individually I am not in good shape as I am out of a situation and embarrassed by the outlook ahead. I hope however to be at work in the spring & to more than gain what I may have lost financially. My own work is progressing finely & I wish that I might be able to keep it up independently of any organization that would require my time" (December 31, 1878). There were rumors of a national geological survey, and he had talked with James T. Gardner, but these comments were just to keep his spirits up, for he spent New Year's Day worrying about the future.

After New Year's Day, however, there was no time for moping. Sister Josie came from Utica to help with the editing and copying over of his manuscript. With her clerical help, Walcott started on another manuscript to accompany the *Triarthrus* study. This correlated the Utica slate to its equivalent rocks in other parts of the country. The paper was based primarily on study of the literature, but reexamination of Hall's Wisconsin fossils and the stop in Cincinnati were of considerable help. Two years earlier, Walcott commented on "a discourse by Prof. Hall on the Hudson River Group of New York geologists. He demands the retention of the name over Cincinnati Group, in which all fair minded men should support his views" (May 5, 1877). Recall that "Group" is a geologic term for a series of formations.

Although there was strong sentiment in Ohio to honor the Queen City on the Ohio River, by December 1878, S. A. Miller wrote Hall: "I have concluded that the Cincinnati Group is a synonym—the Trenton Group exists and is well developed in Kentucky. The Utica slate is represented by the lithological characters of the strata and the fossils from low water mark in the Ohio River to 100 feet or more above—and that above this we have the Hudson River Group. I feel myself compelled to establish this fact and at some future time will write it up in full."[19] Miller also noted that this correlation, with which Walcott concurred, had first been given by Hall in 1842. Miller mentioned J. S. Newberry, and used "Newberryize" as a synonym for plagiarism, for Newberry hardly mentioned Hall's early view on correlation. On the other hand, so far as Newberry was concerned, Miller was a second-rate lawyer and a first-rate troublemaker; so much for the image of the impartial scientist.

Walcott urged use of the term "Hudson River" for all the rocks; years later, he again emphasized the priority of that term. Hall and Walcott lost that argument, for priority or not, in Cincinnati were exposed some of the most fossiliferous rocks in the world, and paleontologists are familiar with the Cincinnatian. Walcott never ruffled anyone's feelings in this matter of what was basically civic pride on accepting one name and rejecting another.

The writing ground along, bringing headaches every few days. Walcott returned to the drawing of fossils, occasionally saw Hall, and met a visiting French paleontologist, Charles Barrois. Walcott was discouraged with his prospects. In an obituary to Walcott, Barrois wrote, "He confided to me, while chatting on the banks of the Trenton [sic], his final hesitation between a business career and the world of trilobites."[20]

On January 31, Walcott sent a letter to Clarence King by way of Gardner, who had been a topographer with King's Survey of the Fortieth Parallel and then with the Hayden Territorial Survey before moving to Albany. Walcott almost certainly wrote to apply for a position with the U.S. Geological Survey, if it were ever formed. A few weeks later, Hall wrote to King:

Charles Doolittle Walcott, Paleontologist

I beg leave to recommend Mr. Charles D. Walcott for a position as assistant on your staff. Mr. Walcott has been with me for two years past, his duties having been chiefly in the field where he has done very excellent work in the collection of fossils and their preparation for the State Museum and for use in the palaeontology of the state. His palaeontological studies up to the present time have been chiefly among the trilobites of his own collections where he has done excellent work. He is now engaged upon some operations of wider character and has in hand already for publication an interesting paper upon the Utica slate, its fauna, its geological relations, geographic range, etc.

In all the work in which he has been engaged I have every reason to be satisfied. (Clarke 1921, 473)

It was a generous letter; the difference between this and that to Regent Clinton is again characteristic of Hall's vacillations.

Despite a flare-up of boils, Walcott finished the article on correlation of the Utica slate, amidst doubts as to its merit; "I am not any too sure of the paper now as a contribution to science but I will study at it until I know more about it than I do now" (February 11, 1879). A few days later, Walcott "After tea called on Prof. Hall & talked over Utica epoch & other geological topics. He expressed himself as pleased with the paper as far as the points at issue were concerned" (February 13, 1879). Walcott renewed his effort on trilobite sections; he also alternated with labeling his collection and packing fossils for exchange. Walcott started drawing, and remarked he had thirty or more sketches to make of sections, new data that appeared in his definitive 1881 paper.

The resurgence of interest in the sections was correlated with republication of his 1877 work, which serves as a representative example of the complexities, expense, and duplication of effort in Hall's operations. The same plate was reproduced, but figure numbers and magnifications were printed on the plate, rather than hand lettered. The entire work was reset in smaller type, so that the five pages already published shrunk to three. Finally, he added another short note on trilobite legs from Cincinnati (Walcott 1879). Under Hall's supervision, papers were not simply written and published, they evolved. Walcott's description of new species from 1877 was also reprinted.

The preprints which issued from Albany in Hall's zeal to grab priority are a librarian's nightmare. The repetition of paragraphs or even pages from one work to another was a trait that Walcott unfortunately picked up from Hall and followed occasionally in a few of his later papers, but at least Walcott, unlike

Hall, never changed wording between a preprint and an official series, nor did he print the words "new species" more than once in connection with the forms he described.

In March Walcott started to prepare descriptions of crinoids from the Trenton limestone. Long after he left Albany, this resulted in another preprinted paper (Walcott 1883); the official printing reset in larger type was dated 1884. Walcott pursued the crinoids off and on all through that spring; between times, he still pursued trilobite limbs. He made arrangements with Hall for publication of his Utica fossils and correlation manuscripts by the Albany Institute rather than the State Museum. Although authoritarian Hall was president of the institute, the members could not agree on how to publish the next full volume, so that once again Walcott was dragged into a preprint.

Phillip Ast put Walcott's drawings of Utica fossils on lithographic stone. This form of printing is a reversal process and the lithographer must draw the opposite of what he sees. All in all, winter and early spring were a fairly busy time, though not the hectic pace he pursued when working for Hall.

Walcott's twenty-ninth birthday passed quietly, but next day brought bad news: "Met Prof. Jos.[*sic*] L. Gardner who told me it was doubtful if I obtained a situation on the U. S. Geological Survey. It will be a disappointment to me if I do not as I wish to build up my future with it" (April 1, 1879). Regardless of that bitter disappointment, on the evening of April 7 he gave a talk on trilobites to the Nature Club. It was good experience, for the following Tuesday he presented his research at the prestigious Albany Institute. "Mr. Walcott has discovered the means of locomotion and the anatomy of these interesting animals, which have been hitherto unknown, as was shown in the discussion following the reading of the paper by extracts from the text books of the most noted geologists of the present day, read by Prof. Prescott."[21]

In the absence of any prospect of employment by the federal government, Walcott turned to his family for financial support. He wrote Uncle William about possible purchase of his collection; that must have been painful. He received a "Letter from Uncle W*m* Walcott in which he states that he does not feel able to assist me by taking my collection. I hoped that he might but still I can get along until another year" (April 21, 1879).

At this point, it is a little hard to place Walcott's standing in the Albany scientific community. Perhaps the best parallel to Walcott's situation is the modern-day graduate student, who having scrimped for years to be able to attend the university, after a few months is more or less abandoned by his major advisor yet still hangs on, hoping to finish his thesis and move on to a better place.

Walcott tried to sell his collection to the American Museum without success. "We would take much to possess your rare collections, but our present obligations to Professor Hall will absorb all and more of our moneys for purchase that we can devote to fossils this year."[22]

That avenue closed, Walcott hoped to sell his collection to the State Museum. He began by calling on Secretary of State Beech and getting him to visit Swan Street to examine the collection. With that first step taken, Walcott jumped on a train to Buffalo to meet Judge Clinton and to obtain letters of support to Secretary Beech and the political powerhouse, U.S. senator Roscoe Conkling from Utica. For Walcott this was quite uncharacteristic Sunday behavior, but he was in a financial bind. On Tuesday, Walcott was back in Albany to attend a meeting of the committee on the museum. They agreed his collection was worth purchasing.

Meantime, Hall was doing his part to obtain these fossils:

> In advocating the purchase of Mr. Walcott's collection by the State I do not do so for the sake of accumulation of specimens for the state alone, but for the reason that his collection of sections of Trilobites has become already a typical collection. A portion of the literature of the Science [*sic*] is founded upon their study and they will be the basis of still further investigation and publication. The collection series showing the development of Triarthrus from the earlier conditions of the body with two segments through its stages of growth till we have it with sixteen segments will soon become the typical and original collection showing the development of Trilobites [*sic*] in the museums of America.
>
> The Museum which contains these collections must for all time, so long as science shall be cultivated, be known and resorted to for the study of such objects and for the evidences of the internal structure and development of the Trilobites.
>
> A simple accumulation of objects of Natural History does not make a scientific museum; it must be by investigation, discovery and publication regarding its collections, that an institution can have a standing and appreciation among men of science.[23]

In 1879, Walcott did not bother to cut the names of the legislators from the paper and paste them in his diary, for after two years of activity in the capitol, he knew many of them well. It was very late in the session to seek an appropriation, but the lobbyist who had trained under Hall and learned a few tricks of his own "Spent the day on my feet about town looking after the bill to be brought before the legislature. I fear we are working on a hopeless job but have faith in trying" (May 5, 1879). Tuesday and Wednesday he was still buttonholing members of the legislature. The next day preliminaries were over for his appropriation bill. "Dr. [J. I] Hayes introduced it in the morning session. It is very late in the day for it but I still hope to see it go through" (May 8, 1879). Monday, he was at the meeting of the Ways and Means Committee recounting details of his fossil collection. "My bill was reported favorably by the way [*sic*] & means committee. Now the fight comes to get it through before the adjournment" (May 13, 1879).

The rest of the week he spent scurrying around the capitol keeping his bill alive in a race against the clock. On Friday "My bill passed the 3*d* reading & and may go to the Senate on Tuesday" (May 16, 1879). By the next Wednesday he wrote, "My bill passed the Senate at noon" (May 21, 1879). This is incredible progress for any bill, especially at the end of session. Walcott had learned how to deal with lawmakers, and if he learned nothing else in Albany, in later years this lesson was worth all the effort he invested for two years.

One more painful lesson had to be learned. After passage, legislation must be signed into law. He tried and failed to see Governor Robinson, although he got as far as the private secretary. He wrote to former governor Seymour, appealing for support in convincing Governor Robinson to sign, but to no avail. "Lucius Robinson was a tight-lipped, economy-minded man. . . . Construction on the new capitol in Albany had started in 1867, and was finally to the point where part of the structure could be occupied. To demonstrate economy, Governor Robinson refused to move his office into that . . . great public calamity" (Roseberry 1964, 41). Irresistible force was stopped by immovable Governor Robinson, who vetoed Assembly Bill 744:

> A full account of all the money which has been expended, and most of it wasted, upon what is called the natural history of the State, would afford little encouragement for going any further in that direction under any circumstances. In the present condition of financial distress the State has too many necessary expenses to warrant the outlay of four thousand dollars in the purchase of fossils. (Robinson 1879, 140)

Once more Walcott's hope of financial security vanished.

Throughout these frantic last days of the session, Walcott went to Hall's establishment to confer with Philip Ast about the lithographs. Late in May, he received 350 copies of two plates, run off the press on the hill in Hall's establishment, and he took them to the printer who was setting type. Walcott read proofs of his two Utica slate papers, and wrote another letter to King, now director of the U.S. Geological Survey:

> Some time since Prof. James T. Gardner kindly offered to speak to you in relation to my obtaining a position on the U. S. Survey. He also forwarded to you a letter sent to him by Prof. Hall and some other papers I gave him. As he has not seen you since your return from the west, I write to inquire if there will be an opening for me another year, if not this? I am willing to do any work that I am able to do that will be of the most service. My desire is to pursue stratigraphical geology including collecting and invertebrate palaeontology, the latter having occupied my attention thus far. Prof. Hall said that he would write you his opinion of what I was best adapted to do.
>
> I wish very much to see and talk with you in regard to this matter. I desire to make this my lifework, and knowing the opportunity that will be afforded by your Survey, I sincerely hope that I may have a trial and then remain or not as my work may decide.
>
> I go to Trenton Fall the 4th inst. to work on my collection as Prof. Hall cannot pay for any work this summer as Museum funds are low.
>
> If you will be so kind as to let me know if there is any prospect for my working on the Survey, and if so when and where I can see you, you will greatly oblige me.[24]

Walcott left Albany and finished proofreading at Utica and the Rust farm; Jessie helped him sort out the Utica slate specimens described in his paper. Walcott had determined that he would put his collection in order, sale or no. There were occasional pauses for breaking rock along the brook, but mostly it was writing labels and pasting them to specimens. June slipped into July, with steady work on the collections. His Trenton fossils were recorded, but he still had work to do on the older material from Troy and St. John.

The two preprints (Walcott 1879b, 1879c) came out before June ended. One copy was inscribed to "Mrs. Cha's D. Walcott with love from her affectionate son Cha's *The stone gatherer*." Combined, they were the equivalent of a thesis from a university. Walcott had demonstrated that he could conduct independent research and bring it to fruition. He had considered both the biological aspects and physical geology of his subject. The seventeen-page paper on the relations of the Utica Shale—Walcott still called it a slate—presented correlations to Ohio and elsewhere in the Midwest that remain essentially unchanged today. "In these papers Mr. Walcott presents some interesting discussions, makes known important facts upon the subjects indicated." (White 1880, 257); Walcott had passed peer review.

As for the "Fossils of the Utica Slate,"

> It is not designed under the above title to present a detailed description of the various fossils found in the Utica slate formation but to give a list of those occurring in it with references to publications where descriptions of the species mentioned may be found; also descriptions of some new species not hitherto known in the formation, and a notice of the development, or metamorphosis as far as now known, of the characteristic trilobite *Triarthrus Becki.* (Walcott 1879c, 18)

This developmental series of the trilobite was based on a study by Barrande, and Walcott's work was only the second trilobite growth series to be described. It was on the cutting edge of science, and in 1884 in his *Annual Report,* Hall noted that his museum exhibited a growth series of *Triarthrus becki,* purchased from collector Charles Haskell.

A skilled worker without a place to practice his skill is a terrible waste. Walcott had no prospects whatsoever. There were no positions in New York and no teaching opportunities had ever been offered him, apart from an occasional Sunday school class. His one tangible asset, his collection, was not an item anyone would buy. He had been a widower for more than three years without any potential bride in the offing. His destiny seemed to be to become a farmer like William, a most gloomy prospect for the aspiring paleontologist.

Destiny took a hand. Late in June, King sent a telegram to Whitfield. "Would Charles Walcott make a promising assistant. Answer normally. Hotel Washington."[25] King had used the American Museum as his headquarters while the reports of the Fortieth Parallel Survey were being written and the two were well acquainted. Whatever Whitfield replied has been long lost, but it must have been a strong recommendation. Walcott's efforts to make peace and protect the insignificant and weak Robert Parr Whitfield from the great and mighty James Hall were more than repaid. There is a moral to be learned in this event.

On July 8 Walcott went to Utica. It was not an urgent trip; he had tea with Ed Hurlburt. "After called on Senator Conkling. He informed me I was appointed to the U. S. Geological Survey" (July 8, 1879). Suddenly, the world was different. He went to Albany and packed immediately, after talking to Hall and Gardner.

Walcott shipped his possessions to Trenton Falls, packed there, and said his goodbyes to the Rusts and to his blood relatives who were summering at Holland Patent. At 10:40 A.M. the train left for Utica and Niagara. "I regret leaving all my friends but my work necessitates it" (July 19, 1879). The sentiments may have been a little overdrawn, but this was a firm close to one chapter of his life and the opening of another, even more so than his move in 1871 from Utica to the Rust farm or from Trenton Falls to Albany in 1876.

When future trips brought Walcott to Albany, he almost always called on Hall. They exchanged letters when Hall needed support to purchase a collection or he thought one of his string of subsequent assistants had betrayed him. When Hall was in his 80s, he sold a substantial part of his collection to the University of Chicago and again created as much of a furor with the legislature as he had with his 1875 sale; Walcott came to his aid. Hall remained his irascible self until the end.

In western New York, the Genesee River flows north into Lake Ontario and cuts though Upper Devonian beds exposed in a series of magnificent gorges that constitute the heart of Letchworth State Park (Roseberry 1982, 47–57). In this setting, a plaque was dedicated in 1915 to Hall by some of his former associates. Walcott is one of the names listed on this tribute. In November of 1878, the professor had not kept his word to his assistant. Nevertheless, Walcott recognized all he had learned in Albany from James Hall and honored that memory.

4

A Grand Beginning: Riding into the Sunset with a Toehold on a Government Mule (1879–1880)

The lofty cliffs of the Colorado Plateau rise east of the desert country
with some of the most spectacular scenery on earth—the grandeur
and colors have to be seen to be believed. Great faults break the
Colorado Plateau into a staircase of lesser plateaus across southern
Utah and into northern Arizona.

Bill Weir, 1988

AFTER SPENDING SATURDAY in Buffalo, Walcott met Sumner Bodfish and
J. H. Renshawe, topographers of the newly formed U.S. Geological Survey.
Bodfish was an old western hand, having made topographic maps of the Colorado
Plateau for Major Powell. Monday morning, with Niagara Falls as a backdrop,
Bodfish administered the oath of office. Walcott was now a federal employee,
number twenty of the USGS, with the title of "geological assistant"; the first *Annual Report* of the Geological Survey lists him incorrectly as "Assistant Geologist," but the starting salary given of fifty dollars per month is correct. Formalities over, they headed west to Utah, a five-day train trip.

To the twenty-nine-year-old New Yorker, the great American West was a dramatic new experience without any breaking-in period, for as soon as the camping outfit was assembled, they left Salt Lake City. Fortunately, J. S. Newberry of
the Columbia University School of Mines was in the city, and he gave Walcott
a few pointers, being the "same kind philosophical man he was three years ago."
Not everyone in American geology had that view of Newberry. Walcott went
south on the Utah Southern Railroad, an experience so vivid that decades later
he recalled "sleeping on the floor of a freight car" (Walcott 1917, 112). The group
took a stage coach west to Beaver, Utah. Even using Trenton Falls as a standard,
Beaver could not be classified as a city.

Charles Doolittle Walcott, Paleontologist

After a few days of reorganization, the budding geologist mounted his mule and followed Bodfish south via Fremonts Pass to Bear Valley on the Kanab Plateau. "Its desert surface of small relief is divided midway by Kanab Creek, the only northern tributary which comes down from the high plateaus of Utah into the Grand Canyon. Even it can scarcely be said to do this, since its middle course in the Kanab Plateau is dry most of the year" (Fenneman 1931, 280–81). The Utah plateaus form a high country, which was dry and hot in August.

Daily mule rides were exhausting, but the scenery was dramatic. At Kanab, some seventy-five miles to the south, they established camp. Bodfish began topographic mapping, and Walcott measured rock thicknesses and collected fossils. It was not easy, and Walcott recorded: "From the past week of experience I think it will take me fully three months to complete the work assigned me & I would like four or five to do it in" (August 16, 1879). Unlike Albany, where Hall watched every action and kept changing priorities, the USGS expected a great deal of initiative from its employees. Near the end of August, Bodfish entrusted Walcott with three mules and Jerry Pickett to cook, and off he went into Sinks Valley on the east fork of Kanab Creek.

Captain Clarence E. Dutton, a decade older than Walcott, was in charge of investigations on the Southwest high plateaus, but he did not visit Walcott in the field. To incorporate observations of Major Powell—a major character in Walcott's future—and publish his own geologic discoveries, Dutton required topographic maps on which to plot the geologic strata. Bodfish was to work in the Grand Canyon District, and his young associate Renshawe set off to map the Unikaret Plateau. Dutton also sought better information on the thickness and age of the various rock units to the north and within the Grand Canyon:

> With these topographical parties a geological party was organized, under Mr. Charles C. [*sic*] Walcott, who was instructed to make a stratigraphic section from the summit of the Pink Cliffs, at the source of the Kanab, along it course through cañons to its juncture with the Colorado. This section embraces a nearly unbroken series of geological formations, from the Eocene Tertiary to the base of the Carboniferous, with unconformable Devonian and Silurian rocks below. It was the purpose of this work to establish a detailed section as a standard of comparison for various subordinate sections previously made in the adjacent country. This work was successfully accomplished. A good section was made, and valuable suites of fossils collected in several formations represented in the section. (Dutton 1880, 29)

In less technical terms, the lowly assistant geologist was expected, without further guidance, to round out details of the geology for the captain. The canyon of Kanab Creek provided a natural cut through the rocks exposing them, just as West Canada Creek had done at Trenton Falls, but on a vastly larger scale. Likewise, there were vertical faults to cause problems for the unwary; near Alton, Cretaceous rock are uplifted and younger Tertiary strata are downdropped. Walcott observed the faults and stayed out of geologic trouble.

He began at the summit of the Pink Cliffs in southern Utah, elevation eight thousand feet, on the drainage divide between the Great Salt Lake and the Colorado River. Measuring the vertical thicknesses as he went, he moved from the young rocks in the northern part of the plateau to ever older ones to the south. For practical purposes the rocks were flat-lying, and by measuring the vertical faces, one could obtain the thickness of each principal layer. In theory, this was no different than noting the *Asaphus* layer along West Canada Creek was two feet thick and below it was the three-inch *Ceraurus* layer. On the scale of the West, the operation was like an ant determining the height of a room by starting at the second floor and measuring down each of the risers on an enormous staircase.

One of the world's best places to demonstrate that axiom of geology, the law of superposition, is the Colorado Plateau. Unlike West Canada Creek, for mile after mile there appeared to be no lateral change in each layer, so the thicknesses measured in one place could be transferred to another. Dutton was particularly interested in erosion of the region, and the thickness of the rocks measured to the north would give an indication of how much strata had been stripped away from the rim of the Grand Canyon.

Captain Dutton was a noteworthy polymath (Pyne 1983). He fell under the spell of Powell, who arranged for him to start an entirely new career as a geologist in May 1875. He remained effectively a civilian until September 1890, setting an army record for length of detached service. In addition to his work in the plateau country, he made impressive contributions to the study of volcanos and earthquakes and was one of the premier geologists of his time. He had a romantic, literary style unique in U.S. government publications. For example, two of his shorter sentences on the Grand Canyon are: "A little, and only a little, less impressive than the great wall across the chasm are the buttes upon this side. And such buttes!" (Dutton 1882, 146). The Grand Canyon had a mystic effect on many who visited it.

Charles Doolittle Walcott, Paleontologist

Walcott's horizons expanded both metaphorically and practically. Not only could one see farther in the great vistas of western America, but desert outcrops were not masked by vegetation and individual features of the various rock units could be observed. Geologically, his horizon also expanded in the vertical sense. Except near the Colorado River, the Colorado Plateau rocks were far younger than any he had studied in New York. The geology exposed to his eye had challenge and opportunity written all over it. He was impressed with the wonder of the area and forever after had just a touch of the poet in his descriptions of the landscape.

Two months after his abrupt shift to the West, Walcott wrote friend Joseph Lintner, the entomologist in far distant Albany:

The stage ride to Beaver, 120 miles, was a tiresome affair as the road was through desert valleys nearly all the way. . . . the most tedious, disagreeable ride I ever experienced. At Beaver we met the pack train and since then mule power has carried me about. I travel every day from ten to fifteen miles and walk along the cliffs and steep places. I have one man with me to cook and look after the stock (four head). Camp as near my work as pasturage and water will permit. . . . My work in general is to construct a detailed section of the rocks of the Kanab Valley ranging in geologic time from middle Tertiary to Lower Carboniferous. An airline of the section extends from the Colorado in Arizona 60 miles north to Upper Kanab. Owing to the windings of the Canon and the traveling incident on hunting up good exposures it will require several hundred miles of travel to accomplish what is desired. I have nine weeks more to give to the section which is little enough.

The section I commence work on tomorrow encompasses over 2000 feet of strata, crosses the mooted boundary between the Tertiary and Cretaceous and carries more or less fossils. A month would work it fairly. I have a week as I devide [sic] my time in order to complete the section. The view from the summit of the White Cliffs is very fine but from the Pink Cliffs, nearly 10000 feet above the sea, the scene is one to be long remembered. To the south the great basin of the Colorado lays before you. The White and Vermillion Cliffs form great escarpments carved in a hundred forms by the numerous canons. Outlying buttes stand like islands off the shore while from around to the south west the blue line of the Kaibab Plateau in Buckskin mountains bounds the horizon and to the south the outline of the great canon of the Colorado is seen in shadowy outline. West the Pink Cliff terrace rises from the plain above the White Cliffs appearing in the morning sunlight as tho' a line of furnaces were in full blast as the pink rock carved in deep recesses and salient headlands is lighted by the strong light. To the north over the devide [*sic*] between the Great Salt Lake & Colorado basins the long line of light colored ledges running west of the Sevier river tell of the fresh water Tertiary limestones above which a hundred miles away two high volcanic peaks may be seen standing like sentinels guarding the northern line of cliffs. The Pink Cliff extends north on the opposite side of the valley until lost to view beneath an immense lava flow which covers it for fifty miles or more to the base of the Wasatch.

Thus far I have enjoyed my trip very much. It is accompanied by many privations but still it will be a good schooling for me in many ways. What the result of my work will [be] I cannot tell. Messers. Powell, Gilbert & Howell worked on the same range of rocks & their reports are published. It is putting me on a severe test to follow in their footsteps. I shall try to render a satisfactory report but it has taken time to get used to the mode of living, the method of doing work, etc.[1]

Walcott ended with the hope that Governor Robinson would be defeated by a Republican, definitely soured on the Democrats after the governor vetoed the appropriation for purchase of his collection. Generally, Hall's *Palaeontology* was financed better by Republican than Democratic administrations. In later years Walcott got on well with politicians in both parties, but he never hid his political affiliations.

Walcott's worries about lack of time to accomplish fieldwork in a proper manner were unwarranted, for he was a careful investigator. In 1892, T. W. Stanton, another USGS geologist worked in the same area and wrote: "Some years ago Mr. C. D. Walcott measured a section in Kanab valley and made a considerable collection of Cretaceous fossils there. . . . The measurements are all Mr. Walcott's" (Stanton 1893, 34). One could hardly expect published critical comments of a senior geologist by a new man, so Stanton's field notes are more significant: "Camped at A. L. Siler's ranch, Upper Kanab Valley, and examined Mr. Walcott's section from the base of the Jurassic to the middle of his Div. II of the Cretaceous. Nearly all the members of Mr. Walcott's section were easily recognized and it was therefore not necessary to make many measurements."[2]

Walcott's principal discovery, in Dutton's eyes, concerned the boundary between the strata of Permian age and the overlying Triassic rocks, to this day a problem for the geologist. It provided the opportunity for Dutton to expound on the methods of the field geologist; the captain, at times, was given to long paragraphs and only a portion of one is quoted here:

Charles Doolittle Walcott, Paleontologist

In the summer of 1879 Mr C. D. Walcott, of this survey, at length found some limestone bands near the base of Powell's Shinarump [Conglomerate], which seemed to establish pretty conclusively their Permian age. But the fossils so far discovered have only a small vertical range, and lie near the base of the group. Above them are many hundred feet of beds which yield no fossils at all. While some of them are unquestionably Permian, it still remains to find the horizon where the Permian ends and the Trias begins. The Trias is as destitute of fossils as the Permian, excepting, however, some which are useless in determining age. In cases like this the geologist finds himself in trouble. He is quite sure that he has beds of two distinct ages; and he must, for purposes of discussion, separate them somehow; if not by a natural and unmistakable dividing horizon, than by an arbitrary and provisional one, . . . he would examine the [Triassic] beds downwards and finding no fossils would pay attention to their lithological characters. Finding no marked difference in the beds, and finding a strict parallelism or "conformity" in the several members, he would infer that they were deposited under conditions which were substantially identical throughout the period of deposition. But if he at length reached a stratum of very different character, say, for instance, after passing down through a great series of sandstones and shales, he came to a heavy mass of limestone or a bulky conglomerate, he would have found at last a "break" in the continuity or homogeneity of the group. Here, at last, is something which he can use. . . . In this way Mr. Walcott seized upon the Shinarump conglomerate as a divisional stratum between the Trias and the Permian. But another perplexing question arose. To which of these two series should the conglomerate itself be assigned? . . . Mr. Walcott settled the question (provisionally, of course) in the following way. The summit of the lower series shows in many places that immediately after it was deposited it was slightly eroded, and the contact of the conglomerate shows an "unconformity by erosion." The contact of the conglomerate with the upper series shows no such unconformity. Now, an unconformity means to the geologist a break in the continuity of deposition, and in the absence of reasons to the contrary, and with no better divisional criterion at hand, it may be used to separate two series of beds. He therefore assigned the conglomerate to the Trias, and the beds below he placed in the Permian. (Dutton 1882a, 92–93)

In his larger report, Dutton (1882, 44) more succinctly praised Walcott's accomplishment of finding a thin band of Permian fossils, but still managed to use more than a page for a paragraph. Duttonian style is no longer a product of the Government Printing Office.

On October 3, geologist, cook, and mules headed south toward the mouth of Kanab Creek. The blistering heat of summer had given way to the raw, bone-chilling rain of fall. What with rock falls blocking the trail, and collecting and measuring en route, it was not until October 21 that they reached the Colorado River, where Walcott found a few trilobites below the great limestone cliffs of the Canyon. Walcott collected until he had sufficient trilobites and other fossils to document the "Primordial" age of these oldest rocks at river level. He then worked back up the canyon, gathering fossils along the way. Between the trilobites at the base near the Colorado River and the cherty limestones of the great shear vertical cliffs he found some fossils of an unexpected age.

A few more days, he "Worked in the beds above the Silurian & which I hope to prove are devonian. Boil broke & neck is better. Not satisfied with work done but as provisions are low must move up the Canon" (October 30, 1879). Devonian-age strata had not hitherto been noted in the Canyon country. Walcott kept observing the rocks as the men moved upstream; on occasion they had to unload the mules to get around rock falls blocking the trail. It was not until November 5 that Walcott reported back to Bodfish in Kanab. According to his notes the mules carried 700 Primordial fossils, 148 Silurian, and 66 Devonian fossils out of the canyon. Added to 500 Permian fossils from the rim limestone and 1,200 from younger strata, it was an impressive load. Much has been written of the horse in western America, but the mule has received scant credit. They are sturdier than horses, carry more relative to their size, and are smarter.

Even with what had been accomplished, King telegraphed Walcott that he could spend another month in the field, though this may be a reflection of the director's quirky sense of humor. For example, earlier King had written Bodfish regarding a young topographer who was sending information on Geological Survey activities to Chicago newspapers: "Should any member of your party have his life or health endangered by overflowings of literary matter, he must relieve himself by venting his lucidations on me in person. Our collection of kindling wood in the central office will thus be enriched."[3]

The snowstorms persuaded Walcott not to accept this kind offer from Director King. In mid-November, with snow two feet deep on the ground, Bodfish and party began six days of cold march to a railway. They thawed out in Salt Lake City; "It is good to get back to civilized quarters again" (November 21, 1879).

On November 28, after four months away, Walcott was back in Utica, and then his Trenton Falls home. He discussed politics with William and rearranged his possessions sent from Albany in July, what must have seemed like eons ago. Always the compulsive investigator, Walcott completed his paper on Trenton Limestone crinoids and started another short manuscript.

Charles Doolittle Walcott, Paleontologist

He and William looked over the farm, stored wagons for the winter, examined his new orchard, and reached a formal agreement pertaining to their fossil collecting business. For the sum of one hundred dollars, Walcott leased rights to the Gray's Brook trilobite quarry. "The said party of the first part reserves the right and privilege for himself, comrades and assistants to work said lands in search of fossils during his the party of the first part natural life."[4] Walcott knew the scientific value of the trilobites with limbs that he had first described in 1876 and which continued to preoccupy him. If being a federal geologist did not work out, this gave him something to fall back upon. William had the right to collect throughout his lifetime. Should Walcott die before William, William had exclusive rights to collect until his death; they were both shrewd businessmen.

Walcott settled down to grind several trilobites sections. However, he was very much at loose ends and, as Walcott phrased his actions at such times, he "fussed about." In mid-December he talked with Hall in Albany and conferred with several of the regents in regard to selling his collection. Christmas was spent in Brooklyn with family and, of course, talking to New York City geologists.

The last week of the year, Walcott was in Washington, D.C., slowing getting organized. He saw paleontologist C. A. White, who had worked for the Hayden Territorial Survey, and discussed the prospects of White describing the younger fossils Walcott collected around Kanab. Walcott visited the Smithsonian Institution and met Secretary Spencer Fullerton Baird (Rivinus and Youssef 1992). He summarized 1879:

> I am much more content than a year ago tonight. My position on the Survey is, as yet, an uncertain one but I hope to make it good by my work. A year ago I was out of employment & not as well as at present. As a whole the year has not been a poor one. If my home life was settled satisfactorily I should be quite at rest but that cannot be. Mainly owing to my own actions, twice I have thrown away my own best good. How I will not say. I welcome the incoming year as I hope to do well during its time. (December 31, 1879)

As was expected of him, Walcott began a formal report of fieldwork to supplement that written in the field to the director. He had measured a section of "13,300 feet of bedded rocks ranging in time from the Lower Tertiary to the Upper Primordial" (Walcott 1880, 221). Part of this report was published as a short paper discussing the mile thickness of rocks from the edge of the canyon to the mouth of Kanab Creek. The upper portion of this great pile was moderately well known; thirty years earlier Meek had identified Permian-age rocks in North America. The rock ledge forming the actual lip of the Grand Canyon is today called the Kaibab Limestone. Walcott had noted that the Permian was separated by slight erosion from the underlying Aubrey Group, which terminates below the Redwall Limestone, the greatest single cliff former in the canyon. He recognized three main divisions of Upper Aubrey, Lower Aubrey, and Red Wall, as had been seen and named by earlier geologists. Today the units have been extensively divided, for there are many more subtle unconformities and changes than Walcott had time to recognize, but the three main divisions are still obvious.

Lower in the section, closer to the river, Walcott added his new findings on the geologic history of the canyon. Below the Redwall Limestone, he had discovered a "plane of unconformity by erosion" and beds of Devonian age, locally varying considerably in their thickness, but never more than one hundred feet thick. He identified the fossils from their similarity to those collected during his fieldwork in central and western New York; he also recognized Devonian fish fragments in sandstone overlying the limestone. Throughout most of the Canyon, the Devonian has been eroded away and it was only by luck that Walcott found these patches, which were mostly preserved between hillocks cut into the underlying limestone on a older irregular erosion surface.

In the pre-Devonian rocks, geologically Walcott was still feeling his way. He recognized two divisions of the "Silurian." The underlying Tonto contained fossils which Walcott identified as "Primordial," the most ancient of fossiliferous rocks, with an archaic name that cropped up later in Walcott's career. A few hundred feet of limestone occurred above the Primordial, but there were not like rocks at Trenton Falls. "The missing Silurian groups may not have been deposited in this region, or, what is quite probable, their representatives were removed in the period of erosion that followed the close of the Silurian times, and has left traces of its action in the hollows and irregular surface over which the Devonian beds were spread" (Walcott 1880, 225). The rock strata along the walls of the canyon succeeded one another like the leaves of a storybook, but part of the chapter on the Silurian had been excised from the book, and for the Devonian only a few sentences remained.

While writing up his field observations, Walcott returned to studying trilobite limbs. In fact, after making calls on his colleagues on New Year's Day, he went home to grind yet another section. Work progressed reasonably well, and Walcott hoped "to get the paper ready this winter but fear I shall not be able to do so as I cannot keep that in my mind & attend to my work in the office" (January 16, 1880). His fear was groundless as the office work was going fairly well; Walcott found time to recount his efforts to Joseph Lintner in Albany:

Charles Doolittle Walcott, Paleontologist

I spent my time working up field notes and getting things in order to give the fossils a suitable reception and due attention. I am left to myself in all matters pertaining to my work and there is nothing to disturb the harmony which appears to reign throughout the building. It is a striking contrast to my experience elsewhere. I expect to be judged by the report I hand in as to my fitness for during future work on the Survey. Prof. King is a very pleasant gentlemen and impresses you very quickly with the force that is in him. Always quiet and under control he has a great reserve force to call upon in an emergency. Major Powell in whose division I am is unlike the Director but is still a man of mind, energy, and many instincts. Mr. Gilbert I have not yet met as he is still at the west. As yet have not been out much. I am pushing along my trilobite work & hope to have it in shape before I go west again.

I called on Prof. Baird and found him to be a very agreeable gentleman.

Prof. Barrande has sent me his valuable volumes on the Trilobites of Bohemia, "In recognition of original work done."[5]

Walcott told his older colleague of a considerable honor. Barrande was the preeminent paleontologist of the day in Europe, and perhaps of all time. During his lifetime he published more tomes than Hall, with far less controversy. For that savant to compliment Walcott on his investigations and especially his study of trilobites was indeed high praise. In particular: "This is gratifying to me as that work was done in some of the darkest years of my life" (January 2, 1880).

When Walcott finally met Gilbert, seven years his senior, he must have immediately impressed him. In a long newsy letter to colleague William Henry Holmes, Gilbert told of the developing organization and of the tenderfoot: "Walcott, a new man from Utica, spent the summer at Kanab & vicinity and made a splendid collection of fossils. He has established my Tonto as Primordial, discovered a distinct Devonian with ganoids [a type of fish], marked out a distinct Permian & found fishes in the Trias."[6]

Walcott's characterizations of King and Powell to Lintner were perceptive. Some background is appropriate to place these men and the Geological Survey in context. According to his friend Henry Adams, Clarence King was the finest example of the educated man, embodying all the best characteristics of the latter half of the nineteenth century; King's name appears repeatedly in Adams's autobiography (Adams 1946). He graduated from Yale University, Sheffield Scientific School, and went off to the West. He ended up in California as a volunteer with the state geological survey headed by J. D. Whitney; being in California, King also avoided service in the Civil War.

King conceived of the idea of a geologic survey of the land along the fortieth parallel from the Sierra Nevada to the Rocky Mountains; in 1867, the young man convinced the War Department to fund this ambitious scientific project (Wilkens 1988). He was an able geologist, an excellent organizer, and a fine judge of men. By 1872, his group completed fieldwork from the California-Nevada border to Boulder, Colorado, and thereafter prepared a series of volumes. King frequented Washington for a number of years while the final reports were being written. Mr. and Mrs. John Hay, Mr. and Mrs. Henry Adams, and Clarence King formed the "five of hearts," the epitome of young intellectual society in the nation's capitol (O'Toole 1990).

John Wesley Powell was about as different from Clarence King as one could imagine (Darrah 1951; Stegner 1954). He grew up in frontier Illinois with essentially no cultural advantages and no schooling after age twelve. He served in the Civil War and lost his right forearm at the battle of Shiloh, but returned to active duty. After the war, he went exploring in the West for two seasons, with token support from the army in the form of rations. In 1869, a few months after the golden spike linked East and West by rail, Powell traversed the last major unknown river in America, taking his boats from Green River, Wyoming, through the Grand Canyon of the Colorado River. He returned a national hero and was able to wrestle from Congress his own modest official territorial survey. For a few years it was under the supervision of the Smithsonian Institution, headed by Joseph Henry. The professor Baird mentioned in Walcott's letter was the second secretary of the Smithsonian, having joined the Institution in 1850, and in 1878 succeeded the great Joseph Henry. The names of two other western explorers who had played a part in the founding of the USGS do not appear in this letter. The first is that of Ferdinand Vandiveer Hayden (Manning 1967; Foster 1994). Hayden had been a volunteer for Hall before the Civil War, traveling west to collect with F. B. Meek, the first of Hall's assistants; as mentioned, Meek came to Washington in 1858 and roomed in the Smithsonian Castle for two decades. After service as a doctor in the Civil War, Hayden, with the help of Baird, received five thousand dollars in 1867 for a geological survey of Nebraska. He parlayed that modest beginning into a major western natural history survey which grew larger almost every year.

The second western explorer not mentioned is Lieutenant G. M. Wheeler of the U.S. Army. In 1869, the year Powell became a national hero, the War

Charles Doolittle Walcott, Paleontologist

Department organized its own western topographic survey under Wheeler (Bartlett 1962). Groups went over some of the same territory and increasingly strident arguments between the Hayden and Wheeler surveys led to the dissolution of both and the founding of the U.S. Geological Survey (Rabbitt 1979).

The new agency was a combination of unequal portions of the surveys organized and led by those four men. The only member from the Wheeler Survey was John McChesney. King wrote: "I have had my eye on that treasure and I believe the tenth commandment says nothing about coveting thy neighbors clerk. There are some geologists of the various surveys whom I do not desire, fearing to covet my neighbor's ass."[7]

Federal support of geology had an interesting political history, long before the four territorial survey were formed (Rabbitt 1979). During the late 1870s, Congress was induced to ask the National Academy of Sciences for advice on how to resolve the conflict between Hayden and Wheeler. Joseph Henry, president of the academy, had just died, and as a consequence O. C. Marsh of Yale, a friend of King, formed the committee to consider the congressional inquiry. The committee, and subsequently the academy, recommended founding a permanent civilian government bureau to investigate geology and replace the territorial surveys operating on a year-by-year basis (Manning 1967; Rabbitt 1979). The civilian scientists stacked the deck to cut out support for Lieutenant Wheeler in particular and the army in general.

On March 3, 1879, the U.S. Geological Survey was established by Congress and somehow has survived to become the sixth longest-lived bureau in the government. The survey was founded by an attachment to an appropriation bill, and it took adroit maneuvering behind the scenes and major lobbying by scientists to get even that (Rabbitt 1979). Who was to become the director became vital when President Rutherford Hayes signed the bill. In January, King moved to Washington to lobby for the bill and for the position. Through the winter, Hayden lobbied long and hard for the post and for the new agency, probably in that order, and was the most obvious candidate (Foster 1994). By 1879, Powell was more interested in ethnologic investigations of Indians of the Southwest than he was in geology. He considered Hayden so poor a scientist that he was as much against his getting the post as he was for King. Hayden directed his attention to ensuring that Powell was not director. Powell, by now a consummate Washington politician, pulled various strings. Partly as a consequence of this infighting, two weeks after the bill was signed King received the position both on the strength of his own accomplishments and strong support from prominent geologists, as well as a compromise dark horse candidate.

In less than two years, King resigned to become a consultant in the mining industry; Powell succeeded him. It is not clear whether Powell and King had an understanding on succession in the directorship, but that seems unlikely. One piece of evidence is in a letter from King to Director A. S. Bickmore of the American Museum, a year after the USGS was signed into law. "Powell has about decided not to go on with his geological work, but to turn it over to Captain Dutton, and to devote himself entirely to ethnology."[8] King was quite successful during his time on the Geological Survey, and there was no scientific reason which compelled him to leave. However, he was personally restless and wanted the potentially large sums of money available in mining geology. Powell was on the spot in Washington and could well have stepped into the vacuum rather than arranging a deal.

Historians of science have considered and reconsidered the origin and early days of the USGS; almost any interpretation of events can find scholarly support. It is sufficient for Walcott that the organization was formed and that King appointed him. As for the future of the two men upon whom Walcott commented, if one may mix scientific and administrative work and throw in a few moral judgments, King peaked early and then went into slow decline from 1881, whereas Powell grew in power and stature before crashing down in 1892.

The Geological Survey was mostly an alliance of King and Powell geologists, though a few of Hayden's scientists came into the bureau. Officially never noticed, there could not help but have been some tension between the Powell and the King men. Fortunately for Walcott, he was one of the few early employees who had no prior allegiance to the antecedent territorial surveys. His first work under Dutton on the Colorado Plateau was important to Gilbert, Powell's staunchest supporter and probably the best scientist within the Geological Survey (Davis 1926). However, his second field assignment was with Arnold Hague, a strong Fortieth Parallel man. Walcott remained friends with those in both camps and stayed out of office politics.

It was not clear whether the new agency was confined to public lands in the West or could also work in the East. To be on the safe side, King opted in 1879 to begin in the West, and he divided the survey into three western divisions. The Pacific Division was to be headquartered at San Francisco, the Great Basin Division at Salt Lake City, and the Rocky Mountain Division at Denver. A temporary fourth division of the Colorado Plateau was set up to complete the geologic investigations started by Powell. "Former national geological surveys have been conducted by means of annual campaigns to the far West. The corps, when driven from the field by the storms of late autumn have returned to Washington, there to wait the accidents of appropriations; and if provided for by Congress to take to the field at the close of the Congressional session" (King 1880, 6). By keeping geologists closer to the rocks, King could get more field time at less cost. Only the accident of being in Powell's division enabled Walcott to return to the East after his 1879 season.

King also became deeply involved with the 1880 census. There was a great need for a better understanding of the scope of the American mining industry. The staff of Census agents he recruited was far larger than that of the survey, and some USGS geologists had dual appointments; King threw himself into organizing and writing. The effort on the Tenth Census was all to the good, and it is still the most comprehensive survey of American mining ever undertaken. Fortunately, this peripheral effort bypassed Walcott, one of the few new employees who had no experience and it gave him more time for science.

With arrival of the western fossils, Walcott's real work started. Some of the genera and most of the species were not familiar to him; much of the necessary literature was scattered in various libraries around the city. For comparative material there were only a few fossil collections at the Smithsonian "Castle," mostly as a result of Meek's work on material sent in from earlier western expeditions, but it was painfully obvious that the national treasures in paleontology were skimpy. Four days after Walcott began unpacking his fossils, King asked if his report would be ready by March 1. "Shall endeavor to have the fossils in shape by that time but hardly anticipate getting much of a report ready" (January 20, 1880).

Walcott found a kindred soul in the Smithsonian Castle. He repeatedly visited William Healey Dall, who had foregone college to pursue geology and mollusks in Alaska. He showed Dall his trilobite sections and gleaned data from the living crustaceans Dall had described. He also, incidentally, went out of his way to convince Dall of the merit of Hall's efforts in paleontology. When he had first entered Hall's service, Walcott had written to Dall for advice on nomenclature so they knew of one another.

Walcott steadily studied the southwestern plateau fossils all day and his trilobite sections in the evenings. He found time to attend several plays, visit the Corcoran Art Galley to admire *The Grecian slave,* play an occasional game of cards, tour the Capitol, and partake of a presidential reception, so the city was not work all the time. Walcott continued to attend church regularly on Sunday, but in one of his errors of prediction, he decided that he would not be in Washington for long and would not affiliate with any particular Protestant church at this time.

Gilbert returned from the West, and Walcott shared an office with him, quite an unexpected plum. Early in February, Powell gave Walcott permission to publish his findings in the *American Journal of Science* and promised that no one would be given access to his data. This was a step forward, but a week later he received a jolt: "Dr. White startled my nerves by stating that he was to work up the Permian fossils & that I was to have the Silurian alone. A pretty kettle of fish he has prepared to cook but I shall have a word ere it is served" (February 12, 1880). Having been able to defend himself against the predations of Hall, any other paleontologist was no match for Mr. Walcott. Gilbert and Walcott went to the meeting of the Philosophical Society of Washington a few evenings later, where White spoke on the Permian Period in the Colorado Valley, "A quiet steal of some facts gathered by myself" (February 11, 1880).

Walcott hurried on with his study of the Permian fossils, but took the last week in February to travel to Trenton Falls: he paused long enough in New York City to report his progress to an enthusiastic King. Several of the regents visited Trenton Falls to examine his collection and again to discuss its purchase for the State Museum. After a few days in Utica, it was back to Washington. In the late stages of his study, Walcott finally had a long talk with Dutton as to the previous season's results. After several changes in plan over the winter, a trip to the West with Major Powell now seemed in the offing, but "Mr. Clarence King told me that I was not to go west at present. I am disappointed a little but more agreeably than otherwise. I can now put my notes in better order" (March 5, 1880).

On March 11, Walcott noted that he had completed his paper for the *American Journal of Science.* His title, "The Permian and other Paleozoic groups of the Kanab Valley, Arizona," indicates he won the battle with White as to whom had jurisdiction over the Permian fossils. Regardless of that squabble, the principal new data was lower in the section. Walcott's paper of four printed pages and a stratigraphic column appeared in September (Walcott 1880).

Meanwhile, in the evenings, Walcott progressed to describing his trilobite drawings. In one playful moment in his diary, they were referred to as his "Bytes." He continued to attend a few plays, stroll with young ladies, and shop around on Sundays through the various churches in Washington. "The days come & go in a most monotonous manner. I presume that I shall soon be started out but at present all is quiet. The N.Y. Legislature has my collection to pass judgment upon. If the money for its purchase is granted I shall [have] a load off my shoulders as the collection as it is a dead weight to carry" (March 20, 1880).

If his private New York collection was to be sold, it was time to firm up his future as a government geologist. Walcott spoke with Powell and Gilbert, emphasizing that he wanted to do general geological investigations and not just be a specialized paleontologist; the dust of western fieldwork had lodged in his throat. The next day, "After a consultation with Mr. King (Director of the Survey) I judge that I may now have some general geological work and also palaeontological investigation to pursue afterward. This was Mr. King's idea of what was best for me" (March 23, 1880). It was exactly what Walcott wanted. The following day he showed his trilobite manuscript to the director, who "thought that in a year or more it might be published in the Survey proceedings. The New York Legislature passed the supply bill yesterday" (March 24, 1880).

King's comment on publication in a year or two reflected the issue of publications this new agency might institute and how long it would take to start them, not the quality of Walcott's study. With the prospective sale of his private collection, Walcott could now see that his future lay with the USGS. When he left the end of the month for New York, it was with expectation of winding up his earlier activities in Albany, Trenton Falls, and Utica. A few months later, July 1, 1880, King promoted Walcott to a permanent position and doubled his salary.

Taking care of business investments for his mother required a few days. Commercial business done, Walcott could take up scientific business at the Rust farm, but disposition of his collection took on a wholly unexpected turn. After the death of Louis Agassiz in 1873, his son Alexander had taken charge of the Museum of Comparative Zoology. Son Alexander had done something that father Louis had never been able to do—he made a great deal of money out of scientific training. Alexander Agassiz turned failing copper mines in northern Michigan into substantial profit makers. Alexander wanted to build up the Cambridge museum as a monument to the memory of his father, an enterprise in which he succeeded (Winsor 1991). The current Professor Agassiz had heard that a fine collection of New York fossils was for sale. He inquired and Walcott responded from Trenton Falls:

> Your letter of Mch 23*d* was forwarded from Albany to Utica to Washington to Trenton Falls, where I found it last evening.
>   I left Albany a year ago and am now an ass't., on the U. S. G. Survey. The season of 1879 I spent in southern Utah & northern Arizona. Having 20 days

leave I came on home to look after my collection. I enclose some papers which will give you information of it. Gov. Robinson vetoed the bill in a very harsh manner and the Committee of the Regents have had the same item inserted in the supply bill that is now before the N. Y. Legislature.

Prof. Hall thinks that it will pass and that he will have the collection. From personal preference I had rather not have him obtain possession of it, and altho' I need the money, it will not be a disappointment if the appropriation is not passed. I had about given up the hope I had entertained of doing any work for the Cambridge Museum. I was strongly attached to Professor [Louis] Agassiz and owe to him the courage and enthusiasm that has enabled me to do what I have done in geology. I went to him discouraged and about to give up my work. I left after a week's association, with the intention of pursuing it under any and all circumstances. Three quarto plates, 50 figures, illustrating the anatomy of the trilobite, are lying on my table. These drawings and the text that is to accompany them is one of the results of your fathers kind and encouraging acts and words. I carry into my western work the same spirit and hope to add to what is already known of the Palaeozoic rocks west of the Great Plains.

If I carry out the plan of work mentioned by Mr. King I shall be occupied for several years to come. From the necessity of obtaining means to carry on my work here, in the past, I have not been able to do anything for the Museum and at present, I cannot assist in the filling up of the gaps in the collections. I wish that I was free to obtain the material and then assist in working it up and regret that I cannot do so at present.

The copy I enclose of the Governor's veto etc is the only one I have so I will request its return as I wish to keep it. I send you this that you may know what the collection is, and, in case Prof Hall does not get it, some arrangement may be made in the future for its going to Cambridge.[9]

The business part of the letter may appear a bit strange, but recall there was no significant paleontological collection in Washington. The Museum of Comparative Zoology was at least a theoretical possibility as a place where a paleontologist might find work, and Walcott was cultivating it by holding out the possibility of building their collection, quite apart from any sale of his own fossils. Walcott may have thought he could manipulate Agassiz a bit, for the same day he wrote that letter, he recorded in his diary: "I wrote Alex. Agassiz respecting my collection. I hope that it may go to the Cambridge Museum if it fails to go to Albany this winter. I would prefer to have it go to Cambridge & remain under my control" (April 4, 1880).

With that out of the way Walcott delved seriously into the trilobite sections: "I now think that the Trilobite's leg is homological with the leg of the lobster (ambulatory). The little arm that has troubled me so much being the epipodite & the leg the endopodite the exopodite not being developed. This point aids me materially & and clears away several doubtful points in my own mind" (April 7, 1880). This may not sound like much to the average person or even to the average paleontologist, but it was insightful on the mode of construction of trilobite legs, and Walcott forged ahead rapidly toward completion of his manuscript.

Putting finishing touches on this paper and preparing restorations of how a trilobite might have appeared in life was hard work. However, progress was so good that Walcott wrote King requesting additional leave to complete the study. He labored onward and in a few weeks, "Completed my present plan of work on the trilobite sections and fussed about getting ready to move out tomorrow. Spent two or three hours on the brook breaking up rock. I find I am restless as soon as my work is up in order and wish to move on" (April 23, 1880). Therein is perhaps one of the clues to Walcott's success. He could not pause, but was driven to move immediately from one completed project to another.

Hall wrote that the appropriation was certain. Walcott proceeded to pack up part of his collection. He broke more rocks looking for trilobites, visited Lura's grave, and helped with farm chores. Alexander Agassiz had written again and it was time to reply:

> I have delayed answering your last letter as I wished to ascertain if the appropriation was passed at Albany. The bill is now in the Senate committe [*sic*] & will not be finally settled under two weeks or more.
>
> I shall report at Washington the 5*th* inst & then, probably, go west soon. I have packed 8 barrels and 21 boxes of fossils, leaving unpacked 3000 or more specimens. These are in my cases & and I shall not pack them unless the collection is sold.
>
> The paper I have prepared will fill about 30 pp. quarto & 3 plates of illustrations. It refers to the trilobite as I have worked its structure out by cutting section. I had spoken to Mr. King about publishing before hearing from you and it may be published in connection with the work of the Survey.[10]

Walcott left the Rust farm for the South. He traveled via New Haven to spend two hours with James Dwight Dana, the doyen of American geology, James Hall notwithstanding. Dana was likewise the editor of the *American Journal of Science,* and Walcott probably talked about his Grand Canyon paper. In addition, Dana knew fossils and had described living crustaceans as part of his labors for the Wilkes Exploring Expedition he had participated in forty years earlier.

Walcott also consulted with two other Yale zoologists about trilobite limbs and rounded off a busy day dining with Marsh, the vertebrate paleontologist. He arrived at the USGS office May 5 to find all was quiet and he might as well have stayed away. Congress was debating whether the USGS should be permitted to work in the East, and until that was clarified, much of the future was uncertain.

The day Walcott arrived in Washington he wrote Agassiz: "I was at New Haven yesterday & saw Prof. Dana, Marsh, Verrill and Smith with regard to my paper on the trilobite. They all said that I had best sent the paper to you and not wait a year or two for publication here. I came directly on and saw Mr. King this A.M. He said that he had no objections to my sending it to Cambridge and though well of it."[11] Walcott concluded by noting, first, that the New York appropriations bill was still pending, and second, that he would try to prepare a set of trilobite sections for the Museum of Comparative Zoology.

There being nothing happening at the moment directly related to his western work, Walcott went back to rewriting the section on affinities of the trilobite. In the midst of this, "Received a telegram from H.D. Cunningham stating that the item for my collection had been dropped from the N. Y. supply bill. If it remains out so be it. To me it may prove of ultimate advantage" (May 8, 1880). Walcott shrugged it off, for Agassiz had written again; he wanted both the collection and the trilobite paper.

By May 28 the manuscript was supposedly done, and even though Walcott wrote a letter transmitting it, he kept tinkering with various sentences through June. "The classification used in the section on the affinities of the Trilobite is the result of much study on my own part and I have also gone over it with Messrs. Verrill, Smith and Gill. They all agree that Limulus and its allies cannot be placed in the class Crustacea."[12] Walcott had consulted the experts and though this reads like gibberish in Latin and Greek, it made sense to Agassiz.

Between bouts with the manuscript, Walcott was pursuing a variety of Washington interests to rest his mind, reading at the Congressional Library on western geology, talking to Smithsonian specialists about crustaceans and trilobites, attending meetings, and socializing. Toward the end of May, he heard that the New York Legislature had put money for his collection back in the bill and passed this information along to Agassiz. By now Walcott must have had affinities for a yo-yo, what with the up and down motion of the legislature. A point that emerges from the correspondence is that Walcott and Agassiz viewed his trilobite manuscript as independent and unrelated to the sale.

Congress had still not clarified where the Geological Survey was authorized to investigate, delaying any western trip, so the first of June saw Walcott back in Utica and then at Rust farm for a barn raising. One might have expected he would have gone to Albany to lobby for the collection appropriation; perhaps he knew deep down that this was a lost cause. Walcott continued to pack his collection, though he decided not the nail the boxes shut until the sale was consummated. The matter was finally resolved on June 9 when he heard that Governor Cornell had vetoed the bill; so much for the state of New York. The next day he wrote Agassiz:

> I have been patiently waiting for six weeks to learn the fate of the item to purchase my collection. Prof. Hall wrote me a week ago that there was no doubt but that he would obtain it. Last evenings paper states that the Governor vetoed most of the Supply Bill, the item of $4,000 among others so Prof. H. will lose it unless he buys it personally.
>
> Owing to Prof. Hall's assurances I packed the collection & now have 9 barrels and 32 boxes ready to ship. As you requested I let you know at once the result from Albany. Have not heard from Prof. H.
>
> Owing to delay at Washington I have been up here a week & hope to remain ten days longer altho subject to orders at any moment.
>
> As to the collection, from the statements I made to the committee I cannot consistently put the price less than $4000. I would prefer to have the collection at Cambridge than anywhere else and would like to arrange to have it go there. I would pay the expense of transportation and add a fine lot of crinoids that never have been included in it. They are from the Trenton limestone but not in this vicinity. Would also spend a month or more next winter if Mr. King would permit in working on the collection.
>
> I enclose a statement that I gave to the governor. Personal feelings I think caused the veto. Prof. H. has many enemies and they have endeavored to defeat his plans many times."[13]

Hall provided his view of these events in Albany:

> During the years 1879 and 1880, special communications were made by the Regents regarding an important collection of fossils, chiefly of the Trenton limestone, belonging to Mr. C. D. Walcott, of Trenton Falls. In 1879, the committee on the State Museum recommended the purchase of the collection, and the legislature made the necessary appropriation ($4,000) for that purpose. This appropriation was vetoed by the Governor, and the collection remained in the hands of the owner. In 1880 the subject was again brought before the Board of Regents, who appointed a special committee to examine the collection and report. The committee made their examination and recommended the purchase, and the Legislature again appropriated the re-

quired sum. The appropriation was a second time vetoed, by the Governor; and the collection was sold elsewhere and lost to the State Museum for ever. It is not my business to discuss the subject in this place; but it is necessary to record the facts, in order that the Museum and its Trustees may be vindicated in the future, as having discharged their duties to the institution and to the sciences which it represents. (Hall 1881, 9)

Hall never lifted a finger in 1879 to help with the appropriation, and it is uncertain how much effort he put forth during the 1880 session. There is more than a touch of irony in the veto by Governor Cornell of the appropriation. After twelve years of anguish and procrastination, Hall had finally published another volume of the *Palaeontology of New York* in December 1879. Volume 5, part 2 (which preceded part 1) was dedicated to Lucius Robinson, who vetoed the purchase in 1879! One would think that Hall might have had the political sense to delay publication a few days until 1880 and dedicate the volume to the new governor. Once Hall produced this volume and finally broke his own self-imposed delay, subsequent volumes of the *Palaeontology* appeared fairly rapidly and Hall's reputation as a major figure in science was assured.

Meanwhile, Agassiz wasted no time. He wrote and he telegraphed, but Walcott had gone to New York Mills for a family wedding. As soon as Walcott was back in Trenton Falls, he replied:

Prof. Hall made no arrangement for the exigency that arose & he has lost the collection. I bear him neither love, malice or fear. I endeavored to serve him faithfully & he failed to carry out his agreements. In the present matter I have acted fairly as the Secty's letter shows.

I will send the collection to the station tomorrow or by Friday P.M. As it is bulky & heavy will send as freight. The boxes are numbered and a list will accompany them that you may be directed in unpacking. I had not tho't of its going to Cambridge & it is packed with reference to having an experienced person open it. As Prof. H. wished to work up much of the material from the Trenton the bryozoans are still buried & protected by the adhering sediment. It was in relation to working this material that I wished to spend time in Cambridge next winter. I will designate a number of boxes etc that contain the finer portions of the collection & unless you wish to see it all out at once would suggest that the other boxes be left until I can get to them. Great care will be necessary in unpacking & subsequent treatment & handling of all portions of the collection

As to payments I have no objection to accepting your proposition except that if is convenient would rather have the last payment made by July 1st 1881. This I leave to you to arrange as you think best & can do. I wish the money to invest that I may derive some income for it & use it in connection with my work. I have been sorely tempted at times to go into business but as yet have not given up my original plan of work & shall not if all well with the U. S. Survey.[14]

The agreed payment was one thousand dollars down and three one-thousand-dollar notes, payable at six-month intervals; the collection was sent off to Cambridge before this last little detail was resolved, but they were both honorable men. Walcott had been an enthusiastic collector since his 1873 sale; in the seventy-two hundred pounds of fossils, Walcott counted 11,857 specimens, each with its own locality label affixed, plus a few hundred more not recorded or labeled:

> Great care will be necessary in unpacking the barrels. The long slabs are packed tightly & will be injured if carelessly taken out. If the collection is placed in drawers, out of the *dust* I will endeavor at the first opportunity after my return from the west to supply any missing labels of locality & formation as well as other information. I wish now that I had a year to give to it & other N. Y. collections in the Museum. I sent by express today the paper on the Trilobite.[15]

It would be almost two years before Walcott had the opportunity to keep this promise.

It is extremely difficult to calculate the price of these specimens in today's market, quite apart from changes in the value of the American dollar over the decades. Natural history specimens are not like paintings in that they are seldom unique, but they do have some similarities in being increasingly rare. No one in the museum field dwells on buying collections. If scientists had their way, everything would be donated to a museum. The market is restricted and opportunities for sales are few, but when an institution wants material of a particular kind, it may pay well. Add to this the observation that college laboratory supply houses now sell certain fossils which are abundant for five dollars each; at four thousand dollars for nearly twelve thousand specimens, Walcott's were one-twentieth that price.

On the other side of the ledger, considering the actual collecting, preparing, and labeling, Walcott must have had at least a full year's involvement in these specimens. As noted earlier, he had spent one thousand dollars to buy part of this lode from his brother-in-law. He also did some traveling to collect and paid shipping costs for fossils that he had exchanged with other collectors. Even valuing his time at nothing, the four thousand dollars was far from pure profit. Reasonable conclusions are that Walcott did not overcharge and that the Museum of Comparative Zoology received remarkably good value for the money.

Sale of the collection was a time of mixed emotion. Walcott wrote to his entomological friend at the State Museum in Albany:

> You may have learned thro' Prof. Hall of the disposition of my collection. I feel quite lonely here without it as for years it has been my chief care and *object* of *attention*. As I wrote a friend last week I feel quite deserted and hardly know which to do, obtain another collection or get some foolish damsel to accept & to take its place in my heart & life. You will see that my nonsensical vein has not yet run out.
>
> A telegram came last week stating that my instructions would soon be sent on and that I was to go to Central Nevada. I know something of what is to be done there and anticipate a severe test of my powers of doing field work. I had tho't of going back to the *cañons* but a change has been decided on since I left Washington.[16]

The sentiment concerning his collection was sincere. To give another analogy, it is as though a man bought an antique car for restoration and spent six years in the repairing, fine tuning, polishing, and painting associated with this, eventually to be offered a price too good to turn down. Still, unlike one who sells to an unknown party just for money, Walcott's loss was partially tempered with relief that the fossils were in a safe place and he probably could study them later. Regardless of Albany's loss, and Walcott's mixed feelings, his financial condition was substantially better; after all, six hundred dollars or even twelve hundred dollars a year is not a overwhelming salary. With a metaphorical sigh of relief, Walcott relaxed. He wrote a letter of strong affection to a young lady, read novels, admired his now grown-up eighteen-year-old niece by marriage Jessie, played croquet, helped with chores, dug a ditch for a water pipe to the new barn, and observed that Miss Cleveland was a "clear headed intellectual woman." Ever since Lura's death, Walcott mentioned marrying again, yet he always found an excuse not to become to deeply involved with any young lady.

Meanwhile, Walcott continued to break up rock by the brook. Even with assurance of another trip west, he was unsettled: "I am as yet undecided as to getting another collection. The weight of circumstances is most decidedly against it but my position may change so that it will be best for me to collect another" (June 29, 1880). Obviously, the federal survey was still viewed as an uncertain proposition, whereas another sale of fossils could be counted on for future income.

Charles Doolittle Walcott, Paleontologist

Lintner finally received a promotion at the New York State Museum and Walcott congratulated him. "I would like to talk over the events of the past winter with you but at present I do not think that I can visit Albany as my instructions are in New York with the geologist I am to go west with & he may be on at any day."[17] Memory was fading of the harsh times with Hall and was being replaced by nostalgia. To give another analogy, it was like the graduate who was very nearly failed by his professor looking back on his formative years with pleasure. Even with the veil of nostalgia, Walcott always was able to distinguish between Hall the avaricious man and Hall the scientist.

On July 6, Clarence King ordered Walcott to meet Arnold Hague in New York City. Walcott traveled south immediately only to be told that he was not wanted for at least a week; back to Trenton Falls went Walcott. After haying, he spent time at nearby Holland Patent, digging out Utica Shale fossils with Charlie Haskell. He and William took a busman's holiday, leaving on the 5:30 A.M. train to Sugar Mill to collect Trenton fossils. All such interludes must end, and on July 17, Walcott met Arnold Hague and J. P. Iddings in Syracuse for the start of another facet in his career, with fieldwork at Eureka, Nevada.

Before moving to the next phase of Walcott's life, it may be of use to reconsider the New York years as regards fossils and especially trilobite appendages. His metamorphosis from commercial collector to geologic investigator was a major step, for a fundamentally different mindset was involved. No matter how much one is enamored with an object, a professional collector is prepared to part with it for money. The scientist cannot place monetary value on his object, for it is priceless. Even though he may have found the object, it does not belong to him, for by publishing he makes the object public property. A scientific paper and a patent on an invention have little in common.

Quite apart from any lack of formal training, this change in outlook was a formidable hurdle for Walcott to overcome. After 1880, he no longer trafficked in specimens; he did purchase a few fossils, but they were for research. Later he hired professional collectors and arranged exchanges; invariably this was in connection with increasing and improving holdings of the National Museum, never with a personal collection. Today no paleontologist on the USGS payroll has a private collection. The kind of activity involved with private collecting now is simply not done by a federal scientist; past practices have changed.

In Albany, Walcott had a good grounding in the importance of publication. The "type specimen" of a described species was far more valuable than any other specimen of the same kind, though this was not monetary value. Besides learning the fundamental importance of publishing and mechanics of the process,

Walcott absorbed much of ethics and the way science is sometimes really done. He observed how one person might become involved in the work of another and claim it for his own, and he learned how to defend his own scientific frontiers. The trilobite work was not by Hall, or Hall's protégé, but was always the brainchild of C. D. Walcott. Walcott respected Hall's accomplishments and even, with distance between them, admired the old man himself, but Hall was not his mentor in scientific matters.

Walcott had learned a great deal of practical value about fossils while he was in Albany and had made good use of his time in Hall's library and collections. He could look at fossils on the western outcrops and determine where he was in the stratigraphic section. He knew far more about the faunas of older rocks than younger ones, but he was not at a loss when he went into upper strata of the plateau country. His determination of Permian fossils at the rim of the Grand Canyon when he had never seen any previously in the field was no mean feat. His discovery of Devonian rocks was impressive scientifically.

There are fundamentally two different ways to approach the study of fossils, but they almost invariably overlap and mix with a third aspect. The first is that of stratigraphic paleontology, and Walcott's identification of Devonian strata in the Grand Canyon was an excellent example. Nowadays, it is dignified as biostratigraphy, though the name change means little. One learns the fossils in a standard geologic area and compares those found locally to that standard. Examining the contained fossils is the quickest and easiest way to tell the relative age of sedimentary rocks. Walcott studied the rocks in the West Canada Creek gorge and then went to outlying isolated outcrops of the Trenton Limestone. He could place these in the proper stratigraphic position because he knew the complete sequence in the gorge and identified similarities in these isolated fossil assemblages.

In teaching about fossils, many college courses emphasize the second approach to the subject, that of paleobiology. Most fossils which can be seen without a microscope are marine invertebrates, organisms that few people encounter in day-to-day life. Paleontologists learn, for example, how to differentiate the two valves of a brachiopod shell from a bivalved clam. Then one must learn the characteristic morphology of brachiopods and its terminology. Next, one can search the literature to see if this form has been named and if so from where it has been reported.

A major aspect of paleobiology is systematic classification, that is, the relationship of fossils to living organisms. After species and genera are distinguished, there is a natural tendency to place these into larger groupings, as a generalization of sorts. Almost everyone instinctively recognizes the "cat" family. Some few of the public may wonder whether "cats" are more closely related to the "bear" family or the "dog" family. Cat enthusiasts see the relationship of *Smilodon,* the extinct sabre-toothed tiger, to living pussycats. The relationships of most fossils, both to living forms and to other fossils, is seldom so obvious. Arthropods have a hard carapace or covering, composed of several pieces. A lobster and a sow bug are both living arthropods, and a trilobite has features vaguely similar to each. Are all three forms related as being arthropods, and if so what is their interrelationship?

The paleobiologic approach considers the fossil as a former living organism; its geologic age is secondary. Many fossil clams, again for example, look like living clams, but most fossil brachiopods do not closely resemble the few surviving forms. Typically, clams live in the sediment with the valves at a right angle to the bottom, but brachiopods live on the bottom with one valve up and one down. A proper paleobiologic question is which valve of a particular Trenton Limestone brachiopod was on the bottom. Another is whether trilobites had legs, and if so how did they function? Such paleontologic questions fall within the intellectual approach known as functional morphology, often involving speculation about soft parts which have long since disappeared. More to the point as an example, arthropods undergo ecdysis, that is they grow by molting an old carapace and replacing it with a larger one. If trilobites are arthropods and if trilobites molt, is a particular fossil a molted exoskelton or a killed organism? If one deals with a fossil lobster, one can at least look at a living one for reasonably close comparisons. In dealing with completely extinct forms, such as trilobites, answers are never certain and even reasonable speculation is hard to come by.

Functional morphology grades into a third aspect of ecology, or rather paleoecology, for obviously fossils are not now alive. Ever since it was first recognized that fossils were former living organisms and not works of the devil hidden inside the rocks, there has been speculation as to where they lived. Leonardo di Vinci deduced that present-day mountains were formed from rocks at sea level because they contained marine shells; that is a lot of deduction, but it has held up for four centuries. Lobsters live in the sea and pill bugs live on land. Do trilobites have living descendants? If some of these descendants live on land and others in the sea, how does one determine where trilobites lived? Did trilobites live in the water or on the bottom? Was the carapace up or down relative to the bottom?

The paleontologist faces many problems. Why are some kinds of fossils predominate in one type of rock, such as the *Ceraurus* layer at Gray's Brook, and other kinds in another type of rock? Why were trilobite legs preserved only at the brook and not at any other locality where the same layer can be observed? Trilobites commonly show several pieces, but if one consistently finds only single type, such as a head, is it because this particular fossil had only one hard part or is it because pieces of other shapes were swept away differentially by currents? If one finds only heads at one place in a particular bed and only tails at another locality in the same bed, are these parts of the same animal? Why are most trilobites flat, but some are rolled up? There are a multiplicity of questions to ask when examining a fossil, quite apart from the two basic ones of what is it and what is its age.

Walcott's paper in the *Bulletin* of the Museum of Comparative Zoology interpreted the Trenton Falls trilobites in terms of ecology and biology, with attendant classification. The ages of the two species he studied were well known and that aspect of the fossils was hardly mentioned. This publication of thirty-three pages and six handsome lithographic plates is a paragon of paleobiology.

Prevailing concepts always strongly influence what is seen and how it is interpreted. In the 1840s, an eminent German geologist, H. Burmeister, surmised that trilobites swam with the carapace downward, and this became the accepted interpretation of life habit. In one of his first short papers, Walcott observed that at his locality most specimens occurred with the carapace downward in the rock, thereby presumably confirming this view. He maintained that opinion in his 1879 note.

Additional data, in theory, causes a scientist to reevaluate past statements and confirm or modify them. Walcott (1881, 213) discussed a similar British observation and concurred with that author that the carapace-down occurrence was better interpreted as a postmortem effect. If these animals swam, there was no reason to assume it was with the carapace down. Walcott indicated what transpired to change his opinion:

> The prosecution of the investigation during 1874 gave the material from which the notes on the inferior or ventral surface of the dorsal shell of *Ceraurus pleurexanthemus* was written. Judging from the dorsal shell alone the views of Burmeister were given as best explaining the facts then known.
>
> The following year thin sections were cut from both Lower and Upper Silurian rocks. . . . In the upper portion of the Trenton limestone at Trenton Falls, N. Y., a thin layer of dark, bluish-gray, fine-grained, partially impure

limestone was found, that contained many perfectly preserved trilobite remains. On examination of these by cutting sections, it was ascertained that other parts of the animal besides the dorsal shell and hypostoma were present. Specimens from all other localities and formations failed to afford more than the strong dorsal shell and hypostoma. (Walcott 1881, 191)

It would be interesting to know how many localities Walcott tested and how many sections were made before he settled on the *Ceraurus* layer at Trenton Falls. Many of the *Ceraurus* were partially curved or flexed, and some of the *Calymene* he and William collected were rolled up, cephalon covering pygidium. One of the reasons a sow bug resembles a trilobite is that it too can roll up. Enrolled trilobites have been known for centuries, and were, and are, highly prized by collectors. No one before had recorded cutting an enrolled specimen to see if appendages were preserved in it, let alone cutting one that was only partially curved. Walcott recognized the unique nature of the preservation in that one thin rock layer and had the inspiration to employ a novel method to exploit it scientifically.

Having discovered trilobite appendages, Walcott then interpreted them as ambulatory, meaning the trilobites spent much of their time walking on the bottom. Crabs of today swim, but also walk on the bottom. Some crabs follow only one life style and some follow the other, but for many, life habit is an admixture of the two. Most fish swim, but a flounder is flattened to spend most its life on the bottom. Walcott made a fundamental change in the way paleontologists would now think about the way trilobites lived. They were more flounderlike, if one can use analogy to make a point.

Even though Walcott did not know quite what he was involved in when he began, the first step was to obtain material:

> The two species of Trilobites, *Calymene senaria* and *Ceraurus pleurexanthemus,* from which nine tenths of the sections were obtained, are the two most abundant forms in the Trenton limestone of Central and Northern New York. Their remains occur, usually in a fragmentary condition, in nearly every layer of the limestone, and range, above, into the Hudson River group, and below, into the Black River limestone. Their geographic distribution is also very extended, as they occur in the Canadas and at nearly all the exposures of the Trenton group in the Northern United States, as far west as the Mississippi River. The *Calymene* is much more abundant at the West, but at the locality from which the specimens of *Ceraurus* were obtained for section cutting the latter far exceeds it in numbers. The special interest attached to

the occurrence of both species at Trenton Falls, as well as of several other species, is their very perfect state of preservation in a thin bed of limestone outcropping in a small ravine half a mile south of Trenton Falls cañon or gorge. An examination of the same horizon that this bed occupies, for several miles along the cañon, which is but half a mile away at one point, failed to give a single entire Trilobite, and the fragmentary remains are rare. Both above and below they are found, but not with any more of the animal preserved other that the dorsal shell and hypostome. This shows that in the vicinity of the outcrop in the small ravine there is a limited area, which was surrounded by conditions that did not prevail elsewhere in that region, as the topography of the adjacent country permits of a close examination of the strata, and outcrops of the same horizon were examined in all directions in the vicinity for the purpose of finding other prolific localities. (Walcott 1881, 212)

Many hours in the field were needed to demonstrate that the outcrop on the Rust farm was uniquely important. No wonder Walcott was willing to pay William Rust for a lifetime right to return for additional collections.

Walcott interpreted this special outcrop in detail:

The layer of limestone on which the prolific layer rests is thick, and formed of the comminuted remains of Crinoids, Trilobites, etc., indicating the action of shore waves and a distributing current. A change supervened, and this surface was depressed beneath deeper water, or a barrier reef was formed, affording a quiet habitat in which flourished Bryozoans, Echinoderms, Brachipods, Pteropods, Entomostracans, and Trilobites. The remains of all these are now found, in a perfect state of preservation, attached to the lower surface of the superjacent layer of limestone. This appears to have been a deposit of fine calcareous mud or ooze, deposited on the surface of the subjacent stratum, so as to form when solidified a layer from one half to two inches in thickness. (Walcott 1881, 212)

The wording is a little simple for present-day paleoecological analysis, but the information and interpretation can hardly be improved upon.

He went on to observe that bending of several closely spaced laminations in the rock suggested that after the trilobites had flexed or rolled up, they sank partway into the soft mud and were then covered by more sediment. From the presence of viscera and appendages seen in the sections, Walcott deduced that these specimens were the actual animals, not molted carapaces. Temporary foul water conditions on the bottom may have caused the trilobites to roll and then be killed. That appendages are present demonstrates the concept of killed and preserved animals.

Charles Doolittle Walcott, Paleontologist

The significance of Walcott's find is best understood in historic perspective. There had been scattered reports of trilobite appendages, but they were generally discounted. As late as 1870, Billings described material from Canada which seemed to show the presence of the illusive ambulatory legs; Dana disputed this interpretation. A specialist in the British Museum, Henry Woodward, supported Billings; Dana again countered Billings's discovery, based in part on the contour of the dorsal interior. "In fact, legs of such proportions do not belong in the class of Crustaceans. Moreover the shell (if it is the shell of a leg instead of a calcified arch) is relatively thick, and this makes matters worse" (Dana 1872, 221).

In regard to his earlier publications, Walcott wrote: "The discoveries of the writer have been received in about the same manner. So many times the discovery of the feet and other organs have been announced, and subsequently proved to have been based on insufficient evidence, or no evidence at all, that naturalists were disinclined to accept any statement that such discoveries had been made, with absolute proof of their genuineness" (Walcott 1881, 197). When Walcott came to New Haven in 1880 with a manuscript resolving the issue of the presence of walking limbs and went on to elucidate fine details of these appendages, no wonder Dana and his zoological cronies were excited.

One of the shibboleths in American culture is that genius is 1 percent inspiration and 99 percent perspiration. Consider what Walcott contributed in that aspect:

> The soil and rock to a depth of nine feet was removed, over a large area, to obtain the fossils scattered through the thin layer of limestone. From this area there were taken over 3,500 entire Trilobites; 2,200 were in a condition to warrant sections being made of them. Comparatively few had the appendages well preserved and now there are but 270 sections affording more or less satisfactory evidence of their preservation. It was very difficult, after obtaining the material, to cut a section so as to show what might be preserved within the dorsal shell. With a knowledge of the character and position of the appendages, as they were buried in the rock, sections might have been cut at once revealing all that was desired to prove the knowledge to others. But the true conditions were more in this wise. An Arthropod of which little was known as to the structure of its appendages was buried originally in a soft, calcareous mud or ooze. It was subjected to maceration and disintegration by the actions of the water, and also to the attacks of the small scavengers of the time (*Leperditiae*), antecedent to its burial in, and the consolidation of, its muddy bed. In the process of mineralization, calcite replaced the viscera and contents of the appendages, destroying most of the details of structure. Taking a specimen that a fortunate blow of the hammer has ex-

posed unbroken, the section is cut down through a mingled mass of what was formerly the viscera and appendages, if they chance to be present at all: that but one specimen in twenty gave an instructive section is not at all surprising. As the work extended over several years, what is now known of the structure of the appendages is the result of an accumulation of material and facts from time to time and not a fortunate discovery of one or more instructive specimens. (Walcott 1881, 192)

That is an underplayed description of a great deal of hard work. Anyone who has been a participant, rather than an observer, in a shoveling exercise, is aware that the charm of the experience disappears in a few seconds. Consider the hand grinding hour after hour of section after section. As another note on labor, Walcott made sketch after sketch trying to interpret the thin sections. At the last stage, Major Powell arranged for the Geological Survey photographer to take pictures of the thin sections at an enlarged size. Walcott then used these as a base in preparing copy for the lithographer. The scientific illustration is exceedingly accurate; as for aesthetic considerations, some people would not object to having these lithographs framed and hung on their wall.

More important than grinding or drawing of the sections was the intellectual activity of interpretation. Walcott freely stated that his 1876 note was in error and his 1877 paper contained several fundamental misinterpretations. This is the way science commonly works; discoveries bringing the cry of "Eureka" are rare. Walcott did not have all details correct in 1881, but he so advanced this field that his interpretations were unchallenged for four decades. His major error was a concept of the gills as a coiled structure; in partial defence, the thin sections do appear as though they cut across a coil.

Precisely what did Walcott discover? Some Americans are familiar with the horseshoe crab *Limulus* that lives on the East Coast of the United States, for it looks like a strange archaic beast. After exhaustively describing the trilobite limbs, Walcott compared them to those of the horseshoe crab and other arthropods. From that comparison he derived a classification. Along the way, he contributed information on the mode of life of the trilobites and what some of their internal organs were like.

The general results were important; in detail, this kind of information is of interest to remarkably few people. Dana (1881, 79) gave the paper only a one paragraph review. He still did not fully comprehend what Walcott had found and commented, "The series of legs in this restoration looks very doubtful for, if so distinct in the animal, it seems to be incomprehensible that such dissections should have been needed for their discovery." In C. A. White's annual review of invertebrate paleontology, this was simply mentioned as one more paper. However, the zoologist Alpheus Packard (1882) immediately incorporated one of Walcott's reconstructions into a paper on crustacean appendages, and his paper was given an extensive summary in French (Six 1884).

There is another way to evaluate this work on trilobites. One aspect of history is the game of "what if." What if Louis Agassiz had lived a few years longer and Walcott had gone to the Museum of Comparative Zoology in Cambridge, instead of to Hall's establishments in Albany. As a result of this investigation, the companion of Arnold Hague and young Joseph Paxton Iddings, heading west from Syracuse, would have been Doctor Walcott. The reality is Walcott lacked the accoutrements of formal college training and never obtained them. America does not indulge in the British system whereby the homebred worker could walk into a university with a remarkable manuscript and be awarded a degree on the strength of that work. Seemingly this lack of a doctorate diploma never hurt Walcott's future career; his sheepskin from the school of hard knocks was an important credential.

With all the complexities of trilobite limbs and other serious matters, some humor is needed. In the fall of 1879, a colleague from Albany wrote to Walcott in the West:

> Thou man of hammer and the disreputable trilobite I have some what to say unto thee. The hammer is an honest instrument that advertises what it does when it smashes—but for the trilobite ah what shall I say? I say that an animal that used 20 000 eyes must have been essentially a sneak!—not the one to meet a foe squarely but one that would be peeking around in all directions out of some of its headlights to be ready to run at the first sign of an adversary. And then you never know how to class him—he wasn't a mollusk or a fish, and he wasn't a bird nor again an honest square reptile like the gay alligator. And he wasn't an Englishman—well perhaps you dont have Pinafore out among the Utes and the prairie dogs.[18]

It may be just as well to return to the Geological Survey. Director King wrote the state geologist of Wisconsin about the jurisdiction issue:

> The precise condition of our legislative muddle is this: the amendment extending the survey of the states was twice taken out in the morning hour, but in each case only the bitter antagonists of the bill spoke, and delivered themselves against time to take us out of Parliamentary standing.
>
> We are therefore left where we were last winter with the Survey confined to its limits [public lands in the West] and its small appropriation all absorbed in financing work begun last year.[19]

When Congress reconvened, it did not expand the USGS as King had hoped, and the Geological Survey in 1881 remained confined to the West. If an official reason is needed for King resigning, this is as good as any.

After less than a year with the organization, long before this administrative difficulty arose, King was ready to resign according to Arnold Hague, one of King's Fortieth Parallel men, and soon to be Walcott's boss. After telling his colleague S. F. Emmons, another of King's men, that King had left New York, he wrote,

> He talks seriously of resigning and wrote a letter from here to Schurtz [secretary of the interior] on the subject. He says at the best it is only a few months that he will remain—not after the 1st of Dec. His plan is to resign July 1st if possible, and if not, to hold the place only nominally, leaving Washington and serving without pay. He will then urge Powell's name and have him confirmed. Powell is, I suppose, the best man if not the only person who can raise money. At the best however it is a very different thing from having King at the head and I sometimes feel as if I should keep out of the thing.[20]

Walcott had no idea the Geological Survey was on an uncertain footing as to its future efforts and funding. Equally, he had no knowledge that his next assignment was given by a director ready to depart the organization and would be gone in less than a year. He knew that a significant paper on trilobites he had written was in press, and that he had money to invest from the sale of his collection. He also knew that he was heading west again, into a country of marvelous geology. Finally, he knew that effective July 1, 1880, he had become an assistant geologist, rather than geological assistant, and that his salary had doubled to twelve hundred dollars per year. No more hardware stores were in his future.

5

Eureka! Practical Paleontology (1880–1883)

Geology has, for the earliest times, claimed the serious attention
of mankind, by appealing to two entirely different sides of human
character. In the first place, reverence for the mysterious in nature,
which in untutored men amounts to worship, has always been excited
by the secrets of the earth; while, in the second place, the cupidity of
man has always led him to explore the rocks in quest of the mineral
treasures which they contain.

G. H. Williams, 1889

DIRECTOR CLARENCE KING partitioned the new U.S. Geological Survey into
several divisions. Grove Karl Gilbert (Pyne 1980), the principal scientist of Powell's survey, continued research on ancient Lake Bonneville in the Utah desert,
with headquarters of the Divison of the Great Basin in Salt Lake City. King was
nonplussed when, in 1880, Gilbert delayed for several months in Washington;
his study of the vanished lake had no obvious commercial application and was
a concession to pure science.

King's heart was in the geology of mineral deposits; he saw investigations of
mining districts as the best way for the new Survey to prove its worth and gain
support. King dispatched Samuel F. Emmons, a former Fortieth Parallel Survey
geologist, to set up the Rocky Mountain Division in Denver, focusing on geology around Leadville, Colorado, one of the newest of the western mining bonanzas. In 1879, George F. Becker examined mining districts in Nevada and set
up a Pacific Division office in San Francisco for Arnold Hague, another Fortieth Parallel geologist, who was then overseas. The only paleontological work for
the fledgling survey was a study by O. C. Marsh of Yale University. Professor
Marsh was greatly interested in fossil vertebrates, and King had not forgotten

the 1878 report of the National Academy of Sciences, when Marsh was acting president, and the subsequent lobbying for him to become director.

Hague had been reserved a position the previous July when the organization first had funds, but he was investigating mines in the Orient and did not report for duty until April 1880. On July 17, Walcott joined Hague and Iddings in Syracuse, and they were off to Eureka, Nevada. Under Hague's general guidance, Walcott was expected to work out details of the geologic column, which because of uplift, tilting, faulting, and folding was a far more complex problem than in the plateau country; he was also to date the rocks by collecting fossils.

Iddings, a Yale graduate with additional postgraduate training, was hired to map and study the lavas and other volcanic rocks; he later characterized the two assistants as "Charles D. Walcott, fresh from the Grand Canyon, and J. P. Iddings, fresh from laboratory and lecture rooms" (Iddings 1919, 25). The midyear start of the fiscal year may have been fine for parts of the federal government, but not for field scientists. This date had plagued the territorial surveys and continued to plague the Geological Survey. Spring is an excellent time to be in the field, but if there are no funds, there is no fieldwork. Almost every year, field parties were delayed until after the fiscal year began.

The trip was the standard bone-jarring train journey of the times. At Palisades, Nevada, "a hot, dirty little town" a few miles south of present-day Carlin, they left the main line, and at 11:00 P.M. on the twenty-second they finally reached Eureka. The next night, John McChesney, chief clerk of the survey, came into town and took Walcott aside: "Mr. McChesney told me why I had been sent here instead of Kanab, Utah. Reasons that are very satisfactory to me" (July 24, 1880). It is bit mysterious, but one surmises that McChesney emphasized Walcott's experience with fossils of the East. By seeing fossils on the outcrop, Walcott could easily recognize the equivalents of Trenton, Waterlime, Corniferous, and other subdivisions of the New York section. A secondary reason may have been to keep him away from those younger rocks in Utah of interest to C. A. White, an able paleontologist with powerful friends at the Smithsonian Institution.

The desert boom towns, destined in a few years to become its ghost towns, have engendered floods of books on the lure and lore of the Old West. The silver they poured out influenced American politics for decades. Eureka was perhaps the greatest of the lead-silver mining bonanzas in the United States, and an investigation of its geology might lead to the discovery of other major ore bodies elsewhere in the Great Basin. When Hague arrived, this metropolis was

Charles Doolittle Walcott, Paleontologist

at its peak, both in population and tonnage of ore mined. Walcott's sociological observation was that "Eureka is a characteristic mining town & holds all the social strata that occur in such districts" (July 23, 1880).

During the summer of 1879, work had started on a topographic base map in anticipation of Hague's return to government service. With the rudiments of a map on which to plot the various stratigraphic units, Mr. Hague "took the field, accompanied by two geological assistants, Mr. C. D. Walcott and Mr. Joseph P. Iddings, and immediately began preparations by establishing our first camp in New York Cañon, near the eastern base of Prospect Peak and in the immediate neighborhood of the mines which occur along the limestone belt to the southward of Ruby Hill" (Hague 1880, 32). The geologists spent more than a week in town before getting the camp established, and as Walcott noted, that was an irksome way to do fieldwork.

Central Nevada has a continental climate. Summers, while not precisely like hell, approximate that place, being very hot, very dry, and very dusty, with sagebrush, where it can survive, supplying shade hardly fit for rattlesnakes. Distances to outcrops are always longer than one expects, for vistas are deceptive. About four thousand feet of relief separate the dust-choked valley floor from the windswept top of Diamond Peak. The country is rugged; scrambling up rock-strewn slopes to pound on ledges of quartzite and limestone and then down the unstable talus with bags of samples made for a tiring day.

From the geologic viewpoint, the area is structurally complicated and thrown into a series of elongate ridges and troughs. When strata are tilted, the formerly flat upper surface dips downward beneath ground level; field geologists use a simple hand-held inclinometer to measure this dip. A more complex measurement is that of strike, the trend of rock ridges. In Nevada, most ridges trend north-south, but generalizations are of little use. Rather, one utilizes a compass to obtain the precise direction of strike relative to North. A change in the direction of strike may be the first clue to a geologic structure. The inclination of a hillside caused by erosion may make a stratum appear to bend when it is actually striking straight across the hillside, or it may make it appear straight when it is actually curving. Dip and strike of several outcrops collectively provide basic clues to the geologic structure of an area. Good field geologists build up a picture in their mind of the area being mapped as it appears in three dimensions; that is an art.

Under certain kinds of forces, rock strata bend into folds, but under other conditions, the rocks break and the various pieces move about. When one has two fundamentally different kinds of rocks juxtaposed, a fault is easy to recognize. In contrast, when two similar-appearing rocks, such as limestones, are faulted against one another, the fault may go unnoticed until fossils are collected and it is found that organisms of two different ages are involved. Little was known of the Eureka District and the more it was studied, the more complex and subtle were the structures revealed. The unknown structure posed an intellectual challenge and what appeared as a simple continuous ridge could turn out to be a melange of limestones of various ages.

The main rock divisions had been named through the work of the Fortieth Parallel Survey, but that pioneering examination had missed a wealth of important detail. Walcott began his work by measuring the thickness of the rock units in a section to determine the general succession. Then he measured the same units in other areas to determine whether they have thinned, thickened, or remained constant. The faulting complicated section measuring, and subsequent study of Eureka has shown that not all the faults were located in 1880.

The best way to reveal the more subtle structures was to study the fossils and examine the lithology of the rocks in detail and plot the various formations on the map. There is a certain excitement in determining the age of a bed and thereby being able to place a line on a map. That field season, Walcott filled four of Henry Penny's patent improved metallic books with his daily field notes, on dip, strike, thickness, and fossils from various outcrops.

Geologists must simultaneously understand the structure to figure out the succession and determine the stratigraphy to make sense of the structure. Years of later fieldwork have shown that Eureka is just at the edge of the Roberts Mountain overthrust, which moved a different suite of rocks eastward (Merriam 1968). As a result, a few of the unfossiliferous outcrops studied by Hague and his crew did not fit in the general geologic pattern, and to this day their age is enigmatic.

No matter what the thrill of breaking open a rock and seeing a beautiful fossil, a field investigation may become tedious. Walcott recorded comments such as "Spent the better part of the day on the hills to the west of camp. Found them to be formed of limestone of Primordial age. As the mule ran off last night traveled on foot & very tired at night" (August 6, 1880). Commonly each geologist went a separate direction, with occasional days together to coordinate findings. By the end of September, Hague had preliminary results to report, beginning his geology at Prospect Mountain ridge, which rose above their first camp:

> Probably nothing in our summer's work will have so much interest for geologists as the discovery of so great a thickness of Devonian strata, which is shown to exist here in Central Nevada.

It is estimated that there occurs here at Newark Mountain 4,500 feet of

Devonian beds, and the evidence seems quite conclusive that the Devonian hills lying to the eastward of the Pinto Toll road underlie the beds of Newark Mountain. If this is correct, we have a thickness of between 6,000 and 7,000 feet of strata.

At Newark Mountain, from the base to the summit, there occur at intervals, beds carrying *brachiopods* of characteristic Devonian types.

Above the limestone of Newark Mountain occur several hundred feet of black fissile shale, crumbing easily upon exposure. In places, they are more or less arenaceous, and pass into thin beds of sandstone, which finally become a dark compact quartzite, again overlain by black shales. The interesting feature of these shale beds is, that they are the exact equivalent of the black shales of White Pine—a formation that heretofore has never been recognized except at the latter locality.

Here, at Eureka, Mr. Walcott has found several species of fossils, identical with those obtained from the Hamilton black shales at White Pine. . . .

One of the most interesting geological features of this portion of the district is found at Lone Mountain, where the Silurian and Devonian strata occur, perfectly conformable, without any breaks, with both structural and paleontological evidence of their true position. We here have 4,000 feet of conformable beds with organic remains throughout the series. The Devonian beds are easily correlated with the beds to the eastward. (Hague 1880, 33–35)

The mention of Lone Mountain brings forth one anecdote concerning that season:

Walcott has told me that to get in two days' work at Lone Mountain, some 18 miles from Eureka, a start was made one afternoon. The party would camp overnight at a ranch near Devils Gate. Water barrels were filled and hauled to the foot of the mountain the next morning, the geologists going ahead on horseback. With a dry camp that night, field work could be carried on the following day, and then the whole outfit would have to move back to the ranch for water.[1]

This excursion by Hague and Walcott to Lone Mountain was at the end of September, a month after the desert nights had already turned cool. It must have been some trip during the summer.

Hague was anxious to have a thorough geologic investigation. He had been late getting to Eureka, a delay related to uncertainty as to the appropriation for the second year of the survey. Equally anxious to save money, in October King wrote Hague: "Do you really need either Iddings or Walcott east? If not let them also come to San Francisco for the winter."[2]

A few days later, King also wrote Walcott: "Many thanks for your copy of the note on the Kanab section. I knew you would enjoy working in the company of such a broad-minded man and excellent man as Mr. Hague, and that the well exposed section at Eureka would call in play all your power as a turner-up of paleontological evidence."[3]

Hague took a quick trip to the director in San Francisco, pointing out the foolishness of his assistants moving west while he traveled east. He returned with news that in the fall they would go to New York City; King's letter to Walcott may have been to sooth any residual concerns. Meanwhile, the work of examining outcrops and determining their age and how their present position fit into the geologic structure of the area went on and on and on:

> The active field season for geological investigations occupied four months and ten days, from July 25 till December 5, a period far too short for the district, when we consider either its great economical importance as a silver-lead producing region, or its complicated geological structure, and bearing upon the geology of the Great Basin. . . . From this time we were favored with good weather, never forced to stop work for a day, and surveys pushed forward without interruption through summer and autumn. . . . Much time was devoted to paleontological work, and collecting carried on with energy, which was rewarded with success. . . . Field operations were only brought to a close by continued low temperatures of winter, accompanied by high winds and violent snow storms. During the last three weeks of the season the thermometer in camp registered in the region of zero every night, and on one occasion fell as low as −16° Fahr. (Hague 1882, 23–24)

Despite the closeness of camp living, in Walcott's diary reference was always to "Mr. Hague" and "Mr. Iddings," even though Iddings and Walcott were in the same tent. Only on a single Sunday were they out in the field and that in November when they were anxious to break camp. Even that late in the season enthusiasm persisted, and Walcott "Had a interesting day on the great ridge of quartzite trending down from Prospect Peak to 85 [a map topographic location]. Was found to be Silurian age. Heretofore was placed in the Primordial" (November 6, 1880). The geologists moved into town and went into the mines to search for fossils underground to date the ore-bearing beds. When the season ended, Walcott wrote a comment any field scientist would understand: "Regret leaving at this time. Would like a week or more about Ruby Hill & vicinity" (November 21, 1880).

The long field season in the Eureka District should have been sufficient, but to be certain the taxpayers got their money's worth out of the train fare west,

Charles Doolittle Walcott, Paleontologist

Hague packed Iddings off to Virginia City, Nevada, for a few days with George Becker. Walcott was sent to New Mexico to collect Triassic plants near Santa Fe; it took a week by train to get there

The reasons for the New Mexico trip are not clear, although years earlier, J. S. Newberry collected Triassic plants in the area from old Spanish mines. Walcott drove a team and wagon to Abiquiu to search for fossils and returned in a snowstorm. He obtained a few Carboniferous marine fossils, but no younger plants. When Walcott finally left the field December 9, it was after accomplishing very little; about the only noteworthy event was that in Denver Walcott finally met Emmons. He arrived in La Crosse, Wisconsin, at Brother Ellis's home on the fifteenth and was promptly sick for a week, but returned to Utica for Christmas and ended a busy year quietly in upstate New York.

Hague left Eureka for New York City, and Walcott joined him at the start of the new year. During their report writing, King and other geologists of the Fortieth Parallel Survey had enjoyed the hospitality of the new building of the American Museum of Natural History (Hellman 1969). In 1880, there was no place in Washington which had proper facilities to study the rock and fossil samples. The Smithsonian Castle was filled to overflowing and the supposedly temporary building for the United States National Museum next to the Castle was far from complete. Thus it came about that the headquarters of the short-lived Division of the Pacific was in New York.

For Walcott, the American Museum was an excellent scientific location. His old friend Professor Whitfield was the first curator; his paleontological library was close at hand, and he was a potential source of information about some of the enigmatic western fossils. The sixty-five-thousand-dollar fossil collection of James Hall, which the American Museum had purchased, was invaluable for making comparisons of well-known eastern species to similar but slightly different relatives from the West, and the collection was not accompanied by Professor Hall. The offices on the mansard floor above were light and hopefully airy.

Accordingly, it must have been a shock to Walcott when Professor Whitfield was too busy to see him. A few days later "Mr. Hague told me that Mr. R. P. Whitfield said I mailed the circulars directed against his character some years since. Given on the authority of J. Stevenson. As yet have never seen a copy of the circular or know anything of its publication or circulation" (January 12, 1881). Stevenson, then on the faculty of New York University after his years in the West, was not a gossip monger and if he told Hague that Whitfield was upset, it was true. This was this sort of innuendo, hurt feelings, and grudges which had made life in Albany so difficult. Fortunately, Walcott was able to straighten out the affair immediately.

Even better than Hague's official report on Mr. Walcott were his comments to Emmons:

> We have large collections in Primordial, Silurian, Devonian, Lower Coal Measures, Upper Coal Measures. We have a larger collection than the entire "40*th* Par[allel Survey]" can show. Indeed, I think the Devonian collections would surpass the entire "40*th* Par" exhibit. From the Devonian we have nearly every family represented but the fishes which are so very rare in the Cordillera region. Walcott found them however in the 250 ft of Devonian in the Kanab country. Strangely enough, Walcott who was examining the Devonian fauna of the 40th Par on breaking open the rock carrying fossils from your small collection from Hot Springs Tucumbits mountain found a very good fish spine.[4]

There is no accounting for luck.

Once the geologists had settled in, they began plotting up their field notes and sections. The fossils and rock samples arrived late in January and from then on, it was nonstop work to derive some results at the same breakneck pace that marked the fieldwork. Walcott had to unpack and arrange the collections, examine each of the fossils individually, compare them to specimens in the museum, search the literature for other related species, and write his comments. By the end of summer, he had averaged identification of essentially a new species a day. To find that a particular form resembles one described from, say, New York and Iowa, but differs from it in having a few more ridges on the shell requires a grasp of the literature, as well as a keen eye.

Walcott began with a quick look at all the collections, starting with the oldest, for geologists naturally go from bottom to top in sequence. "Slowly but surely the general results are coming out of great interest as the Quebec Group and Primordial pass into each other and give a large & interesting fauna" (February 14, 1881). He then went though all the fossils a second time in more detail, again in stratigraphic sequence. He named the forms he could identify and selected specimens for illustration of the new species. Walcott was deep into the problem at hand and not interested in what had been done last year, a mindset which characterizes many scientists. When the printer's proof of his trilobite paper arrived, his reaction was: "Wish the paper was out & well received as it has cost me much time & labor & it hardly pleases me owing to the hurry of its final preparation" (March 17, 1881).

Even before Walcott arrived in New York, events which ultimately shaped his future began. Director King was restive, and the previous fall Hague, just after he returned from San Francisco, wrote to Becker for help: "I believe that the Director expects to make you a visit on his way East. If at that time or at any other time the subject of his resignation should come up, I hope you will do all you can to impress on his mind the duty he owes to science, his country, or whatever you may choose to call it, to remain at the head of the Survey."[5] The pleas of his colleague did not prevail, and on March 11, 1881, King resigned, a week after President Garfield was inaugurated.

The resignation shocked the younger geologists. "Did not work well as the news of Mr. King's resignation of the Director of the Survey was received. Am very sorry that he should resign both on personal & public considerations. Major J. W. Powell is nominated by the President to fill the position. Trust that he will be confirmed" (March 15, 1881). Within a week Powell was director, a position he held for thirteen years.

How much influence King had on the later development of the Geological Survey depends upon which historian one reads. King and Powell were both important as scientists and administrators. When it comes to the finer details, each had and has supporters and detractors. In broad outline, King was a person with many advantages who showed brilliance early but failed after leaving the survey; he was a genius or a charmer, or both. Powell started with nothing and grew throughout most of his career; he was an opportunist or a visionary, or both. Powell's approach to administration and views of science were drastically different from those of King. No doubt those involved with mining investigations could not help but wonder what about their future under a director preoccupied with arid land problems.

Clarence King was a complex man and a great surprise in a biography of this bon vivant bachelor was that he had secretly married a negress, or rather tricked her into thinking it was legal. However, King's interest in the ladies was quite well known; Emmons confided to Becker: "I can imagine H.[is] R.[oyal] H.[ighness] after a bout among the dusky fair ones of Mexico,—he has a peculiar weakness for color, and especially, when it is on a fair cheek."[6] One school of thought is that the unwillingness of Congress to extend the domain of the Geological Survey into the East, where there were no public lands, caused King's resignation. Another is that King wanted more money and the chance to travel to mining areas where Henry Adams and his other cultured friends would not be peering over his shoulder.

Walcott generally did not indulge in office gossip; perhaps, then, it is appropriate to leave probing of King's personality and return to geology. Geologists in the 1880s had a view of a world much younger than accepted today, but they still dealt in millions of years, sufficient time for many past events to have occurred. If the underlying and overlying fossils in a sequence of strata are of quite different ages, the field geologist will want to reexamine the contact more closely, to see what transpired before the overlying layer was deposited. Perhaps there is evidence of weathering, perhaps there is channeling, or perhaps there is a slight unconformity. Mining geologists were beginning to understand that former events, such as these, affected where ore minerals occurred; they were not deposited at random. Study of the ages of the rocks was eminently practical research.

To bring this into perspective, in the Grand Canyon at Kanab Creek, Walcott had found channels in the underlying rocks filled with Devonian rocks and above this irregular surface a few hundred feet of flat-lying Devonian beds. At Eureka he found thousands of feet of Devonian in a section seemingly continuous from the underlying Silurian. The Devonian geologic history of the two places was strikingly different. The early ideas on the age of a few of the outcrops developed in the field were discarded when more detailed plotting of the sections or the fossils showed the presence of an unanticipated disconformity or the possibility of an overlooked fault.

Near the end of March, Walcott jotted a few lines to William Healy Dall in Washington: "I am doomed to board around much as I dislike it. . . . I am busy on field notes & collections of the past season. Have about 100 n. sp. from the Cambrian & Devonian of Nevada."[7] In May, Director Powell and Chief Clerk McChesney came to New York to meet with Hague and King; Walcott also had a heart-to-heart talk with the director. Allaying their fears, Major Powell did not scuttle the project. Indeed, there was even financial support so that in the summer of 1881, Hague could return to Eureka for a month to check his map where laboratory results suggested problems or errors.

In April, G. B. Simpson visited the American Museum. Despite his relieving Walcott of bryozoan eye-strain in Albany, Simpson was primarily a scientific illustrator and when Hall did not have funds, he could contract out for work.

Charles Doolittle Walcott, Paleontologist

Simpson was to take Walcott's sketches and the specimens back to Albany and execute finished drawings of the Eureka district fossils. They concluded an agreement for 250 pictures at $2.10 each.

Simpson was one of those spear carriers who keep the scientific enterprise going, but who hardly rate an obituary when they die. In addition to the legacy of his drawings, he wrote several papers, and a few species were named for him by his friends, but otherwise he has vanished. A century later, Simpson is being recognized as a pioneer who looked more analytically at bryozoans and corals than Hall did, both groups whose important characters are on the interior, not the exterior (Oliver 1987).

Illustration is the lifeblood of a descriptive science and before photography came to be perfected, the illustrator could make or break the paleontologist. Hall's monographs describing the fossils of New York became standards for the profession (Blum 1987). In Simpson, Walcott employed one of the last of a steadily improving line of skilled specialists. In some instances, one can draw a line between commercial art and fine art, but scientific illustration does not fall easily into either category. The criterion a scientist uses to judge an illustration is whether it accurately portrays the specimen, and Simpson certainly did that.

For Walcott, examination of the western fossils was steady, intensive work, but certainly not drudgery. He had congenial associates who cared about his opinions. Even more, this year in New York may have been the most pleasant socially ever passed by widower Walcott; no work from the office occupied the evenings. In January, he had a new lady friend to dream about at Holland Patent; like the others whom he did not pursue vigorously, he eventually lost her. He found a nice place to live and a congenial roommate at Mrs. McConnell's; at twelve dollars a week for room and board, he had plenty of money in his pocket. Mother and Josie came to New York for a few months; there was opera and theater to attend. Life was better than it had been in Albany or Washington.

Late in March, some interesting news came north from Washington. Walcott reflected: "Events show a tendency to some changes in the personal [*sic*] of the Survey, especially in the appointment of a palaeontologist. This may or may not interfere with my work but I trust not as I have but one field I wish to occupy & and there is plenty for all who go out into practical work in the west" (March 28, 1881). To translate, C. A. White was now officially a full-time government paleontologist, whereas Walcott was a field geologist who was studying fossils. Fortunately, White was interested in the younger Mesozoic and Cenozoic, and Walcott was interested in the older Paleozoic, so there need not be any conflict.

In the spring, Walcott spent a weekend at the New Jersey home of his volcanological colleague. It was "Iddings" or "Joe" thereafter in his diary, though still "Mr. Hague." He went to Albany to check on the progress of drawing and to compare specimens. Hall was both cordial and helpful; a month later, Walcott again took a steamer up the Hudson. Walcott kept mentioning to Hall the manuscript on Trenton fossils left in 1879, and two years later he finally got around to publishing it—as a preprint (Walcott 1883)—but at least these fossils were illustrated.

The big-city idyll began to be marred by the summer heat, which somehow was worse than in the western desert. In his office, the temperature was recorded as 88 degrees; no doubt the thermometer was broken. Hague returned refreshed from the field, and the work kept moving ahead. The heat persisted, and by mid-September it was 101 degrees; someone had obtained a better thermometer. Walcott escaped for few days to visit family; of course, this included a bit of collecting in the Utica Shale with William Rust. It was so hot that even Walcott quit, though his brother-in-law continued digging. This episode resulted in a one-page paper, enough to let the profession know that he was alive and well (Walcott 1881a). It was back to work, and nine months after the laboratory studies started, Hague reported to Director Powell on Walcott's effort and the importance of fossils to the field investigations:

> The collections made by the Eureka District survey number about 4,500 specimens. . . . it is, so far as I know, very much the largest collection of paleozoic fossils ever brought in from any equally limited area in the Far West.
>
> Accompanying my report upon the "Geology of the Eureka District" will be Mr. Charles D. Walcott's report upon the paleontology of the district. It will, I think be accepted as a valuable contribution to our knowledge of the geology of the Great Basin.
>
> Mr. Walcott's detailed study of the paleontological material shows three hundred and fifty-nine species in the collection. Of these three hundred fifty-nine, two hundred ninety-nine have been specifically determined, the remaining sixty receiving only a generic name, as they are either imperfectly represented, or, as in the case of the Trenton fauna and the Devonian corals, it appeared best to await the collecting of more complete material before attempting to illustrate them.
>
> During the preparation of Mr. Walcott's report he has written descriptions of one hundred and twenty-three new species, and made notes, more or less full, upon one hundred and sixty species, which presented in their characters or geographical distribution information not heretofore published.
>
> It will be seen, therefore, that the report embraces a fauna from the

Cambrian, Devonian, and Carboniferous. It will be illustrated by over three hundred accurate drawings of fossils, arranged on twelve plates. Four plates represent the fauna of the Cambrian, five that of the Devonian, and three that of the Carboniferous. (Hague 1882, 28–31)

Simpson's drawings had to be copied onto lithographic stone for reproduction. Early in October, Walcott went to the lithographic firm of Thomas Sinclair & Son in Philadelphia to look at proofs of the first four fossil plates. Once again, Walcott was lucky, for Philip Ast from Albany, who had helped him with his Utica Shale illustrations, was now working for the company. Again, he got one of the best artisans in the business to reproduce the plates.

After the first examination of fossils, and next the preparation of faunal lists, the third step was to write out detailed descriptions of the species. The descriptive work in turn led to some corrections and changes in identification. Walcott decided that a few of the species he had identified really were new species and a few others were finally assigned names already in the literature. About the only statement of taxonomic philosophy given was when Walcott was "Reviewing a few species & reduced one to a variety. Wish to be as conservative as possible in making new species" (November 4, 1881). By and large, the similarities and differences that Walcott saw have been confirmed by later studies. Walcott also provided a rather detailed study of a species of *Olenellus,* an early trilobite, a diversion into biologic paleontology rather than stratigraphic paleontology; he even drew the illustrations for this fossil.

Retired director King set up offices in the museum, and later Emmons and Becker were on hand. It made for marvelous luncheon conversation, quite apart from the opportunities to discuss the geology of different areas with experts. In December, King sensibly advised Walcott to turn over to C. A. White his notes on Kanab, Utah; Walcott sensibly followed his advice. After a brief holiday visit at Utica and Trenton Falls, it was back to work.

A week after 1882 started, Walcott "Completed writing out des[cri]pt[ions] of plates. My report is practically ready to go to press" (January 7, 1882). However, on January 13, for those who believe in numerical omens, Walcott made a paleontologic error. He wrote to Dall in Washington for assistance with literature: "Not trilobites this time but land & fresh water shells. It is necessary for me to study up on this subject & I wish to obtain Binny & Bland on Pulmonates. . . . My report on the Eureka District is nearing completion. Hope to see you in the spring."[8]

This led to some concern and confusion in Washington, which was resolved in another letter:

> Do not I beg you, suppose that I think of studying the L[and] & F[resh] W[ater] shells as a study. I discovered a few species (3) in the Carboniferous rocks of Nevada & consequently took up the subject in a general way & called on friends for assistance. . . . Have 125 n. sp. & over 80 species of the east identified west of the Plains for the first time. 13 plates, 335 figures. Paleozoic geology & paleontology will be my life study if I have my own choice.[9]

Walcott had collected from a much younger Cretaceous fresh-water limestone deposited in a lake, plastered onto the outcrop of Carboniferous limestone in such a way that it appeared to be interbedded with the marine strata. Geologists at the time were unaware of Cretaceous beds in that part of the Great Basin. Carboniferous nonmarine snails were enough of a novelty that they warranted a special brief notice (Walcott 1883a). It was an error in dating which stayed in the literature for about half a century. Discovery of another locality in 1938 and restudy of its fossils resolved the age of these outcrops "hundreds of miles from any previously known Cretaceous rocks" (MacNeil 1939).

There is one major error associated with the Cambrian work. The genus *Olenellus* is Early Cambrian in age, not Middle Cambrian, but that was not known for some years to come. As a consequence, several faults in the Eureka District were not recognized until later remapping, and there was some mixup of the sequence of Cambrian faunas.

Walcott did not delve into the bryozoans in the report, and he considered the corals only superficially. As mentioned earlier, study of both groups was moving away from consideration of the external form to include the inner details; that required preparation of thin sections to study these internal features, and Walcott simply did not have the time. Hague was interested in the age of the outcrops, not a total description of all the fossils and Walcott could obtain as good determinations of geologic age from the trilobites, brachiopods, and mollusks, which did not require such elaborate preparation. Only decades later was detailed stratigraphic sense made out of the profuse Devonian coral assemblages (Merriam 1973, 1974).

Early in January, in the midst of finishing study of the Eureka fossils, an unusual fossil arthropod from the Utica Shale came Walcott's way. He immediately sent off a paragraph reporting the find (Walcott 1882), and by March, a description (Walcott 1882a). The specimen was a fragment of a eurypterid, and in his first letter to Dall, he thought that it might be about eighteen inches long if complete. At a few localities in the Silurian limestones overlying the Utica Shale, eurypterids are common. Not only was this the first from the older Utica beds, it was by far the oldest example reported in the world. Eurypterids look something like lobsters in having two claws, but the posterior is more like a scorpion; as regards their biologic position, they are about second cousins to the trilobites, have about as many parts in the exoskeleton, and are just as extinct. Good specimens are much prized by collectors, so much so that when a state fossil was selected for New York, the honor went to a Silurian eurypterid.

After this quick foray into eurypterids, it took Walcott about a month to be satisfied with the classification of the nonmarine western snails and to finish other details. Then he and Hague considered the main stratigraphic divisions to be used in the Eureka report, including whether to use the term "Primordial" or "Cambrian." Walcott had consistently used Primordial in his field notes, but now preferred Cambrian; Hague changed to it in his third annual report.

Primordial will come up again, but for now it is enough to know that in the 1840s, the great Barrande had recognized three distinct faunas in Bohemia: first, Primordial Silurian; second, Lower Silurian; and third, Upper Silurian. Walcott wrote him:

> I brought the question of the use of the term Cambrian before the geologist who has charge of the geology and maps (I have the paleontology) and after long argument and effort we agreed to restrict the name Cambrian to the 1st fauna. He strenuously objected as the line between the Cambrian and Silurian is drawn in a continuous section where there is no stratigraphical break and to the stratigraphical geologist it seems difficult to establish great divisions as such a place, but it is now done [and] printed on the maps.... Whether we call the strata of the 1st fauna Cambrian or Primordial Silurian is not of initial importance. It is the recognition of the 1st, 2d, and 3d faunas that concerns all geologists especially in a new and great country like that of the western United States.[10]

Once use of Cambrian in the report was settled, Walcott took a few days off to visit family upstate. Of course, this included looking at fossils from the Utica Shale. Walcott succumbed to temptation and "agreed to take W.P.R.'s collection of Utica slate at $400" (February 25, 1882). Ever since his fossil sale of 1880, Walcott had corresponded with Alexander Agassiz. Earlier, he had offered to help the Museum of Comparative Zoology obtain Devonian fossils, and he now brought Agassiz up to date both on his promise to curate the collection he had sold and his latest acquisition:

> The Utica slate material I have has cost about $500. Will not recommend it be purchase [d] by you until after the collection you now have has been care-

fully reexamined. My material is packed up at Trenton Falls. Havent [*sic*] any Trenton fossils but secured the control of a collection by buying the Utica slate portion & another large collection owned by a lawyer in Utica [E. Hurlburt], a personal friend, is also held open to my use. The first collection can be purchased by me, the second is not for sale. Why I endeavor to keep control of the material I will tell you in person.[11]

Hall may have been interested in describing the Trenton fossils, and Walcott wanted to forestall him.

The discussion with Hague on the use of Cambrian prompted others concerning the ages to be assigned to overlying rocks at Eureka. "Owing to a change in the nomenclature of the Pogonip limestone reviewed matters pertaining to it" (March 2, 1882). Late in the field season, working northeast of the Dunderberg mine, Walcott wrote in his field notes that

From this horizon up to the Receptaculites beds the fauna gradually changes from the character of the Primordial to that of the Upper Quebec. Owing to no distinct boundary line being present in the fauna & that a partial & distinct change occurs at the close of the Hamburgh shale the position of the Hamburgh beds & and the beds up to the Silurian quartzite is within the Canadian division of the Lower Silurian.[12]

In brief, Walcott had recognized that the geologic history of the area was more complex than had been recognized. When he persuaded Hague to use Lower Silurian rather than lump many beds under the broader term of Silurian, it was a step forward. That was the beginning of an argument which lasted for two more decades on the terminology and correlation of the Lower Paleozoic rocks of America. The notion of "passage beds" wherein an older fauna changed gradually to a younger fauna was an indication that dramatic changes of fossils distinct in Bohemia might not be so obvious in western America, as witness Hague's concern with an age boundary in the middle of a section which appeared to be continuous. The faunal differences Barrande observed were partly the result of discontinuities in the rock section, as the "passage beds" of the West seemed to show.

The Eureka investigations were nearing an end. Iddings and Hague completed their study of the volcanic rocks of Eureka and compared them to collections from other parts of the West made by the Fortieth Parallel Survey; Walcott was writing out labels for the collections. It must have been a shock for him to be told "My report is not to be printed until after Mr. Hagues [*sic*] so I shall be kept in New York until late in the season" (March 20, 1882). Precisely why is not clear, but four days later, Walcott took an overnight train trip to Washington, and "Settled matters very satisfactorily with the Director" (March 25, 1882). According to the preface, *The Paleontology of the Eureka District,* in its original state, was transmitted for publication May 1, 1882. Because it was not immediately printed, Powell may have considered offering Walcott the prospect of another field season to add to the Eureka work. He also discussed plans for Walcott to continue his investigations on the Kaibab Plateau and Grand Canyon.

In his official report for the fiscal year to Director Powell, Hague was unstinting in his praise as he had been in the past year:

> Mr. C. D. Walcott's full report upon the paleontology of the Eureka district, a brief sketch of which, indicating the scope and importance, appeared in my last letter, was completed in the spring and is now ready for the printer. It embraces a rich fauna from the Cambrian, Silurian, Devonian, and Carboniferous. Over three hundred careful drawings of fossils, illustrating the new species, have been arranged on thirteen plates, which have already been engraved in a most satisfactory manner. (Hague 1883, 10)

After Walcott's meeting with the director, the pace of life slowed. He had a photograph taken and celebrated his birthday the end of March, more secure in his position with the Geological Survey than during the previous year. Having finished all of his assignments, in mid-April Walcott was permitted by Hague to go to the Museum of Comparative Zoology and arrange his former collection. While in Cambridge, Walcott had a long discussion with A. S. Packard about arthropods, paid a courtesy call on Jules Marcou, to talk over geology, and spoke to the natural history club. There was time to examine Cambrian fossils in the Museum and collect trilobites at Braintree, Massachusetts. It was a fine couple of weeks.

In early May, Walcott further broadened his western horizons by looking in more detail at the Fortieth Parallel fossil collections stored at the American Museum. He made a flying trip to Utica and Trenton Falls to bid farewell. Then it was back to New York City for "Packing up and getting ready to go to Washington. . . . Regret breaking up as I have enjoyed living within reach of friends" (May 17, 1882). This was to be a lifelong move; for nearly forty-five years thereafter, Washington was his home. Secretary Baird of the Smithsonian Institution, who was also director of the United States National Museum, wrote him, "I have the honor to state that your name has been placed upon the roll of museum officials as honorary assistant curator of fossil invertebrates. You will be entitled to all the privileges with the regular officers of the museum."[13]

Walcott, the practical man, put it a little differently in his diary: "Made arrangements to work on the paleozoic collections of the National Museum & and settled down to it P.M. Found it in a dirty bad condition" (May 20, 1882). During its early days the Geological Survey moved several times, and it has been erroneously stated that headquarters for a time was in the National Museum. This was not so, for Walcott almost always distinguished between the time he spent at the survey office and at the museum building.

Walcott marked time and after a week of limited scientific activity, he "returned to room to read and work on sections of trilobites. A new start in an old work" (May 25, 1882). The last week in June he left Washington to check on the progress of the Philadelphia lithographers, and stopped to see Hague at the American Museum.

He went on to Trenton Falls and "spent most of the day in the brook searching for trilobites to cut up for study of the appendages. Poor success" (June 28, 1882). However, William, always helpful, showed him a specimen with one eye peculiarly developed that was worthy of publication (Walcott 1883b). The note was short, but interesting enough that a British journal republished it. The paleontological world was beginning to pay attention to Mr. Walcott.

That spring Walcott had contacted Charles Haskell of Holland Patent, and wrote Alexander Agassiz: "Mr. Haskell will go out in the field collecting this season for $40 per month and expenses. I know of no better man for the work. . . . If you wish I will engage Mr. Haskell to accompany me as your assistant, as per the understanding between Major Powell and yourself."[14] This was a marvelous opportunity for Haskell to see the West. Even the career of the artist Simpson is infinitely better documented than that of Haskell. Where and when he was born and died and what he did for a living besides selling an occasional fossil is unknown.

Earlier, Walcott had purchased a few specimens of *Triarthrus* from Haskell for the 1879 study of Utica fossils; he had even mentioned in print the "persistence and diligence" of the man (Walcott 1882a). Thus, he was getting as an assistant for the trip someone he could count on and who was already a skilled collector. By having Haskell travel with Walcott, Agassiz was certain to receive a large number of fine western fossils at a considerably lower cost than if they were for sale on the open market. As for Powell, first, he obtained a field assistant at no expense to the Geological Survey, and second, he did a favor for Agassiz, who was a significant force in the politics of science. For all parties, it was an attractive arrangement.

Charles Doolittle Walcott, Paleontologist

Agassiz agreed and Walcott immediately sent an estimate of travel costs, only to find that the figures were too low. He wrote again with an estimate of $537. In a masterpiece of logistic understatement he noted, "Going to Kanab, Utah adds about $175 to the expenses but at the same time increases largely the value of the collections and the lower part of the Grand Cañon will not be visited by collectors very frequently, if once a generation."[15] The new estimates were acceptable; for those who care about comparative prices and good bookkeeping, in 1882 the total cost of travel and meals from Utica to Eureka was $152.82. From the Devonian and Carboniferous rocks of Eureka the Museum of Comparative Zoology received 1,200 labeled specimens representing nearly 140 species. It was good value for the money, especially when an unknown number of Cambrian and Lower Silurian fossils were added to these upper Paleozoic invertebrates.

The end of June, Walcott met Haskell to make final plans for their trip. The federal fiscal year dawned bright on July 1 without a financial cloud to worry the USGS, and that evening Walcott departed with Haskell; the trip west was much the same as that in 1880 with Hague and Iddings. Inside a week the two were in Eureka. On the evening of the eighth, S. E. Tillman arrived and the next evening Midshipman E. E. Hayden reported. By the tenth, they were camped just west of town; for most of the season they rented horses and took their meals in town, thereby avoiding the more onerous aspects of tenting, such as having to cook after a hard day in the field.

Tillman was a U.S. Army engineer, two years Walcott's senior, who had graduated third in his West point class of 1869. He spent several seasons in the West with Lt. Wheeler's Topographic Survey, and in 1882 was the professor of chemistry, mineralogy, and geology at West Point; in later years he had little contact with geology. During the First World War Tillman was called back to service as superintendent at West Point. When he left Eureka five weeks later, Walcott was "Sorry to see him go" (August 13, 1882). Knowing Powell's style of operation and the minuscule size of the Geological Survey appropriation, it is probable the major talked his army cronies into assigning Tillman to a season in the West at no cost to the bureau.

Midshipman E. E. Hayden, eight years Walcott's junior, was a graduate of the Annapolis class of 1879 and was paid by the U.S. Navy. Just why he was in Eureka or how he made contact with Walcott is not clear. After the 1882 field season, he spent two more seasons with Geological Survey parties. He lost a leg from a field accident in the Cascade Mountains, but even with this handicap was recalled to the navy and retired as a rear admiral. Hayden was quite able as a budding geologist, but more than that, the presence of a midshipman in the desert generated legends which still persist. The first myth was that for years the USGS had a program to teach surveying to young naval officers. The second is that three Midshipmen were out with Walcott and all they did was spend the season as social lions in Eureka society. The third and best is that there was a whole corps of midshipmen. Walcott assigned each a square mile to crawl over and collect fossils, and to this day a few overlooked piles of fossils can be found under the sagebrush where they were placed to cool from the desert heat. It is remarkable what word of mouth and time can make of one young man enjoying field geology.

Walcott knew the stratigraphy around Eureka and which localities to collect for the additional fossils he needed to improve his monograph. Once some critical points among the older rocks were settled, Walcott concentrated on the Lower Carboniferous beds. In particular, he spent more time on the stratigraphically spurious fresh-water fauna, yet he never saw his error, for a second locality seemed to confirm the stratigraphic position of the fossils found in 1880. They were an enthusiastic crew, the weather was good, and the rocks yielded fine specimens. Hague's evaluation was that even though Walcott brought back large collections,

> there is, with the exception of the fauna from one new horizon in the Carboniferous, but little material that is entirely new, and nothing which necessitates any change in my conclusions and deductions formed from observations in the field. The result is especially gratifying, as it shows how well the paleontological work had been carried out during the survey of the district. (Hague 1884, 17)

As the season progressed, the geologists employed a teamster and a cook and moved camp to investigate the White Pine District, and especially the outcrops of black shale. Tillman and Hayden measured rock thickness, Haskell collected, and Walcott roamed the outcrops seeking the best places for future study. They examined the rocks on Pogonip Ridge and moved again so that Walcott could restudy the Lone Mountain section. Collecting continued to be superb; in all 2,415 pounds of fossiliferous rock were shipped east. After Tillman left, the three took the train across the Piñon Range to the summit, where they spent the day collecting graptolites in the railroad cut and slept out that night under the cedars. Graptolites, which commonly resemble dark pencil marks on dark shales, were not uncommon in the East, but at that time were almost a novelty among the western rocks. For the finale, "with horse went to base of N.W. end of Raven's Nest & discovered it to be Devonian and not Carboniferous as given by Mr. King" (August 21, 1882). Very nice, indeed.

Walcott received further orders from Powell, as had been discussed in Washington, and on August 23, he, Haskell, and Hayden moved on to Kanab, Utah, a tedious eight-day journey, by train, coach, and wagon team. They recovered the worn camping outfit Dutton had left, collected some Triassic fish remains, and then searched the area for places to measure the thickness of the Triassic sandstones, though with indifferent success. They moved south and did well in collecting Permian fossils. Because the boundary between the rocks of these two ages is also the boundary between two larger groupings, namely the Paleozoic Era and the Mesozoic Era, they concentrated on the contact of the Triassic with the underlying Permian. This was of considerably more significance to the geologic history of the West than just a change from beds of limestone to beds of sandstone, both of which were lying nearly horizontal.

The party moved southwest of Kanab, obtaining water from the temporary pools. Then they traveled across the Kaibab Plateau to House Rock Spring in Arizona, named by the major during his exploring days. "The road over the mountain and plateau is very rough & we lost a saddle out of the wagon" (September 18, 1882). The party chief is responsible for field equipment signed out in his name, but McChesney was the sort of intelligent administrator who could make a decision that the saddle was worn out and discarded; nothing further mentions if Walcott paid for the loss. Near the spring, they made a good collection of Paleozoic fossils.

The geologists moved camp back north to where the Shinarump Conglomerate outcrops across the landscape. Eventually they discovered in an outcrop the cross-section of a cliff cut into the Permian rocks and subsequently covered by the Triassic, "a remarkable confirmation of the view of the unconformity between the Permian & Triassic" (September 22, 1882). Captain Dutton's faith in Walcott's earlier findings was vindicated. Still following the boundary, the party circled around and returned to Kanab. They then traveled south again, collecting fossils from the underlying Permian limestone and examining its character.

After Midshipman Hayden picked up the mail in Kanab in mid-October, Walcott discovered he had been raised to assistant geologist at eighteen hundred dollars per year. The geology continued to be of interest, but by now it was cold at night and there had been several snows; a six-inch snow kept them in camp one day. They pushed south to the Grand Canyon rim between Shinimo Amphitheater and Muav Canyon, where they had a magnificent view before returning to Magnum Spring. After more fossil collecting in the limestones, in an effort to distinguish the Carboniferous from the overlying Permian, the party went back to Kanab; the end of October, Midshipman Hayden left, a camp hand and three horses taking him north to Silver Reef, Utah. ". . . our little party felt the loss of his cheerful presence at the camp fire" (Walcott 1884, 46).

Three days later Walcott was notified by George C. Shutt, Powell's assistant, to assemble a camp party and meet the major at House Rock Spring. Walcott came down with a chill and spent a day under blankets. He pushed himself to keep moving, and by November 9 Walcott was at House Rock Spring, though Powell was not for another two days. The weather turned to a chilly rain, and his condition became worse; "Throat bad & obliged to lay in log cabin of Judd Adams" (November 10, 1882). The next day, when Powell arrived, he was a bit better. Years later, when he recounted this incident to his family, Walcott's recalled he lay in bed with what he diagnosed as diphtheria, hardly breathing as phlegm built up in his throat. He spotted a bottle in the rafters of the cabin, and a young boy sitting with him clambered up to fetch it; Walcott uncorked the bottle and took a swallow of turpentine which burned the membrane from his throat.[16] Walcott recovered from this effective, but grim, frontier self-doctoring, though he spent almost a week resting up. When the party started south, he was still so weak he had to be driven to the first camp by buckboard.

Powell aimed to build a trail to the Colorado River. The descent was into Nankoweap Canyon, northwest of what is now Point Imperial in Grand Canyon National Park. Walcott and his party could then work through the winter, for they would be about four thousand feet lower and thereby warmer. In later years, it was on the slopes of the Grand Canyon that scientists of the original Biological Survey formalized the concept that life zones, that is changes in the fauna and flora dependent on climate, could be expressed in terms of either latitude or altitude. On December 31, Walcott recorded that winter in the canyon depths was like Trenton Falls in the autumn.

Before getting into the major's scheme or into the depths of the canyon, it may be helpful to consider the broader aspects of the canyon itself. The Green River runs southward from Green River, Wyoming, where the major started his river voyage through the canyon in 1869, the year the continent was joined by rail. In southeast Utah, the Green joins the Colorado, which then flows southeast. In southern Utah and extreme northern Arizona, large faults weakened the rocks and helped dictate the course of the river.

After the Colorado flows into Arizona, it turns abruptly west below where the Little Colorado joins it on the east bank; the river then continues west through Granite Gorge. This bend is an area of stream capture, where one river has eroded headward and cut into another, changing the second's direction of drainage. The capture is related to uplift of the Colorado Plateau some ten million years ago. The plateau is both raised and gently arched into a broad anticline. The ancestral Colorado River moved across a plain when the uplift occurred. Uplift increased the gradient of the river so that the waters flow rapidly, and it has since cut down ever deeper in the same bed (Rabbitt et al. 1969).

The crest of the uplift and the position of the river do not quite coincide, and it is for this reason that the north rim is higher than the south rim. Most rainfall on the south side flows away from the Canyon, making the south rim a steep drop to the river. In the 1880s, there was more of a trace of western man near the north side of the canyon than near the south. At the north rim itself, water drains south into the Canyon, and this side is serrated like the teeth of a comb (Wallace 1972). As a result, to the southwest of the Marble Canyon section of the river are three steep valleys, the Nankoweap, Kwagunt, and Chuar, and for part of their length the streams within these valleys actually contain water; recall this is desert.

Desert erosion shapes the canyon landscape. In a dry climate, a shale will weather to a slope, whereas a horizontal lying limestone will form a vertical cliff. Sandstone also tends to form cliffs, but it is less resistant than limestone. The Shinarump or Chocolate Cliffs mark the edge of the Triassic sandstones, which millions of years of erosion had stripped back from the underlying Permian limestones that formed the upper surface of the Colorado Plateau after its uplift. The loose sand grains were used by the river in sawing down through the limestones. The difference between erosion of limestone and of shale is what makes the dramatic shapes within the chasm.

In a geologic sense, as one moves southward through Utah, the river cuts through ever older rocks, piled on top of each other in neat stratigraphic order. Walcott had measured the thickness of most of these during his 1879 season. The rocks are nearly flat-lying and the river does not cut to a great depth. It is only on the margin of the uplift that the canyon becomes deeper. The prime component of the canyon is the walls rising because of the slight tilt of the uplift;

as slight as one degree of tilt will cause apparently flat-lying rocks to dip ninety feet in a mile's distance. Time is a strange dimension for most people to grasp, but as one goes deeper into the canyon and more and more of the underlying strata come into view, it is obvious that one is traveling from younger to older. It is also obvious that a large amount of time was required to deposit and harden the many layers.

Before the Civil War, J. S. Newberry had examined the rim rocks on the south side; in 1869 Powell was on the north. Part of the mythification of the Grand Canyon began here. One of helpers wrote: "Major Powell in his ghastly fright whispered 'My God, boys, its true, we've struck the end of the world!'" To this comment, the artist W. H. Holmes, who accompanied Dutton, appended, "The Major was never frightened."[17]

After Walcott published the results of his 1879 field season, by the standards of the time one could say that the top of the canyon was well known; the canyon depths were another matter. In 1869, Powell had looked at the rocks within the canyon, mostly as his boat swept past them. His second voyage, two years later, still permitted little time for detailed geology (Fowler and Fowler 1968). The upper limestones, the red shale, and the lower limestones, stained by water from the shale to make the Red Wall, were broadly sketched out. The geology became more complex where the river turned west. Within the chasm, a V-shaped valley, the Granite Gorge, contained both the worst rapids on the river and contorted and tilted ancient rocks which were tough and difficult for the river to erode. One prime question was the age of the rocks below the Red Wall and above the metamorphics of Granite Gorge. Major Powell thought they were Silurian; Dutton looked down from the distant rim above and concurred.

By the early 1880s, the major was deeply into the study of American Indian ethnology and historians have suggested he had lost interest in geology; according to this scenario, he headed the Geological Survey in an administrative, but not a scientific sense. That interpretation contains a grain of truth, yet it was the major who invested federal funds and time in trail building. In 1884, the major was still out on the Chautauqua circuit, speaking about the Grand Canyon (Powell 1884).

> During the month of November, 1882, the Director of the Survey had constructed under his immediate supervision, a horse trail from the brink of a lateral cañon on the east face of the Kaibab Plateau, Arizona, down to the more level cañon bed of Nun-ko-weap Valley, 3,000 feet below. (Walcott 1883c, 437)

Charles Doolittle Walcott, Paleontologist

The party consisted of Charles H. Haskell, collector; John Brown, cook; Joseph Hamblin, packer. Provisioned for three months and provided with nine saddle and pack mules to transport the party, necessary supplies, and camp equipage, the work was at once begun by a detailed study of the Tonto Group. A mass of limestones passing down into sandstones below the Tonto was speedily proved to be of Cambrian Age throughout, and to underlie the Carboniferous red-wall limestone conformably by dip, but unconformably by a line of erosion.

The strata beneath the Tonto Group was studied first in Nun-ko-weap Valley, then in Kwa-gunt, and on to Chuar Valley. Trails were built over the high ridges separating these valleys, as it was found impracticable to follow along the shore of the Colorado River; and the Great Buttes, separating the river from the inner cañon, forced us to cross the ridges connecting them and the walls of the Kaibab Plateau to the west.

The third camp was in the upper portion of the Chuar Valley—a name proposed by you [Powell] for the second large valley south of Nun-ko-weap Valley. At this camp Mr. Haskell succumbed to the feeling of depression resultant upon living in the depths of the cañon, and I was obliged to send him to Kanab and thence home, Mr. Hamblin and the Indian mail carrier accompanying him to Kanab. Mr. Haskell is an excellent collector, and I regretted his going at this time, as I was left with but one man for two weeks, and was obliged to undertake many dangerous climbs on the cañon walls alone. (Walcott 1884, 46)

The casual mention of an Indian mail carrier—his name was José but no more detail is known of him—is an indication of the position and importance of the desert natives, six years after the battle of the Little Big Horn. Mail also brings up the matter of the monthly report. Shortly after he became director, King required a written statement each month. Geologists complained and continued to complain for more than a century, but the reports were sent in. Picture if you will, Walcott, in perhaps the most remote part of the nation, following survey orders by writing to Washington about his activities. With his promotion to assistant geologist, Walcott also had to contribute to the annual report.

The day after he entered the canyon, Walcott scribbled a note to Alexander Agassiz, which Powell carried out to civilization. "Haskell said he could not remain out at $40—so I have obtained permission of Major Powell to retain him at $50—in case you did not think it best to keep him as your asst. after Dec. 1st. I could not replace him with another man & he would not remain at $40."[18] The next time he wrote, as indicated in his official report quoted above, the situation had changed.

One letter from the semiliterate Haskell was retained by Walcott, who later had sent him some photographs of the canyon. "Well I was down to see friend Edy [Hurlburt] the other day & took down the pictures to show him & we had a boss old tyme. I wish that Edy & William [Rust] & you & me could take a trip to the grand canion."[19] They must have parted as friends, regardless of the potential difficulty his leaving presented to Walcott.

Walcott wrote Agassiz:

Illness brot on by homesickness rendered him unfit for work. This is a very lonely, quiet place. No life & nothing but cliffs & cañons. Rocks-rocks-rocks. To me it is intensely interesting & worth a year of exclusion from the outside world. Three weeks of search in the Grand Cañon group has given but one fossil—a *Stromatopora*-like form. Haskell is only a collector & his ill success united with the desire to return home broke him down. Shall send another man out in a few days from the same cause.

The collections of the spring & summer will be merged into those already obtained & I shall select as good a series of the fossils for you as tho' Haskell had remained. Shall give special attention to collecting after getting thro' in the Cañon (probably March) as the Director wishes me to report on the Paleozoic fossils of the Plateau Province.[20]

It took several years for Walcott to deliver the fossils to the Museum in Cambridge, but he did fulfill Major Powell's part of the agreement. No one can blame Charlie Haskell for leaving and certainly Walcott did not. The season in the West had already been a long one, the descent into the depths of the Grand Canyon and its solitude was more than had been expected, and, for the final straw, there is nothing so disheartening for a collector as looking day after day for fossils without success.

On the other hand, Walcott was having a great time. He measured the thickness of the section with his Locke level and described the individual rock units. In tallying up, he had studied two and a half miles of rock thickness deposited after the schists of the inner Granite Gorge were folded and eroded but before the Tonto Group was laid down. There were some snows and rains and one day it was so cold that the ink in his pen never thawed, but this was balanced by the thrill of being where no geologist, and indeed no white man, had ever been before.

The stratigraphy was in layer cake arrangement, but more complex than anticipated, for within the area the Butte Fault trends parallel to Marble Canyon. It dropped the cliff-forming Paleozoic rocks down to near the river edge and exposed the older rocks behind it. These down-dropped younger blocks forced Walcott to climb high up the canyon walls to move from one valley to another as he measured his section. Differential movement on the fault occurred in different places, so matching up strata on either side of the fault was intellectually stimulating.

> On January 2, 1883 Joe Hamblin returned, bringing with him B. L. Young and Achilles Brown as substitute for John Brown, the latter returning to Kanab. After this the party was not broken up until disbanded at the close of the field work.
>
> Camp was moved down to the shore of the Colorado, below Chuar outlet, early in January, and for the first time we were in the Grand Cañon, the inner cañon valleys forming a great amphitheater between the Kaibab Plateau and the Buttes stretching along and forming the west side of the lower portion of Marble Cañon. From this point a detailed study was made of Chuar Lava Hill to determine the character and thickness of each flow of lava and also the relations of the hill to a great fault line which had been traced from its inception in Nun-ko-weap Valley along the west base of six great buttes where it forked, passing each side of the lava hill. It was here the data were obtained showing that the Tertiary fault had been superimposed on an old pre-Tonto fault, with a reversing of the throw of the latter. (Walcott 1884, 46–47)

During his stay in the Grand Canyon, Walcott's experience gained with Iddings and Hague in examining lava flows and interpreting structures was put to good use. Walcott's observation that the major ancient Butte Fault moved again at a later time, but in an opposite direction is extremely perceptive. He had been sent into the canyon to find fossils so as to date the section, but since virtually none could be found below the Tonto, he was studying other aspects of the geology. It is an excellent example of improvising when the original research idea fails.

> Moving back to the lower end of Chuar Valley, a trail was made up on to the ridge next south, advantage being taken of the one break in the Tonto cliff, up through which a trail could be built. When on the Tonto terrace (2,200 feet above the Chuar camp), we followed along its edge for several miles, camping the first night in a little cañon, beside a few water pockets. The following day a heavy wind, accompanied by snow, compelled our remaining near camp, as the danger of falling off the cliff was greatly increased by the light, loose snow covering the crumbling *débris*. The wind quieting down, I went up to the summit of the Tonto group and was delighted to find a narrow belt of Devonian sandstone between it and the Carboniferous. Obtaining a few fish-scales and several brachiopods, the return to camp was hastily

made, as the temperature rapidly lowered with the clearing away of the clouds. During the night the water in sandstone water-pockets was frozen solid, and we were compelled to build large fires and pile the ice about them in order to obtain water for the animals. (Walcott 1884, 47)

So much for Major Powell's theory of good winter working conditions. As an added footnote, finding Devonian rocks here was even more of coup than finding them at the mouth of Kanab Creek.

The flat area atop the Cambrian Tonto Group, on the south side today called the Esplanade, is the highway on which one can travel the canyon's length, and on the north side, it is still an avenue of sorts. Walking along the river is not feasible, for in many places there is no bank. Walcott evidently had several barometers with him. In a barometric survey, a person in camp, commonly the cook, reads the barometric pressure to calibrate the field readings. Subtracting one from another gives a difference in barometric pressure which is then converted into the elevation at the field man reading. This is inexact because weather and air pressure may change rapidly, but the method is more reliable than one might think. The investigation was not easy:

Starting out, a trail was cleared as we proceeded, sometimes along the level terrace and again on the brink of the cliff, where a stumble or a false step would have sent man or animal over a cliff from 300 to 800 feet in height and down a terraced slope 1000 feet or more. Heading the cañon of Un-kar Valley a broken place in the Tonto cliff permitted a trail to be worked zigzag down to the cañon, and as night closed in we camped at the upper end of the narrow, dark inner cañon through which the Colorado flows in the Kaibab division of the Grand Cañon. From this camp the Lower or Grand Cañon Group of the pre-Tonto unmetamorphosed rocks were studied, including the interbedded lava beds, a displaced portion of which forms Chuar Lava Hill. To reach the Archaean, south of Vishnu's Temple, the Tonto terrace (2,200 feet above camp) was scaled and followed along for several miles to a narrow cleft which gave a passage down to the Archaean 1,700 feet below. This terminated the work in that direction. The animals were getting weak from hard work and poor pasturage. The supplies were running low, and the building of a trail further was impractical with the men and tools at hand. (Walcott 1884, 47)

Because of the inclination of strata, minor structure, and slope of the river, the oldest beds, the Archean, are in Granite Gorge. In 1879, Walcott had descended to the west of the Gorge and at Kanab Creek found Primordial, that is Cambrian, fossils in the Tonto. Working to the east this season, he began at the

Charles Doolittle Walcott, Paleontologist

Tonto and measured down once more, but found essentially no fossils. When he finally reached Archean, he could not continue his section; it was time to stop.

The logistics of getting to this part of the Grand Canyon remain difficult, yet starting in the 1920s, geologists continued to look for animal remains in the section decade after decade, but without success. The Unkar and overlying Chuar Groups have been modified by the insertion of a Nankoweap Group between the two (Van Gundy 1951). This group is bounded by two obscure disconformities, and is a prosaic revision in the stratigraphy; in the absence of most fossils to indicate how much time is represented by the disconformities, the importance one might place on an obscure break is a matter of opinion.

There is an unlikely story and two tangible mementos of Walcott's months in the Grand Canyon. After Walcott became secretary of the Smithsonian Institution, he read all manuscripts prepared by staff members, including a report by a young anthropologist working for the Bureau of American Ethnology. Evidence of a hitherto unknown tribe of Indians had been found in the Grand Canyon; the evidence consisted of stone fireplace rings. Walcott commented that these were from his campsites and the manuscript disappeared. Before the turn of the century, prospectors came down the Tanner Trail on the south rim, and ended up opposite Chuar Creek, where the river was easier to cross (McKee 1928). Indians had made the same trip earlier, and ancient dwelling sites are in the area. Still, Walcott's camps were mainly not where any sensible Indian would have lived and finding them would have excited an anthropologist; just possibly, the tale is true.

One tangible trace is found in the geologic literature. While "Walcott Glen" does not appear on any topographic map, it was bestowed on a northwest branch in the lower part of Kwagunt Canyon, southwest of Nankoweap Butte. The strata exposed in the glen and the upper part of Nankoweap Butte constitute the type locality for the Walcott Member of the Kwagunt Formation of the Chuar Group (Ford and Breed 1972, 8). Even if Walcott at first considered the rocks Cambrian, this unit is an appropriate marker of his stratigraphic investigations.

A second tangible trace is on the geologic map of the Grand Canyon (Huntoon et al. 1986), where a structural feature has been named for the man. Under some circumstances of confining pressure and rock strength, a vertical fault may split and further along come together; the block of rock between the two branches of such a fault may be raised or dropped. Near the edge of the Walhalla Plateau is the downdropped block of the Walcott Graben. This is to the west of where Walcott worked, but the name is a fitting tribute to his investigations of the structural effects of the Butte Fault.

In 1882–83, Walcott may have measured the longest single stratigraphic section studied during the nineteenth century. In measuring, geologists occasionally will "offset," that is move laterally along strike to a better local exposure. The Tonto ended one segment of thirteen thousand feet in 1879 and Walcott "offset" to the east and continued downward. By this reckoning Walcott had measured from Archean to Tertiary, from the nearly the youngest to nearly the oldest nonmetamorphic rocks in the world, in as close to a straight line as is possible. Measuring this five-mile-thick pile of rock is surely a record which will be difficult to beat.

> January 25, camp was broken in Un-kar Valley and the back trail was taken to the water pockets. A short stop was made in Chuar and Nun-ko-weap Valleys to review the original observations made on the lava beds. February 5, the camp was moved up to the trail leading out of the cañon, and the following day we reached the old wagon camp on the slopes facing House Rock Valley. In going out one mule was killed outright and two badly injured. (Walcott 1884, 48)

The return trip was even more difficult than indicated in the official report: "Bid Chuar Valley a final farewell & at night camped in Kwa-gunt valley. The total asent [sic] for the trail is 3600 feet & descent [sic] 2800 feet in a distance of 10 miles" (February 2, 1883). "Up on the divide east of Nun-ko-weap butte. Met with good success & cleared up the last missing link in the Butte Fault line as far as I know. Camp moved up foot of trail in Trail Cañon" (February 5, 1883). "Went out to buckboard camp. Bad luck killed Old Beck. Crippled Marse & had a tough trail generally. Left half of packs at Jacob's ladder. Reached camp long after dark. Feet frostbitten" (February 6, 1883). It must have been quite a trail and dreadful weather.

After a day of rest, Walcott traced the Cambrian beds to where they disappeared upstream in Marble Canyon, while the boys went back down the trail to pick up the samples that had been left. The mule Satan had a bad fall and was crippled; horses could not do what the survey mules accomplished. It took a couple of more days to get all the material to House Rock Valley and then to Kanab, where Walcott was "Glad to get back to P.[ost] O.[ffice] & people in houses once more" (February 12, 1883). A few days were spent in working on the map, and repacking samples, before he set out again with a couple of fresh assistants, heading west to Pipe Spring, and then Virgin City, traveling more or less at the foot of the Vermillion Cliffs.

En route, he observed two different sets of lava flows and "Noticed on east side of the Hurricane fault a conglomerate made up of fragments of Carboniferous

ls. capping the Carboniferous. Evidence of a change of level at close of Carb."
(February 22, 1883). The Hurricane fault marks the western side of the Colorado
Plateau. Walcott's observation of movement on the fault during the Carboniferous was again an interesting point that earlier geologists had missed. Thanks
to his work the previous fall, he had no difficulty distinguishing Permian from
the underlying Carboniferous. Where there are no long sections in cliffs, this
is more difficult than one might imagine.

The wagon moved on to Toquerville, a small enough place that they camped
in the street. They went north and Walcott observed the Carboniferous and Permian beds folded by drag on one side of the fault. They drove over terrible roads
from Cedar City to Minerville, hard work for the poor team. Eventually, on February 27, they reached Milford, Utah, where boxes of samples could be sent east
by rail. Thought of more fieldwork as Walcott had outlined in his December letter to Agassiz had vanished.

Walcott took off his field clothes and caught the evening train for Salt Lake
City. He spent the following day at Survey headquarters getting his accounts
in order and visiting with the geologists. The next morning he was on the Ogden
train and the first leg of the long ride back to the East; after so many months
in the field, sitting on a train for days must have been difficult. In Buffalo, he
missed the morning train, but late on the evening of March 6, Walcott was finally in Utica.

After a couple of days of catching up with his family and friends, he was off
to Trenton Falls. Once there, in snow which covered the fences, Walcott, "Spent
the day looking over various things & also fossils from the Trenton and Utica
slate" (March 9, 1883); after all that barren rock in the canyon depths, seeing
William Rust's latest prizes must have been a treat. He stopped for a day in New
York City on his way south and "Found Mr. Hague and Iddings at work and met
the old mess table circle" (March 13, 1883).

His first day at Geological Survey headquarters in Washington, Walcott found
that "The Director wishes me to work in Washington & collect all material at
the National Museum from the Paleozoic rocks" (March 14, 1883). The following day he back on a train to New York. July 1 to March 14 is a long season, but
Walcott showed no evidence of slowing down.

The next month passed rapidly. He packed up the Fortieth Parallel collections
at the American Museum and got his notes in order. Walcott took a quick trip
to Albany, and availed himself of the power saw to cut some sections; he chat-

ted with Hall and compared a few specimens from Nevada with those from New York State. Back in the city, he finished packing and shipped twenty-seven boxes of fossils to Washington.

Once in the nation's capital, Walcott "Began working on Grand Canon notes" (April 21, 1883). "At survey office laid plans of future work before the Director. They included charge of the Paleozoic collections, the completion of the Paleozoic section in the Grand Canon & Ditto Great Basin & the working up of the 1st fauna to the base of the Trenton" (April 23, 1883). During the next decade, Walcott managed to complete the first and third of these projects, but a complete study of the Paleozoic of the West was too much for any one person, even a Walcott.

The process of setting research priorities concerns modern philosophers of science, and one can analyze Walcott's procedure to gain some insight. He concentrated on the Grand Canyon work because it was clearly circumscribed and the dearth of fossils meant that the amount of illustration needed would be relatively small. He worked on those field notes because there was simply no place to unpack his collections; sometimes simple explanations are better than more complex ones. However, on May 8 he finally moved into the National Museum.

Shortly thereafter, J. C. Gentry came to assist with the general work and later the typing. In June, he was also able to hire a professional assistant, Cooper Curtice—of whom more later—to help with the Eureka fossils, having gotten a modest sum from Arnold Hague for salary money. This support enabled Walcott to increase his research productivity. "I now have two good, cool working rooms in the National Museum a long way from the office where I am quiet & retired. Two assistants relieve me of mechanical work & I hope to add to the report in Mr. Hagues volume & bring some other good points."[21]

If one may leave Washington for a brief excursion into geology, Walcott's investigations in Arizona had created quite a stir. Dutton wrote to one of his favorite correspondents, Archibald Geike of the Geological Survey of Great Britain, about how the classification of rocks below those with Cambrian fossils disturbed official organizations on both sides of the Atlantic:

Last summer [sic] a frightful trail was built into the head of the cañon & Mr. Walcott a young palaeontologist & splendid fossil hunter went into it. Above this unconformity for some 500 feet or more he found an abundant fauna most decisively or unquestionably Cambrian & of many decisive types. But what are the beds below? There are over 12000 feet of them as little affected by metamorphism as any mesozoic beds. Walcott spent over two months hunting for fossils but found only a single limestone band three feet thick which yielded one kind only of large fossils which close examination proved to be Stromatopora closely resembling forms which occur in the middle & upper Silurian & Devonian of New York. "Only this and nothing more." Anywhere Walcott cannot find fossils I pity anybody else who tries. Of course the stromatopora means nothing at all. [Originally thought to be a coral-like fossil of no utility in dating rocks]. . . .

Now we have both in Wisconsin & in the Grand Cañon two series of un-metamorphosed beds separated by a strong unconformity. The upper series is unequivocally Cambrian. Is the lower series Cambrian also? I give it up. When the enormous Cambrian deposits of the Wasatch & Great Basin come to be studied they may throw more light upon the subject. Quite likely the Grand Cañon group and the Lake Superior copper rocks are lower Cambrian. Selwyn [Geological Survey of Canada] suggests as much for the latter. At present I have no opinion. I am however under the principal necessity of correcting a statement (doubtfully expressed I am glad to say) in my Gr. Cañon monograph that the lower beds are probably Silurian or Devonian. And I have colored them so on the maps, but with a reservation. . . . In this country the Cambrian system is as yet very obscure and presents problems of a very peculiar nature.[22]

In interpreting the past history of the earth, geologists distinguish between an unconformity and a disconformity. At an unconformity, strata were deposited, tilted, and planed off by erosion, before the overlying strata were deposited; it was an obvious break in the record and had been understood for a century. At a disconformity, the beds are all horizontal or uniformly inclined, but some geologic ages are missing. Rocks of the missing ages may have been deposited and later eroded or may never have been deposited. The absence of "Silurian" in the Grand Canyon indicated a major disconformity in the geologic column. The Silurian may never have been deposited. The irregular upper surface of the Devonian limestone with low hills buried by Carboniferous limestone, which Walcott had seen to the west at Kanab Creek in 1879, was powerful evidence of erosion at that disconformity. As Walcott termed it, it was "a plane of unconformity by erosion, not dip" (Walcott 1883c, 438).

Dutton was wrestling with the concept of isostasy, the elevation of rocks of different density, combined with the notion of great movements of rock masses which may have created the disconformities. A few years later, after he studied the 1886 Charleston earthquake, Dutton formulated the concept of major vertical uplifts in past times. Certainly the elevation of the Colorado Plateau and the differences between the geologic section there and the Great Basin influenced his thinking. Vertical uplift could explain disconformities of great regional extent. Eventually the concept came to suggest that continental blocks stayed in one place but, relative to sea level, moved up and down through time. In contrast, European geologists were much influenced by the structure of the Alps, where apparently horizontal pressure formed great folds of rocks and moved them laterally. The earth reacted both vertically and laterally, and these two great geologic concepts were to clash decades later in battles over continental drift.

Walcott's collection of brachiopods and trilobites, plus more of their tracks and burrows from the Tonto Group, confirmed Gilbert's guess of Cambrian age for these rocks and it was an important accomplishment. There still remained the sequence below the Tonto Group, separated by a disconformity, but it was no greater a disconformity than that which Walcott had found between the Permian and Triassic in 1882 or the Devonian and Carboniferous in 1879. In addition, one of the remarkable points about the rocks in the depths of the canyon, which Dutton touched on, was how fresh they appeared:

> In fact there is no evidence of metamorphism throughout the 12,000 feet of conformable beds than there is in the evenly bedded strata of the Trias and Cretaceous groups of southern Utah. Ripple marks and mud cracks abound in horizons, but not a trace of a fucoid, or a molluscan or annelid trail was observed. But for the discovery of a small discinoid shells, a couple of specimens of a Pteropood allied to *Hyolithes triangularis* and an obscure Stromatopoa-like group of forms, the two and one-half months' search for fossils in these groups would have been without result. They serve, however, to retain the group within the Cambrian. (Walcott 1883c, 441)

The interpretation of unmetamorphosed rocks of great age deserves a few historical comments. In the early history of geology, a classification developed centered on the northern Europe mining areas. The core of mountains was composed of masses of ancient, twisted, complex rocks called primitive; layered, hard rocks, were tilted up to flank the mountain core. Further from the core were more layered rocks, softer in composition and nearly flat lying, and these were succeeded by still less indurated deposits that graded into river bank sands and soft clays of the sea shore (Laudan 1987).

Once geologists got away from the notion of deposition of all rocks by a universal flood, these divisions above the "primitive" of the mountain cores, became the primary, secondary, and tertiary aggregations. At about the same time, early geologists recognized that different age rocks contained different fossils. Later, the terms Paleozoic, Mesozoic, and Cenozoic, basing those names on the concept of ancient, middle and young life came into use.

The geologists of the new USGS knew the value of fossils in dating rocks and they certainly did not judge the age of a rock by its hardness or composition. On the other hand, they also instinctively knew that rocks which had been on earth for vast intervals of time were changed. Ancient rocks, Archean or Azoic—without life—were not supposed to look fresh, and in fact they almost never do. Further, the discovery that metamorphic rocks could actually contain fossils was to be made a few years in the future in Norway by Hans Reusch. The fresh appearance of the rocks and the few fossil remains were good evidence that the Cambrian sequence of the Grand Canyon continued on down for two and one-half miles of thickness. If these rocks were primitive, older than Cambrian, they should have looked older and should not have yielded any fossils at all.

So much for theory. Back in Washington, work blowing theory to pieces progressed on both Grand Canyon geology and Eureka fossils; evenings, Walcott returned to grinding sections of trilobites. Early in June, he was elected to the Cosmos Club. The Cosmos Club had been founded by Major Powell and others as a place for the scientists to relax; not only did this election provide for more social interaction, it marked that he was a fully accepted professional on a par with other scientists in Washington, even without any college degree.

In mid-June, Walcott rode a bicycle outdoors for the first time; velocipedes had come to Utica in the late 1860s, but this was a major improvement over the old bone-shaker. Although he fell and hurt his leg, Walcott mastered the machine. He moved to rooms a little further uptown and thereafter commonly biked to the Museum. It was good transportation for a man in a hurry.

When the new fiscal year came around on July 1, 1883, the major appointed Walcott as a paleontologist, a recognition of where his greatest talents lay. There was more to the story than that, for reform of the Civil Service was finally taking place following President Garfield's assassination. Congress specified the number of permanent positions in the survey and the salary to be paid each. Two of the permanent positions were for paleontologists, and these were filled by O. C. Marsh at four thousand dollars annually and Walcott at two thousand. From six hundred to two thousand dollars in four years was satisfactory advancement, and from temporary to permanent employment was heaven; Walcott had found his niche. Congress left the USGS a loophole of engaging temporary employees and Powell showed his consummate political skill in shuffling the lists so that excellent experienced people were placed where an appeal later could be make to make them permanent. For example, Iddings and White were among those who were now "temporary."

Throughout the spring and summer, Walcott alternated between adding to the Eureka report and writing up his Grand Canyon investigations. In addition to measuring the thickness of the rock section, describing movement on the Butte fault (which he named) made for an interesting study. By late July, Walcott completed the map he had compiled in the field, and on August 2, he turned in manuscript and map to the director. No grass grew under his feet. The next day Walcott left hot and humid Washington for the field. That work in the Taconic Mountains of the Northeast forms a separate phase of his career and is discussed later.

By December, Walcott published a short report concerned with Grand Canyon stratigraphy in the *American Journal of Science* (Walcott 1883c). However, his study of the Butte Fault waited five years and his map languished even longer before publication. The first *Bulletin* of the USGS appeared in 1883 and one might think that Walcott's report would have been appropriate as a short study. On the other hand, Dutton's *Monograph* appeared the year before Walcott crawled out of the canyon, and to show errors so soon after a definitive work might not be good politics. In any event, Walcott was either satisfied with the arrangement or too busy to worry about publication of only a small portion of his results.

After returning to Washington in mid-October, Walcott estimated that it would take two weeks to complete the Eureka report, an only slightly optimistic statement. Shortly thereafter, "It is decided that my part of the Eureka Rept be printed separately" (November 9, 1883); study of the fossils would be a distinct monograph from Hague's report on geology. Walcott's summary age determinations had been included in Hague's preliminary paper in the third *Annual Report*. Walcott's report, which was large and growing larger every day, would stand alone to provide the documentation for Hague's map and report. There was also an agreement, almost certainly at Walcott's suggestion, that the fossil collections from the White Pine Mining District be included. With this addition, he estimated the report would include more than four hundred species.

Walcott continued hard at work on the Eureka fossils during most of November. A collector wrote him to inquire about the Trenton crinoids. Walcott told him of the sale to Agassiz and that if he could visit Cambridge and receive permission to separate out the crinoids, they would be sent on. As regards Eureka, "I now have over 450 species of Paleozoic invertebrates 150 n. sp. but not a crinoid represented except by plates of the column."[23]

He took a few days at the end of the month to study a remarkable trilobite with legs, important in itself, but not germane to the Eureka report. By mid-December he was "leading a quiet uneventful life at the office during the day & calling or working in the evening" (December 12, 1883). He ended the year with a cheerful summary in his diary.

By mid-February, he was "arranging plates and figures for Eureka Rept" (February 11, 1884). Compared to the report he had submitted two years ago, "eleven plates of illustrations and nearly double the amount of text have been added" (Walcott 1884a, ix). The new plates bring up John C. McConnell, another of those shadowy-figured artisans about whom little is known. Walcott called him Doctor, but officially he was a clerk; "Jn McConnell is an exceptionally skilled draughtsman, and an artist in color whose work is at times of great value to the [Army Medical] Museum."[24] He doubled as an occasional natural history illustrator, and drew pictures of a few fish, but his largest amount of work was portraying shells for Dall, and probably Dall directed Walcott to him. They got on well and Walcott spend a few evenings and Sundays at the McConnell home.

McConnell's drawings were on woodcuts which allowed flexibility in their placement on a plate and permitted Walcott to include figures in the text of the report. These were reproduced by electotyping, that is copper was electrolytically precipitated on the lines of the drawing, which was then inked. In contrast to earlier methods of printing, many more copies could be run off without a change in the quality of reproduction. The method had been around since about 1840, but had been improved in 1870 (Ringwalt 1981, 152–55). Powell wanted to try electotyping as an experiment, and technologically it was a success, though some art critics will judge Simpson's lithographed drawings more pleasing to the eye. To be fair, after an engraving is made, the printer touches it up with an engraving tool so a few of the lines and curves may not be precisely where McConnell had drawn them. The two illustrators worked in different ways, thereby making comparison difficult, but in final analysis, McConnell was a draftsman and Simpson was an artist.

Though the Eureka report is two parts pieced together, except for differences in the plates, there are no discontinuities; one has to read its history to be aware of this point. From the start, Walcott treated the fossils of each principal geologic age separately, using a biological arrangement within each fauna. With such a framework, he could add or delete species or genera as necessary without upsetting the whole work. Judging from the plates, most of the new material was of Devonian age and most of the added fossils were mollusks. With so many new species to name, Walcott generally used place names or descriptive terms, but there are a few patronyms. A species is named after Iddings and one for Hague. There is also a new species named after C. A. White; presumably Walcott wrote this up in 1881 or 1882 and designed it as a peace offering.

The actual printing finally started and by June, Walcott was busy reading proof. Hague's letter transmitting the report to Director Powell, a governmental formality set in type, is to the point: "Mr. Walcott's intimate knowledge of the district lends additional weight to his own special labors. I regard his report as the most important contribution yet made to the invertebrate paleontology of the Basin Ranges, and of great value in its bearing upon the geology of the Cordillera" (Walcott 1884a, vii).

A letter of transmittal is hardly the place to be modest and one might dismiss Hague's comments as hyperbole. However, his remarks are accurate. Eminent geologists who restudied the area wrote: "For fifty years the monographic studies of Hague and Walcott remained the most significant references on Paleozoic history and paleontology of the Great Basin, in fact of the entire Far West" (Nolan, Merriam, and Williams 1956, 5). *Monograph* 8 is the only work to treat the Paleozoic fauna as a whole that was ever produced for the rocks of the West. Later studies refined and modified identifications of various fossil groups, and the ages of the stratigraphic units are now more precisely known, but overall Walcott's descriptions of new species or referral to previously described species have stood up well.

In one historian's view, "By fossil correlation, one could integrate the landscape geographically; by fossil successions one could integrate it historically.... As a result, paleontology became the mathematics of geology and stratigraphy, the first specifically geologic subject ordered by fossils, became its mechanics" (Pyne 1979, 168). Walcott had written the basic text for fossils of the West; his monograph is still the first place to look when trying to identify an unknown Paleozoic fauna. Not only had he documented the age of the rocks at Eureka, he had demonstrated that the geologic column, the thickness of the rocks of different ages, in central Nevada was fundamentally different from that in the Grand Canyon.

Government geologists at this time had two official outlets for larger works, either as papers appended to the annual report, or as distinct monographs; the monograph series was part of Clarence King's legacy. Dutton's *Monograph* 2 on the Grand Canyon District, off the presses in 1882, was the first published of the series and set the tone. *Monograph* 1 was reserved for Gilbert, but it did not come out until 1890. It was fortunate for Walcott that his research was separated from that of Hague, for *Monograph* 20, *Geology of the Eureka district, Nev.* was not published until 1892, long after the mining boom had peaked and Eureka became ghostlike.

As often happens at the Government Printing Office, there was a delay. Although the *Monograph* has a date of 1884 and a few volumes were officially delivered then, most copies were not distributed until 1885; the National Museum did not record receipt of a copy until August 25. The Government Printing Office issued three thousand copies of *Monograph* 8 for the U.S. Geological Survey and fifty for the author; another one thousand were printed for distribution by Congress.

The volume received notice in the leading American scientific journals, though no critical reviews were published. A Utica paper gave it nearly a full column under "Literary Matters": "The contents of this important volume are the results of personal work and observations on the part of Mr. Walcott. . . . Probably no geologist in this country was better equipped for this special work, and it is very certain that no one would have devoted to it more careful and conscientious labor."[25] That may be a little overdrawn, but Walcott was a local boy who had made good, and Uncle William was a pillar of the community.

Until *Monograph* 8 went out of print, the Geological Survey sold this book for $1.10. Even with the large number printed, it is now rare. The few copies which are on the market today commonly fetch $100 to $125 each. For a specialized paleontological audience, this is still a most important work. If Walcott published nothing more than this monograph and his earlier paper on trilobite limbs he would still be remembered as an important paleontologist.

After a final draft is submitted for publication, most scientists tend to lose interest and move onto another problem. By the time the Eureka report finally came out, Walcott had already devoted more than a year to another more complex geologic problem, that of the age of the rocks in the Taconic Mountains of western New England.

6

Potsdam: Start with What You Think You Know (1883–1886)

I had hoped ere this to have been able to go to press with a completed work, and could easily have done so but for the impossibility of getting from the various paleontological authorities (to whom we were obliged to commit our collections of fossils) any lists. It is the misfortune of geology to be more or less dependent on this branch of specialists. Without their specific determinations, the geological maps, even, cannot receive their ultimate color-designations, nor can reports, which like ours, involve a wide range of stratigraphy, be safely written. So it has happened, in spite of every effort on my part, that these scientific autocrats, although abundantly promising, have again and again disappointed me and caused a wearying delay in the publication of our report.

Clarence King, 1875

WALCOTT ARRIVED IN Washington in March 1883 and was assigned an office in the new United States National Museum building. For a field geologist, excitement and fun reside outdoors, not in the office. There was much to be done with the Eureka fossils to enlarge his report, but at this stage the effort was more mechanical than intellectual, even with new species to describe. Since his first days in Albany, when Walcott ground sections of trilobites at night while assisting Hall during the day, he had learned that an element of success was to pursue more than one project at a time. Now, given an opportunity, Walcott started a major new project before the old one was finished. To add to his pleasure, he also had funds to hire a fossil collector in Wisconsin.

The politics of this new project concerned the geologic map of the United States. Under King, the Geological Survey was confined to public lands of the

Charles Doolittle Walcott, Paleontologist

West. Though an adroit political ploy, Powell had a minor amendment passed which could be interpreted by lawyers as giving the Survey national scope (Rabbitt 1980, 64–67). King had fired topographers, but Powell hired them and immediately began a program of topographic mapping in New England. Walcott was only one of several geologists who began work in the East, but Walcott's effort were critical in regard to the major stratigraphic units of the county, as shown below.

Walcott (1912, 253) claimed that at age seventeen, his curiosity was aroused by fossils from older rocks. He already had a fair knowledge of geology when he joined the USGS, and in measuring the geologic sections in Utah and Arizona and in studying the Eureka, Nevada, rocks he was given a great deal of latitude. Nevertheless, these investigations were assigned by senior men to whom he had to report. Even in the months in the Grand Canyon, he had not been entirely his own master. On every assignment, Walcott had produced significant scientific results. As a consequence, now he was in part able to pick his own research interests.

If given a chance to shape his own project, why would Walcott agree to an eastern area, rather than returning to the West, where outcrops and chances for discovery were abundant? It may have been based on the old principle of better the devil you know than the devil you do not. Also, Walcott would be involved in a problem which had bedeviled geologists for forty years; younger people are often certain they can solve problems that their elders could not.

One of the best ways to resolve any scientific problem is to start at the known and move gradually into the unknown, rather than jumping into the middle of a morass. In New York, everyone knew exactly what was meant by Trenton Limestone. That rock unit provided a datum plane for Walcott to start investigations of the underlying rocks, including the Potsdam Sandstone. (NOTE: Capitalization is a relatively recent phenomenon, the change taking place during Walcott's career; so, for example, the use of both "Trenton Limestone" and "Trenton limestone" does not mean that all proofreading has been ignored. For the most part, however, modern capitalization and word treatment have been used. One exception is in an earlier chapter in which Walcott worked on what he called the "Utica slate," which today is called "Utica Shale.")

Potsdam, New York, is a small town to the north of the Adirondack Mountains whose only claim to fame is as the type locality of the Potsdam Sandstone. West and east of Potsdam, a vast deposit of sandstone occurs in a crescent surrounding about one-third of the Adirondack dome and extending down state in the Champlain Valley to about sixty miles from Albany.

The Potsdam Sandstone is the base of the New York System, a usage that carries a considerable weight of history. During the 1830s, many of the eastern states instituted geological surveys primarily to provide information for raw material discoveries, including coal, iron ore, and precious metals. The most elaborate of these was the Natural History Survey of New York, which began in 1836 (Merrill 1920). This survey was organized into four districts, each with its own geologist, and included additional specialists to describe the minerals, fossils, and flora and fauna.

"The New York survey gave to American geology a nomenclature largely its own; it demonstrated above everything else the value of fossils for purposes of correlation, and, incidentally it brought into prominence one man, James Hall, who was destined to become America's greatest paleontologist" (Merrill 1924, 187). Only through the stubborn determination of Hall to describe all the fossils of New York did the Natural History Survey persist after the district reconnaissance stage. Though the legislature in effect abolished the survey organization several times, Hall simply ignored that body and kept on working (Fakundiny and Albanese 1988).

A digression is needed to explain what geologists mean by "system." Like "catalogue" in a library, the concept behind the term has changed fundamentally. During the early days of geology, "system" had a geographic meaning, such as Alpine System. In other usages, it meant a series of rocks which had the same general composition, such as the Oolite System or the Cretaceous (Latin for "chalk") System. Commonly, there was also a structural component clearly separating one system from another. Systems were consonant with these various usages in western Europe, and relationships among them were seldom apparent. As noted earlier, one of the great geologic challenges was to systematize, literally and figuratively, the "transition" rocks near the base of the geologic column.

Two pioneering British geologists, Rodrick Murchison and Adam Sedgwick, began to make sense out of the transition rocks. In 1835, Murchison proposed a Silurian System on the western border of Wales; the same year, Sedgwick named the underlying Cambrian System in northern Wales (Secord 1986, 69–109). Moving to Devonshire, in 1839 they jointly named the Devonian System as a new system above the Silurian (Rudwick 1985, 276–300) and below the Carboniferous. The distinctions of these systems were based partly on breaks in the sequence, as well as occurrences in different areas. Murchison also characterized his Silurian by a unique fossil fauna, instituting modern usage of the term; British geologists also characterized the Devonian by its own particular fossils.

Charles Doolittle Walcott, Paleontologist

In the New World, in their major final publications, the four principal New York geologists agreed that the series of rocks that were stacked up from the Potsdam as the oldest to the youngest, the Chemung and Catskill, constituted a system, a sequence of rocks without any obvious major structural breaks during deposition. In a sense, the New York System was like the transition rocks divided by Murchison and Sedgwick in Great Britain, in that the strata were above the Primitive in the Adirondack Mountains, to the north, and below the Secondary, near the Atlantic Coast to the south. Given the understanding of earth history at that time, the New York geologists were justified in their proposal of a system. Unfortunately, they were just a few years too late, for Silurian and Cambrian had already been named.

At the start of the New York survey, Timothy Conrad was one of the four principal mappers, but after one season he abandoned fieldwork and took the position of paleontologist; James Hall, who had been an assistant to Ebenezer Emmons mapping in the East, moved up as principal geologist in the far western district. From the scraps of information trickling across the Atlantic, he was immediately able to recognize from similarity of the fossils that the New York System included Silurian rocks, and later he noted the upper part of the system included Devonian rocks. It may have been unfortunate for geology that Conrad was correct in his brilliant correlation. After a few decades, the New York System disappeared to be replaced by the British terms. The British names were based on weaker scientific ground, but had priority, and priority is an overriding principle in almost every argument.

Even with agreement on the New York System by the four principal geologists, there was trouble in that Garden of Eden of flat-lying rocks dripping with fossils. In some versions of subsequent events, the role of the serpent was played by Ebenezer Emmons. In 1838, like the others, he saw the Potsdam as the oldest rock in New York, the sandstone being followed by a succession of overlying strata. Further investigations brought a change in his thinking. From the Hudson River eastward and into Massachusetts and Vermont, the rock sequence is terribly contorted and quite thick; the lithology of the rocks does not particularly resemble anything on the eastern flank of the Adirondack region (Fisher 1977), or west of the Hudson River. In the rocks of the Hoosic Mountains of Massachusetts and extending westward through the Taconics, Emmons saw another geologic system:

> To this series, which Emmons conceived to be older than the Potsdam, he proposed in 1841 to give the name Taconic, after the Taconic range, elevating

it to the dignity of a system. . . . Unmoved by argument, to the day of his death Emmons adhered faithfully to his "system," although from the very first he noted its most inherent weakness—that in no case had the Potsdam sandstone been found resting upon any of its members. That this system was actually an older, lower-lying series was indicated only by the fact that neither were any of its members found intercalated with the overlying series. (Merrill 1924, 596–97)

Few fights and feuds in American geology equal that concerning the Taconic System. No sooner did Emmons suggest the system than Henry Darwin Rogers, the Pennsylvania state geologist, vigorously opposed it (Schneer 1978). Three years after his first proposal, Emmons reversed the order of strata he had first presented. After that, the rock sequence was interpreted and reinterpreted and rereinterpreted. More than just a sprinkling of politics and personalities was involved. Both Emmons and his former assistant Hall wanted permanent positions at the close of the Natural History Survey. When the dust finally settled, Hall was state paleontologist and Emmons, state agriculturalist. Eventually, Emmons left the state to live in North Carolina, but he continued advocacy on the issue.

Local geologists in Vermont found a few fossils at several localities, especially at the strangely named town of Georgia, Vermont, that caused more difficulties with the Taconic System (Eagan 1987). Canadian paleontologist Elkanah Billings reported a peculiar sequence of fossils near Quebec which he thought indicated that the Taconic System extended northward. This led to more name calling (Yochelson 1993). Between Emmons being forced out of New York and the onset of the Civil War, after two decades the Taconic controversy eventually simmered down for a while.

The Green Mountains and Taconic area extended into eastern Canada, and T. Sterry Hunt of the Geological Survey of Canada took up argument for the Taconic System. Jules Marcou, who resided at the Museum of Comparative Zoology, also became a proponent of Emmon's system. In the 1870s, James Dwight Dana began investigations that convinced him the Taconic System was spurious. Controversy reached a new peak of invective. In almost each passing year after Emmon's death, some geologist wanted vindication for him and another refuted his work. With each new discovery, the region was found to be more complicated than had been previously assumed. Whatever view any protagonist or any antagonist might take on the Taconic System, some fact or interpretation would support that position.

Charles Doolittle Walcott, Paleontologist

In 1879, the year Walcott joined the U.S. Geological Survey, Dana wrote a thumbnail description of the region to fellow geologist Archibald Geikie in Great Britain: ". . . the degree of metamorphism is more and more marked as you go south from Vermont to Connecticut, and as you go east from the Taconic range. West of the Taconic Range the schist and limestone becomes but less crystalline, and for the most part the schists are hydromica schists, and what has been called clay-slate" (Gilman 1899, 334–35). Complicated metamorphism of rocks and complex structure need not necessarily be related, and many geological regions are affected by one or the other. New England has both, a horrendous combination for geologists in the last part of the nineteenth century.

Long before Walcott moved into eastern New York, most proponents spoke of upper and lower parts of the Taconic System. One issue was the age relationships of the Lower Silurian, or the newly proposed alternative term Ordovician, to the Upper Taconic. This paled beside the question of the relationships of the Cambrian and the Lower Taconic; some thought they were the same, some thought the Taconic was older, some thought it was younger, and some thought nothing of the original idea made sense. Powell had no use for either the Taconic System or the new Ordovician System proposed in 1879. Still, if the USGS was to publish a geologic map of the United States, the problem of what names to use for these rocks had to be resolved. Relationships and correlations of strata below the Trenton were very much up in the air, and Walcott's aim was to sort them out.

In July 1883, Walcott vacationed with friends at Asbury Park, New Jersey, the seashore being far preferable to Washington summer. Naturally, part of his time was devoted to finishing up the Grand Canyon map and notes. Early in August, he was in Utica to check on Mother and Josie and then to collect fossils at the Rust farm with William and with Ed Hurlburt.

In mid-August, Cooper Curtice and Walcott in Utica went off to Saratoga Springs; the geologists moved to Vermont in late September. The Taconic wars were going on full force when Walcott arrived at the outskirts of the battle zone, and he was intelligent enough not to venture unprepared into the battlefield. The Saratoga Springs fossils, which had engendered Walcott fall from grace with Hall, provided a first clue in sorting out the rock relationships. They went out "Collecting fossils from Hoyt's quarry. Fauna Potsdam in character" (August 14, 1883). "From the past season's field-work, it was discovered that a massive limestone, containing a typical Potsdam fauna, overlies the Potsdam sandstone of New-York geologists in Saratoga county, N.Y." (Anonymous 1884, 136–37). The next generation remarked: "Walcott's work was, of course, a great advantage over everything that preceded. We differ from his conclusions chiefly in regarding the Hoyt limestone as of the horizon of the Calciferous rather than of the upper part of the Potsdam . . ." (Ulrich and Cushing 1910, 101). Today's paleontologists consider the limestone Late Cambrian, just as Walcott indicated.

Walcott also established that the Potsdam Sandstone of the upper Mississippi Valley was the same age as the limestone. During Late Cambrian time as the sea gradually inundated the continent, it deposited a great sheet of sand which became progressively younger toward the center of North America; in other words, limestone in New York was the same age as sandstone in Wisconsin. Walcott hired a local geologist, L. C. Wooster, to collect that summer and had a large number of new fossils on which to base this opinion.

In that summer of 1883, "field work was begun . . . in the vicinity of Saratoga Springs, and continued north along the eastern base of the Adirondack Mountains into Warren, Essex, and Clinton Counties. Crossing the lower end of Lake Champlain, a careful study was made of the Cambrian formations in Franklin County, Vermont. Many sections were taken in both New York and Vermont, and a large number of paleontologic specimens were collected."[1] The "large number" filled five barrels and nine boxes.

East of Lake Champlain, the rock sequence was complicated and the time spent in Vermont and northeastern New York only laid a foundation for the future. In the official published report, Walcott skimmed over the point that a few days were spent at Phillipsburg, two miles north of the Vermont border; rocks do not recognize international boundaries, but there was no sense waving a red flag for the politicians. Fortunately, Chief Clerk McChesney paid more attention to easing the way for geologists to do their job than to pointing out the potential illegality of a federal geologist collecting in Canada.

In his monthly report, Walcott noted to the chief clerk, now James C. Pilling, that "Curtice proves to be a good man in the field and an active worker."[2] In contrast to collector Charles Haskell, who left Walcott in the Grand Canyon, went west with Walcott in 1882, Cooper Curtice was well-known during his time and is still dimly remembered in a few scientific circles, though not in geology. Curtice's versatility stretched from paleontology to parasitology.

There were similarities in background between Walcott and Curtice. Curtice was born in 1856 in Connecticut, but for part of his life lived in central New York (Butts 1953). He descended from a family in Salem, Massachusetts, by 1640. Like Walcott, he lost a parent at age two, though it was his mother, not his father; his father had a loose foot and Curtice moved five times before entering Cornell University. He was president of the Natural History Society of the University his senior year, studied zoology and veterinary medicine, and took a course of paleontology from H. S. Williams. After graduation in 1881, he and his sister went to medical school at the University of Michigan for a year. In 1882, Williams came for a visit to the American Museum and recommended Curtice to Walcott. After the move to Washington, Walcott hired him in June 1883. Curtice tied up the loose ends of the Eureka fossils and Walcott was not about to let such good help leave.

Curtice had come to Washington in 1882 to attend Columbia Veterinary College. During his survey career, he continued schooling part time and earned the degree of doctor of veterinary science; in later official reports, Walcott referred to him as Dr. Curtice. In August 1886, Curtice transferred to the Bureau of Animal Industry as their first staff zoologist and also entered National Medical College, Columbian University, now George Washington University. His varied early research concerned sheep parasites in Colorado; his report brought international fame to the bureau. Curtice then studied Texas tick fever until he resigned in 1891. In 1894, Curtice was reappointed as an inspector, only to be dismissed after two years (Logue 1995).

The principal cause of Curtice's dismissal was the issue of cattle tick fever. Because he had investigated the life history of the tick, Curtice was convinced that the parasite could be eradicated and the fever wiped out. The prevailing view, and especially that of his bureau boss, was that infected cattle should be quarantined to curb the disease. Curtice experimented on tick eradication, in addition to his assigned duties, and campaigned for a policy to destroy the ticks in a manner which varied from unpolitic to fanatic—that is, Curtice's activities, not the actual destruction of the ticks. Curtice never stopped lecturing and writing on the subject. To parasitologists he is still known as "Dr. Ticks." In 1896 at Walcott's request, the secretary of agriculture allowed Curtice a USGS interlude to search for fossils in California; once more Curtice performed beyond expectations.

Curtice next became state veterinarian of North Carolina, where he began a tick eradication program. 1900 saw him on the faculty of Rhode Island College of Agriculture and Mechanical Arts. By 1906, he was back at the bureau, following a special congressional appropriation for cattle tick eradication. Time proved him correct. Curtice is one of the persons responsible for the low cost and abundance of beef in the United States, though he never received proper credit for his contributions. He also started a program to eradicate tuberculosis in dairy cows, put production of poultry on a sounder basis, and investigated diseases of turkeys.

Walcott occasionally used the phrase "promising young man" when referring to an assistant or someone he worked with, a phrase that may well have started with Dr. Curtice. "His integrity and outspoken conviction of what he considers right is unsurpassed. . . . When with me he always accomplished the work given him & obtained larger results with the same amount of money than one man out of ten."[3] In turn, the last of the seven Curtice children, born February 14, 1907, was named Charles Walcott Curtice. When Curtice joined the USGS, he donated more than fifteen hundred Devonian fossils to the National Museum, and as late as 1926, less than a year before he died, Walcott recalled the donation and the manifold collections Curtice made for the Geological Survey.[4]

A further digression concerns how Walcott obtained an office in Washington. The tale of the Smithsonian Institution has been told many times (Oehser 1949; Carmichael and Long 1965), and only a few words are needed here. Briefly, James Smithson willed a fortune to the United States of America to found an establishment for the "increase and diffusion of knowledge among men." Except for specifying that this was to be in Washington, no other directions were given. Smithson died, then an heir without issue, and the money came to America. It took two years to collect the money and another eight to decide what to do with the funds.

Congress, on August 10, 1846, set up the Smithsonian Institution, giving it the broadest kind of charter. The board of regents in turn queried various prospective heads as to what they thought Smithson meant. Joseph Henry of Princeton University, perhaps the outstanding American scientist of his time, was chosen as secretary. Even then it was not obvious what the institution should do. Against Henry's wishes a building, the Smithsonian Castle was built, for the regents argued that without an imposing home the Institution would never command respect" (Hafertepe 1984). Henry convinced the regents to use only half the interest for construction and between 1848 and 1855 the place was slowly built. Even though Henry detested the Castle, he was a good soldier, and for the remainder of his life he and his family resided in the east side of the building. This was partly symbolic and partly to save money.

Smithson money was important to Henry as a sacred trust given to the country and he was determined not to squander the endowment. There were battles galore in the early days about the course that the Smithsonian should follow.

Charles Doolittle Walcott, Paleontologist

Some wanted a museum, some a university, and some a national library. One of Henry's guiding principles was that the Smithsonian should not be doing anything that another organization could do. The first battle, over a national library, Henry won. Though the Smithsonian developed a large library, it did not make that a major preoccupation and the books eventually were deposited in the Library of Congress, except for those that the Smithsonian deemed were needed for its own work.

The museum story is much more complicated. The standard version is that Joseph Henry was opposed to museums and the notion of displays was forced upon him. What Henry was opposed to was dissipation of the endowment. As soon as the Castle opened its doors, there were a few public displays. In the various histories of the organization, such emphasis is placed on the endowment that it is seldom noted that Smithson also left his library, his traveling chemical laboratory, his large collection of minerals, and even his clothing to the United States. From day one onward, the Smithsonian Institution was in the museum business. During its first decade, the Smithsonian was given other objects of art and of natural history.

The United States Exploring Expedition of 1838–1842, headed by Lt. Charles Wilkes (Stanton 1975), brought back many specimens and these were housed in the second major government office building in Washington, on F Street between Seventh and Ninth. The terrible handling of these specimens became a matter of national embarrassment. In 1856, Henry was asked to take charge of that material. The secretary stipulated that he would accept the Wilkes collection only if the government would pay for transport plus cases to house it and provide money on an annual basis to maintain the specimens. The next year a deal was struck, and ever since federal money has come to the Smithsonian annually.

Four years after Henry's appointment, he hired Spencer Fullerton Baird as assistant secretary. Baird was a diligent, classical naturalist, still well known for his investigations of birds, mammals, and fish. He was a prodigious collector, and when Baird came to Washington, his private collection filled a railroad freight car; these specimens were donated to the Smithsonian long before the Wilkes material was transported to the Castle. Understandably, Henry turned the museum function over to Baird. Baird knew of Henry's aversion to anything that would eat up the endowment and his skepticism that collections were worth what they cost to support. Accordingly, he kept a low profile but accumulated specimens to such an extent that in a couple of decades the museum tail wagged the Smithsonian dog. Baird may well have been the greatest collector in the history of museums, not so much through his own efforts as through the network of government and private individuals he enlisted to send specimens to Washington.

At the Philadelphia Centennial Exposition, Henry formally appealed to the exhibitors to contribute their material to the Smithsonian. As a result of this bonanza, an old, four-story former armory building used for storage was packed to the rafters with unopened boxes. The elderly Henry died full of honor in 1878, and Baird was immediately appointed secretary. Congressional funds lent the exposition were repaid, and in 1879 a congressional appropriation for a museum building was passed. The physical entity of the United States National Museum finally came into being (Yochelson 1985). When the new structure was completed, one of the staff joked that it suffered from the same defect as the Pension Building, namely that it was fireproof and therefore the Smithsonian was forced to keep it.

It was a square squatty affair of red, blue and yellow brick, exteriorly an architectural horror; interiorly a barren waste. . . . no partitions, no ceilings, nothing but acres of space interrupted by vertical columns and overhead a network of iron rods to support the roof. Light streaming in from high windows producing shadows and reflections everywhere but where wanted. The quadrennial period of silliness for which Washington is noted come on early in 1881. A place must be found for the inaugural ball on March 4 [President Garfield], and as there was no other place, the museum building was selected. . . . A board floor was hastily laid on joints in grooves dug in the soft black earth. On these the boards were nailed. . . . These shoddy floors were allowed to remain until the occasional breaking thru by rotting necessitated their replacement. . . . One early summer I recall such a host of newborn termites bored their way thru rotting floors and attacking the woodwork of the cases.[5]

The building had four entrances, each flanked by rooms on either side of the doorway. Walcott's office in 1883 was on the south side and occupied a space about twenty feet square. It was divided into laboratory and office proper by a wall. There was a window to the outside on either side of the partition and smaller windows on the interior wall opening into the museum display area. Collections were placed elsewhere in the building. A high ceiling was a saving grace in the summer. This was smaller than the space Walcott had at the American Museum in New York, and there he had worked alone, not with two other people. Still, the place was infinitely better than no space at all, and by government standards of the day, the office was not cramped. The Arts and Industries Building, as it is known today, came full circle, for in 1976 it housed a reconstruction of the Philadelphia Exposition.

Now Walcott's narrative can resume. When he and Curtice returned from New England, one of his first acts was to write his colleague H. S. Williams: "I have seen Prof. Hall & you had best keep a careful outlook in his direction as he will strike you in everything he can."[6] The grand old man of American paleontology was incensed that anyone dared work on New York fossils without his blessing and, probably, his senior coauthorship.

Even with Mr. Gentry available for typewriting—a fantastic technological improvement over writing out a clean copy for the printer—the Eureka report required nearly full time and attention, with descriptions of new fossils to prepare and integrate into the existing text. By extra effort, Walcott completed two abstracts summarizing the past summer's work and presented a paper to the new Biological Society of Washington on fossils in a sedimentary rock superficially resembling granite, sent in by a field geologist.

More important, late in the year he gave a talk before the Philosophical Society of Washington, the most prestigious local scientific society. It was a sketchy first attempt to discuss the Cambrian of the United States and Canada. Walcott used the terms "Acadian," "Georgian," and "Potsdam" to subdivide the Cambrian into lower, middle, and upper series, respectively. He correlated across several thousand miles and equated the Tonto Sandstone of the Grand Canyon with the Potsdam. His treatment of the older parts of the Cambrian had problems, for in both the upper Mississippi Valley and the Grand Canyon, he assigned considerable thickness of rocks below the Potsdam to the Cambrian; these eventually turned out to be much older.

Uncertainty as to the age of unfossiliferous rocks was one kind of problem, but there was a more pervasive one. In reading Walcott's work, one must remember that Lower and Middle Cambrian reversed in usage after 1888, as Walcott's knowledge of faunas and stratigraphy grew. In the Philosophical Society paper, his conclusions on stratigraphic order, like those of his predecessors, were wrong, despite new data from Nevada. Interestingly enough, the still-novel concept of evolution mislead him. "Below the Potsdam horizon [in Nevada] there occurs a distinct fauna, characterized by a considerable development of the trilobite genus *Olenellus*, a genus that in the embryonic development of several of its species proves that it is derived from the *Paradoxides* family and is consequently of later date" (Walcott 1883d, 100). Confusion on Lower and Middle Cambrian reigned for another five years.

Late in November, Walcott squeezed in time for trilobite appendages. A remarkable specimen had been collected in the Cincinnati area. Walcott wrote in haste to Alexander Agassiz at the Museum of Comparative Zoology: "I am now studying the Ohio trilobite that shows so many well preserved legs. It was described by Mickleborough & the figure reproduced in the Amer. Naturalist. It is a genuine & fine specimen. I have the original Billings specimen from the Canadian Survey here & the Ohio specimen is far superior."[7] Walcott did some cleaning and preparation before redescribing and illustrating it (Walcott 1884b). The owner lowered the price from $500 to $150, but in spite of Walcott's further urging, Agassiz declined to purchase the fossil; eventually it came to the National Museum.

Along with his own scientific investigations, promotion from geologist to paleontologist in July 1883 brought new duties. Walcott directly supervised Curtice and Gentry, and he also arranged for paleontologic investigations of others. At Cornell, H. S. Williams was collecting and studying the Devonian of New York as a part-time federal employee. Walcott continually received fossils for identification from USGS geologists measuring sections in the central and southern Appalachians. The large collections from New England and Wisconsin caused space problems.

By mid-December Walcott summed things up: "Leading a quiet uneventful life. At the office during the day & calling or walking in the evening" (December 13, 1883). He moved again, this time to 1214 K Street N.W. "The year terminates with all moving nicely in my little routine of life. A year ago today in the wilds of the Colorado Cañon. Today in possession of the position aimed for five years ago at Washington. As a whole the year has been a pleasant & profitable one to me" (December 31, 1883).

Despite the gloomy months of January and February, completion of the Eureka report in the latter must have helped to keep up scientific spirits of the group in the museum. Further, Walcott's mother and sister Josie came for an extended visit and Walcott told the Biological Society about the Ohio trilobite with limbs preserved and spoke to the Travel Club on his trip to the Colorado River.

In 1884, Walcott developed another front on his attack on the Cambrian. To discuss this properly, it is necessary to digress once more and review some of the basics in paleontology. Today when one describes a new species, it must also be properly illustrated to be considered valid by other workers in the field, but as late as the first part of the twentieth century, natural history specimens were still being described without any illustration. Illustration really is the heart's blood of natural history, but because drawings were expensive to make and

Charles Doolittle Walcott, Paleontologist

difficult to reproduce, many fossils were originally described without any accompanying sketches; Walcott wrote papers of this sort while working for Hall. As the number of fossil species and genera kept increasing, later workers could not comprehend what their forebears had written. To make his old study of the Saratoga Springs fossils more useful, Walcott assembled a plate of drawings to illustrate the Potsdam fauna in New York which he circulated to colleagues; it appears that no copies of this remain.

To cite one germane example of the lack of illustrations, in the early 1860s the fauna described by C. F. Hartt from St. John, New Brunswick, established that rocks outcropping there were Cambrian; Hartt's paleontologic work was the basis for the Acadian, the oldest subdivision of the Cambrian in North America. Shortly thereafter, Hartt pursued geologic work in Brazil, became a professor at Cornell University and died in 1878 at the young age of thirty-eight. Walcott (1886c, 10) complained, "It was with great difficulty that more than the common species could be identified from the descriptions and the few illustrations given."

Williams was determined to build a great department at Cornell University, and late in 1883 he convinced the administration to buy Hartt's collection. Walcott wasted no time in borrowing this material from Cornell; by February he was studying it. Late in April, Walcott went north and called at the American Museum to look at their Cambrian collections; he chatted with his Eureka colleague Iddings and called on John S. Newberry at the School of Mines. Being in Washington, Walcott was isolated from the academic community of geologists, and the professional contacts he maintained were important.

From New York Walcott visited Alpheus Hyatt at the Boston Society of Natural History. Although this was a quick trip, Walcott also went to the Museum of Comparative Zoology, partly to borrow some of his 1878 specimens from New Brunswick, and partly to borrow fossils from N. S. Shaler of Harvard, who was studying the Cambrian rocks of Massachusetts. It was a year before he returned them, but he added additional Cambrian fossils. At that same time, Walcott sent along Agassiz's share of the Eureka collections which Charles Haskell had gathered in 1882. Finally, Walcott also spoke with Jules Marcou, almost certainly about the Taconic System. Walcott returned via Scranton, where a certain Miss Maggie showed him the area.

Even before his trip to Cambridge, Walcott corresponded with G. F. Matthew, who had given him field advice in 1878. In 1860, L. W. Bailey had become professor at Fredericton, New Brunswick. Bailey, with his student Hartt, and assisted by Matthew discovered and documented Cambrian rocks in Acadia. Fossils were Mr. Matthew's avocation and he published prolifically in scientific journals:

> We shall be very glad to obtain a representation of any species that you can send as the National Museum collections have nothing from the St. John's group. I have made a preliminary study of Prof. Hartt's material, and shall have drawings made of all of his type specimens before June and publish them all with a copy of his descriptions and a few remarks, as some of his descriptions are very short. . . . Your work on the Paradoxides group is very fine and I hope that will have the time and energy to carry through your original plan of monographing the fauna. Although working in the same field just now, I think we can assist each other very materially.[8]

Almost immediately after he started on the Hartt collection, "the writer learned for the first time that Mr. Matthew was engaged on a monograph. . . . The plan of illustrating the entire fauna was at once changed so as to include only the Hartt collection" (Walcott 1884c, 10). The project moved rapidly, and as it progressed he kept Matthew fully informed: "The plates of the Hartt collection series are made up with the exception of a few figures. Will send them to you about July 1*st.*"[9] "I send you photographic prints of plates of St. John & Braintree faunas. Any remarks you have to make will be acceptable."[10]

Walcott supplemented the Hartt material with a section on fossils from Braintree, Massachusetts, and on a strange fossil from Georgia, Vermont. Walcott published this eclectic collection in the new *Bulletin* series of the survey, begun in 1883 to contain investigations that did not fit well into annual reports or monographs. Each was supposed to "contain but one paper and be complete in itself." Walcott stretched the rules a bit with three separate paleontologic items loosely related, but they were all Cambrian.

In a proof copy, the printer had one of the trilobites upside down, but that was corrected in the final printing. The drawings were adequate, if not as elegant as those in the Eureka report. This research was not artistic, without the fancy lettering G. B. Simpson put on the first set of Eureka plates. No delineator of the drawings is mentioned in the text or listed on the plate. It was and remains the custom of the Geological Survey to give little recognition to technical support. As was stipulated by Congress, three thousand copies were printed for official use. Walcott bought one hundred to distribute to colleagues; *Bulletin* 10 sold for five cents.

In five years, the United States Geological Survey had gone from a limitation to study the rocks on public lands to international activities. Fortunately

Charles Doolittle Walcott, Paleontologist

Congress had other things on its mind than this fledgling bureau. Walcott's re-description of Hartt's species was basic to understanding the Cambrian of North America, but one would have been hard pressed to justify this to those in Congress who wanted only "practical" geology.

During the spring of 1884, Walcott also began the accumulation of large collections. He publicly announced his willingness to cooperate with other collectors and non-government geologists. "It is very desirable that large quantities of material should be brought together from all the Cambrian groups; and the survey would be glad to receive collections, whether large or small, from all portions of the country. Care should be taken in packing and a record kept. Correspondence has begun with numerous collectors in Wisconsin, in order to obtain material from the Potsam group" (Anonymous 1884a, 582).

The material from Wisconsin was part of a research plan to characterize all the various faunas from the Potsdam Sandstone up through the equivalents of the Trenton Limestone in Minnesota and Wisconsin. In view of the decreasing age of the sandstone toward the center of the continent, detailed correlation was a tricky problem. To this day, the precise relationships of a particular limestone or shale to the section at Trenton Falls is still vexing, but Walcott's general picture was correct and provided the key for more detailed investigations.

> During the months of July, August, September, and October Mr. Cooper Curtice, paleontological assistant, made extensive collections of fossils from Central and Western Wisconsin and Eastern Minnesota, besides taking notes on the geologic sections and on geographic and stratigraphic distribution of the Potsdam or Upper Cambrian fauna. Mr. Curtice's collections embraced thirty barrels and seventeen boxes of specimens that add materially to our collections, and will give much valuable data in studying the Potsdam fauna. . . . Mr. Cooper Curtice has had charge of the preparatory work on the collection, and has rendered most efficient service in preparing for study the various collections of the Middle Cambrian fossils and those of the Upper Cambrian of Texas. (Walcott 1885, 75, 77)

Other difficulties with decentralized paleontology were the dissipation and duplication of effort. Hall had described some fossils from the upper Mississippi area and they were in Albany, as were those from Walcott's first published and nonillustrated work for the professor. Whitfield described species that were housed in New York City. The type specimens of other described forms were with the state geological surveys in Madison and Minneapolis. Professionals and amateurs throughout the United States had nibbled further at the fauna in scattered descriptive papers. To make sense of the overall picture required recollecting the localities of described fossils to have topotypical specimens for comparison. Synonyms among the names could be then weeded out before looking for new species. Fossils properly named and from known stratigraphic levels could then be more precisely compared to the New York section.

In addition to reference material from those localities, Walcott wanted as many new localities as possible, with detailed stratigraphic investigations to ensure that the fossils were in the correct sequence. The beds are nearly flat-lying in this area, but "nearly" is just enough to complicate matters. Outcrops are scattered and one has to pay close attention to get the sequence correct. Curtice did all this and more. During his four months in the field, Curtice wrote Walcott almost every week, in addition to submitting his more formal monthly report, and enjoyed life to the hilt:

> I think someone ought to hold me down. I am getting wild, wilder than I ever thought that I would become over old bugs and clam shells. . . . I found here several fragments which indicated that with time perseverance and blasting powder one might get track of something new. I reached the point by boat from Madison, and as it was my first day I got fairly well sunburnt and blistered my hands rowing. My boat was a small one, and the wind blew a gale. I have dried off since and of course did not drown as I half expected to.[11]

When the pygidium of a trilobite that he could not identify turned up he punned, "In that material there is a tail that would a tale unfold."[12]

There are still many fossils to be found in the sedimentary rocks of America, but Walcott's era was the great heyday of fossil collecting. The railroad cuts provided many exposures and as the fresh rock began to weather, fossils were easier to extract. Building stone and agricultural lime came from small quarries operated by hand; Curtice provides insight:

> At Mazomanie [Wisconsin] I found a Mr. John Murrish who was at one time State Geologist and is at present an enthusiast on the fossil question. He said that he collected the first that were ever found at Mazomanie, sent some to Prof. Hall who afterward came out to collect and examine the locality. Before he came on Mr. Murrish watched his opportunity and when a large space in the quarry had been cleaned off from over the fossil bed he wrote for Mr. Hall. This was the way Prof. Hall came by his nice specimens.[13]

Curtice unpacked and prepared the collections on his return to the museum. They were invaluable for reference, but now that the Potsdam fauna was under control, if not understood to the last detail, Walcott could pursue the older fossils in the underlying rocks. Twenty years would pass before the key trilobites of this interval were monographed. As Walcott later wrote: "Many years ago I planned an investigation of the genus *Dikelocephalus,* but under the pressure of other studies and administrative duties it was delayed. Dr. L. C. Wooster in 1883, Dr. Cooper Curtice in 1884, and Dr. Charles Schuchert in 1896 all made extensive collections from the Cambrian of Wisconsin and Minnesota, and it from this material that many of the illustrations in this paper are taken and the association of species determined" (Walcott 1914, 346). In the large scheme of things the delay did not matter, as fossils are not harmed by sitting in a museum, where specimens can accumulate and be retained in safety until they are needed for a particular scientific investigation.

Throughout the spring and the first days of summer of 1884, Walcott, as usual, was going several different directions at once. He labeled the Devonian fossils from Eureka and put on another hat: "As honorary curator in charge of the collections of invertebrate Paleozoic fossils of the United States National Museum, attention was given, at various times during the year, to the arrangement of the collections, and a large amount of material collected by the Geological Survey has been labeled and transferred to the Museum" (Walcott 1885a, 54). Once identifications were made, more than three hundred labels had to be written. When this curatorial work was combined with the science, it had been almost as busy a time as when he first went to New York City with Hague.

During the final stages of the Eureka study, he added eleven plates after comparing the Nevada Cambrian fossils to the fossils from the Tonto Sandstone in the Grand Canyon and the 1883 collections from New York. All this while completing the study of the Hartt material. The manuscript for *Bulletin* 10 was submitted June 30, 1884, the end of the fiscal year. In contrast to monographs, bulletins were supposed to be prepared promptly, and this one certainly was up to specifications. No matter how restricted the study, February to June is fast time. June was spent proofreading the Eureka monograph. When fieldwork came, it was a relief.

While Curtice traveled to the Northwest during the summer of 1884, Walcott went to the Northeast, via Scranton and Miss Maggie; as usual, there was a pause at Trenton Falls. The flatlands, near the Adirondacks, had provided as many data on the strata and fossils as they were likely to yield in the immediate future, so Walcott concentrated on the more complex rock sequence east of Lake Champlain. By staying north, close to the Canadian boundary, Walcott skirted the metamorphosed rocks of the Taconics in a strict sense and, likewise, avoided the associated arguments. The sequence he studied was confused by faulting and thrusting, but the rocks themselves were little affected. Fossils near Phillipsburg, Quebec, tend to be a bit stretched by the forces which broke and stacked up the strata, but they are abundant and well enough preserved to determine the stratigraphic level. One question was were these rocks more or less the same age as the flat-lying ones west of Lake Champlain?

In 1883, Curtice had worked for a few days at one place in Vermont, digging down to bedrock to collect. Walcott scribbled a note to him in Wisconsin:

> The puzzlement about the rocks of Highgate [Vermont] was solved in one days tramp. At Swanton [Vermont} took fossil from the upper black slate. The first day of work on the "Parker Ledge" bro't out *8 Bathynotus*, one with head spines in place. Now have two holes down in solid rock for the large trilobites. In the shale found a *Serpularia* new to the horizon. Dug a little above where you and Lewis worked.[14]

Walcott hired local men to do the heavy digging and Ed Hurlburt came out from Utica to help collect trilobites.

Just when Walcott finished at the trilobite bed on the Parker farm and moved south to Burlington, his New England geologic work was abruptly interrupted. A settler in the Arizona Territory had started a small coal mine which, unfortunately, turned out to be on an Indian reservation. Once the correct boundary was determined, who was to get the money for the coal mined? Settlers, Indians, and the U.S. government never have mixed well.

The secretary of the interior appointed two official commissioners to look into this problem and propose a solution. After expressing surprise at seeing Walcott, the clerk, Gentry, wrote Curtice: "I learn that after waiting for some two weeks to decide upon the right man, our Mr. Walcott was selected upon the part of the Survey, and is to partly represent the Land Office."[15] This could be a politically hot potato, but Curtice was so naïve in the ways of the world that he wrote congratulating Walcott on what he thought was an honor. With experienced mining geologists already in the West, it is strange that Powell selected Walcott; the appointment indicated considerable trust in his judgment.

With the exquisite sense of timing so often displayed by the Geological Survey in its field assignments, in late August Walcott was in the Deer Creek valley of the White Mountain Indian Reservation, better known as the San Carlos Reservation, pursuing a Carboniferous coal. One day Arizona was 110 degrees, and Walcott had not been on a horse in two years. Still, in spite of heat and hard riding, all went well and in about two weeks, the job was finished. Walcott (1885b) noted the underlying rocks, and of course, their fossils, the presence of faults and the quite limited amount of coal present. This was not basic science, but it was a workmanlike report and everyone, or at least the secretary of the interior, was pleased. The amount of coal on the reservation was too small to cause a fuss.

On his way back to Washington, Walcott visited the Llano uplift in central Texas, three weeks more to his liking. Although sediments of Cretaceous age cover most of the region, in a small area they have been eroded away. The older rocks are exposed in a bullseye pattern, like a mini-Adirondack dome. Walcott found Carboniferous, Silurian, and Cambrian, and he collected from the Upper Cambrian, the oldest rocks with fossils that he could find. Years earlier a few fossils had been described from here, but the Llano uplift was a poorly known area. The section of fossiliferous strata is much thinner than in the Grand Canyon.

"All the localities where the base of the Potsdam was observed, it rests *unconformably* on a great formation that is stratigraphically the equivalent of Powell's Grand Canon series (Grand Canon and Chuar groups) that are overlaid by the Tonto group, a series of rocks, in both lithologic and paleontologic characters, singularly like the Texas Potsdam group."[16] Emphatic mention of an unconformity may have been the first hint that there were well preserved strata in western America significantly older than Cambrian. This sequence, which Walcott recognized as similar to the beds he had seen in the fall and winter of 1882 and 1883, was named the Llano Series (Walcott 1884d).

After telling Curtice of Walcott's success in the Potsdam terrane of Texas, Gentry wrote, "I agree with you most heartily in the hope he will take a vacation this fall and rest up a little; for he has had a long and tiresome journey and should not be unmindful of his health."[17] Walcott was a leader who inspired the loyalty and concern of his assistants. The remark about vacation went unheeded: "Walcott is now looking 'fresh as a rose' yet he said when he reached Washington, he felt about 'used up.' He will leave in a day or two for a short trip to New York."[18] Walcott wrote:

> I returned to Washington October 14, and at once took up the study of the Middle Cambrian faunas, and also attended to the completion of the publication of Monograph VIII, Paleontology of the Eureka District, and Bulletin 10, Preliminary Studies of the Cambrian of North America. Both of these publications were completed in December, 1884, and a few copies secured, but owing to unavoidable delays, the main edition was not delivered until April, 1885. (Walcott 1885, 76)

In November, he was along the Hudson River with S. W. Ford, trying to unravel the rocks near Troy, New York; these were germane to the problem of the Taconic System. Coming and going, he paused in Scranton with Maggie.

When he returned to the office, Walcott seriously studied the Cambrian fossils from Troy and Georgia. Opening up another front, he arranged for Ford to be paid for making drawings of fossils and for geologic mapping. Ford was a jeweler by trade and fossils were his avocation; in the early 1870s he found Cambrian trilobites and other fossils near Troy. This was an important area, as far west in New York as one found fossils that old.

Next, Walcott labeled older collections gathered by the territorial surveys which preceded the USGS, and documented the need for more drawers, a perennial cry of curators when collections are growing. He spoke to the Biological Society on his Cambrian work: "It was without notes. The substance is the 10th Bulletin."[19]

Walcott spent Christmas at Scranton, and referred to the young lady as Margaret. Back in Washington, he was "Tired & out of tune. Lonely & wishing for a home of my own" (December 27, 1884). Still, he ended the year on the note of all's well that ends well.

At the end of September, while Walcott was in Texas, a great event took place in the history of the Geological Survey, in renting space in the Hoee Iron Building; the name came from the cast-iron facade, then the rage in commercial architecture. The Hoee was on F Street N.W., between Thirteenth and Fourteenth; it occupied part of the site on which the National Press Club has been built. Eventually, the Survey filled the entire building, and until 1916, this was the principal home of the organization. On payday, headquarters was an easy fifteen-minute walk from the museum. Offices in the museum were vacated by some geologists, and chemical labs were installed. A physical lab which had gone from Washington to the American Museum to Yale University returned to Washington. As a result, a different group of scientists socialized during the day. His friend Iddings was now in Washington, and occasionally they ate together; those who live in boardinghouses seldom use the word "dine."

There may have been some socializing at the office, but life in the boardinghouse was fairly quiet. Attending the Biological Society meetings every other Saturday and dropping into the Cosmos Club covered most of the distractions, apart from church. Reverend Bartlett, married to his cousin, had come to the Church of the Covenant in 1882 and stayed for the next thirteen years. In mid-February, Walcott returned to Scranton for sleighing with Margaret; he attended Grover Cleveland's Inaugural Ball until almost midnight. On Saturday, March

14, 1885, at 3:30 P.M, Walcott presented a public lecture at the National Museum, "Searching for the first forms of life," illustrated with diagrams he hung around the lecture room.

In 1885, Walcott completed his study of the trilobites that he thought to be of Middle Cambrian age, helped Survey colleagues by identifying fossils, and started study on Cambrian brachiopods. The fossils have two shells and look like clams to the uninitiated. Walcott estimated for the director that he had about twenty-five thousand fossils in his laboratory and the museum collections contained about twice that number; most of these Walcott had collected or at least identified before transferring them to the museum.

The year 1885 appears to have been relatively unproductive for Walcott from the standpoint of publications. He sent three short notes to the *American Journal of Science.* The first concerned a new genus of Cambrian brachiopod (Walcott 1885c). The second considered an unusual new trilobite from Georgia, Vermont; Walcott had a fragmentary specimen, but Ed Hurlburt had collected a complete one in 1884 and gave it to Walcott (Walcott 1885d). The third was a potpourri of rare Cambrian and Ordovician forms that did not fit in well anywhere in the animal kingdom (Walcott 1885e). Annual reports to the survey and museum added to the total, but these were administrative, not science.

Walcott now had a grasp on faunas of the Upper Cambrian, or Potsdam, and a start on the older Cambrian through his study of the New Brunswick fossils. With that background, he concentrated in New England on the rocks he thought of as Middle Cambrian:

> Finding it necessary to obtain some additional data in connection with the study of the Middle Cambrian faunas, I spent a few days, in May, at Swanton, Vermont, and also visited and examined the collections of the Geological Survey of Canada at Ottawa. Through the courtesy of Dr. A. R. C. Selwyn, director of the Canadian Survey, and Prof. J. F. Whiteaves, paleontologist, a number of typical specimens were loaned to me for illustration, and twenty species were procured for the National Museum collections. The material thus obtained has been of great service in the identification of species from Vermont. (Walcott 1885, 76)

Part of the trip, not mentioned in his report, was to Troy, where he and Ford again struggled to understand the sequence of Georgian and Quebec group rocks exposed near the Hudson River. At Swanton, Vermont, Walcott "Discovered a fault line that cuts off the upper portion of the Georgian group as I had previously known it" (May 15, 1885). With each season, the rock relations in the field were becoming harder to understand, rather than the other way round.

Walcott instructed the gem of a person, Curtice. "A small box of fossils shipped yesterday contains Georgia g[rou]p. fossils. A number of young Olenellus etc. Examine each bit of rock carefully & put pointers to all the little trilobites & shells. The specimens are from two localities. Handle with care."[20] Walcott could not have worked as fast as he did without this able assistant.

The trip to Canada was important at this stage of his research. Some of the fossil species from near the border were first described by Elkanah Billings, and Walcott had to examine them critically. The rocks of the Quebec Group trended south and their relation to the geologic mess in Vermont was a key point. Ever since 1860, when Sir William Logan, based on Billings's evidence from fossils, had proposed that a presumably normal sequence of rocks actually had been changed by faulting (Eagan 1987), geologists had argued about the Quebec Group. Walcott needed firsthand experience with those rocks and faunas.

Back in Washington the first of June, Walcott worked steadily on the trilobites from various places in Vermont and New York which seemed to be the same as those from the Georgia locality. Scientific visitors were increasingly in Washington and he spent time with H. S. Williams from Cornell, T. C. Chamberlin from Wisconsin, and others. Now and again Powell had him come over to the main office to discuss problems and progress. June passed into July, and Walcott celebrated Independence Day by writing plate descriptions for another manuscript.

Late in 1884 and into the winter and spring of 1885, another major event took place. In writing to Williams, Walcott mentioned "unavoidable delays" in delivery of his monograph and bulletin. This was a mere ripple from what could have been a tidal wave of catastrophe. A congressional investigation, which has come to be known as the Allison Commission, began with the Coast Survey and widened to include other federal scientific bureaus. Major Powell became the spokesman for government scientists (Rabbitt 1980). Part of the investigation was a result of interagency fighting, part of it was inspired by Edward Drinker Cope, the vertebrate paleontologist once connected with the Hayden Territorial Survey, and the last part stemmed from Alexander Agassiz. Agassiz had the use of Coast Survey steamships whenever he desired, yet this rich autocrat insisted that the government should not be involved with science.

Charles Doolittle Walcott, Paleontologist

In the end, the head of the Coast Survey, in ill health after forty years of faithful service, was fired (Manning 1988). The USGS emerged as a dominant government bureau and Powell was the man of the hour. Basic science for the benefit of the people could be pursued. This is a good story with villains and heroes, but the hearings did not directly concern Walcott, and there is not a serious mention of them in his diary.

Of more concern than delay of *Bulletin* 10 was how his colleagues might react to it. Concern about nomenclature pervades science. Are objects, be they stars, elements, rocks, or fossils, being referred to by the appropriate name? Battles over nomenclature occasionally are as nasty as those over priority. Walcott created one in Canada when he discussed nomenclature for the rocks which had yielded Hartt's fossils. Walcott wrote to Professor Bailey of Fredericton, New Brunswick, who held his university post from 1860 on into the twentieth century and was not a man to be antagonized. Baily, Matthew, and Hartt had contributed to Sir William Dawson's book *Acadian Geology,* the Bible for the Maritime area. In redescribing Hartt's fossils in *Bulletin* 10, Walcott did not step on any toes, but he came close:

> I send you today copies of some of my recent publications. Will you read the note on page 9 of Bulletin 10, and tell me if I have been, in your opinion, unjust to Sir William Dawson.
>
> I regret that I imputed unfairness to him, as he may have acted without such intention. In a recent letter to me, he says: "The name (Acadian) was proposed with concurrence of the gentlemen concerned in the discoveries made and with whom I was in communication, and that of St. John was dropped, but not for the reasons to which you refer, which are sufficient, but also because we had written of the St. John rocks in a wider sense before the *Acadian* fossils were found; and because I felt that the discovery was so important and so far ahead of anything else that had been done in America, that it deserved a name more befitting it that of St. John, a mere local name, which I and other had used loosely." He says further: "It has been proposed *now* that Mr. Matthew has established other fossiliferous groups of the Lower Cambrian, to extend it the whole Lower Cambrian as developed in New Brunswick and to reserve St. John for the species horizons so well studied by Mr. Hartt."[21]

Several things are apparent from this letter. First, unlike the West, the rocks of eastern North America had already been examined by several generations of geologists; one had to pay close attention to the literature. Second, new discoveries were less likely than new interpretations; one had to be a little cautious and not plunge ahead. Walcott did not forget these lessons.

Starting in the early nineteenth century, there was a gradual shift to standardize nomenclature to the extent of naming rocks from geographic areas. The Potsdam was a fine example of a geographic name for a formation, in contrast to the overlying "Calciferous"; eventually that became the Beekmantown, named from exposures at Beekmantown, New York. Some sedimentary rocks also contain fossils, organic objects which change through time; as stated repeatedly by paleontologists, physically identical limestones or sandstones may contain markedly different fossils.

From the pragmatic standpoint, the Cambrian system began in 1835 by the naming of a rock sequence in north Wales (ancient Cambria), and later represented a geologic interval during which rocks containing certain kinds of fossils were deposited. Cambrian became a time term, rather than a rock term. The Potsdam Sandstone was in New York, and when geologists in Wisconsin spoke of Potsdam they meant another sandstone not quite the same age. It was confusing to have the same term for both a rock stratum and a segment of time; with two separate terms there was less chance for misunderstanding. Walcott continued to use "Potsdam," but increasingly for a time unit, and eventually he proposed another term for this portion of geologic time.

The name "St. John" was originally used in New Brunswick for certain rocks. Dawson came to realize that a time term, "Acadian," was needed for the part of the Cambrian known from that area. The rocks at St. John and in some other places were deposited during the Acadian. The concept of names for intervals of time, not rocks, most certainly was not obvious to many nineteenth-century investigators. When Walcott questioned Dawsons's usage of Acadian rather than St. John, he was in troubled waters; fortunately, no hard feelings were generated and the matter passed.

Early in July 1885, just after the fiscal year began, Curtice went south to Alabama, Georgia, and Tennessee, chasing the Cambrian strata and searching for fossils. He was out until late November—no short field seasons for this collector. Now that Curtice knew what the Potsdam fauna was like, Walcott moved him into areas where both older Cambrian and post-Potsdam rocks occur. Curtice's discoveries in the southern Appalachians would fill several books. It is appropriate to note that Walcott later named a trilobite species after him.

Walcott was also away for the summer, beginning with two weeks at Scranton to see Margaret. Then, it was off to Utica and to Trenton Falls, where

Charles Doolittle Walcott, Paleontologist

William Rust and he collected more Utica Shale fossils. It was back to see Margaret, and back to Utica and Trenton Falls. Whether Walcott was truly vacationing, trying to sort out in his mind both his relations with Margaret and the New England rock sequences, or waiting for Powell to send orders is not clear; perhaps all three were intertwined.

Finally, on August 17 he was on his way to the West, despite important field-work in the East uncompleted. Part of the explanation lies in a tantilizing discovery made by King's Fortieth Parallel Survey. At the Pioche, Nevada, mining district Cambrian fossils had been collected; Pioche was not a household term like Comstock or Eureka, but it had produced its fair share of the nation's riches. Walcott was after topotype specimens and any new Cambrian fossils that might turn up; he also had to compare the Highland Range sequence to that at Eureka. Further, he wanted to visit other Cambrian localities in Utah. New information from the West might shed some light on the complications in the East.

During the months of August, September, and October. . . . The results obtained were—

(1) The discovery of a great series of Devonian strata . . . more than 3,000 feet in thickness, and carrying a characteristic Devonian fauna. . . . At the base the Devonian passes down to the Upper Silurian and this to the Trenton horizon of the Lower Silurian.

(2) In the Highland Range a connection was made . . . with the Silurian of the Eureka District, Nev., and the section carried down through the Upper and Middle Cambrian to the Great Cambrian quartzite. A large collection of fossils was obtained from different portions of the 6,000 feet of strata . . .

(3) Crossing from Pioche to Toquerville, Utah, via Hebron and Saint George, the only data obtained was the evidence of the non-presence of the Paleozoic strata of the Great Basin system.

(4) Southeast of Toquerville, Utah, a section was measured of the Permian formation and numerous fossils were collected. This completes my study in the field of the Permian formation between House Rock Spring, Arizona, and Toquerville, Utah, and north of the Grand Cañon of the Colorado.

(5) The examination of the Wasatch Cambrian section gave nearly the same thickness of strata as that obtained by the Fortieth Parallel Survey (12,000 feet). The paleontologic data, however, is of the greatest importance, as it locates the horizon of strata which have been referred to the Quebec group . . . as Middle Cambrian.

With the data we now have, most of the Paleozoic fossil horizons collected in the entire Rocky Mountain region can be referred to their true strati-graphic horizons, but it is desirable that further study should be given to the

Cambrian strata of the Uinta, Oquirrah, and Tintic Ranges, as we know nothing of the fauna that preceded the Middle Cambrian in the Rocky Mountain region. (Walcott 1888, 115–16)

Despite the heat and dust, it must have been sheer heaven for Walcott to return to the West. The rocks are exposed, not covered with vegetation, and in places fossils still littered the ground begging to be picked up. This was a hard trip, but it paid large dividends in new information obtained. Walcott never published a study of the Permian as he alluded to under his fourth point, though later he did return west to search for more Cambrian fossils in Utah.

It may be a bit cavalier to dismiss three months in the field with a few words, but one cannot note every detail. Still, to give credit for help received, Walcott's assistant was a J. Edward Whitfield; his relationship, if any to Professor Whitfield at the American Museum is unknown. The cook Arthur Pipe received forty dollars a month. Walcott paid six dollars a day for the heavy wagon, four horses, and driver, but after a week found another person to do the work for five dollars. Walcott covered many miles and saw some fine exposures of Devonian and older rocks. Naturally the group made large collections of fossils; in the Wasatch Range, they collected in a snowstorm.

One consequence of his trip was more stratigraphic information for Arnold Hague. "As you will see from the Quartz Peak section, I found the Trenton fauna above the quartzite, but the fauna is not so extensive as I expected to find it. There is very little doubt that the Eureka quartzite belongs to a Trenton horizon and that there is both above and below it characteristic forms of the Trenton fauna."[22] When Hague's monograph finally came out, it included an appendix on fossils obtained from this investigation in southern Nevada. The age of the Eureka Quartzite has been accepted since Walcott's pronouncement that Trenton fossils were above and below it.

After the western excursion, the train ride back east was pleasant, but at Utica his old headaches came back and he spent several days taking electric treatments. He stopped in Albany to ask the paleontologists about their experiences with photolithography, and called at the American Museum after a detour to Miss Maggie in Scranton.

On November 6, Walcott was finally settled in his office, and started examining the western Cambrian fossils. Late in November, when Curtice returned from the field, the pace of work increased; Walcott began adding the data from latest collections to his *Bulletin* manuscript. As the year wore down, the manuscript for *Bulletin* 30 came close to an end. Christmas day he cleaned his bicycle

and had dinner with his cousin. "1885 leaves me unsettled in relation to marrying. Doubt if it is best. Am getting along fairly well in my work. Feel the need
of better training and more mental energy to do what I wish. Work may help
the defects" (December 31, 1885).

Despite a nice snow, the first week of the new year 1886 was dismal. The last
stages of a major work go very slowly, the significant conclusions are known and
most of the forms have been described, but the last 10 percent seems to take 90
percent of the effort. Walcott was now studying the Cambrian sponges, a group
that for most paleontologists is far less interesting than trilobites; actually, these
were not true sponges, but an extinct group with a few more unusual features.
He wrote to Margaret concerning the "unfortunate state of affairs between us"
(January 6, 1886); this ended some of his personal turmoil.

Walcott brightened up and attended a few concerts and plays. Utica, Albany,
and New York City connections from times past, combined with his membership in the Cosmos Club, gained for him an entré from the world of science into
the world of politics. He was gradually building a power base of influential
friends in Washington, but he focused on Cambrian fossils, not politics. Walcott did not aspire to any position on the Geological Survey other than the one
he occupied. He had fossils, time to study them, and assistants, and he wanted
nothing more.

By mid-February, Walcott transmitted the manuscript and plates for *Bulletin*
30, removing one load from his mind. He headed north for the funeral of old
Mr. Rust, William's father. Not one to ever miss a chance for fieldwork, he spent
a couple of days in the field with W. D. Dwight from Vassar College chasing the
Cambrian along the southern part of the Hudson River, and he visited with R. P.
Whitfield at the American Museum.

Back in Washington, it was time to catch up on all the odds and ends which
had been put aside to finish the bulletin. Old collections were labeled and turned
over to the museum. The pleasant social life of attending scientific talks and calling on friends continued. Just before his thirty-sixth birthday, Walcott wrote a
paper on the Cambrian System of the United States to present at the coming
meeting of the National Academy of Sciences; one participated only by invitation, and this indicated Walcott's rising scientific stature.

Page proof for part of *Bulletin* 30 came in and was returned promptly. In mid-
May, Walcott examined Silurian and Devonian fossils from central Nevada. He
worked on his section of the *Annual Report* before deadline and the end of the
month went off to the field. It began with a familiar itinerary of New York City
and Albany. Then he went eastward to Williamstown, Massachusetts, to see

Ebenezer Emmons's original fossils from the Taconic System, and Saratoga Springs, where Mother and Josie joined him. Next, he was back in Utica spending a day or so with Ed Hurlburt. He went north to Theresa, New York, to examine Potsdam Sandstone. He rowed up the river to see the overlying Calciferous and its contact with the Chazy Limestone. Walcott took the steamer up the St. Lawrence to Ogdensburg and Potsdam. Still moving rapidly, he worked his way east to Lake Champlain and collected fossils at Isle La Motte.

Walcott went north to Beauharnois, Quebec, just south of Montreal, to see more Potsdam Sandstone:

> Mr. Walcott, of the United States Geological Survey, is at present in this town, examining specimens of rocks. He has found several turtle tracks in the sandstone, and some shells of that in the limestone. Although not quite so good as those taken out by Sir William Logan, some years since, he says they are very good of their kind. He has visited the Museum at Ottawa, from which he intends taking plaster casts of those placed there by Sir William Logan. These, together with his own, he will deposit in the National Museum at Washington.[23]

Sir William Logan had indeed found a very strange track, which he named *Climactichnites;* to this day, the origin of this fossil is uncertain, but all paleontologists agree that it was not made by a turtle (Yochelson and Fedonkin 1993). Those who visit the Natural History Museum in Washington and walk into the paleontology wing see these enigmatic trails collected by Walcott.

Walcott studied Dawson's collections at McGill University in Montreal and arranged to ship the trail-bearing slabs; it had taken four men nearly a week to pry them up. Proof of the index of *Bulletin* 30 and of his talk before the National Academy of Sciences awaited him at Chazy, New York. From there it was back to Keeseville and through Au Sable Chasm by rowboat to examine more Potsdam sandstone. Walcott reviewed the same ground as in the past years, now looking at the relationships from the standpoint of the rocks of southern Canada and northern Vermont. At Keeseville, he collected three slabs bearing *Climactichnites* tracks from the city sidewalk and went east to Burlington, Vermont, and then back west to Whitehall, always looking at the relationships of the Potsdam to the overlying rocks. He worked along the lake shore, then walked the railway to and from Fort Ann, piecing together the geologic section. Outcrops are scarce in this landscape covered with glacial debris.

After a weekend break at Gloversville, with more familiar rocks around, he then went to the slate mines at North Granville, New York. Although it was almost too hot to be in the field, Walcott "Discovered Middle Cambrian fossils

2 P.M. beneath roofing slates of Middle Granville" (August 11, 1886). This was a new find, not in *Bulletin* 30; luck held and he found one more slate belt fossil locality before going to Trenton Falls.

Walcott changed from field geologist to conventioneer and traveled to the AAAS annual meeting at Buffalo, where he reported that within the Taconics, in a thin limestone interbedded in the slates, "a fauna occurs that is identical, as far as known, with the fauna of the Middle Cambrian or Georgia formation as it occurs in Canada and in Renselaer county, N. Y. . . . The extensions of the slates to the north and south are of the same age; although in parts of Washington county, slates of a later geologic age may exist" (Walcott 1886).

One advantage of attending a nearby AAAS meeting was that it allowed a break in field routine. This session also provided the opportunity to present new data. In those days, the interval from scientific discovery to announcement actually was shorter than today. A geologic tour of Niagara Falls and collecting in the waterlime quarries were other attractions; Walcott had gathered fossils from these quarries for Hall nearly a decade earlier. All in all, this year AAAS held a first-class meeting.

After Buffalo, Walcott studied Bald Mountain and the uncertainty of the western edge of the Taconic Mountains. "After dinner went out to the east end of the Town of Greenwich & found Hudson River gp. graptolites. This makes a bad mess of my section" (September 13, 1886). Walcott added to the proof of his AAAS abstract that the red slates on top of the Granville had definitely been dated as Hudson River formation, a much younger unit. He started to grasp the notion that several slate units of different age were in this area. Without fossils to provide information on age, most field geologists would assume that only one thick shale was present.

Walcott moved to Salem and luckily found both Cambrian and Silurian fossils. He started traversing back and forth from New York to Vermont, examining the rocks along each road. He found fault lines and began to trace them north; light was starting to emerge. Walcott worked north to Whitehall, then traversed to Vermont, to Albany, to Greenwich, to Whitehall, to Utica, and to Trenton Falls. The Potsdam Sandstone had been reported to the southwest at Canajoharie, but it was an incorrect identification, and he went south in the rain to Vassar College. When the weather relented, he went out with Prof. Dwight and they found the Georgia group on Stissing Mountain near Poughkeepsie. He spent a couple of days in New York City.

In early November, Walcott was back at his same old rooming house and at the same table where he boarded, four blocks away. Curtice had left in August for a position with the Department of Agriculture, but even without his help Walcott cleared up accumulated mail and started two new projects. He studied the Potsdam fauna which Curtice had found during the summer of 1885 in Georgia, the state, that is, not the town in Vermont. The second was a map and geologic account of Washington County, New York, a most confusing place. He had a good start on both before the first of December when Mother and Josie came down to Washington for the winter.

December 2 brought a new assistant, Dr. R. R. Gurley. Not much is known of him or how he came to be in Washington. Gurley may have been paid by the National Museum, in contrast to Gentry who was employed by the Geological Survey. The following day, Walcott and assistants "Began moving contents of office and laboratory from old rooms to larger rooms in S. W. corner of museum" (December 3, 1886). Curtice could never be replaced, but the new help was promising. Once he was settled in the new office, Walcott started a manuscript on the granular quartzite of Emmons, hoping to end the Taconic controversy on some sort of compromise. The snow melted and unexpectedly he was able to ride his bicycle to the museum.

Late in December, Walcott went with Gilbert, McGee, and Diller for a day at the annual meeting of the American Society of Naturalists in Philadelphia. He traveled on to New York for a chat at the American Museum and caught the train to New Haven and several days of long and complex discussion with Dana as to the disposition of the Taconic. Dana strongly opposed any usage of the term; Walcott thought some of the rocks which Emmons had designated as the Taconic System should carry that name. Back in Washington, he ended the year on this most unsatisfactory note.

Nevertheless, 1886 was a year of major accomplishment. *Bulletin* 30 (Walcott 1886a) came out in the fall of the year with the statutory printing of three thousand. It cost twenty-five cents, five times as much as *Bulletin* 10. Whereas *Bulletin* 10 had seventy-four pages, this new work contained 369 pages. The former had ten plates, the latter thirty-one plates and ten figures. Just on size, the difference in price may be justified. A few of the fossil drawings were by S. W. Ford, the jeweler from Troy, but most are done by J. L. Ridgway. Ornithologists today might remember Robert Ridgway, who drew and monographed birds of this continent for half a century, first with King's survey and then at the Smithsonian and the National Museum, but no one recalls the other Ridgway, a superb draughtsman and a mainstay of USGS publications. A drawing of a natural history object is supposed to be a precise rendition of what one sees, nothing less and absolutely nothing more. If one compares the work of Simpson and McConnell in the Eureka monograph with these drawings, Ridgway's skill is apparent. His drawings of fossils are art.

In contrast, *Monograph* 8, Walcott's first major government publication, documented fossils from one area, going up the geologic column from bottom to top. It is to be classed with the older paleontologic volumes that delineated the broad stratigraphic groups of this country. The new bulletin was a regional study of fossils from a far more restricted slice of time. In a stratigraphic sense the *Monograph* was extensive, and the *Bulletin* was intensive. The *Monograph* was limited geographically, whereas the *Bulletin* gathered all data then known on distribution of North American Cambrian fossils. Fundamental to each were the illustration and description of the fauna.

There are no perfect papers in paleontology in the sense that one can write an equation in physics or record a chemical reaction and have it endure. Paleontology is an accumulative science building on prior data. Once the broad features of a stratigraphic or biologic group are outlined, increased precision brings changes. Changes in the names of fossils come about in two different ways. First, in winnowing through the literature or in collecting better topotypes of a described species, one may determine that forms thought to be different are the same or, contrariwise, forms thought to be different are identical. Second, in finding fossils from new localities and in making a more intensive study of a group new forms may be distinguished. To overgeneralize, the first results in change of the names of species and the second results in change of the names of genera. Most of Walcott's generic names in *Bulletin* 30 remain in the literature. Some species are now placed in other genera, but few of the new species he named have been relegated as synonyms.

Not only do species and genera change through time, different major groups of fossils vary in abundance and diversity in different geologic periods. Thus the large variety of fossils in the *Monograph*. Nature is so arranged that trilobites are particularly characteristic of the Cambrian. About half of Walcott's systematic section in the *Bulletin* is devoted to trilobites, and half to all the other groups of fossils he encountered. This included the material from eastern Canada that Walcott restudied; some of those forms were not well represented in his collections. In addition to generic and specific descriptions, he discussed the curious sponges and included a new classification of mollusk or mollusk-like forms which do not fit into either the snails or clams.

This brings up one jarring note in the text. At the end of the text in *Bulletin* 10, Walcott added an unusual fossil from the Georgia locality. He repeated that procedure in this bulletin and discussed and illustrated *Matthevia*, a Saratoga Springs fossil named after G. F. Matthew, the collector of customs and paleontologist in New Brunswick. Walcott had named it earlier in a short paper, and added virtually nothing new to the text. The illustrations are much better than those first used and that could have been why it was included. This is a strange fossil and obviously it intrigued him. A century later, the morphology and systematic position of *Matthevia* is still being argued, and the genus is one of the points in a protracted scientific argument about evolution of the mollusks.

In the opening seventy pages of the *Bulletin,* Walcott reviewed the geologic sections he had collected, and summarized the fauna described in the latter part of the work. In keeping with his earlier views, he called the time interval which contained this fauna Georgian and he gave its age as Middle Cambrian. That would soon be shown as an error. but an understandable one, supported by two lines of evidence. First, the fauna was not actually Potsdam and had been found without too much question in beds older than Potsdam. On the other hand, it was not Acadian and that fauna by consensus was considered the oldest Cambrian in North America. Nowhere had beds containing Acadian fossils and those containing Georgian fossils been found in contact in a continuous sequence. Walcott knew that in the Grand Canyon, the Llano area, and the upper Mississippi Valley Upper Cambrian rested on vastly older rocks with none of the earlier Cambrian strata intervening. It was logical that there must also be regions where the Acadian did not underlie the Georgian.

Second, there was the biologic evidence alluded to in his paper to the Philosophical Society of Washington. Here, in his discussion of the key trilobite genus *Olenellus,* he elaborated. "Olenellus is the representative of the group of Paradoxides of the Lower Cambrian in the Middle Cambrian, and expresses, in one of its species at least, the decadence of that branch of the type. The example is *O. Gilberti,* where, in the retention and great development of the embryonic stages of growth by adult individuals, we have an example of the loss of power in the larger number of the individuals of a species to develop to the adult form. In other words, it is an instance of retrogression toward the earliest forms of the family to which it belongs" (Walcott 1886a, 166). Whitfield had written that he was not so certain of this succession, Ford agreed with Walcott. Both biologic and geologic evidence were in accord that the Georgian should be younger than the Acadian.

Whether the Georgian was Middle Cambrian or not, Walcott had carefully documented the fossils. Another geologist or paleontologist, finding a new locality, could determine by comparison of his fossils whether they were the same and therefore the same age, or they were different and therefore younger or older. That is what stratigraphic paleontology is all about. The more detailed the study of fossils, the more precise can be determination of similarities and differences in age.

Science reviewed the *Bulletin* for nearly a full page:

> Mr. Walcott's studies lead him to the same results reached by the English geologists; namely, the division of the early paleozoic series (omitting the supposed pre-Cambrian) into three systems,—the Cambrian, Ordovician (lower Silurian) and Silurian (upper Silurian). . . . In the Cambrian system Mr. Walcott recognizes three series, a lower, middle, and upper,—which correspond respectively to the St. John's group, the lower and upper Potsdam of Sir William Logan. The lower Cambrian fauna is not known to occur "west of a line passing north-east through eastern Massachusetts, New Brunswick and Newfoundland"; being kept out of the internal basin, Mr. Walcott believes, by a barrier extending from Lake Superior south to Texas, and west to Arizona. The middle Cambrian fauna would seem to be peculiar to America, not being represented in Wales, Scandinavia, or Bohemia. . . .
>
> Only a beginning has been made in a great undertaking, but it would be difficult to exaggerate the value of the work already done, which now offers a series of well-defined questions for solution, instead of the chaos which reigned but a few years ago. (Anonymous 1887, 545–46)

Bulletin 30 received a one sentence review in the *American Journal of Science:* "A very large and elaborate contribution to Cambrian Paleontology, with numerous excellent illustrations on the 33 plates" (Anonymous 1887a, 158–59). One would hope three years of hard work merited a little more than that. However, shortly before the *Bulletin* was released, in August the *Journal* had published a long paper by Walcott based on the National Academy of Sciences talk (Walcott 1886b). Many junior scientists today would seriously contemplate selling a member of their family to obtain publication in only five months; times have changed.

The *American Journal* paper had several additional cross-sections from Texas and northern Wisconsin. It also had a map and another hypothetical cross-section. In the *Bulletin,* Walcott had shown the Grand Canyon series as Cambrian on a diagram, but in the text suggested these this might be pre-Cambrian. He now developed this concept briefly, suggesting an ancient land of Keweenaw against which the older Cambrian sediments were deposited; it was not until the time of the Potsdam that the entire continent was submerged.

Paleogeographic maps outlining the past distribution of land and sea had been published for about fifty years, but were uncommon. Walcott's was one of the first in North America and set the stage for more to be drawn around the turn of the century by other paleontologists. He also touched on the notion that the Grand Canyon rocks, those in the Llano, and in northern Michigan formed a Keweenaw series, quite distinct from the Cambrian. This idea was to mature for a decade and become significant later as his career moved along into studies of older rocks.

Because his monthly reports had been fragmentary, near the end of 1886 Walcott summarized where he had gone in the field and provided insight as to how he was attacking the problem of the of the Taconic rocks; reading this recapitulation in full exhausts one from the scope of Walcott's movements and activities:

> On the 9th of June I began the study of the Potsdam formation about the Adirondack Mountain in Jefferson Co. N. Y. Thence I passed through St. Lawrence, Franklin, and Clinton Counties. . . .
>
> From the 1st to the 7th of July I was engaged in taking a section of the Chazy formation on the Isle la Motte, Vt. . . . I then went to Beauharnois in the Province of Quebec. . . .
>
> I next studied the Potsdam formation at Ausable Chasm and in the vicinity of Keeseville, Essex Co., N. Y. . . . The next section was taken at Whitehall in Washington Co., and from there a reconnaissance was made to the eastward partially across Washington Co. . . . On returning an examination was made of an outlier of Potsdam sandstone from the west side of South Bay, at the head of Lake Champlain. . . . I next examined a section crossing the town [township] of Greenwich in the southern part of the county and there obtained good results, as there was one locality already known from which Cambrian fossils had been obtained that could be used as a starting point in a section.
>
> I decided to make an examination of the Cambrian formations in Washington Co., and to map their lines of outcrop. This was continued up to Oct.

21st. I rode over 600 miles on a buckboard within the limits of the county and examined many areas between the roads by crossing them on foot. The results of the work was the discovery of 82 localities of Cambrian fossils within the county and 8 localities of Hudson River fossils in strata that were faulted in amidst the areas of Cambrian strata.

Three great fault lines were traced across the county and the limits of the Cambrian and Silurian (Ordivician [*sic*]) rocks determined on both stratigraphic and lithologic evidence. The examination of the strata was carried across the State line into Vermont sufficiently far to identify the great belts of strata that pass across the line. Two localities of Cambrian fossils were discovered in strata colored Hudson River group, on the geologic map of Vermont (1861).

I examined three reported outcrops of the Potsdam formation in the Mohawk Valley. . . .

I then proceeded to Poughkeepsie, N. Y., and examined the outcrops of Cambrian rocks north and south of the city with Prof. W. B. Dwight of Vassar College. . . . the so-called Potsdam sandstone contained fossils from the Middle Cambrian fauna and that it should be referred to the Georgia horizon of the Cambrian

I am now preparing a map showing the distribution of the Cambrian formations in Washington Co., and their connection with the Cambrian formation in Vermont.[24]

Phew!

Walcott's contribution to Vermont geology in *Bulletin* 30, with its detailed documentation of the Georgian fauna, is clear. He chose to write only briefly about the geology, for it is exceedingly complex:

At the base of the section are more than 4000 feet of Lower Cambrian clastic and calcareous rocks. The Middle Cambrian, most of which is slate, is nearly 3000 feet thick. The Upper Cambrian includes several hundred feet of Franconian and possible Trempealeauan limestones and shales. The Lower Ordovician is about 3000 feet thick. . . . Structurally, the St. Albans area is part of the large overthrust sheet called the Rosenberg slice, which has been folded into an asymmetric, northward-plunging syncline. The western limb of the syncline dips gently to the east, but the eastern limb is vertical or overturned and has been pushed westward (Shaw 1958, 522–23).

Like his work on the Permian of the Colorado Plateau, nothing appeared by Walcott on the geology of the Champlain lowland to the west of the lake. Walcott is not mentioned as one who worked in this area (Rodgers 1937), yet he labored there long and hard. His measured sections and observations would have made several good papers, yet he did not take to time to write them up. He was after bigger game, both in trying to document the Cambrian and in physically moving in on the Taconic type area, having skirted it to the west and to the north. Some of what Walcott learned was published in *Bulletin* 30, but much remained undone. Large collections of fossils reside in the National Museum, but they are the only documentation of all this effort in Vermont and New York.

7

Domestic and International Relations: Getting Down to Basics (1887–1888)

> It has been ten years since I published my last paleontologic work.
> In that work I proved that despite a difference in facies, the Olenellus
> zone, in North America as well as in Norway, represents the oldest
> trilobite zone, older than the Paradoxides schist, while the American
> paleontologists, in particular Matthew and Walcott, were long
> unwilling to admit this.
>
> W. C. Brøgger, 1895

For Walcott, 1886 closed as it began: "Still unsettled in relation to home life. Scientific work progressing in good form" (December 31, 1886). The following year brought a step in settling his home life; for his career, 1887 was a complex interval. It was also a watershed year for the Smithsonian, with the appointments of G. B. Goode and S. P. Langley as assistant secretaries; after Dr. Baird's death later that year, Langley became the third secretary (Oehser 1949).

The workaday routine of fossil identifications and writing in the office resumed for Walcott. He answered his mail, identified Silurian fossils, served on the admissions committee of the Cosmos Club, and attended the Biological Society of Washington; of course, every Sunday was spent at the Church of the Covenant with Josie. Some evenings he squired sister Josie to a concert, the local Literary Society, or a friend's home.

At the museum, Walcott progressed with his major problem. During the winter, by studying the collections lent by several New England geologists, he wrote, "I was enabled to arrive at positive conclusions respecting the geologic age of the lowest member of Emmons' Taconic System and to correlate the entire Upper Taconic System with the lowest formation of the Lower Taconic."[1]

In *Bulletin* 30, written prior to his 1886 field season, Walcott reviewed Emmons's work on the Taconic and views of others: "I have been influenced by a desire to do justice to the work of the author of the 'Taconic System' and to retain a name proposed by an American geologist. It is with regret that I find myself compelled now to use Cambrian in preference to Taconic, especially as the Middle Cambrian fauna of this paper is the fauna of the Upper Taconic of Emmons" (Walcott 1886a, 65). On the same page, Walcott emphasized the difficulties under which Emmons had worked and praised him for what he had accomplished.

"Cambrian," originally based on the rocks in Wales and later their contained fossils to mark this time interval, was preferred over "Primordial." The three great faunas which Barrande differentiated in Bohemia clarified the older fossil-bearing rocks, but their utility was passing. The boundaries of the three faunas began to blur; at Eureka, Walcott had described "passage beds" through which the Cambrian fauna changed gradually in character to the Lower Silurian fauna. A more precise standard for comparison defined the rocks, and the standard was Cambrian. Primordial appeared a few more times in American literature, but the use was at best a curiosity; Cambrian was a better term.

This leads to the question of priority, and when it is invoked, almost invariably arguments become nasty. Taconic in outline form was named and defined by Emmons in 1841, six years after 1835 use of Cambrian by Sedgwick. Emmons completely reversed his sequence in 1844 and described Taconic fossils that year. Did one accept his original concept or to his subsequent work? Did one pay attention to how later workers defined the rocks, using fossils from Vermont rather than from the type area? The 1844 fossils were not recognized as Primordial until years after Primordial fossils in Great Britain were equated with Cambrian rocks (Yochelson 1993). Who had priority and priority in what?

Cambrian had clear priority over the Upper Taconic and because the faunas were the same, Cambrian should be used. As for the Lower Taconic, more detailed fieldwork was knocking the props out from under it. The chauvinistic argument that an American author should be supported because American work deserved international recognition was not one that Walcott even deemed to discuss.

On January 15, 1887, Walcott spoke to the Philosophical Society of Washington; an abstract, published in the *American Journal of Science*, received more attention than usual for a local talk (Walcott 1887). He emphasized his discovery of Middle Cambrian or Georgian fossils in Washington County, New York, and pointed out that fossils demonstrated that several shales were the offshore time equivalents of the sandstones. Walcott confirmed Dana's interpretation that some of the major limestones were Lower Silurian (Ordovician). There was not a great deal left for Emmons. "Of the strata referred to the Taconic System in the Taconic region, the granular quartzite and the Upper Taconic still remain in it as pre-Potsdam formations, and the Stockbridge and sparry limestones and the superior hydromica schists are referred to the Lower Silurian (Ordovician) system" (Walcott 1887, 154). Still, it is one thing to make pronouncements in Washington and quite another to convince one's geologic colleagues outside of town.

"Some progress was made on the preparation of material for the study of the Upper Cambrian faunas, prior to February 15, but after that date, owing to the want of an assistant to do the mechanical work, very little was accomplished" (Walcott 1889, 175). Cooper Curtice was sorely missed; Walcott had properly called him "a valuable assistant." Except when funds were extremely scarce, Walcott always had help, and later he had other full-time assistants, but none were up to the standards of Curtice. Walcott started sending key specimens to his brother-in-law to prepare out of the matrix in the evenings after William completed farm chores.

T. Sterry Hunt of the Geological Survey of Canada dropped in to chat, and Walcott discussed the Taconic question with him. Hunt was first an opponent, but then a strong proponent of the Taconic System, and his opinions could not be ignored. The last week of the month, Walcott went off to Boston and Cambridge. He saw Hyatt's collections and gave two popular evening talks on his adventures on the Colorado. Walcott took the time to call on Jules Marcou; with Hyatt present, they discussed the Taconic question for five hours. In print, Marcou (1887) propounded a chauvinistic view and ridiculed Walcott's interpretation of priority. After the Marcou meeting, Hyatt went with him to Amherst College, where they searched the collections for more Cambrian fossils. Then it was south to call at the American Museum, and home to Washington.

One scientific morsel resulted from this trip. Marcou showed Walcott an error, no doubt with glee. A few of Billings's fossil names had been published four years in advance of his major book for the Geological Survey of Canada, and Walcott had missed them. Because of priority of publication, this had an effect on a name to be used for one of the curious Cambrian sponges (Walcott 1887). Walcott took a copy of *Bulletin* 30, placed blank pages between the printed ones and for a few years kept track of all such corrections.

Work was coming along steadily, and his Washington County, New York map was being drafted. When not otherwise involved, Walcott was "studying the Taconic, Cambrian, and Silurian question" (March 17, 1887). March 17 lists no mention of St. Patrick, but it was a cause for at least minor celebration when Ira Sayles reported as a new assistant to replace Curtice. Sayles had a weak prior career and had been reduced in salary before Walcott took him on; after Sayles left the Survey, he built his reputation in mining geology.

A few days after Walcott's thirty-seventh birthday, he completed an important paper, documenting the "Upper Taconic" fauna he has found in Washington County, showing it to be like the Cambrian fauna described in *Bulletin* 30 (Walcott 1887b). Only one page was devoted to general discussion, the rest describing and illustrating species with fairly exact locality data. Dana published the manuscript six months after Walcott finished it. In April, Walcott took a quick trip to see Dana, probably bringing him that manuscript.

On his return, he conferred again with Hunt, still in Washington, and "Read a paper on the 'Taconic System of Emmons' to the National Academy of Sciences" (April 21, 1887). This was the second year in a row he had spoken before the academy. Walcott was some years away from being a member of that august body, but being invited to give a paper was a step toward possible election; the talk was well received.

However, Walcott had other work besides the Taconic problem: "The results of my field observations on the Silurian, Devonian, and Carboniferous formations of southern-central Nevada was reviewed, written out, and transmitted to Mr. Arnold Hague to be incorporated into the volume on the 'Geology of the Eureka District.' This course appeared better than to publish the matter in bulletin form, as it combines the information on the geology of Nevada in one volume."[2] This procedure was also quicker for Walcott; his interests now were squarely in the Cambrian and the younger western rocks were just a distraction. It was a wise decision, as Hague frittered away five years before finishing. Mining geologists remarked that the sure sign a district was played out was that the government report on it was published.

Walcott became ill with a kidney stone, but once that had been passed, life was better. Mid-May brought a major conference on geologic nomenclature attended by the principal government geologists. Powell, Gilbert, Hague, McGee, Dall, and White were full-time employees, and Captain Dutton might just as well have been. R. D. Irving and Raphael Pumpelly came to the city to attend. Walcott was in with the cream of American geology. The significance of this gathering requires a tangential discussion.

Charles Doolittle Walcott, Paleontologist

The geopolitical issues of 1887 behind this meeting go back to 1876, the Centennial of the United States (Rabbitt 1980, 131–36). Geologists assembled for their section of the AAAS in Buffalo, inspired by patriotic zeal, laid the groundwork for what became the International Congress of Geologists, first meeting in Paris in 1878. Having reached its prime objective of an international meeting, the American Committee became moribund. Few Americans attended the 1881 Bologna meeting, at the Berlin Congress of 1885, a number were present, and several proposed holding a session of the congress in North America. In January 1886, the American Committee was revitalized (Frazer 1888). Director Powell was tied up with a congressional investigation and W J "No-Stop" McGee represented him and the Geological Survey. McGee may have been the most egotistical and least diplomatic geologist ever in federal service.

One of the actions of the second meeting in 1886, to which Powell did not send an envoy, was to set up subcommittees on nomenclature of geologic systems. The Berlin Congress focused on this matter, and several of the Americans who attended were anxious that stratigraphic terminology in America be regularized and conform with European usage. Meanwhile, federal geologists were preoccupied with the Allison Commission hearings in Congress and the Charleston earthquake. During 1886, geologic nomenclature was hardly a priority concern in Washington.

The USGS already had a color scheme for its geologic maps, given in the second *Annual Report* by Director Powell. The major was not about to be dictated to by Europeans on the proper color of maps. He told McGee to compile and hand color a geologic map of the United States to present the Survey position, and when McGee could not do this promptly, Charles Hitchcock of New Hampshire was hired to assist. By October 1886, Hitchcock felt impelled to point out that USGS usage was at variance with that recommended by the International Congress. In December, at its third meeting, the American Committee accepted the usage for geologic systems of the Berlin Congress and urged American geologists to follow it. They also decided that subcommittees should compile the views of the American geological community as to stratigraphic subdivisions to present at the 1888 London congress.

In April 1887, the American Committee met again for discussion. Henry S. Williams of Cornell was a voice of sanity in trying to differentiate between the activities of stratigraphers and those of paleontologists, and the necessity for different kinds of nomenclature. Rock units needed names best based on geographic localities where the rocks were exposed. On the other hand, paleontologists were concerned with organic change and correlation of events from place to place; too rigid a scheme would be counterproductive. They saw the continuum of time, rather than focusing on rocks at a unique geographic location. Powell's meeting of government geologists in May 1887 was a reaction to the April gathering of the American Committee.

At this April meeting, N. H. Winchell of Minneapolis was appointed "reporter" for the Lower Paleozoic, taken to be the interval prior to the Devonian, that is the Silurian and Cambrian as they were generally used in the United States. In addition to a general call for information, Winchell specifically solicited the opinion of a few leading geologists, Walcott included. After Walcott spoke on the Taconic System to the National Academy of Sciences, "a short abstract of it was sent, June 8, 1887, to Prof. N. H. Winchell" (Walcott 1888a, 232n.). Dates become critical to trace Walcott's actions.

In August, the American Committee had another public meeting. At Powell's request no votes were taken on the various reports. The following week was the annual AAAS convention; Powell was association president and Gilbert the vice-president of the geological section. Gilbert delivered an address on his view of the function of the International Congress. "Its proper field of work lies in the determination of questions of technology; it is a trespasser if it undertakes the determination of questions of science. It may decree terms, but it must not decree opinions" (Rabbitt 1980, 135). This was followed by a tedious discussion of the American Committee reports and an attempt by Powell to increase the size and pack the committee. Everyone was upset, but eventually the committee was formally thanked for its work, and the reports were designated as the individual views of the various reporters. Regardless of whether the action of Powell, and to some extent that of Gilbert, was justified scientifically, this was high-handed in the extreme, and left bitter feelings. Now it is time to return to Walcott and his pursuit of the Taconic in the field.

Late in May after the big pow-wow on geologic nomenclature in Washington, Walcott went to Ithaca, New York, to check on the fossil collections made by Williams; as expected, all was in order. Visiting family in Utica, he also made some observations on a well being drilled on the farm of Mr. Campbell, his late grandfather's partner in the woolen mill. After a quick call at Albany and a visit to Schoharie to examine a collection, Walcott went to Whitehall, New York. William joined him for collecting in eastern New York and Vermont. This collecting confirmed earlier ages, but nothing new or dramatic resulted. Walcott went on to Middlebury College in Vermont and then back to Utica.

Charles Doolittle Walcott, Paleontologist

June 27, in retrospect, turned out to be a critical date, for Walcott went to a baseball match with Mr. and Mrs. Timothy Griffith and a Miss Helena B. Stevens who was visiting her aunt at Scanandoa, east of Oneida. The next day they all drove "to Richfield Springs & thence to Cooperstown. Dined at Hunnicliff's on Lake Otsego. Returned to Utk. at 9 P.M. A beautiful day & most enjoyable trip" (June 28, 1887). Walcott does not say so, but this day he was smitten by Miss Stevens. After another day at Trenton Falls, he returned to fieldwork.

"July 1st, 2½ miles east of Bennington, Vt. in the town of Woodford, characteristic Middle Cambrian fossils were found *in situ* in the quartzite where an extended section is exposed. This quartzite extends south into Massachusetts, is the basal member of Emmons' Taconic System and occupies the position assigned it by me in the paper read before the National Academy of Sciences, April 22nd, 1887."[3] The antique phrase "red letter day" applies, for there is nothing like the satisfaction of a scientific prediction confirmed. After several more days, Walcott left for Massachusetts, Vermont, and eastern New York to wind up his work.

Walcott returned to Washington during a very hot July, so hot that almost nothing could be done. He stewed in the heat while Powell decided whether he was to go west or to continue in New England. July 27, Walcott left again with assistant Robert T. Hill for Massachusetts, only to have Hill recalled to Washington after a few days for proofreading duties; Hill spent some years with the USGS and then moved to the Texas Survey to become the "father" of geology in that state (Alexander 1976). For Walcott, the climbs up hills were hard, the wagon broke, and all in all it was a difficult few days in the field.

Occasionally hard work and determined looking will pay off, especially if one is lucky: "Found fossils in the ls. (Taconic) ½ mile north of Vt. state line in Hoosic valley" (August 5, 1887). This was more than a red letter day, for this find was fundamental to solving the Taconic problem. Fossils in rocks correlated to the Taconic did not have the significance and authority for dating the Taconic as fossils in rocks which every warring party agreed were truly Taconic, as defined by Emmons. The fossils in Taconic rocks which Walcott found were Lower Silurian in age, not ancient forms. Thus, on both west and east sides of the high Taconics, formed of contorted and enigmatic schists, Walcott now had younger fossils and therefore the Taconic rocks between them were also younger. The problem was resolved.

Walcott geologized his way west to the Hudson River and took a steamer to the AAAS meetings in New York City, where he gave two talks. One concerned the stratigraphy in the deep-water well (twenty-three hundred feet) drilled near Utica. Walcott could not be there during the entire drilling, but the able lawyer Edward Hurlburt collected chips brought up by the drilling rig. "This is the first known section in the Mohawk Valley, where the strata between the base of the Oneida conglomerate of the Silurian and the gneiss of the Archean, have been measured and the relative thickness of the formations determined. Fossils were found in the chips from the Trenton limestone, but not from the rocks beneath" (Walcott 1887c, 212). Subsurface data had been used before in America, but this little study shows that Walcott was aware of what the new dimension of depth could contribute to geology.

His paper the following day reported discovery of fossils in Lower Taconic strata. He first discussed the quartzite, followed by his find in the Hoosic Valley:

> The discovery of determinable fossils in the quartzite and the Eastern limestone of the Lower Taconic united with the data obtained from the Western limestone and the Taconic slates in Washington county, practically puts at rest the question of the geologic age of the Taconic system. We now know positively that the quartzite series and the Upper Taconic are Cambrian age, and the limestone series with the overlying schists are of Lower Silurian (Ordovician) age. (Walcott 1887d, 213)

It was eleven days from field discovery to public presentation. No grass was growing under Walcott's feet. The AAAS was also the first time Walcott had been face to face with most members of the American Committee. As a result of Powell's May meeting of Survey geologists in Washington, a message was clear that the USGS was not about to be dictated to regarding the nomenclature of the rocks. Now, out of left field as it were, Walcott, who had been sympathetic to how hard Emmons had labored, shattered the Taconic System. Conspiracy theorists of the time might have conjectured that Walcott was doing Powell's bidding in trying to destroy an *American* geologic system.

Walcott went back to Washington County and met Ira Sayles, a new assistant, to collect fossils. Secretary Baird died on August 19, 1887, but Walcott did not hear the news for some time. After a few days on the local geology, they traced the Cambrian north to North Granville. Then it was a return to Whitehall to complete the geologic traverse and to North Granville and to Fort Ann to trace the boundaries of limestone and shale. Then east and west, back and forth several times to visit the various units, traveling between twenty and thirty miles a day. By early September, a geologically confident Walcott went to Utica for a few days break.

Charles Doolittle Walcott, Paleontologist

From Utica, Walcott went to Albany and then east once more into the confused terrane "looking for fossils to close the gap in the Greenwich section" (September 17, 1887). He kept on the move from town to town, "trying to straighten out the Cambrian & Hudson terranes" (September 21, 1887). Both rock sequences are similar-looking dark shales and, without fossils, it was almost impossible to differentiate one from another. Combining the trip from Washington with his zig-zag course, he had traveled more than twelve hundred miles. The first of October, Walcott went back to the simpler carbonate rocks of Whitehall, detouring to see a graphite mine in the hard rocks of the Adirondack; this entailed rowing nine miles and walking eight. Then back south again to the tangled rocks, mapping contacts where possible, finding a few trilobites and finishing his mapping at Glens Falls. After a few more days in the field and a quick call on Hall, Walcott was back in Utica to attend to family business and clean up the map. He also had personal business to pursue.

"At 11:40 left for Oneida where H. B. S.[tevens] & Mrs. H. B. Sanford [aunt] met me. Drove to Scanandoa the home of Mrs. S. Visiting—" (October 28, 1887). The following day he walked twice with "Miss Helena B. S.," and again the next day. The following day it was "Miss Helen"; he was entranced with this lady—no other word is expressive enough. Walcott returned to Utica to talk to his family and back to Scanandoa three days later, where he passed a delightful evening. Miss Stevens's mother came into town the following day. Walcott went to Trenton Falls, spoke to William and wrote to "H. B. S." After a few days he went to New York City for a meeting of the National Academy of Sciences and called on Mrs. Sanford, who was in the city; he was firmly hooked.

Finally, on November 12, Walcott was back in Washington. As soon as he disposed on his mail, he wrote a long report to the director on his fieldwork which led to the demise of the Taconic System, except as an historic curiosity. There were to follow a couple of years of harsh words among geologists, but once the elderly Marcou died, the Taconic essentially vanished from the literature, though years later various structural interpretations caused more difficulties.

> The stratigraphy of the eastern portion of the Taconic system was found to be essentially as described by Dr. Emmons, but the finding of fossils in the quartzite on the east, and, also, in the overlying limestone proved that he had misinterpreted the geologic horizon of the greater part of the Lower Taconic. The study of the strata included in the Upper Taconic by Dr. Emmons proved that he had included a great mass of the Hudson Terrain in the Upper Taconic and, also, that he had founded the Taconic system on errors of ob-

servation along the line of contact of the rocks of the Champlain Terrain with those of the Upper Taconic. At all localities given by him I found that the Upper Taconic rocks were thrust over on to the Champlain rocks, and in no instance did I find the Champlain rocks, either by original deposition or by subsequent dislocation, above or on strata belonging to the Upper Taconic Terrain.

The summing up of the results of my study of the Taconic system is, that it was founded on an error of stratigraphy, that a large portion of it belongs to the Champlain series, and that the portions which we now know to be pre-Potsdam were not placed at that horizon on stratigraphic evidence that could be subsequently verified. The paleontologic evidence upon which we now place the strata of the Upper Taconic as pre-Potsdam was not obtained until long after the publication of the Taconic system in 1842, '44, '47, and '55.

Another result of the study of the Taconic area has been the determination of a thickness of Cambrian strata greater than all sedimentary rocks heretofore known in the State of New York. Near the base of the Taconic series I found and identified a trilobite belonging to the genus Paradoxides. This, united with certain genera and species which I found during the field season of 1886, definitely identifies the Lower Cambrian horizon near the base of the sixteen thousand feet of Cambrian strata in Washington County, New York. As far as known to me this is the first positive identification of this fauna in America east of Braintree, near Boston, Mass.[4]

Walcott had cracked the Taconic problem, but he still thought of *Paradoxides* as Lower Cambrian; that error would be resolved the following year. After this Taconic exposition in the monthly report, he should have put a paper into print as soon as possible, laying his new information before the geologic public. Total disavowal of the Taconic was a dramatic switch for Walcott and one that he had to document promptly to convince his peers. Walcott did work hard, but, interestingly, he left his geology at the office and spent his evenings calling on his cousin and other friends, going to meetings of local scientific societies, and writing to Helen.

Just before the end of the year, the American Committee met in New Haven. A week prior, the comments of Walcott were "withdrawn owing to the field work of the season of 1887 having negatived and rendered obsolete several of the conclusions therein expressed" (Walcott 1888a, 232n.). If, as with Darwin's career, one looks for psychological causes for illness, the strain of this formal withdrawal of opinion may have been the cause of a brief illness in mid-December which called for electric treatments. Walcott recovered enough to travel to Utica for Christmas with Mother and Josie. The sleighing was good.

Charles Doolittle Walcott, Paleontologist

He went to Oneida, that is Scanandoa, for two days and back to Utica. December 31, Walcott sent his geologic map off to the printers and caught the train back to Oneida. "Watched the old year out with Helena as it closed the first chapter in the history of our acquaintance, one leading to a fuller richer life I trust in the year to come" (December 31, 1887). Perhaps moonstruck is the word to describe Walcott. This was indeed a lovely personal note on which to end this year wherein a major scientific problem had been solved. Of course, a problem solved and an issue resolved are not necessarily simultaneous.

After two more days with Helena, Walcott returned to Utica for electric treatments, dental work, and manuscript writing on the Taconic problem. That was enough of a combination to send him back to Scanandoa and Helena for several more days. He wrote a bit more and took Josie to see his lady love. The first part of the Taconic paper was sent off and he escorted Helena to Syracuse. The second part was more difficult to write, and he settled down at Utica for a week. The paper started, he went to Trenton Falls to see the material William Rust had collected in the Champlain Valley. "I found the collection to exceed my expectations. It will be of great service in the review of the faunas below those of the Potsdam and Trenton terranes."[5] Rust was a collector's collector; he had taught Walcott and could still impress his brother-in-law. In all, Rust obtained more than six thousand specimens, very good value for the government funds paid him.

Late in January Walcott still wrestled with his Taconic paper and had both stomach trouble and headaches; Mrs. Shepard's electric treatments did not help, and he went to a sanitorium for a few days. Meeting Helena in Rochester helped, but it was back to the sanitorium for a week and then to Rochester again. Walcott took Helena to see Ward's Natural History Establishment, which should have given her a foretaste of his interests and how strongly he pursued them. Somewhere along the line, Helena became formally engaged, but Walcott did not mention it in his diary; in some matters he was very private, even to himself.

Not until late February was Walcott back in Washington, reading proof on the first part of his Taconic paper, which appeared in the March, April, and May issues of the *American Journal of Science* (Walcott 1888a). The geologic map of part of eastern New York, western Vermont, western Massachusetts, and northwestern Connecticut, was included; none of his mapping west of Lake Champlain ever was published. The forty-five-page text could have been a USGS *Bulletin,* but there is no question that Dana could publish faster than the Government Printing Office. The paper included drawings of the fossils Walcott found in the Hoosic Valley on the east side of the Taconics. The map shows all of Walcott's fossil localities. Between this and his earlier paper on the Washington County fossils, anyone who desired could recollect his localities.

Walcott first discussed his fieldwork and then reviewed what Emmons and others proposed before giving his final conclusions. This report is clear and succinct: "I endeavored to make, in 1886, an argument for the use of the name Taconic for the Middle division of the Cambrian System, but it failed in the light of later results of field work; and now I think that geologic nomenclature will be benefitted by dropping the name entirely. Based on error and misconception originally, and used in an erroneous manner since, it serves only to confuse the mind of the student, when applied to any formation or terrane" (Walcott 1888a, 394). Walcott emphasized that his was not simply a laboratory investigation of fossils, but fieldwork of a geologist in the type area of the Taconic System, and that both approaches showed the original concept of a distinct geologic system to be in error.

Not every geologist accepted what he read and not every geologist read the *American Journal of Science.* Dana now had some competition. Powell's actions at the AAAS meeting in August caused exceptionally bitter feelings, and one immediate consequence was the founding of a journal, the *American Geologist,* in 1888. With an increasing number of geologists in America, another outlet for geological papers was appropriate. The new journal wanted free exchange of views and its editors "had serious misgivings as to the result of the influence of the national geological survey in extending its operations into the settled states of the Union, and especially into states in which official surveys are in progress, fearing that by the concentration of all authority and control at the national capital, and by the extensive accumulation at one centre of all the material illustrating the state and local geology of the country, the local interest may die out, and that ultimately the weight of public sentiment favorable to geologic investigation may suffer diminution" (Calvin et al. 1888, iii).

The academics and the state geologists who did not receive largess from the USGS felt themselves ignored and scorned by the federal/eastern establishment clique. Blaming the government for one's troubles is nothing new in America. To be fair, however, once the editors vented their spleen, the journal performed a valuable function. It appeared monthly until 1906, and increasingly N. H. Winchell was its mainstay. Considering its origin, this journal was the obvious place to publish the nomenclature reports of the American Committee.

Charles Doolittle Walcott, Paleontologist

It was also the place for Marcou to take another shot at Walcott (Marcou 1888). Marcou's later remarks were privately published, a blast at the workers on several geologic systems who had not given him his due. He began by noting that Billings considered Hall and Hunt to be against the Taconic. "I shall add several other names: Messers. W. E. Logan, James D. Dana, the two Professors Rogers [William and Henry], and C. H. Hitchcock. The part taken by these seven united adversaries of the Taconic system is inexcusable, and even odious" (Marcou 1888a, 7–8). In at least a dozen copies of this tract the "seven" has been replaced in ink by "eight" and "Chas. D. Walcott" has been written in. Jules Marcou was a very determined man.

In his own mind, Walcott had good scientific reasons for his switch from use of the Taconic, though people such as Marcou would never understand such a change. To some persons the timing of the dramatic change of views made it appear as yet another machination of the federal Survey to dictate the course of geologic studies in America. However, insiders distinguished between Major Powell's organization and Walcott as a scientist, even if they did not approve of Walcott's conclusions.

Early in 1888, N. H. Winchell wrote his older brother Alexander, professor at the University of Michigan, a sketch of the latest Taconic controversy:

> I would particularly call your attention to the view taken by Prof. Dana in his investigations, that the Taconic contains only 2nd fauna rocks, because *mainly* it contained only those at the time Emmons first announced his Taconic System (though his typical system extended also over primordial strata). Not allowing Emmons to remodel and establish his system on new evidence in 1844–6, Dana ignores entirely the primordial aspect lately brought out by Walcott & Ford saying those rocks were not in the Taconic *at first,* & hence have no right to be used as a basis in 1844, nor in 1888. This seems to me very absurd when it is remembered that it [is] the reverse from the fundamental idea of Emmons. He wanted only to include strata below the second fauna and aimed to do so. He expressly omitted all second fauna strata from his system when he described it. Now I dont [*sic*] see by what hocus-pocus of philosophy Dana can content himself in the position he holds. It can be made very ridiculously embarrassing for him when put in such a light in the manner it seems to me to deserve. I want to deal with the question in a respectful & dignified way, however, and I want all the backing I can get. I feel sure the Taconic is going to win, notwithstanding the admission of Dana to the Committee.

I have written to Jules Marcou for a statement and I shall recast my report, necessarily after Walcott's withdrawal of his letter, and considerably amplify the *advocacy* of the use of the term—this latter for the benefit of European geologists rather than American.[6]

The major had not been all wrong in objecting to the American Committee reports.

A month later the younger Winchell wrote again, giving his views of the federal geologists and their director:

We are willing to "support the survey," but we ought to insist on some changes in its methods, and be free to criticize it in its mistakes. If you mean by "support the survey" that we are to laud it through thick & thin (which I dont understand you do) I should demur. The survey under major Powell has overgrown all reasonable dimensions, and has too imperious a way of dictating all geological opinion and geological methods. Powell is a smooth politician and ambitious operator rather than a candid earnest working geologist. Those qualities have made the survey grow wonderfully but I think it is liable to totter from the highth [sic] it has mounted to, and I think the greatest good of geology in the U.S. will come when the survey is more modest and more restricted to geological investigation without seeking to build up an aristocratic club, and trampling all outsiders who do not bow to its orders—orders which generally emanate from Powell himself. They hang together as if under military discipline.[7]

Winchell went on to complain about slights rendered to him by the major. Powell's policy of hiring some professors for temporary work gained him their support, but he did not hire everyone. Some of the sentiments expressed by N. H. Winchell are much like those of the present generation when a grant proposal to the National Science Foundation has been rejected; unless the scientific bureau is a source of funds, what good is the government?

Another letter a month later was more specifically germane to the problems of New England geology:

I shall make liberal extracts from your paper [reviewing the Taconic] for my report to the Am. Com. Int. Cong. of Geologists, to be presented April 2 in New York. I have a brief letter from Dana, & he adheres to his old views and recommendations respecting the use of the term Taconic. Walcott's "new discoveries" seem to be not new, except perhaps in the conclusions he will draw from them. His March paper (Am. Jour. Sci.) is *a strong Taconic paper,* but I anticipate an antitaconic conclusion on nomenclature from him. He has not sent me any communication since the withdrawal of his former one, and I shall have to rely on his later statements for my knowledge of his views.[8]

The brothers Winchell had little direct interest in fieldwork in New England. In their respective states, the Potsdam sandstone lay atop a vast thickness of sediments and lavas. The Winchells correlated these to the Taconic and thus were proponents of its use. Alexander Winchell's paper, summing up the Taconic once more, is laudatory toward Walcott's efforts, in contrast to Marcou's diatribes:

> American geology owes Mr. Walcott gratitude and honor for what he has accomplished. But I am inclined to the opinion that it is the very severity of his scientific method which prevents his due appreciation of the bearing of all the facts which he has been foremost to bring to light. Mr. Walcott has gone further than a comprehension of the elements of the Taconic question requires. He has followed Taconic history too far, and with too much minutiae of criticism for a broad, judicial contemplation of the essential problem— though not I repeat too far for the ends of science. (A. Winchell 1888, 360–61)

Winchell concluded that Emmons should be praised for stating there were rocks older than the New York System, but was not bothered by the fact that these older rocks were so scrambled in with younger rocks, that it was an accident that a small part of the Taconic System was actually of Taconic age. Concepts and definitions can be trimmed and modified through time, or they can be abandoned as having been too vague originally to be of use. Alexander Winchell was for the former, and Walcott was now strongly for the latter.

N. H. Winchell's Lower Paleozoic report of the American Committee was published with the following caveat: "Your reporter finds it difficult to divest himself of his personal predilections" (in N. H. Winchell 1888, 193). The introduction refers liberally to Walcott's work, especially his conclusions in *Bulletin* 30, long since superseded. A footnote dated May 24 after the last part of Walcott's Taconic paper had appeared, gives the text of a brief letter on the Taconic matter which Walcott sent to Frazer, the committee chairman. "This must not be considered as a report from me, but simply as a suggestion to you" (N. H. Winchell 1888, 215). Walcott's comments were followed by four pages of Winchell's views, rather than a true summary.

"The foregoing remarks on the late results of Mr. Walcott are demanded at this place, because of the importance of the investigation which Mr. Walcott has been engaged in, and because the recommendations of the body of report B were based largely on his first stated opinion" (N. H. Winchell 1888, 224). Winchell's four pages leading up to this final comment are less than judicial in tone. After stating that the discovery of fossils in the Hoosic Valley was simply an extension of occurrences elsewhere, Winchell moved into innuendo: "Aside from this no facts are stated not previously known to Mr. Walcott; and with slight exceptions they had all previously been published by him. . . . What may have been the other considerations which have thus induced Mr. Walcott to reverse his opinion he does not state" (N. H. Winchell 1888, 220). That is downright nasty, though mild by the standards of Marcou. The Taconic System somehow made passions run high. These polemics were presented to the London meeting in the fall of 1888 and republished three years later.

Walcott wrote Marcou he had never accused him of any ulterior motives and insisting that he stick to facts and not insinuation. Walcott never made any public comment about the way Winchell handled his change of opinion, though he did write a manuscript which Gilbert critiqued. "This article treats first of Mr. C. D. W. and his opinions, and second of Mr. N. H. W., and his opinions. These two subjects are unquestionably of interest to these gentlemen and a small circle of their personal friends, but they are of no interest to the world at large. It is my judgement that by the publication of this article you will diminish the reputation you have made by investigation chiefly but also in part by discussion of the Taconic question. . . . I trust you will excuse my extreme plainness on the ground of my cordial friendship."[9]

Walcott had the good sense to listen. Gilbert was right, for to argue further would weaken the case. The geologists who knew the area accepted Walcott's findings. H. A. Seely of Middlebury College summed it up:

> It seems to me that Walcott's extensive and apparently careful work must set this matter definitely at rest. No theoretical considerations can overthrow patiently observed facts. . . . Emmons was right in the idea that there were fossils lower down than the Potsdam. He however seems to be altogether in error in his stratigraphy grouping into his ideal Taconic formations of various ages.[10]

From New Hampshire, C. H. Hitchcock wrote Persifor Frazer: "I accept Walcott's paper as *affording the best interpretation of the structure that has yet been given to us*—and if you wish to refer to me the above is my opinion."[11] The Taconic System was gone and it was time to move on to other issues.

Charles Doolittle Walcott, Paleontologist

Walcott returned to the more routine work of preparation and identification. There was plenty of this to keep Sayles and Gentry busy, but they also began work on a card catalogue of species. There is nothing much more difficult to justify to an administrator than clerical help and financial support for a reference list, compiling each time a species name is used is the literature; there is nothing much more important to practical stratigraphic use of paleontology. One way or another, Walcott kept his catalogue up to date throughout his lifetime. It still is an invaluable, though unpublished, guide to the Cambrian literature of the world. That spring the National Museum actually provided some help and the collections made in the West before the USGS was founded were put in order for the first time.

One group of specimens which came to Walcott that spring of 1888 were some fossils from Mount Steven in the Northwest Territory of Canada (Walcott 1888b). Walcott determined their position relative to a section he had measured in the Highland Range, a correlation of a thousand miles. The fossils were important enough for him to give a talk to the Biological Society of Washington, and two decades later they would lead him to the Canadian Rockies in his pursuit of the Cambrian.

Work on Cambrian and on problems of classification of the Lower Paleozoic rocks filled the days. A great break for him came in April: "Telegram from Helena that she may go to Ne[w]f[oundl[and]. with me in July" (April 21, 1888). He rushed to Oneida to see the fair Helena. They made plans, and he went off to Harvard University and out into the field with N. S. Shaler. North Attleborough, Massachusetts, had yielded a fair number of fossils, still thought to be Middle Cambrian. He even called on Marcou. There was also a quick look at collections in the Museum of Comparative Zoology and Yale Peabody Museum.

Back in Washington, Walcott examined specimens from Montana for A. C. Peale; earlier Walcott had identified the first Devonian fossils known in the northern Rocky Mountains. He identified Colorado fossils for Samuel Emmons, and participated in a major USGS meeting on geologic nomenclature. Near the end of May he was off to New York City; his old roommate Dr. Eddy pulled a molar. Fieldwork near Poughkeepsie took away a little of the pain. He met William Rust at Troy, and they went to Greenwich Township, Washington County, New York. "We found an entire Olenellus ? asaphoides which shows the species to be the same type as the Swedish & Russian species beneath the Paradoxides beds" (June 2, 1888).

The section was carefully reexamined, and fossils collected from several horizons where none were known in 1886–87. One object of the work was to obtain evidence bearing on the stratigraphic succession of the Cambrian faunas, as the investigations of Swedish and Russian geologists pointed to a different succession from that heretofore published in America. The data obtained in Washington County goes a long way towards substantiating their view—that what I have called the Middle Cambrian fauna is, in reality, beneath the Paradoxides or Lower Cambrian fauna. The evidence is not conclusive, as there is not any known stratigraphic connection between the strata carrying the two faunas, nor do their typical genera, Olenellus and Paradoxides, occur in the same geologic province, as known to me today.

The question involved is an important one in its bearings on the geology and paleontology of the Lower Paleozoic rocks, and I shall follow it up, during the present field season, to the extent of crossing the line into the British Provinces. That field gives promise of furnishing the data necessary for settling the problem.[12]

Light had finally dawned on the succession of Cambrian trilobite-bearing beds. One can almost sense the great excitement of the chase, hunting for the key fossils. Even if these proved Walcott wrong, having the sequence of trilobites determined once and for all would clarify investigations throughout the continent.

There was another cause of excitement for, finally, more was going on in Walcott's life than paleontology. He was seriously engaged in affairs of the heart. Walcott in 1888 was thirty-eight, and Lura had been dead for more than a decade. He slipped away from the field in mid-June. Josie went with him to Chicago, and on June 22, a Friday, Charles married Helena Burrows Stevens at the home of her parents, 383 Ontario Street. After the reception, the couple left to begin their honeymoon, otherwise known as fieldwork. Walcott at least had the sense to first take his bride to Toronto and then by river steamer to Montreal, where they called on Sir William Dawson and saw the Redpath Museum. It was a full three days before Walcott was back on the rocks at Highgate Springs, Vermont.

"June 28th, a most important datum point was secured in the discovery of the Potsdam sandstone and fossils at the base of the Phillipsburgh series of strata on the shores of Missiasquoi Bay. This and other data now being collected will prove fatal to Prof. Jules Marcou's theory of 'colonies,' which was founded so largely on the Phillipsburgh section."[13] If one can send in a monthly report from the wilds of Arizona, one can surely do it while on a honeymoon, or at least while in Vermont with a new bride as field assistant.

To understand the Phillipsburgh work, recall that Barrande, the great paleontologist in Bohemia, distinguished three major distinct faunas in succession within the Lower Paleozoic rocks surrounding Prague. In 1850, Barrande visited England and identified a trilobite without a label as being a member of his "primordial" fauna. Strange as it may sound, Barrande was the first to equate the earliest faunas and the rocks named Cambrian in north Wales. When Barrande later noted that Emmons's Taconic fossils were also primordial, matters really became complicated.

Like human affairs, nature is never simple. A few places near Prague simply would not fit into this grand sequence of three faunas. To accommodate localities where the fauna was unexpectedly younger than the fossils in surrounding rocks, Barrande developed a theory of limited areas wherein precursors or "colonies" of organisms lived ahead of their time, so to speak, before blossoming forth in the next younger rock unit. Barrande humorously named the various colonies after those who opposed this notion.

The colony concept assumed a normal stratigraphic sequence, but unfortunately in places near Prague, faulting has confounded the simple stratification. This structural explanation was first worked out by a British geologist, John E. Marr. Today all the colonies are explained as tectonically displaced slices of rock that have been dropped down into the midst of older rocks, not as biologic precursors.

Marcou applied the concept of colonies to explain the sequence of faunas in northern Vermont and southern Quebec. By the late century, geologists were aware that rocks could be folded and overturned and in that way older rocks are over younger one. They also were learning that a sheet of rock could break and be pushed so that older rocks were over younger ones, though the magnitude of such movements was still highly speculative. Sir William Logan had first applied the notion of a major fault to explain the rocks around Quebec, when Billings reported that the sequence of fossils was wrong. That rocks could be moved for miles and that there could be multiple slices of rock piled atop one another were difficult ideas for some geologists to accept. The presence of "colonies" seemed as good a way, if not better, for the irascible Marcou to explain a strange sequence of fossils (Yochelson 1993):

> The fact that such an expert in finding fossils and in paleontologic work as
> Mr. Walcott is, has hesitated to determine the ages of the groups of strata

contained in his Calciferous-Chazy-Trenton, twice as thick as the Champlain System, and lithologically different, shows plainly that it was too much for him, even with the help of his overlapping fault and other faults so easily and freely used since Logan discovered them in his Montreal office on the new year's eve of 1861. (Marcou 1888, 70)

Regardless of the strident tone, this was emphatically not a silly argument, just one that was years too late in the development of the science. If Barrande was correct about precursors in older rocks, determining the age of rocks by their contained fossils was in jeopardy. On the other hand, if the fossils correctly dated the rocks, there were several different stacks of rocks at Highgate Springs. Discovery of the Potsdam Sandstone by Walcott showed that he was right in placing faults in the area. On almost every subject Marcou touched in later life he was wrong, but the man did have a way with words, even if it was poisonous. Proving Marcou wrong was like shooting fish in a barrel—there was not much sport—but Walcott was on his way to resolve far more important matters.

In his published *Annual Report* to the director, Walcott skirted his fieldwork: "Early in July I made a preliminary examination of the section near the boundary line between Canada and Vermont for the purpose of determining the stratigraphic succession of the rocks and their contained faunas between the shores of Lake Champlain and the village of St. Armand, Canada" (Walcott 1890, 160). A few lines later: "On my return from the field, in November. . . ." Not a word is written on Walcott's manifold travels and discovery during this interval. Perhaps the USGS had been advised not to mention work in British Canada and abroad.

From Vermont the newlyweds returned to Montreal, though without even time to see Sir William or look at collections. July 5 they took a cabin on the *Bonavista* and steamed down the St. Lawrence River through increasingly rough seas. They touched at Grand Banks on the southern coast of Newfoundland and then sailed into St. John's, then and now the largest city on the island. "We were glad to get on land" (July 13, 1888). They dined at Government House with Governor Blake and Lord Fitzgerald, and two nights later they were in the wardroom of HMS *Emerald*.

Vermont had given Mrs. Walcott a tiny taste of field geology, but lots more was to come. In the 1860s and 1870s collections had been made in eastern Newfoundland and studied by Elkanah Billings and later George F. Matthew. Walcott had looked at the same fossils in the museum of the Geological Survey of Canada, and these indicated to him the collecting potential of this area. The earlier work and correlations, based on little more than faith, suggested that *Para-doxides* was the oldest fauna, as Walcott had also documented in his Eureka *Monograph* and *Bulletin* 30. However, several European papers had described Cambrian trilobites from the Baltic region, and, in particular, the Norwegian Waldemar Brøgger insisted in 1886 that the sequence described in America was wrong:

> As the two zones [*Olenellus* and *Paradoxides*] nowhere come in contact with each other, it would seem that the foundation for this relation in age is rather uncertain, and under such circumstances it would seem that a comparison should be with other occurrences, where exactly corresponding deposits are found. Now we find here the remarkable circumstance that in Scandinavia, where the relations in regard to age between the Olenellus zone and the Para-doxides zone has been established with perfect certainty both by myself at Ringsaker and by Nathorst at Skåne, the former is undoubtedly the older, the second the younger. (Brøgger 1886, 193–94)

Brøgger thoroughly surveyed the American literature, pointed out several mistakes in Walcott's identifications, and even used Walcott's faunal lists for Hague to argue that in Nevada *Olenellus* indicated the Early Cambrian.

After reading Brøgger, Walcott sensed that Matthew could be wrong in his interpretations in New Brunswick and wrote him. "Go slow on correlating horizons until more data is in. I look to you for the links between the Paradoxides and Olenellus horizons, but make them pretty sure as Brogger is on the war path and will scalp you if he can, as it will not agree with his theory."[14] The trilobite collecting Rust and he did during 1887 in eastern New York gave a stronger indication that Brøgger was correct.

Matthew's investigations in Newfoundland warranted another letter from Walcott: "I have just laid down your paper on the Cambrian faunas in Newfoundland. I suppose that Olenellus occurs at Topsail Head, but have you found the genus anywhere below the Paradoxides zone? There appears to be little if any doubt that it occurs below in Sweden, as shown by Brøgger and Holm, but I cannot place it there from my work in the United States."[15]

Fieldwork was imperative to resolve the issue, and Walcott sought the advice of J. P. Howley, the government geologist in St. John's. Howley replied:

> The nearest outcrop of the Primordial Silurian [Cambrian] is at Topsail Head in Conception Bay where a narrow ridge rests unconformably against the Huronian of the Head. The limestone & shale here contains numerous fragments of trilobites &c. They extend along shore to southwest towards

Manuels but are for the most part concealed. At Manuels River below the Old Bridge a good section of the shales is seen where I have no doubt a careful search will well repay you.[16]

Mr. and Mrs. Walcott moved to the hamlet of Topsail, about ten miles to the west on the east side of Conception Bay. The Glover Hotel accommodated the new couple, and it was time to look at the rocks and fossils:

> There remained but one section known to me where the Cambrian rocks rested on the Huronian "gneiss" and the stratigraphic succession of the beds continued unbroken up to the unquestioned Paradoxides horizon. This was on Manuel's Brook, one-and-a-half-miles west of Topsail Head. A coarse conglomerate rests directly and unconformably upon a syenitic gneiss. Along the line of the brook the conglomerate is conformably subjacent to a belt of greenish shale which is succeeded by a band of red shale subjacent to a thin stratum of limestone, which is followed by greenish shales, and these in turn by black shales carrying an abundant Paradoxides fauna. This section being conformable, a careful search was made for fossils in the beds just above the conglomerate. They were first found about 1,500 feet north of the brook, in a railway cut, in some irregular masses of impure arenaceous limestone resting on the conglomerate, and subsequently in red and green shales resting on the conglomerate. In the reddish argillaceous shale a large fine species of Olenellus was found that may be referred to the sub-genus Mesonascis. It is allied to *O. (M.) asaphoides*, and I propose to call it *Olenellus (Mesonacis) Bröggeri*. (Walcott 1890a, 378–79)

By the 1880s, biologists recognized that one should not propose a new name without giving an adequate description or illustration, but Walcott might be forgiven this lapse. He had been wrong in his earlier work and by using Brøgger's name for a new species, he was both admitting his earlier mistake and honoring the one who had resolved the puzzle.

Manuel's Brook, a small stream that has cut a remarkably deep valley, exposes more than five hundred feet of black Cambrian shales before the stream reaches the seashore. Rather than sit alone all day, Helena helped with the collecting or she sketched. Several times the couple went trout fishing. It was an idyll, in spite of all the time Walcott spent splitting shales and Helena devoted to wrapping fossils. They moved to Brigus Harbor, a sail of sixteen miles, where Walcott "Found Olenellus beneath the Paradoxides horizon" (August 9, 1888), though seemingly neither he nor Matthew actually found specimens of *Paradoxides* at this locality. Then they sailed back across the bay to Topsail Head, and Walcott got very serious about the business of stratigraphic paleontology.

Charles Doolittle Walcott, Paleontologist

Given all the skill in the world, luck plays a tremendous part in the finding of fossils, and perhaps nowhere was it better illustrated than at this world-famous locality. To rephrase Walcott's description, the Holyrood Granite was eroded shortly before the Cambrian was deposited, and huge cobbles occur at the contact of granite and overlying sediments. This cobble beach covers a slightly irregular erosion surface, and as it was gradually inundated by the sea, the swales were filled with sediment first. Next, a considerable thickness of rock was deposited and later tilted to the west; Manuel's Brook cuts through this sequence. The railroad builders laid track on the relatively level areas underlain by soft shale and wherever possible the engineers avoided the hard granite. A fossil swale lay to the north of Manuel's Brook so that the railroad cut exposed shales older than those in the river valley. Everywhere else, the Manuel's Brook sequence lies directly on the coarse boulder conglomerate.

In this cut, Walcott found his *Olenellus*. Just to add to the luck factor, the railroad was a narrow gauge. Had it been full-scale, the curvature of the track might not have exposed the oldest sediment. Walcott knew what he was looking for, he knew where to look, but most importantly luck was with him. During the past century, only one other artificial exposure (for a house cellar) in this area has yielded *Olenellus*. Had the little Precambrian valley not been quite so deep, had the rail right-of-way been a few feet different in its alignment, or had the railroad been built a few years later, the argument over the sequence of *Olenellus* to *Paradoxides* would have continued.

One fine day in July, the new couple went sailing with a fisherman to Great Belle Island, where Walcott examined the outcrops on the eastern side of the isle; a later attempted trip was thwarted. In spite of the interval covered by water, these rocks were younger and in a normal stratigraphic sequence with those exposed at Manuel's Brook. In about three weeks Walcott had managed to collect enough fossils to fill ten barrels and two boxes. It is a wonder that Helena saw anything of him. The outcrops in Manuel's Brook not only established the principal sequence of trilobites, but allowed him, after study of the fossils, to recognize subdivisions within the Middle Cambrian zone of *Paradoxides*. In congratulating a younger paleontologist who later investigated the Manuel's Brook section in more detail (Howell 1925), Walcott wrote:

> It brings back vividly to mind the collecting work that I did there thirty-seven years ago. I wished then to make a thorough study of the section, but my time and means were so limited that it could not be done. If I had remained a week longer I would have found the iron mines on Great Belle Island, and probably not been troubled about finances for research for the remainder of

my life. I endeavored to reach the outcrops of ore twice with a fisherman who told me about their being there, but we were driven back by northeast gales of wind and rain and had to give up.[17]

A newspaper report of Walcott's honeymoon was far more dramatic than even his own account of the discovery of *Olenellus:*

Newfoundland has contributed a great impulse to geology. C. D. Walcott, of the U.S. Survey, found there the key to the order of the Cambrian beds. He spent the greater part of his time at Topsail, twelve miles from St. John's, on the south shore of Conception Bay, and there made a large collection of fossils—chiefly trilobites—some of a very large size. Here too he found the "missing link," of which he was in search of, which settled the order of succession of the Cambrian rocks. So important were his discoveries that he was requested, by the chief of his department, to proceed to London to lay them before the International Geological council.[18]

When the fossils in the railway cut confirmed the *Olenellus* zone as oldest Cambrian, Walcott sat down to write up his discovery. It was as dramatic as finding the fossiliferous limestone in southwestern Vermont which had destroyed the Taconic System. After four days, he finally "Decided to go to London meeting of International Geological Congress. Leaving St. John's Sept. 5" (August 21, 1888). After all, why not? This was a fundamental discovery with many ramifications, St. John's was already nearly halfway to London, and finally the influence of a honeymoon, even on a determined fossil collector, should never be underestimated. "In the six weeks' search for the Olenellus fauna about Conception Bay, Mrs. Walcott was my constant companion and efficient assistant, and shared with me the pleasure given by the finding of the fauna on Manuel's Brook" (Walcott 1890a, 382, footnote). The Newfoundland expedition cost Walcott more than two thousand dollars. From the standpoint of geologic work, it was money well spent. From the standpoint of his personal life, the trip was like a perfect fossil—invaluable.

The Walcotts spent a few more days collecting and packing fossils, before moving to the Atlantic Hotel in St. John's, a three-story structure burned in the great St. John's fire of 1892. Mrs. Walcott was given two days in relative luxury while Walcott squeezed in a talk on the Grand Canyon to a local group. They boarded the Allan Line steamer *Carfian,* and immediately Walcott was ill for four days, though Helena was fine. They landed on the thirteenth at Liverpool, and Walcott's first act was to go to the city museum; the next day they were in London.

Charles Doolittle Walcott, Paleontologist

There are two stories as to the origin of the International Congress of Geologists. One gives credit to Italian geologists, but the more generally accepted history, presented earlier, traces this gathering to 1876 with the prime mover being T. Sterry Hunt of Taconic fame or notoriety. The 1878 Paris Congress was a success in its own right, and served as model for international gatherings of scientists in other disciplines. Despite interruptions by world wars, the slightly modified International Geological Congress still meets regularly.

At the second congress in Bologna, the group endeavored compilation of a geologic map of Europe, which immediately raised the problem of what units to use on the map. The third congress in Berlin in 1885 delved further into this Pandora's box, and according to Marcou was the site of a plot to discredit the Taconic System. Following Berlin, an increasing number of geologists realized that the international gathering had achieved stature and deserved their attention. As a result, the London session became one of the jewels of Victorian science.

One hundred forty foreign delegates attended at London and about half again as many from the British Isles. Only one other wife accompanied the twelve United States geologists, Mrs. G. H. Williams of Baltimore, a cousin of Walcott's. The only other foreign wives were from Russia and Romania. The handful of lady geologists attended were preoccupied by the meeting. It could have been a dull time for Helena, but, a few wives and daughters of London geologists showed her the sights of this great city.

The congress started at the University of London, then located at Burlington Gardens. The first Jack the Ripper murder had occurred on August 31, yet nothing of this horror intruded on the congress. After a formal opening and reception, mornings were devoted to science and afternoons to scientific sightseeing at institutions around the city. Most of the intellectual effort centered on problems of correlation and what terminology to use for the major rock units.

One of the first items was the nomenclature of Cambrian and Silurian rocks. The *Times* noted that "Mr. C. D. Walcott (of the United States) gave some account of his observations on the stratigraphical succession of the Cambrian faunas in North America."[19] Walcott's diary entry for the day is cryptic: "Session of Geol. Congress in the morning—Debate on Cambrian, Silurian, etc. Spoke in favor of Cambrian" (September 18, 1888). Because the First Congress had been held in Paris, the official acts were printed in French. The sessions themselves were an admixture of French and English; Walcott's contribution was in French (Walcott 1891), perhaps a testimony to his lessons in Washington. Within a couple of weeks, a summary of his report was published in a British journal (Walcott 1888c), along with a footnote addition based on a British trilobite.

For Walcott, this congress could not have been better. His Washington colleagues Dall and Gilbert were there to hear his presentation, and he knew almost all of the American geologists who attended. The day after he spoke he was appointed to the Council of the Congress and, the following day, to the American Committee planning the next congress.

Because he had spoken early in the congress, many of the geologists became aware of him, paving the way for informal discussions. He became acquainted with British workers on Lower Paleozoic rocks and fossils and met F. Schmidt from St. Petersburg, who had helped clarify the Early Cambrian by describing an *Olenellus* from the Baltic region.

Walcott also visited scientists at the new British Museum (Natural History) (Stern 1981). In South Kensington, he examined the techniques used for public displays and looked at the magnificent fossil collections. If he had been like any other Survey geologist, he would have compared administrative foibles of his organization with colleagues in the Geological Survey of Great Britain.

In the 1888 Washington, D.C., city directory, Walcott was recorded as a clerk with the Geological Survey, but in the congress list he was, according to British spelling, a palaeontologist. Walcott had arrived, so far as the international geologic scene was concerned. Burlington House, the home of the Geological Society of London, of world renown despite its local name, was a sight that interested him. Late in 1886, even before the Taconic problem had been resolved, Dana and four other American fellows proposed him as a prospective fellow of the society. Three eminent British workers added their names as sponsors, and he was duly elected. During the congress he met his British sponsors and even had his picture taken for the society files.

There was one minor annoyance for the Washington group. Frazer saw to it that the subcommittee reports of the American Committee were printed as an appendix to the *Compte Rendu;* that could have been why the state geologist of Pennsylvania characterized the London Congress as "a mere discussion club" (Clarke 1921, 518). It was one thing for Walcott to have his few remarks on Archean rocks, first printed in 1888 repeated (in Frazer 1891, A-69, A-70). It was another to have his refutation of his earlier support of the Taconic System and N. H. Winchell's refutation of his refutation dragged out again, but the *Compte Rendu* was not published for another three years, and by then geologists, Marcou excepted, were concerned with other matters.

Charles Doolittle Walcott, Paleontologist

Throughout the congress week Walcott observed British arguments on the Ordovician System, proposed in 1879 by Charles Lapworth, partly as a compromise zone between the overlapping boundaries of the Cambrian of Sedgwick and the Silurian of Murchison. Walcott had used the term in America two years before the London gathering. The congress did not adopt Ordovician, of which more will come later, but Walcott made a lifelong friend in Lapworth.

In regard to the congress, Archibald Geikie, director of the Geological Survey of Great Britain noted years later:

> Attempts were made at some of the business meetings to draw up and enforce a uniformity of stratigraphic nomenclature, but they met with no general concurrence. Those of us who did not believe that any such unification could be of universal application, except only for the larger divisions of geological time, were not a little amused at the evident disappointment and vexation of some of the older terminologists, who came for the most part from small countries. (Geikie 1924, 223–24)

In 1903, Ordovician was adopted by the British Survey, after Sir Archibald retired.

Nine months after the congress, Walcott wrote Brøgger:

> I regretted not having the pleasure of seeing you at London. . . . It may have seemed strange to you that American geologists did not accept the work of the Swedish geologists on the Olenellus Zone, but when you consider that *Olenellus kjerulfi* was first described as a Paradoxides and then not fully illustrated until Holm's paper appeared, it is not strange that they objected to identifying it with Olenellus thompsoni. In fact, it belongs to a subgeneric group which I have now included under Mesonacis. There is also another circumstance and that is the presence of a peculiarly marked Middle Cambrian fauna in the great sections of the Rocky Mountains. There the Paradoxides is absent and the characteristic genera are Olenoides, Asaphyscus, Bathyuriscus, and Karlia. This group of genera is far more closely allied to the second fauna than to the first, as you will fully appreciate when you see the illustrations of the species which I am now having prepared.[20]

The old issue of priority surfaced again here. Walcott felt that the one who recognized the significance of the fossils was more important that the original collector. This is consistent with his views on the Taconic problem. Emmons had fossils in 1844, but Barrande recognized their significance in 1859. *Olenellus thompsoni* was the significant fossil from Georgia, Vermont. If Emmons had started there first, which he did not, and if Americans had recognized this species as akin to one from Sweden, which they did not, the Taconic might have been recognized and a decade of confusion on the second problem of zonation might have been avoided. Both ifs never happened, but at least they were resolved in 1887 and 1888, respectively.

After the congress closed on Saturday, the Walcotts went by rail to Chester to participate in a congress field trip. Dr. Henry Hicks, a medical doctor specializing in mental diseases, led the trip. He had collected with William Salter, a brilliant but erratic paleontologist, and also treated him as a patient (Secord 1985). Hicks, an avid amateur, probably knew more of the geology and paleontology of the region than anyone else. The group went off to Carnaveron, Llanberris, and Portmadoc. These are not tourist spots, but the names gladden the hearts of geologists interested in the Lower Paleozoic. Hicks wrote the guidebook, and notwithstanding lack of agreement at the Congress, he used the subdivisions of Cambrian, Ordovician, and Silurian; Walcott was to see typical Ordovician rocks and fossils and take that knowledge back to America.

The Walcotts left the organized party and went to Bettus-y-coed where a local collector, Griffith Williams, guided them across the hills near Blauau Festimog. The Walcotts looked at slightly younger rocks at Bulith, the Lower Silurian, the cause of controversy for decades. They went back to older rocks at Haverfordwest and St. David's and Solva. Walcott recorded an unusual field phenomenon for Wales: "First clear day in two weeks & only partially clear at that" (October 10, 1888). The rocks in Wales are not particularly fossiliferous, and one wag commented that most of the fossil finds were made by geologists simply hammering on the rocks to keep warm. After a couple more days in the damp, they arrived in London.

Walcott talked in detail with Dr. Hicks, and cemented relations with other professional geologists. He spent hours at the British Museum and the Geological Survey; most evenings the couple retired early, glad to rest after the socializing of the congress and the thorough soaking in Wales.

After London they went to Cambridge, where John Marr, who was to resolve the Barrande "colonies," met them at the train station. That work eventually led to his becoming professor at Cambridge; years later Walcott named the genus *Marrella*. From Cambridge, the couple went to Birmingham for a day, where the Lapworths were equally hospitable. Walcott and Lapworth talked until 11:00 P.M. The next day, they entrained to Liverpool, and at the end of October the Walcotts were on the *City of Chicago* bound for New York. The trip was "rough, tedious, & altogether unpleasant" (November 10, 1888).

Charles Doolittle Walcott, Paleontologist

No doubt at all that England had been a triumph for Walcott. Not to spoil another's triumph, but one more geologic remark should be made about Manuel's Brook. Brøgger had commented that *Paradoxides* was confined to the eastern border of North America, and Walcott confirmed this interesting observation. He also had noted that the Manuel's Middle Cambrian beds contained some British species and later work found the strata "of unusual interest because a large proportion of the many species which they contain are found also in the contemporaneous beds of northwestern Europe" (Howell 1925, 9). Recently geology has adopted the notion of plate tectonics, moving parts of the crust from place to place. The present interpretation is that Newfoundland is composed of several pieces, welded together at different times. The Avalon Peninsula, where Walcott labored, during Cambrian time was effectively linked to England. In other words, Walcott had demonstrated on what had been a piece of Europe that the Cambrian trilobite succession developed in Europe was correct! Nevertheless, the sequence Walcott worked out and confirmed resolved many stratigraphic puzzles throughout North American because *Olenellus* is widespread. From today's perspective, Walcott may have been right for the wrong geologic reasons, but he was right; if that is not luck, what is?

After disembarking, the couple visited relatives, Walcott went to a fall meeting of the National Academy of Sciences in New York, followed by a planning meeting for the 1891 Philadelphia Congress, and finally to Scanandoa, where they packed Helena's belonging. When Mr. and Mrs. Walcott returned to Washington just before the end of November, they lodged at 1521 I Street and took their meals at the Gramercy. Late in 1879, the first experimental electric lights in Washington were in this area, a sawmill team engine generating the necessary power. Stately mansions were being constructed nearby and Washington was enjoying good economic times. For the former bachelor field geologist, life now was fundamentally different. Not only did he finally have a home and companionship, he was going to be a father. Probably it was in Newfoundland, rather than on board ship, that their first child was conceived.

They immediately went house hunting and found a small place at 418 Maple Avenue in Le Droit Park, a neighborhood some distance from the museum but near a horse car trolley route. In the midst of this, Walcott was trying to catch up at the office, but ended in bed with an inflamed tooth and general malaise. The household goods arrived, and it was December 19 before Walcott began to think about the Newfoundland fossils. Two days later they were in their new home, and shortly thereafter Walcott was "Settled so as to use my 'den' for the *first* time" (December 26, 1888). Life was very sweet at that moment and Walcott understated: "The year has been a most eventful one to me & full of pleasant happiness" (December 31, 1888).

Although Walcott was now further from the museum and was to be more of a home body for a time, he still fit comfortably into the local "scientific-social" scene, an admixture of dinners and meetings with other scientists. The web of communication of these groups had already helped his career and would increase in importance over the years. Home life caused him to miss a few more meetings than in his bachelor days, but there was less of a change in routine than had Walcott been a younger man when he married.

Walcott was a member of the Philosophical Society of Washington, the oldest and most august of the local scientific societies, founded in 1871 by Joseph Henry (Flack 1975). In contrast to the Geological Society of London, the scientific groups with Washington in their title did not have much prestige outside this city. One standard interpretation of history of science was that from the 1880s onward, scientists were abandoning local societies for national organizations (Kevles, Sturchio, and Carroll 1980). That may well be correct, but in Washington the time from after the Civil War to the First World War was the heyday for local groups, and they grew in influence when they were able to publish a journal. Perhaps this difference from the general pattern was a consequence of the relatively large number of scientists in government employ within the city.

Membership in the Philosophical Society was considered an honor. Most members wore evening clothes in the early days and the speaker was absolutely expected to appear in formal dress, give a proper presentation, and be prepared for vigorous discussion. Joseph Henry assumed that members were there for intellectual enhancement, not fun, and even after his death in 1878 his spirit lingered on. Since the Smithsonian Institution helped with publication of the *Proceedings,* it was wise to follow Henry's precepts. The custom of "adjourning" after the last paper to a saloon around the corner on D Street had become a common practice for some of the younger members and lightened the evening.

Walcott played a minor role in society affairs, though he had given several papers to the members. His attendance at meetings was irregular because of the wide spectrum of papers delivered. In March of 1889, he presented his findings on the position of *Olenellus,* serious business to a group of broadly interested scientists who steadfastly refused to specialize.

If Joseph Henry was the guiding spirit of the Philosophical Society, John Wesley Powell held the same position in the Cosmos Club. This was a social club for a small number of select scientists and other professional gentlemen (Anonymous 1904). Almost immediately, it was perceived by some as a threat to the Philosophical Society, though adroit footwork allowed members of the society to join the new club. Finances were delicate at first, but club rooms were opened on the third floor of the Corcoran Building at Fifteenth and Pennsylvania Avenue, a structure replaced by the Hotel Washington.

The club remained solvent and moved uptown. By June 4, 1883, when Walcott was elected, the Cosmos had been at 23 Lafayette Square for six months. The initiation fee had just been raised to thirty-five dollars, ten dollars more than the annual dues, and membership in Washington was limited to two hundred men. By 1886, the club was rich enough to purchase the Dolly Madison House and to construct an Assembly Hall, with a separate entrance, of course, to avoid any possible disturbance to club members. The club invited the various local societies to meet in the auditorium. Understandably, the club imposed its own rules, permitting Cosmos Club members to attend any meeting which was held and requiring a two dollar fee for the janitor. Originally, the Philosophical Society provided the chairs, but after a few years, their furniture was donated to the club.

The scientific power structure in Washington centered in the Cosmos Club, and Walcott's election to membership signaled that he was a man on his way up. Reading in the library and playing billiards may not lead to any major scientific discovery, but it was the games partner and the person in the next chair at the club who decided that a new discovery was indeed major. In addition to science, the issues of government bureau jurisdictions and congressional appropriations were always discussed. For years, the Cosmos was known as the In and Out Club, as these were the only signs on the driveway; if you were a member you knew where it was, and if you were not, there was no need for you to know the location. Walcott prospered in the atmosphere of the Cosmos Club, especially after his return from England. From 1890–94, he was a member of the Committee on Admissions, the gatekeepers to this temple of science. In 1895 he was one of the three club managers. In 1897 he was vice-president, and the following year he was the nineteenth president, not a bad record of service to this organization.

Only a few months separated the founding of the Cosmos Club from the founding of the Anthropological Society of Washington in February 1879. Powell was never in the forefront that year, though later he was essentially the perennial president of that organization. Without question, the organization was an important force in development of the profession. Even more, formation of society must have helped in passing the Sundry Civil Appropriations Bill in 1879; in addition to founding the U. S. Geological Survey, this bill also provided for a Bureau of Ethnology. Every vote was critical for a bill which was in trouble. Emphasizing anthropology by forming a society at that particular moment was lobbying with a delicate touch. Once the new bureau was signed into law, the obvious man to head it was Powell. This is not a cynic's view of the timing, but it violates no confidences to state that Powell was a realist in politics.

Under Powell the Bureau of Ethnology prospered, as did the Anthropological Society of Washington. Its formation marked the start of distinct local specialization, for the Philosophical Society stood for viewing science as an indivisible entity. Walcott rarely attended regular meetings, but he often went to the annual presidential address, for the major was always worth listening to.

Motivation for formation of the Biological Society about a year and one half later is not so apparent. Secretary Baird had allowed the anthropologists to organize and meet in the regent's room of the Smithsonian Castle, and he extended the same privilege to his fellow biologists (Aldrich 1980). Late in 1880, they organized and, appropriately, elected Baird as the only honorary member in the history of the society. Finances were difficult enough for the biologists so that when Walcott joined the society, three years after it was formed, the initiation fee had already been doubled and was now two dollars.

In the fall of 1880, the biologists in Washington were scattered through a number of government agencies, and this new group helped draw them together. The stern and forbidding Philosophical Society judged that few biologists were rigorous enough scientifically to be in their midst, but the Anthropological Society had demonstrated that a new scientific group could form and prosper academically in Washington. The new United States National Museum was about to open, thereby simultaneously providing both a nucleus of biologists in one location and a meeting place in the northwest pavilion of the building.

Almost immediately various sections were formed in the new biological society to satisfy specialists, but to little avail. By 1884, the Entomological Society of Washington split off; in 1901 the botanical section broke free to become the Botanical Society of Washington. Coincidentally, the Chemical Society of Washington also began in 1884. Neither of the 1884 groups held much interest for Walcott at the time but one provides an excuse to relate an item of what scientists judge to be humor. According to the story, an out-of-town member of the National Academy of Sciences came to Washington for the annual meeting. On the street he passed Frank Wigglesworth Clarke, a USGS chemist who had offices at the National Museum along with Walcott. The visitor had heard of the new local group and asked Clarke, "How's the Comical Society?" Clarke responded, "Fine. How's the Notional Academy?" The visitor was so indignant that for several years, Clarke was blackballed from membership in the academy.

Early in 1888, while Walcott was busy writing the epitaph of the Taconic System and thinking about Helena, the National Geographic Society was founded; former Midshipman Hayden of Eureka fame was one of the organizers. The society had grand pretensions, and in couple of years was able to start a journal. However, for the first few years, this new group was still mainly devoted to presenting local lectures, not unlike the other Washington societies with less impressive titles.

That completes the list for 1888. There is not one devoted to geology; it is curious lacuna, considering the size of the USGS. This gap was to remain until 1893 when Walcott took an active roll in forming another society.

The Philosophical Society and the Biological Society each provided Walcott with a forum at which to present his research activities. In addition, they often published a short account in their proceedings of meetings, prior to a larger publication. If one could survive presenting a paper before the Philosophical Society, one could easily appear before any group. No matter how good the results discussed might be, delivery of the words was important, and Walcott learned how to cultivate an audience.

The Biological Society had become more to Walcott than a place to present an occasional talk. The society met on alternate Saturday evenings when the week's work was over. One could go out with a few friends from adjacent offices, have a nice meal and good conversation, and finally gather with twenty or thirty kindred souls for an hour or two to hear some papers, an occasional scrap of scientific wit, and perhaps show off a curious specimen to one's peers. The more Walcott learned about live animals and how they were classified, the better he could interpret his long-dead forms.

One of the first acts of the Biological Society was to join forces with the Anthropological Society to offer a course of free public lectures at the National Museum; the Philosophical Society declined to take part in such an attempt to educate the masses. These lectures, first given in the spring of 1882, brought in audiences of five hundred to eight hundred people. As mentioned, Walcott gave a lecture March 4, 1885, on his Grand Canyon search for early fossils. He became a member of the standing committee on lectures the following year. The series was reconstituted a year or so later when the Philosophical Society finally decided to join in sponsoring the effort. Saturday lectures at the National Museum remained a tradition in Washington for years.

For a small group, the Biological Society of Washington had a great deal of governance—president, four vice-presidents, treasurer, two secretaries, and five councilors. Therefore, almost anyone who attended more or less faithfully would be a officer, and if they stayed in Washington for more than a few years they would be recycled. In 1885 and 1886 Walcott was on the council and the next year was a vice-president. In 1889 and 1890, Walcott was back on the council and on the committee on communications, that recruited speakers. On occasion, some of the local societies were so desperate for talks that they would elect a non-attender to office just to get him to participate.

Following Secretary Henry's tradition, Baird helped both the Anthropological Society and the Biological Society print the proceedings of their meetings. Walcott was chairman of the committee on publications in 1890, 1891, and 1892. That first year the *Proceedings* stayed as before, a brief account of the meetings and a presidential address. In 1891, the number of pages increased significantly when several of the talks were printed. From that point on, the journal of this local society became larger and increasingly important. The duty of the committee was not so much one of editing as it was of finding money to pay the printer, and Walcott excelled.

Walcott would never claim presidency of Biological Society of Washington as one of his honors. In 1891 he was one of the four vice-presidents and was re-elected to this "august" post successively four more times. He gave his last talk to the society in 1896 and thereafter vanished from the index of the publication. He attended meetings from time to time and he always had a warm spot in his heart for the group, but other matters were then taking his time.

To go back a few years, the gathering in of various societies at the Assembly Hall of the Cosmos Club resulted in a period of good feeling. A joint commission of the local societies was formed in 1888; a decade later, the commission metamorphosed into the Washington Academy of Sciences. The commission started a joint membership list and exchanged meeting announcements. The innovative and unexpected action was the commission issuing an invitation to the American Association for the Advancement of Science to hold the Fortieth annual meeting in Washington in 1891. Acceptance of the site meant a lot of hard work, but it also meant that science in Washington was no longer a minor, local affair.

The American Association for the Advancement of Science was an early, and for a long time the only, national organization of scientists. Interested laymen attended to a minor extent and were called on for services and support when the association descended on a city, but it was primarily a gathering of scientists. "It is a prime function of the American Association for the Advancement of Science, fully recognized by its leaders, that it brings men into personal relations and thus promotes mutual appreciation" (Gilbert in Anonymous 1904, 40).

Geologists felt at home in the AAAS because the association owed its origin to an early association of state geologists that became a group of geologists and naturalists, and in 1848 was transformed into the AAAS. The association weathered the Civil War and was going strong during the 1870s. The AAAS was, and still is, divided into a series of a discipline-oriented sections. Section E, Geology and Geography, was one of the principal parts of the association. Walcott attended a number of annual meetings, and in 1887 he had presented his victory over the Taconic System under its auspices.

By 1891, when the meeting was held in Washington, AAAS was not quite such an important an organization as it had been a decade earlier. Specialization in the sciences was catching up with AAAS on a national scale as it caught up with the Philosophical Society of Washington. For Walcott's career, the specialist society was the Geological Society of America.

For years after the AAAS was formed, geologists had talked about having their own organization. Committees formed to investigate the matter and they languished to be replaced by new committees. In the spring of 1888, as part of the complaint against Major Powell's high-handed actions on stratigraphic nomenclature, the newly founded *American Geologist* issued a call for a distinct society, and that broke the log jam. At the Section E meeting that summer, the first steps were taken and in December 1888, the Geological Society of America began (Fairchild 1932). For about a dozen years, the society met biannually, in the summer with Section E and in the winter, but it was an awkward arrangement. Once the geologists concentrated on their own society, they practically vanished from the inner workings of the association and it was decades before Section E again became significant to geologists.

While the break from AAAS was in the air, Walcott was in New England. When the first steps were taken, he was in Newfoundland with bride and with *Olenellus* and had other things on his mind. Fellows of the AAAS, as distinguished from mere members, could become fellows of the new geological society, but the deadline was the first of January 1889. Late in December, Walcott paid his dues and became an original fellow of the Geological Society of America. It was a nice finale to his year of scientific triumph and of marital change.

8

Settling In: Home Fires and Political Fires Are Not the Same for a Field Paleontologist (1889–1892)

> The position of the base of the Cambrian system is not in dispute in widespread continental areas where Cambrian rocks younger than the *Olenellus*-zone lie on the eroded surface of much older igneous or metamorphic rocks of obvious pre-Cambrian age. But in geosynclinal areas such as those in the Appalachian or Cordilleran provinces, the fossiliferous Lower Cambrian is underlain in many places by unfossiliferous sedimentary or volcanic rocks. In the geosynclines, the question posed by Walcott remains in dispute to this day.
>
> P. B. King, 1949

In 1888, the ornate State, War, and Navy Building next to the White House was completed. The National Zoological Park was established under the Smithsonian Institution in 1889, and in 1890 John Philip Sousa composed "The Washington Post March."[1]

Sousa's march was months away, but on January 2, 1889, Walcott was in his office furiously writing on the stratigraphic position of the *Olenellus* zone; he must have still been operating on the intellectual high from the London Congress. Near the end of the month he participated in Major Powell's conference on map coloration and nomenclature; being invited was a mark of accomplishment from his associates. Further, having a wife and a home with an heir on the way must have seemed miraculous to the hardened widower. Life was good.

In late February, Walcott presented the *Olenellus* zone research to the Biological Society of Washington. In early March, the city filled with visitors for the inauguration of President Benjamin Harrison. As might have been expected with a parade, it rained all day; the Walcotts watched festivities from the Willard Hotel on Pennsylvania Avenue. On March 12 Walcott sent the *Olenellus* zone manuscript to the *American Journal of Science*. James Dwight Dana knew an important paper when he saw it; the first part was published in May and the second in July (Walcott 1889a). Walcott switched gears and lectured to the Philosophical Society on structural geology of the fault he had studied in the Grand Canyon. He may not have been addicted to the lecture platform, but he enjoyed public speaking. In April, he presented his views on the *Olenellus* zone to the National Academy of Sciences and attended the organizing committee for the next International Congress of Geologists.

In a companion piece to the *AJS* manuscript, Walcott described a few Middle Cambrian fossils in an unillustrated paper (Walcott 1889b). As they are perceived by the public, scientists are objective and rational, but in this work Walcott named a genus *Helenia;* derivation of the name was not given, but Helena knew. This preliminary note was in the James Hall tradition of rapid publication. A large paper takes a long time to move through official channels; a short paper presenting the core of a fauna comes out much faster. By publishing through the National Museum rather than the Geological Survey, Walcott avoided the delays of the Government Printing Office.

While these two manuscripts were being prepared, Walcott also compiled his paleontological study for the tenth *Annual Report*. Each year the agency was required to document its activities during the past fiscal year. After the first slim volume by Clarence King, Powell seized on this outlet to progress reports or papers too short for the *Monograph* series; Powell's report eventually grew to five extremely thick volumes. By June's end Walcott's comprehensive discussion on fossils in the *Olenellus* zone was submitted to the mercies of the USGS editors.

That spring also produced a field instrument classic in what was almost a throwaway two-page paper. In measuring sections, Walcott (1889c) developed the idea of placing a clinometer on a pole, setting the clinometer to the dip of the strata, and sighting straight ahead. The stratigraphic thickness is measured in pole lengths. In appropriate terrain, field geologists still use the "Jacob's staff" described by Walcott; some small discoveries have just as enduring effects as large ones. This manuscript was from a talk to the American Society of Naturalists and is the only note on technique he ever published. Walcott's speeches to scientific audiences invariably appeared as published papers. Much more commonly today, an abstract of a talk appears, but not a publication, and that is a waste.

During this first half of the year, Walcott temporarily got his hands on another good assistant. T. W. Stanton unwrapped and arranged Cambrian fossils from Wisconsin, probably collections of Cooper Curtice. When Walcott reorganized the agency, less than a decade later, Stanton was in charge of paleontologic matters, and eventually became chief geologist. Joseph F. James also shifted from teaching at the University of Maryland to the USGS. After his stint with Walcott, James transferred to the Survey library and then left the organization. He died young, and his claim to fame was as the son of Uriah James, the grand old man of amateur collectors in Cincinnati.

As mentioned above, Powell convened a meeting to regulate geologic names for the Survey. These rules appeared in the tenth *Annual Report* and were developed by a committee of eighteen "geologists and lithologists" with the addition of "a member of the paleontologic branch whose recent work has been stratigraphic." The USGS was orientated mainly toward mapping, and it was evident to field men that one can best map formations based on their physical characteristics. From this viewpoint ensued a whole series of regulations concerning designation of a typical locality for a formation, the name to apply to the formation, and even spelling and capitalization.

Any particular formation has geographic limits:

> For instance, the Potsdam sandstone of New York has its type locality at Potsdam in St. Lawrence County, where it can be readily identified. To say that it is identical with the Upper Cambrian or St. Croix sandstone of the Upper Mississippi Valley, with which it has been identified, and to speak of the latter as the Potsdam sandstone, is to practically state they are synchronous. The use of the name St. Croix does not imply this. It enables the geologist to mention the formation without a correlation that he may or may not believe in. (Walcott 1891b, 18)

Thus, after the various lithologies were mapped locally, the larger problem was correlation. In the early days of geology, all sandstones were thought to be the same. Even before the late eighteenth century discovery that particular kinds of fossils can tell the relative sequence or age of a rock, the repetition of rock types in the geologic record was apparent. Prior to the end of the nineteenth century, it had been established that the Potsdam as used in the upper Mississippi Valley was Cambrian, but a finer time subdivision was needed. The USGS mapped each area separately and applied a different set of formation names to the rocks in each area, a presentation of facts presumably without any bias, while the paleontologists examined the fossil faunas. If the faunas were the same in two regions, the formations were the same age. Not all Cambrian sandstones were laid down at the time the typical Potsdam was deposited. For another complication, not all rocks deposited when the Potsdam sands began to accumulate were sandstones; Walcott correlated the fauna in the limestone at Saratoga Springs, New York, with the upper Mississippi "Potsdam" sandstones.

The committee regulating geologic nomenclature recognized that correlation was intertwined but distinct from naming formations. The Survey organized a Division of Geologic Correlation under Gilbert and had specialists prepare summaries of correlation for various time segments. The 1891 congress provided a good target date for these compendia. H. S. Williams wrote on the Devonian and Carboniferous Systems in *Bulletin* 80, a classic in tracing development of thought on the distinction between time and rock. Walcott was assigned two topics, the Cambrian and Silurian Systems. The committee decided that the time interval which some geologists, including Walcott, called Ordovician, did not warrant recognition as a geologic system.

Joseph James read all the published literature in North America which discussed the Cambrian. He compiled cards giving the formation names and the fauna in each, and wrote up historic summaries, region by region. A significant portion of Walcott's *Bulletin* 81 is acknowledged as James's effort. The next step was to determine from their faunas which Cambrian formations were of the same age; usage of names of fossils may have changed from one author to the next. Geological correlation is as much art as science, and Walcott was becoming expert at it. Once accurate correlations are made, synthesis of regional changes in lithology and in thickness comes next.

Decades earlier Hall and Dana had noticed the difference between thick rock sequences in eastern mountains and thin sequences in flat-lying areas. However, the USGS correlation program had greater precision than any single geologist could muster. Proper age determination of the rocks is the key to understanding the structure of a region. Indeed, Williams maintained that if the view of the field geologist on age conflicted with the paleontological data, the opinion of the paleontologist should prevail. That was powerful support for the practical importance of fossils. So much for rocks, at least at this point.

For most ladies of the time, confinement was a private experience; not so with the fair Helena. In late April, she and Walcott planted trees in the eastern part of the city. On the thirteenth and fifteenth of May, Walcott took her to baseball games. Two days later, Walcott was "At home with Helena—A boy born at 12:32 P.M. She & the boy in good condition at eveningtide. Baby weighs 7½# Length—19 in. Girth of head 14 in. C. D. W. Jr" (May 17, 1889). The next night Walcott was off to the Biological Society meeting.

The first of June brought terrible rains and flooding on Pennsylvania Avenue, minor compared to the tragedy of the great Johnstown flood. He worked steadily, except for a brief social call on the president; it is hard to imagine how small Washington was in those days. Walcott spent the couple's first anniversary two-thirds ill, possibly psychosomatic; the large *Olenellus* work was completed and the correlation study hardly begun.

The new fiscal year, on July 1, brought the congressional appropriation. Walcott went off to New York for the field season with Helena, Charles Jr., and an accompanying nurse. He left his family at Holland Patent, the little village just west of Trenton Falls, and spent a few days with William Rust examining the Trenton Limestone and overlying Utica Shale. He moved his family west to Clifton Springs, New York, and went to the northeastern flank of the Adirondacks to collect and measure the sedimentary rocks with Rust. They worked their way eastward to Vermont, when family illness called William away.

Walcott continued to measure sections and collect, moving east to Phillipsburg, Quebec, and met R. W. Ells of the Geological Survey of Canada. During one era of American geology there was an interesting phenomenon of structural geology, known as the "state line fault." When adjoining states produced maps, sometimes the lines of the formations did not match. By the geologists examining one another's sections, a mismatch could be avoided at the international boundary. At Quebec, Director A. R. C. Selwyn of the Geological Survey joined them.

The geologic problems around Quebec City mainly centered on the age of the Levis Conglomerate, which had indirectly figured in arguments over the Taconic System (Eagan 1987). Walcott "Saw bowlders [*sic*] embedded in strata containing Calciferous fossils that contain Potsdam or Upper Cambrian fossils" (August 4, 1889). The Levis was a melange of older beds and collections from the boulders gave different ages. Even Lower Cambrian rocks occurred in the Levis Conglomerate. Years later, a Geological Survey of Canada assistant wrote: "Prof. Walcott . . . credited Dr. Selwyn . . . with discovery of this fossil [*Salterella*];

but perhaps my name got detached from the specimen" (Weston 1899, 104). The matrix was significantly younger than any of the huge pieces it cemented; light was starting to dawn.

Walcott reported his Point Levis trip to British colleague Charles Lapworth, proposer of the Ordovician System: "I found an interbedded layer of limestone of 30 feet in thickness and upwards of 500 feet in length, which contained fossils of the Middle Calciferous zone of the New York section, placing the graptolites below the Chazy horizon and in the Calciferous."[2] Graptolites resemble pencil marks drawn on dark shales and are unexciting fossils to collect. However, during Ordovician and Silurian time graptolites changed rapidly and are extremely important fossils for age determination. Walcott had earlier written to Albany to borrow specimens: "I find it is necessary to take up the study of the Graptolites in connection with the study of the Hudson River rocks."[3] In recognizing Levis graptolites as younger than the embedded boulders, Walcott had gone into a classic geologic area and found something new.

Walcott and Ells moved east traversing the Sutton Mountains, the Canadian extension of Vermont's Green Mountains, and back to Phillipsburg; Director Selwyn rejoined the expedition. One contrasts the ease of this trip with the paperwork required today for a federal employee to perform fieldwork in Canada. The group moved back and forth across the border until each understood the lithologic divisions being used by the other. Several thrust sheets repeat parts of the section and it was many years before the complications of structure and stratigraphy were resolved. Selwyn and Walcott went to the Vermont marble belt and tried to determine where these metamorphic limestones fit into the section. Late in August, Walcott finally rejoined his family at Rochester.

A few days with family, and Walcott left for the AAAS meeting in Toronto. The brand new Geological Society of America was meeting twice a year, in the summer with the AAAS and elsewhere at the end of the year. Walcott participated prominently in this first GSA scientific meeting, presenting a paper based on his winter in the Grand Canyon (Walcott 1890b; Yochelson 1988). The long section he had measured was broken by a major vertical fault. The two sides of the fault had moved several times and not always in the same direction. Later mapping (Van Gundy 1946) showed that Walcott had interpreted the fault correctly.

Walcott revealed another facet in a talk to AAAS section D, engineering, speaking on benefits of the sharpnecked roller joint in railroad journal boxes, as specialized a subject as any in paleontology. Walcott had ridden on a lot of trains and talked to a number of train crews; it also transpires that Sidney A. Stevens, related by marriage, was secretary of the company producing this new joint. Later Walcott wrote from the field to the president of the Canadian Pacific railroad: "I wished to meet you & see your collection of Potsdam fossils & also call your attention to a car journal box that bids fair to do away with *hot boxes, all oil* & *accompanying attendance* & also to save more or less *motive power*."[4]

When Walcott returned to Rochester, Mother and Josie were there doting on young Charlie; more often than not through the coming years, these ladies were with Helena as Walcott moved hither and thither pursuing rocks and fossils. He and Helena went to several baseball games and he wrote up notes on the Quebec group. Walcott left for fieldwork on the west side of the Adirondack dome. "Mr. Walcott's working plan was to trace the formations from the undisturbed regions in the northwest and west into the regions of disturbance" (Ruedemann 1901, 507).

Overlying the Utica Shale is the Lorraine Shale, which is succeeded by the sandstones and limestones of the Upper Silurian. It was important to determine if these two shales contained different fossils. These nearly flat-lying rocks have been fractured, and streams exploit these zones of weakness to form small canyons called "gulfs," a geographic term that found its way over from Great Britain to New York. At Lapham gulf, once again Rust found important collections, including graptolites. They returned to Trenton Falls, where Walcott had more than a thousand specimens to examine; these proved the distinctiveness of the Utica from the Lorraine. The broad divisions of an older generation of geologists were steadily being refined.

Walcott met Helena in Syracuse and brought the family to relatives at Scanandoa. Then he was off to the field around Greenwich in eastern New York. Despite almost constant rains, he was in the field each day. Walcott stopped in Albany and New York City and got to Washington one day before the family arrived. If the railroads had the equivalent of a frequent flyer program, Walcott would have qualified that summer.

Several days later, he "Talked with Mr. G. K. Gilbert over my work in connection with the Geological Survey" (October 3, 1889). He was working extremely hard, with no change in salary for a number of years. A new wife and child increased all expenses, not just extra railroad tickets. Whatever Gilbert said, Walcott quickly settled into office routine, repairing the damage editors had done to his *Olenellus*-zone report. He took Helena to see the Capitol by moonlight. Romance seldom is as good as it seems at the moment, and Walcott became ill with a kidney stone, possibly from the moonlight.

Six months into fatherhood Walcott was still pleased, as he wrote J. M. Clarke, the assistant who finally survived Professor Hall and succeeded him: "I congratulate you most heartily on your recent accession. If as much pleasure to you as mine is to me it will worth all the fossils extant and a big margin over."[5] Using "accession" is one of those scientific attempts at humor.

Walcott had drawings made of fossils collected on the Canadian trip to be added as text figures to the tenth *Annual Report*. In mid-October he was off to Hot Springs, North Carolina, joining two USGS mappers, Bailey Willis and C. W. Hayes, both astute field geologists. In 1879, while Willis was waiting for an interview in King's office about joining the new Geological Survey, Raphael Pumpelly (Champlin 1994) offered him a position with a railroad survey and he took it on the spot. When the Northern Transcontinental Survey went bankrupt (Merrill 1924) Willis joined the USGS and was one of the rising stars. Hayes started in 1887 and was another rising star.

The party went up the French Broad River and across the Unaka range (now the Great Smoky National Park). They moved into Miller's Cove; a cove is a more or less flat area surrounded by mountains. These isolated coves are the only places locally which could be farmed and they were the heartland of Appalachian Mountains culture. The group went on to Chilhowie Mountain in eastern Tennessee, and in shales interbedded with a quartzite, "Dr. Cooper Curtice found a few fossils . . . and in 1889 I found a few specimens" (Walcott 1891b, 302). The new enigmatic fossil he took to be a crustacean which indicated Early Cambrian. Subsequent generations doubted that this occurrence was reported correctly. Half a century later, a USGS geologist based in Knoxville spent years looking at each outcrop on the mountain before he duplicated the original discovery. Once again, Walcott was lucky, for this sequence is virtually unfossiliferous. In eleven days Walcott was back in Washington; it was a trip that would have killed a strong horse.

The new crustacean was shoehorned into a plate of the *Olenellus* report which was so close to publication that a blank for the museum catalogue number was never filled in. Walcott reestablished his writing routine and October passed into November. Mid-November brought a visit Philadelphia for the fall National Academy of Sciences meeting. Walcott was not yet a member, but he was a faithful attender. There was more discussion about the coming International Congress in 1891.

Back home, he came down with a rheumatic shoulder and while laid up, wrote a long review of Ells's latest report (Walcott 1890c). Ells's work on the Quebec region effectively ended all use of the term *Quebec Group* and that received high praise; in this review, Walcott recounted collecting from boulders at Levis and finding older fossils than those in the matrix. Writing reviews was not an activity which appealed to Walcott and he wrote only one other in his career, a short summary of a report from the New York State Museum (Walcott 1890d). After a few days rest, Walcott's shoulder improved. Following the Thanksgiving holiday, Walcott (1889d) gave a short talk to the Biological Society on an unusual brachiopod from Trenton Falls, given him by brother-in-law William. He named it *Conotreta rusti*, an honor long overdue.

With that quick note away, Walcott began a manuscript on the Hudson River Group for the first annual meeting of the Geological Society of America. Early in December, Helena's grandmother died. Walcott moralized in his diary as to the loss of a good Christian woman; he and Helena attended the funeral and returned in time for him to complete the text of his GSA talk. Walcott (1890e) picked the subject directly from his assignment on correlation, as it involved the issue of stabilizing the name to be adopted for a major subdivision of time.

The Hudson River beds are contorted, but occasionally yield a few graptolites which were dated as early Lower Silurian, that is, Middle Ordovician in present terminology. The name "Hudson River" was employed in the early 1840s by the New York State Survey. Hall later abandoned usage of the term, but still later resurrected it and insisted the beds at Cincinnati, Ohio, belonged to the Hudson River Group. The original Hudson River outcrops are older, but it was Hall's notion to add both Utica Shale and Lorraine Shale in the Hudson River Group. In such a broad usage, the beds around Cincinnati were of Hudson River age.

When disposing of the "Taconic System," Walcott had been concerned about priority and about original definitions. This involved the same set of arguments on a smaller scale. The original Hudson River was not the same age as the modifications Hall had included. Priority is the basic tenet regulating names in biology. Two or more scientists may independently apply different names to the same organism, but the first to publish carries the day. Walcott applied this principle to Hall's stratigraphy, but it required considerable effort in view of Hall's several changes of mind. The paper is an historical review with only a small amount of new data from Walcott's graptolite study. Geologists, unlike paleontologists, are more concerned with common usage than with priority. By 1890, considerable literature had been published on Cincinnati rocks and fossils. As a result, Walcott failed to sway opinion, and today Cincinnatian is known worldwide as a term for the time of the Late Ordovician.

The year 1890 opened quietly enough with work on his two manuscripts for the coming volume 1 of *Bulletin* of the Geological Society of America. On January 4 Walcott examined Ordovician fossil collections which Stanton had obtained at Cañon City, Colorado; they were suggestive of Trenton age, but more specimens were needed. Although in the official eyes of the USGS, Ordovician did not exist, Walcott used this term in his diary. A week later, he noted an "attack on Powell & Marsh in New York Herald" (January 12, 1890).

Walcott had the sequence of targets correct in what is a bizarre incident in American science (Shor 1974). Edward Drinker Cope (Osborn 1931) of Philadelphia was a vertebrate paleontologist affiliated with Hayden's territorial survey. O. C. Marsh (Schuchert and LeVene 1940) of Yale also worked on vertebrates, though with King's territorial survey. After the USGS was formed, Cope was out and Marsh was on the staff as a part-time employee. Marsh prospered scientifically under Powell, whereas Cope could not get the manuscript on the last of the Hayden collections published.

An enterprising reporter kept circulation rising as he went from one group to another for statements. For a few days, the quarrel over old bones and waste of government funds made great copy. The proverbial tempest in the teapot disappeared in a week, but was a forerunner of more serious problems. Walcott wrote to Winchell at Michigan: "I received a letter from Prof. James Hall on yesterday. He is very much annoyed by the use that Cope and Frazer have made of the American Association Committee of the International Geological Congress in their attack upon Powell and Marsh."[6] After the United States was selected for the 1891 International Congress meeting, the Americans at London in 1888 unanimously recommended Philadelphia. Walcott was a member of the organizing committee formed later that year. By the second committee meeting in November 1889, problems were developing about Philadelphia. Persifor Frazer wrote the European organization asking for a postponement, upsetting some committee members. Next, Frazer and Peter Lesley, state geologist of Pennsylvania, had major arguments. It was against this background that accusations by Cope and Frazer of corruption in government science filled a page of the *Herald*. Once publicity died down, life at the museum returned to normal. There was work on the Potsdam zone fauna, a son to christen, and talks to the Biological and Philosophical Societies.

In mid-March, Walcott managed to bruise his leg badly; it was twelve days before he could leave his bed. The ill health of Charles Darwin is well known, but there may be a more general phenomenon of illness induced by intense scientific activity. Walcott finally got on his feet and back to the museum and the Survey, where he "Talked to Major Powell about artesian well boring in the west" (April 11, 1890); again, this was prophetic of coming events.

The National Academy of Sciences came to Washington in April for its annual meeting. Along with the scientific proceedings, the committee on the International Congress met. As a consequence of the fossil feud, the decision was made to abandon Philadelphia. After the meeting, J. J. Stevenson of New York University wrote:

> Cope has distributed another pamphlet; if half of what he says about Marsh be true and if half of what Marsh says about him, they are a pair. I met Cope on the street in Washington after the adjournment of the Committee's meeting and we had a frank but perfectly pleasant talk about the matter. I told him that he had put some of us into a box by publishing that material at this time so that we were compelled to vote as we did not wish to vote; I told him that to send the Congress to Philadelphia would be simply to give the impression that the Committee condemns Marsh and Powell—a position that no one of us wants to take any more than some of us want to be put on the other side—that of defending those men. I told him the matter should have been kept in abeyance until after the Congress.[7]

An editorial in the *American Geologist* suggested the USGS forced the vote against Philadelphia, and this provoked another outburst from Stevenson: "My mind was made up instantly when I read the Cope and Frazer material at the time of our N. Y. meeting; it was perfectly clear to me that these men cannot be trusted; their integrity, I am not questioning, but their good sense I am questioning; there is no knowing what they might not do during the meeting of the Congress."[8] Stevenson insisted he was not a particular fan of Powell and that he voted as he did for the good of the science. Thus, in 1891 the International Congress met in Washington, and Philadelphia continued to decline as a seat of power in American geology.

During 1890, the Potsdam-zone publication on Upper Cambrian mollusks and trilobites appeared. In examining the collections, Walcott (1890f) found new forms from New York and Texas which he had collected earlier, along with some of Cooper Curtice's fossils from Wisconsin and Minnesota, plus an older collection from the Black Hills. This hodgepodge built up understanding of geographic distribution and stratigraphic zonation. The paper was another stepping stone to bigger things, quickly executed and quickly published.

Meanwhile, the new house was proving unsatisfactory. Helena and Walcott rented 1736 P Street N.W., about twenty blocks west of their first location. A few days later, the little family and nurse went off summering in the Helderberg Mountains. When he joined them near the end of July, Walcott did what any paleontologist would do: he and Helena collected fossils in the neighborhood. Soon he was on the east flank of the Adirondacks with Rust and part-time USGS colleagues Pumpelly and Charles Van Hise, examining the older rocks of the mountains. They looked at a graphite mine to see if this carbon accumulation gave any indication of former early life, then moved east to the overlying rocks which Walcott had studied a few years earlier.

In mid-August Walcott was called to Washington by a telegram from the major. He got together a budget, read more proof, answered the mail, and finally rejoined the family at North Granville, New York. He became ill again, and then struggled out to examine a fault and find a new graptolite locality. All through early September Walcott was in this difficult slate country, "driving all day over the Lower Cambrian rock of Salem. Found all the slates so plicated & faulted that the section cannot be accurately measured" (September 8, 1890).

About this time, another facet of Walcott's life appeared. He bought twenty-five hundred dollars worth of stock in "the curved railroad spike & safety joint co." of Washington, D.C., and for a time served as company secretary. By the following spring, he had taken out patents on two different designs of railway spikes. The railroad spikes eventually turned out to be a loss.

Walcott went off to Vermont with Helena to reexamine the famous Parker quarry that had yielded *Olenellus*. "Found fossils of the Olenellus fauna almost to the base of the section" (September 15, 1890). New England and extreme eastern New York are lovely in the early fall. Then the rains come and miserable is the appropriate word to substitute for lovely. Fieldwork among poorly fossiliferous, monotonous rocks continued, but eventually drew near a close. "Filling in some odds & ends on the section crossing thro M. granville. Out all day despite rain in afternoon. H——— accompanied me" (October 4, 1890). Wife as helpmate has a somewhat different meaning in the family of a geologist than it does in the family of an accountant. Two days later, Walcott bundled up the family to go south.

He was now working steadily on the Cambrian correlations and for the next month there was only one break from routine. "The Director, Messers. G. K. Gilbert, Arnold Hague, S. F. Emmons & C. D. Walcott met in Director's office & talked over the meeting of Int. Geol. Congress next Aug. in Wash-n" (November 6, 1890). He was now part of the innermost circle of the USGS.

He had moved far enough along on the Cambrian correlation paper that Walcott could start the second part of his assignment, a summary of the American Silurian. His first step was to review a few fossils and once more serendipity struck his career. "At my office working over collections from Cañon City. There is an unusual combination of genera and species and apparently fish remains beneath the Trenton fauna" (November 28, 1890). The fossils were, indeed, real fish remains, significantly older than any other vertebrates then known. Five days later, Walcott was on a train to Colorado. December is a poor time to go to the mountains, but occasionally the east slope of the Rockies has shirt-sleeve weather just before the heavy winter snows. Once more Walcott was lucky, in two weeks finding more fish remains and conclusive proof of their age (Yochelson 1983). He eliminated all possibility that these vertebrates were in younger beds that had been moved downward by faults, though arguments as to whether these beds were marine or freshwater raged for years (Spjeldnaes 1967); they were marine. Walcott was home three days before Christmas.

The Geological Society of America met in Washington after Christmas, and Walcott was prominently present. The very first scientific paper of the organization, presented by Dana in the summer of 1889, noted a comment by Walcott. The first *Bulletin* has two discussions by him and the second, five (Yochelson 1988). After a few years, discussions was not recorded, but for the time they were noted, more often than not his remarks were flattering and amplifying to a speaker rather than critical.

On New Year's Eve the Walcotts held a dinner party. Both Alexander and N. H Winchell were there, along with J. J. Stevenson and others. Those in the power structure of the GSA approved of Walcott, and it was a most happy ending to the year.

Walcott began his work for 1891 with good help: "At my office a.m. Mr. S. W. Loper began work. Prof. J. F. James, Mr. J. W. Gentry & Miss Latimer at work in laboratory" (January 2, 1891). Like Rust, Loper had been a farmer who developed an interest in fossils. In 1888 be entered Wesleyan College in Connecticut as a graduate student and from 1893 until his death in 1910 was curator of the natural history museum. He had worked for Walcott the past summer and proved to be a good collector.

Such assistance explains in part how Walcott published so many papers during his career. From the time he came to Washington, after his stint in New York, the USGS provided technical assistance. It is poor economy for scientists to perform the manifold routine tasks which form the basis of any investigation. Another factor in publication lies in technology. Just as Walcott had been an early member of the USGS to take a camera into the field as standard equipment, he also was one of the first to use a dictating machine. Poor Miss Latimer earned her salary as the volume of letters and manuscripts increased.

There were distractions from research. Gardiner G. Hubbard, a prominent lawyer and president of the National Geographic Society chaired the local committee for the coming Congress. Iddings, his field companion from Eureka, was treasurer and Walcott was secretary. In addition, he was refurbishing some fossil display in the National Museum to show the visitors. "[E. D.] Cope came in 9:30 and talked until noon on Cambrian & Taconic. Stated that C. A. White told him of discovery of Silurian fish remains in Colorado" (January 29, 1991). Those ancient rocks were of about as much interest to Cope as was granite, but he could not ask to see the newly discovered vertebrates without going through the proprieties.

By the first week in February, the fish work had progressed to the point that Walcott spoke to the Biological Society. The leading American scientific journals reported this news, and a German abstract was published (Walcott 1891a). Several weeks later he told a National Geographic Society audience of his investigations of the North American continent during the Cambrian and how the sea had gradually encroached on the land.

In March, Walcott took Helena to Rochester to see land relief models. Making three dimensional representations of a region is almost a lost art, but this was the period of its heyday. Most geologic exhibits displayed one or more and they graced the walls of college departments. Gilbert's friend E. E. Howell was the leading craftsman in this field; shortly after this, Howell moved to Washington and for years made physiographic models for the Geological Survey. Walcott also squeezed in a lecture on his Grand Canyon geology to the Rochester Academy of Science, and to an audience of 250 at Cornell University.

The couple entrained to Albany and, it being a Sunday, they relaxed by looking at rocks around Lake George. Then it was to Boston to see Alpheus Hyatt and present another talk. The next stop was O. C. Marsh at Yale and still another lecture. At each place, Walcott inspected collections of the Geological Survey.

Powell had been embarrassed by the newspaper accounts of federal material poorly cared for and he was not to be caught again. In New York and Philadelphia, they visited more paleontologists.

Walcott got home in time to be sick for his forty-first birthday. He recovered, started plans for the Chicago Columbian Exposition, and came down with a bad case of boils. Notwithstanding that discomfort, work on the major Cambrian summaries continued. By early May he was nearly finished with his draft for the twelfth *Annual Report*. With research under control, personal affairs became more important, and the Walcotts decided to buy a new house; furniture was stored and Helena and son went north for the summer while Walcott, lonely, toiled on for a couple more weeks. "Helena my own dear darling wife. I miss you & want you so much. I can hardly realize but that you will soon be in. How strange it is to think of you as far away from me & at the dear old place where we learned to love so well."[9]

Survey finances in 1891 allowed for spring fieldwork, and Walcott went to eastern New York to meet T. N. Dale of Williams College and a part-time member of the Geological Survey. One of Dale's assistants, A. H. Foerste, a Harvard graduate student, found some additional fossils in the slates. Walcott checked these new localities and added a couple more (Dale 1894).

The slate was economically important and the quarries needed information on the geologic structure. Slate requires a special uniform shale, which to begin with is not a particularly good environment for fossils. Folding and application of pressure to form slaty cleavage comes next. It is the cleavage which causes slate to break into thin pieces. About the only places where fossils are not destroyed is where cleavage and original bedding are parallel. Only a few beds made good slate and it helped quarry owners to know where those occur in the section.

Walcott was called to headquarters to prepare the allotment for paleontology as part of the new budget. Many pages of proof were read for his correlation *Bulletin,* and he had to revise the manuscript for the twelfth *Annual Report* and check the new museum exhibits. After the new fiscal year, Walcott "Rec'd appointment as Chief Paleontologist" (July 16, 1891). It was about time. Previously, each paleontologist was head of his own division.

Next, Walcott returned to the Colorado fossils. He gave Loper instructions and sent him off to collect more fish. Loper performed well and even brought back a partial skull. Though Walcott added a footnote documenting this find, several decades passed before a specialist studied the specimen. Twice in his diary Walcott refers to the age of the fish as Ordovician. When he published this

Charles Doolittle Walcott, Paleontologist

work (Walcott 1892) the age in the title was given as "Silurian (Ordovician)." One prime feature of the Geological Survey was a freedom to express opinion. Walcott could not use Ordovician in a government publication, for the Committee on Geologic Names had spoken. However, if he wished to submit his work to an outside journal, so long at it was authorized—not approved, but authorized—for publication, he could present his views. Some in academia viewed the USGS as stifling independence and forcing a lock step mentality on its geologists, but they did not understand the system. Case after case can be cited of federal scientists who were allowed to publish heretical ideas which later became gospel.

A break in chronology is in order, as the "Fauna of the Lower Cambrian or *Olenellus* zone" was left hanging. Officially the tenth *Annual Report* of the U.S. Geological Survey was issued in 1890, and few win an argument with the Government Printing Office. The eighth and ninth reports are mentioned in 1890 issues of the *American Journal of Science,* but not the tenth. The first review of Walcott's paper, by J. James, did not appear until August 1891; had the paper come out sooner, it would have been reviewed sooner. James was no longer working for Walcott so there was no conflict of interest in his reviewing. The *American Journal of Science* did not mention the work until October 1891. Still later, a British reviewer (Anonymous 1891, 32–36) remarked, "We heartily congratulate the author upon having had the honour to bring together so admirable a Monograph." Finally, a letter from J. J. Stevenson, written in September 1891, in Walcott's copy, notes a few corrections. The indirect evidence suggests that Walcott 1890, is really Walcott 1891. It is of such small details that some careers have been built. Fortunately for priority, all the species, save the strange little form from Chilhowie Mountain, were named earlier.

This work is 265 pages long and includes twenty-five text figures and six plates of maps and sections; the heart of it is 150 pages of fossil descriptions and forty-nine plates illustrating them. It was another magnum opus, if it is possible to have more than one in a career. A detailed summary of the literature and historical review was followed by an area by area description of geologic and geographic distribution. The conditions of deposition and biogeography are mentioned; in spite of the official views of the Geological Survey, the term "Ordovician" crept into some of the discussion. Only after all various summaries are given is the detailed paleontology presented.

The plates are a lesson in changing emphasis and changing methods. The Cambrian was the prime time for trilobites, yet only about one-third of the plates are devoted to this group. Many illustrations are pen and ink drawings that appeared in *Bulletin* 10, *Bulletin* 30, and *Monograph* 8. There is not a single plate of older drawings which has not been rearranged and modified. A few brachiopods, bivalved shells which are not clams, are illustrated by pen and ink drawings, but others are by photographs. Many photographs are retouched and this type of enhancement eventually developed into a minor art form.

The illustrations of worm trails and burrows included were uncommon in the literature of the time, but the biggest change from Walcott's earlier Cambrian work was greater emphasis on what he called Actinozoa. These fossils have been called sponges and corals, but probably are a major group unrelated to either. They are illustrated primarily by photographs, both of entire specimens and sections. This had been done by others, but not on such a large scale. The group lay fallow for half a century and another twenty-five years ensued before the importance of these fossils for zonation of Cambrian shallow water deposits was recognized.

Walcott obtained 110 copies of his paper from the government printer and distributed them throughout the world. A modest price for the extra copies was one of the advantages enjoyed by a government scientist, though this seldom made up for the frustration and delay in the official printing process; one simply had to learn to live with that. So much for the tenth *Annual Report*.

Loper was off to the west, and Gentry kept papers moving, so Walcott west to Rochester and Utica and "at 225 left for N. Granville in response to call of telegram. Found Helena ill—Little baby not alive when born. Bad luck for us" (July 30, 1891). Helena was extremely ill, and Walcott stayed close to the house; finally, after a week she began to show some improvement. Walcott went to Utica to meet with Rust on the sale of property along West Canada Creek for a power development. They went one last time to the trilobite "diggings" for old times' sake. Another thread to the past was broken.

Walcott returned to North Granville and Helena for another week. He traced faults, took photographs, and collected a few more fossils; fossiliferous beds are still scarce in that geologic province (Theokritoff 1964). Saturday, August 22, the Walcott family went south to the Potomac River, where it was damp and hot. The geological festivities were about to begin, and preliminaries were well underway.

This International Congress in Washington was elaborately scheduled. Arrangements had been for the AAAS to meet the preceding week. Before the AAAS adjourned, the Geological Society of America held its two-day summer meeting. Each was planned to entice more geologists, especially from foreign countries, to attend. Both organizations made front page news in the local papers. The *Evening Star* thought the AAAS one of the most important scientific bodies in the world. The paper also reported President Benjamin Harrison touring New England, a war in Chile, and several train robberies.

Walcott's speech at the GSA on vertebrates far older than anyone had suspected created a sensation. Consider how Henry Adams reacted:

> Seeking some impersonal point for measure, he happened to see what had happened to his oldest friend and cousin the ganoid fish *Pteraspis* of Ludlow and Wenlock, with whom he had sported when geological life was young; as though they had all remained together in time to set the Mask of Comus at Ludlow Castle and repeat "how charming is divine philosophy." He felt almost aggravated to find Walcott so vigorously acting the part of Comus as to have flung the ganoid all the way off to Colorado and far back into the Lower Trenton limestone, making *Pteraspis* as modern as a Mississippi garpike by spawning an ancestry for him, indefinitely more remote, in the dawn of organic life. (1946, 399)

As at the fourth congress three years earlier in London, Walcott's name was on everyone's lips. More than seventy foreign and nearly two hundred American geologists heard his careful account of the vertebrates and their age; a great deal of favorable discussion is recorded. His Middle Ordovician fish stood as the oldest record of vertebrate for about ninety years.

The scientific sessions of the International Congress, following immediately, were at Columbian University, today George Washington University. "In case any foreigner, or American, either for that matter, should enter the building and not be inclined to ask questions, the corridors were addressed with announcements of various kinds, both in English and French. . . . scientific men are by profession cosmopolitan and are familiar with several languages and are constantly coming in contact with foreigners."[10] The reporter saw that the well-known practice of standing in the halls and talking was well established.

Because Congress president Newberry was too ill to attend, his duties were divided between Powell as director of the USGS and Joseph Le Conte of the University of California, newly elected president of the AAAS. The honor of presiding at the opening ceremonial session went to T. M. Hughes of Cambridge University. According to an *Evening Star* reporter, "He has a tall, rather spare figure, and has a quick nervous manner." Le Conte welcomed and addressed the

delegates. Gardiner G. Hubbard welcomed them on behalf of the local committee. Secretary of Interior Noble welcomed everyone again with a talk mer-
cifully short. The major made remarks, as did Hughes and Gaudry, and the congress was ready for business.

Each morning the congress council met at ten. Scientific sessions began an
hour later, broke for lunch, and reconvened at 2:30 P.M., unlike the frantic pace
of present-day meetings. Classification of the Pleistocene, that is the time of
glaciation, and standardizing of colors for geologic maps were subjects of lectures and symposia, but most time was devoted to less formal comments and
remarks; newspaper coverage was detailed, despite the technical nature of the
congress. For those wearied of talk, a display of maps was on hand, including the great coal map of Pennsylvania and some striking ones from Mexico.
The Cosmos Club opened its doors and local guides led visitors to public
buildings and laboratories. Professors Emmons and Wilson held receptions
at home, and the U.S. Marine Band played a special concert, always a good
event for a hot Washington summer evening. The delegates rested Thursday,
but on Friday the National Museum held a reception, and Saturday, a trip to
Mount Vernon was offered.

Sunday morning a boatload of sixty geologists traveled down the Potomac.
"The first stop was made at Fort Washington. Here the little army of stone
hunters, each armed with a bag and tiny hammer, disembarked and began the
search for specimens . . . and did not return to the city until after midnight."[11]
Monday night Director Powell and the geologists of the Geological Survey received them at the Hoee Building. Final adjournment was the next day, but the
grand finale was a trip by steamer to a festive dinner at Marshall Hall on the
Maryland side of the Potomac, opposite Mount Vernon. Not until 1933, and
then again not until 1989, would the renamed International Geological Congress return to Washington.

Those on field trips to Lake Superior or the West left happy. Walcott prepared
two little sections of the guidebook and produced two pages of remarks for the
Compte Rendu. Seeing that visitors were shown fossils of interest in the museum
was a full-time job for him, and ensuring local arrangements went off as scheduled was another full-time job, but he did both. Walcott's reputation as an organizer was assured. The icing on the congress cake for him was *Bulletin* 81,
which "has been sent to all members of the Congress" (Emmons 1893, 170n.).
Five hundred copies were ordered by the USGS for free distribution, to sup-

plement the print order of three thousand. *Bulletin* 80 by Williams has the same print order and must have been given to the delegates. On occasion, the curse of the Government Printing Office can be a blessing, for the price of each bulletin was twenty-five cents.

Bulletin 81 contains 447 pages of closely printed material. James was credited for compiling the literature and preparing summaries, but the original writing was by Walcott. "This work is a review, by one who is working in the Cambrian field, of the work of his predecessors, and of the results they and he have thus far obtained as he interprets them" (Walcott 1891b, 15). A reviewer in *American Geologist* (Anonymous 1892) gave the essence of this work. He noted it was mainly a historical treatment, because so few of the rock strata that were being placed as Cambrian had been accurately assigned until a few years previously. The upper Midwest outcrops were thought to be Lower Silurian in age, and the rocks near Boston were considered "Primordial." The reviewer noted with admiration that Walcott called this compilation an "unfinished memoir."

In this publication, perhaps as in no other, is visible one of the reasons for Walcott's scientific success. He had a grasp on virtually all the literature in his field, and showed a keen understanding of his predecessors' accomplishments. From this data and his own observations, Walcott could synthesize, but he was never carried away with sweeping generalization. He was aware of gaps in knowledge and eleven pages were devoted to anticipation of future problems on both a local and regional level.

As another reason for success, Walcott built on his earlier efforts. His first brush with the Cambrian had been his 1877 vacation trip to New Brunswick. He elaborated on that experience with *Bulletin* 10. Field investigations at Eureka, Nevada, of the Cambrian, and collecting in the northeast led to *Bulletin* 30. The paleontologic determinations were satisfactory, though he incorrectly assigned *Olenellus* to the Middle Cambrian. Once he saw that error, he publicly corrected it—never an enjoyable experience—and assembled all that was known of the early fauna in one major paper. Now he had summarized that information, plus all details on the overlying beds, in both a geographic and a stratigraphic framework. Walcott compartmentalized a major research program and produced a number of short papers on various faunas along the route to the final product. Thus, this synthesis was not burdened with details on fossil discoveries.

Walcott assimilated new ideas without discarding that which was tried and true. At the International Congress, he stated that "the principles of correlation were essentially the same as those used by the New York Survey prior to 1847, and that the only essential modification made in them has been through the influence of the theory of evolution" (Walcott 1893, 168). He repeated this view in slightly more detail in *Bulletin* 81.

Walcott divided the Cambrian into three series. He noted that the lower and upper part had essentially uniform faunas throughout the continent, whereas the middle was marked by two distinct genera of trilobites, not found intermixed; these "Atlantic" and "Pacific" faunal provinces were first mentioned by him in 1889. Walcott observed that Lower Cambrian rocks are confined to the margins of the continent and that through the Cambrian, the continent was increasingly inundated. A century later, no one has modified these basic observations.

Bulletin 81 contains three maps, one of outcrops, one of relative length of stratigraphic sections in various areas, and one of the hypothetical flooding of the continent by the Cambrian seas. The second and third were repeated in the twelfth *Annual Report* (Walcott 1891c), the former with minor additions to the legend. That paper distilled the essence of the *Bulletin* in a nontechnical manner. It is paleogeography for the intelligent layman, much as Walcott must have presented it originally to the National Geographic Society meeting. The *American Journal of Science* (Anonymous 1893) gave it one good sentence of praise.

Five days after the Congress adjourned, Walcott left for nearly two months in the southern Appalachians. The mapping program needed paleontologic support as the age and relations of rocks on the east flank of the Shenandoah Valley were far from resolved. Walcott met Bailey Willis at Natural Bridge, Virginia. The main object was not that touristic wonder, but the rocks to the east. Were they Silurian, Cambrian, or pre-Cambrian? The map patterns in the Southeast were making little sense; as it turned out, one reason was that ages were incorrect and another was that thrust faults repeated some rock units.

The first stop was on the James River at Balcony Falls, where the section of sandstones had already been measured several times and were regarded by geologists as Potsdam. If they were Upper Cambrian, the overlying rocks must be Lower Silurian, that is Ordovician, in age. Their true age became clear when Walcott "found the Olenellus fauna in the upper quartzite & Upper Cambrian faunas in the shale series above the quartzites" (October 9, 1891). With that new data, the rest of the geologic section fell into line. Walcott later commented that Balcony Falls was the key to the structure of the Appalachians.

Charles Doolittle Walcott, Paleontologist

Some years later Willis wrote:

Walcott, as it happened, was once out for trilobites in the quartzites of the Blue Ridge in Virginia. Many good fossil hunters had looked for them in vain. We broke the ringing rock, where it was exposed in the gorge of the James river, for hours but found nothing. The rock broke across the fossils, if there were any, and they were too thin to be seen. The next morning we looked across the Valley of Virginia to the Blue Ridge, four miles away, and could trace the low ridge formed by the quartzite across its face. Walcott called my attention to the ravine of a small stream, which crossed it, breaking the even ridge crest by a gap which lacked the sharper features of the river gorge. "The trilobites are waiting for us there," said Walcott. "They have been waiting a long time. Let's go." And there we found them in abundance in the weathered rock shown by the gap, which split parallel to the bedding planes on which the trilobites had died. (Willis and Willis 1934, 293)

The two examined sections in southern Virginia before moving to northwestern North Carolina, where they investigated several mountain coves. They geologized into eastern Tennessee and near the town of Cleveland, Walcott identified Upper, Middle, and Lower Cambrian faunas on the outcrops. With the stratigraphic sequence arranged, difficult structural problems were partially clarified; Willis and Walcott recognized some thrust faults, though several which cut through the shale units at a very low angle were missed at this time. For paleontology, it was one grand success after another. Near the end of the trip, a letter from Ed Hurlburt cast a shadow in reporting the death of William Rust, born October 2, 1826, and died October 4, 1891.

Back in Washington, the new house was still unfinished, and there were collections to unpack, sort, and label. Walcott was on the publications committee of the Biological Society and that took several afternoons and evenings. Notwithstanding his own research, plus accumulated mail, Walcott extended his sphere of activity by dating fossils from eastern California. December 2, the Walcotts finally moved to 1746 Q street N.W.; this was to be the family home for a number of years.

In mid-December Walcott went to Trenton Falls. William had willed some land to Walcott and other family members, but one boundary was not clear and eventually the matter had to be taken to court. Affairs dragged on and on, leading to a break between Walcott and Ed Hurlburt who was neglecting law for liquor. The Rust kin helped him pack fossils to take to Washington, and there must have been thoughts of long-departed Lura. He stopped in New York to see R. P. Whitfield at the American Museum and called on his old chief Clarence King.

In Washington, C. E. Beecher visited briefly. Beecher, six years younger, first met Walcott in 1878 in Albany while Hall was in Paris attending the First International Congress. After Hall's return, Walcott was either fired or not rehired, depending on how one viewed Hall's action. One possible factor was that Hall could not afford to pay both men, and he kept Beecher, who was more pliable and less expensive. Beecher stayed ten years in Albany before moving to Yale University. He had worked on trilobites and brachiopods while in Hall's employ. Just now, he was looking at Cambrian brachiopods.

Before the Christmas holiday, Walcott again broadened his geological horizons by starting a paper for the *Annual Report* on pre-Cambrian volcanic rocks collected a decade before in the Grand Canyon. Just as the newspaper feud earlier in the year had portended ill tidings, curiously enough this was a harbinger of another phase of Walcott's career on rocks below the Cambrian.

Eighteen ninety-one had been a banner year, as good as 1892 was to be bad, though it did not appear so at first. "It was a happy new years day for our little family in our new house" (January 1, 1892). "Began work on Middle Cambrian fauna of the Appalachian trough" (January 2, 1892). He noted that eastern Newfoundland and the Boston area yielded trilobite faunas different from those in western Newfoundland and in the Appalachian Mountains. Cooper Curtice in 1886 and 1891 had obtained excellent material to document this difference in faunal provinces. Walcott was short of field collectors and when problems had arisen in California, he requested the Department of Agriculture to detail Curtice to the USGS. In his superb fashion, Curtice made the critical collections to resolve the age of these rocks; more recently Walcott had again asked for his help in the south.

Walcott also moved to a position of power in "the old boy's network" of Washington as a member of the admissions committee of the Cosmos Club. Though the club occupied some of his nights, other evenings at home he worked on lavas of the Grand Canyon, surely a strange relaxation for a paleontologist. That January, he also joined the Sons of the American Revolution. Ancestors on both the Walcott and Doolittle sides of his family had been in General Washington's army and Walcott was a stalwart patriot. Besides, G. Brown

Charles Doolittle Walcott, Paleontologist

Goode, assistant secretary of the Smithsonian, in charge of the National Museum, was one of the organizers of the Washington Chapter; how could Walcott say no?

By mid-February, Walcott was engaged in preparing the USGS display for the Columbian Exposition, which was to show the rocks and fossils of America in stratigraphic order. This exhibit was to take up increasing amounts of time as the 1893 opening date approached. At the moment, he was occupied with Trenton-age material from Wisconsin. A few days later, perhaps by coincidence, perhaps not, T. C. Chamberlin dined. Chamberlin worked part-time for the USGS in charge of glacial studies, but he was also state geologist and president of the University of Wisconsin. Chamberlin was to academia what Gilbert was to the Geological Survey, a very big thinker. It was a pleasant evening and then back to more routine investigations; after completing this segment of the exposition display, Walcott returned to examining the Tennessee Middle Cambrian fossils.

Helena took him to the Daughters of the American Revolution celebration on George Washington's birthday, where he heard Persifor Frazer's address on the importance of patriotism. He took several trips to the Patent Office about his railroad spikes. Routine at the National Museum was increasingly interrupted by calls to the Hoee Building. Walcott visited Philadelphia, to promote his new spike to the Pennsylvania Railroad. Richard Rathbun, then of the Fish Commission, convinced him to give a lecture at the Unitarian church on his Grand Canyon adventures to benefit the YMCA.

In March, in addition to his efforts on the publication committee of the Biological Society, he rewrote the society's constitution, an exercise he would find useful in the future. It was only fair that he give time to the Biological Society, for he had published short notes in their *Proceedings* and he had another half-page note out that year, documenting a fossil locality near Boston. In late March, Walcott started seriously on the Grand Canyon manuscript and then, following a long-established pattern, he became ill. After he finally shook off the fever, Walcott gave two lectures at Johns Hopkins University and called on the chief engineer of the Baltimore and Ohio Railroad; if there was money to be made with the new design of the spike, Walcott was out to make it. At the Survey, Henry Fairfield Osborn came down from the American Museum in New York to see Powell about Marsh; that did not bode well. Still, there were more immediate chores; Trenton fossils from New York were finally arranged for the Chicago exhibit. Spring was marked by the annual meeting of the National Academy of Sciences, and of course Walcott attended.

The end of April, Charlie and nurse went off to relatives while Helena and husband enjoyed a spring field season together, a rare event for a paleontologist. They left for Colorado via Chicago; Walcott inspected the exposition grounds for the USGS display of rocks and fossils, and naturally he collected some of the local fossils to incorporate into it.

From Denver, they went to Colorado Springs and Cañon City. By mid-May, the couple was encamped at the upper end of Garden Park. They moved to Webster Park, Hot Springs, Beaver Creek, and Trunk Creek. Walcott found older Ordovician strata, but saw no vertebrate remains in the overlying Harding sandstone. The fish-bearing bed was restricted to the Cañon City area. Their trip ended in Williams Canyon, where Walcott had gone in 1890. This was a fine excursion for the couple and provided an important datum for the planned Silurian correlation paper.

Even in Colorado, they were aware of ominous events at Washington. Before they took the train back to Chicago, Walcott scribbled off a somewhat desperate personal letter to Alexander Agassiz at the Museum of Comparative Zoology. To open, he noted that he had collected one partial fish and then got to business:

> I learn that the House of Representatives struck out the item for paleontology at the request of Mr. Herbert who based his arguments largely on your advice & letter of Dec. 2d, 1885. While I shall not take issue with you on some points I will in regard to what I call practical paleontology in connection with a geological survey. During the past ten years I have been studying the formations in the field, collecting fossils from them & building up standard sections in various geologic areas or basins for the use of the geologists engaged in areal work & mapping. Incidental to that I have published several papers on geology & paleontology. By being connected with the Survey & having time & money I have correlated the section of various geologists & areas and bro't order out of the lower Paleozoic rocks, where confusion & error prevailed. Such work must be done by someone who has the opportunity to handle all the material collected & to study all doubtful sections in the field. During the ten years mentioned scarcely a month has passed without my being called upon to work on some problem requiring paleontological & geological training. I am endeavoring to train young men into such work & if the paleontological branch of the survey is run according to my views it will be a practical & necessary branch of the Survey. I refer to my own work as it illustrates the point I wish to make. Can you not approve of such work & if so will you not write Mr. Herbert to that effect?

Charles Doolittle Walcott, Paleontologist

I know how you feel in regard to certain work & publications but I fully believe that as a practical business & scientific man you will understand my position. Three-fourths of my time is given to field & office work that bears directly on areal geology & mapping. I should like very much to talk with you but cannot get to Cambridge soon. I am deeply interested in my work & do not wish to be driven from it because Mr. Herbert & others think it is all of little or no use.[12]

Walcott had good cause to be concerned about the views on fossils of Alabama congressman Hillary Herbert. Seemingly no other branch of science had been so singled out for ridicule or had had legislation introduced to forbid its study by the federal government. According to Herbert, "There is no end to paleontology, there is no end to geology; and when the morning of resurrection shall come, some paleontologist will be searching for some previously undescribed species of extinct beings, and some geologist will be pecking away at the rocks to find some characteristics which have never before been ascertained. There is no end to it" (Darrah 1951, 345).

At Chicago, Walcott met Powell, and the two went on to the University of Wisconsin. "Dined at Prof. Chamberlin's. Had a long talk with Major Powell & also Profs Van Hise and Chamberlin. A proposition to join the Chicago University geological staff was made by Prof. Chamberlin" (June 15, 1892). Now that was a surprise! Walcott returned to Chicago with a great deal on his mind. He called on W. R. Harper, president of the newly forming institution. For someone without a day in college to be invited to the University of Chicago sounds like a Horatio Alger story of making good by hard work. Notwithstanding the honor, twelve days after the dinner, Walcott declined.

This was a serious decision, especially in the light of major problems developing in Washington. A bit of comic relief is called for. It was Walcott's habit to include in his diary, small newspaper squibs that once were used for fillers at the end of columns. Early ones concerned romance or duty; after he met Helena, they were about true love. Now young Charlie's influence was felt in a nonsense rhyme for small geologists:

Trilobite, graptolite, Nautilus pie,
Seas were calcareous, Oceans were dry.
Equecene, miocene, Pliocene, tuff,
Lias and trias. And that is enough.

The couple returned to hot Washington in mid-June, and a week later O. C. Marsh came into town. Walcott lunched with him at the Great Basin Mess. This is the first time he mentioned that group in his diary. It was inconvenient to go to the Hoee Building for a weekly lunch and then back to the museum; Walcott was always busy. This luncheon group was started in 1881 by Gilbert for a few of the western hands (Pyne 1980). Gradually it grew in size and added a few younger people. The only picture is of the 1894 farewell luncheon for Powell and from that has grown an interpretation of catered lunches and a clique within the Geological Survey. Out of necessity Gilbert was frugal, having an invalid wife, and the elaborate luncheons were a myth. As to the clique, that could well be, for some notable geologists did not participate in the Great Basin Mess. Like any organization, the USGS was not always one big, happy family. As soon as Marsh left, Walcott was up on Capitol Hill seeing senators and congressmen and meeting with the major. There is an interesting diary entry in early July: "At my laboratory A.M. Lunched at survey & talked to men about geol. work, etc." (July 6, 1892). Powell was leaning on Walcott for advice and help and he was propelled willy-nilly into an administrative position.

He was at the Capitol on almost a daily basis. Congress normally never stayed in session this long, and July heat and humidity did not help anyone's nerves. In mid-July, the family left for Holly Springs, Pennsylvania, where the weather was a bit cooler. On July 19, the sky fell in: "The House of Rep's agreed to Senate amendment cutting Survey appro. about $140,000" (July 19, 1892).

With that, the Geological Survey faced immediate disaster and the potential of total destruction. Thirteen geologic parties were recalled immediately to Washington. Elimination of some statutory positions caused both downgrading and dismissal among the scientists. Gilbert, Willis, and McGee were demoted, but Becker, Emmons, and Pumpelly were let go. Pumpelly was independently wealthy (Champlin 1994) and could forego his position; for the others it was a hardship. Emmons and Becker had never been staunch supporters of the major and that may have partially influenced his choice of whom to keep and whom to cut loose. Several geologists left for universities.

To understand the complex story one has to start at 1888 (Rabbitt 1980). The issue of irrigation for western farmers had been simmering for some years. The election of Senator "Big Bill" Stewart from Nevada made a legislative push irresistible. The major had been concerned with proper use of arid lands for a

Charles Doolittle Walcott, Paleontologist

decade and he was ready with a plan. A March 1888 joint resolution presented Powell his opportunity, though funds were not appropriated until October. Powell and Stewart had a brief lovefest in 1889 and toured the West together (Stegner 1954).

Irrigation activity was novel and to accommodate new duties, Powell consolidated geologic investigations and shifted their responsibility to Gilbert. Early in 1889, the USGS opened a training camp in New Mexico to instruct budding hydrologists in measuring the water flow of streams. The Irrigation Survey was in business, scientifically speaking. Not everyone was pleased with these developments. Arnold Hague gossiped to George Becker: "What do you think of G. for Chief geologist? I can find no warrant for the appointment and certainly the appropriation does not provide for it. . . . Powell is wholly given over to Indians and irrigation. The irrigation of arid lands is a most important matter but hardly a question for the geological survey to take up."[13] Such mutterings from within were ignored by the major.

In Powell's judgment, the primary need was topographic maps of potential reservoir sites. Most of the irrigation money and some Topographic Branch funds went to that purpose. Mapping did not proceed rapidly, and the slow pace of locating reservoir sites was far, far slower than Stewart wanted. To make matters worse, speculators followed the surveyors and staked land claims adjacent to the potential reservoirs.

The drought of 1888 solidified support for irrigation, but it was worse in 1889, and still worse in 1890. Despite funds appropriated by Congress, to date Powell had done nothing to make conditions better. After all, if money is given, results should come, and that the Irrigation Survey did not control the weather was no excuse. The entire economy began to suffer the effects of farm problems, free silver problems, and tariff problems. Some in Congress insisted that artesian wells were the solution for the western farmer, in spite of USGS data as to their temporary nature. By April 1890 the Department of Agriculture—not the Geological Survey—was commissioned to report on this approach.

The fate of the Irrigation Survey became worse when Clarence Dutton testified to Congress that, in his opinion, topographic maps were not needed. Through a quirk in the original law, money for the USGS was appropriated in a lump sum; in 1882, shortly after he took office, Powell was appointed a special disbursing agent by the secretary of the interior allowing him to allocate budget money as he saw fit. Stewart brought this freedom of operation with government funds to the attention of Congress; thereafter, the Survey budget had to be itemized. The General Land Office decided that because of the authorization of the Irrigation Survey, no land claims could be patented until certified by that Survey, and this legal judgment was made retroactive to 1888. Worse still, Powell talked to a newspaper reporter and tried to rally public opinion, but he irritated more congressmen with remarks about lobbyists and special interests. With all these forces combined in opposition, the political pressure was too much.

Chamberlin wrote a colleague on events in Washington:

> The senate amended the Sundry Civil Bill by striking out the Irrigation appropriation. They however increased the appropriation for geology & topography. Gilbert thinks that irrigation will be lost in the conference, and that in view of this, Powell will urge his friends to move for an increase [in] topography of the Survey program. It would appear that he is still strong with Congress and that the Survey proper may be a gainer rather than a looser by the fight over irrigation. This impression, however, comes from the Survey side.[14]

When the 1890 appropriation finally passed in August, the Irrigation Survey was dead. Gilbert had the obvious prediction correct, but in reading the tea leaves of the congressional brew, he was sadly lacking as a prognosticator. Powell had seen this survey as the golden opportunity to preserve the small farmer and prevent farming in areas where it was doomed to fail. He was shattered, and this man, who six years before was a hero when he defended science in government for the good of the people, now became a villain. He was accused of many things, including mixing the staffs of Bureau of Ethnology and USGS, and irregularities in filling Survey positions. The one point that he could not wiggle away from was the diversion of funds to topographic mapping. Still, even his sworn enemies, of whom there were many, never accused the major of any attempt at personal gain. After a century of western irrigation activity, the general conclusion seems to be that Powell was basically right in his approach. It was the political climate that was all wrong for an altruistic social welfare government policy.

Though destruction of the Irrigation Survey was bad, the Geological Survey did not immediately suffer. Cope and Frazer in 1890 had attacked Marsh and

Charles Doolittle Walcott, Paleontologist

Powell, and while many historians view this as part of irrigation fiasco, it makes as good sense to consider it part of the skirmish over the 1891 Congress. After all, whatever else Marsh was doing or not doing with bones collected on federal funds, they had no effect on irrigation. In 1891, the Geological Survey was still going along as usual and actually got a small increase, though itemizing and clarification of salary rolls brought up some embarrassing items. Besides, the International Congress of Geologists was in the city and that provided a favorable light for the USGS. Powell was prominent at the congress, but it was a last hurrah; by then, he had lost his support in Congress.

The recession getting worse, 1892 was a grim year. Congress was out to save money by cutting all frills. In the economically bad year of 1884, the Coast Survey had been attacked and nearly destroyed, but Powell emerged as the chief spokesman of government science. Along with all the new enemies that Powell had garnered, some old ones were out to settle the score. The merits of the Geological Survey were questioned. Indeed, all federal science was now suspect; even the Smithsonian Institution trembled (Manning 1988). Ever since the first of the year, Walcott had been putting in time at the Hoe Building and on Capitol Hill for Powell could no longer cope with the situation. Longtime chief clerk James Pilling had retired. Colonel Rizer, who replaced him, was quite able but lacked experience and threw more of a burden on the tottering director.

Perhaps Powell should have resigned as director in 1890 when he was crushed. Still, there was the prospect that the coming International Congress would redeem his reputation. Some Survey stalwarts, such as his protégé, W J "No-Stop" McGee, who always had the major's ear, convinced him to stay on and fight the good fight. If Powell left, it was uncertain who would take over; some parties harked back to the good old days under Clarence King and wanted the former director to return.

The concept of Civil Service was in its infancy and many government workers had no job protection. With each change of administration, lots of staff were replaced. Still, those not in conventional patronage jobs could assume that life would be on a more or less even keel. Naturally, there are good times and bad times for government workers, depending on the state of the economy and the mood of Congress. Even so, no one anticipated this frightful turn of events, and although Congress warred on the Executive Branch from time to time, it had seldom been so personal and directed at a single bureau. Part of the savagery was vengeance directly against the major, but the attack went far beyond that and a congressional inquiry was planned. No doubt about it, the sky had fallen in.

Walcott wrote "at laboratory A.M. and Survey P.M.—Arranging for running work on basis of $14000 in paleontology instead of $51700" (July 20, 1892). As always happened at a crisis of activity, he had health problems, this time a toothache. He was almost constantly at the Hoee Building, but in the midst of reorganization Walcott did spend a few hours with Cooper Curtice discussing the southern Appalachian Cambrian collections; research went on regardless of catastrophe. Walcott shared his troubles with Professor Chamberlin:

> These are trying times with the Survey—not alone the cuts in the appropriations, but the underlying causes of them. Many of the Director's friends, as well as his enemies, both in the Senate and in the House, are in doubt about his manner of managing the Survey. . . . The Director is not strong and well, and I doubt if he fully realizes the condition of things. I desire to be loyal to him; but I wish to see the Survey put on a business, as well as on a sound scientific. basis, and shall do all I can to contribute to that end.[15]

Walcott asked Chamberlin if he would be a candidate for director, even though others had assured him this was unlikely. Chamberlin had his own department at the new University of Chicago, relieving himself of the responsibility as president of the University of Wisconsin (Fisher 1963, 4–5), and he had no interest in coming to Washington. Chamberlin crossed letters with Walcott, noting that he was hiring Iddings, and would still like Walcott to teach several six-week terms.

The first week in August, Walcott finally left the maelstrom to see his family. As might be expected, he was "Out on the quartzite rock in Mt. Holly Gap. Found fragments of the Olenellus fauna" (August 6, 1892). He dictated a three-page reply to Chamberlin:

> This is a cool sleepy day & it is an effort to brace up & write. The hot weather & nervous strain incident to Survey matters about used me up. . . . Your letter was received an hour before I left the city. I spoke to the Director & he said "If you decide to do that you had best give up your place in the Survey"—This is a radical change of view from that represented by him in Madison. . . . As you well know he likes strong personal loyalty from those nearest to him. This with me is secondary to loyalty to the Survey & its work & hence since the disagreement about Cambrian-Huronian etc in 1885 I have felt that I did not have his full confidence. . . . I do not, however, wish you to keep the place open for me—if it causes you any embarrassment. I should like to be with you & would if conditions were the same as when I was at Madison.[16]

Charles Doolittle Walcott, Paleontologist

For those who argue that history does not repeat itself, consider Hall not renewing Walcott's contract and Powell insisting that Walcott not take a short leave to teach. In both instances, those who needed assistance reacted against the person willing to help. Consider Walcott in 1877 defending Hall's work on the *Palaeontology* of New York and in 1892 defending the USGS. Walcott was cursed with a strong call of duty and conscience. Others fled Washington, yet he stayed. His family weekend over, Walcott was back in the city. August was tense and just how tense is shown that on several Sundays Walcott was at Hoee building writing, rather than at church. In that dreadful summer Walcott had his chance to leave before the catastrophe and declined. In large measure he may have remained because there were scientific problems to pursue and the USGS was still the best place to pursue them.

Early in the year, the younger Winchell had written to friend Frazer commenting indirectly on the situation in Washington: "As to Marcou, he is bitter, personally, and tho' fundamentally he is right in his criticisms, in detail he does not produce the effect that he deserves."[17] During the dog days of August, Walcott wrote the counterpoint. "Someone suggested to me yesterday that Senator Carey had read Marcou's pamphlet and had cut down the Survey organization so as to conform to the views expressed therein. I think that is hardly the case, but, at the same time, there is no doubt that some Congressmen were influenced by his statements; all of which will undoubtedly do the old man's heart good."[18]

When the sky has fallen and there is no hope, one can either wring one's hands or continue pursuing science. Last fall's field investigations in the southern Appalachians had shown Walcott that discovery of the position of the *Olenellus* fauna was the key to unraveling structural complications. He was determined to apply this powerful geologic tool in the central Appalachians, come what may. Besides, there was little more he could do once Congress adjourned, and nearby fieldwork was a chance to escape the heat and humidity of the simmering city.

In mid-August, Walcott was in York, Pennsylvania, with Prof. Wanner, superintendent of city schools, whom Walcott honored in the naming of *Olenellus wanneri*. They were joined by Arthur Keith of the USGS who had mapped in the southern Appalachian and was moving north. The field party went east to the Susquehana River and west to Emigsville, northeast of York. Walcott "Discovered Olenellus fauna beneath limestone. Also traced it to New Holland from Emigsville & also found it above Hellam quartzite" (August 18, 1892).

They returned to Chiques rock on the Susquehana River at Columbia, Pennsylvania. Fifty years earlier, a local iron master had described a curious worm tube from the quartzite at this locality and it was then the oldest known fossil in the country. This was confirmed when Walcott found the *Olenellus* fauna overlying, both in the quartzite and in the so-called upper limestone of the Pennsylvania survey. There were major errors in the earlier assignment of the ages of rock units which Walcott was clearing up in rapid order.

Walcott moved south to Maryland: "With Keith drove across South Mountain *via* Monteray Station W.[estern] M.[aryland] R.R. & thence north along west side of Mtn. & at night to Smithburg. We found the Olenellus fauna in quartzite & limestones at the western side of the mountain 3–4 *mi* west of Waynesboro" (August 23, 1892). They continued south to Keedysville, Maryland, now both an antique town and a town known for antiques. They moved to Mechanicsville across Blue and Catoctin Mountains. They doubled back to Monteray, where Walcott found Cambrian fossils in quartzite about two miles west of the station. They confirmed the findings by working south to Harpers Ferry, West Virginia. From that Civil War site, it was only a couple of hours by rail to home and family. The end of August, Walcott reported in at the Survey office, started on the mail, and following his custom, was laid up with a severe headache.

Chamberlin was still pursuing Walcott, who still declined, but hoped Powell would change his position when he returned to Washington. "I do not know what the policy of the Survey will be after the present fiscal year. It is my impression that decided changes must be made in it, or its existence will be threatened. There is a powerful party both in the House and in the Senate, who appear determined that there shall be a change in the directorship and if this is not done, to cutt [*sic*] off the appropriation."[19]

Walcott summarized politics and fieldwork for a colleague in California:

You doubtless are aware of the present precarious condition of the U.S. Geological Survey, and that it will meet with more or less opposition and danger in the ensuing session of Congress. I fully believe, unless there is a thorough reorganization in the method of administration, there will be greater danger of its final collapse. . . . The Director had also requested me to investigate the Harper's Ferry problem and, also, that of South Mountain, in Pennsylvania as a number of map-sheets, representing these sections, were nearly completed and it was essential that some positive evidence should be obtained of the age and structure of the Blue Ridge and of South Mountain:

so, instead of going to Rochester, or working in my office, I took a team and buckboard, and made a study of the eastern ridges of the Appalachians, from the Susquehana to the Potomac. The result was somewhat disastrous to the views of Frazer, Lesley, and Keith, since I found all of the quartzites belonging to the lower Cambrian, also, an unrecognized belt of limestone, 900 feet in thickness, and two or three series of shales. Two horizons of lower Cambrian fossils were found in the quartzites and two in the limestone. The structure is complicated by sharp folding and thrust faults; and strong cleavage in the quartzites and limestones in many places. . . . I now propose to push forward an exhibit to be made by the Survey at the World Columbian Exposition, to show the stratigraphic succession of the faunas, from the Algonkian to the Quaternary, accompanied by a series of more or less typical rocks. It will be very much such a series as a lecturer on stratigraphic geology would use in connection with a college course, as the space is too limited for a full exhibit. After that is ready, I will to take up the preparation of a memoir upon the middle Cambrian rocks of our continent. At present geologists and paleontologists do not appreciate the extent of this division of the Cambrian.[20]

The display for the Columbian Exposition was finished on time, but the Middle Cambrian study was not to be a Geological Survey activity.

Walcott's interpretation of the ages of the rocks in Pennsylvania and Maryland was correct and has remained unchanged. He did not mention to his correspondent that his discovery of *Olenellus* at Holly Gap before the trip started enabled him to be sure that the fauna was present in the rocks. The hardest single effort for a field paleontologist is finding the first fossil in a particular unit. Once it is established that the creatures are present, a great deal of rock pounding may be needed to make a useful collection, but that is not the same as breaking rock for hour after hour with no certainty that any fossils will be found.

After a week at the office, Walcott had immediate problems resolved, mail answered, and "Spent the day on the Penn. L. Cam fossils. Col Riser, Chief Clerk, dined with me & we talked over Geol. Survey matters" (September 7, 1892). At odd moments, Walcott started on a paper recounting his latest Appalachian discoveries, but mainly he was "At Survey office all day working on plan of organization & estimates from Geol. Survey" (September 11, 1892).

On September 21, the day after the Grand Army of the Republic paraded in Washington, Powell left for Denver as Walcott wrote to Chamberlin:

He is not well & may remain west for a month or more. He retains the same view in relation to my taking time for lectures in Chicago & wishes me to give all of my time & energy to the Survey. As he is putting in the estimates for next year on the basis that I have asked for & one that will put the Survey on a business & scientific basis I cannot consistently ignore his wishes. He has also asked me to assist in getting ready for the investigation committee.[21]

Powell had listened to Walcott, which means that Walcott was a most persuasive talker. Walcott had received all he wanted for the organization, not for himself, and felt honor-bound to stay; what an old-fashioned word is honor-bound. To make administrative changes, Walcott started a routine of half time at the museum and half time at the Hoee Building. Even so, by the end of the month, he "Sent paper on results of work in Penn. & Md. to Prof. Jas. D. Dana" (September 29, 1892). This work (Walcott 1892a) reinforced his efforts in Virginia (Walcott 1892b) on unraveling the Cambrian rocks. Together these are prime references on stratigraphy and major structural geology in the eastern United States, not the sort of effort one associates with a describer of fossils; field mappers have a mind set that paleontologists are not true geologists, yet they did not think that of Walcott.

Walcott returned to office politics in another letter to Chamberlin:

If the Director contemplated resigning he did not manifest it by word or action before leaving here. Mr. King will undoubtedly accept the position if the Major resigns & and it is proffered to him. The western mining men who are fighting Powell have confidence in King & the drift appears to be towards him. My desire is to keep the Survey in as good shape as possible. I have not tho't of the directorship for myself. If those most interested in the welfare of the Survey thought it best to recommend such a course I would then consider it. At present it is not probable from my point of view. If Van Hise were chosen & appointed I would support him most cordially. The estimates for 1893–94 will go to the Secty of the Interior tomorrow.[22]

Walcott worked hard to prepare the budget estimates in so short a time. A post-script to this latest Chamberlin letter is a plaintive "*I wish you were here.*"

In response to a request from his California colleague for some fossils for teaching purposes, Walcott responded:

I wish very much to send you a lot of fossils, but cannot do so at present. Our accommodations are so limited for laboratory work that the duplicates are all packed and stored in the old "Armory" building. My laboratory is full of middle and upper Cambrian fossils, with the exception of some material that is being prepared for the World's Columbian Exposition.

Charles Doolittle Walcott, Paleontologist

> When the Director left for the west, last week, he requested me to do no other work save that of preparing material for the investigating committee, which will meet in November. I have been very busy during the past two weeks in connection with the preparation of estimates for the Survey appropriation for the fiscal year 1893–'94. If these estimates are adopted, without any material change in the wording, the U.S. Geological Survey will be practically reorganized.[23]

Fossils waited; Walcott was now "At Geol. Survey office all day working on data for statement of work of Geol. Survey 1879–92" (September 30, 1892).

In August, while Walcott was in the field, rather than attending meetings in Rochester, he was elected vice-president of Section E of AAAS. This may have been the consequence of his not being present to demur. More likely, it was the doing of H. S. Williams, then current chairman of the section, to honor a colleague and perhaps show support to the floundering USGS.

Just how badly his own activities had been affected, Walcott explained to G. F. Matthew in Canada: "You may have heard of the reduction in the appropriations for the Geological Survey by Congress. The Paleontological branch was much crippled. Of twenty-eight men, who were employed in this branch in 1891, but *seven* remain, and it is probable that the force with be reduced to *five* before the first of January next."[24] The seven included Gentry and a laborer. Several paleontologists were transferred to the museum staff, but the group was shattered.

Both high and low suffered. August Foerste, the Harvard graduate student who found some new fossil localities in the Taconics, was dismissed as a part-time assistant. He went on to teach school and study mid-Paleozoic cephalopods. All part-time professionals were eliminated, and in the turmoil some of the actions were brusk; Walcott tried to sooth hurt feelings and wrote Marsh:

> I do not think that the Director intended that the letter of dismissal should be sent to you as it was, and I cannot conceive after all the support that he has given your work, that he would intentionally place you in such a position. When he was here he was sick and unfit to think of, or transact, business which necessitated recalling matters, or planning for the future. . . . I expect that he will return here the latter part of the month or early in November, when I will speak to him at once about your matter.[25]

Chemistry and physics in the Survey were nearly as bad off as paleontology and went from twelve employees to three chemists and a laborer. Carl Barus, who had been elected to the National Academy of Sciences in April, was fired in August. In later years during one his waggish moments, Frank Wigglesworth

Clarke declared that the Geological Survey kept Steiger because he was the cheapest chemist, Hildebrand because he was the best chemist, and Clarke because he was the chief chemist.

Walcott's annual salary in the USGS had been unspectacular after his first year rise from six hundred to twelve hundred dollars. In September 1882, he received an increase to eighteen hundred dollars; July 1, 1883 he reached the position of "Paleontologist" at two thousand dollars per year. In May 1888, the Geological Survey awarded his back-breaking efforts with an increase to twenty-four hundred dollars. One result of the Irrigation Survey fiasco was Powell appointing Walcott as chief paleontologist in July 1891 at three thousand dollars. This placed an administrative burden on him when he wanted to monograph the Cambrian fossils; it was an astute move on the major's part, and Walcott took on the reorganization of that segment of the agency. Now he was doing the job that former chief geologist Gilbert did, plus preparing data for a major congressional inquiry, and without authority reorganizing the agency, but doing it anyway, still for three thousand dollars.

Reorganization of the USGS was not the only upheaval in sight and the reason for a new home became clear. Walcott took the day off from the office, not even to look at fossils, and was "At home except for taking walks for exercise. At 4:40 P.M. Helena was delivered of a male child. Mother & babe doing well at 9 P.M." (October 2, 1892). The babe was Sidney Stevens Walcott, the second of his children and the longest lived. Important as this personal event was, it was only a pause in his efforts to shore up the agency.

Former director King came to town and Walcott had a long talk with him over USGS matters. Repair efforts continued, with Walcott "at Survey office attending to various matters connected with its work. Spent the evening at the Cosmos Club. Talked over Survey & Major Powell with Dr. Welling" (October 10, 1892). Welling was president of Columbian University and a regent of the Smithsonian Institution, a man who knew what was going on. The next day, Walcott called on Secretary of Agriculture Rusk and met him several evenings that week. When Congress had formed the Weather Bureau in 1890, it was assigned to that department. Congress might well disband the Geological Survey or transfer it from the Interior Department to Agriculture.

Life went on. Sunday Walcott "went out to Zoological Park with Charlie in the morning at home P.M. Sidney two weeks old today. He is growing & keeps well & Helena is beginning to sit up" (October 16, 1892). Walcott reported to Chicago on the boiling political pot:

Charles Doolittle Walcott, Paleontologist

I learn, on what I consider good authority, that if the Director resigns and takes up the Bureau of Ethnology the committee will make the investigation a reconstructive one; still, they will look into the methods that have been pursued and also those that are recommended by leading geologists of the country, and then recommend in their report what they consider to be the true line of administration for the Survey. This is dependent largely upon a consideration that it is to be understood that the Director will turn the Survey over to some other person.

As you stated in a former letter, King is probably the man who will be chosen by the Major. I find that his friends—King, Emmons, Becker, Marsh, and others feel that the Major is in danger and that the Survey will go down with him, if his enemies in the Senate have the opportunity to push forward the investigation in a personal manner. Their remedy is for the Major to resign and turn the Survey over to King. Granting that their first opinion is correct, I find among other leading men here a feeling of uncertainty as to the result if King should take charge. It was well expressed to me by Van Hise last winter when he said he was very doubtful of the outcome. I have recently talked with King; and he will accept the position, if it comes without a fight. Personally, I admire him very much, and feel that no friction would arise in connection with my work; but I fear that he will not stick, if appointed, and get down to hard work and avoid the tendency to make the Survey *what* the Fortieth Parallel Survey was. As a leading scientific man here said of him the other day and of his friends: They never cooperate with any scientific enterprises, pay no attention to the American Association, or mingle with other scientific men or societies.[26]

Walcott touched a number of bases in the volatile politics of the attack on the Survey. "Called on Gardiner Hubbard in the evening. Mr. H. tho't C.[larence] K.[ing] unfit to be Director" (October 17, 1892). As president of the National Geographic Society, let alone all his earlier Washington connections, Hubbard could sway opinion. Enough ugly rumors about King's mining activities were floating around that it was now less likely he would come riding in as a knight in shining armor to save the Geological Survey. "At noon had a talk with Prof. S. P. Langley & G. B. Goode on the Geol. Survey & Bureau of Ethnology" (October 18, 1892). The clerical staff of the USGS had to be disengaged from the Bureau of Ethnology and administering Ethnology was a burden which the Smithsonian Institution simply had to assume.

Columbus Day brought the proof of his *American Journal of Science* article, three weeks after it was submitted; in those "primitive" days of science, publication was far speedier than today. The nurse left, Walcott presented a talk to the Philosophical Society, and at the end of the month, Helena gathered her strength and came downstairs for the first time since Sidney was born. Walcott took a quick trip to the fall meeting of the National Academy of Sciences in Baltimore to look for support for the USGS. Almost continuously, he was "At Survey office during the day attending to various odds & ends connected with preparation of maps, etc. etc." (November 3, 1892). He stole time to work on the Columbian Exposition display and noted the presidential victory of Grover Cleveland. This major political change was among the factors which fortunately delayed the congressional investigation.

Walcott pulled all the strings he could to gain help. He wrote to John C. Branner at Stanford, who was also the state geologist of Arkansas, for advice on reorganization. He did not neglect to add:

> I think you can help us at the present time if you will tell Senator Stanford just what you think of the Geological Survey and the desirability of having it continued. Do you know Senator Felton? I understand that he feels inimical towards the Survey and has criticized both its work and the desirability of continuing it. This has come to me indirectly; but I think it would be well for some one who has the interests of geology at heart to talk with him upon the subject.[27]

Delay of the hearing gave a breathing space. Walcott "Resumed work at Geol. Survey office. A mixture of semi-administrative duty and the preparation of data relating to the work of the Geol. Survey" (December 5, 1892). At odd moments he prepared his manuscript on Grand Canyon volcanics, but it was a small intellectual diversion from troubles. Congress was back and Walcott called on senators and representatives trying to gain support. This was like his old days in Albany when he lobbied the state legislature for James Hall's funds, but the stakes here were much higher. He poured out his worries to Van Hise:

> The Director has not yet returned and I think it is quite probable that he will not be here before December 15. It looks now as though the Investigation Committee might begin its work by that time. There is trouble ahead for the Survey, unless the Director succeeds in over-coming the strong feeling against his administration of the Survey, that now exists in the House and Senate. This is not personal to him out side of a few Members and Senators. There is a wide spread belief that he has used political methods in obtaining appropriations, and been extravagant in the expenditure of them. I think there may be added to this, among a considerable number, a feeling that he has not been fair in his dealing with the scientific men of the country, espe-

cially in relation to the vertebrate paleontology. I should not be surprised if there should be a change of Directorship as a result of the present condition of affairs. When he returns he may be able to counteract the present tendency of things, and I sincerely hope such will be the case. It is very dangerous to undertake to swap horses when you are crossing a bridge.[28]

"Major J. W. Powell returned to the office at 11. A.M. after 2¾ months absence. Reported estimates etc. etc. to him" (December 16, 1892). Walcott also spent most of the next day talking with him; much had been done during the Major's absence. During December, Walcott recorded only part of one day at the museum. Despite the pending hearing, Christmas was pleasant, with Mother and Josie helping to distribute presents:

The year closes with our family well & happy. Mother Walcott, Sister Josie are with us. Helena is getting ready for a short social season. Chas. Jr. & Sidney are growing rapidly and both are well. I am feeling well and working steadily every day at the Geol. Survey office. Major Powell has given me many things to look after in relation to the Survey & the threatened investigation. This prevents my attending to my personal work at the laboratory in the National Museum. The necessity of getting the Survey in shape to commend its work to Congress and to place it in condition to do thorough scientific & economic work is what appears to be the first duty of each & every member of it. (December 31, 1892)

Walcott the child, about age one. *Smithsonian Institution Archives*

Walcott the youth (ca. 1855–70). *Smithsonian Institution Archives*

RES. OF Wᵐ. P. RUST, TOWN OF RUSSIA.

The William P. Rust farmhouse and barn. The house and the barn in the center of the drawing are still in use. From *History of Herkimer County, New York* (1879).

"William P. Rust, Collector U.S. Geological Survey." This photograph was taken in 1889 in Topman's Gulf, Jefferson County, New York, northwest of Utica. The rocks behind Rust are the horizontal shales forming part of the Late Ordovician Lorraine Formation. *U.S. Geological Survey, Denver*

Lura Rust Walcott, about age thirty. *Smithsonian Institution Archives*

Walcott the widower, age twenty-seven. *Smithsonian Institution Archives*

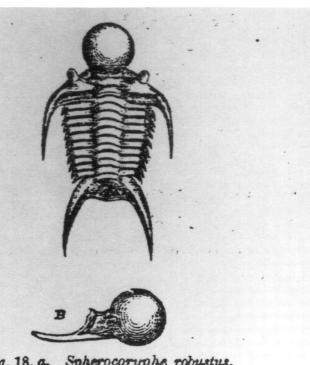

Fig. 18, a. Spherocoryphe robustus.
Fig. 18. b. Spherocoryphe robustus; section of glabella.

Spherocoryphe robustus Walcott, 1875. From C. D. Walcott, "Description of a New Species of Trilobite" (1875) his first publication. The illustration was probably drawn by Walcott.

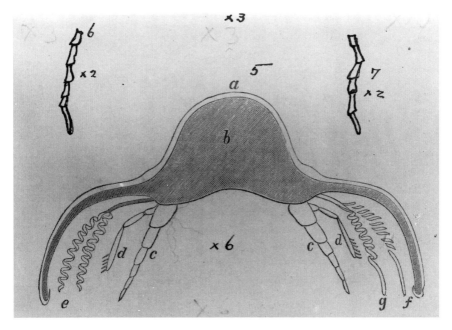

"Transverse section of the thorax of *Calymene serana* partially restored." From C. D.
Walcott, "Notes on some sections of trilobites from the Trenton limestone" (1876).

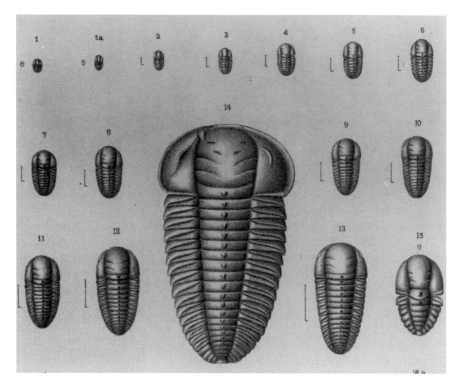

Above. Growth stages of the trilobite *Triarthrus becki.* From C. D. Walcott, "Fossils of the Utica Shale and the Metamorphosis of *Triarthrus becki*" (1879).

Opposite. Exterior of the United States National Museum, currently the Arts & Industries Building just to the east of the Smithsonian Castle. The date is unknown, but it is about the beginning of the twentieth century. Although Washington, D.C., was a segregated Southern city, the Museum was open to all; at least one African American couple may be seen in the foreground. *Smithsonian Institution Archives*

ZEUGLODON
AN EXTINCT WHALE

9469

Fossil display within the USNM, date unknown but after 1896 when the toothed whale hanging in the background was collected and about the turn of the century when bird plumes were still fashionable on ladies' hats. The whale, a turtlelike mammal behind

the table, and a giant ground sloth to the far right are partially or completely plaster models. Specimens of these fossils are currently on display in the Natural History building. *Smithsonian Institution Archives*

"Looking after Paradoxides. Manuel's River, Conception Bay, Newfoundland 1888. Mr. & Mrs. Walcott." Helena on her honeymoon collecting Middle Cambrian trilobites from the rocks above those in which Walcott found *Olenellus*. *U.S. Geological Survey, Denver*

"Charles D. Walcott and Helena B. Walcott at Belmont, New Jersey, August 1896."
Smithsonian Institution Archives

"Eastern Point, New London, Conn., 1897. Mother, Charlie, Sidney, Helen & baby Stuart. Mary Hardy, Agnes." Helena is holding baby Stuart, with Helen beside her. Sidney is on the stool and Charlie sits with his legs crossed. Behind are Mary Hardy, the nurse, and Agnes, the cook; Agnes may be the figure to the right. *Smithsonian Institution Archives*

"Anticlinal fold in sandstones and shales, near base of Upper Silurian; C.[hesapeake] & O.[hio] Canal, 3 miles west of Hancock, Washington Co., Md. From south side of the Potomac, May, 1897." *U.S. Geological Survey, Denver*

"Section of synclinal fold in sandstones and shales, near base of Upper Silurian; C. & O. Canal, 3 miles west of Hancock, Washington Co., Md. C. Willard Hayes sitting on syncline, May 1897." Below Hayes and to the right, the slaty cleavage in the shale is prominent, approximately at right angles to the curved bedding planes of the rock strata. *U.S. Geological Survey, Denver*

"Effect of fire on base of large pine trees, near Tioga Road, Yosemite National Park. C. D. W. on fallen tree. Sept., 1897." *U.S. Geological Survey, Denver*

"Forest on road from Lewis Lake to Snake River station, 1898." The figure is not iden-tified by Walcott, but it must be the patient Helena, who accompanied her husband on this trip. *U.S. Geological Survey, Denver*

"C. D. Walcott, John Wesley Powell, Archibald Geike." This photograph was taken at Harpers Ferry, West Virginia, May 1896, when the director-general of the Geological Survey of Great Britain visited the United States. By this date, Major Powell had been officially full time at the Bureau of Ethnology for two years. *U.S. Geological Survey, Denver*

"Summit of Harney Peak, Black Hills, S. D., Aug. 12, 1897. J. A. Holmes, C. D. Walcott, and Henry Gannett." Holmes became the first chief of the new Bureau of Mines in 1910. Henry Gannett had been placed in charge of the Topographic Branch by Walcott in 1894, and in 1897 he was given responsibility for surveying the boundaries of the new forest reserves. *U.S. Geological Survey, Denver*

Director Walcott at his desk in the Hose Iron Building. In the right foreground and behind him are trays of fossils. On the wall is a geologic map. Date unknown, but probably in the early 1900s. *Smithsonian Institution Archives*

"Teton Mountains, looking westward—Grand Teton left of center. Jenny Lake is at foot of the Grand Teton. Plains in foreground. Jackson Lake would be to the right end of this view. Teton County, Wyoming, 1903." *U.S. Geological Survey, Denver*

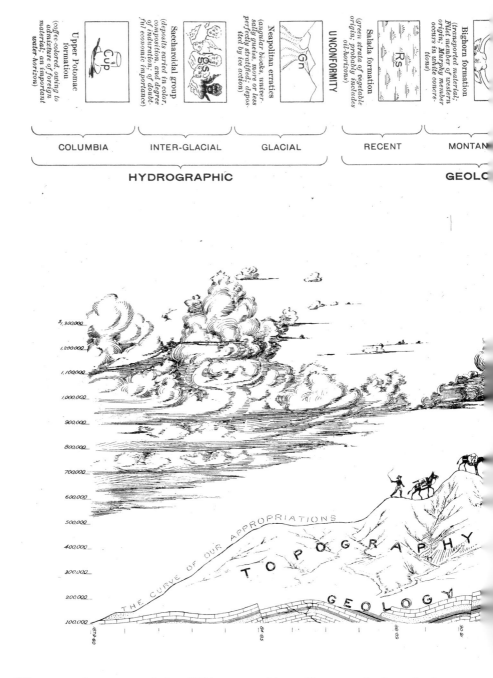

"The curve of our appropriations." This topographic profile accurately charts funding of the U.S. Geological Survey from $100,000 in fiscal year 1879–80 to $1,300,000 in 1903–4. Dollar sums are to the extreme left and years are below. In 1892–93 the Survey mule fell into Congress Canyon (a name used in the Grand Canyon) and was

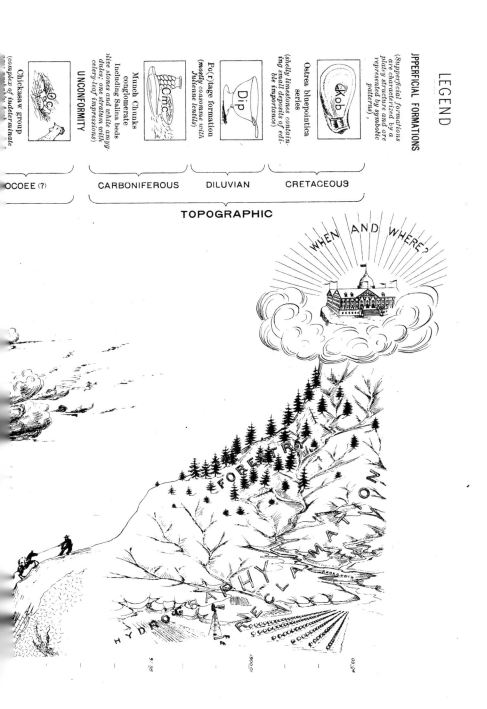

pulled out by Walcott. The break in strata at this point in the depths of the canyon is titled "Whose Fault?" Above the clouds is a dinner menu, divided by branches of the Geologic Survey, with each subdivided in a parody of the geologic time scale.

U.S. Geological Survey Library, Reston, Virginia

"Under the west face of the House Range, Utah, north of Dome Mountain near the end of a long hot march. Sept, 1903." Probably Walcott was behind the camera, F. B. Weeks was driving the buggy piled high with hay, teamster Dan Orr was driving the wagon, and Arthur Brown, the faithful summer cook and winter messenger, was standing at the rear. In a nearly identical picture taken moments later, Arthur Brown has stepped beside the wagon and the dog has moved up near the buggy. *U.S. Geological Survey, Denver*

9

The Director: Administrators Administrate, but Directors Set the Direction (1893–1894)

> Again, because a geologist can see only parts of the features he studies
> and must forever deal with partial information (he constructs geologic
> maps primarily to bring large features down to a comprehensive scale
> at which he can integrate the parts and visualize the whole), it is most
> essential that he be able to visualize, in three dimensions and with
> perspective, processes that may have gone on that will help to
> reconstruct events of the past.
>
> W. H. Bradley, 1963

JANUARY 1, 1893, was stormy and portended a stormy year, as the postponed congressional inquiry was a very real threat. On January 2, Walcott called on Senator Wolcott of Colorado, no relation, a determined foe of the non-economic aspects of the USGS or, at the least, an enemy of Powell, who was to be committee chairman for the impending investigation. Walcott spent many following days "attending to administrative matters under direction of the Director." On January 10 he was back on Capitol Hill and called on Moses Stevens to show him a geologic map prepared by the USGS; he was back several times to speak to other representatives. He and Emmons talked to one of the senators from Wyoming; Emmons had lost a permanent position in 1892 and was no friend of Powell, but he volunteered to assist the Geological Survey. Walcott snatched a few days time for the Columbian Exhibition and "Called to leave maps with Sen. Catchings of Miss. & Judge Oates of Ala." (January 28, 1893). His diary contains a list of senators, as it did when he lobbied for Hall in Albany, fifteen years earlier.

Willis wrote his mother concerning the early geologic folios. "At the Survey I hear indirectly the recognition of the value of the maps in the fight for the preservation of the Bureau. Walcott, who has argued successfully with some of our opponents, has found them his principal weapon and the Director said to me yesterday: 'When we have a hundred of these folios published we will stand on a foundation that cannot be shaken.' It will be ten years before that is accomplished however."[1]

In his *Annual Report,* Walcott noted: "In January I also took charge, under your direction, of a part of the administrative work relating to geology and continued it to the close of the fiscal year" (Walcott 1893a, 253). "At survey office A.M. Wrote Sen. Wolcott respecting Survey appropriations & went up to the capitol to deliver it to him. Left it on his desk in committee room. Returned to Survey office. Prof. O.C. Marsh called to talk on Survey matters" (February 7, 1893). All the while, the opening of the World's Columbian Exposition was approaching and Walcott rushed to complete the display. The intense lobbying efforts with Congress focused when Walcott "went with Major J. W. Powell before Senate appropriations committee" (February 9, 1893). Senator Wolcott wanted to cut funds for topography but was willing to give a small increase for geology.

The fall and winter of 1892 and 1893 marked a struggle, in a sense, between Walcott and McGee, Powell's special assistant, as to who would provide direction to the disorganized organization. In December at the GSA annual meeting, McGee presented a paper for Powell on the role of the Geological Survey in regard to mineral resources, "but the paper was not written by Powell or by McGee, both of whom had a rather florid style. . . . The author may have been C. D. Walcott" (Rabbitt 1980, 215–16). McGee had a rare talent for stirring up difficulties and at the Rochester AAAS meeting in the summer of 1892, he started an argument about the age of early man in North America, involving the USGS in untimely controversy and collecting a few more enemies.

On July 1, 1893, the start of the new fiscal year, McGee left the USGS for the Bureau of Ethnology. McGee was a lightning rod for controversy, no matter where he was located. Among Emmons's papers are typed notes on Survey publications and personalities, including McGee:

> The Director [Powell] gauges men rather on their own opinion of themselves than by that which the experienced geologists would have of them, and as McGee's strongest characteristic is unlimited confidence in his own ability, he has been advanced in a most surprising way, and although possessing undoubted natural ability, through want of control and of balance acquired by previous study and familiarity with the work of older geologists, he has

made many mistakes and brought discredit on the Survey in some case where he represented it. . . . He is a zealous worker, but hasty and impulsive. In his writing he is so fond of using unusual words peculiar to himself, that he becomes unintelligible.[2]

When Powell died in 1902, Ethnologist-in-Charge McGee was not made head of the Bureau of Ethnology, even though according to legend he asked Langley for the position at Powell's funeral while dirt was being shoveled onto the coffin. Langley chose William Henry Holmes to head the renamed Bureau of American Ethnology, and a bitter fight ensued. McGee became ill, and his wife wrote Walcott. "Intimations have come to me recently, from different directions, that reports are being circulated to the effect that Mr. McGee's resignation from the Geological Survey was not altogether voluntary. Also that his geologic work is criticized, on the ground that he published matter which afterwards proved incorrect."[3] She asked Walcott to state the circumstances of McGee's departure. The reply is a note on the bottom of the letter: "Walcott replied in person." A reasonable surmise is that McGee was asked to leave the USGS, though not by Walcott.

In a larger context, it was ironic to have Walcott thrust into a leadership position when factions in Congress were so opposed to esoteric science, as symbolized by paleontology. Of course, paleontology for politicians was equated with vertebrate paleontology. It was hard to see any value in dinosaur bones or swimming reptiles, and "birds with teeth" earned the most scorn; Congress did not foresee the dinosaur craze and commercialization of the 1980s and 1990s. Since Walcott was able to date sequences of fossiliferous rocks, he was not a paleontologist in the sense that others saw Marsh and Cope as the epitome, or perhaps nadir, of the science. In anticipation of the hearing, Walcott had prepared a sterling account of the accomplishments of Survey paleontology.

From a different perspective, the senior geologists were Gilbert, Hague, and Emmons. Gilbert was so happy to leave administration that he had moved to another floor in the Hoee Building. Hague was well respected, but his papers took years to complete and, if that is any indication of reaction time, he could not respond to crisis. Emmons had resisted closing the USGS office in Denver and that had not endeared him to Powell. Other key geologists were Becker and Willis. Becker had professional college training, but he had been long stationed in California and probably did not know the Washington political circuit. Becker also was critical of the major, and if Powell was willing to dispose of Emmons, he equally would not trust Becker. Willis was a little too young and a

Charles Doolittle Walcott, Paleontologist

bit too cocksure to be in charge. Topography was under strong attack, and no topographer would be shifted over to run geology. Viewed from negatives and positives, Walcott was the only scientist Powell could really count on to pick up the pieces.

A measure of the seriousness of the times is that for three Sundays in a row after the hearing, Walcott was writing at the office, not at church. During the days he gathered the lithologic part of the USGS exhibit now that most of the fossils were arranged. His real work was at night, at the Cosmos Club, chatting with those who could help influence Congress or calling at home members of Congress to persuade them the USGS was worth supporting.

Because the investigating committee had not be able to meet while Congress had been adjourned, on February 20, Senator Wolcott indicated there would be no investigation; that session of Congress would be short, ending with the inauguration of President Cleveland (Rabbitt 1980). This announcement was a fantastic relief and a breathing space. Nonetheless, as one might have predicted, the organization now had as many internal problems as those imposed from outside. Geologists could hardly be expected to concentrate on report writing when employment might be terminated at any minute.

Something had to be done to raise morale and Walcott did it in one week. "Called on Major Powell, Sen's Teller & Davis.—At the Senate until 11:00 A.M. & then at the Survey office until 5 P.M. Meeting of geologists to organize Geol. Soc. of Wash-n 4 to 5 P.M." (February 21, 1893). "Washingtons birthday. At the Survey most of the day talking with Major Powell. Attended meeting of Sons of the American Revolution 1 to 2 P.M." (February 22, 1893). That was entertainment to Walcott's taste, for he never really unbent, except maybe when fishing. "At the Survey office during the day. . . . Held a meeting of Committee to organize Geol. Soc. Wash-n. C. D. Walcott S. F. Emmons W. H. Holmes G. P. Merrill J. S. Diller. At home in the evening" (February 23, 1893). "Busy about the Survey office during the day" (February 24, 1893). "Spent much of the day preparing for the organization of the Geol. Soc. of Washin. At 3:00 P.M. those interested met & adopted a Constitution & Standing Rules, after which officers were elected. C. D. Walcott, Pres't. S. F. Emmons & W. H. Holmes vice "s. Arnold Hague Treas. J. S. Diller & Whitman Cross Secy's" (February 25, 1893).

The investigation of the USGS did not occur in part because of the limited time in the short session of Congress, and in part because Walcott turned around criticism with a new plan for the organization; a more general inquiry of the Executive Branch was held by the new Congress (Rabbitt 1980, 223). In the face of the dramatically worsening national depression, the Geological Survey funds were appropriated on the last day of the session, just before Cleveland was inaugurated. Walcott spent that day "Looking up seats for the inauguration 9 to 11. At survey the remaining portion of the day attending to various matters connected with the running of the geological work after July 1'/93" (March 3, 1893).

Powell received more money, but it was mainly for engraving and printing. Twenty-thousand dollars was transferred from topography to geology. Walcott wrote Chamberlin:

> The conference struck out $12000 of geological salaries that the Senate added. If the Director had followed the plan I wished in the Senate Committee I think we would have had from $15000 to $30000 added to the geology. Why he did not I do not know. I gave him reasons from my point of view and from that of members of the House & Senate who were interested in the Survey. As matters now stand Emmons & Becker will be dropped. The two $4000 places will probably go to Hague & Gilbert. Other high places must be made temporary appointments.
>
> Although the Major wishes me to help him in administrative matters of geology & paleontology and may be willing to follow suggestions I do not feel encouraged. At the present time his time & thought is not given to geology but to ethnology & psychology. His attention & grip on the geological survey work appears to be of a sporadic character and a thing to be endured rather that enjoyed. Much as I dislike to think of a change in the administration of the Survey I cannot rid myself of the conviction that it would be best for the interests of science and the people of the United States to have some such person as yourself at the head of the Survey. . . . I feel very much like leaving the Survey & would very soon if it were not for the work I have locked up in it that I wish to complete and the still stronger claim made by men, whose judgement I respect, that I can be of greater service to geologic science by remaining here than in accepting a university position.[4]

Two persistent intertwined myths are that Walcott was handpicked by Powell to be director and that the major spent two years grooming him for the position. These myths do not accord with Walcott's letter to Chamberlin. Despite the major seeming to listen, in the end, he had ignored most of Walcott's advice. Walcott eventually would have the authority to do what he had been doing for months and to do what he was trying to do, but it would nearly two months more before this action even became semiofficial, when he "Took possession of permanent rooms at Geol. Survey office" (April 27, 1893).

These were discouraging times, and no one would blame Walcott if he were to slow down, but after a brief respite at the museum, he was "At the Survey all day talking over plans for Survey work in geology & consulting with men of the Survey about their work. Attended meeting of Geol. Soc. Wash-n. in evening" (March 8, 1893). One would think that the first session of the new society over which he presided would elicit more comment than that. The Geological Society of Washington established a pattern of meeting at the Cosmos Club on the second and fourth Wednesdays of each month during fall, winter, and spring, and has maintained itself for more than a century (Robertson 1993). Some of the local societies founded earlier now have monthly meetings or even only an annual meeting.

The speed in founding this new society shows that Walcott had clearly defined objectives. In 1893, the society functioned well in providing the geologists an opportunity to talk about geology rather than fret over budgets and investigations. Whatever might have been the original reasons for founding this group, it has served as an excellent venue for presentation of new ideas in geology and vigorous discussion of them. If a speaker can survive questioning at a Geological Society of Washington meeting, he can survive in front of any audience.

A few more comments from Willis to his mother help to explain the mood in Washington and why Walcott felt it necessary to push the geologists into a local society to talk about their science: "The topics of chief interest in the Survey are allotments of money for the coming fiscal year and the course Mr. Cleveland may take in regard to the directorship. . . . As to the directorship Powell says he has nothing to fear from Cleveland and he intends to stay. I trust he may."[5] "Major Powell remains Director with the intention of holding his place. Either Mr. Cleveland or a more inexorable ruler, Death, may remove him at any time but he fears neither one nor the other. The talk about a successor has subsided and the old forces continue to run the Survey. I shall not criticize, I am stating facts."[6] "Our helmsman, the Director, is silent and no one knows what course we are steering. He is not yet in touch with the Secretary and Mr. Cleveland and does not know his own future, I imagine."[7]

Walcott continued lobbying, talking with Senator Cary of further work in Yellowstone Park by Arnold Hague, who had been in that area since he completed fieldwork at Eureka, and "Planning work for the next field season Geological— by request of the Director" (March 13, 1893). Two days later, Walcott was in a delegation from the National Geographic Society which called on President Cleveland; ease of access to the White House in those days of small government is mind-boggling. He gave a talk at Johns Hopkins University, worked on his Grand Canyon manuscript, and celebrated his forty-third birthday the end of the month by taking Helena, her aunt Helen Sanford, and sister Josie to the theater. After all, it was because in 1887 Helena visited Aunt Helen at Scanandoa, which is not that far from Utica, that their lives crossed.

The allotments had been made for the field parties in the coming fiscal year. As another positive step, the World's Columbian Exposition display was finally finished:

> The plan is to include a representation of the typical faunas of each geologic terrane (the term "terrane" being used in its broadest sense to include the larger divisions of the various groups—Devonian, Carboniferous, etc.), also an exhibit of some of the rocks of each terrane. As arranged in the Exhibition hall the fossils will occupy open table cases reaching along one side of the room for 100 feet or more, as the assignment of space may determine. Each terrane is to occupy a little more than a square yard of space for the fossils, and the rocks are to be exhibited in a shallow upright case, projecting about one foot above, and extending the entire distance of the table cases at their back margin. Immediately over the line of upright cases a diagrammatic geologic section will present a sketch of the rocks of each terrane from the Archean to the Quaternary inclusive. Over the terranes forming a group a map will show the geographic distribution of each such group on the North American continent as far as the data at hand will permit its preparation. (Walcott 1892c, 139).

It was an ambitious scientific display.

"In April Mr. Stanton went to Chicago and installed the entire collection in the exhibition cases. This collection includes over 2,000 species of fossils represented by upwards of 7,000 specimens, and the rock series numbers between 1,500 and 1,800 specimens" (Walcott 1893a, 254). In describing the proposed display in the earlier *Annual Report,* Walcott emphasized how important the systematic sets of fossils would be for future work of the Geological Survey. When the hammer blow by Congress threatened to destroy this partially completed work, Walcott obtained funds from the exposition to keep Loper engaged and to hire one or two local collectors to obtain needed fossils.

This same busy spring, Walcott wrote two popular articles for *National Geographic Magazine* which were published in mid-July. The first described the Natural Bridge in Virginia, where he and Willis had tramped in 1891 (Walcott

1893b); his photograph of the bridge is a classic. The second discussed his investigations of the Cambrian in Maryland that past fall and put them in the larger context of development of the Appalachian Mountains (Walcott 1893c). These articles came when the USGS needed all the favorable publicity it could obtain and, like the formation of the Geological Society of Washington and the coming display at Chicago, were the most subtle kind of lobbying.

In early April, Walcott took a hurried trip to the Taconic slate belt in eastern New York to investigate several new fossil localities. There was still much uncertainty about even major subdivisions. The previous fall he had written to a New York geologist: "If I were asked to give an estimate of a purely provisional character I would say that about 2,000 feet of upper slates in Washington county may be of *middle* Cambrian age. To the north, in Rutland county, the *middle* Cambrian occurs, if at all, in the great limestone belt beneath the marble. The data I have, however, is too limited to place any satisfactory estimate upon."[8] Without fossils, the mass, or mess, of rock simply could not be understood.

Two weeks later, Walcott "Began to look up data relative to testimony of the sedimentary rocks on the age of N.A. continent. Only a little time as there were many questions in relation to survey work" (April 28, 1893). Walcott's comment on testimony of the rocks introduces the topic of the length of time involved in the earth's geologic processes. Long before the 1890s, most geologists agreed that the biblical interpretation of six thousand years was far too short for the earth to have formed, rocks and fossils deposited, and the surface modified. This discovery of geological time tended to move man out of a central place in nature (Albritton 1980), and it indirectly aided acceptance of the general concept of change through time, evolution. Partly as a result of this concept, Darwin had asked for virtually unlimited time for evolution to pursue its course.

Nevertheless, geologic time of indefinite length was unsettling to some scientists. In particular, William Thompson, later Lord Kelvin, reacted strongly against what he considered wild excess in scientific thought. Using assumptions on formation of the earth and calculations on the rate of cooling, he derived a span of about one hundred million years for the age of the earth, and most geologists tacitly agreed with that figure (Burchfield 1975). Kelvin kept refining his calculations, with each publication reducing the theoretical time span to the point where it seemed impossibly short to the earth scientists. European geologists studied rates of erosion and deposition in an attempt to oppose Kelvin's shorter and shorter estimates of the length of geologic time, centering around one hundred million years as the age of the earth, though assumptions of geologists were no match for the apparent precision of the physicists' formula and calculations.

In January 1893, Clarence King published essentially his last paper, taking data that Carl Barus had accumulated on the melting of certain igneous rocks and using it to derive an age of the earth of about twenty million years. It was an important paper in the sense that King was the first prominent geologist to side publicly with the physicists on a shorter rather than a longer time span. King's work provoked such a negative reaction that the second and third meetings of the new Geological Society of Washington were devoted to criticism of this paper. Having been elected vice-president of Section E of the AAAS in 1892, Walcott was faced with the duty of delivering an address upon retirement from office. This could take any form, but the subject at the AAAS meeting ought to appeal to other scientists and interested amateurs, as well as to sectional members. The age of the earth was a "hot" topic and Walcott decided to pursue it. The investigation was to keep him busy that summer.

In May, Walcott collected another assistant, Charles Schuchert. Schuchert was the ultimate self-made man in American paleontology. He grew up in Cincinnati, but he never even completed grammar school. A father who had a furniture factory and drank heavily, combined with several fires in the factory, forced the youth into the furniture business. In his early teens he was the sole support of his family, and his only diversion from drudgery was collecting the fossils so abundant in the area. James Hall saw Schuchert's collection when he visited Cincinnati in October 1889. As the story goes, Hall tried to have the collection given him as a gift, but when that failed, because the professor had no money for purchase and Schuchert was watching him too closely to allow Hall to steal, the professor offered Schuchert a place in Albany; of course, the collections went with him for Hall. Hall's temperament and treatment of his inferiors had not changed since Walcott's day, and Schuchert survived at Albany for two and a half years. He then worked temporarily in Minneapolis, writing a monograph which came out coauthored by N. H. Winchell.

In 1890 [Walcott] visited Albany for a conference with the Great Oracle. In the course of this visit, Hall expressed the fear his funds would be cut by the State legislature so that he could not retain Schuchert. Walcott then assured him if this should happen there would be a place waiting for him.

Charles Doolittle Walcott, Paleontologist

The appropriation was not cut . . . in 1893 when Walcott . . . needed an understudy to care for the collections, Schuchert was offered the position. (Dunbar 1943, 221)

Despite the dire financial position, Walcott knew the fossil collections had to be cared for and he could not do that while acting for Powell. Walcott had confidence his new assistant could handle routine matters, so he took a new departure with the little time that he had for fossils. "At Survey office during the day & at odd times worked on medusa casts from Middle Cambrian" (June 5, 1893).

A medusa is a form of jellyfish. In 1885, Curtice had found strange lumps in shales of northeastern Alabama. More had been collected and now Walcott was certain, as improbable as it might seem because of the absence of hard parts, that these lumps were casts of jellyfish. If paleontology and esoteric science in general were suspect in Washington, this was surely a foolhardy investigation to pursue. Any congressman who ridiculed studies of birds with teeth would have an oratorical field day with dead jellyfish. Fortunately, the enmity toward the Geological Survey had dissipated and the geologists and paleontologists could go back to doing geology and paleontology, with an occasional dash of a curiosity-driven investigation, a category for the jellyfish.

Walcott's family left for New York state, and he was lonely. A geologist expected to endure solitude when in the field, but family leaving him behind was a different matter. On their fifth anniversary Walcott wrote,

My dear, loved wife, No letter from you to day but then one will come tomorrow. How much I wish that I could be with you and talk over the five happy years that have passed so swiftly, & yet, looking back, they cover a long & eventful portion of the life of each of us. A new life so unlike that which preceded it. A life so full that all that went before is lost in a mist of doubt as to whether it was enjoyed or not. To me the five years have been those in which happiness & contentment have reigned supreme. Small trials have come & gone like bits of clouds over a summer landscape—serving only to outline the greater features. Love has dominated and to day it is the master of the situation. My hope is that as each anniversary comes around the conditions will remain the same except to grow stronger and broader in all its relations & in our relations to each other, our children & those with whom we come in contact day by day. I love you Helena with all my being.[9]

Charlie, as he signed it, went on to some Survey business and chitchat about the heat, but he had poured his heart out in that first paragraph. Perhaps another secret of Walcott's success was that he was a person who, though he might not always express his innermost feelings, was sincere in his convictions. He loved Helena, and that comes through his words; he loved the USGS, and his sincerity had convinced Congress. July 14, 1891, Walcott had become chief paleontologist; now, on July 5, 1893, he became geologist-in-charge of geology and paleontology. The two years of turmoil and increasing paper work had seen his annual salary rise from a munificent three thousand dollars to a dizzying four thousand. If Walcott celebrated, it was by finishing the painting of his roof, a job for the early mornings before the Washington sun blazed.

Actually, Walcott did celebrate by taking a week in mid-July at the New Jersey shore to consider his coming address and to see if jellyfish were tossed on the beach. He stopped at Rutgers University on his return to see W. S. Valiant, who had found a locality between Rome and Holland Patent where trilobites with appendages occurred. Beecher may have mentioned the find to him last December, but Walcott's communications with Utica were good and any number of people could have told him of the discovery. These trilobites had been overwhelmed while living on the sea floor, like the material he had sectioned from the Rust quarry. It was his old friend *Triarthrus becki* with the legs preserved on flattened and flexed specimens; no sectioning was needed.

Walcott hurried to complete his Section E address and the first week in August returned to the Empire State. He collected at the new trilobite locality, paid a quick trip to Rust farm, and met Helena at Rochester. They went on to Chicago and the fair, where Walcott pronounced that "The Exposition grounds & buildings are superb & very creditable to all concerned with the exposition arrangements" (August 13, 1893). The next day it was on to Madison, Wisconsin, and the annual AAAS meeting.

"Flags are floating on the capitol and leading hotels today in honor of the coming of the scientists, many of whom have already arrived, while each train brings additions to the number."[10] For the couple, this was a pleasant meeting, and Vice-President Walcott's talk was well received. The AAAS ended with a day excursion to the Wisconsin Dells, after which the couple returned to Chicago. As an auxiliary to the exposition, the "World's Congress on Geology" had been organized. Chamberlin, now at the University of Chicago, was chairman and Walcott one of the organizing committee for this mini-extravaganza. Walcott spoke on the ancient geographic outlines of North America, amplifying his paper in the twelfth *Annual Report*. From Trenton Falls, on September 7, he sent his Section E address to the publisher. Walcott spent a few days in the Taconic

Charles Doolittle Walcott, Paleontologist

slate belt with Dale and agreed a topographic map was needed for plotting finer details of geology. By mid-September he was at the office, exhausted.

In August, a milestone was passed in that, with the vice-presidency of Section E, Walcott had held his first office in a national scientific society. Although his address has been analyzed nearly to death (Yochelson 1989), a short survey may still be in order. It consists of three parts: a summary of views of various authors on the age of the earth; Walcott's data on the amount of sedimentation in the western United States; and his conclusions. Walcott began realistically: "Of all subjects of speculative geology few are more attractive or more uncertain in positive results than geologic time" (Walcott 1893d, 639). He ended: "In conclusion, geologic time is of great but not indefinite duration. I believe that it can be measured by tens of millions, but not by single millions or hundreds of millions, of years" (Walcott 1893d, 676).

The first step, as with so many of Walcott's projects, was to comb the literature. Most earlier estimates of the duration of geologic time concerned rates of erosion of strata and rates of deposition of recent sediments. Walcott added nothing new in methodology, but he produced the most authoritative set of data ever used for this form of calculation. He reasoned that the region which showed the fewest effects of uplift and erosion would provide the best record. He also reasoned that the more limestone in the total thickness, relative to sandstone and shale, the more complete the sequence would be, which led him immediately to the western Paleozoic rocks. Walcott separated the clastic rocks, shales, sandstones, and conglomerates, from limestones, and compiled the thicknesses of each in different sections, deriving average thicknesses for the region.

Walcott made pertinent observations as to why the sediments were interpreted as deposited in shallow water, were not strongly affected by deposition from any major ancient rivers, and why the sandstones within the section were deposited relatively rapidly compared to those at the base. He considered past climates and past geography, all of which were somewhat speculative, but he did not make any unreasonable assumptions. The information is written in a nontechnical manner and anyone with even a slim knowledge of science can following the reasoning.

Using the data on the thickness of the Paleozoic rocks, he calculated the volume of original sediment. Walcott used what was known of present rates of sedimentation and erosion to deduce the amount of time needed for deposition of the Paleozoic. He hardly mentioned the overlying Mesozoic and Cenozoic, yet he derived the relative lengths of all three in precisely the same ratios used today, which were quite different from the ratios presented by leading textbook writers of the time.

The two principal sources of error are that he did not realize present-day rates of erosion and deposition are atypically fast and, coordinate with that, there are long intervals of nondeposition in rock sequences. Nevertheless, the answer he derived of about one hundred million years for deposition of the sedimentary rock column was squarely in line with the thinking of most geologists and it rested on a solid data base.

Ten years after Walcott wrote, radioactivity was proposed for use as a geologic clock. The first dates derived from radioactive rocks gave numbers in the billions of years, and some geologists reacted against such inordinately large numbers. It was not until about two decades after Walcott published that there was agreement that hundreds of millions of years separated the Cambrian fossils from the organisms of today.

Walcott's talk, with an abbreviation of the historical section, appeared in volume 1 of the *Journal of Geology*, one of Chamberlin's new ventures at his new university. Immediately thereafter, the *American Geologist* printed the paper in full; probably N. H. Winchell heard the talk and asked to publish it. In 1894, it was published again in the *Proceedings* of the AAAS. Finally, the *Annual Report* of the Smithsonian Institution republished. The Smithsonian distributed this widely, and it was also printed as a congressional document distributed by congressmen to yet a different audience.

In all, perhaps fourteen to fifteen thousand copies of this lecture were reproduced in journals and annual reports. Walcott distributed reprints from the journal printings and the Smithsonian *Annual Report*. It is hard to imagine how any English-speaking geologist did not see a copy of the paper or at least know it existed. Withal, there were no comments in the literature, and the paper was hardly cited. One interpretation is that this work confirmed the view of most geologists that geologic time was fairly long and, accordingly, no comment was needed.

With "geologic time" finished, Walcott pursued more practical interests. After a talk with Secretary of the Interior Hoke Smith, he went off with the state geologist of New Jersey and once again found the *Olenellus* fauna where its presence had been suspected but never before discovered (Walcott 1894). Nice as it was to get out of Washington in the beautiful fall weather to break rocks for a couple of days, this only postponed office problems. Walcott "Called on

Charles Doolittle Walcott, Paleontologist

Prof. Langley 4:15 P.M. who wished to speak of Major Powell" (October 2, 1893). The USGS director at this point was a figurehead and simply was not in charge. An objective observer would judge that either he would resign soon or be replaced. Friends were rallying to convince him to resign and avoid the disgrace of dismissal. Powell could devote his career to the Bureau of Ethnology, where McGee would handle the administrative burden. Langley was a friend, and when he dined with Powell the secretary cut up the food on the plate for the one-handed veteran.

In mid-October, Walcott left Washington for a quick week's swing through eastern Pennsylvania with Wanner, covering the area between the Susquehana and Delaware Rivers (Walcott 1894a) but concentrating around York. October 23, six days after returning to the office, Walcott wrote up the results of his latest investigation, which were published in January. Although the paper is only three pages long, and his remarks on Green Pond Mountain in New Jersey, which came out in April, is only five pages long, these are fundamental papers. The *American Journal of Science* had done well in speed of printing.

As the result of his work from 1889 onward, Walcott could write with some pride that he had confirmed by stratigraphic paleontology that the sandstones from Alabama to Vermont "were all deposited in lower Cambrian and that they contain the characteristic Olenellus fauna throughout their geographic distribution" (Walcott 1894a, 40). He had put a base on the Paleozoic along the entire length of the Appalachian Mountains and distinguished the true Upper Cambrian Potsdam Sandstone from the older sandstone unit. Almost invariably in the basal sandstones the fossils are rare scraps, because the high energy environment in which sandstone is deposited is not conducive to good preservation and require a diligent collector.

His was a major accomplishment, for the position of the *Olenellus* fauna affected interpretation of the limestone sequence of the Shenandoah Valley and its topographic equivalents to the north. If the sandstones were "Potsdam," or Upper Cambrian, the overlying limestones were "Trenton," or Ordovician in age. In fact, much Cambrian and Ordovician time was represented in these limestone deposits. "The superjacent limestones carry the Olenellus in their lower portions, in northern and southern Vermont, eastern New York, New Jersey and Pennsylvania. To the south of Pennsylvania the lower portions of the limestones appear to be represented by shales, and the upper and middle Cambrian faunas are found in the lower half of the Knox dolomite series of Tennessee" (Walcott 1894a, 40). This was a powerful generalization, confirmed by a century of ever more detailed investigations. Walcott pointed out the difficulty in drawing the boundary between Cambrian and Ordovician in this great limestone sequence, another prescient remark.

Walcott's body caused trouble, and he was back at the dentist, but hardly paused in his activities. He saw Secretary Smith, and "Major Powell returned from west A.M. Busy attending to survey matters with him during the day" (October 28, 1893). He briefed Powell on what had transpired during his long absence and, because travel money was still available, went back into the field. November 1, Walcott met Arthur Keith in Knoxville. Both the rocks below the sandstones with the *Olenellus* fauna and the overlying limestones were continuing to cause difficulties for the mappers. Age determinations were needed. They spent two weeks, a significant portion of it hammering in the rain.

Walcott showed his political acumen on this trip. He returned home via Atlanta, where he called on state geologist, J. W. W. Spencer. Secretary Smith, a new political appointee in Washington, was from Atlanta. Through the state geologist, Walcott saw the governor and spent two days meeting members of the legislature. It was subtle and it was a shrewd way to have someone tell Smith what nice folks were on the Geological Survey.

Walcott got back to his office November 18 and cleaned up accumulated matters in short order. Meanwhile, the fossils he had collected in August were burning a hole in his pocket and he "Took up study of trilobites from Rome, N.Y. in addition to ex—[executive] work" (November 22, 1893). That idyll did not last long, for a severe cold developed into "la Grippe." Confined at home, Walcott "Began writing a paper on intraformational conglomerates" (December 8, 1893). Although he was sick and rushed for time, neither factor is evident in the paper.

In science, the solution of one problem almost always gives rise to another. Walcott had found that a great thickness of limestone in the east was older than had been thought, and noticed something most peculiar about them compared to the younger limestones. The eastern Tennessee field trip with Keith crystallized his thinking: "He took me to exposures of Knox limestone showing sandstone containing limestone pebbles resting on limestone" (November 8, 1893). The question was the meaning of the limestone pebbles in the sandstone. At the December GSA meeting Walcott was listed on a paper as "By title only," a phrase conventionally used to tell the geologic public that a subject was under active study a publication would be forthcoming. This one came out in February 1894:

Usually, the presence of a conglomerate in a stratigraphic series of rocks is a matter of considerable importance to the geologist. He naturally infers the

presence of a break in the continuity of sedimentation; an orographic movement of greater or lesser extent; erosion of a prëexisting formation. He sees,
in his mental review, the waves sorting and depositing sand, pebbles, and
bowlders [*sic*] derived from the uplifted land. The idea of the lapse of a period of time of considerable and often long duration is formed as he recalls
orographic movement, erosion and unconformity of deposition. If the conglomerate is near the base of some formation or series of formations, he
views it as almost conclusive evidence of the marked change that introduced
the new deposit. This is all fair induction from observed facts, and it is the
general and approved experience of geologists. (Walcott 1894b, 191)

That statement still applies.

What Walcott had observed was quite remarkable. The older limestones contained conglomerates composed of limestone pieces with the same fossil biota
above and below the conglomerate. These "intraformational conglomerates,"
Walcott's new term, thus did not indicate great time breaks in deposition. This
was a phenomenon not previously noted and one contrary to experience with
the more conventional conglomerates. Walcott also emphasized the occurrence
of limestone fragments of all sizes in shales, like the huge chunk he had collected
from in the conglomerate at Levis, Quebec:

> The relation of the bedded limestones to the superjacent conglomerates
> proves that the calcareous mud which was subsequently consolidated into
> the limestones solidified soon after deposition. This is shown by the presence
> in the conglomerate of rounded pebbles and angular fragments of limestone
> with sharp clear cut edges. The presence of the conglomerate above the lime-
> stone beds, from some portion of which they were derived, leads me to be-
> lieve that the sea-bed was raised in ridges or domes above the sea level and
> thus subjected to the action of the seashore ice, if present, and the aërial
> agents of erosion. (Walcott 1894b, 197)

He had part of the problem right in demonstrating rapid consolidation of limestone and the extreme shallow water aspect of subsequent erosion. The present
view of these vast lime-depositing seas is that the limestone was deposited in
extremely shallow water, from a few inches to a few feet. Mud flats exposed to
drying by low tides would crack and the fragments could be moved by storms.

Large boulders and slabs were a different aspect of the intraformational conglomerates. The notion of sea ice was wrong but was the only mechanism then
known for transporting boulders to exotic locations. A concept has developed
in marine geology of an earthquake-triggered slump sweeping down a slope
carrying boulders in a slurry of mud. Walcott was studying the steep outer

edge of the lime mud bank where processes occurred of which no nineteenth-century geologist could be aware. Conglomerates around York, which Walcott illustrated, eventually led to the interpretation of these strange Lower Cambrian rocks as falling off the edge of the continental shelf (Rodgers 1968).

Near the middle of the month, the still-sick Walcott lurched back to the office and caught up on paperwork. At the Geological Society of Washington annual meeting, he was reelected president. After half a day looking at fossils, he was once more on a train. The lawyer Ed Hurlburt in Utica was in financial straits, along with the difficulty he was causing Walcott trying to settle Rust's estate. With USGS problems, Walcott did not need several years further aggravation to resolve a simple boundary line. He hurried home to become another sick member of a sick household. Christmas was quiet. The last week of the year was busy as a result of two trips to the office of Secretary Smith, combined with work at the Survey and at the museum.

The last day of the year, Walcott spoke with Chamberlin at the Cosmos Club. Having failed to recruit Walcott as a permanent faculty member, Chamberlin persuaded him to be a nonresident member of the faculty as professor of paleontologic geology. For two years, he, along with Van Hise of Wisconsin and William Henry Holmes, were listed as members of the department. As the stipend for a couple of weeks of lectures, Walcott was to receive five hundred dollars, a substantial addition to his government salary. However, "on account of the persistent ill health of the Director of the U. S. Geological Survey, Professor Walcott, who has been practically directing the affairs of the Survey during the Director's illness, will not be able to [give] the course of instruction contemplated without injustice to the survey."[11]

Walcott's summing up for 1893 is curious. He noted that the family was recovering, but the country was in difficulty and "the times are 'hard' for poor & rich." However, his biggest concern was that Hurlburt may have been dishonest. Personal loyalty was a prime concern. There is not a word concerning Walcott's struggles with Congress, his promotion, or any scientific matter.

New Year's Day was devoted to formal calls. Walcott saw Secretary Smith, Vice-President Stevenson, and a few friends. Most of January was strictly business, although Whitman Cross dined with the Walcotts several times. The middle of the month Secretary Smith directed Walcott to meet with Indian commissioner Daniel M. Browning. The Indian Territory, now part of Oklahoma, was becoming a plum for settlement, and perhaps the USGS could find a niche in that region. He spent in a day at Johns Hopkins talking to W. K. Brooks about jellyfish fossils (Benson 1987).

Charles Doolittle Walcott, Paleontologist

Life became more complicated by month's end when Chamberlin would not take no for an answer. He wrote that if Walcott moved to Chicago, supplementing the directorship of a department at the brand new Columbian Museum (now the Field Museum), the University would pay one thousand dollars for a twelve-week lecture and laboratory course arranged so as not to interfere with his other duties: "You know so much about the situation that I do not think it necessary to write elaborately about it. We have our hearts set on your coming."[12] Chamberlin had engineered this offer after their meeting in Washington, and, for Walcott's interests, it was even more of a tempting offer to join to a new museum than the faculty of a new university. Walcott "Called on Major Powell & Dr. Bartlett A.M. to talk over my going to Chicago. At Survey P.M. Told Mr. Skiff that I could not accept his proposition" (January 30, 1894). This opportunity to leave Washington was very much a moral dilemma, for otherwise why would Walcott have gone to his minister, relative or not, for advice?

Walcott ended January by calling on Secretary Smith. Next Walcott was "At Geol. Survey during the day. Called on Sect'y Smith at 1 P.M. to convey message from Major Powell" (February 1, 1894). Walcott as go-between and mediator was not a new role for him and apparently he handled it well; recall Whitfield and Hall in Albany. This form of communication is not the best way to run a government bureau. Meanwhile, there was a change of heart about Chicago; it would be nice to know what message Powell transmitted to Smith and whether it caused the change. Chamberlin wrote: "I was very gratified to receive your letter of some days since indicating a preliminary acceptance of a directorship in the Columbian Museum. I sincerely hope it is for forerunner of a permanent relationship."[13]

Skiff offered to pay his expenses for a trip to Chicago. Walcott suggested that he should examine some museums in route; Walcott never wasted time or opportunity when traveling. The university asked that he look at Pumpelly's library with an eye toward its purchase. He went to Chicago via New York City and thence New Haven. At Yale, Walcott had a meeting with the aging Marsh and for the last time with Dana. He discussed *Triarthrus* with Beecher and saw his old friend Williams at his new position. At Newport, Walcott examined Pumpelly's library, and he looked over Hyatt's collections in Boston. At Cambridge, Walcott talked to the faculty members, most of whom had been employed part time by the Geological Survey. Walcott paused in Albany and Rochester and arrived at Chicago on March 5.

Walcott spent five full days in Chicago. He spent most of his time at the Columbian Museum, and several evenings he dined with his Eureka tent mate Iddings. The trip was a triumph, and he impressed one and all in Chicago both personally and with his grasp of museology. On his return, he touched at Rochester and at Utica to check on friend Hurlburt, who was ill. Though Ed had failed him, Walcott was still loyal.

Chicago was such a temptation that Walcott almost succumbed, "almost" being the significant word. Chamberlin wrote:

> I have been thinking over and over an idea that came into my mind as to the result of your suggestion regarding the giving of part of your time to the Columbian Museum and the rest to your work in Washington. This did not impress me favorably as a permanent arrangement, but in thinking upon it, it occurred to me whether it might not meet the several phases of the situation if you were to propose to give as large a fraction of your time as you can to the Museum for the coming year, beginning with your next visit or with the first of May as you please, with the understanding that it is an arrangement simply for the year, leaving the future arrangement for later determination.[14]

Chamberlin kept trying to convince Walcott, though fortunately using shorter sentences: "I was at the museum (Columbian) [the university had the Walker Museum] the other day and things seem to be moving along briskly. You created the impression of being a hustler, and I think you made a very visible impression upon the proceedings."[15] Not one to quit when the issue was still in doubt, he later asked, "Can you give me your latest thought with reference to what university work you would be able to do in case you should accept the position at the Museum?"[16]

On April 21, Chamberlin wrote that the museum should open in May as planned. There is little question but what Walcott could have moved his fossils to Chicago, and could have retained a formal connection with the Geological Survey, as Chamberlin had for years. Ultimately, it all came down to the point that if Walcott left, the USGS would be in grave difficulty. Loyalty to organization won out over both personal gain and greater freedom for research. This might be the place for a noble statement, but Walcott's decision is eloquent enough.

Major Powell's political difficulties were now compounded by physical ailments, and the rumor mills were running. Only a couple days after his return, Walcott was back to calling on senators and congressmen, in addition to the day-to-day affairs of the Geological Survey. Despite all this, somewhere he had found time to write up his research results, and on March 24, he gave two papers to the Biological Society of Washington, skipping from the lowly jellyfish to the lovely trilobite.

The material on the Middle Cambrian medusoids can be considered later, but the short paper on trilobites deserves comment. Just as an aside, the same paper was published twice. Because there are matters of classification and priority, the date is important. On March 30, 1894, the paper appeared in the *Proceedings* of the Society (Walcott 1894c). Walcott had sent a manuscript to the *Geological Magazine* in London, where it was published in May. That journal had several sections in each issue for "Recent Literature," professional news, and so forth. Walcott's paper was published under "Original Articles"; the joke, such as it is, was on the British.

Trilobites were very much of a puzzle in regard to their position within the zoological kingdom. Systematists look at similarities and differences among various living and fossil forms. Once they determine that several forms are distinct from each other, they then study possible interrelations among these different forms, trying to clarify the degrees of similarity and difference. The higher the level of distinction, the less likelihood there is of concurrence of views, especially in the early stages of study of a group of animals or plants.

The soft tissues which interest many zoologists are almost never preserved in a fossil. Accordingly, paleontologists and zoologists are more likely to talk at one another than to one another. Yet another fundamental problem is that the closer one looked at organisms, both living and fossil, the more complicated become the relationships. Darwin's concept of evolution set some systematists scurrying around looking for "natural" relationships among groups, rather than old-fashioned artificial relationships. Classifying whales with fish is artificial; putting them with other mammals is natural. "Artificial" and "natural" tend to change over time as different investigations come up with varying notions as to which features are more significant than others.

There are more kinds of arthropods than all other kinds of animals combined; there are almost as many forms of living beetles as there are all other animals. Arthropods are animals with jointed limbs, and by the last half of the nineteenth century, paleontologists and zoologists concurred that even though limbs were not known, the trilobites probably were Arthropoda; where they were to be placed within the Arthropoda was another question. Although

Billings described scraps of legs in 1870, most people did not accept his findings. The proof that trilobites had jointed legs, and therefore were Arthropoda without question, did not come until 1876 when Walcott described the thin-sections he had cut at Trenton Falls. His 1881 paper was the definitive work on trilobite limbs and gills, for he had virtually all the material in the world on the appendages. The contributions which Walcott made in the field of paleozoology tend to be overlooked when compared to his stratigraphic investigations, but they were significant.

A prime morphologic feature for subdivisions within the Arthropoda is the structure of the jointed limbs. From the time that Walcott first began cutting sections through the trilobites, he was concerned about details of the leg segments and he changed his mind several times as new sections provided better data. Later, he compared his material with the appendages of living arthropods. In his 1881 paper, Walcott's general conclusion was that fossil trilobites formed an order and that fossil eurypterids, and living (*Limulus*) and fossil horseshoe crabs, formed two other more closely related orders all within a class Poecilopoda; this class name was not original with Walcott. The three orders, in two subclasses, were all to be associated near but not directly with the class Crustacea; shrimps and lobsters are delicious representatives of crustaceans.

Eminent French zoologist and doyen of crustacean studies M. H. Milne Edwards prepared an eighteen-page summary of trilobite studies and devoted fourteen pages of it, with three plates, to details of Walcott's 1881 paper. He emphasized the importance of this contribution and extolled its virtues. He added a long critique on the morphology of eurypterids, horseshoe crabs, crustaceans, and other arthropods, and ended with his own views on their interrelations: "Un groupe composé des Trilobites, des Limulus et des Euryptères, serait, à mon avis, complètement artificiel et inadmissible dans une classification zoologique naturelle" (Milne Edwards 1892, 33). The arrangement Walcott suggested was "artificial," not the way the relations were supposed to be nature. From the time of Walcott's earlier 1881 work, zoologists continued to describe living arthropods, but there were no major changes in high-level classification.

The specimen with limbs Walcott described in 1884 from Cincinnati merely added another genus to those he had studied. Less than a decade later, the material from near Rome provided exciting new detail. Columbia College had bought some specimens, about the same time that Walcott collected in 1893. W. D. Matthew, a graduate student, described antennae, not previously known to be a feature of the trilobites. This Matthew was the son of G. F. Matthew, the New Brunswick geologist, and had a distinguished career in vertebrate paleontology (Colbert 1992).

Beecher obtained other specimens from Rome and wrote two short papers in 1893, one describing a larval stage and a second a preliminary description of the limbs. Beecher wrote many more papers on this material, so that the locality became known as Beecher's trilobite bed; Valiant, who found it, was forgotten. Beecher's tentative conclusion in 1893 considered trilobites to be crustaceans, or at least closely allied to them, at variance to Walcott's view.

Classification is based on a Linnaean hierarchy. Species fit within genera, genera within families, families within orders, orders within classes, and classes within phyla. Study of nature's complexity began with the living flora and fauna. The more the recent organisms were investigated, the more complexity was revealed. Linneaus had four phyla and this number had more than doubled by the time Walcott began writing on trilobites. It continues to grow at an irregular rate. Paleontologists came late to the scene in terms of major classification. Although many extinct species and genera had already been described, it was generally assumed that most fossils were to be placed within the higher-level groups—often families and orders, but always classes—that the zoologists had already established. Another century would elapse before paleontologists began to seriously discuss classes and phyla based entirely on extinct organisms.

What Walcott did in a few pages was to compare the general form and limbs of *Triarthrus becki* with those of the trilobites he had described earlier. He remarked on the great diversity within the trilobites, and given the limited amount of data from trilobite limbs, this was a grand generalization. Others saw close similarity to the living crustaceans, but Walcott declared, "I am not yet prepared to abandon the position taken in 1881, that all these groups should be arranged under one class and not as an appendage to the Crustacea, as proposed by Dr. Lang. . . . I would go still further, and form a class of the Trilobita and one of the Merostomata" (Walcott 1894c, 93–94).

The word "class" was used in the sense of a major group, more important than an order and just below a phylum. Walcott was clear in stating that trilobites (and merostomes—eurypterids and horseshoe crabs) were as different from the Crustacea as Insecta were from Arachnida (spiders to the uninitiated). This was a significant change in classification and conceptually a great leap forward. Walcott added two major subdivisions to the Arthropoda, one of which (trilobites) was completely extinct and the other (merostomes) with only one living representative. Walcott may not have been the first to delineate a class based entirely on fossils, but he certainly was among the first.

It would be nice to report that other paleontologists and zoologists agreed, but classification is a matter of opinion and taste. Shortly thereafter, trilobites were considered by the textbooks, the ultimate authority on classification, as a subclass, and Beecher's view that they fell within the Crustacea prevailed. It was not until well into the twentieth century that Class Trilobita was generally accepted, but even that belated recognition paved the way for recognizing other extinct classes and even extinct phyla. It was as fundamental to paleontology as Walcott's determining the base of the Cambrian near Balcony Falls, Virginia, a few years earlier, was to stratigraphy. Unfortunately, except for identification of specimens to confirm the age of a rock, this was to be Walcott's last work on trilobites for a long time.

To leave the trilobites now, one Sunday, the family took a ride on the new electric trolley to Glen Echo. That was the biggest excitement recorded for the month of April, except that on the last day of the month Clarence King dropped in to see Walcott, and returned two days later. As May began, Secretary Smith had a talk with Walcott. Walcott wrote that the "Major is not well. He wishes me to take charge of the Survey" (May 4, 1894). This was the first indication in Walcott's diary of Powell's future aims. Walcott went back to consult with Smith. On May 8, Director Powell submitted his resignation. Gilbert hastened to write Dutton. "I am sorry to say that Major Powell's health has gone from bad to worse, and he has at last given up his work. He sent his resignation to the Secretary yesterday. This is for the present confidential, but will probably be in the papers by the time my letter reaches you. I suspect that the coming man is Walcott, who has done much administrative work during the past year and shown himself efficient."[17]

Walcott was "Studying law relating to the Geological Survey. Called on Senator Teller in the evening" (May 10, 1894). For once events moved swiftly in Washington. "At Geol. Survey all day, The president sent nomination as Director of Survey to the U. S. Senate. Major Powell resigns to take effect July 1 '94" (May 11, 1894). Chamberlin wrote, "Your note is at hand. The outcome is clearly foreshadowed and I congratulate you on the coming honor, and predict a brilliant success for you."[18]

Gilbert wrote, "Friday his [Powell] resignation was accepted and Mr. Walcott was nominated as his successor. The next day the lunch mess invited all the older members of the Survey and chiefs of division, making an assembly of 48 persons, to bid *bon voyage* to the Major who is to go to Baltimore for a surgical operation on his arm. There were a number of speeches, and the occasion was very impressive."[19]

There was some gossip, not all with Chamberlin's enthusiasm. Emmons quoted to Becker remarks he had received from King:

> Meanwhile Hoke [Smith, secretary of interior] has put in Walcott and really I hardly know what else he could do, for the men who know any geology are all dismally unfit to grapple with the populist Congressmen and that is the paramount need. Walcott has no education, & knows little geology, but he is staying and has the confidence of a government mule. If his stomach does not revolt at the smell of a Congressman and he has the American "Get There" quality—If he will not be jealous of the superior abilities of Becker and Emmons but give them any opening, he can make a record.[20]

In contrast, Iddings, writing from Chicago to his fellow petrologist Cross, was unrestrained. "Whoop-ee!! Three cheers for the U.S.G.S.! Something has surely dropped. Hurrah for C.D.W.! and the rising generation. '*Business before pleasure*' will now be the motto for the Geological Survey."[21]

Walcott immediately took charge of all the bureau efforts. He talked to Secretary Smith, lunched with Langley, and attended a farewell dinner for William Henry Holmes, who had decided to cast his lot with the Columbian Museum. "The U. S. Senate confirmed my nomination as Director of U. S. Geological Survey" (May 28, 1894). Walcott took the oath of office on June 30th, but he had already instituted some sweeping changes.

Biographers of Powell pass swiftly over the years between the demise of the Irrigation Survey and Powell's resignation. If nothing else, the major showed grim determination as he hung onto his office. In this he blocked early attempts to return King to the directorship. He also prevented any great groundswell of support for a scientist outside the USGS to assume control of the agency. Some geologists both within and without the organization did not like him, but his integrity was respected. No geologist wanted to appear to be moving in and thereby provoke a fight with the feisty major. In contrast to the custom of later administrations, Powell did not resign when Cleveland took office; he hung on. As awkward as it was for Smith to have Powell as director, to fire a wounded veteran who had explored the last unknown river in America and still had the support of much of the scientific community would have been even more politically awkward for Cleveland. The salary of the director had been fixed at six thousand dollars, but during 1894 Smith arranged for legislation to reduce it to five thousand. In April, Powell testified in favor of a bill transferring the Geological Survey to the Department of the Agriculture. Whether these two items are interrelated is inconsequential. Somehow between mid-March and the end of April, Powell and Smith reached an accommodation.

Not by any stretch of the imagination was Walcott heir apparent to Powell. He was invaluable as geologist-in-charge of geology and paleontology, but his duties were circumscribed. Walcott was quite interested in the Columbian Museum position. If in January he seriously thought he would be USGS director, Walcott would not have planned a trip to Chicago. If in early March, he thought that he would follow Powell, Walcott would not have proposed part-time effort in Chicago and part-time effort in Washington. Who can say what might have been whispered at the Cosmos Club or Capitol Hill early in 1894, but Walcott never openly campaigned for the office. The closest to any political activity were Helena's tea parties.

Walcott sacrificed much to remain with the Geological Survey. He would have had more time for research at the Columbian Museum. Teaching at the University he would have had students and, knowing Walcott, they would have worked on aspects of lower Paleozoic faunas and stratigraphy in segments of a master plan to provide all the necessary geological details. His children would have been close to grandparents. There was one other twist of fate. In Congress Cannon pointed out that the salary cut was designed to encourage Powell to leave, but that a new man was coming in as director. Logic dictated that he should get six thousand dollars, but economy in government, not logic, prevailed. For several years, Director Walcott worked for the salary he would have received in Chicago. More personnel problems, more paper shuffling, and virtually no time for research were the fruits of Walcott's decision to continue to assist Powell for another year after the disappointment of 1893. Loyalty to organization is the only explanation to Walcott becoming the USGS director.

Powell did not have his arm amputated at Johns Hopkins University Hospital. The doctors removed part of a nerve and trimmed the rough and ready surgery done earlier. Inside a week he was released and his library was then moved to the Bureau of Ethnology (Rabbitt 1980). On June 9, the major and Walcott called on President Cleveland. For the next eight years, Powell receded further and further from the affairs of the USGS.

Walcott's appointment received good newspaper publicity when it was announced. Half a dozen major papers had a favorable story on the USGS and Powell's western exploits. The Hoee Building was near Washington's "Rotten

Row," where most of the newspapers were located. Just as Walcott during the years courted members of Congress, especially when he did not need them, he courted the reporters. Lessons learned in Albany under Hall, or rather by watching what that man did wrong, paid off and continued to be of great service. Walcott wasted no time. The same day he was at the White House, Walcott suspended A. H. Thompson, Powell's brother-in-law, as head of Topography and placed Henry Gannett in charge. "Attending to many & diverse matters at Survey. Will have many matters cleared up by July 1"" (June 23, 1894). Walcott took the oath of office on Saturday June 30 and now had the authority to do what he had already accomplished in his reorganization.

It was a strange time for Walcott and family. At Sudley Spring on the new Tenleytown Road trolley a colony developed to escape the heat and humidity of Washington. They had a room and two tents, and director-designate Walcott lived in a tent. How bizarre to spend the evening at the Cosmos Club and then take the streetcar home to a tent. Washington has changed!

Early in July, Helena and the boys left for Rochester. The new Director was sanguine. "I had some trials in reorganizing, but am now looking forward to a few months of comparative quiet after Congress adjourns. The Secretary of the Interior is strongly interested in the Survey and is supporting it in every way."[22] The Geological Survey was out in the field where it should be, and once Congress left Washington, the director could return to his role as geologist. A week later, Walcott suffered a political setback: "Committee on Public Lands voted not to have Survey do work on Public Land surveys" (July 16, 1894). One can be too sanguine. Walcott lobbied to no avail, got in a few hours with his Cambrian fossils, and took a long weekend at Asbury Park. In early August, Walcott had his first victory in Congress. Money for topographic mapping was cut, but a new responsibility and additional funds were provided. The USGS Survey was to gauge streams and determine water supply, including artesian and other underground water, implying that Walcott would not repeat the mistakes of Powell.

Fortunately Walcott had exactly the right person for the job. In 1888 the hydraulic engineer, F. H. Newell had been hired and he had trained young men for the Irrigation Survey in the methods of measuring stream flow. When the Irrigation Survey was wrecked, Newell was assigned to the Census of 1890, and then tucked away in a tiny hydrographic section among the USGS topographers. Now he was ready for serious effort, and almost his first act was to pick Arthur Powell Davis, the major's nephew, as his assistant. This was not merely the old boy's network in action for Walcott, Newell, and Davis were to make a remarkable team in the future.

The Geological Survey was alive and functioning. The nature of Walcott's achievement is shown by contrast to the situation in the Coast Survey, which had also been under attack. F. W. Clarke, the chief chemist with a facile tongue, is remembered as saying, "The government will spare neither time nor expense in the pursuit of economy," and that certainly applied to the gutting of the Coast Survey under the first Cleveland administration. This time around, in 1894, Superintendent T. C. Mendenhall retired because of ill-health and was replaced by a political appointee. Employees were dismissed or demoted more or less at whim. The comparison reinforces what a miracle Major Powell performed in stubbornly surviving from 1890 to 1894.

In mid-August, Walcott went to the AAAS meeting in New York City and stuck another newspaper clipping in his diary. It was titled "A contented man." He then went on to his brother-in-law in Rochester. "With Holmes B. Stevens examined some real estate of the estate of M. B. Holmes. Writing part of the day & attending to correspondence. At 5:25 P.M. Helena gave birth to female child. A fine vigorous baby. All quiet at 9. P.M." (August 20, 1894). The new father did show emotion, for the first "P.M." is scrunched in, forgotten until he had completed the entry for the day. The little girl was named Helen Breese.

A week later Walcott was back to the business of geology. Between trains to Granville he called on Hall and on Hurlburt. "Out all day on Cambridge Atlas sheet with Mr. Dale. Found fossils at critical points and verified geologic boundaries" (August 31, 1894). Walcott's earlier work in the area held up well in the light of more detailed investigations. He found an unusual fossil known from Great Britain but not previously found in North America (Walcott 1894d).

Walcott took the steamer down the Hudson and the train to Washington. "Busy at Survey office attending to various duties. Called on Sect'y of Interior 3 P.M. approved on my going west. Also settled the editorship question by approving of dropping Mr. Croffut & spent the evening at Camp Sudley" (September 4, 1894). Thereafter all ran smoothly in the USGS printing rooms. Four days after official approval for the western trip, Walcott was in Rochester bidding farewell to Helena, the two boys, and infant Helen.

In Chicago, Walcott called at the University and was late for his train connection. With the extra time, he "Wrote letters & dictated note on Survey work for Geol. Journal" (September 15, 1894). The journal editorialized on the need for work on road construction materials and the part the USGS could play. This was a clever initiative at this time in the country's development. In December 1893, a petition of 150,000 names, on a roll seven feet in diameter, was presented to Congress asking for a roads department; Walcott was on top of the trend.

Charles Doolittle Walcott, Paleontologist

At Denver, Walcott met Emmons, consulted with Newell, and sent F. B. Weeks, a junior employee, westward to obtain a camp outfit. Walcott and Emmons spent a few days in nearby mining camps. The newspapers gave his visit favorable publicity. They saw Senator Teller and the mine barons and "worked" them for all it was worth. Walcott went on to Reno, south through Carson City, and ultimately into southeastern California. On September 24, he met Weeks at Big Pine, an obscure town about halfway between Mono Lake and the north end of Death Valley. The White-Inyo Mountains are part of the Basin and Range province. From a geological standpoint, extreme eastern California really belongs in Nevada.

Walcott's investigations in both the east and the west had shown a pattern of older Cambrian on the margins of the continent. By going west of Nevada, he might find the oldest Cambrian. A trip to build political support and plan new work in the far West gave him the reason to be close to this area. In effect, he took a few weeks from his official job to pursue research. Good scientists do what they are assigned but steal time for their own scientific interests, and often that which is done sub rosa turns out to be most significant.

Weeks and Walcott moved up several canyons from the west side of the range to measure sections and collect fossils. It was unsettled, barren and dry in the mountains, but exposures were excellent, and Walcott was satisfied that they had made a satisfactory beginning on the geology of the range. "The principal results of the two weeks work are the discovery of the Cambrian rocks in the White Mt. range and the folding of the strata in the Appalachian type" (October 8, 1894). They went north to the railroad and parted, Weeks east and Walcott west. The pair returned twice more to these fascinating outcrops (Yochelson and Nelson 1994).

December 22, Walcott "Began working up notes on California." A week later at the GSA meeting in Baltimore, he presented two separate talks on his results. The death from typhoid fever that summer of George Huntington Williams (Pettijohn 1988), who was a rising star in American geology, cast a pall over this meeting. One of Walcott's talks was printed the following February (Walcott 1895) and the second in March (Walcott 1895a), six months from fieldwork to publication, not bad for a full-time administrator.

So far as the Cambrian rocks were concerned, the White Mountains were big news. Previously, only a single Mesozoic fossil was known from the region. Walcott measured a section nearly a mile thick, containing limestone, quartzite, limestone, and an overlying shale. In one area of the upper limestone he found archaeocyathids, the spongelike fossils, "so abundant in the limestone that it practically be called a Lower Cambrian coral reef." . . . "So far as known to me, this is the oldest of the Cambrian faunas known in the western United States. Just what its relations to the Olenellus fauna of central Nevada and British Columbia are I am unable at present to state, except that I believe it to be older that the Olenellus fauna of central Nevada" (Walcott 1895, 144). This was a remarkably significant observation, accurate in spite of the limited time for study in the field and laboratory. This is one of those sections below the *Olenellus* fauna that is enigmatic but probably Cambrian; the rare fossils which have been found do not include trilobites.

In his second paper, Walcott discussed his observations on the structure of the White Mountains, and generalized:

> As seen from the western slopes of the White Mountain Range, the next range to the eastward, Silver Peak, is apparently a monocline facing westward; but from the known structure of the Great Basin ranges, such as those of the Eureka District, Nevada, the Oquirrh range, Utah, and others illustrated by the geologists of the Wheeler Survey, it appears that in the broad Paleozoic area between the Sierra Nevada on the west and the early Paleozoic shoreline on the east (Colorado) a period of folding and thrust faulting was followed by a period of vertical faulting, which displaced the strata that had been folded and faulted in the preceding epoch. The extent and character of this disturbance can be determined only by a careful study of each of the mountain ranges for a distance over five hundred miles east and west and probably a thousand miles north and south; and the great geologic problems will not be fully solved until the areal geology of the region between the 109th and 119th meridians have been mapped. (Walcott 1895a, 174)

This was an agenda that has kept the Geological Survey busy ever since.

After leaving Weeks, Walcott spent a week in the San Francisco area. He called at the University of California in Berkeley and twice at Stanford. It was a replay of the Colorado junket, this time with Senator Leland Stanford as the prize. He moved north to Seattle, spoke to the chamber of commerce, saw Senator Dolph, and moved to Portland for more chamber of commerce activity. It is likely no coincidence that in 1895 one of the senators from Washington introduced legislation providing funds for the USGS to begin fieldwork in Alaska.

Having touched the politically sensitive spots in Washington and Oregon, he headed to Boise, Idaho, and spent a couple of days with prominent mining men. The route may be followed by newspaper accounts of the work and plans of the

Charles Doolittle Walcott, Paleontologist

Survey. "Director Walcott has been making a tour of the west for the past two months for the purpose of meeting the leading business men and securing information that will assist him in laying out his work for the coming year. With that end in view Mr. Walcott visits Boise. He will remain in the city until tomorrow afternoon."[23] Finally Walcott headed home, with a few days of train travel to think over what he had accomplished. He stayed in Chicago for a day to talk with Iddings and Van Hise. The end of October he was with Helena and the growing brood. Two months away was long, but not atypical; those involved in mapping were often out for four to five months.

November was occupied with organizing the *Geologic Atlas of the United States* for publication. One of Powell's schemes was to have a combination of both topographic map and geologic map of an area published under one cover. The concept was grand, but execution of the first one was long delayed. The previous year a *Journal of Geology* editorial congratulated the USGS on releasing the first four sheets, but it was not much of a achievement considering the effort which had been expended to get that far. Besides, what else would Iddings (1893) have done except praise his old organization. As it happens, these four maps were not really part of the *Geologic Atlas* as it finally was produced.

Within the USGS were arguments as to how much text to include, what nomenclature to use, how much editing of the maps should be done, and so forth. Walcott and colleagues got it all straightened out in short order and the first of the folios came out. Economy was still the watchword in Washington and issuing a new series of publication may have seemed foolhardy, but it resulted in praise for the Survey. More than two hundred folios were eventually produced, exceeding what Willis had predicted to his mother. Although they never came close to reaching the objective of mapping the entire country, these folios are one of the great landmarks of scientific literature and from some aspects are the finest product of the Geological Survey. During Walcott's tenure, the folios kept rolling off the presses.

On a more personal note, in mid-November Walcott bid adieu to cousin Amah and the Reverend Bartlett, who was retiring from the New York Avenue Presbyterian Church. Within a few Sundays, Helena and Charles were regularly attending the Church of the Covenant on Massachusetts Avenue, a few blocks from their home. Closer to the office, that past spring Secretary of the Navy Hillary Herbert, the old nemesis of government science, tried to have the Coast Survey abolished. In December, President Cleveland urged this action, and it was as dismal a time for the Coast Survey as it had been a year earlier for the Geological Survey (Manning 1988). Walcott was "Looking up matters in relation to consolidation of national surveys & attending to routine business" (December 11, 1894). There was just a chance he might have new duties soon, and it never hurt to be prepared.

December 18 Walcott delivered the first presidential address before the Geological Society of Washington. His topic was "The United States Geological Survey." He gave some history, but concentrated on current work, explaining the rationale and practicality behind all the varieties of activity. He mentioned once more the need for highway construction material research and pointed to USGS efforts already being done by N. S. Shaler at Harvard. The address was printed in full in the only volume of *Proceedings* issued by the society (Walcott 1895b). More important, a slightly abbreviated version appeared February in Appleton's *Popular Science Monthly* (Walcott 1895c).

Christmas was a happy day. After the GSA meeting in Washington, old friends Cross, Iddings, and Williams came to tea, along with a new young friend F. D. Adams from McGill University in Montreal. "The year 1894 has been a severe one for the American people—owing to financial disturbances & poor crops. The outlook is for continued disturbance until financial conditions are improved by wise legislation. With my family all has gone well. A little daughter came Aug. 20" 5:30. No deaths or serious illness. All well today" (December 31, 1894). Walcott got the time of Helena's birth wrong by five minutes, but that was his only mistake in what was politically and personally a most complex year. During 1894, Walcott was elected a corresponding member of the Imperial Society of Naturalists in Moscow, though he made no note of it.

That would seem to take care of all matters for 1894, except for a paper in the fourteenth *Annual Report*. Igneous rocks do not contain fossils, and for a paleontologist to write on ancient lavas requires explanation. To begin at the beginning once more, early geologists developed subdivisions of Primitive, Secondary, and Tertiary; later they added Transitional and Quaternary. Working backward, Quaternary marks the deposits made during the latest of the earth's times of glaciation. Tertiary is now called Cenozoic, and the strata contain fossils comparable to present-day sea shells. The lower limits of the Secondary were argued for years but eventually came to be equated with the term Mesozoic, wherein the rocks contain abundant life forms somewhat different from those of today. The lower part of the Secondary became the late Paleozoic and the

Charles Doolittle Walcott, Paleontologist

Transitional ultimately became the early Paleozoic. By working out the *Olenellus* fauna, Walcott put a base on the Cambrian, the oldest period of the Paleozoic, the era of ancient life.

This left the Primitive, or Pre-Cambrian, as it was then spelled, a difficult terrane to untangle. The implication of the latter term denote rocks and time prior to the earliest fossils (Hamilton 1989). How to subdivide and classify these rocks and how to correlate them from one region to another were major geologic problems. Their scale is daunting, for dating by decay of radioactive minerals shows that about nine-tenths of the earth's history is in the Precambrian (Cloud 1988). Radiometric dating gave the geologists a powerful tool for correlation, and Precambrian time is finally being interpreted in some detail.

Increase in knowledge goes at an irregular pace, as the late nineteenth-century history of the Precambrian shows. In spite of great effort, only the broadest outlines of the geology of the ancient rocks were deciphered, for the critical element of a reliable means of correlation was then lacking. In sedimentary rocks of the Paleozoic and younger eras, fossils have been the means to resolve both major and minor problems of structure and correlation. For the nineteenth-century geologist, there were no Precambrian fossils to speak of, save one dubious form from Canada named *Eozoon Canadense* in 1864 by J. W. Dawson. It had vigorous defenders and outspoken opponents as the candidate for the earliest form of life (Woodward 1907, 217–18). In a curious effort at truth by consensus, at the London Congress there was a vote on whether this form was really a fossil. Walcott, one of the few who had actually seen specimens, voted for organic; the 1881 majority voted for inorganic, but that did not influence present day general agreement that "Eozoon" is no fossil.

Canada has a great deal of Precambrian rocks and the first useful subdivisions of the Primitive were made there. Sir William Logan recognized the Laurentian series of gneisses intruded by granites, over which were the Huronian series of slates and other sedimentary rocks, metamorphosed, but not quite so badly treated by geologic forces as those below (Eagan 1989). The northern parts of Michigan and Minnesota, geologic extensions of Canada, are important to the understanding of concepts of Precambrian in the United States, but another place that influenced thought was the Grand Canyon.

Walcott went into the canyon in 1882, specifically to study and to date the rocks exposed near water level at the right angle bend below Marble Canyon. The highly contorted schists, called Vishnu, were ancient, but the lower part of the overlying pile of rocks that ended in Permian at the top of the plateau was in question. As has been recounted, Powell thought them Silurian in the broad sense, whereas Gilbert, from one scrappy fossil, gave the opinion that they were Primordial in age. Walcott confirmed the sandstone was Cambrian and then measured his way down through two and one-half miles of sediments to the schists of Granite Gorge. He found almost nothing of organic life in this sequence.

He did, however, see bands of black igneous rock. A few years earlier, Clarence Dutton, looking down from above, likened them to coal beds and though that the section just might be Carboniferous and Silurian, even more of a wrong guess than that of Powell. In his systematic way, Walcott sampled these beds and brought part of a mule load out of the canyon. They sat in the museum for a decade before being studied in detail by Iddings. Igneous rocks are of two sorts, intrusive, meaning they cooled under cover of overlying rocks, and extrusive, meaning they came to the surface before solidifying. Feeder pipes of igneous rocks come up more or less vertically from below, cutting across layers of sedimentary rock. Under some circumstances, the molten rock may force its way between two sedimentary layers. This feature is a sill, an intrusive igneous rock; the west bank of the Hudson River opposite New York City is a huge sill about one thousand feet thick.

Distinguishing between a thin sill and a lava flow is one of the classic problems in field geology. Walcott made all the correct observations to demonstrate these old igneous rocks in the Grand Canyon were lavas, not sills. He found the sediment below slightly baked, but that above not affected by heat. In a few places he found bits of lava incorporated into the overlying sediment. He even noted the larger number of vesicles or holes near the upper surface of the lava compared to the lower surface; a sill cools more uniformly, not nearly so fast as the upper surface of a lava.

"Rarely has the geologist an opportunity to study such a series of contemporaneous interbedded igneous rocks as that dissected and laid bare in the walls of the Grand Canyon. The igneous rocks of the pre-Cambrian (Algonkian) Keewenawan terrane of the Lake Superior basin are more or less clearly shown, and those of the classic Silurian localities in Wales have long been studied; but the Grand Canyon series remain unexcelled in completeness of exposure and certainly of stratigraphic position" (Walcott 1894e, 503).

Following Walcott's discussion and description, accompanied by a geologic map and a number of field sketches, Iddings gave a four page detailed discussion of the composition of the lavas. He pointed out that there were virtually no differences between the Tertiary-age lavas which litter the western landscape and these ancient lavas. Had there been an obvious difference, it might have provided a means of correlation of the old lavas from one region to another. This was a significant finding for a large part of science is involved in collecting negative information.

Despite the title, "Pre-Cambrian igneous rocks of the Unkar terrane," the principal part of Walcott's paper is concerned with the geologic section he had measured. A point made here and repeated in earlier papers is how fresh the rock appeared. One cannot tell the age of a rock by its physical characteristics as the geologists had discovered by the early days of the nineteenth century. Still, old rocks ought to be more deformed and changed than younger ones; more often than not, this is so. The Grand Canyon was one of the nots.

In his original description of the section, Walcott had assigned all the sediments below the trilobite-bearing sandstone to the Cambrian. It was a reasonable assumption and there was an indication of fossils, scanty though it was. When *Bulletin* 30 was published, Walcott changed his mind: "In the table the period of erosion is represented as having removed all the strata between the Upper Cambrian and Lower Cambrian horizon, but I now think it would be better to classify all the pre-Tonto strata as pre-Cambrian" (Walcott 1886a, 41). One writer (Yochelson 1979) speculated that the anomalously great thickness of this section if it was interpreted as Cambrian may have lead to the change. Whatever the reason, in *Bulletin* 81, published in 1891, these rocks were ensconced in the literature as older than Cambrian.

The tenth *Annual Report* established that Cambrian time began with the rocks containing *Olenellus;* in the sense of the geologists in the early part of the nineteenth century this was the base of the transition beds. The "Primitive" rocks below were pre-Cambrian, but like the younger part of the column it was important to subdivide them. Investigations into the Primitive were dogged for decades while geologists argued over the origin and age of granite. Now a consensus was starting for an older strongly metamorphosed group of rocks, the Archean, overlain by a younger less strongly metamorphosed rocks called by some geologists Algonkian, Walcott's term. In part, it was the evidence of such a long stratigraphic column in the pre-Cambrian which caused geologists to be so opposed to Kelvin's short time scale for the age of the earth.

Where Algonkian ended and Paleozoic began was the question. It is still an issue. The value of stratigraphic paleontology is demonstrated by the great advances made in understanding of the Paleozoic, relative to that of the underlying rocks. Van Hise (1892), of the University of Wisconsin, wrote the correlation paper on Archean and Algonkian. In retrospect he probably did an injustice to Canadian work in supporting the term Algonkian rather than Huronian for the sediments below the Cambrian (Eagan 1989). This work simply could not draw a general picture in the same way that Walcott did, for there was no way to link the isolated outcrops of Precambrian rocks.

Chamberlin wanted information concerning these early rocks more widely known, and was equally anxious to develop the *Journal of Geology,* He wrote: "I should like particularly to publish the article because I see that Dana in his manual has not given sufficient weight to the probable equivalents of the Lake Superior Keewenawan in other regions."[24] Walcott (1895e) complied with Chamberlin's request. As time permitted in the future, Walcott would study more of the Precambrian, but for the immediate future events in Washington were not likely to allow the new director much time for research.

10

Following a Goode Man: If You Want Something Done, Ask a Busy Person (1895–1898)

> A finished museum is a dead museum, and a dead museum is a useless museum.
>
> G. B. Goode, 1891

AMERICA lacks royalty, though it has titles, and one of the most important is "boss," the person in charge. Even titles have changed through time, and the concept of boss in industry has given way to president, and that, in turn, to chief executive officer. In old-line government agencies a preferred title was "director"; "administrator" marks the modern ones. The distinction between one who administers and one who directs is profound. When Walcott was at the head, the Geological Survey had direction under a director.

Whereas 1894 had been a year in which Walcott had to respond to problems not of his own making, he approached the 1895 with more assurance. He began with a call on President Cleveland, and later that day Helena received at home. "The new year appears favorably with me both officially & at home" (January 1, 1895).

With Congress in session, January was one of the busiest of months, even though not all political power was concentrated in Washington. When Walcott was given the opportunity to address the Engineer's Club of Philadelphia on the Geological Survey, he grabbed the opportunity. Walcott's lecture shows his ability to give an audience exactly what they want, in nontechnical, crystal-clear words. The bulk of it concerned topographic maps, and he used lantern slides to make his points. Although Walcott emphasized topography, he spoke of the hydrologic work authorized in the autumn of 1894, mentioned road-building materials, and touched on geological investigations. He ended with a few scenic views of the West and, when the lights were back on, offered extra copies of the maps to the engineers.

Near the beginning, Walcott delivered his real message:

> There is one fact that should be borne in mind when considering the scope of its work, and that is that the Geological Survey is a bureau of research. Its function is, to a large extent, the discovery of unknown facts and principles and the scientific coordination of them and all previously known facts and inductions that fall within the scope of its work, in such form that they may be useful alike to government and people. (Walcott 1895e, 46)

Near the end he defended science as part of the federal government and not the sole province of academia.

His speech was published in full, and one map specially printed with all control points indicated to show how carefully the mapping was done. The publication includes two fold-ins of maps, a considerable expense. His presidential address to the Geological Society of Washington in December was to appear soon in *Popular Science Monthly,* as well as being published by the society. From these works, influential citizens were absorbing Walcott's message that information gathered by the USGS was of practical value. He took the message of value in government science to Capitol Hill and appeared before the Committee on Printing. By good fortune, this was also the time the Geological Society of London announced that the Bigsby Medal had been awarded him. Walcott was only the third American to be so honored. The medal might not have much practical value, but if the Britishers thought Walcott was an outstanding man, this could have had a favorable impression on more than one congressman. Walcott got more money for printing.

Keeping Survey activities moving occupied Walcott fully, yet in spare moments he served on the Admissions Committee of the Cosmos Club, went to dinners, to a reception at the White House, to the Church of the Covenant on Sundays, to Vassar College for a lecture, to Albany to institute a cooperative program with New York state for a geologic map, to the Committee on Indian Affairs, etc., etc., etc. One representative January day sums it up: "At capital A.M. looking after printing bill. Called on Sec'y of Interior & ret'd to my office 2:00 P.M. Dined with Mr & Mrs. G. G. Hubbard, Mr. & Mrs. Stawon of Washington State, Mrs. A. G. Bell, Miss Jackson, Gypsy, and my own dear Helena at Mr. Hubbards" (January 28, 1895).

Charles Doolittle Walcott, Paleontologist

February was as busy as January, but never overlooking an opportunity, Walcott found time to lecture in the church chapel on the subject of mapping the United States; there were enough members of Congress and the Executive Branch in the congregation to make this a most effective forum. As a sort of spare time activity, he agreed to Professor Chamberlin's late February request for an article on the ancient rocks in the Grand Canyon. This was published in the April–May issue; talk about a fast pen.

In mid-March, Walcott and Helena took a break from the busy social life of attending and giving dinner parties and went to Staunton, Virginia, visiting Dr. and Mrs. Campbell. It was a working vacation, for Campbell was one of those who did geologic mapping for the Survey when not teaching. Walcott gave a lecture on the Survey to students and joined the Campbells at Natural Bridge. The couple then went to Richmond, where Walcott spoke to the chamber of commerce. Virginia once had a state geological survey, though it was abolished many years ago: there was no harm telling businessmen what the USGS did and what a new state survey might accomplish for them.

In the midst of this activity, came a tangible political coup. The Indian Territory, which evolved into the state of Oklahoma, was to be opened for homesteading. It needed surveying, and the Geological Survey—not the General Land Office, the Coast Survey, or any new group—obtained the job. Chamberlin wrote, "I congratulate you on the Congressional act. Certainly it is everything that could have been reasonably expected under all the adverse conditions."[1] The secretary of the interior asked Walcott how this surveying might be carried out, Walcott just happened to have a plan which the secretary approved immediately. Other achievements were funding for geologic investigations in Alaska, and money for stream gaging.

A mark of busy 1895 was a comment in late March that Walcott started a review of the Cambrian brachiopod *Lingulella;* it was the first mention of fossils in his diary that year. The interlude of science was brief, for the Irrigation Board met to discuss plans for hydrologic work. A thought of lost time for science may have flickered when Chamberlin wrote him advice as to whom should be appointed paleontologist at the University of Chicago: "We once knew of just the man to fill it, but you ruthlessly took him out of our hands"[2] Walcott's forty-fifth birthday passed quietly with hardly a comment.

In early April, Walcott delivered two large public lectures, for he was known as a polished speaker and was much in demand. He spoke on his early adventures in the west covering a trip through Utah and the Grand Canyon. Four nights later at the National Museum, he lectured on the North American continent during Cambrian times, based on his 1891 paper in the *Annual Report*. It is hard to see how such a subject could attract that most elusive of all audiences, "the intelligent layman," but it did. What evenings were not spent politicking, he went to the Biological Society, the Philosophical Society, and prepared testimony for congressional committees. The patriarch James Dwight Dana died that month, and Walcott was one of those who signed a letter of condolence from the Geological Survey.

Near the end of April, with a satisfactory appropriation assured, he could relax and return to geology. Extracting a favor from Department of Agriculture colleagues, Walcott borrowed the inestimable Cooper Curtice for a couple of weeks to reexamine localities Curtice had collected in 1885. The two headed south.

After a quick look at the Atlanta exposition, they were in Cave Spring, Georgia, where the two, with Professor Yates from Georgia, met Eugene McCaully, an Alabama geologist. The rocks of the Appalachians are in diagonal belts and the geology is not controlled by the artificial boundaries of states. Field conferences wherein geologists of one state look at the rocks in an adjacent state have done wonders in resolving problems; it never hurt to have an impartial third party, such as Walcott, on these trips, for geologists can be as possessive of the names of their rock units as any scientist can be of his own pet ideas.

The end of the month saw them in the Coosa Valley of northeastern Alabama. "The section of the Cambrian is very much folded and broken" (April 29, 1895). In 1885, Curtice collected some lovely Middle Cambrian trilobites from the shales, but now increasingly refined correlations of the strata demanded that these faunas be better dated within the geologic section. Besides trilobites, Curtice brought back strange cobbles which might have been inorganic, but then again might have been fossils. More cobbles came in from the valley and by 1893, Walcott was convinced they were the casts, that is the internal filling, of jellyfish. Almost as soon as they were at the locality, Walcott found a compressed jellyfish, or medusa, which helped prove these strange shapes were organic. It was another remarkable insight, for everyone "knows" that jellyfish have no hard parts and therefore cannot become fossils. Once again, in finding key specimens, Walcott was lucky as well as smart.

The party moved on to Piedmont, Talladaga, and Sylacauga, where E. A. Smith, head of the Alabama Survey joined them. To put things in plain terms, Smith hated Powell with a passion; much of the material used by Alabama

Charles Doolittle Walcott, Paleontologist

congressman Hillary Herbert to attack the USGS must have emanated from him. Whatever Walcott said or did with Smith on this trip was in the right vein, for thereafter harmony prevailed in the south.

After several more stops in Alabama and Georgia, Walcott returned home the ninth of May. All was well in Washington, but this had been a quick, hard trip and Walcott was ill three days before he was administering at his office. A week before the month ended, Walcott spent three hours looking at the cobbles and squeezed in a few more short sessions in May. Pursing research between conferences and writing memoranda is not the best way to proceed, but by now, after a couple of years of only interrupted scraps of time for science, Walcott had become skilled at making the most of such moments for research.

Summer was still officially nearly three weeks away, but the city was already hot. The family left for Noyes Beach, Rhode Island, though entourage is a more accurate word. There was Helena, Charlie, Sydney, baby Helen, Mary the nurse, and Agnes the cook, with luggage, bags, and parcels. For a solid week, Walcott actually vacationed—apart from photographing ripple marks and looking at jellyfish on the beach and in the water. He completed his *Bulletin* on the Cambrian of Pennsylvania (Walcott 1896a). Short as the paper was, it received a full-page review (Williams 1896). The forty-three pages and fifteen plates cost five cents.

With that manuscript off to the editors, the following day of vacation Walcott began revision of the inside cover text for the folios. A digression is needed to explain "folio" in more detail. As director, Powell had a vision of the mission to develop a geologic map of the United States. Divide the country into rectangles bounded by a degree of latitude and a degree of longitude. A topographic map would be made and the geology would studied and plotted on a copy. These, with derivative maps and a page of text, would be published as one component of the national geologic map. Geologic mapping could be done where circumstances dictated, yet each would fit as part of the grand scheme.

It was a bold, fine notion, but, like Powell's concepts of irrigation, it had practical difficulties in the topographic mapping. A map is relatively easy to construct in flat country, but the more rugged the terrane, the more difficult it is to do a topographic survey using one man with a plane table and alidade, and another with a stadia rod. With exceptions, flat areas are not of as much interest to geologists as rugged areas where the rocks are generally contorted and better exposed. Part of the problem also lay with Powell, who kept modifying and elaborating details, worrying over appropriate colors and printing

patterns, when it would have made much better sense to put out almost anything to quiet his critics. Congress wanted a scientific product promptly; Powell
wanted it perfect.

Finally, the folios began to come off the presses, an impressive achievement
Walcott could point to with considerable pride. After the first few, details of general explanation had to be clarified and this was Walcott's chore. When he was
back in the office, his "brain trust" of Chamberlin, Van Hise, Emmons, and Willis
went over the revision. All agreed to the changes and they further agreed that the
first twenty folios should list Powell as director. That was a generous act.

Two weeks away from Washington was about all Walcott could spare. Going
south, he had stopped in New York City to settle on sale of the property in Russia Township, one of his last ties to Trenton. He dropped by the American Museum to see his old friend Whitfield, a new friend, Henry Fairfield Osborn, and
Director A. S. Bickmore. After all details of the folios were resolved, Walcott, appropriately on a Sunday, summed up the first half of the year: "This closes my
first year in chg. of the Geological Survey. Apparently it has been successful &
certainly no more wearing than the year before" (June 30, 1895).

For the *Annual Report* he wrote:

> Having been a member of the Survey since its organization (July 1, 1879) and
> geologist in charge for some time previous to his appointment as Director,
> he was familiar with the policy and administration of the Bureau under his
> predecessors, King and Powell, which he believed to be, in the main, wise and
> efficient, and hence he had not found it desirable to make any radical
> changes, either in policy or personnel, The changes made by have been in the
> nature of readjustments intended to meet new conditions, and, if possible,
> to bring the Survey more in touch with some of the economic and educa-
> tional interests of the country. (Walcott 1896, 7)

In reality, Walcott had reorganized topography and forced senior geologists to
stay in the office to write rather than continue fieldwork, but this was private,
not public.

Like last year, Walcott was spending the summer in the bizarre lifestyle of
camping near Washington. July 4 was a "damp camp" at Sudley's, but otherwise
camp did mitigate some of the heat. Bicycling back and forth to town gave him
time to meditate on larger issues for the USGS. "Am considering placing of the
Geol. & other scientific experts under the classified service" (July 8, 1895). That
was a phenomenal step forward for the government scientists; no matter what
the field, job security is important. Bureaucracy sometimes moves slowly,

though not in this case. By July 15, the professionals were placed under Civil Service system, and by the following May all USGS employees, except laborers, had this protection against the political spoils system. If Walcott had done nothing else for the agency, he would have been noteworthy for this administrative step.

The medusae study was going well and Walcott selected specimens for illustration before leaving for the north. His first stop was at Martha's Vineyard to speak with Shaler. Shaler had been the state geologist of his native Kentucky and now was one of the part-time USGS workers. Walcott arranged for Shaler to investigate road-building materials, and a laboratory was opened at Harvard, but unfortunately Shaler was to die in five years and this early effort at engineering geology died with him. Along with the study of materials, Shaler became interested in swamps (mud) and beaches (sand). An *Annual Report* article he wrote on them was one of the most popular ever printed.

Martha's Vineyard is of glacial origin. Loose rocks were brought south by the ice and Walcott spent a few days finding Cambrian fossils in pebbles, which he noted were unlike any he had seen except on Great Belle Island in Newfoundland. It was food for thought, as were the modern sand dunes they examined. He went back to Rhode Island with his family and photographed more trails on the beach. This was a typical family seaside vacation for the children, apart from father looking at drawings of long-dead jellyfish.

Again Walcott left for New York, this time with Helena, to see Mother and sister Josie, and then to Rome, New York. The limited time he spent in 1893 collecting at Cleveland Gulf had produced a few sensational *Triarthrus* with their appendages preserved. Walcott wanted more and hired four men to move the overlying layers with pick and shovel for six days. "Removed about 365 cubic yards of shale and obtained 274 sq. ft. of the 'Trilobite' layer, in which *Triarthrus becki* occurs preserving antennae and legs. The trilobites occur in a layer that averages 2 feet in thickness with its capping of ¼ in. to ½ in. of hard sandy shale. Most of the trilobites are in the lower ¾ of an inch of the layer, associated with bits of graptolites, young *Triarthrus* and *Trinucleus.* Found 75 to 100 trilobites, in taking up the layer, and packed up *six* barrels of shale for shipment to Washington, to break up in the laboratory."[3]

He left Helena with her family in Rochester, hustled to Washington for business, and then headed west for a strenuous field season. His route was to Chicago and thence St. Paul, with just enough time between trains to call on one of the Minnesota Senators, for this kind of activity never hurt. F. B. Weeks and Walter Weed, librarian and economic geologist respectively, joined him on the leg to Great Falls, Montana. On a "busman's holiday" they examined the young

Fort Union beds; arguments raged as to whether these were of late Mesozoic or early Cenozoic age. From Great Falls, they went fifty miles south to Neihart, where Weed had mapped. Around the "town" were Cambrian rocks, as good a reason as any to come to the middle of nowhere. "The limestone has the appearance of being brecciated before consolidating and at the time of deposition. The layer of calcareous mud hardened when the tide was out, was broken up by the incoming tide, and the fragments heaped together, many of them being rolled and rounded."[4] Today, many geologists today give the same interpretation.

A long sequence of rocks outcropped below the Cambrian beds. "Spent the day with Weed & Weeks searching for fossils in the Belt formation south of Neihart. None found. The rocks resemble those of the Grand Canyon Series of Arizona" (August 24, 1895). Walcott's paper on the Grand Canyon rocks had been published that spring and the details of the 1882–83 field season were fresh in his mind. They went south another thirty miles to White Sulphur Springs; the Cambrian rocks yielded little in the way of fossils, and the Belt rocks, nothing. In Montana, the terms "Precambrian" and "Belt" are practically synonymous.

They traveled to Helena and to Butte, Montana. Emmons joined them and he and Walcott courted a brace of senators on Labor Day, always a prime time for politicians. The mines in Montana and Idaho were booming and Emmons was shifting his attention away from Colorado. They moved to Spokane and more mines; the USGS should be at work in this region. Topographic maps were needed and Emmons and Walcott agreed a base line should be established. In triangulation, the first step is to measure a long straight line, some miles in length. The other two sides of the triangle can be established by instruments measuring an angle at each end of this known distance. From this first triangle, a series of other triangles are developed. Putting in a base line is tedious, measuring and remeasuring that first critical distance, but it was the crucial step in making an accurate map in the days before aerial surveys. The Geological Survey did produce elegant and accurate maps (Thompson 1979).

Emmons and Weed left, and the other two took the steamer up river to Coeur d'Alene, Idaho, and from there to Kalispell, north of Flathead Lake in northwestern Montana. At Columbia Falls, Walcott scribbled a note to Hall: "I leave here tomorrow with a pack train tomorrow for a ten day trip to eastern front of the Rockies. There is a great series of almost unaltered pre-Cambrian beds. Measured over 4000 feet in one unbroken section yesterday—not a trace of life in limestone shale or sandstone."[5] A pack train consists of a string of pack horses tied tail to nose like railway cars behind a locomotive.

Charles Doolittle Walcott, Paleontologist

The party went to Belton and on toward Nyack. Many maps omit Nyack, as the name is the type that railroad crews gave to water tanks, switches, and signal posts. In present day terms they were near the southern boundary of Glacier National Park. Building the Northern Pacific right-of-way had produced the most continuous exposures in cuts and they walked the track for sixteen miles. From this, they decided that the geologic section measured along the Flathead River was incomplete and moved on.

Walcott and Weeks aimed for the continental divide hoping that the section of rocks in the Nyack amphitheater would be better, but a snowstorm drove them back and forced them to move camp. The season was nearly over, so once again Walcott broke his rules and worked on a Sunday. Worked perhaps is an understatement; to examine the section along the railroad they rode seventeen miles and walked seven. Not much had been accomplished, but at least Walcott had his first brush with these tremendously thick sections of old sedimentary rocks.

On the first day of fall, Walcott headed east. He paused in Madison with Van Hise and in Chicago with Chamberlin, but his goal was his in-laws, the Stevens in Rochester. He went to Rome to check on the trilobites and to Utica to see friends and relatives and settle the last details of Rust's estate. He got home at midnight on October 5. Geologists' wives become accustomed to erratic arrivals and departures.

There was a much to do at the Survey, but it had to wait while he read a letter from Hall: "Mr. Dewey has made under oath the charge that I have stolen and sold state property in the amount of $70,000; that the collection which I sold to the American Museum in New York was the property of the state. Various other charges are also made."[6] Eventually the mess was straightened out and Hall received more honor and glory from the legislature. Still, one must but wonder what prompted the man to bring up this sale from twenty years earlier. It must have been more substantial than Hall lacking a twinkle in his eye. Walcott's thoughts are unknowable, but he might have taken some small joy that not all troubles begin and end in Washington.

Walcott met with the public printer. The printer was a virtually unmovable roadblock in the path of publication; even with the most cordial printer, limited funding caused delay. No matter who was director and what was tried, USGS publications languished. The *Annual Report* for fiscal 1894 came out in 1896. Walcott was able to have the fiscal 1895 printed the same year, but that remarkable accomplishment was not enough. Printing delay became a tradition and remains one; not every aspect of being a government scientist is rosy. For an example, consider the speed of Walcott's *Bulletin* on the Cambrian of Pennsylvania against the manuscript sent to Chamberlin.

Fortunately, in 1893 Powell obtained the appropriation for engraving and printing, the last word being legally critical. The USGS had earlier received authority to print its own maps, and this wording was the rationale to produce folios entirely in the Survey printing plant. The text was on paper the size of a map sheet and bound in with the maps. Good administrators always find a way to comply with legal limitations and still get a job done, and production of the folios is a sterling example. Powell was just too late getting that product out for Congress to see. With the folios under control, Walcott rented a family pew at the Church of the Covenant and took Charlie to the zoo. He "Secured 3 hrs for work on Cambrian medusae. In the other hours attended to administrative duties of Survey, correspondence, etc" (October 29, 1895).

In mid-November, he and Helena had a break from Washington and family. They took the train to the Atlanta exposition and pronounced it good. At the seaside town of Brunswick, Georgia, the water was too muddy to see much, so they continued south through Tampa to the Indian River. Walcott was "out on the water at day light after medusae. Caught a number & later made cast in plaster. Packed up & left at 1. P.M. for St. Augustine" (November 23, 1895). In St. Augustine he noted his father's visit there in 1851. Had Walcott's father not been in such ill health and died the following year, the chances were Walcott would be owner of knitting mills in New York, rather than a paleontologist staring a jellyfish. Helena and Walcott packed up and were back in Washington for a family Thanksgiving dinner. That soothed the body and presumably he soothed his soul by presenting a talk on pre-Cambrian rocks of North America.

November passed into December, and Walcott was off to the Brooklyn Institute, repeating his talk on the pre-Cambrian. In Washington the Irrigation Board met. As a change of protocal, congressmen called on him rather than his going to Capitol Hill. The word continued to spread that the USGS produced information on rocks that was useful for a state. Indeed, life was relatively so quiet that Walcott secured—his word—another three hours to study his jellyfish.

Part of the change in attitude resulted from the content and size of the *Annual Report*. Powell had expanded it, but Walcott pulled out all the stops and had four volumes, the second on economic matters and two on mineral resources. Congress ordered extra copies printed of selected papers. Besides the usual administrative materials, the first volume included papers of a more theoretical nature, one of which was by Marsh on dinosaurs. The fuss over use-less paleontology had died down, but it was an act of scientific courage for Walcott to include this work.

Two weeks before the year ended, the director wrote the secretary of the interior concerning the nation's forest reserves. The Fourth Irrigation Congress expanded its concerns and recognized the necessity of preserving forests as a way to regulate the flow of streams and rivers. Almost any intelligent observer can see that vegetation absorbs rainfall and releases it later; forests are more effective in retaining water than are grasslands, and grasslands are more effective than deserts. To end this year, Walcott would "Trust 1896 will be as fruitful in happiness as 1895 has been" (December 31, 1895).

Eighteen ninety-six began like the last one by wishing President Cleveland a happy new year. The tradition of such visits to the White House vanished long ago. The rest of the day was a round of other official calls, before returning to the business of paying close attention to Congress and running the Survey, in that order. Both were doing well, so the second Wednesday in January, Walcott "In [the] evening spoke on trails & markings on Ancient & Recent seashores before Geol. Soc. Wash." (January 8, 1896). Even vacations ended up as grist for his scientific mill.

About the only other noteworthy event that January was a meeting of the Forestry Association. The fate of America's forests was finally becoming a public concern. Walcott went back to seeing congressmen and those who knew congressmen and might put in a good word for the Geological Survey. February was half over before he even had a free evening for jellyfish, yet near month's end Walcott slipped off to Rochester for several days to investigate a real estate investment with his brother-in-law. He returned in good time to gather up Newell and see Kansas senator Baker. With Newell present, the conference had to be on water resources. All funds for gaging streams had been expended, and Walcott asked for and received a deficiency appropriation.

Not only was Walcott doing well with water, topographic maps suddenly took on a life of their own. Congressmen wanted them for constituents, so Walcott had to explain why topographers mapped where they did and not everywhere simultaneously. In this favorable climate he obtained authority to put in monuments, markers set to indicate elevation and position of a particular point. Walcott told the House Appropriations Committee, "In my report I have said that I think it would improve the service at least 100 per cent" (Walcott 1896c, 114). Powell repeatedly asked for this authority but had never obtained it.

The *Denver Republican* took a dim view of topographic maps, basing their view on the Hayden Territorial Survey efforts. Walcott's reply filled three columns, describing topographic work, costs, mapping methods, and advantages of monuments. "I have written you at length as I do not care to have the opinion spread abroad through so important a journal as the Republican, that the topographic work of the Survey will not be of service in engineering and mining work, as well as in the geologic work."[7]

When the congressional dust finally settled, the Geological Survey appropriation was fifty thousand dollars more than was requested. In 1896 dollars that was big money; Walcott had a terrible toothache when appearing before the Appropriations Committee, but it had not cramped his style. The time Walcott invested in personally explaining the mission of his bureau to as many congressmen and senators as he could corner had paid off handsomely.

Walcott knew exactly what to say to Congress. Consider this exchange a few years later on topographic maps when Walcott was defending his efforts before the House Appropriations Committee:

> MR. CHAIRMAN: The reason I am asking this question is that a constituent of mine was vigorously urging me to see if we could not get a topographic map in Illinois, and I could not see any use of topography in a level country. What is there?
>
> MR. WALCOTT: The only thing I can say in regard to what has been done in Illinois is that along the line of the drainage canal about Chicago some work has been done and a little to the north. You have over most of Illinois deposits of clay and gravel from which your domestic water supply is largely taken, and a map of this and a map of the sources from which your minerals are obtained are entirely based upon a topographic map. You have a rolling country that is not perfectly flat, and upon the topographic map you must delineate carefully the distribution of the different coal seams, beds of clay, and whatever there may be of geologic interest. Now, in England, they started out with a map, like the map we are making. They have had all the geologic formations topographically mapped in just as flat country in places as in Illinois, and they are now surveying on the basis of 6 inches to the mile—a scale which costs fully eight times as much as the maps we are making in this country—in order to get information as to their economic resources in coal and iron. (Walcott 1899, 110)

Walcott got funding because he could answer inane questions in respectful, yet authoritative, dollars-and-cents terms.

Charles Doolittle Walcott, Paleontologist

A Saturday in mid-April, Walcott went off Baltimore to chat with Brooks at Johns Hopkins, who probably knew more about soft-bodied organisms than any biologist in America. Walcott consulted with him throughout his study of the fossil jellyfish and named a Middle Cambrian jellyfish *Brooksella*. It was a mutual admiration society, for in speculating on a change in life-style of animals from floating to bottom dwelling, Brooks wrote, "The paleontological side of the subject has been ably summed up by Walcott in an interesting memoir on the oldest fauna which is known to us from fossils" (Brooks 1894, 12). Brook's ideas in turn greatly influenced Walcott's thoughts on development of life and early changes in the fossil record. Their discussion went well, for that night Walcott presented his findings of ancient jellyfish to the Biological Society of Washington.

Walcott's diary records: "Was elected member of Nat. Acad. Sciences today" (April 23, 1896). This honor in the scientific establishment warrants a brief explanation. During the Civil War, a few Union military men realized scientists could answer very practical questions and some scientists wanted to help the war effort. Other scientists wanted to make their activities more professional and get rid of charlatans, and a few wanted the self-aggrandizement of an elite group equivalent to the Royal Society of London. Whatever the reasons, the National Academy of Sciences was chartered by Congress in 1863 (True 1913).

Historians concur the most important effort in the first half-century of the academy's existence was the 1878 report laying the foundation for the U.S. Geological Survey. Involvement in the growing controversy on destruction of the nation's forests was probably the second most significant act of the academy during the interval. Mainly, the academy was asked to advise the government on trivial issues. There was prestige in membership, but prior to the first World War, the academy was basically another forum to deliver a paper and listen to others present a current theory. The government was not much interested in advice on scientific matters from an outside body.

The annual spring meeting of the academy was in Washington and the fall meeting traveled. The group had no home and became an informal appendage of the Smithsonian once Joseph Henry took over as president in 1866. What day-to-day business occurred was carried out from the Castle, and almost all early Washington meetings were held on its premises. From 1884 to 1897 the annual meeting was in the National Museum. Walcott was no stranger to the group long before his election.

On scientific merit, Walcott might have been elected in 1892 after his dramatic discovery of ancient fish remains. He might have been elected in 1893, but perhaps the academy had enough trouble with its members Cope and Marsh feuding in public to steer clear of government geologists. He might have been elected in 1894, but the fate of the Geological Survey was unsettled and rumors floated that Walcott might leave Washington. He might have been elected in 1895, after appointment as director. One must keep in mind that the academy members do not increase their numbers lightly, and, after all, Walcott did not have a college degree, let alone a doctorate. Robert S. Woodward of Columbia, but with a long career in Washington, was the other new member elected in 1896; Woodward will reappear.

The election process to the academy is secret and complex, with eminent scientists in and equally eminent scientists out. Three years after Walcott was elected, Van Hise wrote him, "Of course we were pleased with the election of Comstock [astronomer at University of Wisconsin] to the National Academy. While Beecher [paleontologist at Yale University] has done some good work, it does seem as if the methods of choosing new members were far from satisfactory when he is elected, and such men as Chamberlin and Jordan are not members."[8] Van Hise did not become an academician until 1902, and Chamberlin did not make it until 1903. David Starr Jordan, ichthyologist and university president never became a member. Commenting on academy elections continues to be a springtime diversion for American scientists.

Honors do not substitute for continuing work. With jellyfish out of the way, on May 1, Walcott began study of Cambrian fossils Arnold Hague had collected in Yellowstone National Park. Since completion of the Eureka report, Hague had been spending his field time in Yellowstone. This geologic wonderland deserved comprehensive investigation and the fossils were a small part of the package. The rest of the month was dull, except for part of one day at the museum looking at fossils. In mid-May, the family again escaped to the countryside: "Spent today moving out to Stott House. Put up tent & settled family well by night. Helena & children in house" (May 16, 1896). Walcott bicycled to and from the train.

May flowed into June with more letters. Meetings involved the Fish Commission, the Civil Service commissioner, and the commissioner of Indian Affairs. There did not seem to be a common thread, though in the offing was a possibility of a move to the U.S. Post Office building, a granite monolith on

Charles Doolittle Walcott, Paleontologist

Pennsylvania Avenue. Others wanted the building more than Walcott did, and he resolved matters when he pointed out that the USGS would require at least three floors; Congress then allowed him to rent more space in the Hoee Building. Walcott was winning in committee meeting and enjoying the country life. Add to that, the director got in three days research on the Yellowstone Cambrian fossils.

In late June, he soothed an anxious and very pregnant Helena; between times, he studied Cambrian brachiopods. Four days after the fireworks on the glorious Fourth, Helena called him at 1:00 A.M. He bicycled to Washington while Helena rode in a wagon; "At 6:30 A. M. Baby boy 10:45 A.M. all well" (July 8, 1895). Benjamin Stuart came on the scene and the Walcott family was complete. Regardless of the new addition, Walcott had to get on with the *Annual Report* and with the Yellowstone fossils. There was a little more to do on the medusae and as always the never-ending flow of Geological Survey paper. Along with administrative chaff, manuscripts were examined in his office.

Walcott escaped from Washington in early August and met T. N. Dale in Vermont. Dale's summer job was detailed mapping in the Taconic region, to gain a better idea of the slate beds, as well as to unravel the geology. Walcott looked over the section and saw an overthrust near Burlington. They moved to St. Albans, but between a sick headache and persistent rain, fieldwork was a less-than-satisfactory outing; it rained at the other sections too. Walcott left for Lake Champlain, where J. F. Kemp from Columbia was another academic doing Geological Survey work. Finally, at Asbury Park, New Jersey, he rented a house for two and a half months, and got back to Washington and forty galleys of proof to read for the *Annual Report*. The end of the month, Walcott moved the family up to New Jersey and actually did a bit of fishing.

The first week in September, Walcott was in Washington "Busy at office A.M. & called on Sec'y Francis at 11:30. Attended funeral of G. Brown Goode in the afternoon. A fine man gone & one in whom I had a strong friendship. Busy at home in the evening." Two points need clarification. First, Smith had left as secretary of interior at the end of August, and Walcott now had a new boss. Second, Goode was a year younger than Walcott and, friendship aside, his death must have worried the mildly hypochondriac director.

Goode graduated from Wesleyan at nineteen, spent a year at the Museum of Comparative Zoology, and returned to Wesleyan as curator in a new science building. In 1872 he met Baird and became a volunteer for the Fish Commission (Oehser 1949). The winter of 1873 he came to Washington to arrange fish collections. After several years of volunteering, Baird gave him a paid position. Baird knew talent and Goode helped develop the Smithsonian display for the Philadelphia Centennial. When Baird became secretary in 1878, Goode was his right-hand man.

Goode put on Smithsonian displays in the many expositions America was holding. He lived for the National Museum, treating it like a mother with one chick, and kept the place going on what was a broken shoelace of an appropriation. Natural history objects have some sort of built-in display scheme, following Linnean classification and Darwinian evolution if nothing else. Increasingly, Goode moved into history, for a major problem was what to do with the artifacts of man, and man himself in terms of exhibits. Concordant with expanding his ideas on displays, Goode was a detailed "nuts and bolts" man. He made sure watchmen knew their duties, files were in order, and no collections left the building without proper paper work. His specifications for trays, storage cabinets, and display cases were used throughout the country. He worried about the size of labels and penmanship. "Every officer of the Museum is required to have upon his desk two kinds of ink" (Goode [1880?], 25). As a rough comparison, Goode was to public display in museums what Walcott was to the research in them.

He was considered the best museum man in America and possibly the world. Goode broke new ground in the philosophy of what a museum should be and his writings are still worth reading. Like so many of his generation, he was a workaholic. Goode smoked furiously though what finally did him in was the fiftieth anniversary of the Smithsonian Institution. He organized the event and wrote and edited a testimonial volume which turned out to be his memorial (Goode 1897). Unfortunately, Goode was not promoted to assistant secretary until January 1887, when Samuel Pierpont Langley was also given that title. Later that year, after Baird died, Goode was bypassed for the more prestigious Langley. A marvelous "what if" is the possible course of the Smithsonian had the regents been daring enough to appoint the man who deserved the position of secretary.

Several days after the funeral, Walcott left the city, this time for the far West. On September 15 he was in Reno, Nevada, "Feeling tired after 4¾ days on the train" (September 15, 1896); the term jet lag may be relatively new, but the concept has been around since the long-distance train trip was developed. The next day he moved to Carson City, had dinner with a friend, with whom he left his watch for safekeeping, and moved to Hawthorne. "Left Hawthorne 6. A.M. &

went by train to Candelaria & from there *via* Columbus to Silver Peak—by stage 46 *mi.* F. B. Weeks met me 8:40 P.M. & we went to our camp near the spring" (September 18, 1896). The 1894 trip had shown good reason to return to the region for more Early Cambrian fossils.

Walcott and Weeks concentrated on the coral-like archaeocyathids for a day or so. Silver Peak was a mining area for precious metals and they examined the geology around the mines before riding back to Columbus to look at coals in the younger Cretaceous beds; Walcott found a workable seam. They moved camp several times and in this dry country the teamster had to travel for water. They measured more rock thickness, found fossils below the archaeocyathids, but in spite of much hard work had generally poor paleontologic results. Walcott logged four hundred miles cumulative of daily horseback rides.

The camp wagon moved south, and Walcott and Weeks rode along the eastern flank of the Inyo Range puzzling out the rocks. The outfit eventually crossed the Inyos and into Owens Valley. One diary entry gives the flavor of the trip back into the mountains: "All day on the road towards Saline Valley a 16 mile grade rising 3600 feet. Kept the team busy until 5 P.M. Camped 20 miles out of Big Pine. Made a study of lake beds on way up Waucoba Canyon" (October 16, 1896). On the way to the summit, on a Sunday, Walcott found a long section from Cambrian to Carboniferous, but the season was too advanced to study it. Going out Waucoba Canyon, Walcott again looked at the beds from the vanished lake and had the essence of another paper.

It had been a busy, full month in the field. The pair got back to civilization, more or less, at Hawthorne, Nevada, and then to Reno and real civilization on the shore of the Pacific. In San Francisco Walcott and Weeks met R. U. Goode, one of the chiefs in topography. After other business, they called at Berkeley and Stanford. There were no fences to mend, but a courtesy call on colleagues never hurts.

Topographer Goode accompanied them to Los Angeles and from there they entrained for El Paso, Texas. Walcott wanted a geologic section of the rocks in the Franklin Mountains. Although the area is well exposed and not very rugged, this was not so easy, for the closest place to stay in this desert was twenty-two miles from the outcrop and they were not equipped to camp. Goode and Weeks both worked, and one may guess that Goode used an instrument while Weeks went out with a stadia rod to the outcrop that Walcott indicated. It was an efficient way to measure a long section of gently dipping rocks and simultaneously have a third person collect. In three days fieldwork was completed, and the end of the month they were in Ft. Worth, where the faithful Weeks left them to travel to Kansas. Goode and Walcott spent a couple of days in Indian Territory with the surveyors to see how the mapping was progressing, now that setting permanent markers was a new part of the effort.

Walcott went to Chicago, via St. Louis, for consultations with Van Hise and Iddings, probably on how to describe igneous rocks in the folios. He got back to hearth and home after being away for two months, and inside of a week was presenting a paper to the Philosophical Society on the dried-up lake he had found. This was one of the farthest west of these former glacial lakes, but much more important than that, the tilting of the lake beds indicated movement of the Inyo Mountains only a very short time ago, geologically speaking. Total fieldwork that season was looking at the lake beds from the Sierra and seeing them from horseback one day up the canyon and one day down. The paper was published in the *Journal of Geology* the following year (Walcott 1897), and still has all the salient points correct.

This investigation may have started Walcott musing along lines other than fossils and stratigraphy, for Chamberlin wrote: "We shall be very glad to consider your possible paper on the faulting of the Basin Range. The subject is one of very great interest to me from the dynamic standpoint."[9] That paper never appeared and Walcott's ideas on moving of the earth's crust remain unknown.

With the excursion into recent uplift out of the way, Walcott studied the laws which applied to the National Museum and the Smithsonian Institution, for Goode's successor and the future of the National Museum was still unresolved. Walcott met with Langley for two hours, though he did not record the subject. The last week in November Walcott went to Boston, where he saw Agassiz and Shaler; no doubt some of the talk concerned the vacuum created by Goode's death. Walcott also found time to look at Cambrian brachiopods in the Museum of Comparative Zoology. He spent the night with Hyatt in Boston, saw the Public Library, and thoroughly enjoyed himself. Walcott dropped down to New Haven to see H. S. Williams, who had left Cornell and was a replacement for Dana. Again there was talk of museums and how to run them. Sunday, he was in New York. Visits to the American Museum the following day and then to Columbia College which maintained collections, further broadened his insight into museology. When Walcott returned to Washington, Langley called on him, though again the subject is not noted.

Charles Doolittle Walcott, Paleontologist

Mid-December brought a surprise, but it might not have been all that much of a surprise. "Had a talk with Prof. Langley 4:30 5:30 P.M. respecting Asst Sect. S.[mithsonian] Inst. He offered the place to me. Talked the subject over with G. G. Hubbard in the evening" (December 12, 1896). It is interesting that Walcott consulted a confident who was Smithsonian regent, president of the National Geographic Society, and a longtime friend rather than any geologist. Walcott declined the position. Perhaps he did not want to leave the USGS while it was doing well and even had an expansion in a new direction; recapitulation may help.

In 1888, Newell was hired to organize a training camp to teach stream gaging to personnel of Powell's Irrigation Survey. He survived that wreckage by getting a pittance in 1891 from the Topographic Branch to continue measuring stream flow. By the dreaded spring of 1894, funds were so short that Walcott warned Newell he might be cut from the rolls. Newell also knew his way around Capitol Hill and at the very last minute, after the appropriation bill had already passed the House, he convinced a senator to add an amendment funding water investigations.

Before success, Newell called on Senator Hale one evening to seek support, who replied: "I have been very much interested in what you have told me but I am not going to support your project. If it once starts, nothing can stop it and I do not favor an endless expense to the Government" (Follansbee 1938, 70). Despite that individual rejection, twelve thousand dollars, which the Senate had added, survived when the committee met to iron out differences in the House and Senate versions.

Since 1890, Newell had the services of C. C. Babb, the Victorian equivalent of an electronic wizard. Topography under Henry Gannett was in financial straits who pointed out that since topographic funds had saved Newell, there was a debt to be paid. Topographer Arthur Powell Davis, the major's nephew, became a hydrologist overnight. These three founded major studies American water resources. Babb designed equipment, while Newell and Davis ran around setting up gaging stations and recruiting volunteers to man them. They met with great success, for everyone wanted to know about the streams and rivers of his area.

In 1895, Walcott took the sensible step of moving water work into the Geologic Branch. It did not fit well there, but it was a better match than with the topographers. The gaging stations sprouted and the data accumulated in the files. In 1896, the first of a new series of *Water Supply Papers* was published. By 1897, there were nine, and they proliferated at a speed which would impress a pair of rabbits. Senator Hale was correct in that this work was unending. Some geology departments built the walls of graduate student cubicles from USGS water supply papers.

The information has proved invaluable and will continue to be of merit as concern about climatic change increases. Many minerals can be substituted when in short supply, but water is priceless and one has to know how much there is. Others may have had the notion of gathering statistics, but it was Walcott who got Congress to agree to fund a new series of publications. Printing is watched closely by Congress and new series are not commonly authorized. These dull as dishwater columns of figures were not as exciting as the first fieldwork in Alaska, but it was another bravo accomplishment for 1896.

The holiday season moved in with its dinners, the load of correspondence increased, and Walcott was sick for a couple of days. Christmas came and went and the annual meeting of the Geological Society of America brought friend Williams into town. The "Year closes with little family well except colds. Survey matters appear to be in good condition. Financial matters dull & not promising for the immediate future" (December 31, 1896). If one does not count two *Annual Reports,* scientifically it was also a dull year, for though the *Bulletin* on the Cambrian rocks of Pennsylvania finally came out of the clutches of the Public Printer, the only really new item was the three-page paper on the Cambrian medusa (Walcott 1896b).

On January 1, Walcott went to church, left Williams at the train station, and paid his courtesy call to President Cleveland. Thereafter, he followed his bureaucratic routine of running a growing organization and courting Congress to insure it would continue to grow. Outlines of the process have been given and it is enough to state that, eleven months later, for the first time that year Walcott recorded he was examining Cambrian brachiopods; so much for research.

Early in January, Walcott was out of town briefly, lecturing in Brooklyn on Cambrian geology; it is hard today to visualize Brooklyn as the center of scientific interest that it once was. Added to his daily routine, even more of his evenings were taken up. Walcott had been rising through the hierarchy of the Cosmos Club, and he spent 1897 serving as vice-president.

He appeared before the Committee on Mines and Mining and prepared an extensive statement suggesting a division of mines and mining within the USGS and providing solid reasons for its establishment (Walcott 1898). He also suggested a museum of practical geology, thirty-thousand square feet in size, as an adjunct to the Geological Survey. Asking is the first step toward getting.

In mid-January, Van Hise arrived and Walcott took to the Smithsonian Castle to meet Langley, as Goode's position was still vacant. Van Hise returned to his own ivy-covered walls and wrote, "Reaching a decision has been a more difficult matter than I had expected, for the opportunity of working with you in Washington to build up the National Museum is very attractive."[10] Van Hise said no.

Meetings of the Smithsonian Board of Regents were big news in Washington and this year brought speculation of argument between Secretary Langley and Regent Hubbard. Ten possible candidates for Goode's position were mentioned and newspapers rumored several had contacted the Regents directly rather than the pompous Langley. Potential argument fizzled when Langley pulled a rabbit out of a hat and read a letter from Walcott:

> I am willing to look after the interests of the museum while your search is being continued to find a suitable person to nominate for the permanent position, but it must be with the understanding that I can give relatively little time to details of its administration. These must be attended to by permanent members of the staff. I think that the title given should intimate the temporary character of the service, while at the same time give the authority necessary for the general administration under the direction of the Secretary of the Smithsonian Institution.[11]

On January 27, 1897, Walcott became acting assistant secretary in charge of the National Museum; so much for a bad pun in the title. He offered to act on a voluntary basis, but the regents agreed with Langley that an honorarium was appropriate. Bureau heads Goode and Walcott were paid five thousand dollars annually, but Goode received an extra five hundred dollars from Smithsonian funds. With due respect to Goode, Walcott had a far larger staff and budget to handle; the regents gave him an honorarium of two hundred dollars per month.

The journal *Science* commented: "Mr. Walcott's selection for this post seems an eminently fitting one in view of the unusual executive abilities which he has shown himself to possess since he assumed the Directorship of the Geological Survey in 1894" (Anonymous 1897, 223). Walcott wrote,

> Nevertheless, when, after Professor Goode's death, the Secretary of the Smithsonian Institution, Dr. S. P. Langley, requested me to take temporary charge of the Museum, it was only after much hesitancy that I concluded to

assume the responsibility, my reluctance rising chiefly from the fear that, owing to official duties previously assumed, the comparatively small amount of time I could devote to the Museum would not be sufficient for the proper care and advancement of its interests. (Walcott 1899a, 3)

This extra duty did not benefit the USGS and occupied what time he might have found for research. As old-fashioned as it sounds, the most logical explanation for his taking on this burden was loyalty to organization. Duty called and Walcott responded. A Washington bureaucrat wrote to a friend: "On Sunday last I dined with Mr. Langley at Mr. [Henry] Adam's. I had not seen him before for a long time. He is looking better than I expected to see him. I asked how affairs were getting on at the Museum. He said he thought they would be all right if he could succeed in retaining Walcott."[12]

Walcott obtained a little relief from daily chores by convincing Congress of the need for a Geological Survey editor. This freed up Bailey Willis to become his assistant. By early February, the USGS Survey was so well in hand that Walcott could call a staff meeting to announce Willis's new position and discuss the appropriation. If the bureau had been moribund from 1892–94, it was satisfactory by 1896, and vigorous by 1897. Like Walcott's personal finances, the accounts of the organization were in meticulous order.

The finances of the National Museum were in order, but the place had other difficulties. One of Walcott's first actions was to bring Holmes back to Washington. The artist-geologist-ethnologist installed the Bureau of Ethnology exhibit of Indians at the Chicago Exposition, liked what he saw in the windy city and in 1894, took a museum position. His personality conflicted disastrously with that of the director of the Columbian Museum.

Late in March, Walcott wrote Holmes that the Museum appropriation would soon be passed: "This, of course, will permit our carrying out the plans we discussed for the National Museum, and your coming to Washington. I will write to Professor Langley on the subject within a few days."[13] "You need not feel disturbed about the Civil Service matter. Under the law some kind of examination must be held. I shall recommend that it be mainly the presentation of evidence of ability, as shown by works published, and positions filled."[14] The Civil Service wanted a written examination, besides publications. "I suggested the writing of an essay on the administration of the division of Anthropology in order that it might bring out your views in relation to the same."[15] A month later Walcott wrote, "You have passed the Civil Service at probably the highest ratio of any one who has ever had any form of examination. The Committee consisted on Major Powell, an officer of the Commission, and myself."[16] When Walcott steered, the ship never went aground.

Seldom is emphasis placed on the tiny numbers in government bureaus of that era. In 1893, the Geological Survey had a total staff of about 150, and the National Museum had about one-third that number. That estimate does not give an accurate picture of the weakness of the National Museum. From the time the Museum building opened in 1881, Baird and Goode welcomed government agencies to help fill the offices. Even under Henry, there had been "honorary" appointments, that is persons who were unpaid but were given an affiliation in return for services they provided; for all his efforts in curating museum collections and organizing displays, Honorary Curator Walcott never received a penny. Well into the twentieth century, honorary curators outnumbered paid staff.

> The ... scientific staff ... number in all 63 persons. . . . Of these 26 are compensated for their services and the remainder serve gratuitously, being for the most part connected with other bureaus of the Government. The system of honorary curatorship, . . . is a disadvantage when carried to the present extent. Such a system has a disintegrating effect upon the organization, as the men are not entirely at the command of the administrative officers and are not obliged to serve at definite hours or under ordinary restrictions of the paid curators. The number of honorary officers should be reduced by the substitution of a larger number of salaried officers. (Walcott 1900, 10)

Walcott may not have had much time for new administration, but when the new fiscal year started, he had reorganized the National Museum into three departments.

Holmes became one of the three head curators in the National Museum. Museum humor tends toward the bizarre, and for years a joke in anthropology mentioned head curators and curators of heads. F. W. True headed biology, and G. P. Merrill was head curator of geology. After Walcott became director, Schuchert was transferred to the museum staff. Walcott detailed an assistant to help him. In the new system, in theory, the assistant reported to Honorary Curator Walcott, who reported to Assistant Curator Schuchert, who reported to Head Curator Merrill, who reported to Acting Assistant Secretary Walcott. That chain of command was never used, but it was clear who reported to whom.

Walcott's reorganization on July 1, 1897, was a fundamental step forward for the National Museum. He went on to report the need for more assistants, a perennial cry, and one seldom answered. Walcott could not obtain a larger museum staff during his tenure, but at least he brought the problem out in the open; Goode minimized it, and Langley ignored it. It is a wonder he had time to think about the difficulties of the museum, for larger problems appeared. On February 22, the 165th anniversary of George Washington's birth, the stew about American forests boiled over. This triggered a complex series of events and their presentation is better delayed for a few pages.

March 4 was Inauguration Day, seeing William McKinley take up residence in the White House. The chiefs of scientific bureaus may have heaved a sigh of relief when the Cleveland administration left. Pressure of government economy for the sake of economy, regardless of the consequences, had eased. For Walcott, it meant a new boss when Secretary of Interior Bliss took office. Walcott was thought of highly, but ongoing programs and any new ideas had to be justified and "sold" to the new management who hailed from the "Show Me" state of Missouri.

Mid-March brought an unexpected break in routine. Walcott took young Charlie on the overnight steamer down Chesapeake Bay to Old Point Comfort. They examined Fortress Monroe, went around the Hampton Roads by boat looking at the ships, and had a good day gathering fiddler crabs on the beach. A week away did wonders for Walcott in thinking through forest issues.

With the positions Walcott held, he was in constant motion. One day detailed in the diary, he "called on Public Printer Palmer 9 A.M. Senator Perkins 9:30. Returned to Survey at 10:A.M. Called on Ray Bliss [secretary of interior] 1. P.M.—Museum, 1:20–3. P.M. Survey 3:15–4:35 P.M." (April 14, 1897). There are tales of Walcott tearing around the city on a bicycle.

Somewhere he slipped in the time to send a two-page paper to the *American Journal of Science* (Walcott 1897a) considering the proper name to use for a few species of brachiopods. It looks for all the world like a couple of pages completed as the first systematic part of a larger paper, but sent off on the assumption that there was no prospect of completing the work. This makes for the driest possible reading, of interest to remarkably few people and one wonders why the editor printed it.

Sir Archibald Geike, since 1882 the distinguished director-general, not mere director, of the Geological Survey of Great Britain, was lecturing at Johns Hopkins, and Walcott took Helena to a dinner in his honor; they had met in 1888 at the London Congress when Walcott was still a youngish man on his way up. The next day Geike and party took a boat trip to Annapolis. Following that, a party of forty-nine geologists entrained with him and toured the Appalachians for three days. A classic picture taken at Harpers Ferry includes almost every distinguished geologist or soon-to-be distinguished geologist in America.

Geike recalled:

> Leaving Baltimore on the morning of 3rd May, with the heartiest good wishes of my friends there, I went on to Washington to fulfil several engagements. Of these one of the most interesting was to pay a visit to the office of the Geological Survey of the United States—a much more extensive establishment than ours in Jermyn Street. I found that besides the geological staff, it included a large corps of topographers, engravers, printers, as well as the officials who superintended national irrigation, water-supply, and forest-lands. With the Director of the whole organization, Mr. Walcott, I had long been in correspondence, and I had formed a high opinion of his ability, both as an original man of science, and as a director of the work of others. What perhaps interested me most, as evidence of his personal character, was a small room, full of boxes, cabinets, books, and papers, with hardly space left in which to turn around. To this little sanctum he retired whenever a few moments could be snatched from the day's work, in order to resume his labours among the Cambrian trilobites—a department of palaeontology in which he has become the highest authority. (Geike 1924, 287)

The USGS laid on a reception for Sir Archibald on May 5, impressive enough to be mentioned in the papers. The Mrs. Hayes, Walcott, and Willis greeted 350 guests while the U.S. Marine Band played. During his time in Washington, Geike was staying with Hague and one afternoon Theodore Roosevelt popped in for tea and overwhelmed them with his energy. For good measure, Walcott dragged Geike to the White House to shake hands with McKinley.

When the noise quieted, Walcott and Van Hise went back to Hancock, Maryland, looking particularly at folded rocks. For years, Walcott's photograph of an anticline was the standard illustration in textbooks. Then he was off to Boston, via the New Jersey shore, partly to look for a summer place, and partly to examine lithographic techniques for the expanding production of maps. The last half of May, Walcott spent planning the field parties. The family left for New London, Connecticut, at the end of the month, and Walcott relaxed enough to go to a baseball game. He used the next month running to and from various offices, but finally was able to go to New York City with his old field comrade Iddings and take the steamer to New London.

It was vacation time for Walcott, the time he worked on the USGS *Annual Report*. Then he read about the Nicaragua Canal for relaxation and finally gathered his thoughts to dictate a popular account of the recent events concerning the Forests Reserves; several administrations later, the designation was changed to National Forests.

Mention American forests and the name that comes to mind is Gifford Pinchot. The name Walcott rings no bells and comment concerning the Geological Survey causes puzzlement. When Van Hise wrote his book on conservation in 1910, Walcott was ignored. In the classic study of forest policy by Ise (1920) both Pinchot and Walcott are mentioned as having studied forestry in Europe, clearly an error, and, except for one paragraph in that book, he is otherwise ignored. In Hays's conservation tome, the USGS has a bare mention about coal investigations, and Walcott's name never appears. In studies of the conservation movement which swept America, he is the forgotten man.

Four hundred years earlier, trees were an impediment when European settlers came to America; destruction of the eastern forests to provide farmland was a major task. By the time of the Civil War there were a few voices pointing out the folly of cutting down all the trees. Mostly no one cared and it took about two more decades before committees began to form and pass resolutions of concern. The concern finally reached a high level in 1896, when Interior Secretary Smith asked the National Academy of Sciences to appoint a committee. One of the five members was Arnold Hague; the very young Pinchot was secretary of what was called the Forestry Commission. Hague was keenly aware of the forest destruction in and around Yellowstone Park. He had a number of social contacts and his talk, a few years earlier to the Boone and Crockett Club, a group of New York millionaires who fancied themselves as hunters, might have been as important to the start of the conservation movement as any other single action.

Who started the National Academy of Sciences activity is not clear, but in his autobiography Pinchot gives full credit to Pinchot for convincing Smith to ask the academy for an opinion and even for drafting his letter. Pinchot has harsh words about the chairman, who was a mere Harvard botanist and not a forester, though he did consider Hague the most valuable member of the commission. Pinchot reveals much of his own character in writing that he was invited to the "Great Basin Mess" and proceeded to eat with the group every week, and then commenting that the regular members were too polite to tell him that attending was a one-time honor.

The land laws passed for a century encouraged settlement and the further using up of trees. Almost by accident, Congress in 1891 granted the president

Charles Doolittle Walcott, Paleontologist

authority to set aside government lands as forest reserves. By the end of that year, sixteen reserves of about 17.5 million acres were established. President Benjamin Harrison did not much care about trees, and the last reserve had been designated in September 1893. In fact, designating reserves was a paper action, for logging and setting fires to increase grazing land went on unchecked.

When Cleveland returned to Washington for his second term, he too was not much interested about deforestation. Education at this level takes time. The Forestry Commission toured the West in 1896 and set down to write a report. "Dr. Charles D. Walcott, Director of the United States Geological Survey, had supplied our committee with much valuable material and the Commission with office room in Washington. Without the Survey, then and later, the Commission would have been up a very tall tree" (Pinchot 1947, 93). The commission recommended setting up thirteen new reserves in the West.

In later years, Pinchot insisted that the chairman virtually sabotaged the committee by not producing an early report so that Cleveland could mention it in his state of the union message. That is the viewpoint of a zealot, for in all likelihood, any publicity would have backfired. As matters eventually evolved, on February 1, months before the final report was completed, the chairman sent a letter to Secretary of the Interior Francis with the recommendations. Francis was a new short-term appointee in a lame duck presidential administration; Cleveland, defeated and then reelected, would be out of office a second time on March 4, 1897. Francis surely made his mark on Washington by forwarding the letter and urging action. On February 22, 1897, Cleveland established by proclamation new forest reserves of 21,379,840 acres, more than doubling the size of these reserved areas.

Cleveland's proclamation may have been based on altruism, it may have been based on foresight, it may have been a political ploy to complicate life for the next administration. Regardless of the underlying motives, this was a bold step and an important one for conservation. When the Forest Reserves were proclaimed, like Queen Victoria, Congress was not amused, and that is putting the matter as politely as possible.

Public meetings were held, petitions were sent to Congress, and an amendment was tacked onto the Sundry Civil Bill; Congress had no time to act under the Cleveland administration. When McKinley called a special session for March 15, the storm of protest resumed and Congress was determined to discuss more than the tariff. After interviewing Walcott, Ise wrote:

In the meantime, Charles D. Walcott of the Geological Survey, seeing that the forest reserves were in danger, went to Senator Pettigrew and convinced him that there was an opportunity to do a great service to the country by securing the passage of legislation for the protection and administration of the reserves. Walcott drew up a bill using the McRae bill (H.R. 119) as a basis, and after talking it over with Secretary Bliss of the Department of the Interior, with the forestry commission of the National Academy of Sciences, and even with President McKinley and his cabinet, asked Pettigrew to introduce it as an amendment to the Sundry Civil Bill. (Ise 1920, 132)

Diary entries support the accuracy of this summary. After returning from his trip with Charlie, Walcott had a "Busy day at Survey & Interior Dept. mostly concerning forestry & the Forest Reserves. At home in the evening" (March 29, 1897). Four days later he "Spoke on the 'Forest Reserves' to President McKinley & his cabinet" (April 2, 1897). Walcott "spent most of the day with the 'Forestry Commission' & the 'Forest Reserve' question at Dep't of Interior" (April 5, 1897). Twice in April he met with Senator Pettigrew.

Important as the Executive Branch of government is, Congress makes the laws and holds the money. The draft bill Walcott prepared was modified, especially in allowing mining groups, and particularly the Homestake Mine, to continue to cut timber. A key point brought out by Rabbitt (1980, 272), biographer of the Geological Survey, is that Senator Pettigrew, from South Dakota, the home state of Homestake, lived next door to Walcott. When the bill finally passed, in effect Congress gave the USGS a full year to begin surveying boundaries and get a grasp on the problems of what areas to reserve. The rationale was to have the forested areas in drainage areas of streams to help regulate the flow of water; this was not quite the full emphasis on harvesting forest products that Pinchot wanted. At the end of the year of grace, even though there was some minor modifications of boundaries, the forest reserves had been saved.

This was an incredible victory, for almost certainly Cleveland's proclamations would be nullified. The new Republican president had to be convinced to support, and strongly support, the unpopular action of a past Democratic administration. In the face of a large number of upset western voters, Congress had to be convinced to provide money to examine the reserves. Senator Pettigrew had been the most outspoken opponent of Cleveland's action, yet he introduced the amendment which saved them.

It might be helpful to go over the ground once more with Pinchot, for he adds color:

Charles Doolittle Walcott, Paleontologist

Walcott, a man of first-class ability who knew Congress like the back of his hand, must have known of this shift [against Cleveland's proclamation]. He was familiar with the work of the Commission and believed in it, and began to consider what he could do to keep it from being destroyed. . . .

On March 29 Walcott had a conference with Bliss, who was with him in wanting to save the Cleveland Reserves, but doubtful of the outcome. Nevertheless, Bliss put the forest question up to the president. To quote further Walcott's own account, "On Friday, April 2, I was called to the White House, and on arrival was ushered into the Cabinet Room, where President McKinley was seated with members of his Cabinet. He explained to me that Secretary Bliss had told him of the proposed legislation, and asked me to explain it to him and to the Cabinet. I did so, and before leaving was assured that it met with his approval." (1947, 114–15)

As stated, it sounds so very simple.

April 5 was another critical point. Walcott advised the commission as to what to say to selected senators. A compromise was struck in that the lands would not be withdrawn from the public domain for a year. By June 4, the amended bill was signed, and four days later Bliss approved Walcott's plan of action. The USGS received $150,000 to survey boundaries. In a way, this was a mirror image of earlier events. Powell obtained the reform legislation he longed for in irrigation and was sandbagged when all land claims were suspended while the Survey surveyed. Walcott, by seeking a delay, saved a reform for the public good. What a change in Congress! Survey interaction in less than a decade.

Much footwork by Walcott and his nimble tongue brought the package together before it was introduced in Congress. Once the pieces were in place "Willis & Pinchot dined with [us] & in the evening others came in: Baker, Gilbert Thompson, Renshaw, Hayes, Douglas, Goode, Wilson, Rizer, Newell & Diller" (April 7, 1897). Those who have not been previously mentioned as USGS geologists or hydrographers, were topographers or administrators. Pinchot was the only forester in the bunch. This group determined how the forests were to be surveyed and studied. All were more or less illustrious in other ways; none has been noted for their efforts on the forest reserves, with the possible exception of Gannett, yet all did outstanding work.

Pinchot was offered a position as special agent of the Land Office at twelve hundred dollars. He declined. Walcott and Hague had him appointed as a confidential forest agent at ten dollars per day, and he accepted. For Pinchot it was the title, not the money. Walcott liked this young enthusiast, fifteen years his junior, and invited him to speak to the National Academy of Sciences under his auspices. Walcott even nominated him for membership, but he was never elected, for he lacked scientific credentials.

Walcott was too shrewd to tell the public of presidents educated, congressmen soothed, and compromises reached. In his account, Walcott discussed the history of forest reserves, where the new reserves were located, how they were to be surveyed, and then went into a detailed justification of the advantages of the reserves:

> If the reserves are judiciously selected and honestly administered, and thus made to commend the policy to the American people, the difficulties met will be of little moment. That the reserves will be of great benefit to the communities to which they are tributary is absolutely certain, and it is also certain that in time the policy of forest reserves will develop into one of the most popular, beneficial, and valuable institutions of the Government. (Walcott 1898a, 15)

With this statement sent off to *Appleton's Popular Science Monthly,* where it appeared the following February and garnered favorable public opinion toward the forestry efforts, Walcott returned from vacation. Instituting Civil Service for the National Museum was a complex business, and loose ends required his attention. Walcott returned north the end of the month to kiss Helena and the children goodbye.

On August 1, Walcott stopped in Holland Patent to see Mother and sister Josie. Then it was westward with the traditional stop in Chicago to see Chamberlin; the faithful Weeks joined him. By the fifth, they were in Deadwood, South Dakota, and had two days on the outcrop to measure sections and collect Cambrian fossils. They went to visit Homestake, the largest gold mine in the United States, and the next day, they were joined by geographer Gannett and J. A. Holmes. Holmes, formerly state geologist of North Carolina, early on volunteered to gage streams for Powell and he was the nucleus of what would eventually separate from the USGS as the Bureau of Mines. The group looked at forest reserves, mica mines, and had their picture taken, probably by Weeks, sitting on Harney Peak. It was a successful politico-scientific venture, and leaving Holmes to his mica, the three pushed on.

"With Gannett & Weeks left Sheridan for the Big Horn Mts. by the Hyattsville road—camped 16 *mi* out at the foot of the grade. Took along 4 horse team, 2 horses on buckboard & one saddle horse" (August 16, 1897). The buckboard team was not up to the job and Weeks had to take them back to town. Notwithstanding that, a section was measured on Big Goose Creek. They moved on to Yellowstone National Park, where Walcott looked at the layout of the park roads, talked to army officers running the park, and considered the trees, while others admired the geysers.

The next year on December 6, the secretary of the interior asked for information on the region south of Yellowstone National Park, and by December 12, Gannett had completed a large report on the forests, along with printed maps, and Walcott a short general statement. They could have worked very hard for a few days, but it seems far more likely that this report was organized in a back room in the spring of 1897. Walcott put matters quite clearly about the winter range of big game in the area. "Will the Government prevent the shooting of game within the Yellowstone Timber Reserve and the Teton Forest Reserve? If it does not, the rifle and the shotgun will as surely exterminate the game as will the destruction of their winter pasture" (Walcott 1898b, 5). He suggested formation of a Teton National Park, for "in my judgement there is nothing that exceeds in natural beauty the valley of Jackson Lake and the Teton Mountains" (Walcott 1898b, 6). The present National Park was not formed until after Walcott died and the land was bought by private money.

Walcott and Weeks continued west to Spokane, where he found a "favorable spirit" toward forest reserves. They moved to Seattle and Walcott noted the rain with an underline and used two exclamation points in his diary. The trip went sour abruptly. "At 11:20 A.M. a telegram came from brother Ellis telling me of my mother's death this morning. Am sorry I was not with her. She was a good mother and I loved her. Age 76" (September 3, 1897). Her death was "not unexpected, but a great shock. Am too far away to attend funeral" (September 4, 1897).

They looked at forests around Mount Shasta, then went to San Francisco and to Yosemite National Park. Walcott and Weeks toured and camped with the army, observing on behalf of Secretary Bliss. After a week they left and traveled over the crest of the Sierra Nevada "45 miles of sandy roads to get to Big Pine [California]" (September 16, 1897). Walcott had done enough field examination of parks for the Interior Department and forests for the Geological Survey to last a while. He wanted to study the geology and paleontology of Cambrian rocks. Walcott, being director, was able to arrange his schedule so as not to be out in the western deserts during summer.

They rested a day in Big Pine before tackling the Inyo Mountains. Weeks was busy with camping gear, and Walcott caught up on correspondence and wrote a report on Yosemite. They rode eastward to the summit between Deep Springs Valley and Waucoba Canyon for a scouting trip. They returned to the eastern side of the Sierra Nevada and worked their way upward to get a view. The next day brought another difficult climb, but Walcott had not lost his sense of wonder: "Scene superb. Counted 25 glacial lakes from one point" (September 19, 1897). They went back to the ranch where they had stayed, for the camp wagon was missing. Eventually they found the teamsters only just leaving Big Pine and ended by setting up camp at night in the dark.

This was not an easy area, and it was stiff day's work to lug a camera to the 10,700-foot summit; there was compensation in excellent fishing near camp. Again, it was up 3,500 feet to look at the forest reserves from above. They went back down the Sierra to Big Pine and moved across Owens Valley to Waucoba Mountain. A couple of locals, Smith and Cuddington, were employed, so the pack string had eight animals. Weeks and Walcott geologized while the packers moved camp closer to the outcrop. Walcott found nice *Olenellus,* just as family illness required Weeks to leave.

The fieldwork continued unabated, camp being moved almost every day. The lower part of the section was cut off by an intrusion of granite, but at the head of Saline Valley, Walcott "Measured nearly 4000 feet of the Olenellus zone" (September 29, 1897), not a bad days's work. Cuddington found himself a temporary geological assistant. The next few days were not nearly so pleasant, what with wind, rain, and unanticipated faults breaking up the sections. Walcott kept going and added five hundred feet to the lower part of the stratigraphic section. He was delighted to find the oldest fossils he had ever collected in the west.[17] They moved down the west side of the range, closer to Independence, California. The geology there was mainly post-Cambrian rocks, but Walcott was pleased with the Ordovician and Silurian fossils; it was a nice ending for the season.

The outfit moved into Alvord, where he paid off the men and took the stage to Mojave, a jolting all day trip. Walcott finally got to Los Angeles and in a reprise of the last year met topographer Goode, plus a few other Survey folk. They took a quick look at the forest reserve in the San Gabriel Mountains and in mid-October headed east. The party crossed Arizona, New Mexico, and part of Texas, and four days later they were in Denver. The surveyors working in the Indian Territory were gathered there for the winter and showed off their maps for part of the day. Walcott pushed on to Chicago; as trustee for a deceased relative he had to explain the estate to one of his many cousins. He pushed on to "Washington 11:55 A.M. Helena & Sidney met me at the station. All well at home. In the afternoon we (Helena & I) sold our Q St. & 16*th* street houses, taking 1323 13th Street in exchange" (October 21, 1897).

Walcott did not pause to catch his breath before getting back onto the Washington treadmill. He had Langley over for dinner the following night, and no doubt one topic was final arrangements for a dinner in four days to honor the Norwegian explorer Nansen, though the budget estimates were equally pressing. The second of November they moved from 1776 Q to 1323 Thirteenth Street, where the family would stay for two years. Walcott's various housing moves had been toward ever finer neighborhoods and each real estate transaction was a profitable one. Even before the family unpacked, he was off to Utica to see Josie and begin settling his mother's estate.

A few days later, Walcott was back in Washington and before Thanksgiving was squeezing in a few hours to study Cambrian brachiopods. Another short work on they fossils appeared, far more meaningful than his two-page effort earlier in the year. This paper illustrates the need to collect widely for years before writing. In one genus, he described new species from Quebec and Arizona which he had collected and another new species collected by a colleague in Montana. A new genus contained a species from Pennsylvania and second from New York; yet another new species was from Alabama. Twelve printed pages plus two plates is a worthwhile endeavor. "This is the first of a proposed series of preliminary papers on the Cambrian Brachiopoda, to be published in advance of a memoir on the subject. Owing to administrative duties, only a small part of each year can be devoted by me to paleontologic studies" (Walcott 1897b, 767). That was an understatement, but other papers in this series did appear in later years in the *Proceedings of the United States National Museum*.

The second Wednesday in December, the Geological Society of Washington met, where Walcott told of latest discoveries in the Inyo Mountains. He gave one talk in 1893 when the GSW started, four the next year, two the following year, and one in 1896. With a large geologic community now in Washington, the society was running well; only occasionally would he appear on this platform. What satisfaction there might be in a talk well presented and well received dissipated, when longtime older friend Gardiner Green Hubbard died, full of years and honors.

In mid-December, he accompanied Helena to an evening meeting of the Woman's Washington Memorial Association. This association is sort of a will-of-the-wisp. It was chased by Walcott for four years until unexpected good fortune changed his goal, though he never abandoned the organization. It has been intermittently chased by historians and thereby given an importance that the organization may not deserve.

More serious matters came in late December: "Survey A.M., Museum P.M. Talked with Prof. Langley about my relations to Museum & Smithsonian. A misunderstanding has arisen that may settle matters very quickly" (December 24, 1897). Langley and Hall shared the same character trait of treating subordinates as underlings. Consider the private letter of micromanagement Langley wrote Walcott on budget estimates to be sent to Congress:

> You know that last year I made a personal appeal to Mr. Cannon for an increase of the item for Preservation of Collections, with special reference to obtaining $10,000.00 to be used to increase salaries, and rather (as I told him) of the higher salaries than the lower. I did in fact obtain an additional $5000.00, which enabled the Museum, among other things, to gain the services of Mr. Holmes. The Chairman will probably remember the impression of this still-urgent need, which it was so strenuously sought to create; and it would be perhaps desirable to lay more stress on this in the present year than has been done.
>
> I should like to consider also whether it is desirable to have so large an increase in the number of items, which are made to fall this year under 14 heads, instead of 8.
>
> I should like to discuss these separately with you before they go to the Treasury, and when I am called before the Committee, I shall be glad to have you with me, and to have in advance a perfect mutual understanding of the most urgent needs to advocate.[18]

That Langley would be concerned over a budget listing fourteen items rather than eight is insightful. Walcott knew that the more items, the smaller each one would be and thus less likely to be cut. This time, Walcott must have had a serious disagreement with Langley, for there is a later diary entry the same day in a different pen and a bit steadier hand pointing out the family had a living Christmas tree on Christmas Eve. Walcott ended the year by noting that all was well with his little family.

Like every new year, 1898 showed promise. Walcott started this one a bit differently by not calling at the White House. Instead, Langley and Walcott talked over matters and presumably reached an understanding. Three days later he spoke to the Philosophical Society of Washington generating more support for the forest reserves. "Busy with museum & survey matters during the day. At annual meeting of the Cosmos Club in the evening was elected president of the club" (January 10, 1898). Walcott served as a vice-president of AAAS in 1893, and on the council of the Geological Society of America through the trying period from 1893–95, and he was involved with the National Museum, quite apart from the USGS and the forests, but that was not enough. This man could no more decline an office offered than a knight of King Arthur's round table could spurn a maiden in distress.

The following evening, he was at a meeting of the joint commission a development from the Washington scientific societies (Flack 1975, 143–64). The first cooperation between local groups in 1882 evolved into representatives of each meeting regularly to exchange information. A directory of members of the societies was published, and conflicts in scheduling of meetings avoided. Occasionally a few of the societies would hold joint meetings or assist in hosting a distinguished visitor.

More might be done. The joint commission was enlarged to include the officers of all the societies, and that did not work. A suggestion came for the Geological Society of Washington to change the commission into a local Academy of Science. Comments began to stir when Walcott was elected to the National Academy of Sciences and stirred more vigorously when he was vice-president of the Cosmos Club, where the local scientists came to drink at sundown.

The fifth of February, Walcott set out to persuade the Philosophical Society of Washington, the oldest and most conservative group, that a Washington Academy of Sciences should rise from the foundation of the joint commission. This was a key point in the formation of the academy and naturally after Walcott explained it, the Philosophical Society voted favorably. "The policy of the new Academy and the choice of functions to which special prominence shall be given are yet to be determined; but its progress will be watched with interest and expectation" (Anonymous 1898, 255).

Early in February, Walcott and Helena went to New York for a few days to see relatives and give another lecture at the Brooklyn Institute, but mainly to look at buildings of the American Museum and Columbia University. At least two prospects for new structures were simmering in Congress, and Walcott wanted to be prepared; he always tried to stay a step or two ahead of any future developments. While they were away, he was elected a member of the board of trustees of the Church of the Covenant. This was important enough to warrant a separate slip of paper placed in his daily diary.

Buildings were very much on the mind of the acting assistant secretary, for the National Museum was a shoddy structure. Walcott was forceful in noting deficiencies. "The present museum building, though large in extent, is over-crowded. It was built with the cheapest materials and under the cheapest sys-tem of construction. Its lack of architectural dignity and the indifferent char-acter of the materials of which it is constructed give it the appearance of a temporary structure and tend to cheapen the effect of really good cases and the very valuable collections which it contains. The visitor is everywhere confronted with rough walls, unfinished ceilings, and obtrusive trusses and supports. It should also be remembered that a considerable portion of the collections are still in the Smithsonian building, where the crowding is scarcely less than in the Museum building" (Walcott 1900, 10).

Secretary Baird may have been proud of this structure, originally constructed at a cost of nine cents per cubic yard. If one adds the cost of roof repairs and continual maintenance, this most economical of government buildings has now become one of the most expensive. Today only minimal exhibit space remains; the bulk of the building is offices, all thoroughly rebuilt from their original con-dition. The roof still leaks.

Stories abound in Washington.

Charles D. Walcott, Powell's successor as director, was less of a fighter than the old Civil War veteran in his relations with Congress. He was more diplo-matic. During his administration "Uncle Joe" Cannon was Speaker of the House, and it was his habit after a fatiguing session to walk up Pennsylva-nia Avenue. Walcott, as if by chance, would draw up beside the curb with a fast-stepping bay and a light buggy and suggest a drive in Rock Creek Park, but during those rides he never mentioned business. On one occasion "Uncle Joe" paused, his foot on the step and said: "Walcott, you may have a building for the Survey or one for the National Museum, but you can't have both." And Walcott took the Museum. (Willis 1947, 32)

There was no choice, for as cramped as the USGS was for space and as much as rent cost, the bureau was still better off than its poor relation on the Mall. The New National Museum building opened for business in 1910.

Early in March, Walcott explained the work accomplished so far on the for-est reserves to Secretary Bliss, and the same day shifted gears to discuss plans for USGS investigations in Alaska with the secretary of war. Alaska had formid-able logistical problems, but the Survey men who went north did a remarkable job year after year. A few days later, he shifted gears again to escort the prince of Belgium through the museum. The epitome of his ability to shift his attention instantaneously may have come when Walcott appeared before the Committee on Appropriations and ". . . at odd moments worked on Cambrian brachiopods" (March 14, 1898).

Walcott plate of responsibilities overflowed and for the topping, Alexander Agassiz wrote him. Over the years, Agassiz had developed harassment of government scientists into an art form. Walcott responded:

> I do not know who the scientific men are that you speak of as protesting against my remaining in charge of the Geological Survey and the National Museum. I do know that some of the strongest scientific men in Washington and elsewhere have urged me to continue in charge of the museum until the reorganization which went into effect July 1, 1897, has been placed on a sound footing.
>
> It may have been a mistake, personally, for me to have taken charge of the Museum, but those upon whom I depended for advice considered that it was the thing to do for the good of the scientific interests in Washington. I myself felt that there were men who were better qualified to take up the work, but at the time of my appointment it did not appear practical to secure any one of them.
>
> The administration of the Museum has been thoroughly reorganized, and also, to a large extent, the system of exhibits. . . . I have a strong interest in the Museum and its future, but, so far as I can see, my work should be, at least for the present, with the Geological Survey.
>
> My Appointment as Acting Assistant Secretary in Charge of the National Museum is a tentative one, and will cease as soon as certain matters that I have in charge are consummated.[19]

On July 1, 1898, Walcott reverted to being an honorary curator, and one cannot help but wonder why he wrote Agassiz that his future was with the Geological Survey. As assistant secretary, he would have had more time to pursue paleontology. The Survey was running well throughout geology, topography, and hydrology, and the forest work charmed the Congress. If one has to guess, the reason lay in Langley. He could be difficult to subordinates and Walcott's temperament was not that of a subordinate. Better to be carry a killing administrative load and be one's own boss.

Walcott did accompany Langley to the 1898 Appropriations Committee hearing, but that was an exception for the secretary. Traditionally, Langley came alone into the hearing room, leaving his various minions outside. When posed a question, Langley would ask to be excused, go into the hall, get the answer, and return. It got to be quite a game in the hearings to see how many times the secretary could be made to leave the room. This was not Walcott's style. Walcott remained friends with Langley, but only because he was not under him.

Before Walcott left administration of the Smithsonian, he initiated one more event which affected the Institution throughout the remaining years of Secretary Langley's tenure. For several years trouble was brewing with Spain, or at least that William Randolph Hearst and his newspapers were pushing for a fight. After the *Maine* sank in Havana Harbor, the result was Theodore Roosevelt's lovely little war. Before that incident, on March 21, Walcott had a long talk with Langley. In 1896, Langley successfully launched a steam-driven model aerodrome. Thereafter, he publicly retired from the mundane problems of making a machine to carry a man. In fact, he was seeking money to continue investigations (Crouch 1980). Possibilities were here, and Walcott never overlooked possibilities. He was a patriot and this new machine might be of service to his country. Langley asked Walcott to pursue matters, saddling him with several difficult requirements, including total secrecy and complete control of funds by the secretary.

If the prospect of a new secret weapon was in the offing, there was no time to waste and Walcott began at the top. "Called on President McKinley at noon & talked with him about Prof. Langley's flying machine, Had a long talk with Prof. Langley 1:30 2:30 P.M." (March 24, 1898). "Busy with survey matters. Called on Ass't Secty's Rosevelt [*sic*] & Miekeljohn about Prof. Langley's flying machine & later on Prof. Langley" (March 25, 1898). Walcott had had prior dealings with Roosevelt. Whatever there might have been about Civil Service matters or New York state social ties, they were professional colleagues of a sort. Roosevelt gave a talk to the Biological Society of Washington on the classification of mammals from the standpoint of a big game hunter; it was a silly, but rousing, performance.

As with almost anything in Washington, a procedural step is to appoint a committee. Thirteen days after he spoke with the president, Walcott "Met with Prof. S. P. Langley, Graham Bell, Col. Davis & Cap't Colt Craig U. S. A., Commander Davis & Prof. Brown U. S. N. for the purpose of looking into flying machine" (April 6, 1898). That is spectacular time for launching any new project in Washington and considering the highly speculative nature of man, who has no wings, flying, it is remarkable.

Charles Doolittle Walcott, Paleontologist

Walcott inquired periodically to keep things moving along. He was "At War Department most of the morning looking after report of Board on the Langley flying machine" (May 26, 1898). Again, this is fast action on a report. Langley on his own would never have brought his machine to the attention of the military, and even he had, without Walcott's push and know-how of federal corridors, the military would not have responded. Walcott was "Busy at the Survey most of the day. Called at the War Dept. A.M. in relation to Prof. Langley's flying machine. Prof. Langley called to say goodbye for the summer" (June 13, 1898). Langley was off for his annual trip to Europe.

Walcott's concept of urgency and Langley's notion of it were not the same. In a similar set of circumstances, Walcott and any other person would have plunged immediately into the problem of manned flight. The story from this point on is well known. The Spanish-American War was over quickly, but notwithstanding that, Langley received a great deal of money from the government and in 1903, his machine failed a few days before Orville and Wilbur Wright succeeded. As a measure of the span of his interests, Walcott noted spending April 9 on the forest reserves and the flying machine. When the National Academy of Sciences met, Walcott mentioned, "I was elected Treasurer of the Nat. Acad. Sci. today" (April 20, 1898).

Congress was near the end of its term and, surprisingly, Senators Pascal and Pettigrew called on Walcott. That afternoon Walcott went calling on the honorables Allison and Cannon. The forest reserves designated by Cleveland were about to become a permanent feature, but a few legislative details had to be attended to. He and Pinchot went calling on Agriculture Secretary Wilson to make sure that the Departments of the Interior and Agriculture were of a like mind.

Throughout most of this busy spring, Walcott's father-in-law had been living with them, just to add another complication to an already heavy burden. One knows exactly the sentiment when in mid-May he wrote "Helena's father left for the north in the morning. We are alone in our home with our four children" (May 17, 1898). All that was missing was an exclamation mark.

The first of June, Walcott was off for a week's fieldwork with Arthur Keith in the Shenandoah Valley. They went to Balcony Falls, where Walcott had first found the Early Cambrian *Olenellus* fauna in the southern Appalachians. The federal geologists moved to Lexington and joined forces with Campbell to measure the section Walcott had explored last year, In this country most of the mapping was done by plotting the elongate hills and valleys. When the distance between them changed from that in the measured section, one looked for structural complications. Walcott had a grand time collecting Middle Cambrian trilobites which he compared to his 1888 Newfoundland material. When he returned, Congress was still in session. "Called on Mr. J. G. Cannon A.M. & urged him to support appropriation for publications of the survey" (June 20, 1898).

Several days after their tenth wedding anniversary, Helena and Walcott had a little trip, to Rhode Island to look for a summer place, then a day in New York City, and finally to Utica. On June 30, accompanied by friends and relatives, Walcott traveled southwest of New York Mills to Clinton, New York, for commencement exercises at Hamilton College. That afternoon C. D. Walcott, LL.D., returned to his home town in triumph; why others received the more appropriate D.Sc. is a minor mystery on no consequence. Truly, this is the story of a local boy making good. At a grand party afterward, the only sad note was that Mother was not there; she was always so proud of her little stone breaker. This was an outstanding way to end the fiscal year.

11

Big Sky: Eastern Geology Has Its Challenges, and Western Geology Has Its Challenges, but Those in the West—Like the Land Itself —Are Larger (1898–1901)

> Science has no explanation for the origin of Life. The living
> organism instead of being a product of physical or chemical forces,
> controls these forces for its highest forms.
>
> J. D. Dana, 1895

THE FISCAL YEAR started hot, and the next day was hotter, reaching 101 degrees. The family, including Agnes the cook, went off to Rhode Island, and Walcott went off to confer with Pinchot on the forest reserves. With no major problems to be resolved, by midmonth Walcott "Put in several hours on Cambrian brachiopods & rest routine" (July 14, 1898). Five years earlier, when Helena and Walcott were apart on their fifth anniversary, he wrote a love letter, quoted earlier. She kept that epistle and, now, though he missed the anniversary by a month, he added in the margin "Ten years after. More than true."

Inspired by love to finish the odds and ends so he could meet Helena, Walcott polished off the *Annual Report* of the Geological Survey plus the *Annual Report* of the National Museum. He finished his brachiopod manuscript on the twenty-fifth and sent it for publication by the National Museum; relaxation was a bicycle trip to Cabin John on the Potomac a few miles north of Washington. Helena and Charlie returned from the sea shore, and the end of July the three left for a great western adventure.

The first stop was in La Crosse, Wisconsin, to see brother Ellis and his wife Josie. The paths of the two brothers had not crossed for years, and little sentiment was noted: "After dinner went out on bluffs east of city & found a lot of Cambrian fossils—Obolus mostly" (August 1, 1898). *Obolus* is a brachiopod, not nearly as impressive to the eye as a trilobite.

By August 4, they hired stock and equipment in Livingston, Montana, and were under canvas in camp ready to go south into Yellowstone Park. In addition to Weeks, the nearly perennial field secretary and assistant, Arthur Brown was along, and that is a surprise. Washington was a southern town, and segregation there was as strong as anywhere in America. At some time between fiscal year 1891 and 1893, Arthur Brown, classified as mulatto by the 1920 U.S. Census, joined the USGS as a watchman. He survived the maelstrom of 1892, and by 1895 was a janitor. As of fiscal year 1897 he was an assistant messenger. These were increasingly better jobs, though all at a six hundred dollars per year salary. He must have displayed considerable initiative for Walcott to take him west. Oral tradition from two decades later testified that he was a fabulous camp cook, a position requiring a plethora of skills.

It was a glorious month, and the well-watered landscape was a contrast to the semidesert Owens Valley the previous year. The Walcotts kept on the move and eventually recorded twenty-one camp sites, each nicer than the last. Charlie saw the geyser basin and helped collect samples of geyserite, They rowed across Jackson Lake and collected Cambrian fossils in the Grand Tetons. Walcott "With Mr. Weeks went to summit of Gros Ventre range—a long hard day's work. All the range should be included in the Teton Forest Reserve" (August 18, 1898). Those who have been south of Yellowstone know how spectacular is the country, and those who have not, have missed a thrill. They went back though the Park to Livingston, and the luxury of one night in a hotel.

Yellowstone National Park was not the park of today. There were no rangers of the National Park Service; what protection the Park had from tree and wildlife poachers was provided by the United States Calvary (Bartlett 1985). Walcott wrote a short report to the secretary of the interior:

> Unlike last year the roads were muddy rather than dusty, in accordance with the rule that a dusty road also makes a muddy road. . . . The principal complaint of the private campers was the annoyance caused by the incursion of bears into their camps at night. . . . teachers, students, and people of moderate means who find that the cheaper rates and additional time given them

Charles Doolittle Walcott, Paleontologist

by the Wiley Company more than compensate for the more elaborate hotel and transportation companies.[1]

Walcott recommended: some concessions be given more than a year-to-year lease, more road work be done, everyone be allowed the opportunity to tour Yellowstone Lake by boat, and a U.S. Army engineer be appointed as superintendent or assistant superintendent.

Train service being what it was, the group went west to Bozeman in a freight car; "Helena & Cha's are well & strong" (September 5, 1898). They had a last family camp on the Gallatin River, where there were lots of Cambrian fossils. No fine time lasts forever, and Charlie had to attend school. Once again, it was a freight train for the director's wife. "Miss them greatly after our six weeks in train & in camp" (September 11, 1898).

The reduced group moved camp twice and "Near mouth of [Deep Creek] canyon found traces of fossils in the siliceous Belt *shaly* slate" (September 14, 1898). "Collecting in Belt slaty shales all day. Only found a few bits of a crustacean suggestive of a limuloid type" (September 15, 1898). This remarkable new material was being compared to the horseshoe crab *Limulus*.

The term "Belt" was mentioned in the 1897 season. Belt Mountain itself is composed of Cretaceous rocks, which include a thick coal seam about two-thirds of the way up the hillock, making this the hill with a belt around it. The feature inspired naming the Little Belt Mountains and Big Belt Mountains, formed by an immense pile of Precambrian rocks, wherein the sections are measured in miles, not feet. Exposures in northern Montana and Idaho add more miles to the thickness of the Belt Supergroup.

The rocks have undergone some metamorphism but in places are little changed. This is why Walcott originally commented on the shaly nature of the slate and the next day made the same outcrop into a slaty shale; the degree of metamorphism observed was partially a state of mind. The Belt rocks were not as fresh-appearing as those in the Grand Canyon, but they were not contorted gneisses and schists. The less metamorphosed the rock, the greater the likelihood of finding fossils and the less metamorphosed, the younger it might be. This latter is a vague rule with many exceptions, but in the days before rocks were dated by radioactive decay, there was no way to know the Belt rocks were about twice as old as the oldest Cambrian strata.

As for fossils, Walcott had scoured the section in the Grand Canyon, he had looked at metamorphosed rocks in central Texas and the Adirondacks, he had searched diligently in the Taconics and in Maritime Canada. Searching and find-ing do not necessarily go hand in hand, but if anyone was entitled—if one can use that word in science—Walcott was entitled to find the oldest fossils in the world. The puzzling objects were thin, black scraps on gray slaty shale. In the Silurian of New York state, whole eurypterids are rare, but fragments of these beasts, which look like a cross between a lobster and a scorpion, are locally com-mon. The color and texture of fragments in the Belt was like that of eurypterids and horseshoe crabs, limulids. Many scraps were irregular and obviously bro-ken, but a few resembled pieces of a head or body. In a theoretical sense, it was disturbing to find complex organisms in ancient rocks when the concept of evo-lution suggested that simpler forms should come earlier. Nevertheless, this was the first real evidence of any fossils in these older rocks, and who could say what they should or should not be.

They moved camp twenty-three miles to Sawmill Canyon, collecting Cam-brian fossils en route. The first day of fall saw Walcott "Studying sections of Belt Rocks in Sawmill Canyon. Found a lot of fragmentary crustacean remains (Eu-rypteroid) on shale *above* the limestone" (September 21, 1898). The season was getting late and rains began as they moved north along the eastern side of the Big Belt Mountains to White Sulphur Springs. That was the thirty-first camp of the season.

Walcott packed his fossils and tried a sulphur bath; he was sick at night with what he diagnosed as renal colic. He was then sick enough to travel to Helena and spend the following day in bed. Whatever the attack was, Walcott recovered enough so that by the end of the month he was "out all day studying Cambrian and Pre-Cambrian rocks with L. S. Griswald. Found an unconformity between the Flathead Sd & the Belt Terrane" (September 30, 1898). The Flathead Sand-stone contained Cambrian fossils, not unlike the Tonto Sandstone of the Grand Canyon. This unconformity proved that the underlying rocks had been tilted and partially eroded before Cambrian rocks were deposited and was final proof that the fossils from the Belt were indeed Precambrian.

October began with weather to miserable too be out in, so Walcott wrote an article on the forest reserves and that evening spoke to the local mining club about the economic work of the USGS and the need for forest reserves. The little party moved to "Gates of the Mountain" on the Missouri River, then to Beaver Creek, and then a fifty-mile drive to the Big Belt Mountains where Griswald wanted to show Walcott the outcrops. Then the travel was a difficult fifty-four miles to Townsend, where they collected more of the presumed fossil remains. It rained on the eleventh to end Montana fieldwork on a dreary note. Walcott moved to Butte and took the time to call on local newspaper editors.

Walcott hopped a train out of Butte and ended up in Collinston, Utah, at 5:30 in the morning. Colliston is an absolutely obscure place west of Logan and east of Great Salt Lake, about forty miles south of Malad City, an equally obscure place in Idaho. He hired a team and drove to Malad Canyon. Walcott spent two full days collecting and noting the similarity to the Cambrian rocks along the Gallatin River in Montana. He was a tired man when he returned the team. After five days and multiple changes on trains, Walcott was home. "I am happy to be here" (October 25, 1898).

He caught up on accumulated papers and conferred with Langley. Walcott again recorded one of those great diversities of interests: "Took up notes on Pre-Cambrian rocks of Montana. Called at Navy Dept. Board Ord. & Fortifications to see about Prof. S. P. L. bringing subject of flying machine before them" (November 2, 1898). Walcott was still pursuing funds for a flying machine. It is characteristic of the standoffish Langley that he expected Walcott to lay the groundwork for him.

In mid-November, Helena's father became ill and she rushed off for two weeks. The only noteworthy event of this interval was Walcott stealing part of a day to study the Belt fossils. During this slack interval, it might be appropriate to mention three different publications of the year which give a perspective on Walcott's efforts.

The first was a description of USGS activities in the southeastern United States. Walcott aimed to show the practical nature of the bureau, and began a short article with:

> Starting on a bicycle trip from Chattanooga to Knoxville and the mountains of North Carolina it would be worth 5 cents to have a map of the road for the first thirty miles, and if for each thirty miles [of] your journey you could be furnished with such a map the investment would become more and more satisfactory as you proceeded into regions less well known. (Walcott 1898c, 117)

Only a confirmed bicyclist would have chosen such an example. Walcott used it as a springboard to put all of the Survey's efforts into equally understandable words for the layman.

The second publication is Geological Survey *Monograph* 30, a substantial publication of 201 pages and 47 plates (Walcott 1898d). Historians of science tend to place great emphasis on publication of major works, as perhaps they should. On the other hand, for many scientists, after the thrill of the first few publications is over, the time for satisfaction is when the manuscript is completed, critiqued by colleagues, and turned into the editor; from there to publication is drudgery. Walcott almost never mentioned in his diary when his publications came out, nor did he in this case. Just when in 1898 "Fossil Medusae" was published uncertain and hardly worth pursuing for the names of fossils had been published in 1896. What is more important than the month in which it was published is that three thousand copies were printed and that the tome was for sale for $1.50. Enough copies still exist and so few people are interested in fossil jellyfish that supply still exceeds demand. However, many a paleontologist would be willing to pay a few times more than the original cost just to have a copy to keep on the shelf. The AJS gave it a two-paragraph review, but a Belgian colleague devoted a dozen pages to it (Meunier 1899), another measure of scientific worth.

The chief aim of *Monograph* 30 was to document the fossil jellyfish found in the Middle Cambrian of the Coosa Valley in Alabama. During the 1940s a few paleontologists had reservations concerning this interpretation, but the discovery of older faunas dominated by soft-bodied forms has removed that doubt. About one-third of the publication was directly concerned with these fossils. Approximately another third of the text detailed Lower Cambrian specimens from New York and from Europe; Walcott gives full credit to those who first made this interpretation of soft-bodied forms in old rocks and led him into the inquiry. The last third is concerned with Permian and Mesozoic accounts of genera and species assembled from the literature; that summary of scattered literature alone would make this study worthwhile. Problems of preservation are discussed and Walcott described his experiments of putting jellyfish in plaster of Paris. The Society for the Prevention of Cruelty to Animals seemingly has never had particular interest in these lowly creatures.

Naturally enough, the most important part of the monograph are the plates; there are even two printed in color. About one-third of the illustrations are drawings and a few are copies from the literature. However, in a further evolution of depiction of fossils, more than half the plates are photographs. Granted that some are retouched to emphasize subtle details, this was still a major step forward in scientific accuracy.

The plates also bring up, indirectly, the issue of trace fossils, that is the indication of activity of animals. During the summers on seashore family vacations, Walcott observed and photographed marks made by algal fronds and jellyfish tentacles dragged along the beach by waves. Most specimens which

Charles Doolittle Walcott, Paleontologist

Walcott thought might have been fossilized tentacles marking are now reinterpreted, but it was a good early effort in this particular branch of paleontology.

In contrast to the uncertainty as to which month *Monograph* appeared in 1898, for date of the third work discussed is November 19, 1898. Priority of a scientific name of a newly named organism depends on the date of publication and the National Museum was always careful about the precise day a paper was distributed. This was a very much smaller work, not in the same league as *Monograph* 30, but at least it provides the opportunity to bring in the point concerning publication dates. The subject matter was solid brachiopods, in contrast to the vague outlines of jellyfish:

> In continuation of the study of Cambrian Brachiopoda, all the American forms of *Obolus* known to me have been considered, and those that may be referred to *Lingulella*, which is a somewhat more doubtful subgenus of *Obolus*. A few species from the Lower Ordovician rocks are added, as they form a part of the passage fauna between the Cambrian and the Ordovician faunas. (Walcott 1898e, 385)

To give a partial translation, the fossil *Obolus* had been named from Cambrian beds in the Baltic area and four species were known from North America; Walcott added another six. The bulk of the work was description of twenty-nine new species and two varieties of *Lingulella;* these are all in alphabetical order, an arrangement easy to follow, though not particularly scientific, but then this was a preliminary paper. An interesting tidbit is in the use of "Ordovician," a name not accepted officially by the Geological Survey for another five years. Another interesting tidbit is the recognition of gradual transition of faunas. This was a long intellectual step from the early part of the century, when each geologic period was judged to be characterized by a unique assemblage.

In what was a wildly optimistic comment, Walcott stated: "The figures illustrating the new species are now made up as plates for a monograph of the U. S. Geological Survey, and will be transmitted for publication probably during 1899" (Walcott 1898e, 385). Walcott also mentioned: "All of the material was carefully prepared by Dr. George H. Girty, who made a preliminary study of the type and other species of the genus when superintending the preparation of the drawings" (Walcott 1898e, 395); the drawings are three plates showing details of the shell interior of several species. Girty had been hired in 1895 as a USGS paleontologist, and within a few years, he grew to despise Walcott, one of the few to speak ill of him. It may have begun with his receiving what he considered meager credit for his scientific contribution. However, Girty also had difficulties with other colleagues later in his career.

Most of December was unextraordinary, though Skiff of the Field Museum came to discuss a mining show to be held in Paris in 1900; mining was increasingly on Walcott's mind, quite a stretch for a paleontologist. Christmas Day was marred with the death of Helena's father, and they hurried to Oneida for the funeral in zero-degree weather. There was nothing more to be done in Oneida, and Walcott went to New York City for the end of the Geological Society of America meeting, where Walcott gave a major report on the pre-Cambrian rocks he had studied mostly in Montana.

"The results of my investigations were the discovery of a great stratigraphic unconformity between the Cambrian and the Belt formations; that the Belt terrane was divisible into several formations, and that fossils occurred in the Greyson shales nearly 7,000 feet beneath the highest beds of the Belt terrane" (Walcott 1899b, 204). Combined with his observations in 1895, he had the data to show that below the Flathead Sandstone, different parts of the Belt were exposed in different areas; it was a classic demonstration of an unconformity. "I think than an unconformity to the extent indicated is sufficient to explain the absence of lower Cambrian rocks and fossils and to warrant our placing the Belt terrane in the pre-Cambrian Algonkian system of formations" (Walcott 1899, 215).

Walcott went on to summarize similar relationships in the Grand Canyon, the Llano region in central Texas, and the Avalon Peninsula in Newfoundland, all of which he had investigated, and the Great Lakes region studied by Van Hise. The aim was to lay a solid geologic foundation for the presence of great thicknesses of sedimentary rocks below the Cambrian, and thereby at least indirectly establish the antiquity of the fossils, before the fossils themselves were described. He also took the occasion to dispose of a few names which had been given to Precambrian objects that he now considered to be inorganic. Finally, he got to the paleontology as he then understood these fossils.

Before discussing this paper further, some backtracking is in order. From at least the time he was in Albany with Hall, Walcott was a correspondent of Sir William Dawson at McGill University. In 1884 he wrote him:

I have packed up and sent to you this day, by express, specimens of the Stromatopora-like forms from the Potsdam limestone, Saratoga Co. N.Y. and also specimens from the Lower Cambrian of the Grand Cañon of the Colorado, Arizona. Use the material as you may see fit and let me know the result of your investigations, that I may incorporate it (as coming from you) in my report of the Cambrian Fauna.[2]

Charles Doolittle Walcott, Paleontologist

Dawson responded quickly, but unfortunately the original is lost and the draft copy is almost indecipherable. In reply, Walcott mentioned that Hall had just given the name *Cryptozoon* to the Saratoga Springs cabbagelike structures and asked for a reexamination of the Arizona material. Dawson answered: "I have had other slices made of the Grand Canon fossils? and have puzzled over them a great deal; but cannot make out any certain structure."[3] Dawson also expressed reservations about the Saratoga Springs material being organic.

New information results in new interpretations of old material. Fourteen years later Walcott wrote:

> This past summer I was so fortunate as to find some fairly well preserved Pre-Cambrian fossils in Montana. They embrace beautifully preserved annelid trails and fragmentary remains of a large crustacean which recalls Eurypterus and Pterygotus rather than any of the trilobites.
>
> I am preparing a paper on my present information in relation to the Pre-Cambrian fossils, and in this connection have referred to your note on the Stromatopora-like fossils in the Grand Canyon of the Colorado which I sent you in 1892.[4]

Letters are missing, but Walcott must have sent the Grand Canyon material back for another look. In 1897, Dawson described a new species of *Cryptozoon*, though he still had doubts as to it really being organic.

Walcott had no doubts about this structure as a former organism:

> When collecting material in the Chuar terrane in 1883 I was strongly impressed with their resemblance to the forms occurring in the upper Cambrian rocks of Saratoga county, New York, which Professor James Hall subsequently described as *Cryptozoon proliferum*. There were certain differences of occurrence, however, that were noted at the time. These were that the Chuar forms in the Grand Canyon were more elevated and were not semispherical as most of the Saratoga forms are. (Walcott 1899e, 234)

One result of the 1899 paper was that this Grand Canyon material became the first authentic Precambrian fossil to be generally accepted. Walcott also described *Chuaria circularis* from the Precambrian shales. Picture a tiny dried grape, smaller than the smallest raisin; flatten it further and one has a *Chuaria*. For more than half a century, this almost nothing of a fossil was ignored until it began to turn up worldwide in the Precambrian. Walcott thought incorrectly that it might have been a brachiopod.

His interpretation of the Montana fossils was worse. Most of the annelid trails are now judged to be filaments of algae which coiled when they fell to the substrate; one of them is probably inorganic. The supposed crustacean was named *Beltina danai,* surely to honor the late professor. Walcott did express surprise that the fragments resembled those of eurypterids rather than trilobites, but he had described fragments in the Utica Shale of the oldest eurypterid then known and thus had a solid basis for his interpretation. For what it is worth, Walcott cautioned that this was a preliminary description. Still, he added a full plate of pictures of eurypterids so comparison could be made to the fragments. Current thinking is that these are the remains of some kind of frondlike alga, or possibly part of a thick organic scum floating on water, but not any animal.

Everyone can make mistakes and in retrospect *Beltina* may have been Walcott's biggest one; applying hindsight to science is easy! Wrong as the identification was, given the nature of the material and the state of knowledge of the Precambrian, it was logical. Even with that error, this paper was important, for it took Precambrian paleontology out of the realm of near mythology and made paleontologic inquiry into ancient rocks respectable. "Mr. Walcott has brought together in this valuable contribution more information than most geologists would suppose to be in existence regarding clastic formations, clearly pre-Cambrian in position, and yet as clearly of sedimentary origin, and probably fossil-bearing, situated in various regions on the North American continent" (Williams 1899, 78).

So much for pushing back the frontiers of knowledge. On New Year's Day 1899, Walcott dined with Clarence King, his old chief, and Henry Fairfield Osborn, a new power in vertebrate paleontology at the American Museum (Rainger 1991). Helena came into town that evening; the following day he gave another lecture at the Brooklyn Art Institute, after which the couple went back to hearth and home in Washington.

Business for the year began. "Called at War Dept & Navy Dept about Dr. Beckers work at Manila. On Public Printer in relation to printing Survey reports. Secty of Interior on matters of Survey—At White House saw Secy Porter—At Survey 2 to 5 P.M. At home in evening" (January 5, 1899). The first item is unusual. With annexation of the Philippine Islands after Spain was humiliated, there was a dire need for information as to just what America had annexed. George Becker, geologist, and Henry Gannett, geographer, were sent off to the Orient.

Charles Doolittle Walcott, Paleontologist

After seeing some members of the Cabinet, it was back to Capital Hill for Walcott, "looking after a resolution establishing division of Mines and Mining" (January 12, 1899). Walcott earlier had gone after an increase in funds to compile statistics on mining production; now he was after a separate department or at least a separate bureau, but it was not to be this year (Rabbitt 1980, 291). About a week later he was testifying again concerning a proposed national university, one aspect of the elusive George Washington Memorial. This was followed by a "Meeting of Wash-n Acad. Sci. 8–10 P.M. Elected President. Reception at A. Graham Bells" (January 18, 1899).

At the end of this busy month, Walcott presided at the first formal meeting of the Washington Academy of Science; whether this society would accomplish anything novel partly depended on the start it received. To make a long story short, as an annual event Walcott kept being elected president of the Washington Academy of Sciences until 1910.

Early February was busy but not noteworthy, as becomes the generally nasty character of this month. The poor weather of February exceeded itself on the thirteenth when a blizzard brought more than two feet of snow; Walcott was up on the roof shoveling off snow. The heavy fall did slow the pace of life, and Walcott "Secured two hours for work on pre-Cambrian fossils of the Belt Terrane of Montana" (February 17, 1899). This was the same day that a Committee on Geologic Formation Names was formed.

Ever since, the names committee has been misunderstood by geologists outside the USGS for seeming to attempt to dictate to the entire scientific community, when actually its scope was limited to USGS publications. Ever since, until it was abolished in 1995, the names committee was cursed by Survey geologists who have had manuscripts delayed or—worse—modified by its rulings. On balance, the committee worked well. Walcott had taken an important administrative step in further improving the quality of Geological Survey publications.

The month went fairly quickly after that. He heard Hague and McGee deliver presidential addresses to local societies, went with Helena to a Daughters of the American Revolution reception, appeared at a Senate Appropriation Committee hearing with J. A. Holmes and filled in evenings seeing a few congressmen. It was a well-known routine, one resulting in obtaining a larger appropriation than was requested (Rabbitt 1980, 290).

The following month Walcott was lobbying again, but to a different group. In Baltimore, he had lunch with President Gilman of Johns Hopkins, Secretary of Agriculture Wilson, the Maryland state geologist W. B. Clarke, and others. The drive for a national university in Washington, based in part on government departments, was slowly rolling, and Wilson was a man to be wooed. From Baltimore, Walcott took the train to Harrisburg to talk to the state legislature. In mid-March, he "Spoke on the U. S. National Museum before Washington Academy of Sciences 8:15 to 9. P.M. Reception or social meeting followed" (March 15, 1899).

"A national museum should be the center of scientific activity in the country in which it is based" (Walcott 1899c, 491). From this fairly obvious base he gave a quick summary of the founding of the museum and the reorganization he instituted in 1897. He discussed pros and cons of removing the museum from the Smithsonian Institution: "The museum is a child that by its vigorous growth already overshadowed the parent institution in the extent of its buildings, its expenditures, and its direct influence upon the people of the United States" (Walcott 1899c, 493). Henry and, to some extent, Baird were of the view that the Smithsonian should institute new approaches and then leave them to the others; the Weather Bureau and the Fish Commission were good examples. Walcott concluded that the museum should be under the care of the institution, but separate enough so that it did not interfere with the main Smithsonian goals.

He went on to elaborate the idea that the museum ought to function as an element in national education, adding that with the present inadequate building, that was virtually impossible. There was an appeal to civic pride in pointing out the growth of the American Museum of Natural History in New York, compared to the sad state of affairs in the nation's capital. He then mentioned his philosophy of how exhibits should be arranged for educational purposes; this is still worth reading. His final thrust was for special displays for children. Langley has received credit as a lover of children and a nicer person than the written record would suggest because the Smithsonian Castle later opened a children's museum at the south entrance. All well and good, but it is appropriate to put the record straight as to where that particular idea originated. This article was one of the pushes toward funding of the "New National Museum," and like most of Walcott's projects, it was eventually successful.

A few days after this talk, Walcott was on the train to New Haven with Langley, both to be pall bearers at the funeral of O. C. Marsh. That marked the end of an era and the start of a problem in sorting out government collections from those belonging to the university. There was mumbling in the scientific community that Yale kept specimens gathered at federal expense. Walcott took the trouble to publish an 1891 report on his visit to examine collections, and another concerning the transfer of five freight cars full of vertebrate fossils to the National Museum, plus a formal response from Langley (Walcott 1900a). The funeral and accumulated business was enough to convince him to take a few days off. Helena had gone to Atlantic City to meet Aunt Helen Sanford and he joined her.

They were back in the city on April Fool's Day. A week later Walcott presided at a Saturday lecture; the Washington Academy of Sciences was continuing the tradition of the local societies helping to educate the public. Less than two weeks later, the academy performed another one of the functions Walcott had in mind, when the group hosted a formal reception for the National Academy of Sciences; heretofore it had been up to the local societies or individuals to bear this burden and sometimes the annual meeting of the academy resulted in local social embarrassment when nothing was done. Between these goings on of the new academy, Walcott concerned himself with USGS matters "and at odd times working up in my den on the Cambrian brachiopoda" (April 10, 1899).

Near the end of the month he went to New York with C. Hart Merriam of the Biological Survey, a part of the Department of Agriculture. Merriam had found an angel in E. H. Harriman, the railroad magnate, and they discussed with him the finishing touches of Harriman's expedition taking a coterie of scientists to Alaska. Walcott lunched with Osborn and the subject was vertebrate fossils. Marsh had procrastinated and never produced what he should have for the Geological Survey; as events finally turned out, Osborn was even worse a procrastinator, but there was simply no one else to work up these collections. With that taken care of, or at least started, Walcott took a quick trip to Williamsport and Wellsboro, Pennsylvania, to look at oil wells.

May is a good month in Washington. There is little rain, flowers and flowering trees bloom, and the humidity is low. Shad migrate up the Potomac, and "planking" these fish by nailing them to a board and cooking over a fire is a local tradition. "After lunch went down the river with Charles as guests of Prof. S. P. Langley. A very pleasant afternoon. Shad dinner at Marshall Hall" (May 5, 1899). Langley could be a gracious host for those who were not under him, and the pleasant glow of spring continued. "Resumed work on the study of Cambrian brachiopods as the Survey plans etc—are well in hand" (May 6, 1899). The Washington Academy of Sciences had a large number of board meeting for Walcott was wasting no time setting a course for that group.

The geologic and water efforts surveys were doing well; one need only count the numbered folios of the *Geologic Atlas* and the *Water Supply Papers* pouring out. Most citizens were pleased with the work in the forest reserves, and topographic mapping was equally well in hand. The brachiopod work was proceeding apace without any need for a great push to complete the final stages of a paper. Life was fairly good.

Walcott even had another title to add to his list. The tome on Yellowstone Park, Hague's continuous work since he finished in the Eureka District, was finally out. Hague did not write quickly, and the forest commission had been important, but still it was a distraction from his geologic activity. *Monograph* 32 was the largest published to date and would hold the record until H. F. Osborn published decades later. Girty wrote on the younger Paleozoic, and the paleobotanist Frank Knowlton described fossil floras. Walcott's modest effort in this multiauthored work was on the Cambrian fossils.

> Preliminary examinations of the collections were made from year to year as the specimens were brought in from the field and reports were made to Mr. Arnold Hague. When it was found possible to make a detailed study, I requested Mr. G. H. Girty to prepare the brachiopods contained in this collection, and I am indebted to him for assistance rendered in this direction.
>
> This fauna is more intimately related to that of the Black Hills and the Upper Mississippi Valley in Wisconsin and Minnesota than to the Middle Cambrian of Nevada or British Columbia. There are no indications of the Lower Cambrian or Olenellus fauna. (Walcott 1899d, 441)

The absence of Lower Cambrian rocks in Wyoming was in keeping with Walcott's demonstration of gradual encroachment of seas from the continental margins. Comparisons to other regions was further sharpening of his ideas on faunal provinces, different fossils in different regions, though his notion of the dividing line between Middle and Upper Cambrian was to be modified later.

This is not earth-shattering data, but the paper was a respectable contribution and, after all, that is what most scientific publications are. Many building blocks are needed to construct a synthesis, and still more have to be emplaced to fill in a structure once the main beams were in place. Six plates and thirty-eight printed pages in large format is nothing to ignore.

At the pace Walcott operated, spring was a relatively quiet period, and he "Gave an hour to looking up matters pertaining to an apartment house at 1323 13th" (May 15, 1898). Shortly he was "Cogittating [*sic*] over plans for apartment house in the evening" (May 18, 1898). To jump ahead, the plans and location

Charles Doolittle Walcott, Paleontologist

were superb, and that fall Walcott "organized the Iowa Apartment House Co. with S. F. Emmons, E. Watkins, I. L. Schneider, A. M. Mclachlen" (October 11, 1899). The Iowa is pictured in a compendium on Washington apartments (Goode 1988, 162).

Things were so well in hand with the bureau that Walcott could devote field-work entirely to his own special scientific interests. On May 27, Walcott kissed Helena goodbye and took off for northeastern Canada, not the western United States. He spent the next day in Boston and Cambridge and made contact with Loper, who collected for him in 1891. Walcott named *Obolus loperi* "in recognition of the difficult and persevering work of Mr. S. Ward Loper, curator of the Museum of Middlebury College, who made a large collection of fossils, under the most adverse circumstances in the mountains of Colorado" (Walcott 1898e, 390).

As to the why of this trip, G. F. Matthew had a different view of the Early Cambrian than Walcott. Coincidentally, his paper was reviewed in the *American Journal of Science* immediately following Walcott's pre-Cambrian publication: "This paper describes a series of strata beneath the Cambrian in New Brunswick, Canada, and Newfoundland, which unconformably underlie that system" (Williams 1899a, 79). Walcott either wanted to obtain these fossils, older than his Cambrian but younger than the new material from Montana, or show that Matthew was in error in his interpretation of them as older than Cambrian.

Loper and Walcott left Boston and spent "A very pleasant half day in St. John with G. F. Matthew" (May 29, 1899). For more than twenty years, they had been in contact with numerous letters between visits. Walcott had asked to examine many of Matthew's fossils and Matthew had readily lent them. Matthew still was at the Custom House, not employed as a geologist, and no matter how much effort he put into publication, there was a certain stigma of nonprofessionalism. Add to that, no one in Canada really worked on Cambrian and could fully appreciate his efforts. No wonder Matthew and Walcott got on well.

Walcott and Loper went on to Sydney, Nova Scotia, and took the ship to Port-au-Basques on the southwestern tip of the island. This was a far shorter sea trip to Newfoundland than that he and Helena had taken to Newfoundland eleven years earlier. In 1898, the narrow gauge railroad had finally been completed across the island, making access a great deal easier. By the first of June the pair were in a sailboat on Smith Sound, an inlet on the western side of Trinity Bay, in pursuit of Matthew's Etcheminian. "I visited Smith sound, and at Smith point found the Olenellus fauna 369 feet below the summit of the Etcheminian, and one of its types *Coleoides typicalis* in the basal beds of the Cambrian on the south side of Random Island. This retains the Etcheminian of Newfoundland in the Lower Cambrian, to which the strata representing it on Manuels river were referred in 1888" (Walcott 1900, 3). They spent several more days confirming the demise of the Etcheminian Stage in Newfoundland. It is good to have a witness when a dramatic wrench in the geologic column is taking place, especially when one is a guest in a foreign country doing damage to the ideas of a native son. On July 5, J. P. Howley, the provincial geologist, joined them, and "for seventeen days we worked on the Cambrian and pre-Cambrian formations about Trinity and Conception Bays" (Walcott 1900b, 3).

"Icebergs and 'growlers' were everywhere present, and the average temperature of the sea did not rise about 38 degrees while he was on the island. The geologic work and collecting were done under adverse conditions; living in a small skiff, landing on rocky shores, on rough water, in rain and fog, clothed in oilskins, rubber boots and hat, transporting collections over slippery rocks to place them in an open boat, fended off by boathooks from the cliffs, requires an enthusiasm such as is found only in a devotee of the work in hand."[5]

The day Howley arrived they had to spend the night in a cove on the northern shore to get out of the wind. The following morning opened with "Snow squalls 5 to 6 A.M. Returned to work section on north side Smith Sound. Found Olenellus fauna in Matthews Etcheminian beds, *Olenellus—Agraulos—Microdiscus—Obolella?*" (June 6, 1899). One more day and a final judgment was rendered on the Etcheminian of Newfoundland, "base is lower Cambrian and the upper portion Middle Cambrian" (June 7, 1899). Two decades later, the fisherman still remembered the visit of "Prince Charles," their term for this tall, impressive man.

The geologists sailed to the slate quarries on Tilton head, out into Trinity Bay and south to Random Island, where they collected more *Olenellus,* and had a fine sail up North West Arm. "Passing around Random island to Hickman harbor, on Random sound, a section was found east of the harbor showing the Signal Hill sandstone and conglomerate, and, resting conformably on it, a series of sandstones, quartzitic sandstone, and sandy shales extending up to the base of the Cambrian. The Cambrian section extends up to the Hyolithes limestone of the Smith Point section. For the terrane between the Signal Hill and the Cambrian Mr. Howley and I agreed upon the name Random" (Walcott 1900b, 4).

The Signal Hill was named for rocks on Signal Hill in St. John's, locally famous as a station for Marconi's wireless. By everyone's definition, the Signal Hill rocks were Precambrian. Rocks above these strata on Random Island and below undoubted Cambrian should still be Precambrian, so here was another series of sedimentary rocks bridging the gap between old and trilobite-bearing young. Howley measured them to be 415 feet thick. Near the top "In number 4 of this section I found several varieties of annelid trails, including a variety about 3 millimeters broad, a slender form ½ millimeter broad, and an annulated trail 2 to 3 millimeters in width" (Walcott 1890b, 4).

The issue of the boundary of Precambrian and Cambrian is not yet fully resolved. Some parties place great store in the observation that trace fossils occur below the trilobite-bearing beds and would consider these trace fossils to indicate Cambrian. Walcott was no stranger to trace fossils but never studied these forms because there were so many Cambrian shelled fossils to describe. Walcott knew the difference between what he called annelid trails and marking made by trilobites, and had any trilobite indications been present in the beds he examined at St. John's, he would have mentioned them.

They sailed out southward into the windy waters of Trinity Bay and made it to Gannetts Cove and then Hearts Delight Harbour. By now, the Walcott party was on the southern shore of the bay and got into the more protected waters of Chapel Arm Bay. The weather was bad, but the boat made it safely to Spread Eagle Harbour and finally to Dildo Harbour. The geologists examined rocks exposed along the shore; sailors worry about the shore, not the sea, and the captain must have been nervous.

The three geologists went west by train and north up the eastern side of Conception Bay to Manuels, a few miles west of St. John's, where Walcott had found *Olenellus* in 1888. Luck was with them, and they collected more specimens and measured a section upward into the younger Cambrian. The weather was good one day and terrible the next. Leaving Loper to collect *Paradoxides,* Walcott went over to see the iron beds on Belle Island; many decades later, iron deposition was interpreted in the light of knowledge about similar beds in Wales, but at this time no one thought of continents breaking and moving apart. On Sunday, Walcott "Took a walk down to beach A.M. & returned by Manuels river. Note Olenus above Paradoxides on the N. W. bank" (June 25, 1899). Walcott thus had a complete sequence of Lower, Middle, and Upper Cambrian trilobite zones at one place.

Loper and Walcott took the train back to St. John's and then went far south along the coast to Ferryland with geologist Hawley to look at slates. "A collection of the form known as *Aspidella terranovica* was made from the Momable terrane of the Avalon series. It proved the supposed fossil to be spherulitic concretion, and this removes it from among the possible pre-Cambrian forms of life" (Walcott 1900b, 5). That was a little tidbit to add to the store of knowledge, and they went back to St. John's to pack up eleven boxes and two barrels of fossils.

Walcott and Loper left July 2 for a narrow gauge railroad trip of twenty-seven and a half hours. After the ferry ride back to Nova Scotia, Walcott stopped in Grand Narrows to see Alexander Graham Bell, who annually headed north, but by the sixth, they joined Matthew and the three went overnight to Hanford Brook, a key outcrop north of St. John. Full credit should be given Matthew for cooperation, as Walcott was, at best, dubious as to the status of the Etcheminian even before his trip to Newfoundland. On Sunday, Walcott rested up, but "Took a short walk & noted that the supposed unconformity between the Cambrian & Etcheminian is a break within the basal bed of the Cambrian St. John quartzite" (July 7, 1899). The next few days were devoted to looking for fossils in poorly fossiliferous rock. Eventually they found "*Coleoloides typicalis* & *Iphidea labradorica* in the 'Etcheminian'" (July 13, 1899).

That was sufficient for his purpose of proving these rocks to be Early Cambrian in age. Walcott was right and Matthew was wrong in his proposal. Fast forward to the 1950s and to new work on the earliest Cambrian of Siberia, called the Tommotian. When dissolved in acid, rocks below those that contained the oldest trilobites yielded a cornucopia of tiny forms. Matthew was at least partially correct; he had the right idea at the wrong time and lacked the methodology to prove his point.

Tommotian-like rocks have turned up in the Placentia Bay region of southeastern Newfoundland, an area Walcott never investigated. In the great game of "what if," Walcott might with some difficulty have found a few fossils, but he would have placed them in his *Olenellus* zone and therefore Early Cambrian. His view was that rocks that were conformable with those having trilobites, that is the same dip (geometric position) and were not separated by a conglomerate were essentially the same age. It was just a case of breaking enough rock until an older trilobite would be found in these underlying beds. To this day, the position of the oldest trilobite and the position of the base of the Cambrian are argued. For Walcott's day, he had the correct interpretation.

In mid-July Walcott left St. John for Wakefield, Rhode Island, where Helena and the children were summering. The busy field season was not without its toll; "Have been about used up with lame back & limbs since Sunday" (July 21, 1899). Regardless, Walcott had to return to Washington to oversee the *Annual Report*. He continued to have difficulty with rheumatism and a lame side. Except for a quick visit by Williams, it was a lonely time. "Began writing a paper on the Atlantic Coast Province Cambrian" (August 2, 1899)

The *Annual Report* was on its way to the printer, and Walcott paused in Harrisburg to see the Pennsylvania Survey Commission. He met Helena and young Charlie in Boston, and the three left for Quebec. They journeyed to Trois Pistoles on the south bank of the St. Lawrence River and "Began searching for fossiliferous limestone in conglomerates A.M. Located them in the afternoon when we were driven in by rain" (August 17, 1899). Sciatica returned and was not helped when Walcott noted very little return for a hard day of work.

There were no Cambrian beds as such in the area, only the pieces that had been incorporated into younger conglomerates. Just why he was at Trois Pistoles was not clear, but in 1890 Walcott was studying fossils from the Levis conglomerate lent him by Sir William Dawson. Perhaps he wanted to obtain more from comparable conglomerates. Less likely, this venture might have been tied to a find of brachiopods in a similar conglomerate in Rhode Island (Walcott 1898f). They moved on to Bic and to Bic Harbor, still with poor collecting in the conglomerates, made more miserable by lots of rain. They moved again to Little Metis and began collecting younger fossils with Sir William, who had come out from Montreal; as a good geologist wife, Helena sat and split some of the younger shale searching for sponges.

Having exhausted the immediate prospects for Cambrian fossils along the river, and vice versa, the three left by train for St. John, New Brunswick. The collecting was better, and part of the time Matthew accompanied them; in spite of differences of interpretation about the Cambrian, relations were cordial, if not quite so warm as in past years. Lest this leave a wrong impression, in 1904 at Matthew's request, Walcott was urging the purchase of his collection by the National Museum. On Long Island and Caton Island they made fine hauls. Walcott sent back eight boxes and four barrels, and though the size of each container cannot be known, that was a large collection of fossils.

Helena returned to Rhode Island to collect her brood, and Walcott went to consult with Beecher about his trilobite work. Before September was two-thirds over, the family was home. The rest of the month and October passed quickly enough. Except for a fast trip to New Haven to attend inauguration of Yale's new president, Walcott stayed at home. With the material from the field season, there was plenty to supplement administrative chores. The family moved to another house and Walcott went to the fall meeting of the National Academy of Sciences in New York.

December began with a lecture by Gilbert on Alaskan glaciers visited by the Harriman expedition. Harriman attended and Walcott passed a few words with him; it never hurt to know monied people. He started a manuscript on his Canadian fieldwork and finished it by the ninth (Walcott 1900c).

In mid-December the GWMA commemorated the 200th anniversary of the death of America's first president; this anniversary to loom as a goal to aim for in providing more resources for American science. With Helena Walcott as a vice-president of the association and with Walcott as president of the Washington Academy of Sciences something tangible might come of the GWMA, just possibly a national university. A short two-page comment on Washington's efforts as surveyor and explorer appeared (Walcott 1900d). Surely there is a connection between this little piece and the GWMA meeting. Washington's exploration is extolled, but the main emphasis was on trade, the need for maps, and vision for the future, all strings Walcott was plucking.

In a larger context, Walcott had a role as the publicist for broader government functions. In *Popular Science* he had brought the Geological Survey to public attention when it needed support, next he had urged support for the forest reserves, and finally he had given support to the National Museum when a new building was being considered. This little piece on Washington was part of a pattern Walcott had established for his nongeologic activities. *Popular Science* exists today in a specialized form, but during the last century it was the voice of science for the public.

December 25 was "A happy pleasant Christmas. Boys up 5 A.M." Two days later, the GSA came to town. Second vice-president Walcott was busy with council meetings, but the Washington Academy of Sciences was now thoroughly trained by him and the group hosted a reception. Walcott recounted his summer's fieldwork on the Cambrian of eastern Canada to the geologists.

Less than two months later, Walcott published this material in volume 1 of the *Proceedings of the Washington Academy of Sciences*. Why there rather than a geologic outlet, is hard to understand. The new journal may have been short on manuscripts and he was helping the editor, or perhaps he felt that this would demonstrate the *Proceedings* were to become a significant journal. The publication is easy to read with a minimum of jargon, and anyone can follow how he quotes the papers of Matthew and then refutes them with new field data. Still, it is the writing by a geologist for a geological audience; included are five nice pictures of outcrops, but pictures of rocks seldom excite the general scientific public.

Charles Doolittle Walcott, Paleontologist

The Etcheminian was sunk and a threefold division of the Cambrian, against the twofold division of Matthew, carried the day. Walcott wrote in a straightforward manner with no malice, but even so it could only have been extremely painful for that gentleman. Hidden in the midst of the stratigraphic sections, descriptions of unconformities, and faunal lists is a nugget of philosophy. In one of his works, Matthew had pointed out that the Etcheminian fauna was of a somewhat different composition than the *Olenellus* fauna. Walcott's partial response was to cite great thickness of strata in the West and the Southeast through which this fauna occurred.

"To the geologist the position of the Olenellus fauna is well assured. Theoretic biology may question the facts of stratigraphy, but, as many paleontologists have learned in the past, it is dangerous to base broad generalizations on the relatively small amount of biologic data available from the older Paleozoic rocks" (Walcott 1900c, 338). Recall that earlier Walcott followed Matthew in the view that *Olenellus* was younger than *Paradoxides,* based in part on assumptions as to possible changes in morphology through time. Once burned, twice cautious.

Two developments of mid-twentieth-century paleontology would have particularly interested Walcott. The Tommotian fauna found in the lowest Cambrian has been mentioned. In rocks below the Tommotian is the Ediacaran fauna, which, unlike the Tommotian, contains larger animals; apart from "jellyfish," these animals are unlike anything in the Paleozoic. These too have been discovered in Newfoundland. The Belt rocks are far older, but no one at the time knew they were so much older. Again one can play "what if," but if Walcott had been aware of two different stratigraphic levels, each with a strikingly different and diverse fauna, between *Olenellus* and "Beltina" he might not have been quite so quick to classify his Belt fossil as a eurypterid.

This may be time for a personal note, just to indicate Walcott's growing stature. Walcott was generally privately immune to any honors received and almost never mentioned them in his diary. In 1892, he had been elected an honorary member of the Rochester Academy of Sciences. That was nothing compared to his election as a foreign member of Imperial Academy of St. Petersburg in 1895. The American Philosophical Society elected him to membership in 1897, and the American Academy of Arts and Sciences elevated him to associate fellow to fill the vacancy left by the death of James Hall. One might think that filling his former chief's footstep would be worthy of note, but it was not. In 1900, the Christiania Scientific Society in Oslo, Norway, and the Royal Physiographic

Society, in Lund, Sweden included him in their ranks. The oldest scientific society in the world, the Academei di Lincei in Rome tapped him. Not one word did he write in his diary.

Against this background, it is interesting that the first item in his 1900 diary was a pasted-in list of the Geological Society of America slate with his name as first vice-president. It was truly remarkable for someone with no formal training in geology to reach this level of professional respect. Foreign honors are based on publications, but this was a recognition by his peers who knew him of scientific and administrative ability, combined with a good personality.

New Year's Day, Walcott noted going with Pinchot to call on President McKinley and the wives of the cabinet members, a quiet day. January 2, however, included four meetings during the day concerning USGS matters and presiding at a board meeting at night: "A busy day—typical of Washington in winter" (January 2, 1900). For entertainment in the evenings when there were no board meetings, he read proof on the forthcoming paper based on the Canadian work and delivered a speech, warming the public toward the concept of a national university.

January 10 brought another trip to New York and a lecture at the Brooklyn Institute. He spoke about his trip to Newfoundland, and at least two of the local papers gave the talk extensive coverage. Walcott seldom spoke at universities, and just what the connection was with Brooklyn or why Walcott spoke there so often is not clear. He saw Osborn and they discussed completion of Marsh's monograph and what to do about describing the fossils Cope had collected. The next day he was back in Washington, briefing Secretary Julian on the status of the forest reserves. "Annual meeting Wash'n Aca., Sc. 4:15 to 5:30 P.M., was re-elected president" (January 17, 1900). There were no surprises here. Late in the month he was working on the bylaws of the GWMA. It was one chore to organize a scientific society, or even a group of scientific societies, but more tricky to get academic, feminine, and patriotic notions all straightened out and headed in the proper direction. One possibility would be a new building which could house the local academy, provide a permanent office for the National Academy of Sciences, and generally serve as a focus for scientific activities. Perhaps the women's organizations could be made to see that as a suitable memorial.

The third week in February, Walcott read a paper at the meeting of the American Institute of Mining Engineers and the following night attended their reception at the Corcoran Galley of Art; the Washington Academy of Sciences sponsored the social affair. In his published paper an impressive four-color map

Charles Doolittle Walcott, Paleontologist

showed areas of topographic, hydrologic, geologic, and mineral investigations in the United States since the Geological Survey was founded, and a list of studies of mining districts published to date was included. These items were the work of others, but the gist of the paper was remarks by Walcott on what the agency was doing and what it was not doing, a restatement of the prohibition against consulting for individual gain. There are some general comments worth quoting:

> In government organizations depending upon the will of so complex a body as Congress, it is often difficult to carry out a policy outlined in advance. Usually the policy is modified by considerations, not of what is abstractly best to do, but of what it is possible to do. This compels the administrative officer to aim at the nearest attainable approximation of the desired object. (Walcott 1901, 12)
>
> The results already attained by this single bureau of the government form a monument to the intelligent interest taken in its work by Congress and the hearty support given it by the several Secretaries of the Interior. It is my belief, founded on years of experience, that the American people, as represented by Congress, desire to do what is just and right for governmental scientific organizations. Individual mistakes and narrowness of concept and action will occur at times, but as a whole the outlook is good, both for science and for the people of the nation.
>
> I have been made to make the preceding observations because it is not uncommon to hear and read criticism of Congress and of governmental methods of doing things. Governments, like individuals, oftentimes learn and act slowly. (Walcott 1901, 23–24)

It is small wonder that Walcott got on well with Congress. Not only did he say all the right things in a forum where they were certain to be relayed to Senators and Representatives, he believed what he said.

However, this was Walcott's last effort for a time. The machine broke down from overwork, and by February 24 he was in the Glen Spring Sanitorium at Watkins Glen, New York. Walcott endured salt rubs, vapor baths, and electrochemical baths in what he described as a most monotonous life. He wrote Williams that he was there for a two-week cure. Toward the end he was up to doing a bit with the Cambrian brachiopods, but otherwise Walcott was inert for more than three weeks. His fiftieth birthday passed without comment.

In April, Walcott testified before the Subcommittee on Appropriations; it went very well, especially since a new secretary of interior had been appointed in 1899. To be certain, he just happened to see Mr. Cannon that evening to clarify a few points of his testimony before presenting it to the committee.

On stream gauging (Congress and the Geological Survey differed on the spelling):

MR. WALCOTT. There is a very strong demand for an increase in this work, but I did not submit to the Secretary an increase in the appropriation; on the contrary I stated, when the matter was brought to my attention by petition and otherwise, that until the demand for it was so strong that it amounted to a public request to have an increased appropriation made though Congress, I should do nothing in the way of recommending an increase. (Walcott 1900e, 240)

On topographic maps:

MR. WALCOTT. There is a great pressure of topographic work from all our states, and last year the appropriation was raised.

THE CHAIRMAN. This appropriation seems to have been raised from $180,000 to $240,000?

MR. WALCOTT. I have not asked any increase this year.

THE CHAIRMAN. Do you think you want the full $240,00?

MR. WALCOTT. Yes, sir. (Walcott 1900e, 241)

On geological surveys:

THE CHAIRMAN. In 1898 you submitted an estimate of $150,000 and you had $110,000 last year, and for the next year you submit $135,000. Is there any special reason for that submission?

MR. WALCOTT. Yes, sir; there is a most marked reason for that. The increase for geology I asked a year ago, in sending my estimate to the Secretary of the Interior, was to $150,000.

THE CHAIRMAN. That is 1898 you asked that?

MR. WALCOTT. I asked it last year, but it did not reach the committee; it was cut down at the Department, and the present year I asked the same appropriation and it was reduced to $135,000. (Walcott 1900, 241)

Walcott got his $150,000 for geologic investigations and more: "In the eight years since that bleak August of 1892, the total appropriation had more than doubled, water-resources investigations were firmly established as part of the Survey work, funds for Alaska had increased twelvefold in 5 years. Only paleontology remained at the 1892 level" (Rabbitt 1980, 302). Quite an accomplishment in six years; at Langley's annual shad party, Walcott could relax for the coming fiscal year.

Near the end of April, Walcott went to Baltimore to attend a lecture by Waldemar C. Brøgger. It was Brøgger who had first pointed out that the Cambrian trilobite zones were misinterpreted in America. Johns Hopkins University had established a lecture series in memory of G. H. Williams. Sir Archibald Geike had been the first lecturer, Brøgger the second. The Norwegian geologist was taken into the field in Maryland for a few days by Walcott and others and then came to Washington for a lecture; it was a replay of the hospitality for Geike. Just what the two spoke about is not recorded, but both had moved far beyond the stratigraphic position of *Olenellus* in their concerns.

Mid-May saw Walcott appearing before the Appropriations Committee of the Senate. As usual, the director got what he wanted for the Geological Survey. Next it was a "Meeting of Committee on building Washn acd. sci. 4:30–6 P.M." (May 18, 1900). His sciatica flared up again and kept him housebound for a day, but he hobbled off to Philadelphia to meet with S. Weir Mitchell; Philadelphia was going to celebrate Benjamin Franklin's birthday, and he was a member of the committee.

Late May brought an interesting scientific diversion. J. E. Watkins had his own railway car, ideal for any small-scale expedition. Secretary Langley, Assistant Secretary Rathbun, and Walcott were guests on a trip to North Carolina. On the twenty-eighth, a total eclipse occurred and a good time was observed by all.

June was busy, especially as Walcott was trying to get ready for fieldwork. The GWMA held a meeting. A congressional request for information concerning water investigations was pointing the way toward a national effort in irrigation. Osborn came to see about the old bones, and Van Hise arrived to talk about fieldwork. Meanwhile, a plan was evolving to reorganize the Geologic Branch into seven divisions, each with a scientific head; Walcott would still control the administrative details. The plan and budget were sent to Hitchcock and came back approved the next day. Because of all this activity, Walcott spent a Sunday morning in his office, a most unusual event; the afternoon was for his family, and he measured Charlie at just over five feet—thirteen inches shorter than his father.

On midsummer's day, the Walcott family left Washington for the Midwest. They established themselves at Picnic Point, not far from Madison, Wisconsin, with Helena's brother and his family. Walcott left Helena with the three younger children, took Charlie with him, and went on to Helena, Montana. The camp party consisted of W. N. Smith from Madison, a budding geologist, and Arthur Brown. By July 5, the outfit pulled out for the "Gate," Gates of the Mountain on the Missouri River, and then headed up the northern side of the Big Belt Mountains; the familiar Flathead Sandstone was like that along the Gallatin River, studied the previous year. As the years had progressed, it was increasingly difficult for Walcott to leave a desk and plunge into fieldwork; after a couple of days on horseback, he was lame enough to comment on his condition.

They looked at the shales and limestone of the Belt, noted that the Cambrian shales overlying the Flathead Sandstone were broken by faulting, collected a few Devonian corals, and took photos. Eventually the party reached the Dearborn River more than fifty miles north of Helena and in the shadow of Scapegoat Mountain. They measured more than sixty-seven hundred feet of the Belt (Walcott 1906, 8–9).

Walcott wrote Williams:

Today we are camped in the Dearborn river cañon in the Rocky Mts. of Montana. I am greatly interested in the Paleozoic section and in the pre-Paleozoic Belt series, both of which are wonderfully well developed in the region.

It is not probable that I shall return East before Sept. 20th. The outdoor life and bracing mountain air have had a very beneficial effect on the sciatica.[6]

Walcott started another section on the northeastern side of Lewis and Clark Pass. Here they were only able to measure about twenty-five hundred feet of rock below the Flathead Sandstone, but it was different from that along the Dearborn River (Walcott 1906, 9–10). Arthur Brown moved the camp several times keeping up with the geologist and stayed busy while Smith, Charlie, and Walcott climbed Mt. Dearborn. As a break from wilderness living, they drove to Augusta one day for mail.

On August 12, after a hard twelve and a half hours, they completed the geologic section on the Dearborn River of four thousand feet of limestone above the Cambrian (Walcott 1908, 200–201), but then Walcott broke a tooth and had to travel to Helena to have it drilled. They moved a couple of more times and paused from geology to examine the boundary of the Lewis and Clark forest reserve. The party went to the North Fork of Sun River, almost due west of Great Falls, and back to Wolf Creek. Walcott had to go back to Helena to have his bad tooth extracted. Four days later, he was up to climbing Haystack Butte and determined that it was one of those curiosities, a syncline, rocks bending down structurally but standing up topographically.

The group moved west across the continental divide to a nearly nonexistent place called Ovando. From here, they packed into the mountains, looking for a good place to measure; this is now the Scapegoat Wilderness area. They moved northwest up the west side of the mountains to Holland Lake, near the western end of the Swan Range; this is now the Bob Marshall Wilderness area. Here they measured five thousand feet of the Belt (Walcott 1906, 10–12). On a "Fine day. Took a long climb—6 *mi* 3700 feet up.—Obtained a fine view of the Mission range & glaciers of Mt. McDonald. Out 7:30 A.M. to 8:20 P.M. Cha's went with us & did nobly" (September 2, 1900). Walcott dragged his camera up and back. They moved south toward Ovando, and then east to near Elliston on the Little Blackfoot River. All this is rugged territory.

Walcott wrote to Hayes:

> I have met with some superb physiographic problems on the eastern and southern sides of the Lewis and Clark forest reserve, also with a very difficult problem in relation to the pre-Cambrian rocks of the same region. It would require at least three months work with a pack train to work out the latter problem; and some time with a buckboard to accumulate data in relation to the different peneplains and orographic movements that have taken place on the eastern slope between the mountain fort and the Missouri river.[7]

Walcott's observations of tilted lake beds in Owens Valley had sharpened his eyes toward interpreting relatively recent movements of mountains; a peneplain was supposed to be a flat surface cut by streams, and tilting of this surface would indicate movement. There were more than enough problems to keep one busy.

The tenth of September the Walcott party drove to Helena and broke up camp for the year. The following day Arthur Brown and Charlie left for the East. Walcott took Smith to Confederate Gulch, but the section was broken by plications, tight angular folds, in the shale, and there was little point searching for fossils. Part of another day was spent looking in the Belt, and for his last day, Walcott "Worked over a large amount of slaty shale 8. A.M.–3. P.M. but found few fossils. Rain began at 4:00 P.M." (September, 15, 1900). Walcott returned to Helena, for enough was enough, even for him. Two days later, Walcott Emmons, and Weed, the promising geologist specializing in copper, met with vice-presidential candidate Roosevelt in Butte.

This had been a hard season both physically and scientifically. Whereas in the Inyo Mountains in eastern California the rocks were beautifully exposed, here most places were covered by vegetation or soil. Although the Inyos were no picnic, the term "rugged" does not apply as it did in the north. Add to that, this part of Montana was a region poorly known topographically and unknown geologically. A good beginning had been made on the stratigraphy of the Precambrian, though this field season would not lead to any quick publication.

The Flathead Sandstone was established as Middle Cambrian in age, and along the Dearborn River Walcott obtained "A fine collection of annelid and trilobite trails much like that from the Tonto sandstone of the Grand Canyon, Arizona."[8] This formation was a reliable datum all over the area from which to look at the underlying rocks of the Belt. There was at least one generalization which could be made:

> In 1900 I crossed the Belt Mountains and endeavored to trace the connection, north of Helena, of the Belt terrane and the pre-Cambrian rocks of the Rocky Mountain "front" at Lewis and Clark pass and north of the south fork of the Dearborn River. It was evident that a great series of strata extended westward beneath the Cambrian that was in general similar to the Belt terrane, but quite different in detail. (Walcott 1906, 2)

In St. Paul on September 20, Walcott called on a senator. The next day he stopped in La Crosse to see brother Ellis; Ellis wanted to show brother Charles his cemetery lot! Then it was to Picnic Point and a far more cheery family gathering for five days, some time spent in packing, but mostly in fishing with the boys. They were home just before the month ended.

October 1 was a "mixed-up day," but then what can one expect after being out of the office for so long. There were problems with the Public Printer, and Walcott smoothed them; there were always problems with the public printer. Construction on the new apartment house was in its final stages, and he took Helena to see it. He left for Boston to attend the inauguration of H. S. Pritchett as the new president of the Massachusetts Institute of Technology. On his return, Walcott "Kept busy with study of faulting & folding etc." (October 26, 1900), one of the few studies that he never brought to publication, though it did result in a talk at the fall meeting of the National Academy of Sciences.

Some of Walcott's activities were never recorded in his notebook. The International Geographical Congress was in Berlin in 1899, and Walcott (1901a) had a paper in the *Proceedings* outlining USGS activity in topography. This might have been compiled by the staff, but it is concise and reads much like his other works. The statistics as to what had been accomplished were impressive.

In October, friend Williams sent him a check for thirty shares of stock in a slate company:

> There has been nothing printed in relationship to the Newfoundland Slate Company. . . . The Sound at the quarries is land locked so that storms cannot interfere with the loading of vessels. . . . The supply is practically inexhaustible. . . . It is anticipated that by the use of electric power the quarries will be producing sufficient slate in two years to pay fully 10% on the investment. If this anticipation is correct it will be possible to sell the whole of the stock at par or above, which make a very profitable investment for the original stockholders.[9]

Interesting!

By the first week in November, twenty families had moved into the Iowa Apartment House—it has forty-nine apartments—and Walcott had another success. He went downtown for the latest election news, and McKinley was re-elected by such a landslide that the contest was over before 11:00 P.M. Next, Walcott traveled to Providence, Rhode Island, visiting Pumpelley and Hague. They did what geologists do and looked at the local rocks; Walcott carried his camera most places, and he took photographs of the conglomerate. They washed off mud and gathered at the fall meeting of the National Academy of Sciences, the main reason for this trip, and then home he went. Life was harried.

December is another dull month, busy but dull. Washington, D.C., marked its centennial, as minor an event as was its bicentennial celebration a century later. Walcott appeared before the Subcommittee on Appropriations for a deficiency appropriation, and, as usual, gave a satisfactory performance:

> THE CHAIRMAN. Now for furnishing the new addition to the Hoee Building?

> MR. WALCOTT. That is another item. At the last session of Congress there was an appropriation made of $5,000 for additional rent, and the building has been completed, and we are occupying it as best we can temporarily and using any material which we have for desks, and we use boxes and cases and everything of that kind, but we have no furniture for it, no material for covering the floors, and material for installing the library in the new addition. To do that we want to put in fireproof or steel book racks, which are not a permanent fixture to the building, but which can be used indefinitely for the shelving. If we use pine, it simply furnishes material for a bonfire in that room, and we wish to put in improved book shelves, and this $12,000 is to

cover the cost of the book stacks, the desks, and the necessary furniture for that building.

THE CHAIRMAN. What does that do, put on any style?

MR. WALCOTT. Not at all; we have done away with rosewood furniture and everything of that kind and we use hard pine and the ordinary type desk, as is used in the Interior Department." (Walcott 1900f, 76)

As the year ground down, the Washington Academy of Sciences and the GWMA met jointly, with Walcott steering them along, to determine how to promote postgraduate education in Washington. "Began work on the Cambrian fossils collected by S. W. Loper on Cape Breton Island" (December 18, 1900). The family had a good Christmas and immediately thereafter Walcott left for the Geological Society meeting in Albany. In a day or two he would be president; it was a fine time to see old friends and receive congratulations. "A very busy day at office attending to routine matters. A quiet evening at home.— All well. In most if not in all ways we are in better condition than Jany 1 ' 1900" (December 31, 1900).

There was a new year and a new century, but if one process stayed the same it was that the workload Walcott undertook always increased. Granted some jobs were thrust upon him, but for many others he could have said no or left projects to others to initiate. Even though running the Geological Survey and the forest reserves were more than full time activities, they gave the illusion of occupying relatively little of his concern this year. For example, being president of the GSA entails some effort to keep the organization growing, though there were relatively few council meetings. In contrast, Walcott's presidency of the Philosophical Society of Washington this same year required him to preside at both council and regular meetings. The Washington Academy of Sciences had fewer regular meetings than the Philosophical, but in 1900, the academy had twenty-five board meetings and the same number were recorded for 1901. He was still treasurer of the National Academy of Sciences, and wrote a debtor: "Of all the investments in my hands for the National Academy of Sciences, this is the only one at present that is delinquent in the payment of interest."[10] The man paid! To add variety and keep Walcott from being confined to science, he was reelected a trustee of the Church of the Covenant for another three years.

The first week in January, Walcott was at his USGS office five days, presided at an evening lecture, helped dedicate the new church, went to two dinners, and gave a talk in Brooklyn about forest reserves, pointing out that trees conserved the water from running off, a connection of forests to western irrigation.

Charles Doolittle Walcott, Paleontologist

"Dinner at Arnold Hague's with H———— & later 10:20 P.M. went to Cong. Newlands to listen to talks on irrigation" (January 8, 1901). "At survey office 9–12 A.M. Meeting of Board of Iowa Apt. House Co. 12:15–2.P.M. Survey 2:10–3:10 P.M. Conference at Sety Interior office on San Francisco Mt. reserve 3:15–5:20" (January 10, 1901). Five days later, he was involved with the charter of the GWMA, and two evenings later, he "Talked to a lot of men at A. Graham Bell's residence on movement to utilize scientific & other bureaus in Wash'n to aid in education" (January 17, 1901). To prove he was human, three days later Walcott collapsed with the flu, which suspended operations for a more than a week. He got up, went to the USGS and Congress as needed, and picked up as though nothing had happened.

February was, well, February. Most of it was USGS routine with ditto marks in his diary day after day. There were only about three events worth recording; the appearance before the Senate Appropriations Committee was routine. Walcott and Newell got together about the various irrigation bills floating around Congress. None were going to pass that year, but sentiment was strong for government irrigation in the West, and it was better to be prepared. In less then a decade the pendulum had swung back toward the subject that had destroyed social reformer Powell.

The most far-reaching item of the month was a joint meeting of the committees of the Washington Academy of Sciences and the GWMA. Walcott was running one organization and masterminding the other, like playing both sides of the net in a tennis game. This was closely followed by a "Meeting of Wash'n. Acad. Sci.— G. W. M. A. & Am. Ass. Ag. Colleges Committee at Mrs. George Hearsts 8–10. P.M." (February 13, 1901). The GWMA had as one of its original objectives the founding of a national university, but Walcott persuaded the organization to amend their charter and drop that aim, the better to have it pursued by others. GWMA was now in the position of lobbying for national support from the various educational groups for a national education center.

By now the Washington Academy of Sciences was very much a going establishment. The society was publishing *Proceedings,* had money in the bank donated by patrons, and was buying a lot for a permanent building. There was some concern expressed by a few members to what this local group was doing, and Walcott distributed a form letter to reassure nonresident members who were also in the National Academy of Sciences:

The Washington Academy may consider such questions affecting the relations of science to the government as are not taken up by the National Academy, and which affect the entire scientific body in its relations to the Government. It may also consider the interrelationship of the various scientific
organizations that unite to form the scientific body, and give such assistance
that may be in its power to the correlation of scientific work and the advancement of scientific interests in the country. It was reasons such as these
that led me to favor the development of the Washington Academy of Sciences. . . . I have given a great deal of time and attention to this organization the last year with the belief that it was well spent. At the same time I
should take pleasure in aiding in any way in my power in the advancement
of the interests of the National Academy.[11]

When the aim was to be obtuse and obfuscate the issues, Walcott could do that
too. In simple terms, the National Academy of Sciences was mainly honorific,
and to move it to action was a time-consuming, cumbersome effort. It was easier to have a scientific lobby at hand in Washington that knew how to take instruction from Walcott as to what it was to lobby for.

Despite their disparate interests, the Washington Academy of Sciences and
the GWMA formed a strange assemblage that actually was moving forward.
Under prodding from them, the Smithsonian Institution's board of regents
passed a resolution asking Congress to permit postgraduate study and research at various federal facilities. Lo and behold, on March 3, 1901, the last
day of the session, Congress passed legislation which opened federal facilities to students. A few students had been in federal laboratories earlier, but
there were no policies and the general attitude was that only government employees should be in government buildings. This legislation was a significant
step forward for training scientists in America. Such events do not happen on
Capitol Hill without considerable coordination and guidance, yet nowhere
does Walcott's name appear.

The following rainy day brought the second inauguration of President
McKinley. Despite the soggy start, reelection gave promise that the USGS would
continue to prosper and that the extracurricular activities in education would
gather more force. Late March, the higher education bandwagon rolled a little
further. In New York Walcott consulted with Nicholas Murray Butler and President Seth Low of Columbia University, and had the opportunity to meet John
D. Rockefeller Jr., Mr. Payne, and other figures of wealth.

Charles Doolittle Walcott, Paleontologist

April 1 marked work on USGS plans for the summer, and other Survey and forest chores kept the pressure on. He slipped away to Baltimore for a meeting with faculty members at Johns Hopkins and spent the night with President Gilman. "At Survey 9–10:15 A.M. 2–5 P.M. Meeting of N.[ational] A.[cademy] Sci. 10:30 1:45. Presided at lecture of Prof. Alpheus Hyatt 8:15 9:15. With Helena to reception at Hearsts 10–12:30" (April 17, 1900). One of the most difficult chores for a scientist is attending a scientific meeting in one's own town; the office somehow always interferes.

The Washington members of the National Academy of Sciences sponsored a dinner at Raucher's Restaurant for their out of town colleagues. Simon Newcomb wanted to invite members of Congress, but Walcott gave him sound advice: "It would be unwise to invite any Senators or Representatives as it might lead to the feeling among those present that they were invited for the purpose of influencing in some matter their action in Congress."[12] Near the end of the month, Secretary of Interior Hitchcock and Walcott performed their annual ritual. Walcott would submit plans for the year, and a day or so later they would come back approved. Insofar as one can tell, Hitchcock never changed an item. Hitchcock had a reputation of being a cold man, but he and Walcott got on well throughout his eight years as secretary.

As much for the need to get away as to collect a few more brachiopods, Walcott took two days in May to meet Professor Wanner at York, Pennsylvania. They went to York Haven and Emigsville, and "We worked south on outcrops of shales & ls until 4 P.M. & rode in on bicycles to York. Look at outcrops about York 7–8 P.M." (May 4, 1901). This was hardly a horseback ride in the high mountain country, but it removed a few office cobwebs.

The middle of the month another piece of the educational effort was emplaced. Walcott dashed off a letter to President Gilman in Baltimore:

> At a meeting of the joint comittee [sic] of the G.W.M.A. & W.A.S. held today it was decided to incorporate the Washington Memorial Institution at once. Can you come over and be one of them? We will meet at my office at any hour you can be present tomorrow— (Thursday) or Friday before 4. P.M. The incorporators here will include Merriam [chief of Biological Survey]— Wright [commissioner of labor]—Sternberg [Surgeon General]—Mrs. Archibald Hopkins—Walcott. Dr. A. G. Bell is unfortunately away. The incorporators will have to formulate the byelaws and elect 15 trustees. The bye laws are in shape & most of the trustees practically agreed upon. Next week 23*rd* I go to New York to meet the N.E. A. committee—Harper—Low— Elliott—Butler & D*r*. Curry. D*r* Hudley will work with us if necessary as a trustee. In haste.[13]

As with past activities, Walcott formulated a plan, had the different pieces such as bylaws and agreement by individuals to serve in hand, and then moved rapidly to cement the organization. Walcott became president of the trustees of the WMI, and Gilman was elected director. Walcott, on the twenty-fourth, had written a long letter to Gilman indicating the steps to be taken and asking advice. Having done that, he then moved ahead without waiting for comments.

A local paper reported the first meeting of the Washington Memorial Institution (WMI) a few weeks later: "The object of the Institution is to render the scientific and other resources of the government in Washington practically and continuously available for advanced study and research, and to co-operate with the universities, colleges, and individuals to this end in the use of such resources. This is in conformity with the law approved March 3, 1901, providing that facilities for research and study in the government departments be afforded to duly qualified individuals, students, and graduates of institutions of learning in the several States and Territories and District of Columbia. The institution, however, is to be entirely independent of government support or control."[14] Although the writing is pure Walcottiana, the only places where Walcott's name appears is his election as president of the board of trustees and as host to a trustees luncheon.

By now Walcott had gotten out of the habit of speaking to the Geological Society of Washington. However, to ensure that things kept moving forward, he organized a symposium the society held on governmental cooperation in science. Next, Walcott went to New York for the meeting with the powers of the National Education Association, came back, and, almost as an afterthought, had the Philosophical Society of Washington incorporated.

Helena and Walcott went to Buffalo to receive guests when the Mines Building opened two days before the formal start of the Pan-American Exposition. Displays by the USGS at expositions helped keep the name of the agency before the public. This one in particular, with its emphasis on minerals and mining, was another step in Walcott's campaign for a federal mining agency.

Chamberlin wrote on another matter: "My Dear Walcott, If you can be present to receive it, I am sure the Senate and Trustees of the University would be glad to confer upon you the degree of LL.D in token of their appreciation of your scientific contributions and the executive ability you have displayed in the conduct of the Geological Survey, the National Museum, and other public interests committed to your charge."[15] Walcott was "Busy with letters of allotment at Survey & daily routine. Have little time to work on Cambrian brachiopoda" (May 31, 1901). Without a formal commitment of funds, no field parties could spend funds and this administrative chore had to be completed. Walcott was so frantically busy he recorded starting his speech for Chicago on May 28 and again on June 4.

Walcott left for Chicago and spent a day socializing with Chamberlin. On the seventeenth he read his talk and had dinner with the faculty. Following this, Walcott was "Visiting with Prof. Chamberlin etc. At 11. A.M. went to University with six others rec'd degree of L. L. D. Later at lunch with Univ. faculty gradu-ates etc. met John D. Rockefeller. At 8:00 P.M. left Chicago for home" (June 18, 1901). When the University of Chicago was conceived, honorary degrees were not to be part of its academic activities. The patriotic fervor of the Spanish-American War forced the university to grant a degree to President McKinley. Now, to celebrate the tenth anniversary of its founding, it awarded others. The Utica Free Academy nongraduate now possessed two honorary doctorates.

His speech "Relations of the National Government to higher education and research" was printed in *Science* eleven days after presentation. Walcott used the venue to further the need for academic activity in Washington. He reviewed the growth of universities in colonial America and efforts of several framers of the Constitution to insert specific provisions for educational activities of the federal government. He then went into land-grant colleges and the rising need of the scientific bureaus for trained personnel, heaping considerable praise on the Department of Agriculture for employing temporary student assistants, and discussed the policy of the USGS of employing graduate students during the summer. He started a new section of the talk with the steps leading to forma-tion of the Washington Memorial Institution, as a nonprofit foundation free of any government control. Next, he indicated what the federal government was spending for scientific and research work, surveyed the libraries and collections in Washington, touched on law, diplomacy, and medicine, thereby showing in-directly the advantages of locating an institute of higher learning in Washing-ton, and had a rousing close:

> The relations of the National Government to higher education and research are intimate and complex; but the complexities are already partially resolved, the present is auspicious, and the future outlook is most promising. Long ago the nation recognized its obligation "to promote a higher and more ex-tended policy than is embraced in the protection of the temporal interests and political rights of the individual." The action of Congress in opening the Government bureaus at Washington for study and research is a long stride forward, and if carried out in good faith must result in another and higher standard for American endeavor. (Walcott 1901b, 14)

Walcott was back in Washington for only a few days, to help with packing for a family vacation. Helena had responsibility for Charlie, Sidney, Helen, and young Stuart, but this was an old-fashioned family with at least a fair amount of money; Mary Hardy, the nurse, and Agnes Golden, the cook, were along. A little perspective on costs and current family fortune might help. The house rented in Washington on S Street cost seventy-five dollars per month; the Walcotts maintained that while they were renting the summer place for one hundred dollars a month. This was something of a luxury, but it was possible without scrimping. Recall that in an effort to oust Powell in 1894, the salary of the director was cut from six thousand to five thousand dollars. Finally, at the start of the fiscal year, Congress restored the missing one thousand dollars. Of course, they did not make it retroactive for the seven years of overwork and underpay.

After more than ten hours on the train, the family was in the Finger Lakes region of New York. Walcott wrote to Williams; the abbreviations and missing punctuation are characteristic of Walcott's haste when he wrote:

> We left Wash'n the 22*d* & settled down at beautiful spot on the shores of Seneca lake 8 *mi* N. of Watkins—I was about played out so came along with the family—Expect to remain here most of the summer. Will write up annual rept—Estimates etc—and push along the study of Cambrian brachiopoda— ... Are there any fossil localities in the vicinity to which I can take the boys? The flags & shales along shore here are not at all promising—[16]

Walcott did vacation, of a sort, for the longest time in his career. Mornings he worked on brachiopods and afternoons he wrote letters. Sometimes early in the morning, sometimes late in the afternoon he was out on the lake fishing, often with Charlie. He noted Stuart's fifth birthday, was out for a couple of days with a summer accident cutting his wrist on a boat roller, and lazed around in the hot afternoons. Walcott noted "A very quiet week. Made considerable progress with species of Actrotreta & kept up with large correspondence" (August 10, 1901).

It is perhaps just as well that Walcott took uninterrupted time for this next brachiopod paper. Earlier he had another one of his series published (Walcott 1901), and although it contains useful information, the arrangement leaves much to be desired. In fact, it is a sixteen-page paper with a table of contents showing six different parts; as with most of these shorter brachiopod papers, no illustrations are provided. Some specimens discussed are from Sweden and Sardinia, the result of his exchanges and purchases, some he collected in Idaho and Montana, and some were from Canada, collected in 1899 by Loper. In that sense, it is an up-to-date work. On the other hand, if any additional evidence of going a number of directions from overwork in needed, that paper would seem to provide it.

Walcott took a quick trip to Washington and spent a few days at the USGS, followed by house hunting. Helena came down, but they could not decide on a place. In the neighborhood they liked, the houses were not satisfactory; there are some constants in life, regardless of the year. By the end of August, they were back in the cottage. Later, Walcott took Helena and Charlie to the Pan-American Exposition. The architectural effects and the electrical display received good marks. Surprisingly, the shooting of President McKinley on September 6 received no comment in his diary, nor did his death eight days later, though Walcott rushed down to Washington and, with Pinchot, attended the funeral. He went back to the cottage, and the working vacation continued until the first of October.

In the first days back, Walcott saw the secretary of interior on diverse matters and developed his own diverse matters. "A busy day with survey & outside matters. With Mr. McLachlen arranged for loan to complete Mendota Ap't House" (October 3, 1901). The McLachlen bank was one of the fixtures in Washington for years, on F Street about four blocks east of the Hoee Building. This second real estate venture of Walcott's was a U-shaped structure seven stories high. The Menodota was designed by an architect who had worked in Minnesota and liked the Indian name; it was also the name of a Late Cambrian formation in that state. To give some indication of Washington, the apartment building at 2220 Twentieth Street N.W. was the most northern large structure in the city at the time (Goode 1988, 43–46). Helena and Walcott decided to move to 2117 S Street, two doors from where they had been living; apartment living was not for them. A last day was spent packing and then Walcott began another train trip west.

The first significant stop for Walcott was St. Louis to confer about the Louisiana Purchase Exposition coming in three years. Then it was the long haul across Missouri and Kansas to La Junta, Colorado, where Gilbert joined him. They went to Alberqueque and Williams, Arizona, and from there north to the Grand Canyon. The Santa Fe had completed a spur line from Williams, and the first train was on September 17. From now on the flood of tourists would come to the South Rim.

The first day they went down Indian Garden Canyon to the Cambrian, photographed the rocks, and collected a few fossils. Next they went west to Havasupai Point and the camp of prospector Bass who took them down the Bass trail.

"Crossed river A.M. & with Mr. Gilbert examined section of Unkar pre-Cambrian rocks. Camped at night on Shinumo Creek—Mr. Carkhuff took a number of photo's" (October 16, 1901). Norman Carkhuff was a photographer with the Geological Survey and had accompanied Walcott from Washington. In terms of geography, this was a little to the west of where Walcott had measured his section twenty years earlier. The next generation of geologists in that area had no difficulty in following Walcott's stratigraphy (Noble 1910).

After two days on the north side of the canyon, they came out and met N. H. Darton. He is judged one of the best regional mappers ever produced by the Geological Survey. Eventually he had four state geologic maps to his credit, and he lived to be the last surviving founder of the Geological Society of Washington. The group went east to Grand View Point near the head of the Hance trail and peered into the depths. Gilbert left.

Walcott and Darton went back to Williams and boarded the private car of the chief engineer of the western division of the Santa Fe Railway. They toured the southern edge of the Colorado Plateau by rail, going east to Gallup, New Mexico, and back to Williams. Whenever they wished, the car was dropped at a siding to be picked up later by a passing passenger or freight to suit their convenience. It provided a excellent opportunity to see the geology and was reconnaissance in style and comfort. What a change from a pack train in the mountains.

Darton left and Walcott went on to Bakersfield, California, to look at oil fields. The Director had some experience with coal, but oil was a growing part of geology in which Walcott's background was sketchy. Senator Perkins had to be seen. Mr. Hearst was a usefull man to know, and since there was a question as to who should gather data on gold and silver production, it was wise to call on the director of the San Francisco Mint.

He returned to Los Angeles to look at a few more oil wells. Then it was on to San Diego and up into the hills for several days to examine dams. Again engineering geology was a field that the Director scarcely knew, and if the USGS were to become involved in irrigation, practical study on his part would help. He went back to Los Angeles and spoke to the chamber of commerce; that kind of activity never hurt. The newspapers loved him:

> Mr. Walcott is a quiet, unassuming gentlemen, courteous and simple. His room at the Westminster is a tangle of maps, fishing tackle, shotgun shells, and apparatus which have to do with geology—at least it was last night, for he was packing his trunk. . . . "Our department is a bureau of investigation

and information, and not in any sense of discussion, so, necessarily, we are reticent in the matter of discussing our work. The object of the present trip is to gain information of the irrigating possibilities of the west, through a study of what has already been accomplished in that line by individual effort. Of course, not all irrigation works have been successful, and we are bent on learning the causes of failure and the possibility of success in other works."[17]

The Engineers and Architects Association of southern California tendered him a banquet with more favorable publicity. Walcott could make the complex problems understandable. "Taken together, forest and water form perhaps the most vital of the internal problems of the United States."[18] Walcott was for the government building large public works for irrigation and had a rousing close for reporters. "Looking at it from all sides there is no one question of greater importance to our people than forest preservation, water conservation, and reclamation and settlement of the arid lands of the West by those who will build homes upon them. Throughout our history the success of the homemaker has been but another name for the upbuilding of the nation."[19] Powell might have smiled at Walcott's remarks.

On November 9, Walcott was back at Seligman, Arizona, with an R. B. Burns. They camped in the Chino Valley, a far cry from a private car, and measured a section of the Cambrian. This was only a two-day trip, but Walcott enjoyed it thoroughly and noted he had learned much of practical value from Mr. Burns. One would like to know more of a man who could impress Walcott. Even though Seligman, Arizona, is a long way from anywhere else, Walcott was finally home on the fifteenth of November.

He plunged right into administration, going with Pinchot to see Roosevelt about forest reserves. The USGS kept him occupied and there was a stream of visitors. Add to that, a proposal for another new apartment house on Connecticut Avenue was being discussed. The proposal was interesting enough that Walcott strolled out to look over the ground. Withal, twelve days after he returned, Walcott was "Nearly caught up with Survey administrative matter & put in two hours work on Cambrian brachiopods" (November 27, 1901).

This comment must have referred to the finishing touches on the paper which came out next year: "I had hoped to complete the monograph on Cambrian Brachiopoda before this time, but owing to the large accessions of new material and to increased administrative duties this has been impractical" (Walcott 1902, 577). In contrast to his last paper on the group, this one is well organized as a consequence of his uninterrupted summer. It is a careful treatment of the genus *Acrotreta*, listing all previously described species and adding a number of new ones. As in his past papers, the new species came from widespread material. He described a new genus and named a species after Girty; apparently he was unaware of Girty's dislike for him. A few other species and genera ended this thirty-five-page work.

December 1 was a quiet day, with Sunday school for the children and then a drive with "Uncle Joe" Cannon. Monday was a typically busy day at the Survey, as was most of Tuesday. Mid-morning Tuesday, Pritchett, Wright, Merriam, and Walcott got their heads together about the WMI, quiescent while Walcott was away. That afternoon Andrew Carnegie dropped a bombshell, big enough to be put aside for more detailed discussion to follow; Walcott had a couple of busy days with the Geological Survey and then a conference with Nicholas Murray Butler, C. D. Welsh, C. Hart Merriam, and Marcus Baker to talk over Carnegie's bombshell. The future was promising, though it was not at all clear quite what the promise was.

Walcott always looked to the future, but he acted in the present. During the next week he lined up another patron and another one-thousand-dollar donation for the Washington Academy of Sciences, and made sure that at its annual meeting the GWMA stayed on track. The last full week in December began "At survey most of the day—At dinner given by Mr. Newlands to Irrigation Committee of Senate and House 8–11:20 P.M." (December 23, 1901). Irrigation coming up at this very time was a case of more largess than a body could properly handle, but if opportunities are not seized when they come, they might not come again.

Christmas was a jolly time, and he even took Helena out to an evening party, not a private dinner with political overtones as was their customary entertainment. He went to New York City to wrap up loose ends with Carnegie and got in a couple of days for USGS business at the office before leaving Washington again. The last day of the year, Walcott "Presided at meeting of Geological Society of America at Rochester University during the day—Gave my annual address in the evening as President G. S. A. A snowy, cold night" (December 31, 1901).

His talk "Outlook of the geologist in America" summarized geologic studies in North America during 1901. He considered the national surveys, the state surveys, the amount of publication, and who was working where on what problems. He then devoted several pages to current problems in geology deserving

Charles Doolittle Walcott, Paleontologist

of further study; anyone searching for ideas today could well examine this list. He concluded with a section on the future, pointing out that new problems in science continue to arise:

> Question after question, both local and continental, has come up for investigation. Most of them are still unsolved, and the study will bring a host of others that will line up before the mind of the student like the aisles of pines in the forests of the Sierras—some small and dwarfed, others strong and attractive, that are nearby, and farther away the less defined but silent mass that awaits his coming. We are only on the threshold of the golden era of geologic development in America.
>
> We older men are still endeavoring to do our part, but in a few years all the work will be turned over to the young men of today. Some persons here will look back from 1950 as we look back to 1850. There has been an advance since we began—20 to 40 years ago—and we have full faith that it will be sustained as generation after generation of geologists carry the grand work forward throughout the twentieth century. (Walcott 1902a, 117–18)

It was a bit of blarney, for Walcott did not consider himself old. He was as enthusiastic and as optimistic in private as he was in public. "As a whole 1901 has been a pleasant & prosperous year for Helena, myself & children. The Geological Survey has prospered but now needs more room & men. The bringing to a head of the Washington Memorial Institution that has led to the endowment of an Institution for study & research in Washington is the most important public work in wh- I have taken part. It should be put in shape as a practical working basis during 1902" (December 31, 1901).

12

Big Money: It Is Better To Be Healthy and Rich Than Poor and Sick (1901–1904)

Another exclusive circle within the Survey gates is the Association of Aspiring Assistants which was organized in 1894 by certain younger members in the geologic branch, to promote social intercourse and informal discussion. . . . The Society has been very useful in teaching the younger geologists how to mingle and drink beer.

"Birthday Bulletin," USGS, 2 April 1904

RECAPITULATION may assist understanding. George Washington willed five thousand shares of his Potomack Canal Company to the nation with the hope of establishing a national university. Apart from rhetoric, nothing happened. Near the centenary of his death, in 1897 various ladies organized the George Washington Memorial Association (GWMA) to honor his bequest. A "call" was sent forth and a nationwide organization sketched out. In December 1899, the first annual meeting was in Washington.

One aim of the GWMA was to promote "patriotic interest" in Washington's bequest. A second specific aim was to raise funds by way of small donations to build an administration building. In theory, once this was up, the campus of a national university would follow. Amidst more rhetoric, GWMA had raised about seven thousand dollars. The GWMA was just starting to be noticed about the time the Washington Academy of Sciences was founded. Walcott needed a home for the National and Washington academies, and he also had a case of building fever from his real estate efforts. It was almost a marriage made in heaven. By early 1901, he steered the GWMA and the academy to form the Washington Memorial Institution (WMI); the immediate objective of the WMI was the construction of a building.

The action now shifts to New York City. Andrew Carnegie needs no introduction. This Scottish lad, born in 1835, emigrated to America and made a

Charles Doolittle Walcott, Paleontologist

fortune, the finale being organization of the United States Steel Corporation. Carnegie retired in 1901 and was in the process of seriously giving away money. Church organs, free public libraries, and the Carnegie Institute in Pittsburgh could not use up the dollars coming in.

One of Carnegie's guests at Skibo Castle in Scotland that spring was Andrew D. White, who had been president of Cornell University and was then ambassador to Germany (Madsen 1969). White was not the first to bring Carnegie the idea of a national university, but he was the first to capture his attention on the subject (Miller 1970, 168). Two other men require mention. Just as Daniel Coit Gilman was retiring as founding president of Johns Hopkins University, Walcott nabbed him for director of the WMI. Gilman was a grand old man of American higher education. White wanted him in Scotland, but the proposed trip never materialized. That summer White and Gilman privately surveyed the status of higher education in the United States for Carnegie. In mid-November, Gilman went to discuss matters with the millionaire.

John Shaw Billings, seven years younger, was nowhere near the end of his activities. He had spent thirty-four years in the army, thirty of them at the Army Medical Museum as curator and librarian. Lieutenant Colonel Billings retired in 1895, for a year at the University of Pennsylvania medical school. Billings had built an incredible medical library in Washington, and from Philadelphia he moved to New York City. The Astor, Lenox, and Tilden libraries were to be consolidated into the New York Public Library, and Billings made that happen. When Billings met Carnegie is not clear, but with their interest in libraries, meeting was almost inevitable.

If Andrew Carnegie had a "brain trust" during the last part of 1901, Billings and Gilman were it. The two had corresponded for a quarter of a century, and Billings had a role in organizing the Johns Hopkins Medical School. They were strikingly different in approach, Billings characterized as "army, trained to give orders and to follow orders." Gilman spent his life among warring academic factors, soothing feelings and seeking consensus. When Gilman arrived at the Carnegie mansion, Billings was present and Carnegie asked him to stay. Afterward, Carnegie requested they jointly draft a report on how to spend his money. Next, on November 28, 1901, Carnegie wrote President Roosevelt of a sizable gift to the nation and the story really begins.

What is significant is that both men who helped influence Carnegie knew Walcott well. For at least a decade, Walcott repeatedly visited Gilman in Baltimore. The connection with Billings is more subtle, but just as real. The Philosophical Society of Washington originally met in Ford's Theater, which then housed the Army Medical Museum; Billings and Walcott may have met at meetings. In 1885, the Medical Museum moved to a new building east of the U.S. National Museum; that red brick structure was sacrificed to make room for the Hirshhorn Gallery. Walcott must have gone to the Medical Museum to use the library. Billings, like Walcott, was often at the Cosmos Club. When Billings resigned in 1898 as treasurer of the National Academy of Sciences, he recommended Walcott for the office. For one more thread, Helena Breese Walcott and Mrs. Billings were cousins.

The first Monday in December, Walcott was "At Survey 9–12—1–3 P.M. Meeting of Dr. H. S. Pritchett, C. D. Wright, C. Hart Merriam & C. D. W. 9–10:30 on Washn. Memorial Institute. At 4. P.M. went with Dr. D. C. Gilman to call on Andrew Carnegie to talk over research work etc. in Washington. Dined with Mr. Carnegie, Dr. Gilman, Pritchett & J. S. Billings at the New Willard. Home 9:30 P.M." (December 2, 1901). He added, "Mr. Carnegie stated that he had decided to give ($10,000,000) ten million dollars for research work & post-graduate work in Washington" (December 3, 1901).

Reading between the lines suggests Walcott was surprised. He was thinking of a building for higher education, when funds for research appeared as an unexpected, grand development. White and Gilman were strong advocates of higher education. Billing's interests were more in research, and his view prevailed. To delve into the psyche of a philanthropist, Carnegie had the Carnegie Museum in Pittsburgh and J. P. Morgan had the American Museum of Natural History in New York; that was sufficient for the field, and there was no need to compete with an associate. John D. Rockefeller had founded the University of Chicago and Big Oil was larger than Big Steel. Rockefeller had also ventured into the field of medical research. Carnegie could support other research and keep up with him. Millionaires, like everyone else, seldom deliberately set out to end up second best on a new venture.

Walcott had spent the summer contacting people who might introduce him to Carnegie. By late fall, Gilman knew that large sums could be dispensed, but letters to his friend White indicate that he said nothing to Walcott concerning this matter. Late in November, on behalf of the WMI, Walcott wrote Carnegie and Rockefeller, though seemingly he received no reply. He later wrote a memorandum on his meeting with the great benefactor:

Charles Doolittle Walcott, Paleontologist

Dr. Walcott returned to Washington in November and on the afternoon of December 2, 1901, Dr. Gilman called at the office of the Geological Survey and said that Mr. Andrew Carnegie was the Willard Hotel and would like to see Dr. Walcott. He went down to the hotel with him and met Mr. Carnegie for the first time. Mr. Carnegie said that he had had luncheon with President Roosevelt and he thought it right to tell him that first he intended to give ten million ($10,000,000) as a foundation for a scientific research institution in Washington along the lines outlined to him in a letter that had been sent to him and which had been further explained by Dr. Gilman. After a short conversation Mr. Carnegie led Dr. Walcott to a bay window and said that he wished his dear old friend, Dr. Gilman, to be the first President of the new institution, as he had done a great work at Johns Hopkins from which he was about to retire. Mr. Carnegie spoke of Dr. Gilman being seventy years of age and that not much initiative work could be expected from him. He then asked Dr. Walcott to act as Secretary and to take an active part in the organization and conduct of the institution in its first years at least. This Dr. Walcott agreed to do as far as other duties permitted, as he was then Director of the U. S. Geological Survey.[1]

On the sixth, Walcott had dinner with Surgeon General Sternberg, one of the WMI incorporators. At a meeting the next day, Nicholas Murray Butler of Columbia College, C. Hart Merriam of the Biological Survey, Marcus Baker, a Geological Survey employee who had been detailed to work with Gilman on the Venezuela Boundary Commission, and Walcott discussed the Carnegie gift. What Walcott does not record is that less than a week after he met Carnegie, geologist Becker prepared a memorandum on the need for a laboratory to study geophysics (Yochelson and Yoder 1994). Walcott made plans for the money before Carnegie had any idea as to what he really wanted to do with it. It never hurt to keep as many irons in the fire as could be kept hot, so on the fourteenth, Walcott attended the annual GWMA meeting.

Newspapers were delighted with the story of a gift of ten million dollars to the nation. Butler wrote Walcott: "I have had a long talk with Mr. Carnegie and he has no criticism to make of the publicity that has come so unexpectedly because he knows that newspaper men have all sorts of ways of getting at information supposed to be confidential."[2] Shortly, the news was not going quite the way the Laird of Steel anticipated. The story suddenly became juicy when reporters found that the bequest was to be in United States Steel bonds, not cash. Congress being involved with that corporation was quite a different matter than Congress accepting money. Butler wrote again, "I wish it were possible to ascertain how the Carnegie matter became public, or who gave the story to Wellman, for it has been a serious embarrassment. I am also in some trepidation as to the outcome of the negotiations regards the form of the gift in bonds."[3]

Unfavorably publicity grew stronger and stronger. Teddy Roosevelt invited Merry Andrew to lunch at the White House on the eighteenth and told him gently that there was no way that he would get a congressional charter; the Homewood strike was still fresh and political implications of corporate bonds stained with the blood of workers was too hot to touch. Secretary of War Elihu Root was present at the lunch and hoped that Carnegie would obtain a charter elsewhere. Neither he nor the president had any idea what Carnegie might do after the congressional rebuff.

The sixteenth and seventeenth of December, Walcott was at the dentist, just what was not needed at the moment. Wednesday he was "Talking over matters of institution for research with Andrew Carnegie & Dr Gilman 9:30–12:30 3 to 4:45 P.M. At home in the evening" (December 18, 1901). His memorandum provides detail:

> Mr. Carnegie gave no indication of what he would do about it. In the afternoon Dr. Gilman and Dr. Walcott talked with Mr. Carnegie as to what could be done. Mr. Carnegie said that "as Congress declined to grant a charter, it might be just as well to let it go." Dr. Walcott told him that he thought the work was worth doing and that he would draw up articles of incorporation under the general incorporation law of the District of Columbia, which was a national law and submit it to him. Mr. Carnegie said, "All right; go ahead, and send it over to me."[4]

After the White House lunch, the Carnegie Institution was as good as dead; Carnegie did not care for the word no in regard to his ideas. The organization came into being because, at the last possible second, the right man said the right words to revive the moribund concept. Walcott was correct that because Washington was a territory, federal law applied; his real estate dealings taught him the intricacies of the local government. As the British would say, it was a near thing. Walcott had much riding on his shoulders, but was "At dentist 10 to 1:30 4 to 5 P.M. To [sic] much used up to be useful in the evening. Prepared draft of articles of incorporation for an institute of study & research to be founded by Andrew Carnegie in Washington D. C." (December 19, 1901). Friday was "A busy day at the Survey. Sent Andrew Carnegie draft of Articles of Incorporation & Bye Laws & wrote him at length. At home in evening" (December 20, 1901). Dentist or no dentist, Walcott was not about to let this prize slip away. Besides, he could write articles and bylaws for an organization with one hand tied behind his back. For example, that year as president of the Philosophical Society of Washington, an honor not even recorded in his diary, he persuaded the organization to incorporate, an act that most scientific groups in Washington failed to do for more than half a century.

After the Christmas lull Walcott was "At Survey 9–2:49 P.M.— Left Wash.n. 3. P.M. in a B[altimore] & O[hio Railway]. At Baltimore Dr D. C. Gilman joined me & we went on to New York. At Manhattan Hotel met Dr N. M. Butler. Put up at Manhattan for the night" (December 26, 1901). Friday, he "Went to Mr. Carnegies 9:30 A.M. At 10:30 A.M. met Mr. Abram S. Hewitt of N. Y. Jn S. Billings, Dr. D. C. Gilman at the Andrew Carnegie home. Plan of organization of Carnegie Institution in Washington D.C. discussed & adopted. Lunched with Mr. & Mrs. Carnegie & returned to Washington by 340 train B&O" (December 27, 1901). One major hurdle had been crossed. "A very busy day. Called on the President Secty. John Hay & Justice White in relation to the Carnegie Institution. Messers. Hay & White & Carol D. Wright agreed to serve as incorporators. At dinner given by Asst Secty of State D. J. Hill met many men I wished to talk with" (December 28, 1901). Another hurdle was crossed.

Walcott was even busier that Saturday. Clarence King died on December 24 in Phoenix. King had been in decline, in several senses, for a number of years. After his success with the Fortieth Parallel Survey, King never lived up to his potential; Powell kept growing in stature until Congress cut him down. Director Walcott combined the best features of both. A memorial meeting was in Walcott's office with remarks by Powell and Emmons. Walcott put on record that:

> The present Director's personal relations with Mr. King began in the winter of 1879, and continued to the time of his death. They were of the most cordial and inspiring character. Mr. King's ideals were high, and none could talk with him on any geologic or general topic without receiving valuable suggestions. All of his scientific colleagues on the Survey honored and respected him, both an a man and as a scientist. (Walcott 1902b, 206)

High praise, maybe a little too high, but Walcott was loyal both to his former chief and his organization.

That Sunday there was no church! Walcott "Went to Survey office to meet Alfred Swan of New York with whom I talked about Carnegie Institution" (December 29, 1901). There followed a frantic day at the office, a train trip to Rochester and his GSA presidential address (Yochelson 1988). Walcott took a quick swing through Utica to see sister Josie and sped south.

"Found all well at home. A very busy day Survey & other business. Talked with Mr. William F. Mattingly on articles of incorporation of Carnegie Institution. Called on President Roosevelt at 6. P.M. in relation to his becoming a member of the board of Trustees of the Carnegie Institution" (January 3, 1902); the president declined. On Saturday

> Incorporators of Carnegie Institution met at office of Secretary of State 10 A.M. & signed articles of incorporation. Secy John Hay, Justice White, D. C. Gilman, J. S. Billings, Walcott. Discussed bye laws. Elected trustees—etc. At Survey during the afternoon & home in the evening except for a call on Col. Wright. Sent copies of proposed bye laws to Messers. Gilman, Carnegie, Wright & Billings." (January 4, 1902)

After it crystallized on the eighteenth, in two and a half weeks the CIW was organized by Walcott. The final hurdle had been crossed.

The incorporators were a lustrous group. As to any connection of John Hay with Walcott, it might have come years earlier from Clarence King or Henry Adams. Apart from that, the $600,000 Stoneleigh Court Apartment House in Washington was known as Hay's apartment, but it was Walcott who engineered the deal. Although they moved in different circles, the director and the secretary of state knew each other fairly well.

Monday afternoon Walcott noted a trip to New York City. Almost as an aside he also mentioned meeting Secretary of Interior Hitchcock to talk over irrigation matters. Like the dental problems which came up while Walcott and Carnegie were involved in December, irrigation was an issue not needed at this time, but it could not be delayed. Walcott "Took breakfast with H. S. Pritchett. At 10 30 A.M. met Dr. D. C. Gilman, A. S. Hewitt, J. S. Billings & Carol D. Wright at home of Mr. Andrew Carnegie for conference of Carnegie Institution. Lunched with Mr. & Mrs. Carnegie, Dr. G. & Col. Wright" (January 7, 1902).

Walcott rushed back to Washington, kept the Survey moving, repeated part of his GSA presidential address to the Geological Society of Washington, and gave another talk later that evening at the home of Alexander Graham Bell. He devoted half a day to the USGS, spoke to new president Gilman of the CIW, and looked for a home for the newest organization in town. After some time in a private house, CIW eventually settled on offices in the Bond Building, a few blocks west of the Survey. Walcott then actually had more than an uninterrupted week to attend to the rocks and waters (and trees) of the United States.

On another trip to New York City, he "Took breakfast with Dr J. S. Billings. Called on Abram S. Hewitt, Dr Rossitor Raymond before 2 P.M. Looked over

Charles Doolittle Walcott, Paleontologist

Astor Library & called on Mr. Andrew Carnegie 5–6:30 P.M. Called on Dr N. M. Butler 9–10. Left N.Y. 11:30 P.M." (January 24, 1902); that qualifies as a full day. Back in Washington, his business consisted of calling on senators in regard to the USGS appropriation and other pending legislative matters. Things were at such a pitch that last week in January that after Sunday school, Walcott went to his office for three hours just to find some quiet.

He squeezed in two more days, mainly for the USGS, before Mr. Carnegie came into town for the big event. "Met Mr. Carnegie, Dr Gilman, Abram S. Hewitt, J. S. Billings, C. D. Wright, for consultation—Lunched with Mr. Carnegie's party. At 230 met with Trustees of Carnegie Institution at State Dept & acted as Secty & was elected such later. In the evening dined at Secty John Hay's with the Trustees. President Roosevelt was present" (January 29, 1902). The next day was a morning meeting of the trustees for two hours and an executive committee meeting at lunch and later in the afternoon; between them Walcott scurried to the Survey. The trustees voted that the secretary should receive one hundred dollars per month for his services; little did they or Walcott realize what effort would go into this position.

John Hay lived next to Henry Adams at what is now the site of the Hay-Adams Hotel. They were best friends, but this did not prevent the caustic Adams from commenting on the events: "Our distraction this week has been the meeting of the Carnegie Trustees, twenty-seven contemporaries of mine doddering like me. I could not believe Carnegie so wretched an organizer. Any elderly literary frump would have done better, but I suppose Carnegie gained his object in harnessing respectability to his coach" (Levenson et al. 1988, 333).

Henry Adams notwithstanding, the CIW hit the ground running. At its first meeting, the Executive Committee, or Ex. Com. as Walcott often abbreviated it, agreed to institute a series of advisory committees, commonly one to three persons to prepare position papers on the needs of various fields in sciences and humanities. Billings and Walcott were the driving forces behind establishment of these committees and rapid completion of their reports, but this operation had the support of President Gilman. Walcott and Billings were moving so fast that all but one or two of the advisory groups were proposed and partially staffed by the end of this first Ex. Com. meeting.

February was more or less a blur. The Survey had to be attended to with Congress deep into the session, and the new CIW required another quick trip to New York and several dinner parties to line up the advisory committees. The middle of the month was marked by a meeting of societies in Washington to consider a new building in Washington which might be used for concerts, meet-ings, and so forth; inasmuch as this was not to come from Carnegie money, the WMI still had to be pushed along. To satisfy the curious, Walcott made a pre-sentation to the Geological Society of Washington concerning the Carnegie gift.

On the twentieth, Walcott went to Baltimore to preside at a meeting of the GWMA Trustees, and to see Ira Remsen, the new president of Johns Hopkins University. The next day Walcott wrote, "I rec'd degree of L. L. D. with a num-ber of others" (February 22, 1902). As at Chicago, this honorary degree had extra significance, marking both the twenty-fifth anniversary of the university and installation of a new president. The university prepared a nice citation: "The chief of this survey is a geologist whose administrative duties have not prevented his personal devotion to scientific research in which he maintains acknowledged excellence."[5] A sociologist of science has written of the "Matthew effect"—To them that hath, it shall be given, and to them that hath not, it shall be taken away—explaining that after several honors have been bestowed, others follow automatically (Merton 1968). That may be true in general, but Walcott worked steadily throughout his career to earn medals, honorary memberships, and de-grees that were awarded. On Sunday, Dr. Walcott returned home.

Near month's end, Walcott had a meeting with USGS geologists when ge-ologist-in-charge of geology and paleontology, the office Walcott held under Powell, was reinstituted. Hayes, a great field man and an excellent economic geologist, would run the Geologic Division; Walcott kept control of the rest. After conferring with Gilman, he took a quick another trip to New York. "Took breakfast with Prof. R. S. Woodward 8–9:30 A.M. Talking with Henry F. Osborn 10:30–11:30. Attended breakfast given to Prince Henry of Prussia 12:30 3:00 P.M. Conference with Abram Hewitt 3:30 5:30" (February 26, 1902). Life would be easier if the Ex. Com. of the CIW were in Washington, but nothing could be done to change that. That year the committee met eight times, half of them in New York.

Walcott's plate was still not full enough. He "Attended meeting of organiza-tion of board of directors of Ontario Apartment House Co. 4–5:30 P.M. Was elected president of Co." (March 1, 1902). A few days later he took Emmons and George Otis Smith, a young geologist on the USGS whose wife had money, to see the site. The Ontario is a huge building, surrounded by beautiful grounds, and the McLachlen mansion was torn down to prepare the site (Goode 1988, 59–63). Banker McLachlen financed this structure, as well as the Iowa and Men-dota apartments; he and Walcott made a formidable team.

Charles Doolittle Walcott, Paleontologist

March was even more of a blur than February. A diary entry is: "At survey office most of the day. Conference with Dr Gilman 2–3 P.M. Worked on Carnegie Institution matters after 4 P.M. At home in the evening work plans etc for apt house on Conn. Ave." (March 3, 1902). The apartment house was the Stoneleigh Court; what Helena thought of all the extra activity is not recorded. Sidney and Helen came down with "kine pox," but one advantage of household help was that this did not prevent the Walcotts from attending an evening reception given by the Westinghouses in honor of Earl and Lady Grey.

After a couple of days at the Survey, next came another flying visit to New York City. "Breakfast with Dr. Billings. Meeting of Executive Committee Carnegie Institution at Abram S. Hewitt's 10–1 A.M. 2–4 P.M. Left N -Y at 5. P.M. Home at 11:10 P.M. Lunched at Mr. Hewitt's with Earl Grey & daughter, the Hewitt family, Dr Gilman, C. D. Wright, J. S. Billings, S. Wier Mitchell" (March 11, 1902). Not bad for a farm lad.

By March, advisory committees were nearly all formed and hard at work. Walcott formally announced formation of the CIW in a circular letter to organizations and interested individuals. In April, Gilman sailed to Europe to confer with colleagues and reflect on what course the CIW should take. A great deal has been made of the Ex. Com. running the CIW in Gilman's absence, and of fundamental differences between Chairman Billings and President Gilman (Reingold 1979). All this is true, but during the early meetings of the Ex. Com., Gilman, Walcott, and Billings readily interacted and knew of one another's activities.

Walcott went several times to Capitol Hill, for the USGS appropriation was in limbo and irrigation was uncertain. He took another trip to New York, this time with Helena. On March 25, the Ex. Com. met with Carnegie, and later Carnegie took them to dinner at the Waldorf-Astoria. Walcott had a breakfast meeting with Gilman, Pickering, Hale, and Newcomb; astronomy was to be one major interest of the new institution. That afternoon, he and Helena looked at apartment buildings, a busman's holiday; she seemed to enjoy this as much as he did. After another day in the Big Apple and a few informal discussions, it was back to Washington and mounds of accumulated paper.

Early in April, a break in routine came when Walcott went to Philadelphia to the annual meeting of the American Philosophical Society. The organization had heretofore not occupied much of his time, for in some measure it was honorific rather than professional. In 1897, he had been elected member 2,331 of the oldest learned society in the United States, founded by Benjamin Franklin in

1743. This gathering permitted him to expand his horizons to other fields of science and to the humanities as he wrestled with the issue of how to spend Carnegie's money.

It was back to Washington to the meetings of the National Academy of Sciences. There was enough overlap in the membership of the APS and NAS that by gentlemen's agreement the annual meetings never coincided. The brilliant young astronomer George Ellery Hale was elected to the academy. After four years in office, Walcott resigned as treasurer. He had more than enough to look after.

Near the end of April, Walcott "Worked on estimate for an apartment for Col. John Hayden in the evening" (April 22, 1902). His real estate dealings in Washington would probably make a nice subject for a thesis, without considering any of his other activities. Walcott appeared before a Senate committee and a week later with a tone of exasperation wrote: "A busy week has passed. Congress has not touched survey matters except to agree to Senate Committee amendment in the Senate" (May 3, 1903).

A couple of days later, it was "routine survey and Carnegie Institution work with odd moments given to Cambrian brachiopods" (May 5, 1902); this is noteworthy as being the first diary reference to fossils that year. Three days later, he was out with Secretary of War Root looking over property in northwest Washington. Next he had another quick trip, spending one day looking at apartment buildings in New York City, another at Woods Hole, Massachusetts, to find a summer place, and back to New York, where he talked things over with Chairman of the Board of Trustees Abram Hewitt and met Billings before taking the sleeper back to Washington. Walcott never wasted time.

Still keeping a variety of irons in fire, Walcott met with a committee of the Daughters of the American Revolution (DAR); they had hopes of building some kind of a hall. Just how much of a role Walcott played in the DAR Continental Hall on Virginia Avenue and Seventeenth Street next to their headquarters is not clear, but he was surely involved in the early stages of planning. The next day being Sunday, Walcott was "At church A.M. with Helena & Cha's. After dinner went out with Gen'l David B. Henderson to see ground I have selected as a good site for the Carnegie Institution 3 to 5 P.M. At home in the evening" (May 18, 1902).

By the end of May, Walcott obtained an option on one tract of land, and shortly thereafter on another. It is here that began one of the controversies which marked the early days of the CIW. Walcott believed strongly that the organization should have its own buildings in a campuslike setting. However, no matter how strong his personal conviction, he would not have proceeded in his plans without authorization. Walcott saw Gilman frequently, and he had met with both Chairman Hewitt and Vice-Chairman Billings earlier in May; everyone in authority knew what he was doing.

The future looked rosy, for if the GWMA could not raise funds for a building, certainly Carnegie money was around. The lesson that the Smithsonian's board of regents had crammed down the throat of Secretary Henry was that a building was needed to make an organization important. With a building the Washington Academy or perhaps even the National Academy could assume a more significant role in science policy.

The rest of May was mainly taken up by meetings in a curious mixture of governmental and private business. One evening he worked on plans for the state cooperative program in topographic mapping and plans for the Stoneleigh Court Apartment House. "Called on Set'y Hay 9:30 A.M. with Mr. Jas. G. Hill & Jos E. Fitch. Mr. Hay agreed to arrangements for building his large apt. house" (May 27, 1902). James Hill was the architect for the Mendota and was as important to apartment development in Washington as was the banker McLachlen.

With all of what today would be called "wheeling and dealing," both for Mr. Carnegie and for his own ends, Walcott did not neglect the Geological Survey. One may argue he was able to pursue his extracurricular activities with such vigor because he was heading a small organization. That view is not correct, for by 1900 the USGS contained more than three hundred people, most going in different directions, both geographically and scientifically. Congress loved it all, but especially the topographic mapping program (Rabbitt 1980, 324–26). For fiscal 1903, the USGS appropriation exceeded one million dollars. Walcott noted this milestone in a quaint way: "At Survey. Quiet waiting for Congress to pass appropriations bill.—This gave me time to work on Cambrian brachiopods & and look after odds & ends of administration" (June 2, 1902).

Walcott accomplished another matter of significance with Congress. He obtained permission for a new series to be called *Professional Papers*. The *Annual Report* for 1899 was about eighteen inches thick, that for 1900 was about six inches thick. By setting up a new series for papers too long for bulletins yet too short for monographs, he provided a boon to government authors, to readers, and to the public printer.

Now, a step back is in order. Conservation came to the fore under Theodore Roosevelt and had its beginnings in 1901. "Newell and Pinchot, both of them younger than the new president, had already moved with young men's impetuosity and called on him when he returned to Washington after President McKinley's funeral, even before he had moved into the White House. Newell hoped his first message to Congress would help along his dream of a reclamation service. Pinchot was equally keen that it say the right thing on forestry. Their conference was more than satisfactory; they were authorized to draft what they thought the necessary message say on the twin subjects" (Rabbitt 1980, 320). Impetuous though youth may be, both men were wise enough in government service not to have called on the president without advising their chief. Newell did better with his project than Pinchot, for on March 1 the Senate passed a reclamation bill.

Early in June, Walcott took a quick trip to Pittsburgh to see the Carnegie Institute and to consult with others who had more experience trying to interpret Mr. Carnegie's wishes. Back in Washington, Walcott waited for Congress to act. Friday, June 13, the Newlands Reclamation Act passed the House of Representatives (Anonymous 1919). A decade earlier, a national irrigation congress had booed Powell for his plans to have the government aid the small farmer; this was a vindication of sorts.

Roosevelt wrote Secretary of Interior Hitchcock:

> I regard the irrigation business as one of the great features of my administration and take a keen personal pride in having been instrumental in bringing it about. I want it conducted, so far as in our power to conduct it, on the highest plane not only of purpose but efficiency. I desire it to be kept under the control of the Geological Survey, of which Mr. Walcott is the Director and Mr. Newell the Hydrographer. These men have been tested and tried and we know how well they will do their work. (Morrison 1951, 277)

Walcott recorded: "President Roosevelt informed me that he wished the survey to take chg. of the National Irrigation Surveys" (June 18, 1902).

The previous year Newell had arranged investigations of the Hydrologic Section that would be directly germane to irrigation projects. Newell also came up with the concept of financing reclamation work from the sale of public lands, and he is credited with working harder than anyone else to bring the bill into law. "Walcott's contribution is harder to assess, because, in characteristic Walcott fashion most of it was behind the scenes. It was, however, acknowledged as indispensable by those who were familiar with the many details involved in maneuvering the bill through Congress" (Rabbitt 1980, 327). Walcott wrote a short paper pointing out that concern for irrigation had a long history and that the arid area of the West was huge (Walcott 1902c).

History repeated itself. In 1897, Walcott was directing the Geological Survey, but the Smithsonian Institution badly needed assistance, so he became acting assistant secretary. Shortly thereafter, the forest reserves landed in his lap. In 1902, Walcott was directing the Geological Survey, but the Carnegie Institution of Washington badly needed assistance, so he became secretary. Shortly thereafter, the Reclamation Service landed in his lap. With all these activities that he felt were either his duty to pursue or were placed on him, it is hard to understand how his enthusiasm for fossils remained undaunted.

Walcott took a week off and went to Woods Hole with the family. He set up an office in the old Fish Commission building, was sick for a day, took a sentimental trip to Cooperstown, New York, and was back in Washington before the end of the month. The new fiscal year was noted in that Walcott mentioned in his diary his twenty-third year with the USGS and his eighth as director. Now that the Reclamation Service was tacked on, this was a good opportunity to reorganize the Survey. The Hydrologic Section became the Hydrologic Branch and received the assignment of studying the forest reserves. Some remarks circulated about the USGS being the government's wood and water department.

Newell and Walcott had their heads together making plans. Walcott called on the president for an hour, and Roosevelt talked of nothing but national irrigation. The director spent July 4 "Quietly working on Cambrian brachiopods all day." That qualifies as a busman's holiday, but afterward it was back to administration: "Busy all day at the survey with Mr. F. H. Newell—Talked over plans for National Irrigation with Sect'y Hitchcock" (July 5, 1901). In two days the plans were approved.

With formal approval in hand, Newell started putting the Reclamation Service together, and Walcott headed north to Woods Hole. He stopped in New York to discuss Carnegie activities with Hewitt and inquired about an exhibit by United States Steel at the coming St. Louis Exposition. When he got to Massachusetts, Walcott actually stayed in one place for a month. The Annual Report of the USGS had to be completed and a report prepared for the Carnegie Board of Trustees, as well as beginning the first CIW *Year Book*. There was enough accumulated paper to keep him busy for two weeks, when he started to generate fresh paper.

"At work in my office A.M. Profs. T. C. Chamberlin & C. R. Van Hise came at 11:20 A.M. Also Prof. R. S. Woodward. We worked over paper on propositions for research in geology & geophysics" (July 20, 1902). The next day after a morning fishing trip, Carl Barus, who had run a laboratory for the Geological Survey, and Prof. Michelson, who had destroyed the concept of aether affecting light and was to win a Nobel Prize, arrived "completing committee of C. I. on geophysics. Worked on subject 4–6 — 7:30 8:30 P.M. Voted to favor establishment of geophysical laboratory in Washington" (July 22, 1902). If Woodward has not been properly introduced, he was the Dean of Pure Science at Columbia University. Long before that he had been an astronomer locating positions in the trackless West for Hayden, and later working for the Coast Survey and, still later, the Geological Survey; Walcott knew him well.

The report (Carnegie Institution of Washington, 1903) was carefully constructed of twenty-six printed pages, plus one appendix on specifics of a research program, plus another with strong support from European scientists— but it was only the first step in a long, hard campaign to obtain a laboratory (Yoder 1994). In his anticipatory style, during May, Walcott wrote various authorities to garner letters of support. Just in case the committee decided they wanted a laboratory for geophysics, he wanted to be prepared. Walcott did not railroad through a proposal, but he laid groundwork carefully and chose his committee with equal care. Much advanced planning is needed for proper spontaneity.

Indeed, at the end of January, F. D. Adams had written a long formal letter to the Honorable Charles D. Walcott, secretary of the Carnegie Institution— before news of Walcott's election would have reached him through normal channels—detailing his work on deforming marble.[6] This nine-page letter was not thrown together in an instant. Adams got a grant and he later he also got an invitation from Walcott to revoke his Canadian citizenship and join the USGS. Adams declined that offer.

A phrase Walcott used occasionally was to refer to someone as "a promising young man." Pinchot was one such, and Adams was another. In 1900, the Geological Survey had hired Arthur L. Day, a very promising young man. Day was interested in igneous rocks, and to investigate them one needed a laboratory specially equipped for investigations in high temperature and high pressure, but none existed in North America. One of the aims of the CIW was to support the efforts of the "exceptional man"; this was Carnegie's phrase. Since Walcott already had such a man in hand and since Walcott knew real estate and building, putting this exceptional man in his own exceptional laboratory was logical. Unfortunately, logic does not always prevail, and even when it does, often it is not without a struggle.

The crusty historian Henry Adams reported on geology eight months before Carnegie appeared on the scene:

> If you are bored by politics I will give you some science. Last Friday I had a geological dinner. Frank Emmons brought his colleague Van Hise, and his chief, Walcott, and a young Canadian named Adams, to dine with me. But I am old, you may put up a margin on that! When I was young, geology began with fossils and shells and the signs of life. Nowadays it ends there. Not one of these four men, whose names are all of the highest authority all over the world, will look twice at a fossil except to throw out the rock they find him in. All they touch is granite and things that lie at the bottom. There they have about five times as much rock as above it, and all they study is to know what made it. The youth from Canada has been squeezing it like butter. (Arvin 1951, 224)

Young Adams followed the administrative footsteps of Sir William Dawson and become principal of McGill University; for a time the Geophysical Laboratory had a branch at McGill under his direction. Henry Adams piled on the prose a little bit, for Walcott never threw away a good fossil. Nevertheless, the CIW committees on geology and on paleontology, in both of which Walcott naturally played a role, reported that their scientific needs were met by the current administrative organizations.

That paleontologist Walcott would throw himself so strongly into support of investigations of igneous rocks is remarkable. It marked a major shift in geology from mainly a field science to increasingly a laboratory science. After the first two decades of the CIW, astronomy and the Geophysical Laboratory were the big winners of funds; the money was well spent.

Lest one get too carried away with ecumenism, Walcott received a small slice of the first Carnegie pie. Cambrian fossils were reported from China and Walcott wanted to know more. "The first grant for execution of Mr. Walcott's purpose was made in the autumn of 1902, and Dr. Arthur C. Spencer of the U. S. Geological Survey was charged with preparation of plans, in the expectation that he would carry them out. Later, when Mr. Spencer was obliged to forego the opportunity, I volunteered for the service and the expedition was intrusted to me" (Willis 1907, xi). "Me" was Bailey Willis, assistant to the director. "Meeting me one morning in the spring of 1904, in the hall of the United States Geological Survey in Washington, the Director, Charles D. Walcott, inquired casually: 'Would you like to go to China?'" (Willis 1949, 3). The expedition grant was for twelve thousand dollars, and a year later an equal amount was allocated.

In a revisionist context, this might look like pure pork barrelism. Except in scientific knowledge gained, Walcott did not benefit from this money. Billings's pride and joy at the army medical library was the *Index Medicus*. He got a large slice of the Carnegie pie, for printing was supported by the CIW for nearly forty years. Though this bibliography was important, it does not qualify as research. Any mystery that the final grant given by CIW in 1902 was for the study of venoms disappears when one knows it was a subject of interest to Mitchell; his desires were more modest and satisfied by a small sum to a colleague.

After the assembled scientists left, back at Woods Hole there was plenty for Walcott to do with the committee report, but he stole time for fishing. August 5, he was unhappy at leaving Helena and the children, but delighted to be away from the damp climate which irritated his sciatica. After several days in Washington, he headed for Chicago. Hale presented the report of the CIW astronomy committee and took him to Yerkes Observatory. He paused to see brother Ellis, and then it was on to business for the Reclamation Service.

Walcott met Newell in Helena, Montana, to compare notes. Next day, he and Arthur Powell Davis, moved over from the Survey to be number three man in the service, spoke eloquently to the local businessmen. They moved to Billings and thence to Wyoming, looking at reservoir sites and beating the drum for the latest federal agency. Walcott paused in Ogden and went to Nevada. Metaphorically with one hand he waved to local ranchers and farmers, and with the other he designated reservoir sites. Walcott covered a fair part of the state in two weeks and moved to southern California.

In another two weeks, Walcott covered part of the coast, saw Lick Observatory, met with USGS employees, checked with Professor Branner at Stanford, and headed for home; the whole way east he read letters sent to the Carnegie Institution and framed replies. Walcott was back in Washington on September 24, 1902, the day after Major Powell died. "The body of Major Powell arrived in Washington early in the morning of September 26th. It was a miserable night with a cutting cold drizzle; nevertheless Jack Hillers, Charles Walcott, Dr. David T. Day and Mrs. Alexander Bentley—a friend of Mrs. Powell's—had waited for hours at the Sixth Street depot" (Darrah 1951, 396). "At C.I. office 9–11. Survey

11–12:30—Memorial service and funeral of Major J. W. Powell 2 to 6–P.M. Internment at Arlington. A strange day until 4 P.M." (September 26, 1902).

As shown earlier, Walcott was a man of strong loyalties. When the legislature of New York state tried to make Hall's last years a misery, Walcott had sprung to his defense. When a group arranged for Clarence King's half-brother to paint his portrait, partly as a way of helping out the family, Walcott contributed fifty dollars. Shortly, he would be one of three who took it upon themselves to raise money for a monument to Powell in Arlington National Cemetery, and later another at the Grand Canyon.

One cannot dwell on the past, but must keep moving forward, and Walcott flattered Carnegie a little:

> When in Wyoming, in August, I stopped at the town of Sheridan. Mr. Edward Gillette . . . asked me if it were possible to interest you in giving them money for a public library. I told him that if he would put the application in shape, I would transmit. . . . I was very much pleased with the Carnegie Library at Cheyenne. It stands where, twenty-three years ago, I rode across a sage brush plain. Now the trees and homes surround it.[7]

Walcott left for New York City and "Called on Dr N. M. Butler 9–10 P.M. and talked over W. M.I. matters" (October 2, 1901). Even with no prospect of money, there was still a hope that this group could play a role in higher education. The next day was an "Executive meeting of C. I. W. 10–12 2–4. Gilman, Mitchell, Hewitt, Billings" (October 2, 1902). The meeting continued for another day, and it took Walcott three days to clear up the resulting paper work.

The Walcotts took a quiet trip to Glencoe, New York, where they had spent a lovely summer, and saw relatives in Rochester. Then it was back to the grind until near the end of the month. For a change, the Ex. Com. met in Washington. Hewitt was too weak to travel, but Gilman and Walcott were joined by Billings, White, and Mitchell; Root tore himself away from his cabinet duties to attend. The meeting went on until the following day, but by then they had completed the general outline of a plan to recommend to the board.

October faded into November, and the accumulated papers of the CIW were readied for the printer. After the fall meeting of the National Academy of Sciences in Baltimore, there was plenty of administrative detail to occupy time until the CIW Board of Trustees met. Walcott had his plans firmly laid for the purchase of land and building of an administration building and later laboratories. He had the support of all but one member of the Ex. Com., though he did not have the support of committee chairman Billings (Yochelson and Yoder 1994).

President Hewitt was too ill to attend, let alone preside; Vice-President Billings chaired the meeting. The trustees refused to buy the land, fearing to commit too much of the endowment—at least that is the public reason. Henry Adams had been correct in his assessment of the board as too old; one trustee had already died. Why Billings would let Walcott proceed to obtain an option on land and then be so adamant in his opposition at the meeting defies understanding. Root was in favor of the purchase of land, and was present at the morning meeting, but could not attend in the afternoon. Gilman, who had a note from Root, kept silent about it until the last minute, when it was too late. That afternoon Hay was absent, as was McVeagh, who might have opposed Billings just on general principal.

In addition to the twenty-one active trustees, of whom sixteen attended in the morning, four of the five ex officio members were present. The president of the National Academy was Alexander Agassiz (Yochelson and Yoder 1994), who had bedeviled Powell that science should not be done by the federal government; it should just give money to scientists. He bedeviled Walcott with the same general argument that CIW money should go to established scientists at established laboratories.

Had the trustees followed the advice of their secretary, a shrewd local real estate tycoon, the CIW would have had more than one hundred acres of prime land, worth a fortune. Considering the number of bankers on the board of trustees, it is even stranger that a good real estate deal was turned down. There was a sense that Carnegie did not want to get involved in land and buildings, and while he had no vote, the board was not about to go against his perceived desires. It was certainly a serious blow to Walcott, yet for years thereafter he and Billings continued to work together on the Ex. Com. Walcott's plans failed, yet all he wrote was: "The Institution starts out in a conservative manner" (November 25, 1902).

Other actions of the board brought complaint, as Butler wrote to Walcott: "I regret to see it announced in the morning papers that the details of the appropriations made by the Carnegie Institute Trustees are to be withheld, on the grounds that to divulge them might promote jealousies between individuals and universities."[8] Walcott gave an ample reply.

To my notion the "secrecy business" is a mistake. It has been my policy in the administration of the Geological Survey to cooperate with individuals and institutions throughout the country, and to indicate such cooperation in the Plan of Operations filed with the Secretary of Interior. This report is always open to newspaper men, and is extensively used by them, especially in the localities where work is to be done. The results of the cooperation are also published in the Annual Report. At times hard feelings have been engendered, but the mischief done is not a fraction of what it would be if people were left in the dark as to what was being done.[9]

If Walcott suffered any hurt pride from the actions of the trustees, he kept it well concealed in a talk to the Philosophical Society:

Dr. C. D. Walcott presented a paper on the development of the Carnegie Institution. He pointed out how its location in Washington is a case of natural development, tracing the growth of scientific organization in the city from the early Philosophical Society, through the separate societies, the Joint Committee, and Academy and the Memorial Association until plans for research were formulated clearly enough to attract Mr. Carnegie's attention.

He said sixteen advisory committees, including forty-six members, had been appointed, whose confidentially printed reports, filling over 200 pages, had been presented to the trustees at the recent meeting. Some general principles, both of exclusion and inclusion have been adopted, special emphasis being laid on the man responsible for any research. (Hayford and Wead 1902, 2)

Though organizing the committees, pushing them to meet and write, and assembling reports was a difficult job in the few months allotted to it, this was a beginning, not the end. The CIW was increasingly eating into his time. "At C.I. A.M. & P.M. & Survey during middle of day. Meeting of G. W. M. A.—3 to 5 P.M." (December 10, 1902). Once it was evident that Carnegie's creation was for research rather than education, Walcott might have concentrated on it and abandoned all else, yet he continued to keep the WMI and the GWMA in mind. Their results were limited, but it was not for his lack of trying.

In mid-December Walcott was back in New York. On Sunday, he "Called on Mr. Abram S. Hewitt 11–12 A.M. R. S. Woodward 1–4 P.M. Took supper with Prof. Henry F. Osborn" (December 14, 1902). Now that the trustees had spoken, or at least mumbled and grumbled, the question was what to do next. Carnegie was enamored with the concept of the "exceptional man," yet in all fields of science, team research and great laboratories were looming as the future pattern. Even the humanities were considering a few larger projects rather than individual investigations.

Walcott "Took breakfast with Dr J. S. Billings—At 11:30 called on Andrew Carnegie & and had a very interesting visit with him. Stopped for an hour at the Metropolitan Museum of Art & then went to Abram S. Hewitt's to get ready for meeting of Ex - Com. C. I. tomorrow. Took a cup of tea with the family. Theater in the evening" (December 15, 1902). The next day started with "Breakfast with Dr Gilman 8:15 A.M. Meeting of Ex- Committee Carnegie Institution at Mr. Hewitt's 10–2:50 P.M. Messrs Hewitt, Gilman, Billings, Mitchell & CDW" (December 16, 1902). As soon as the meeting ended, Walcott took the next train back to Helena, waiting at the family hearth.

Thus, Abram Hewitt was still actively participating in CIW affairs. For the game of "what if," had Hewitt presided at the November board meeting, it is unlikely Billings would have gone directly counter to his wishes. The land purchase might have passed and the entire course of the CIW would have changed with a research campus in Washington. However, the milk was spilt and that was the end of that. Walcott had more immediate concerns, running back and forth to ensure that Billings and Gilman were not at total cross purposes all the time.

Even in the week before Christmas, CIW correspondence nearly overwhelmed Walcott. After Christmas, annual meetings of the AAAS, the GSA, and the American Society of Naturalists brought swarms to the city, including colleagues and old friends who wanted to know how Carnegie's money was going to be handed out. "1902 closes with all well in our little family & home life. The most notable event in my personal life is the organization of the Carnegie Institution of Washington. As its secretary I have much to do with its development" (December 31, 1902). Walcott could be the master of the understatement.

"At C-I- office 9–10:30—3–5 pm attending to correspondence, etc. Had a talk with Dr. Gilman about C. I. and his relations to it" (January 5, 1903). The odds are that Walcott told Gilman he should be doing more to run the organization than simply preside at the Ex. Com. meetings. Two days later Carnegie was in town for the opening of the Carnegie Free Library and Walcott had a chance for a few words with him. Anyone who saw the tall Walcott and the diminutive Carnegie side by side would have compared them to the old comic strip characters of Mutt and Jeff.

Carnegie left and it was back to the routine of visiting the CIW office early to dictate letters and late to sign them, with USGS affairs handled between. The Survey was not neglected, for that January a handbook of rules, regulations, and customs was prepared and authorized for distribution by the director. On top of all this were the running the Iowa and Ontario Apartment House companies, and another term as president of the Washington Academy of Sciences.

Charles Doolittle Walcott, Paleontologist

If there was ever to be a laboratory for study of physics of the earth, it was time for serious politicking, so another trip to New York ensued. "With Prof. Van Hise called on Andrew Carnegie 10 A.M. to 1 P.M. & and talked C- I- and geophysical work. At 2:20 P.M. we called on Dr J. S. Billings & at 6 P.M. Dr S. Wier Mitchell in Philadelphia—also Prof. G. R. Barker. Returned home" (January 16, 1903). For a baseball metaphor, this was a home run in touching all the bases, but in achievement, they struck out.

An undated pencil comment by Carnegie might be directly related to this trip. "What I need to know is What means are employed for Geo Physics— ? That do not exist—What does the G. Py do that is not done now—What is he after? What does he propose to arrive at that is useful and adds to our knowledge. Why new chemical laboratories are needed. For what does it require 150 000 $ per year. Its all so nebulous. In the air— No one has given it substance."[10] This was not auspicious for the project; it is curious that other major projects were never so strongly objected to by Carnegie.

Sadly, five days later Walcott returned to New York to attend Abram Hewitt's funeral. Regardless of any help Hewitt might have given to the concept of a geological laboratory, Walcott admired him greatly. Hewitt's name is perpetuated in the Cooper-Hewitt Museum of Design, a fragment of the Smithsonian empire now housed in Carnegie's New York mansion. Walcott passed a few words of business with Carnegie, for the course of CIW was affected by Hewitt's death. Three days later, most of the Ex. Com. assembled in Washington—Gilman, Mitchell, Billings, Wright, and Walcott. Secretary of State John Hay had become a member of the committee, replacing Hewitt, but like Secretary of War Root he was almost never present. Van Hise was given twenty-five hundred dollars to travel and to make plans for a geophysical laboratory; this was one answer to Carnegie's complaint about lack of specifics.

January brought another honor, not noted in his diary, when he was elected an honorary member of the California Academy of Sciences. On the thirtieth, the Walcotts hosted a dinner honoring Dr. and Mrs. Gilman. Whether it was the food, the company, the strain of too much work, or the weather, Walcott fell ill for three days. He struggled from a sick bed to Capitol Hill, where he "Looked a little after Survey appropriations" (February 3, 1903). In two days he was busy as ever.

Mid-February the Washington Academy of Sciences held a memorial meeting for Major Powell, Walcott presiding. This event marked the end of an era in American geology; Newberry, Dana, Hall, King, and now Powell were gone.

For the last decade of his life, the crippled reformer of environmental matters had become as anachronistic as the concept of the American frontier. Later that month, Walcott took Helena to a meeting of the Geological Society of Washington, for the exciting topic of classification of ore deposits. The speakers elicited numerous comments from the audience, and Walcott enjoyed the program. Geologists' wives who are not themselves geologists endure a lot.

After Walcott appeared before a Senate committee, he went back to moving papers and making summer plans. The routine was broken only by another attack of the grippe, but by March 7, 1903, he left plans for five major irrigation projects with Secretary Hitchcock and picked them up approved a few hours later. Bureaucracy need not be slow when those in high position agree on the aims and objectives.

A few months later Roosevelt commented:

> My aim in the irrigation policy is to benefit the small homemaker, and the opposition we have has been nine-tenths from those who want to get great tracts of land, either to be leased or to be used for speculative purposes. Of course Walcott has been fiercely attacked everywhere. For instance, he has been attacked by the Utah Republicans because he recommended work to be done in Nevada, a Democratic State. He has been attacked by many of the Senators, both Republican and Democratic, in the Rocky Mountain region because he recommended work to be done in Arizona which has no representation or influence in Congress, etc. etc. (Morrison 1951, 510)

If any of these attacks troubled Walcott, they were not significant enough for him to write in his diary.

In Walcott's diary is: "Meeting of Board of Philapine [sic] Survey 9– 10:45 A.M. Meeting of Committee on Scientific Work Government in Washn. 11–12:45. Busy with Survey matters P.M." (March 19, 1903). Roosevelt asked the National Academy whether exploration for natural resources should be undertaken in the Philippine Islands, and they responded positively. Thereupon he appointed a board of seven, headed by Walcott. "The board held five meetings in March, May and June 1903, appointed a committee on plans and organization, prepared estimates of expenditures, drafted a bill for the consideration of Congress, drew up various memoranda, and transacted other business" (True 1913, 327). Two years later, Roosevelt sent the draft to Congress, where it died.

Knowing a good man when he had one, Roosevelt set up another committee, and again appointed Walcott chairman (Morrison 1951, 443). After all, he presumably had the USGS, the Reclamation Service, and the Forest Reserves under control; if Walcott chose to be involved in nongovernmental efforts for the CIW, and other societies and organizations, that should not matter when more government duties were required. The only task this particular committee had to do for the president was examine the entire federal government, pick out the parts vaguely concerned with science, and report on how to rearrange them in better order!

Even without these committees, because of the weight of the Reclamation Service and the CIW, Walcott the scientist was slowly foundering. His two publications of the year, apart from official reports, were each less than two pages. One contained his remarks at the Powell Memorial meeting and the other was a result of USGS discussions of nomenclature. Chamberlin wrote: "I am greatly obliged to you for a copy of the rules of nomenclature and classification for the geological atlas of the United States, and especially for your statement relative to a 'New Term for the Upper Cambrian Series,' which we will take pleasure in publishing in the Journal of Geology."[11] After publication, few weeks later, Late Cambrian time in the United States became known as Saratogian rather than Potsdamic.

In the midst of all this, Walcott was trying to convince Carnegie to visit Washington and examine a building site. Carnegie declined in a humorous manner writing about temporary buildings at the base of a waterfall to generate power. Walcott was not amused and a month later from camp wrote a fairly stern letter to one of the richest men in the world (Yochelson and Yoder 1994). Apparently there was no reply from Carnegie.

After a busy day at the office, seemingly without committee meetings for a change, on the evening of March 20, Reclamation Service Chief Walcott, accompanied by Mrs. Walcott, Charlie, and Sidney, boarded a westbound train, and on the twenty-fifth ended their journey in Phoenix; the world did not always have jet airplanes. Walcott commented that the boys were good travelers; certainly this was far better than school. The boys went to a cowboy camp while Mrs. Walcott settled at the Maxwell ranch just outside the small town of Phoenix. The concern was water for irrigation from the Salt River, and the Salt River Valley Water Users Association (SRVWUA) was being organized. Irrigation has many facets besides engineering, so the first item for Walcott was to speak to the SRVWUA and examine their proposed rules. Only then did he travel the region to look at dams built and dam sites proposed, with canals flowing and canals proposed.

The Salt River Valley was in the grip of a drought, and the Reclamation Service was welcomed with open arms; some of the Indians were not happy, but they were in a minority. The Reclamation Service was under Secretary of Interior Hitchcock, but Walcott also wrote to Secretary of Agriculture Wilson. Just to show how attuned Walcott was politically, he was joined by USGS photographer Cartkoff to make certain he could show the powers that be in Washington, both legislative and executive, what was being done.

The two headed east toward the San Carlos reservation and to Globe, Arizona, and then north to the Tonto Basin; after a long tortuous route, the waters of Tonto Creek eventually drain into the Colorado, far to the north. They did not find any likely dam sites.

The pair returned to Globe and were joined by the hard-working Arthur Powell Davis. All went to Benson and down the San Pedro River Valley to Bisbee, but still no good reservoirs sites were found. At Bisbee, Walcott stole half a day when he and Cartkoff collected a few Cambrian fossils. They traveled north to Tucson, where Walcott put on his CIW hat and looked over the desert laboratory and the exotic vegetation. Marcus Baker was holding down the CIW fort and Walcott wrote him. "A spring climate at Phoenix and three weeks strenuous effort to get irrigation matters straightened out, about used me up.—I shall remain here [in the West] until about 5th, and then return direct to Washington. I am sleeping under the pines, at an elevation of seven thousand feet. The air is cold and bracing."[12]

Walcott concluded site examinations, returned to Phoenix, and on the eighteenth again met with the SRVWUA. This project was extremely tricky politically, for there was no public land involved; rather, it was to improve existing private irrigation facilities (Worster 1985, 172). Walcott was able to keep all vested interests happy. The Maxwells were kind, but Walcott, as he indicated by letter and in his diary, was glad to leave; they gathered the boys, with difficulty, and headed for Los Angeles. In Pasadena, Walcott conducted CIW business with astronomer Hale, and they all went off to Catalina Island for an overnight stay.

Back on the train east they went to Williams, Arizona, and north to the Grand Canyon. As with his 1901 trip with Gilbert, this to was the south rim; the canyon depths of his youth, approached from the Utah side, were years behind him. The family went to Grand View, and after a Sunday stroll, the magic of the West caught his pen: "The Canyon is in its gala dress as the afternoon sun went down" (April 27, 1903).

Charles Doolittle Walcott, Paleontologist

The four spent a couple of days collecting fossils along the rim until photographer Cartkoff arrived. They all packed down the Grandview Trail to the Cambrian Tonto Sandstone. Geologists now know this at the Tapeats Sandstone, and hikers know it as the Esplanade, the wide area just above the harder rocks of the inner gorge. There were sections to measure, photographs to take, and fossils to collect. Trilobites were not abundant, but some of their tracks and resting places were also found.

Coming out on a Sunday, as long as they were climbing up, Walcott measured the section from the base of the great cliff maker, the Redwall Limestone, to the rim at Grandview Point. This rock thickness seems never to have been published; it was just an extra bit of information for him to store away. While the family packed, Walcott spent the next day with Francois Matthes, an extraordinary topographer whose maps of the Grand Canyon and of Yosemite are the acme of that profession. Matthes had some hair-raising tales to tell of crossing the river, of cold and snow, and of a mule falling, to which Walcott could certainly relate. This was the end of the West for a while; the family got on a train and a long four days later were home.

"In the spring of 1903 six weeks were given to an examination of the proposed irrigation developments in Arizona, especially with reference to the construction of the Tonto dam on Salt River and the utilization of storage waters in the vicinity of Phoenix" (Walcott 1903, 18). The official report has not one word of fieldwork in the Grand Canyon. That was pure "bootleg research." He wrote a colleague, "I have been accumulating tracks, trails, etc from the Cambrian for many years."[13]

The day after the western travelers returned, the reunited family went to Church, and following that, Sunday or no, Newell came to see Walcott because the Reclamation Service had many questions to be answered. Walcott had one day for the USGS, and then the CIW Ex. Com. intruded. The days involved constant running back and forth between USGS and CIW. Near the end of the month, Walcott took a trip to New York City to check in with Billings and to consult with Messers. Schwab and Galey of United States Steel about the coming St. Louis Exposition. Walcott remarked that he spent Decoration Day peacefully in his laboratory for six hours.

June started quietly with a bicycle ride, but thereafter the Committee on the Organization of Government Scientific Work moved to the fore:

Charles D. Walcott, the exceptionally able and effective Director of the United States Geological Survey, was made Chairman. The members were Brigadier General William Crozier, in charge of Ordnance and inventor of

the disappearing guns in our seacoast fortifications; Admiral Francis T.
Bowles, Chief of Construction of the United States Navy; James Randolph
Garfield, head of the Bureau of Corporations, and afterwards Secretary of
the Interior in T. R.'s cabinet; and Gifford Pinchot, who was made Secretary.
(Pinchot 1947, 241)

This was an oddly assorted committee to review scientific effort, quite effective in its operation. One organizational gathering had been held before Walcott
left for the Southwest, and now they got down to business. Most meetings were
at night in the library of the Pinchot residence; in his modest fashion, Pinchot
dubbed it the "Hall of Science." That summer the committee met thirty times
and reviewed the work of twenty-five government bureaus, scattered through
the Smithsonian, the Interstate Commerce Commission, and six Executive
Branch departments.

The committee found little duplication of effort but did find a "lack of effi-
ciency and of co-ordination" (Pinchot 1947, 241). Mostly the committee recommended a transfer of all activities having to do with land to the Department
of Agriculture. Considering Walcott's admiration for the use of research assistants in that department and Pinchot's drive to run the forest reserves, this recommendation is not surprising. It would have gone far toward making the
Department of Agriculture into a Department of Science, but most of the sug-
gestions were never acted on by Congress.

During June there were two breaks in the killing routine, one sad, one glad.
R. U. Goode died, a topographer so excellent that it was expected that he would
become chief of the branch. "The Geological Survey looses [sic] a valuable
member & I loose [sic] a friend" (June 11, 1903). Six days later, Walcott "Left
Wash.n 7A.M. at Philadelphia rec'd degree of L. L. D. from University of Pennsylvania" (June 17, 1903).

The last week in June, Walcott, with Agnes the cook, Charlie, and Sidney
in tow, left for Seneca Lake in upstate New York. Helena had already settled in
a summer place with Helen, little Stuart, and nurse Mary Hardy. Walcott fished,
fossicked about, fossilized with his boys, and generally did nothing for almost
two weeks, or at least nothing noteworthy he cared to record in his diary, quite
out of character. Perhaps he mulled over efforts of the presidential committee,
for on his return, the committee had six meetings in seven days. The report
is a scant fifteen pages, double-spaced—half lists recommendations for trans-
fers of divisions, and bureaus, and most of the remainder lists which organizations were examined. The philosophy is pure Walcottian in both prose and
approach:

Charles Doolittle Walcott, Paleontologist

The general principle which should govern the coordination and classification of work within the scope of this inquiry has received the Committe's [sic] careful attention. Its conclusions are based upon the theory, which appears to be sustained by the facts, that Government scientific work should be organized upon such a basis that the administrative unit should comprise all the elements necessary for the solution of a distinct scientific problem, or a group of closely related scientific problems, the investigation of which is for the benefit of the people in general. For example—whatever sciences and arts may be required for the investigation of the diseases of cattle should be employed in the various special lines which modern science has assumed under the direction of the Chief of the Bureau of Animal Husbandry. This theory presumes, on the other hand, that the individual sciences and arts should not be segregated in the separate bureaus and offices, unless there exists such a large item or group of items in which a single branch of science or art predominates as to render such separation a matter of distinct economy. The Committee is also of the opinion that research in pure science on broad and general grounds is more properly the scope of private institutions, and that in general the work of scientific research on the part of the Government should be limited nearly to utilitarian purposes evidently for the general welfare.[14]

Historians of science have tended to jump on the remark about lack of coordination in government science and applaud the comment about private investigations. Walcott was practical, but he also had the good sense not to follow his own statements too closely and encouraged some USGS work that had long-range goals. Quite incidentally, the Bureau of Animal Husbandry is a curious example for a geologist to pick, unless his old assistant Curtice had told him about the workings of the Department of Agriculture.

On July 22, Walcott went to Oyster Bay, New York, to present the recommendations to Roosevelt. The report was not published (Dupree 1957, 297), and whether it was an exercise in futility, so very common in Washington, or had some positive results is a issue for others to ponder. Having fulfilled his assignment, Walcott immediately returned to Washington and the next morning was on his way west. The day Walcott was at Oyster Bay, Willis left for China, Carnegie money in hand.

At Billings, Montana, Walcott rented a team and two days was in a camp on the Shoshone River, east of Cody, Wyoming. Walcott did the unconventional and went fishing all day in the middle of the week. Fishing was so good he gave two more days to this task, in the rain. He might also observed stream flow, a consideration in whether a dam and reservoir should be emplaced.

He then rushed east to look at a mining district, more potential than real, and on to Greybull and up Greybull Canyon. There was a Reclamation Service party, and the key word may be party. Newell and Pinchot were present, along with both Wyoming senators, the representative, other dignitaries, and three camp hands. They headed west and crossed the Continental Divide to a tributary of the Wind River. They packed over the Wind River Mountains and came to Jackson. By August 16, Walcott was in Idaho Falls, Idaho, where a dam was under construction. One result of this trip was a magnificent photographic album for presentation to a selected few; another was increasing appropriations for the Reclamation Service.

Walcott took a train south to Salt Lake City. Marcus Baker wrote that "The only thing in Washington at present is about Langley's air ship. The secrecy maintained on the houseboat down the river gives 'The Star' a chance to devote columns to it every day."[15] He also mentioned a new son. After congratulating him, Walcott scribbled, "I am just in from two weeks trip in the mountains. Leave from Park City in the morning & thence to the Unitas. Left Newell yesterday up in Idaho. All well."[16]

A few miles southeast of Salt Lake City in the Wasatch Range, Walcott conferred with a USGS geologist mapping the Park City mining district, and "At 11 A.M. left with camp outfit, Mr. Weeks, Arthur Brown, Dan Orr teamster. Camped out 5 mi above Oakley on Western River" (August 18, 1903). Bibliographer, stenographer, and field man Weeks came west once more, bringing with him the finest camp cook. Judging by present day maps, they must have made close to 20 miles with the outfit, remarkable considering the late start. They traveled along the Weber River into the Uinta Mountains for four days. The structure was a tilted mass of Algonkian sandstone surmounted by Algonkian shale. Cambrian may have been present above the shale, but Walcott was uncertain enough to put a question mark in his notes. Above was a tremendous thickness of Carboniferous, interesting in itself but distracting to one concerned about Cambrian and older rocks. The party retraced the route and camped in Salt Lake City.

On August 27, when it was still hot enough to readily fry eggs on the sidewalk, they headed west and the first day were north of Tooele. Next the geologists went to Stockton bar, not a saloon but a Pleistocene lake deposit made famous by Gilbert. They crossed the Stansbury Range; thrust faults complicate these rocks into what some geologists call "eggbeater structure." The group had a dry camp at Joy, Utah, crossed Whirlwind Valley, and the end of the month were at the northern end of the House Range. These mountains are north of Sevier Lake and south of the Fish Springs Range, convenient to absolutely nowhere.

Gilbert had hastily marched through the House Range with Lt. Wheeler's Survey in 1872, but the mountains were undisturbed by geologists until a second Gilbert traverse in 1901, when topographer W. J. Johnson mapped the range. The House Range is composed of very gently dipping layers of alternating Cambrian limestone and shale. This is "sheepherder structure," rocks so obviously laid out that one of that profession can understand them. A granite intrusion in one area adds a bit of spice. It is classic territory with magnificent exposures (Rees and Robison 1989).

Walcott spent almost two weeks measuring sections and collecting from a dozen fossil localities (Walcott 1908). Weeks left for supplies and water, while Orr accompanied Walcott to the western side of the range. In Dome Canyon, Walcott found some Lower Cambrian, but otherwise all rocks were Middle and Upper Cambrian. According to one story, Orr brought in a magnificent trilobite, stating he thought about where it should be and went there; the trilobite *Orria* is in the literature. The Orr Formation was named after Orr Ridge and the Weeks Formation after Weeks Canyon (Walcott 1908). Formations are named after geographic places and these places happened to be named after people. The presence of Arthur Brown in the House Range is unrecorded.

They moved to Osceola, Nevada, where the rocks of the Snake Range were folded and broken by faults. They came back via the Confusion Range, which had a spring to fill the water barrels, and were able to get in another three days of fieldwork. The southern part of the range had many outcrops, but relatively few fossils compared to the quantities gathered to the north. The autumnal equinox saw them at Deseret, Utah. The next day "The wagons went north in chg of Dan Orr and Arthur Brown—Regret to leave camp life as there is much to be done in the Cambrian & I like the life" (September 22, 1903).

Walcott got a train to Ogden, and then to Butte, Montana. Sciatica was troubling him, but he put a few hours in on Cambrian rocks near town before heading east. In Madison, he saw Van Hise about CIW and USGS plans and visited Helena's uncle. Then on to Chicago, and, ultimately: "Am very happy to reach home" (October 4, 1903). This was not to be an extended homecoming, for three days later Helena had to leave for Madison and her sick uncle.

Walcott and the boys invited Gilman for lunch. While he returning from the wilds of Utah, Marcus Baker wrote:

The present plan is to have a meeting of the Executive Committee beginning October 12. The Dr. [Gilman] has indicated to me his intention in spending very much more time here this winter in looking after the affairs of the Institution. He has been house hunting. Whether he has actually one as yet I do not know. I do hope that you will not be overwhelmed with C. I. business this winter as you were last.[17]

It was a hope in vain.

In accepting Carnegie's offer to assist Gilman, Walcott got a great deal more work than he bargained for. The President commuted from Baltimore on an occasional schedule and the Chairman of the Executive Committee was in New York. Walcott conducted all daily matters and answered the voluminous mail.

One Friday afternoon Walcott took Charles and Sidney to a clubhouse south of Mount Vernon for the night to fish in the Potomac. What is surprising is that Arthur Brown came along. Washington, D.C., was a city of the Deep South, with segregation in full flower, but this did not bother Walcott. Another meeting of the GWMA ensued, and that was not a pleasurable change in routine, for the association simply could not move forward. Finally, after four weeks, Helena returned; Walcott was so happy, he took the train to Martinsburg, West Virginia, and greeted her.

Meanwhile, the geophysical laboratory was still in limbo. The past summer, Van Hise had called on Carnegie at Skibo Castle. That November Walcott wrote Carnegie a long letter repeating the general view that the CIW needed facilities of its own and his specific arguments on what investigation of the earth might mean. There was no reply. Walcott's state of mind is reflected in a letter to William Healey Dall in which he thanked him for a copy of a major publication. "I congratulate you upon being able to prosecute it and publish it. I speak with considerable feeling in this, when I think of the condition of my Cambrian work."[18]

Mid-November marked the one hundredth anniversary of the New York Avenue Presbyterian Church, a very big Sunday, immediately followed by a big Monday at the twenty-fifth anniversary of the Cosmos Club. That same week Director Walcott actually had three days away from all paper work to do geology. He, Hayes, and several other geologists went to the coastal plain on the eastern shore and in southern Maryland. A Paleozoic specialist would hardly dignify this dirt with formation names, but even in mid-November coastal plain geology is far better than no geology.

Charles Doolittle Walcott, Paleontologist

Another meeting of Ex. Com. ensued where Gilman met with Billings, Root, Mitchell, Wright and Walcott. This went on from 9:00 A.M. until 8:00 P.M., and the next day they met again for two and a half hours. Historians have documented the breakdown in relations between Gilman and Billings. For the coming trustees meeting, Gilman wished to submit a statement separate from that of the Ex. Com. and Walcott had advised him against it. Walcott wrote Billings, and Billings was blunt to Gilman (Madsen 1969, 168). It is a wonder that Gilman did not formally resign sooner.

Thanksgiving was the next day, but even then CIW business was transacted, for the *Year Book* had to be assembled. The astronomy report occupied 170 pages; geophysics weighted in with papers of half that length. Relatively small grants were still being given, and some twenty-odd research assistants were being supported, though the institution was heading more toward support of larger projects. The new publishing program was a success.

December did not go well. Interestingly enough, there was no record in Walcott's diary of Professor Langley's dramatic failure to launch his aerodrome. Aunt Helen Stevens died, and Helena rushed off to Rochester, returning ill. Regardless, the trustees meeting was scheduled for all day on the eighth; the idea of a geophysical laboratory was shunted aside; the annual dinner went on until 11:00 P.M. and must have seemed interminable. This defeat was followed by two days of Ex. Com. meetings and then another blow. "Marcus Baker died 6. A.M., A most valuable man in all life's relations. As Asst. Secty of C - I - he has done a fine work & will be greatly missed" (December 12, 1903). It took two people to carry the load Baker had handled.

There was a trip to New York for a rump session of the Ex. Com. with Billings and Mitchell. The next day, Walcott had meetings at Columbia University, lunch at the Carnegie mansion, and another talk with Billings. Walcott did receive a small ego boost in December. Prof. Dr. Eduard Suess's multivolume study of stratigraphy and structure of the world *Der Antlitz der Erde* had been translated into English, *The Face of the Earth*. Suess sent a copy to the USGS. "This other copy is indicated for your private library and I hope you will accept it a sign of the high respect."[19] It was an appreciation of scientific effort as three decades earlier, when Barrande sent the trilobite memoir.

Christmas was jolly with the children around. Walcott was settled in for the nap between Christmas and New Year's, when at "9:30 when word came that Geological Survey building was on fire. Ret'd 1130. Damaged NW top floor of building" (December 27, 1903). It was to be the first of several fires in the fireproof Hoee Iron Building. "The fire burned up our outfit for photographing fossils, but we hope to have it back in operation within a month or six weeks."[20] About all Walcott cared to note for the year was the death of Helena's uncle.

January 1 brought the traditional visit to the White House and other official calls. This was a hard winter, and on the third, the temperature was ten degrees above zero, very cold for the city. The USGS and the CIW were unremitting, though one evening Walcott went to a dinner in honor of the Great Basin Mess, a minor oxymoron, but the only logical way to describe the event.

Walcott returned to the attack with Carnegie, asking for more money to support the astronomical work of Hale and trying to get support for a geophysical laboratory, but the man was not in a mood to fund either proposition. The twelfth brought Carnegie to town for a reception in honor of Governor Durbin of Indiana, and Walcott conferred with him. The next evening, Walcott went to the Archaeological Society meeting, a relatively new interest. The Iowa and Stoneleigh apartment companies took another evening.

Walcott appeared at a deficiency hearing to report on the fire and a few other items. Remarkably enough there was a bit of hostility after Walcott described the loss of photographic equipment used in the map-making process:

> MR. BURKETT: Would it not have been well if it had burned up all this process of making those topographic sheets, so that it could never be made any more?'
>
> MR. WALCOTT: No sir; I do not think it would have been a good thing. We are entirely dependent upon maps for our knowledge of the topography of the country. (Walcott 1904, 96)

Walcott also got some heat for desiring extra money to compile mineral statistics, but "Uncle Joe" Cannon did not let the hearing get out of hand.

Later that year Walcott received more money, for new shelving, for a coal-testing laboratory, and to compensate a topographer who was sued when a horse he hired kicked a buggy to pieces and the topographer had been forced to pay for the vehicle. If that is strange, there is famous story of the harnessed mule who tried to scratch his ear and strangled itself. Herbert Hoover attested to the truth of that one. The hearings were a warmup for two days of the CIW Ex. Com., immediately followed by a tea of Helena's, attended by three hundred people.

The last week of January, Walcott was invited to an atypical Washington dinner, that of the Boone and Crocket Club. This group of rich and mighty hunters became a significant force in the conservation movement. Arnold Hague and George Bird Grinell, the only two nonhunting members, led the effort to have the area south of Yellowstone Park established as the first forest reserve (Reiger 1992). The New York club members held a dinner in Washington so that Teddy Roosevelt could talk to the group he had helped found in 1887. Walcott reported that the president "spoke well and to the point" (January 23, 1904).

January ground on and gave way to February, which ground on and on. The Walcotts gave a dinner in honor of Secretary Hitchcock, and, later in the year, the Hitchcocks reciprocated. This February there seemed to be more social activity than in past years, and an evening at home was an exception. Walcott was reelected a trustee of the Church of the Covenant and was occupied more than full time with extracurricular activities.

"As Secy of Ex-Com of C- I- busy all day. Messers Gilman, Billings, Mitchell, Hay and Wright attended" (February 18, 1904). The next day, the committee continued discussions, or deliberations, or arguments; Gilman had indicated his intent to resign and his presence did not help Billings's temperament. That evening, Walcott talked with Professor Barker, from Philadelphia, about "geophysical projects" of the institution. Some studies of terrestrial magnetism had begun, but Walcott still did not have the laboratory he so desired. Although there were seven on the Ex. Com., Billings, Walcott, and Mitchell made decisions. It is plausible that Mitchell tended to lean more toward support of an individual than toward a big project. Barker was a CIW consultant, and in talking to him Walcott may have been trying to influence a friend to influence Mitchell.

Following defeat of his CIW real estate proposal, it was obvious to Walcott that a carefully laid campaign was needed if a laboratory were ever to be built and equipped. Indeed, months before that defeat, in 1902, shortly before the committee meeting at Woods Hole, Chamberlin wrote asking about reversing the order of the words geology and geophysics in the report and added,

> I fell back into some question as to its advisability. This was considerably emphasized a few days ago by a confidential hint that Mr. Carnegie would not put more money into the general scheme until results were certain. This of course may be another apprehension but it sounds rather business like. If this be the case, it is of course advisable to plan a working scheme which could be adopted and carried into execution at once with the present resources.[21]

Two years later, regardless of the way plans for a laboratory were modified or what letters of support were presented, Walcott's efforts had been fruitless.

Still without enough to do, Walcott attended a dinner of the Board of Trustees of Columbian University. This was the year a new charter was issued and it was renamed George Washington University. That was not what the George Washington Memorial Association had hoped for, as this never became a national university, but simply one in the nation's capital. Walcott was a university trustee for six years, until 1910. He was also involved with the Washington Monument Society, a group that lunched once a year on Washington's birthday and generally oversaw the condition of the monument; there was no park service to supervise the various attractions in Washington. As another strand in the Washington network, Speaker Cannon had been a member of the society during his early days in Washington and must have looked with favor on Walcott for this civic duty.

Even all this did not fully occupy Walcott's evenings, and he was busy with the University Club, just forming (Wilkinson 1954). This club was to be run by a council of a dozen members who would elect the officers from within their number. Walcott, with four honorary degrees, was on the original council. His first job was to contact Chief Justice Fuller, who had been placed on the council and ask if he would run for president. Justice Fuller declined and resigned from the council. Thereupon, Walcott was a committee of one to approach William Howard Taft. Taft accepted and the University Club was launched the last day of February. Walcott was second vice-president for two years, before moving to first vice-president. More often that not, he ran the council meetings.

The end of February brought a tantalizing diary item: "A busy day at Geol. Survey & at Capitol.—At White House 9–11:30 A.M. in conference Prest. Roosevelt, Speaker J. G. Cannon, Senator Allison—Genl. Crozier, Admiral Bowles,—Gifford Pinchot—Jas. R. Garfield" (February 29, 1904). The who and where are given, but the what and why are not; most are members of Roosevelt's reorganization committee, and that is one explanation. On the other hand, the start of the Rooseveltian conservation movement is generally dated from transmittal to Congress of a report of the Public Lands Commission a few days later. Pinchot was one of the three on the commission and was at the White House meeting; Newell was also on that commission. This White House meeting, with its mixture of conservation-minded military, legislative, and executive folk, is worth pondering. Walcott had a nickname which may have originated with Pinchot, who had observed him in action at both the Legislative and Executive Branches. He was "snowshoe Charlie," for where he went he left no tracks. Much has been written on Roosevelt's conservation movement, but those who want to delve further might try to follow the path of Walcott through conservation politics.

On March 1, Walcott was politicking at the Capitol concerning the Geological Survey appropriation. He also went to a reception to formally meet once more Taft of Ohio. The appropriation took some looking after, but there was not much excitement the early part of the month. In mid-March, Walcott presided at a mass meeting of University Club members and a reception for four hundred, which laid the groundwork for their first clubhouse. If Walcott were in an organization, Walcott participated; later, along with his council duties, he was on the Committee on Admissions. He dined at the home of General Greeley, the Arctic explorer, and was again formally introduced to Taft.

Even yet there was more for this man to do; Walcott decided that it was time the family had its very own house. Not a place built by someone else, but one that they planned and oversaw the construction. Inside of a couple of weeks, Walcott had drawn up his plans and began looking for a lot. When the time came to move, no matter what the project, Walcott moved swiftly.

The USGS had been signed into law March 3, 1879. That precise date slipped by, but a month later, Walcott attended a "Dinner on acc't of 25th anniversary of the Geological Survey 7–11:59" (April 2, 1904); after midnight, it was Sunday and no wine or spirituous liquid could be served in Rausher's Restaurant. The toastmaster was chief clerk Colonel Rizer, and an enormous windmill lettered "The Grind of the Colonel" occupied part of the room. Each time Rizer spoke or an invited speaker went on too long, the windmill made a clatter. Members of the USGS were not adverse to practical jokes, and the kernel grinder was the kind of play on words that delighted the group.

"Col. Rizer introduced the first speaker, Director C. D. Walcott, in a happy facetious manner. He spoke of Mr. Walcott starting in the survey, at the foot of the ladder, a quarter of a century ago. The reason he started there, said the toastmaster was because there was no place further down."[22] Walcott spoke on the early traditions of the Geological Survey, giving credit to Abram Hewitt as father of the organization. He also hoped that within two years the Survey would have its own building. Walcott was presented a four-foot-high requisition. "Please issue to C. D. Walcott, for official use, one home for the Geological Survey—not a flat." Colonel Rizer approved the requisition, and "a miniature public building of elaborate, if somewhat fanciful, architecture"[23] was carried around the tables. Seventy years later, the John Wesley Powell Building was dedicated, a building of fanciful architecture.

Several days following the anniversary dinner, Walcott was in Philadelphia in his capacity as member of the Franklin Bicentennial Committee, scheduled for 1906. This led to a bizarre appearance of Mitchell and Walcott before a Senate committee. One does not normally expect to find humor in the hearings on a Sundry Civil Appropriation bill, but it is here. The closing remarks give the tenor of the whole affair:

DOCTOR MITCHELL: Taking him all in all, I suppose, intellectually speaking, he [Franklin] was perhaps the greatest American.

SENATOR BERRY: I do not agree to that. Jefferson was the greatest man the country ever produced, I think.

SENATOR HALE: Jefferson was political.

SENATOR BERRY: We will not agree on that.

DOCTOR MITCHELL: We would disagree very sharply on it.

SENATOR HALE: Washington morally was greater than either. (Allison et al. 1904)

That evening Walcott went to a meeting of the Oriental Society; Gilman had steered his interests in this unlikely direction. Undeterred by the Mitchell event, Walcott went to Capital Hill to check on the appropriation, and to seek out a new USGS building. The former was successful, the latter not. Walcott even "Worked on Cambrian brachiopods for an hour or two" (April 11, 1904); this year was a quarter over before fossils were first mentioned in his diary.

Alexander Graham Bell gave a dinner, and for the fourth time Walcott was formally introduced to Taft. When Taft was elected, they knew each other well, and Walcott's easy access to the White House continued. The National Academy came to town, and after they left, there was another meeting of the CIW Ex. Com.; a change in the institution was in the wind.

On a fundamentally different project, Helena and Walcott went to Baltimore to look at houses for ideas to incorporate into their new home. Before the end of the month, they moved their household belongings "from 2117 S Str, NW to the Ontario Apt, House Lanier Heights. Apartment 405" (May 24, 1904). Walcott's long dream of his very own home was going to come true; once the old house was demolished, construction started on the same site.

The second week in May, Walcott made a quick trip to New York to check with Billings, talk to Root, and become better acquainted with John L. Cadwalader, a new trustee and a long time friend of Billings; he laid the foundation for the next board meeting. "At meeting of Carnegie Institution Trustees 10–12:30. Ex-Com 9:15–10 A.M. 2:30 to 4:30 P.M. Trustees adopted new charter

Charles Doolittle Walcott, Paleontologist

for C- I- Wash,n. 14 Trustees present" (May 18, 1904). The new charter had been written by Root and introduced into Congress by Senator Lodge. The trustees reelected Walcott and Billings to the executive committee for three more years.

Carnegie now had his formal sanction of approval from the Congress. This pleased the millionaire such that Walcott took a trip to New York for receipt of a few hundred thousand dollars worth of railroad bonds; one might view this as a tip for service rendered. He returned to New York in a couple of days, for with the new charter the endowment of ten million dollars in bonds had to be moved from Hoboken to the New York City offices of J. P. Morgan. In connection with writing about these various matters, Walcott took the opportunity to again urge Carnegie for more support for a solar observatory and a geophysical laboratory. Nothing came of either.

After a few days of moving around Washington to tidy up business at the University Club, the CIW, and the USGS, Walcott left for Seneca Lake. Really, no one stayed in Washington for the summer. The British, who had experience worldwide, classified Washington as a subtropical capital; business could be conducted in Bermuda shorts. Seneca Lake was a short vacation for Walcott while he fished, painted a boat, and got his mind in order for return to Washington. "With Helena went down to see Charles off for Washington State. He goes off at 15 years 34 days old to do field work on survey of US & Canadian boundary" (June 19, 1904). As a father, Walcott must have been both proud and sad to see his namesake leave. Charlie's job was probably to fetch and carry for the crew or cut brush for surveyor's lines.

The Walcotts gave a dinner for Dr. and Mrs. W. Cross; he specialized on the details of igneous rocks. Another guest was Joe Iddings, visiting in Washington. No matter how long Walcott knew someone, diary references were formal; Joe was the sole exception. During the 1894 debacle, Iddings left for the University of Chicago and hated every moment of teaching. After a decade he unexpectedly received an inheritance and according to legend walked out of the classroom; actually, he took sick leave.

It was about this time that Walcott lost some scientific support. When he became director, Walcott arranged for Charles Schuchert to transfer to the National Museum and curate fossils. Schuchert served faithfully for a decade, worked hard, and published. Quite unexpectedly, Charles Beecher died, leaving a vacancy at Yale University. Schuchert, who had not even completed grade school, moved north to become the most successful teacher of paleontologists of his generation (Cloud 1987).

The contract was let on the new house and, Walcott, Agnes the cook, and two boys—this time Sidney and Stuart, took a long hot train trip to Glenora, New York. A stenographer came a day later and set up an office in the Union Hall. Walcott started on the accumulated mail and unpacked Cambrian brachiopods, ready to describe more species. At the start of the new fiscal year, Walcott "Began systematic work. Two hours on Survey C- I- mail & then Cambrian brachiopods. Fished a little 6 P.M. on lake, nothing biting" (July 1, 1904).

It was nine until five each working day that month. The brachiopods were pressing rather heavily. One looks for similarities and for differences among the specimens at a locality, and the more closely one looks, generally the more differences one finds. Then one compares the assemblage of species from one place with an assemblage from another. If the assemblages are distinct, perhaps living conditions were different or perhaps the presumed correlation is not correct.

After some years, carrying all the details of morphology and stratigraphy in one's head can become tedious; so much time had already been invested in this project. 1904 marks the nadir of Walcott's career as a scientist, for it is the only year in which no scientific paper or even a speech was published. There is a lag between completion of a manuscript and publication, but it was painfully obvious that the tank was empty and scientist Walcott was running only on fumes.

By the end of July, afternoon fishing improved slightly, Helena carried Helen off for a visit to relatives, and sister Josie, now sixty-two, came for a few days. Walcott took a two-day trip to Washington to check on the house and tidy up a few Survey matters. In early September Walcott left for D.C. and arrived in time to attend an evening reception of the Geographical Congress. The following day he was "At meeting of Internal. Geog. Cong. 10–12 A.M. Spoke five minutes" (September 7, 1904). It was the first time this group had met in America, and Walcott substituted for the honorary president, Theodore Roosevelt.

That chore out of the way, Walcott saw Billings in New York, stopped at the United States Military Academy for advice, and looked at a military school in Peekskill. At Albany, he inspected the observatory for CIW, moved to Oneida to see Helen's aunt, and went back to Seneca Lake, where Charlie rejoined the family. A week later, Charlie left for military school. Walcott was not a disciplinarian, but a loving father who wanted the best in education for his namesake. The end of the month the family left Seneca Lake for home, though Walcott stayed on, continuing with the brachiopods and with the *Carnegie Institution Year Book.*

Charles Doolittle Walcott, Paleontologist

By mid-September, Walcott was back in Washington, facing nothing except administration. Early October brought another Ex. Com. meeting. Billings was there—he never missed a meeting—along with Hay, Wright, and Gilman; even with Gilman retiring, the institution functioned.

Always thinking ahead, Walcott had a "Conference with Mr. Richard Rathbun on the Museum of Arts & Industries" (October 21, 1904). In mid-June ground had been broken for a new major building across from the Smithsonian Castle, and when it was finished, the brick building might be emptied. The new structure would be dubbed the New National Museum, and the old brick box became the Arts and Industries Building (Yochelson 1985). Walcott spent part of another day around the Smithsonian starting his new brain child on its path.

He met with the Executive Board of the George Washington Memorial Association. Spirits were low, but the change in name of Columbian University to that of George Washington gave hope for the future. He called on President Roosevelt, and he watched his new house go up. The month ended with another meeting of the CIW Ex. Com. and virtually for the first time, all seven members were present. The selection of Gilman's successor proceeded, though not without arguments and problems.

Walcott consulted with Secretary Hitchcock on irrigation matters, got paper work under control, "Cleared up a little work on Cambrian brachiopoda" (November 3, 1904), and left for St. Louis. "The first impression of the St. Louis exposition is that its plan & detail have been worked out with greater care than previous expositions" (November 8, 1904). At the Buffalo Exposition, the USGS set up a printing press and gave away topographic maps of the area. For the St. Louis Louisiana Purchase Exposition, a Bulletin on history of the Survey was written. However, the great USGS display in St. Louis, both figuratively and literally, was the coal-testing plant.

Holmes, Day, and Hayes had developed the idea of studying the burning of coal in a scientific manner at industrial scale. Walcott obtained an appropriation of thirty thousand dollars for a building and salaries, railroads donated mileage, companies donated machinery for the plant, and mines donated carload lots of coal. This was a detailed study of the burning qualities, amount of ash, and other critical features of American coals. "Among the government exhibits at the Louisiana Purchase Exposition there is none which has attracted more attention among engineers and technical men generally than the fuel-testing plant of the Geological Survey" (Walcott 1904a, 26). One result was publication of the largest *Professional Paper* until the 1970s; another result was a further step on the road to a federal mines bureau.

Walcott spent a week at the exposition. Midway through his stay, he noted "A day of conferences & looking up odds & ends— The subject of other organization & shaping the policy of the Dept. of Mineral Technology of the U.S. Nat. Museum was the chief subject of discussion" (November 12, 1904). Shortly after Hewitt died, Walcott had raised the point of honoring him with a collection to illustrate iron technology. This was one aspect of his plan, for after the exposition a great deal of display material came to Washington for the National Museum in a repeat of the 1876 experience. "With the view of providing for the oversight of the latter a new department of the Museum, entitled Mineral Technology was constituted under the curatorship of Dr. Charles D. Walcott" (Rathbun 1906, 9).

It was back to Washington in time to leave for New York and the fall National Academy meeting. Walcott had a week of playing musical offices in Washington and then he and Helena forfeited an at-home Thanksgiving to meet Charlie in New York. Walcott went on to Boston to consult with an engineer on reclamation business.

The end of November, Walcott was "Working on Chinese Cambrian brachiopods at my room in morning" (November 30, 1904). Willis and young Eliot Blackwelder had returned safely from nine months in China. Sixty years later, Blackwelder could recall telling Walcott that he had brought back half a ton of fossils and being asked why he did not bring back a ton.

Outside of the University Club council, a dinner with the Civil Service Reform League, and a trustees meeting of the Church of the Covenant, there was little, apart from administration, to occupy the first part of December. The pace quickened when he "With J. A. Holmes went before appropriations committee House of Representatives" (December 12, 1904). They talked about the coal-testing plant and obtained more money to continue the work.

The next day the trustees of the Carnegie Institution met. Robert S. Woodward, dean of pure science at Columbia University, was elected the new president. The struggle between Billings and Gilman ended; for what little it counted, Gilman ended his term with a resounding statement on organization. It also marked a turning point, in that the president's power waxed and that of the

Charles Doolittle Walcott, Paleontologist

Ex. Com. waned. Meanwhile, after nearly three years, Walcott was finally serving a CIW president who also wanted a laboratory for geophysics. The election of Woodward also had Carnegie thinking about future directions for his brainchild. That was all to the good for Walcott's scheme.

Christmas could not have been better. The children were happy and the presents were just what they wanted. For the finale, the family had a picnic supper in the nearly completed new house. There were a couple more days of light work in the office before Walcott was off for Philadelphia and the annual meeting of the Geological Society of America. It had been a quiet year in Walcott's opinion.

13

Big Change: Once One Has Juggled the Maximum Number of Balls without Dropping Any, an Intelligent Person Will Retire Gracefully (1905–1907)

> I am convinced that, at its best, science is simple—that the simplest arrangement of facts that sets forth the truth best deserves the term scientific. So the geology I plead for is that which states facts in plain words—in language understood by the many rather than only by the few. Plain geology needs little defining, and I may state my case best by trying to set forth the reasons why we have strayed so far away from the simple type.
>
> G. O. Smith, 1922

THE NEW YEAR STARTED on a Sunday, so it began with Sunday school and church as usual for the family. Walcott and Helena celebrated privately by looking at the new house; official calls were made the next day, starting at the White House and working down through several cabinet members to a brace of senators. The American Association of Foresters came to the city, and Walcott "At 2:15 P.M. read a paper before the Forestry Congress" (January 6, 1905). In it, he built upon his 1898 remarks on the history of the establishment of forest reserves to explain what had come next. Walcott moved on to the relationship between forest cover and runoff to bring in the reclamation work, added comment on the need for mine timbers, and then added the coal-testing laboratory.

Along the way, he managed to tell this group, mainly industrialists, what a marvelous job the USGS had done in fixing the boundaries of the forest reserves, estimating the amount of timber, and doing scientific work on forest development, fires, and other matters:

> From the point of view of effective administration, I believe that the examination, development, and administration of the forest reserves should be

placed in charge of the Bureau of Forestry of the Department of Agriculture, and that the topographic mapping of the reserves and the adjoining forest areas should remain in charge of the director of the Geological Survey, and be carried on in cooperation with the Bureau of Forestry. (Walcott 1905, 380)

His conclusion to the Congress was appropriate inasmuch as this was not a meeting for facts and figures. According to Pinchot (1947, 254–55), it was "planned, organized, and conducted for the specific purpose of the transfer by the Bureau of Forestry." February 1 the transfer bill passed the Congress, and at the start of the fiscal year, Pinchot had his Forest Service. Pinchot did not like "bureau" in the same way that Powell did not like "-al" endings on words; the major was legally bound to Geological Survey, but the bureau had a geologic branch.

The Forest Reserve studies by the USGS rapidly faded from memory, and eight years of incredible effort receives little attention in the history books. This chapter was completely ignored in an account of conservation activities published by the Department of the Interior (Wilbur and DuPay 1931). Of the fifty-three USGS *Professional Papers* written from the start of the series to the time of transfer, one-third were devoted to the Forest Reserves.

In reply to inquiry from R. U. Johnson, editor of *Century Magazine,* Walcott scribbled a note from camp: "Due in Washington Octr. 3 *rd.* Can send you much data on the forestry movement of 1898— I drew up the present [?] law & supported it before the administration & congress. Am very glad you are to write up the history."[1] When Walcott was in a rush, his handwritten deteriorated; "present" makes sense, but so might other words. Three days after Walcott was in Washington, he mailed a long, typed letter, directing attention to part of his 1905 article:

> There are a number of personal details, such as conferences with different senators, the Secretary of the Interior, President McKinley, etc, that are of interest but which I should hardly care to have published at present. I made a very strong effort to have Secretary Bliss [Interior] permit me to organize the Forestry Service on a Civil Service and business basis, but he preferred to "give the boys a chance," and Binger Hermann [General Land Office] made a first class political machine of the Service up to the time that it was transferred to the Agricultural Department and came under Pinchot's control.
>
> In the spring of 1897 Secretary Bliss said to me that Secretary Wilson [Agriculture] would like to have a conference in relation to the appointment of a forester to succeed Professor Fernow. I became acquainted with Pinchot

while he was acting as Secretary of the National Academy Committee on Forestry, and unhesitatingly recommended him to the Secretary. He asked me to ask Pinchot to come over from New York for a conference. This took place a few days later, and after about twenty minutes' talk the Secretary said to Pinchot, "If you will accept the place, I will give you a free hand and help you all I can." Pinchot returned to New York and soon after accepted the Secretary's offer. The struggle soon began to get the Forestry Service under Pinchot's control, but it was so strongly entrenched as a political machine by Hermann that it took a number of years to dislodge it. Secretary Hitchcock [Interior] realized the condition of affairs, but was powerless to do anything toward reorganizing the Service as long as Hermann remained in charge. The present effective organization is entirely owing to the superb work of Pinchot and his able assistants. The cause of the attack made in Congress last winter and much of the unrest existing in the West I think will be done away with when the proposed new organization of the field service is put in operation. There will be for a long time a certain amount of fault finding by persons either directly interested or employed by interested parties, who wish to exploit the timber on the government lands at the public expense.[2]

In his autobiography, Pinchot writes nice words about Walcott and the Geological Survey, though Mr. Conservation neglects to mention that it was Walcott who got him into federal service in Washington, who tried to have him elected to the National Academy, and who worked hard for many years to have the Forest Service established. Probably Walcott would have shrugged this off as a lapse of memory. Walcott wrote to "Dear Gifford" throughout his life, and Pinchot was almost the only one ever to write to Walcott as "Dear Charlie," so why delve further?

With the trees about to leave Walcott's jurisdiction, the CIW came to the fore. He went to New York, where Messrs. Hay, Mitchell, Billings, Wright, and Walcott met with new president Woodward and former president Gilman. The presence of Gilman at the first meeting of the Ex. Com. was a pretty clear indication of no seriously bruised feelings; kindly Dr. Gilman continued on as a member of the Ex. Com. for several years.

Back in Washington, Walcott had both a busy and a wide-ranging day. In the morning, he discussed current irrigation with Roosevelt. In the evening he acted as one of the Trustees of George Washington University. Between these events the family "Moved into our new house and home" (January 11, 1905). It was the last family move for the much-traveled Walcott, and it was the place in which he would die twenty-two years later. His use of house and home was deliberate.

Charles Doolittle Walcott, Paleontologist

There were briefings to give the secretary of interior, a lecture to attend by Willis on his China trip, and the annual meeting of the Washington Academy of Sciences. "I was elected president" (January 19, 1905). This was the season for the appropriations, and a busy Walcott wrote "At Survey—no time for my personal scientific work" (January 26, 1905). At the appropriations hearings, Walcott had a varied agenda. Among other items, he wanted to run the coal-testing laboratory in St. Louis for another year, he wanted to rent a basement that the USGS was already using and hoping for funds to pay for it, he wanted steel shelves for the library, and he wanted paleontology raised from ten thousand dollars back to forty thousand dollars. Finally, Walcott wanted a promotion for John D. McChesney. Mac began in 1878 as a disbursing agent for Lt. Wheeler. He and Gilbert were the only ones from that survey to be original USGS members; Gilbert had deserted to Powell's survey before Mac was hired by Wheeler:

> MR. WALCOTT. He gets $2,500. This reclamation work has fully doubled his duty, and he gets nothing extra for it.
>
> THE CHAIRMAN. He was working but half time before, then?
>
> MR. WALCOTT. The reclamation service gives him additional clerks, and he has the additional responsibility of making disbursements.
>
> THE CHAIRMAN. Does he work overtime, Mr. Director?
>
> MR. WALCOTT. He works early and late; yes sir.
>
> THE CHAIRMAN. Does he get there as early as 8 o'clock?
>
> MR. WALCOTT. I do not know that he does, because I do not get there myself that hour to see.
>
> THE CHAIRMAN. He is doing a little more work than he did before, but he is not doing it in the regular hours of work?
>
> MR. WALCOTT.. I presume he may be doing it in regular hours, except that I know he is there late, and he is always fully occupied; and in addition to that is the responsibility that he has.
>
> THE CHAIRMAN. Who fixes his salary? How is it fixed?
>
> MR. WALCOTT.. It is fixed by law.
>
> THE CHAIRMAN. You cannot promote him?
>
> MR. WALCOTT. No sir. This additional $1,000 will come out of the reclamation fund to pay for the work he does for the reclamation service and does not increase the appropriation carried by this bill.
>
> THE CHAIRMAN. He is a particularly bright fellow, is he?
>
> MR. WALCOTT. Yes, he is. (Walcott 1905a, 163–64)

Walcott went on to point out that McChesney's accounting system had been adopted by the entire government and that he was considered the best disbursing officer in Washington. Throughout the years, whether committee members tried to bait him or to inject humor, Walcott always responded in a straightforward manner. He never played games when testifying before Congress.

When the appropriations bill came up, the representatives, and later the senators, outdid themselves in heaping praise (Rabbitt 1980, 32–33). The Geological Survey got 20 percent more than the previous year; it was to be the calm before a storm. Senator Henry Cabot Lodge made some sneering remarks about Walcott as the best money getter in Washington, but he had also made nasty remarks about Walcott and the CIW a little over a year earlier shortly before he was elected to that CIW Board of Trustees. Walcott pushed too hard for this aristocrat's temperament.

If February had anything of note, it was a visit to New York. Helena and Walcott had lunch with the Carnegies and then went to Peekskill to visit Charlie. The Ex. Com. meeting went smoothly. March brought some relatives in to see the inauguration of President Roosevelt. The middle of the month, Walcott was on his way north, stopping off to see Charlie. His business was with the director of the Geological Survey of Canada. The channel of the Milk River does not respect the forty-ninth parallel, and for that irrigation project to proceed an international understanding was necessary. The GSC and the USGS have always gotten on well and this time was no exception. Walcott returned to brief Secretary Hitchcock and the president. A year earlier, Walcott had indicated the need for an outside consulting engineer for the Reclamation Service; he got one.

Near the end of March, Walcott the scientist surfaced again. As might be expected, he had a laboratory-office in the new house. One morning he was "At home A.M. doing a little work on Cambrian brachiopods of India" (March 29, 1905). "Through the courtesy of the Director of the Geological Survey of India, I have had the opportunity of studying the collections of Cambrian fossils from the Cambrian rocks of the Salt Range" (Walcott 1905b). From this introduction, he went on to publish a businesslike essay mentioning the genera he had identified and from this data making an intercontinental correlation that has remained essentially unchanged.

In April, Walcott obtained a couple of more days for work at home on the brachiopods. The new place really had turned out to be most convenient to Walcott the scientist, but he maintained and used his laboratory at the Survey whenever he could steal a few minutes. As usual, another meeting of the Ex. Com.

ensued, but Woodward was rapidly taking hold of the CIW and Walcott was easing out of some of his workload. The members of the National Academy came
to town, lectured to one another, and left. After three years, Walcott was off the
council. In the past, the academy had elected twelve members a year to this body.
One action Walcott initiated was a change to a more logical three-year term,
with four new persons elected each year. In his view, even the National Academy should be run on a businesslike basis.

Sister Josie, who had been visiting, left before the city became too hot. The
same day Walcott recorded "at C- I- office A.M. busy with Chinese Cambrian
fossils. Survey P.M." (May 2, 1905). There are another two remarks about work
on the Chinese Cambrian and a comment "Busy on Chinese Cambrian fossils
A.M. at C-I- office. At survey P.M. & home in the evening" (May 22, 1905). The
wording is ambiguous, but seemingly, Walcott had a laboratory at home, along
with the one at the USGS, and yet another at the headquarters of the Institution. At least this way CIW investigations on the Chinese fossils would not be
mixed with federal business on American Cambrian fossils.

As Walcott put it: "In a thoughtless moment, I promised Bailey Willis that I
would work up the collections of Cambrian fossils from China so that he could
have the data for his report by July 1st. The result is that for the past four weeks
I have averaged half a day each day in their study and description. It is most
interesting work to me; but with getting the field plans of the Survey in shape
for the summer and working out a lot of problems connected with the irrigation in the West, I have not had time to get over to New York or anywhere else."[3]

Charlie came for a visit, then left for a summer job in Montana. Walcott took
a quick trip to Rochester to join Helena and, after a family wedding, spent a few
more days on fossils. "Completed paper on Chinese Cambrian fossils" (June 8,
1905). This was published by September, another example of remarkable time
for preparation of more than one hundred pages of descriptions. The paper
gives a thumbnail description of working methods:

> A considerable quantity of material was collected and received in Washing-
> ton in the fall of 1904. The preparation of the specimens for labeling was
> given to Mr. Henry Dickhaut [a preparator at the National Museum], with
> instructions to work them up carefully and secure every species possible
> from the mass of fragments of trilobites, brachiopods, etc. of which nearly
> all the specimens of rock are composed. The material when thus prepared
> was labeled with locality and formation numbers and taken in hand by Miss
> Elvira Wood [secretary at Geological Survey], who separated the species and

selected and indicated specimens for illustration. I first studied the brachiopods in connection with my systematic study of the Cambrian brachiopoda, and published description of 23 species in 1905. Mr. Willis and Mr. Blackwelder informed me that they would like in July, 1905, a list of all the species in the collections in order to use them in the correlation of the various sections and the discussion of the stratigraphic geology. To meet this request, I made a preliminary study of the fauna, and now publish it in advance of the illustrated report, which will not be ready to go to the printer before the spring of 1906. Many drawings have been prepared, but it will require several months to complete them. (Walcott 1905c, 3)

Walcott had learned well under Hall how to use assistants in partitioning out phases of the work for a paleontological publication. This Chinese Cambrian paper was modified in some particulars before it was published with the plates, and one copy retains another clue giving information on working methods. Sections to be copied from the 1905 paper are marked in pencil; those to be changed have slips with shorthand notations attached. Walcott dictated his descriptions and discussions. A modern electronic word processor may be fast, but having someone else do the typing and correcting is even faster. Walcott had come a long way from the New York State Museum, which still has in its archives his handwritten manuscript for the twenty-eighth *Annual Report.*

Actually, Walcott the scientist had reappeared even before his work for Willis was completed. This same year the Museum had earlier published 110 pages of descriptions of brachiopods (Walcott 1905d); it was another paper in advance of the monograph which was so slowly wending its way toward completion. This brachiopod study included a large number of foreign forms, the result of years of contact with workers overseas, though naturally the bulk of the specimens Walcott had collected. Several of the new genera and subgenera named were *Rustella, Curticea, Jamesella, Loperia,* and *Schuchertina.* Walcott did not forget those who had helped him with his investigations.

With those two substantial manuscripts in the press, Walcott headed west with Helena, the three younger children, and Arthur Brown. They detrained in Helena, Montana, and left for Ovada by way of Helmville; that was an easy two-day wagon trip. Two packers and Mr. Collen, a Montana rancher/geologist, completed the party. Not much is known about Collen except that he had some experience or interaction with Weed, the USGS geologist who had worked on the copper deposits at Butte. In the fall of 1903, Collen thought he had found corals in one of the units in the Belt. These turned out to be algal masses, stromatolites, but it was a shrewd observation. When it came time to study these stromatolites, the genus *Collenia* was named. Walcott did not give the derivation of the name, but it would be unlikely in the extreme that this was a fortuitous combination of letters.

Once a base camp was set up near Ovada, Walcott took a pack train up the north fork of the Blackfoot River, "A beautiful camping place" (June 17, 1905). In the canyon were "All Algonkian rock of the Belt Mtn. type. Purple & greenish siliceous shales & bedded rocks overlain by limestones & these by red siliceous shales" (June 19, 1905). While the geologists covered the country on horseback, the pack train moved the camp site every few days. The geology was interesting, even if Walcott had to contend with fog and rain while climbing to the continental divide with camera equipment, and searching for the best place to measure a section. Walcott "Celebrated the [Independence] day by 11 hrs work with Mr. Collen. Rode 20 miles & examined Algonkian limestone for fossils— None found" (July 4, 1905).

Walcott, Collen, and Frank Haun, one of the packers, took the two boys and they measured a section two miles thick, using the dip compass and rod Walcott had described many years earlier. They slept out on the continental divide with a sandwich for supper. It was a great adventure for Sidney and Stuart. The party moved camp several times and went into the Swan Range. In a way, this was a repeat of the former season among the Belt rocks, but a second look at the rocks considerably enhanced Walcott's understanding of relationships. In this area, the section measured was only a mile thick, but it took three days to get to the proper place and return to camp. After Walcott rested and they moved camp again, a couple of days went into collecting Middle Cambrian fossils; after all the Precambrian Belt strata, it was a relief to see rocks containing fossil animals.

Charlie showed up, his job having terminated, and they moved camp to west of Gordon Mountain. Collen and Walcott measured a section of Cambrian and collected a fine mess of trilobites. Measuring rock thicknesses and looking for fossils was what they were there to do and all that there was to do. This was long before the days of radio, let alone television, but the party was so far into the mountains that even if the technology had existed, nothing electronic would have worked. Having rested his soul with the trilobites, Walcott took Collen on another rugged pack trip. When they returned, base camp was moved to a ranch to make certain Helena and Helen would be all right; Helena had been bucked off a horse and was very lame.

The packers, the three boys, Collen, and Walcott headed for Scapegoat Mountain. They were on the trail for three days before coming to a ranch which had a telephone. Walcott called Great Falls to be told that it was impossible for Charlie to get on a Survey party. There were rules and rules were not bent, not even for the director's son. They worked their way back to base camp to rejoin the others. Helena could finally sit on a horse, but Walcott led it to be on the safe side. "A long tedious days march as Helena was lame & sore & discouraged" (August 8, 1905). Horseback riding in the great outdoors is not 100 percent enjoyment.

Once they were in camp near Ovada, the geologic fun ended for a time. It was hot, and the *Annual Report* had to be written. The start of the *Professional Paper* series had slimmed the annual reports after a couple of years and, in addition, the twenty-sixth *Annual Report* was in a smaller format. These changes affected the writing and compilation. Add to that the USGS had been attacked in the papers, and a response was necessary. Of course, a mountain of mail had come in. With all else, Walcott started on a speech for the Irrigation Congress in Portland, Oregon.

The ladies left for a leisurely trip to Ravalli, and the men and boys went on one last pack trip west up the "Jocko" trail and across the Mission Range to the Jocko River. Walcott observed, "Mt. McDonald is formed of the Holland limestone & chert formation & is essentially the same as Mt. Holland of the Swan Range" (August 16, 1905). Despite rain, they arrived safely at Ravalli and measured another half mile of Algonkian rock. The next day, Walcott identified the Holland limestone above eight thousand feet of siliceous beds. He took photographs of the Mission Range, and that was the end of fieldwork for the family; "All well & brown from trip in mountains" (August 20, 1905).

From Ravalli, they caught the train to Portland. While Helena and the family looked over the Lewis and Clark Exposition, Walcott went to the Irrigation Congress to speak and to politic. When that was over, Walcott bid adieu to his family and headed east with Newell and others of the Reclamation Service to inspect several projects. His last stop was at Minidoka, not far from Burley, Idaho, where a diversion dam was being built on the Snake River. In 1903, Walcott had looked at the headwaters of the Snake in the Grand Tetons and at a dam site downstream. In 1904, Congress had allocated two million dollars for construction of the Minidaka project, which was to irrigate about 120,000 acres.

Late in July, bibliographer/geologist Weeks wrote to Walcott from Salt Lake City. He and Burling had been working in northern Wasatch Range, particularly studying and collecting the Cambrian rocks. Clarence King had the rock sequence correct, but it was thicker than the Fortieth Parallel Survey geologists estimated. Before delving into the details of geology, Weeks reported,

> When I arrived here I found my outfit in good shape expect that the saddle horse which we bought in Park City, and you used him two years ago, had his front foot nearly cut off by barbed wire. I concluded to try and cure this cut rather than sacrifice him for five or ten dollars. During the past month since I have been in the northern part of the state they have gotten the proud flesh out of it, and while it has not healed a great deal it is now in good condition to improve right along and I am in hopes that by the time you come down here I shall be able to send to Salt Lake and have him for you to use. I had to purchase another horse in his stead, of course, and have a pretty good bronco, as broncos go, for which I paid fifty dollars. The animals are all in splendid condition and everything else is in good shape.[4]

Healing a horse was all in a day's work, for in addition to geology, geologists do a number of things. Nowadays, when a vehicle does not start miles from a road, one either walks out or repairs; it is amazing what some geologists can do with a hammer and piece of wire. Whether the horse survived is unknown, but at least Weeks was both humane and interested in the taxpayer's property. The Survey mule has been honored by geologists' songs, but the Survey horse has never gotten his due.

For work in western Utah, it was essential that the outfit be in good shape. It is equally essential today, for in this region civilization is still very sparse. Weeks went on to heap praise on assistants: "I have two very good camp men; my cook is the best one I ever had with the exception of Arthur, and if for any reason you should not bring Arthur with you I think you would find this man would fill Arthur's place quite acceptably."[5]

Walcott left the Minidoka project and he and Arthur Brown arrive in Salt Lake City the penultimate day of August. Weeks met them, and presumably Burling departed with Arthur. Walcott lunched with the governor and two senators. Later, Newell assisted while the director talked to newspaper men. The next day was also used to obtain favorable publicity for the Geological Survey and the Reclamation Service.

Finally, it was off to the field. Walcott and Weeks took the railroad to St. John's, Utah, where Dan Orr met them with a wagon and a buckboard, and they camped on the western side of the Stansbury Range. The next night was a dry camp in the desert before they finally reached the Fish Spring Range. "Drove about 12 miles along east front of Fish Spring Range. Examined sections as far as Sand Pass. Found rocks much altered so decided to go to Antelope Spring in the House range & work from there as the strata are in continuous section & not much altered" (September 4, 1905). It was another hard day to get to the House Range; they had to go via Joy, Utah, for water.

From the sixth until the nineteenth of September, Walcott measured sections and collected fossils, assisted by Weeks and Burling, in a detailed reprise of the 1903 season, and this time not in terra incognita. A couple of diary entries show how and why the fieldwork was done. "Worked on section of Cambrian rocks & collecting fossils all day—Measured up to 1100 feet of the section— Mr. Weeks & Mr. Burling collecting fossils on line of section" (September 12, 1905). "Continued work on section about 2000 feet above camp— Continued up to summit of ridge where erosion had cut section off— Very sorry as I wished to take section up to the Ordovician. Will try to the west" (September 13, 1905).

"A magnificent continuous sequence of shallow-water marine Cambrian strata more than 10,000 ft (3,000 m) thick is exposed in the House Range. From a scientific standpoint, the most important feature is that these sedimentary layers contain one of the most diverse sequences of Middle and Upper Cambrian faunas known from anywhere in the world" (Hintze and Robison 1987).

It was a grand trip, but eventually good things end. The outfit moved to Oasis, and Walcott caught the night train east to Salt Lake City, getting in at 6:10 A.M. He disposed of the desert dust, saw the governor again, and answered a mountain of mail before leaving for the Reclamation Service camp at Strawberry Valley in the Wasatch Mountains. Fall began with inspection of a reservoir site and a proposed long tunnel, which was a good scheme. The next day was devoted to inspection of a proposed diversion canal: "The canal scheme is a dream of a visionary engineer—unless there is unlimited money" (September 23, 1905).

Walcott and his Reclamation Service Engineer, Swensden, went back to the main camp and from there to Provo. In Provo, Nunn ran the Telluride Power Company, but he also ran a school and a work-study program; Walcott was interested as to how Charlie might fare at such a place. Next, Walcott was off to Montrose, Montana, and then east to Denver to see the Reclamation Service employees there, and then to St. Louis where the coal-testing plant was still very much in business.

October 5, Walcott was finally home. A couple of days later he was out on his "wheel" interviewing for household help. His second Saturday at home was "A busy day closing a busy week. Have matters well in hand. Called on Presi-

Charles Doolittle Walcott, Paleontologist

dent Roosevelt 11 A.M. & reported on irrigation work in the west. Called on Sec'ty Elihu Root 12:15 P.M. At University Club 9–11 P.M. Introduced Secty Taft who spoke on his trip to the Philippines" (October 14, 1905). That alone was a busy day.

The new week began with a meeting of the CIW Ex. Com. There is another interesting diary entry: "Mr. Burling my new private secty—began C. I. 9:30 A.M. work today" (October 16, 1905). A bit of speculation may be in order. Walcott had completed a draft manuscript on the Cambrian fossils of China, but the final work of minor revision of descriptions, additions, adding illustrations, checking figure captions, verifying references and manifold other details had to be done. In general terms, 90 percent of the science is done in 10 percent of the time it takes to complete a manuscript. The remaining details are slow and wearisome. Burling was an excellent assistant, for he needed a minimum of supervision to put in that kind of effort.

In addition to that principal work, another smaller Chinese Cambrian study had started. "During the summer of 1905 a box of fossils, that had been lost, was received in Washington. . . . It has afforded a number of new species, but has not added otherwise materially to our knowledge of the Cambrian faunas of China, except in the case of the occurrence of the genus *Concinocyathus*" (Walcott 1906a, 565). Not forgetting his manners, Walcott used a new specific name *elvira* to denote the work of Miss Elvira Wood, and named a new genus *Blackwelderia*.

At the moment, China was not particularly on Walcott's mind, for the last part of October and through November he focused on the past season's investigations. "Completed paper on Algonkian rocks of N.W. Montana A.M." (December 1, 1905), which was out by the following May (Walcott 1906). It included eight plates of photographs taken during the several fields seasons by Walcott and another three by Willis, whom Walcott had sent in 1901 to examine the area now encompassed by Glacier National Park. Several photographs were panorama views Walcott took with a huge spring driven camera, which slowly moved around in an arc; it was hell to drag this monster up a mountain.

This paper is primarily a compilation of measured sections from various places in Montana and Idaho. Once those details were given, Walcott proceeded to correlation. Miles-thick sequences with few key marker beds made correlation a formidable task. Had these been marine Paleozoic rocks containing fossils, the job would have been straightforward. Although Walcott does not actually state it, he did use what was available to him in terms of occurrences of "Beltina" and stromatolites, the strange cabbage heads in certain limestones to correlate. Half a century later, Russian paleontologists excited the geological world by using these algal buildups in Siberia for Precambrian correlation.

> The Dearborn section provided Walcott enough continuity to correlate: 1) the Helena with the Siyeh of Glacier National Park; 2) the Greyson, Spokane and Empire formations of the Helena area with the Appekunny and Grinnell of Glacier National Park; and the Newland formation of the Belt Mountains with the Altyn of Glacier National Park, truly a brilliant accomplishment. Walcott also correlated the Ravalli series with the Burke, Revett and St. Regis formations of the Coeur d'Alene district; the carbonate Blackfoot series with the Wallace of the Coeur d'Alene district; and the lower part of the Camp Creek series with the Striped Peak formation of the Coeur d'Alene district, another largely correct, significant contribution. Unfortunately at the same time, Walcott miscorrelated the Wallace-Blackfoot carbonate intervals with the Newland limestone. (Winston 1986, 2)

Anyone who drives in the West knows that Montana is not as large as Texas, but at times it seems like it. Brilliant was the word for such long-distance correlations, and one cannot hope to get everything correct the first time.

Collen wrote from Montana:

> My trip with you last summer in the northern Rockies has given me a broader view of the Algonkian rocks of the West; but I am more fully convinced now than ever that a fuller and clearer conception of the pre-Cambrian times is to be had by a more careful study of the rocks of the Belt Mts. than from anything I saw further north.
>
> In both the Big Belt and the Little Belt Mts. there is conclusive evidence of profound *pre-Cambrian faulting* and subsequent erosion of the Algonkian formations. . . . I hope you will be able to visit this locality again in the near future and thereby get a more comprehensive idea of the conditions prevailing in these early times.[6]

However, there was much that Walcott had to do outside of being a geologist. At a November meeting of the CIW Ex. Com., Mitchell, Billings, Gilman, Wright, Root, and Woodward were present. A majority would be sympathetic toward Walcott's ideas and since December of last year, Wright had been chairman of the committee. No longer was Billings running roughshod over Gilman. Root was a strong voice in Walcott's corner, and Woodward was as good a president as Walcott had hoped for. Woodward had not been Carnegie's choice, but when he was elected, Walcott expressed his satisfaction to Carnegie, and Carnegie expressed his satisfaction that Walcott was pleased.

Charles Doolittle Walcott, Paleontologist

After its first year of operation, the CIW began funding buildings, with a desert station in Arizona, and, later, the Dry Tortugas facility in the Florida Keys, but it was a giant step away from those structures to a full-fledged major laboratory, though that too was coming at Cold Springs Harbor, Maine. In the congressional appropriations hearings of January, Walcott had noted that the CIW had given twenty thousand dollars to assist the Geological Survey in its chemical and physical laboratories. Now was the time to reach for big money. Under Woodward, the publication program burgeoned, and the tide of the CIW turned toward large projects, notwithstanding that some individuals were supported.

Woodward was a strong executive, running the CIW in proper fashion. Walcott commented, "I do not know of anything that is to come up at the meeting of the Executive Committee on December 11. All matters now come through the President, so that I have no information in advance, that is not known to other members of the Committee."[7] That may not be as straightforward as it seems, for Walcott would not have tendered his resignation as secretary to Billings unless the Geophysical Laboratory was assured.

"The great demand made upon my time and energy in connection with my official work and certain research work that I am carrying on, has necessitated my withdrawing from active duties in connection with a number of organizations, the duties of which individually make relatively small demands, but in the aggregate interfere seriously with the principal main work I have in hand."[8] All may have been quite true, for he never spoke to the Washington Academy about the paper on India, and likewise his Precambrian correlation efforts were presented at the GSA meeting by title only.

At the CIW Trustees meeting in December, Walcott spoke forcefully on the need for the laboratory:

> Work was started two years ago, and has been going on very favorably under unfavorable auspices at the Geological Survey. The auspices, I say are unfavorable because the laboratories there are quite unsuitable. Think of putting a laboratory which needs stability on the fourth floor of a building. And the rooms are very much crowded. Now, it seems to me the Trustees should decide one way or another what they will do in regard to this, and they should either abandon the work entirely or sustain it and provide adequate facilities and quarters for it.[9]

Carnegie was present at the morning session, but not in the afternoon, when a vote was taken. Walcott wrote Carnegie a few days later:

I went home Tuesday evening in a very happy frame of mind. This came about as a result of a very harmonious and successful meeting. . . . Dr. Woodward showed himself to be a leader. . . . I do not know whether you have been informed that it was voted to purchase a suitable site for the administration building. . . . Also that authority was granted, and the money appropriated, to purchase a suitable site for a geo-physical laboratory, and erect thereon a laboratory and provide for its equipment, $150,000 being appropriated for the purpose.[10]

Carnegie was shocked:

Yours of December 16th received. I had heard of the money appropriated for administration building, but had not heard of the large physical laboratory. You know my own opinion is that no big institution should be erected anywhere, but the exceptional men should be encouraged to do their exceptional work in their own environment.

There is nothing so deadening as gathering together a staff in an institution. Dry rot and routine kills original work. At least that is the opinion of
Yours very truly, Andrew Carnegie.[11]

Walcott fired back a letter, pointing out that Arthur L. Day was an exceptional man, exactly the kind that Carnegie wanted to support, and that eighty thousand dollars was the "cost for plant to do work and not for the purpose of erecting a building which has not been well planned and thought out." Walcott wrote on, noting precedents of the CIW providing facilities for exceptional men. "This is, as I understand it, the spirit of your great gift for research."[12]

Few ever dared call Carnegie to task, but Walcott did not give an inch Carnegie backed down and had his secretary reply: "Mr. Carnegie desires me to say that he is much pleased with your explanatory note and as he understands it the laboratory will remain the property of the Institution."[13] The laird was leaving for the south and was too busy to write, but conveyed his cordial greetings for the season; the two men remained close.

Obtaining the Geophysical Laboratory was a near thing, for by the next year, Woodward was pointing out that the CIW could not support all it was committed to, let alone take on new projects. With any further delay, the Geophysical Laboratory might not have materialized. The finest thing that Walcott did for the science of geology was save the USGS from destruction in the 1890s. The second finest was to bulldoze his way though meeting after meeting and garner this world-class facility. In a nutshell, the geewhiz lab changed the way geologists thought about inner workings of the earth (Servos 1983).

Charles Doolittle Walcott, Paleontologist

Walcott, the secretary to private money, had grand success. Walcott, the government administrator, had aggravations bound up in the Government Printing Office. He spoke to the printer, appeared before a committee of the Interior Department, got Hitchcock to send a letter to the printer, and ultimately spoke to the printer again to smooth feelings.

Several times in December, Walcott called on the president; once he took Charlie to meet him. At other times, he was involved with Assistant Secretary of State Bacon and the international ramifications of the Milk River irrigation project. Notwithstanding that, the year was pretty much under control. "The close of 1905 finds my wife Helena and our four children, Charles, Sidney, Stuart & Helen all well & happy. The event of the year with us was moving into our home Jany 11*th*" (December 31, 1905).

Before the traditional New Year's Day visit to the White House, Walcott went to the USGS to sort out some papers. After seeing Roosevelt, he stopped to visit Root, Taft, and one or two other cabinet members. As with so many events, increase in government size and increase in tempo of life gradually made the quaint custom of New Year's Day calls archaic. With opening year formalities completed, the next day Walcott spent a few minutes on the Chinese Cambrian fossils before Schuchert of Yale dropped in for a chat. Later, he visited the Public Printer again and in a couple of days was before the Joint Committee on Printing. The Geological Survey wanted quality printing, which is a reasonable request. The Geological Survey wanted prompt publication, which was also a reasonable request. The two together were something else. In general, the Public Printer provided adequate to good quality, but speed varied from slow to glacial. Even protests at congressional committees did not speed the presses.

Walcott spent a few of hours here and there on brachiopods, but one day he had to see Hitchcock about the Salt River project, and the next day about the St. Marys–Milk River project. The Reclamation Service was eating up more and more of his time. Almost for relaxation, and perhaps to make up for not presenting a talk at the GSA meeting in December, Walcott spoke to the Geological Society of Washington on the Algonkian rocks in Montana. Walcott seldom produced a paper without giving a talk on the subject, and he seldom spoke twice on the same subject.

Walcott went before the House Appropriations Subcommittee to tell them of USGS investigations in Alaska and about black sands, grains of dark, heavy minerals concentrated along a shore by wave and current sorting. The appearance went so well that the next day, he "Secured an hour on Cambrian fauna & then busy with administrative work" (January 12, 1906). A few days later, he "Completed descriptions of Cambrian fossils of China. Next correlation & comparisons of faunas" (January 16, 1906).

One evening of note was at the National Society of Fine Arts, followed by half an hour at the White House. Presumably this was a social event without Roosevelt wanting to talk about irrigation. It was off to New York again, where Walcott had a conversation with Billings prior to a meeting of the George Washington Memorial Association. The hoped-for building had not materialized, and perhaps with Billings's assistance he might rejuvenate the project. Then it was back to Washington, and "At survey except for two hours at the office of Secty of Interior. Busy with administrative matters & for an hour on Chinese Cambrian fossils" (January 24, 1906). Walcott was a man who could shift gears in a hurry, another factor in his success.

Irrigation kept bringing up new problems, partly from visiting delegations who wanted consideration for pet projects, and partly from works in progress. It was a pleasure in February to get away to New York for a couple of days. Walcott returned with Osborn and had him present a lecture. Irrigation on the Rio Grande came up, followed by the annual meeting the University Club at which Walcott presided. There was never a free moment.

By catching a night train to New York immediately after that meeting, Walcott was able to spend the next day with Charlie at the Bronx Zoo. They dined with L. L. Nunn, who was to employ Charlie in the summer, and, after the meeting of the CIW Ex. Com., dined with him again. Once Walcott returned to Washington, the Arizona Canal brought problems to his office.

Congress was into its session and a revolt against Speaker Cannon had been crushed, but there was little harmony on Capitol Hill. Seemingly this had no effect on Walcott, who stole a couple more hours for his beloved brachiopods. At the annual University Club dinner, the featured speaker was the president of Princeton University, Woodrow Wilson.

Near the end of the month, Walcott spent an afternoon with Roosevelt. Later that night he returned to speak with the president and Pinchot about administration of the Reclamation Service. The context is not clear, but because forest growth helped control erosion, it almost followed that the boss of the forests also ought to be the boss of the waters, if one reads the character of Pinchot correctly.

Whatever was discussed at the White House, news the next day directed Walcott's attention elsewhere: "Prof. S. P. Langley, Secty of Smithsonian Institution

Charles Doolittle Walcott, Paleontologist

dies at Aitkin, S.C." (February 27, 1906). The 1903 failure of his aerodrome had been a terrible blow. Several times thereafter when Henry Adams had Langley to dinner, Adams commented on how distraught the man looked. In 1905, the institution treasurer was discovered to be an embezzler, and that may have been the final straw speeding Langley's decline. He asked to be excused from attending the regents' meeting in January and hoped that a warmer climate would help. It had not.

There are lots of stories about the imperious and absent-minded professor. He got in his carriage one day and ordered the driver to head south. Langley became involved in watching the flight of a flock of birds and when the carriage stopped, he shouted to drive on. The driver pointed out that if he drove on they would be in the river, and Langley is supposed to have replied that if that was the case, the driver should turn left. Another time, he stormed around the office looking for his hat and it was ten minutes before a clerk had the courage to tell Secretary Langley it was on his head.

Walcott spoke to the employees of the Smithsonian, and he was a pall bearer at Langley's funeral. Eleven months later, Walcott would succeed Langley, but this event was not obvious at the time. When the regents met in March, after some debate, they voted to delay selection of a secretary until the regular December meeting.

In March, Walcott noted three meetings at the White House; Pinchot was at each. Two separate investigations of the coal industry were being conducted at the time and a reasonable surmise is that this subjects was discussed. Both investigations reached the conclusion that the railroads owned much of the coal fields and controlled the price. Apart from a dinner at the Gridiron Club, where the politicians twit one another, and a few odd moments to work on brachiopods, nothing extraordinary seemed to have occurred in the last half of March.

If there was a hallmark to April, it was "A busy day at the Survey. Many people call and matters of administration are up for consideration every day at this, the busiest season of the year" (April 2, 1906). Today, the Executive Branch goes on about its business and the Legislative Branch goes on about its business, in some administrations each seemingly nearly oblivious of the other, but in past times the rhythm of the congressional session orchestrated the activities of the executive bureaus. There were a couple of White House meetings, actually followed by a quiet day in which a few minutes were spent back in the Cambrian. At the Boone and Crockett Club dinner Theodore Roosevelt orated on the American Bison. Quiet time ended.

Walcott spent three days testifying at the appropriations hearings in mid-April, his longest time ever on the grill. He was questioned about two Pension Office clerks who had been detailed to the USGS for years. Questions followed over the need for a librarian in a library not open to the public and concern as to what a cataloguer did. Why were four photographers needed?. When the representatives got to paleontology, Walcott told of studies in Indiana when he a young man. State Geologist E. T. Cox examined coal seams and fossils in Ohio and Illinois and from that data determined the depth to the coal seams in his state.

The committee was upset that money from a new fiscal year was spent the last few days of the old fiscal year; Walcott explained three or four times about estimating expenses for field parties. Topographic mapping, and especially the cooperative program with some states, upset Representative Smith, who wondered that richer states, unlike Nevada, would be mapped, whereas "the possibility of the development of Nevada is largely lost sight of, and only those things surveyed where private enterprise has already made discovery?" Walcott replied,

> I would not like to put a personal statement in here, but in 1896 I left Carson, Nev., and personally made a reconnaissance down through what is now known as the great gold belt, traveling in the desert for two succeeding summers—one summer six weeks, and another of two months. In the fall of 1896 I gave out a newspaper account—a statement which was published—that that was the future gold belt, and that prospecting would probably be rewarded there more than elsewhere. Also at a banquet given me in the city of Carson, Nev. I made the same statement. Shortly after that (whether from that or not I cannot say) prospecting was extended into that region, and soon afterwards these discoveries began to be made. And we send men in that manner, making what we call reconnaissance surveys, in advance of maps, topographic and geologic, and indicating in their reports where it is probable that mineral values will be found so far as they can determine from the geological condition and the reconnaissance. (Walcott 1906b, 485)

Characteristically, Walcott was quick on his feet and could produce right answers to tough questions, or at least deflect them. While the grilling proceeded, the National Academy assembled and the Walcotts entertained 225 people at a reception. Instead of attending scientific meetings, Walcott attended the manifold questions raised by Representatives.

The great San Francisco earthquake hit at 8:30 A.M. Eastern Standard Time. Walcott telegraphed Robert Marshall, in charge of the western topographic division, to move all camp equipment in the Sacramento warehouse to the stricken city. Marshall took a boatload of supplies and became head of the General Relief Committee. For months thereafter, geologists, particularly Gilbert, investigated the disaster. If the earthquake was to occur anyway, it could have struck a few days earlier when Walcott was testifying to Congress.

After the National Academy left, Walcott and Helena went to Philadelphia for the American Philosophical Society meeting, a special affair this year celebrating the two-hundredth anniversary of the birth of founder Benjamin Franklin; Walcott was a member of the planning committee. Once home they had Professor Chamberlin as a house guest. Walcott returned to the Capitol Hill and the appropriations subcommittee. Another White House and State Department call concerning irrigation and April was nearly done.

Walcott was nearly done also, starting May with a chill and a cross temper. Working at home on Cambrian brachiopods and a visit from Van Hise were the tonics he needed. Not only was he up to par for the CIW Ex. Com. meeting, he and Helena gave the group a dinner. Several days later, Walcott even "Put in 6 hours on Cambrian brachiopods" (May 10, 1906).

Once more he went up Capitol Hill. The USGS needed its own building, and congressional action for construction requires a great deal of effort quite apart from the annual appropriation. There were remarkably few government buildings in Washington before the first World War. Preliminary lobbying must have gone smoothly, for the afternoon was devoted to the brachiopods. A couple days later, the family passed a milestone: "Charlie left 5:30 P.M. for Provo, Utah to report to Mr. L. L. Nunn" (May 14, 1906). His namesake had a real job.

For two weeks after Charlie left, life was fairly quiet. Only one visit to the White House was necessary during this interval. Walcott made a business call on Root, who after the death of John Hay, moved from secretary of war to secretary of state, but otherwise there was little to note. The tranquil period gave no indication of future difficulties. "Decoration Day. Spent the day at the office. The bill carrying Geological Survey appropriations was reported with $300,000 reduction. Must get busy—and work on restoration" (May 30, 1906).

In the face of this looming problem, Walcott still could write to a Canadian colleague, "As you learned from my letter to Mr. Walker I am about to publish the report upon the Brachiopoda which has been under way for the past eight years. . . . With the exception of the genus Acrothele the text is completed, but I do not expect to be in a position to take up that genus until after the first of July."[14] Walcott was not a man who panicked.

The deepest cut from the committee was in stream gauging; Congress used the accepted spelling, but those in the Survey still did gaging.

The real cause may be attributed to the persistent lobbying which had been carried on by Survey members, beginning with Powell's administration.... Walcott ... realized the unfavorable impression that had been created ... and prohibited lobbying.... During the latter years of his administration, however, Walcott relaxed his strict attitude and the branch chiefs became active in pressing the claims of their respective activities.... Tawney of Minnesota, who was serving his first year as chairman of the committee, [was] resentful of Walcott's success in building up the Survey. They were, therefore, anxious to curb him. (Follensbee 1938, 181)

The story is more complicated and included organization of a new Congress, discontented with Speaker Cannon (Rabbitt 1986, 181). Walcott was a favorite of "Uncle Joe," and the cut in part may have been directed against the House leadership. Matters became worse where a point of order was raised on the floor against gaging—pardon, gauging—as studying water was not mentioned in the 1879 founding of the USGS. Not until 1909 did a friendly congressman adroitly manipulate the rules through two points of order to establish that water was a mineral and therefore legally could be studied by the Geological Survey.

By day, Walcott called on representatives at their offices and called at their homes by night, virtually nonstop. Yet a week later the main excitement for Walcott was "My monograph on Cambrian brachiopods was for'd to the Department—104 plates 1400 pgs of mss" (June 8, 1906). Overall, it was "A quiet uneventful week—sultry & rainy by showers" (June 9, 1906). The USGS was facing its worst crisis since Walcott took over, and he was savoring the moment of submitting this massive manuscript. "Enjoyment" does not convey what goes through a future author's mind, when such a load of manuscript is shifted to others.

Indeed, once it was submitted, Walcott "Resumed usual work at Geological Survey office. Called at Government Printing Office 11 A.M." (June 11, 1906). There is nothing like talking to a printer to change euphoria to reality. About this time Collen sent in half a ton of stromatolites from the Precambrian of Montana. Walcott was pleased to have the fossils, although this was hardly the moment to worry about moving and storing these specimens, none of which was small.

Walcott's call on the printer initiated a busy week. He spent three days talking to various senators and to President Roosevelt. The brachiopods received a few hours, indicating that some crisis management had been accomplished. Indeed, Walcott went overnight to New York and met with E. C. Harriman. who owned the Southern Pacific Railway. Granted that Walcott had a patent on a railroad spike, the odds are quite high that was not the reason for the visit. Harriman had shown lavish support for a scientific expedition on the Alaska cruise a few years earlier. Walcott was probably laying the ground for a donation, be it a building for the National Academy of Sciences or the Washington Memorial Institution, or direct support of a scientific project.

After this trip, Walcott stole half a day at home for the brachiopods before showing up at the office. Next he "Attended conference at the White House 9:30–10:15 P.M. President Roosevelt, Secretary of Interior Hitchcock, Senator Frank P. Flint of California, Gifford Pinchot & CDW" (June 23, 1906). With a Saturday night meeting at the White House, Roosevelt obviously had something on his mind. This gathering surely must have been related to conservation, for two years later Flint was deeply involved in the National Conservation Committee.

Sunday was hot, Monday was hot, and Tuesday was hot. If there was a chance to leave the sweatbox on the Potomac, no one stayed, and this weather was the final spur. "Congress adjourned P.M. As a whole the Survey has come out in good shape despite determined attacks upon it. *Hot!*" (June 30, 1906). Walcott had friends in the House who used the point of order ploy to benefit the organization, and staunch supporters in the Senate (Rabbitt 1986, 42–45). There may have been a muted cheer from the ranks that things were not worse.

Roosevelt made life worse by ordering an investigation of coal on public lands. Since no one knew what coal was present, almost immediately Secretary Hitchcock withdrew a large amount of public land. A few older Survey members recalled a comparable withdrawal for irrigation and what it had done to Powell.

Even with Congress adjourned, the new fiscal year began on as hot a day as when that year ended; Washington summertime heat may not be unique, but it is unforgettable. Fortunately, the other Walcotts were away: Charlie was in Grace, Idaho, and Helena with her tribe was to arrive in Provo, Utah, the following day. For a few days, it was quiet both at home and at the USGS. The Reclamation Service was being disentangled from the Geological Survey. Newell gave up his position as chief hydrologist at the start of this new fiscal year to devote full time to being chief engineer. In effect, Walcott was now the only official tie to the Geological Survey, and the change made life easier for the director. It was so quiet in Washington that Walcott was able to put in undisturbed time on his brachiopods. At midmonth he reported, "Many survey matters & the attempt to finish up the descriptive matter of the brachiopod monograph keeps me very busy" (July 14, 1906).

More activity on brachiopods is hard to understand, since Walcott had already submitted his manuscript to the secretary of the interior. Walcott knew how long it would be before the manuscript of the *Monograph* moved a next step, and he kept adding new information to another copy. He would not be the first author to submit an unfinished manuscript to gain a little time in the editorial queue. Be that as it may, description of species can be tedious, as one tries to explain subtle difference in shape for which language is ill adapted. Ultimately it becomes drudgery to complete the descriptions, but much more of science is drudgery than the general public realizes. Walcott kept at the work, and less than a week later, he "Completed descriptive work on species of Cambrian *Acrothele* at 5 P.M." (July 19, 1906).

The next morning, Walcott headed west before another memorandum or another collection could arrive on his desk. Four days later, he was examining dry farming methods in Nebraska in connection with an irrigation project on the North Platte River; the Platte has been described as a mile wide and six inches deep. Two days later, delayed by train wrecks on the line, Walcott was in Salt Lake City, where he made plans with Weeks and Burling. He went down to Provo, saw Helena and the children, saw Senator Smoot, saw a power plant, and saw Mr. Nunn; Sidney had grown to where he too could be given a real job, so he was left in Nunn's charge for the season. Before month's end, the reduced Walcott family was encamped in Logan Canyon.

Walcott was immediately out on the rocks, but at first it was more to supervise Weeks and Burling than really perform all the section measuring. He worked on his manuscript and on the mail. Summaries for the *Annual Report* came in, and estimates for next year were prepared; Walcott had the papers headed back east in less than a week. "Have made considerable progress with MSS. but there is much yet to done" (August 11, 1906).

Charlie came into camp for a visit, and a Utah congressman dropped by. It was a happy camp and restful after the struggles with the appropriation. Fishing in the Wasatch Mountains could not compare to that of the Finger Lakes in New York a few years earlier, but, conversely, with so many Cambrian trilobites at hand, Logan Canyon was an excellent spot. The tents were adjacent to the outcrops and fossil collecting was an occupation for the younger children.

Rain delayed fieldwork for three days, but following several more days of examining the rocks, measuring the section, and collecting, Walcott "Reached summit of upper Cambrian 4. P.M.—It is a good section but unfortunately is cut off in places by great masses of arenaceous limestone in wh-[ich] no traces of fossils except annelid borings occur" (August 25, 1906). By the time Walcott published details of the sixty-six-hundred-foot section, descriptions of the rock types and thicknesses were augmented by nearly three dozen faunal lists compiled from the collections they obtained.

Just before month's end, Nunn and several people from Westinghouse Electric Company arrived. The relationship between dams the Reclamation Service was building in the West and the prospects for generation of electricity was perfectly obvious. Walcott and these worthies, with Charlie tagging along, left for Bear Lake on the Utah-Idaho border. They looked at the lake outlet, moved to Montpelier, and then on to admire Nunn's Telluride Power Plant at Grace. The group headed north to Soda Springs and caught a train to Boise.

In spite of having arrived at 4:30 A.M., that afternoon Walcott gave a talk to the Fourteenth National Irrigation Conference on "Relation of government reclamation work to private enterprise." It was a subject bound to attract attention, and one that required an adroit political hand. He spoke first of the Salt River Project in which the government had purchased some of the existing canals and dams:

> The administration of the reclamation service considers the reclamation fund a trust fund and that it is answerable to the people for its wise and economic expenditure. Knowing that the cost of each and every project must ultimately be paid by the settlers, and the price won from the soil by hard labor, it has resolutely antagonized all attempts of corporations, individuals, or their attorneys, to obtain more than a fair price. (Walcott 1906c, 50)

Major Powell, whether in heaven or hell, must have beamed.

Walcott went on to a project turned over to private enterprise, and then moved into forestry efforts, emphasizing the relationship between siltation and irrigation. This was long before the days where clear cutting decimated the forests. He mentioned the USGS hydrographic branch, and told the Irrigation Congress: "The line of demarcation between the geological survey and the reclamation service was sharply drawn on July 1, 1906, the director of the Geological Survey, and its chief disbursing officer only occupying similar positions in the reclamation service. It is not improbable that within a short time the two organizations will be completely separated" (Walcott 1906c, 53).

Walcott sent his remarks to Hitchcock with observations on the congress: "Senator Heyburn and a few disappointed people showed a somewhat ugly spirit toward the Reclamation Service, but when it came to a final show down in the discussion in the evening on the subject of forestry, Senator Heyburn was roundly hissed by the large audience present, and it was evident that the Congress was in sympathetic touch with the administration of the Reclamation Service."[15]

The Irrigation Congress ended with a trip to a new dam near Boise. Then it was back to Logan by train and into camp. With the accumulated mail and a conference with J. A. Holmes, who came to camp to discuss the future of the coal-testing plant in St. Louis, there was not much time to collect fossils. They finally broke camp and went to Laketown, Utah, at the southern end of Bear Lake. Arthur and the camp wagon failed to make it in, so the party spent the night in a hotel. For Helena, it had been more than a month since she was under a roof.

Driving through snow flurries, they went twenty miles north to Fish Haven, just into Idaho on the western side of the lake. The next day it was to Paris, which has the distinction of being a county seat, but not much else to commend it. R. C. Spence, from just over the line in Evanston, Wyoming, joined them. He had given his name to Spence Canyon, ten miles west of Paris, where Arthur made camp. The canyon became the type locality for the Spence Shale, a unit in which Spence had found some remarkable fossils which he first sent to Walcott in 1896.

Trilobites were present in abundance, but one indication of the administrative pressure that Walcott was under is that these fossils languished in the National Museum for years before a study was published. "Shortly after the large collections were made from Spence Gulch in 1906, illustrations of the more conspicuous elements of the fauna were prepared" (Resser 1939, 2). Walcott included some of the material in later papers, but most of the fossils were undisturbed for three decades. Recent work described remarkably preserved soft-bodied forms from this unit.

The first morning in the new camp, ice was an inch thick on the water pail, but fortunately the tents were only a few hundred yards from the outcrop. The weather steadily improved and for nearly a week Walcott and Burling engaged in what can only be described as an orgy of collecting. Finally, they had to wrap fossils and pack boxes. "Broke camp & moved to Franklin on the Oregon Short Line R. R. A rough drive on Paris road. We tipped over once & later broke a wheel—No one hurt. Arrived in Franklin at 8:30 P.M. tired, dusty & hungry" (September 25, 1906). Fortunately, at Franklin the hard traveling was over.

It was the end of the season for Helena. Walcott had a conference in Salt Lake City and then accompanied her to Provo, where Sidney was collected. The family went on to Denver and home; after looking at a new power plant, Walcott returned to Salt Lake City. Following another quick conference on irrigation matters, he went north to Malad City, Idaho, and walked out to Two Mile Canyon, where Burling and Arthur were camped. He had the mail out of the way by Saturday, and on Sunday, Walcott was "out on south side of canyon all day looking over section I measured in 1898" (September 30, 1906). It was late in the season, and the general rule of no fieldwork on Sunday had to bend occasionally.

Possibly as a result of the chilly weather, there was a change in field gear since 1898. A geologist who worked in the region many years later was told by a farmer of a Mr. Walcott. He was alone and worried about rattlesnakes, for this is snake country. Walcott put a section of stovepipe on each leg and apparently the clanking when he walked could be heard for miles. This is a funny story, but probably it is true. Being alone is the field always has an element of risk. A thickness of stovepipe would have stopped any cottonmouth, no matter how upset he was at an intruder pounding on rocks.

Without stovepipes on their legs, the first of October Walcott and Burling were on the outcrop for eleven hours and almost as long the following day. They had rain on the trip southwest to Samaria, Idaho, another virtually nonexistent place. The rain stopped, but it was a forty mile drive to Elwood, Utah. Arthur and the team did not arrive until 8:00 P.M. This area near Brigham City is essentially the foothills of the Wasatch Range and the time spent there augmented the section established earlier. By October 10, they were all back in Logan, Burling and Arthur to take care of the gear and then head east, Walcott to head west.

Geologist Walcott became Chief of Reclamation Service Walcott. He examined construction around Fallon, Nevada. It was on to Hazen and the line of the Truckee-Carson Canal; a dam was going in on the Truckee River. Nevada is a peculiar place to fish, but it had been a long time since Walcott wet a line, so he examined more of the watery habitat. Nevada was really just a pause on the way to California. He examined a gold dredge near Maryville before descending on the politicians in Sacramento.

Conservation, or economics, or trust-busting, or however different schools of history characterize Theodore Roosevelt, was going full blast. Walcott wrote Hayes: "Your letter on the situation in relation to the withdrawal of coal land received. I am very glad to learn that the president has taken such positive action, and the examinations under Dr. Campbell's direction have progressed so favorably."[16] The letter was wildly optimistic, for classifying coal lands was to occupy the USGS for years.

Several days later, Walcott was in the vicinity of Mount Shasta checking a reservoir site. The next stop was Klamath Falls, embarking there on steamer across the lake. He inspected another canal and looked at another working dredge. Walcott ended up in Thrall, Oregon, and had a fine view of the Siskiyou Mountains while going to Portland. From Portland, the trip was eastward to home and hearth, though he paused in Helena, Montana, and again in Williston, North Dakota, on irrigation business. Walcott collected mail in Chicago and spent the last part of the trip answering letters.

The day following Walcott's return, he briefed Interior Secretary Hitchcock and the president. Walcott learned that Hitchcock planned to retire in March. The man was in his seventies, and after eight years he had lasted longer than most secretaries. James Garfield, commissioner of corporations and a member of Roosevelt's "tennis cabinet," was to succeed him, Walcott told him of irrigation matters, and especially how much time it took to run the Reclamation Service. The two were longtime friends and became closer through the years. The next day was election day; Walcott "Worked on Cambrian brachiopods at home" (November 6, 1906).

After letters, conferences, and a tiny little bit of work on brachiopods, Walcott went to Boston for the fall meeting of the National Academy. He listened to a few papers and took time to look at fossils in the Museum of Comparative Zoology. Walcott stopped in New Haven to see Schuchert. He was often a master of timing, or was lucky, or both, and again was in the right place at the right time for the Yale-Harvard football game.

It was good to be home and settled for the remainder of November. Before Thanksgiving, Walcott spoke with Richard Rathbun at the museum as to what might be transpiring with the Smithsonian Board of Regents. It seems unlikely that Walcott was aiming for Langley's position. The extended western trip was a poor time to be away if he was trying to lobby the regents.

In fact, when Walcott returned, his prime concern was not the next Smithsonian secretary, but how best to contend with a public embarrassment. Years earlier, John C. Branner of Stanford University simultaneously had been state geologist of Arkansas, until that survey was abolished in 1893. Preliminary information on state coal beds was released, though maps had not been published when the legislature ended the operation. Branner, employed part time by the USGS and Washington headquarters in 1902, discussed publication of the maps by the Geological Survey at a reduced scale.

Matters languished until January 1906, when Hayes, under Walcott's signature, revived it. Letters were exchanged, with each side becoming more strident. Branner resigned and Walcott replied, in effect asking him to cool off, and presented reasons why the USGS should remap the area. Branner let matters sit from March until late October and then sent all correspondence and his long reply to Walcott to the journal *Science:*

> The above facts make it plain that the true explanation of your course in this matter is not frankly set forth in your three letters. The real reason must be sought elsewhere, and I know of no place to look for them save in the general policy of the U. S. Geological Survey as reflected in its attitude toward the geologists of the country since the present director came into office.
>
> The attitude of the survey toward the geologists of the country has come to be simply intolerable. (Branner 1906, 536)

Six weeks later, Walcott responded with several columns of print: "Not only professional courtesy but also personal regard prompted the offer of cooperation made to Dr. Branner. . . . But I deny his charge that the survey is an undemocratic organization which abuses its power to the disadvantage of state surveys or of individual geologists" (Walcott 1906d, 693). In the same issue, Branner published a long letter which Walcott had written him early in November and his refutation of the points Walcott presented: "Mr. Walcott does 'not think anything is to be gained by a public controversy.' Perhaps not; but it certain that nothing is to be gained by an appeal to courtesy or by a private controversy with a public bureau that has the whip-hand of every working geologist in America" (Branner 1906a, 725).

"Furthermore, this same policy [wholesale discrimination against the universities] is already being put into active operation in the Carnegie Institution and Mr. Walcott is now a candidate for the position of secretary of the Smithsonian Institution, where he could be counted upon to put it in still further practice" (Branner 1906a, 728). The last letter from Walcott, which Branner had made public, mentioned a professor by name and Walcott immediately rushed into print to state that the man was an excellent geologist and ended the exchange with an indirect dig at Branner: "A further point in his favor, and one highly appreciated, is that his results are submitted when promised" (Walcott 1907). Humorist Josh Billings commented that mosquitoes must be a luxury of life, as they were not a necessity, and Walcott may have felt the same about

Branner. Nevertheless, the quarrel was patched up, for a few years later Branner helped organize the Seismological Society of America and was one of the persons who sponsored Walcott.

> In December 1906, Walcott submitted his resignation as Director of the Reclamation Service, but Secretary Hitchcock asked him to stay until the new Secretary assumed office. Within the Survey, Walcott was busy with a full-scale investigation of the Topographic Branch, precipitated by a complaint of discrimination by a member of the Eastern Division, and at the same time arranging a meeting of the State geologists of the Atlantic Coast states, who seemed not to share Prof. Branner's distrust of the Survey, to plan a cooperative survey with special reference to the ground water resources of the Atlantic Coastal Plain. (Rabbitt 1986, 51)

That excellent summary for the last of the year may be amplified by a letter to secretary of the Geological Society of America which provides information on his scientific activities and on his state of mind:

> I have had eighty plates of my Cambrian Brachiopoda memoir brought together on twenty lantern slides. I think some members of the G. S. A. would be interested in seeing them and in hearing what points have already been secured from the study of Cambrian Brachiopoda. If there is room on the program, and you think best, will you not put me down for twenty minutes, as per the accompanying slip.
>
> I am thinking of asking the State Geologists and those interested in the development of geological work to have an informal discussion over the matter brought up by the Branner correspondence. What we need evidently is constructive criticism, not destructive personalities. My great aim since I started work as a boy was to do the best scientific work that I could and advance the interests of scientific men and educational work. If Branner is correct I have evidently failed to a large extent. On this account I should like to get the benefit of unprejudiced opinion where the general welfare and the advancement of scientific interest in America are the motives.[17]

An event of more significance than Cambrian brachiopods or geological tiffs occurred December 7, though it took a few days for Washington to be embroiled. As a result of incredibly poor engineering, the Colorado River broke though an embankment and was drowning part of the Imperial Valley in southern California. The Salton Sea, a watery remnant of an interior drainage basin below sea level, suddenly was becoming larger each day.

Charles Doolittle Walcott, Paleontologist

Unaware of California difficulties, early in December, Walcott delivered an address in memory of the late Secretary Langley; another evening was devoted to the Newfoundland Slate Company. He spent a day at a meeting of the National Advisory Board on Fuels and Structural Materials. At the St. Louis Exposition, a company set up a cement-testing laboratory comparable to the USGS coal-testing facility. When the fair closed, the cement lab was donated to the Geological Survey. Walcott got money appropriated to test more cement in 1905 and 1906. This was stretching the bonds of Survey activity, though the Reclamation Service was using ton after ton of the material and scientific study of good and bad cement was critical. The board evolved from these two labs. Walcott did not want tests indefinitely, but meanwhile useful information was obtained which was at least tangential to geology. Next, he attended the Ex. Com. and the annual meeting of the CIW, important although not so critical as last year.

A more significant meeting than CIW Trustees was that of the Smithsonian Institution Board of Regents. For months, they pondered the matter Langley's replacement. On December 4, they decided upon Henry Fairfield Osborn, vertebrate paleontologist at the American Museum of Natural History. Like so many people, Osborn was a complex character. Words used to describe him are "autocratic" and "highly ambitious" (Rainger 1991). Osborn received congratulations, one of the first being from Assistant Secretary Rathbun.

"This morning the Board of Regents, in the full possession of its senses, elected you *Secretary* of the Smithsonian Institution. You will receive the notification from the Chief Justice who is the Chancellor. . . . What I mean when I said the Regents were in the full possession of their senses was that they did the one good thing that was in their power."[18] Roosevelt offered congratulations, as did others in Washington. Charles Schuchert stated he had repeatedly asked Walcott to "stand for the appointment," but congratulated Osborn. One letter is to "My dear Osborn," handwritten by Walcott from the Cosmos Club:

I am on the fence as to whether to urge you to accept the Smithsonian Secretaryship. For the Smithsonian, yes. For the interests of your great work, no. You are preëminately fitted for the Secretaryship and I am glad that the Regents recognized it, but when I look ahead and see what must be done to bring the Institution and its bureaus up to date so as to make all a strong influence for the advancement of scientific interests, governmental and private, I feel as I told you in Boston that your great work will suffer. It is up to you to decide. We will all welcome you here heartily and sincerely. Personally I can think of nothing better than to have you and Mrs. Osborn in Washington.

Today I am happy at the tho't of being relieved of the "Reclamation Service." This may occur in a few days. I can then devote more time to the Survey and my Cambrian work.

Now I must go up to the Capitol and see what can be done about getting a bill put thru for the Survey building.[19]

Osborn did not have to think too hard about the offer. Supplementing all the support he received from the American Museum was a private salary arrangement with J. P. Morgan. Morgan did not want him to leave. Furthermore, in Washington he could not command the personal power and work force he had to pursue vertebrate paleontology on the lines he dictated. Osborn promoted himself as much as he promoted the science, and that would not be so feasible in Washington. By December 11, Osborn declined, and the issue of the next secretary was wide open. Nothing of a talk with Osborn at the fall meeting of the Academy in Boston, nor the regents meeting, nor Osborn's decision is in Walcott's diary. The main event the day the regents met for him was "Secured a few moments for brachiopods" (December 4, 1906).

In mid-December Walcott had "A busy day at Survey. Saw President Roosevelt twice in relation to Colorado River break into Salton Sea. Also requested relief from administration of Reclamation Service. With Helena attended dinner of National Geographic Society 7–11:30 P.M." (December 15, 1906).

With the Salton Sea rapidly rising, the aggravation over coal on public lands was slowly residing. After Roosevelt conferred with Pinchot and with Walcott, he wrote the secretary of interior, and late in December Hitchcock modified the withdrawal order. Damage had been caused in upsetting many western citizens, and members of Congress were upset. During the last part of Teddy Roosevelt's reign several major conferences on conservation were organized and deemed a great success, but by the end of 1906 the conservation movement began to lose momentum.

To return to water, when an irrigation cutoff failed, the break became a new channel and the Colorado River ran unchecked into the Imperial Valley. The break was actually in Mexico, south of Yuma, providing international complications, separate from the issue of whether the Reclamation Service should be the group to check the flood.

Walcott was called repeatedly to the White House and on several occasions went to New York to consult with E. C. Harriman. His problem was that the main line of the Southern Pacific was being inundated; before the flood was stopped, tracks were shifted six times to ever higher ground. Mexico assured the State Department that something might be done some day. Roosevelt wrote Walcott to "please proceed at once, after whatever discussion with Mr. Harriman may be necessary, to prepare information for me on which I can base recommendations to Congress as soon as that body reassembles looking to the permanent prevention of any repetition of the disaster" (Morrison 1952, 531). This was a manmade disaster, not Mother Nature on a rampage.

The Reclamation Service provided more advice than anything else. The Southern Pacific took charge from the bankrupt irrigation group which caused the difficulty. Carload after carload of crushed rock was dumped into the break before the flow was slowed, let alone stopped. Two months after the break, the Colorado River was back where it had been. Engineers in flood control work tend to ignore this incident, but it is an example of the point that it is better to let a river flow where it wants than where mankind wants.

Meanwhile, as regards the Reclamation Service, Walcott formally wrote Hitchcock:

> The period of organization and of allotment of funds to projects has largely passed and the second step, that of construction is well underway. . . . it is clear to me that the Reclamation Service and the Geological Survey should have separate administrative heads.
>
> I therefore have the honor to request that I be relived of the directorship of the Reclamation Service at an early date.[20]

With his resignation on record, Walcott was in a holiday mood as the year wound down. The Ontario Apartment House board met, and next came "A very happy, jolly Christmas Day. At 9:30 A.M. Helena, Sidney, Helen, Stuart, Aunt Sydney [Helena's half-sister], grandmother Ella Paul Patterson & our 3 servants had Christmas presents" (December 25, 1906). There was never any doubt the Walcotts were upper class, and the presence of three servants proves it. Arthur tended the furnace and served as butler at dinners, as a change of pace from running a western camp. Probably Agnes the cook was one of the other two servants.

Immediately after Christmas, Walcott was in New York for the AAAS meeting, followed by that of the Geological Society of America. The GSA secretary thought it wise to give a former president of the society the twenty minutes on the program he had requested, though how close the subject was to the hearts of many members is a question. The conference of state geologists followed the lecture on Cambrian brachiopods, and for a finale, Walcott participated in dedication of a hall of fame of scientific men. He unveiled a bust and "Spoke on Louis Agassiz" (Walcott 1907a). Even for New York City, that was a full four days. Walcott summarized the year "Our summer in the Rocky Mountains was the most striking event of the year 1906. Charlie going to work for L. L. Nunn of the Telluride Power Company may be the most important event for him" (December 31, 1906).

There is a footnote to the New York trip. A Department of Agriculture biologist wrote a California colleague of ways and means to promote biologist C. Hart Merriam, their candidate for Smithsonian secretary:

> It is probable that he [David Starr Jordan of Stanford] favored Walcott until the scrap with Branner. . . . It seems to me we who are interested in systematics and exploratory biology are at our last ditch and if we don't win here we are almost certainly down and out. The Carnegie Institution has refused us everything so far and at a recent meeting it definitely decided not to undertake any new biological work for years to come. . . . The President's influence with the Regents has been much impaired by his use of the Big Stick in connection with the Freer art collection. Walcott's scrap with Branner has probably injured him somewhat. They say, however, that he was attacked at the Am. Assoc. in New York in public and that he met things very diplomatically.[21]

The Freer reference needs clarification. Last in December, 1904, Charles Freer, a Detroit millionaire with definite ideas, offered his art collection to the Smithsonian. Secretary Langley was ailing, the deed of gift was peculiar, and nothing happened very fast. Freer renewed his offer a year later, and allegedly Roosevelt called in regents and pounded on a table. True or not, he did send them a long letter in December 1905. Roosevelt found Freer's letter of conditions reasonable, he found the proposed donation a remarkable gift to the nation, he urged action, he suggested who should examine the collection in Detroit and ended:

> I hope that the Regents of the Smithsonian will feel warranted to close with the offer for they are the national guardians of such a collection. If in their wisdom they do not see their way to accept the gift I shall be obligated to prevent the loss to the United States Government, and therefore to the people of the United States, of one of the most valuable collections which any private individual has ever given to any people.[22]

The regents could read and accepted Freer's gift.

Walcott started his official calls on January 1 with President Roosevelt, then saw "Uncle Joe" Cannon, the vice-president, and three cabinet officers. Fun was over and the next day he was at the White House about the Salton Sea. The day after, he returned to the White House about the Colorado River, the two topics continuing to merge rapidly. The third day he was back at the White House concerning the Laguna Dam in California. Saturday, at his office, he listened to visiting delegations. "Am thoroughly tired of Reclamation Service as it interferes with Geol. Survey administration" (January 5, 1907).

The first three days of the next week were taken up with the Colorado River, still discharging inland. He had an evening at the home of Alexander Graham Bell, the most powerful of the regents. Nothing says they talked about the secretaryship, but Walcott was a logical choice, and Walcott was sick of what he was doing. Thursday he was on Capitol Hill and then drafted a memorandum for Secretary Root to give to the president. The next day Walcott was at the White House twice, once about the river, and later with Helena for a musical evening. On Saturday, Walcott "Stopped at White House 9 A.M. Made a change in message on Colorado River. At Survey during the day. Put in an hours work on Cambrian brachiopods P.M.—Call on Mrs. Jas. R. Garfield on way home. Spent the evening fussing with odds and ends at home" (January 12, 1907). The second week of the new year was about as unsatisfactory as the first.

The third week of January began not much better. Walcott was at the USGS early and late, with an appearance on the hill in between. The same Monday, he was forced into a theater party and late supper; "Cannot endure many such nights if work to go on well" (January 14, 1907). He went to see Speaker Cannon about his hopes for a new Survey building, and presided at the Washington Academy; he was reelected president again in 1907, but it was so routine that no mention in his diary was necessary.

Walcott went back to the Capitol and to the White House and in the evening functioned as a trustee of George Washington University. He returned to Capitol Hill to see if a bill for a building could go into the House and the Senate, and then to the Interior Building to tell Hitchcock the latest on the Colorado. By Friday, he actually "Put in two hours on Cambrian brachiopods collected in 1905–1906" (January 18, 1907). Walcott needed that break, for the next day, he was back at the Capitol to see Congressman Tawney, who had not mellowed one bit during the past year. The appropriation was to have difficulties.

Monday, Walcott walked downtown with Assistant Secretary Rathbun, who lived on Massachusetts Avenue about fifteen blocks from the Walcotts; there was plenty of time to chat before they reached F Street. After the constitutional, Walcott spent most of the day listening to people talk about the Los Angeles Water Canal Company. He spent the evening working on GWMA papers; compared to reclamation, this was relaxation. Tuesday it was back to Capitol Hill, and then to the office shuttling between USGS concerns and the recalcitrant Colorado River.

Wednesday morning the board of regents met, and after other business ended by electing a new secretary; the brief minutes record a unanimous vote for Walcott.[23]

> It was not definitely known when the regents met that there would be an election. It was generally suspected that Mr. Walcott would be selected for the place if he could be secured, but there had been a rumor that the President had put his foot down and said that he wanted Mr. Walcott to continue with the geological survey, where he was needed and that his name would have to be passed up for that reason. However, it is understood that the brakes were taken off at the White House and that the selection was made in accordance with the original desire of the regents, who wanted to get a man who was not only a recognized scientist, but a man of decided executive ability. Mr. Walcott fills both these requirements.[24]

Interesting indeed! Does "original desire" mean the regents wanted him in December and Roosevelt had said no?

Walcott spent that morning first at the Survey, next a the White House, and then at the Capitol. That afternoon, he was informed unofficially of the vote. The next day he was back at the White House "to report my election as Secty of Smithsonian to President Roosevelt" (January 24, 1907). A formal letter of acceptance was sent to the chancellor, Chief Justice Fuller, amidst his writing replies to the congratulations which poured in. It was a remarkably pleasant time these few days, but in characteristic fashion Walcott was already consulting with Rathbun, Bell, and others concerning his new duties.

On Monday, Walcott called on Secretary Hitchcock at 4:00 P.M. and "handed my resignation as Director U.S. Geol. Survey to latter. Wrote Chief Justice Fuller that I would take charge of the Smithsonian Institution January 31"07" (January 28, 1907). Walcott "Drove to Smithsonian Institution & officially took charge of the Institution as Secretary. Met chiefs of branches etc. Returned to Geol. Survey 1. P.M." (January 31, 1907). For several more months Walcott continued in charge of the Geological Survey and the Reclamation Service. It is hard enough to imagine running two such basically different operations simultaneously, as he had for five years, let alone now adding another disparate administrative entity.

Garfield was confirmed as secretary of interior, on January 15, to take office in two months; Walcott's resignation was a problem. The withdrawal of coal

Charles Doolittle Walcott, Paleontologist

lands had stirred up Congress and Hitchcock was attacked, just to warn the incoming secretary that the real power was on Capitol Hill (Rabbitt 1986, 52). It was better for Walcott to continue until Garfield was settled in office. Walcott's one-sentence letter to Roosevelt noted his resignation as USGS director would "take effect when my successor qualifies, or at such time as you may designate."[25]

After two days in office, Garfield wrote: "I therefore at this time accept your resignation as Director of the Reclamation Service. In so doing I desire to express my hearty appreciation of the service which you have rendered in assuming the burden of the administrative work resulting from the operations of the Reclamation Act. While I have not had in the past immediate personal contact with this work, yet I am aware that much of the success attained has been due to your untiring personal devotion."[26] Newell was the choice for chief of the Reclamation Service; after him, it evolved into the Bureau of Reclamation.

This may be the appropriate place to comment on the Minidoka project on the Snake River near Burley, Idaho. Construction began in October 1904, and by 1907 water was available to irrigate 190,000 acres. This was the first place that the Reclamation Service generated electricity for pumping irrigation water and the plant is a registered historical landmark. One of the first wildlife refuges designated by President Roosevelt is named after the lake behind the dam.

The caption on a photograph in the Reclamation Service files taken April 25, 1907, states it is a view at the outlet of beautiful Lake Walcott. What an appropriate form of recognition to the retiring chief. When the USGS celebrated its centennial in 1979, that appeared a good time to mention Lake Walcott but there is no documentation in Idaho or in the National Archives to link the man and the lake. Supposition that the name came from Newell and Davis, who had moved from number three to number two in the Reclamation Service when Walcott left, is not the same as documentation. Ultimately, the Board of Geographic Names ruled Lake Walcott was named in honor of Charles Doolittle Walcott.

By 1907 the USGS had grown, and for many employees contact with the director was not as direct as it had been in 1894. Water workers did not aspire to directorship. Water had a new chief with the good political sense to change Hydrographic Branch to Water Resources Branch so that Congress could understand what was done. That still did not restore the cuts in money for stream gaging, but it was a first step. The topographers were involved in a discrimination hearing and there was no close association between eastern and western groups. The name of the next director was not of much interest to them.

In contrast, the geologists fretted as to who would be director, for it was a foregone conclusion that a geologist should have the position. Van Hise was the logical choice and he was in Washington February 1, 1907. In a repeat of 1897, Walcott took him to the Smithsonian and to see secretary-designate Garfield. However, Van Hise was happy as president of the University of Wisconsin and declined. There was talk of his understudy C. K. Leith, and of W. B. Clark, the state geologist of Maryland. Through February and March, rumors flew.

The second week in March, while the new director was still unknown, the incumbent was honored. "The members of the Geological Survey gave me a great dinner. Helena and Mrs. Jos. Enfield received 240 guests. Many speakers during the dinner and after—all very kindly disposed to me as Director of the Survey" (March 13, 1907). The dinner began with Blue Point oysters, went through a consomme to planked shad and Smithfield ham, accompanied by appropriate vegetables, and eased into coffee and cigars, via Harlequin ice cream and fancy cakes.

Speeches were equally elegant and demonstrated the wit of the organization. Colonel Rizer served as toastmaster as he had at the twenty-fifth anniversary dinner. Arnold Hague, who supervised Walcott at Eureka, was to talk on "The Director as an assistant" but ill-health kept him away. Bailey Willis represented the geologists and commented on "The "Director's hammer." W. M. Beaman noted "The Director on the level"; this is an inside joke, for the Beaman arc was a major improvement on the topographic alidade. The head of Water Resources Branch, M. O. Leighton, spoke on "The Director on the Water Wagon," another play on words, for Walcott hardly touched a drop of spirits. S. J. Kuble ran printing and engraving and titled his remarks "The proof of the map is in the printing." The last item was reclamation by F. H. Newell on "Blessed is the man who makes two drops of water flow where one 'flew' before." Secretary Garfield said a few words and the director replied. It was a fine affair.

"At 5 P.M. had conference with Secty Garfield and Mr. Pinchot on question of Directorship of Survey" (March 29, 1907). "George Otis Smith appointed Director of Geological Survey—I vacate May 1" (April 5, 1907). Smith was to remain director for more than two decades, and he did not cover himself with glory for much of that interval. Land classification had to be done, but it became nearly the be-all and do-all of the survey, and almost brought the agency to an end-all with the decline in basic geologic investigations.

Smith received a doctorate from Johns Hopkins University in 1896 and joined the USGS; he was just thirty-six when appointed director. Geologist-in-charge

Charles Doolittle Walcott, Paleontologist

Hayes was a better scientist, was well known, and was the choice of Gilbert. Hayes had no doctorate and, more important, lacked Smith's political connections. Pinchot was charmed with kindred spirit Smith because of his insistence on businesslike methods, and probably pushed him to the forefront when Van Hise declined. Smith served on a subcommittee of a Garfield committee, and the new secretary was also impressed with his businesslike facade. Garfield changed Hayes's title to chief geologist; "it is reasonable to infer that the new Director was expected to be the Survey's principal administrative officer but not its chief scientist" (Rabbitt 1987, 56). As an Australian would say, "too true."

A Washington rumor was that the syndicate which built apartment houses was composed of Walcott's brains and Smith's wife's money. That may not be correct in fact, but it was the eventual harsh judgment of Smith's peers. Director Smith did start with the goodwill of old-timer Emmons, who wrote a Mexican colleague "one of the young geologists, whom you met in Mexico, George Otis Smith, has received the appointment. He is an excellent man in all ways, the only thing wanting is experience in Survey work. I think his personal tendencies will be good. . . . Hayes . . . is too much inclined . . . to the popular demand for quick results."[27] In a few months Emmons wrote Becker "Smith is at present very much under the influence of Hayes & his fiscal policy, and Walcott prepared things before leaving in such a way that he really has no initiative now."[28]

Walcott was not coasting during his last few months as director. He saw Congressman Tawney several times, still to no avail in convincing him of the merits of the Geological Survey. The CIW Executive Committee met in New York. There were several trips to the White House, apart from an official dinner. By now the embankment break of the Colorado River was repaired. A standard phrase is "taming a river," but retrospective study of flood control measures shows that no matter how much is spent, eventually the river again floods and costs more in damage than was spent. Today, the Salton Sea is safe, only because river water is drained off for irrigation. One positive result of the flood was a major study published by CIW on the effects of the flood and the gradual decline of water level.

Walcott was "Busy with various matters at Smithsonian & Geol. Survey appropriations by Tawney & others in Congress" (February 21, 1907). The assault was vigorous, yet the USGS made out fairly well (Rabbitt 1986, 52–56). Even in his final brush with Congress as a bureau head, Walcott was trying to obtain a building. For "what if," had Walcott stayed director another year or had Roosevelt not angered some congressmen by withdrawing coal lands, the USGS might have gotten a new home at that time.

Within the Geological Survey, Walcott reviewed the work of a topographic trial board, spoke to the topographers, and made a major reorganization by the third week in March. He next "Settled work between Geol. & Technological Branches of Survey" (April 1, 1907). The following day the Technologic Branch was announced, J. A. Holmes Branch Chief. Three years and much aggravation later, the Technologic Branch would become a part of the Bureau of Mines, with Holmes heading the new agency.

Walcott was heavily involved in his manifold activities. One day he was at the Smithsonian Institution, at the CIW Ex. Com. at the White House, back to his USGS office, and finally to the Interior Department to confer with Garfield on coal lands. In April, Walcott was elected vice-president of the National Academy but did bother to note this in his diary.

The end of the month, Walcott "Called on Secty Garfield 2:30 P.M. & then went to Geological Survey offices. Said goodby to the survey members as today closes my directorship, begun July 1" 1894" (April 30, 1907). Even so, this was not the end with the Survey. On April 23, Walcott was retransferred, the phraseology of a Civil Service clerk, to geologist. He was to receive thirteen dollars per day for occasional duty. Walcott explained to Garfield,

> The object of this appointment is in order that I may be able to carry on and complete certain investigations that I have had in hand for the last twenty years, and upon which I have given more or less time each year during my directorship. A quarto volume is now nearly ready for the printer, and I expect to be able to complete further studies and preparation of material in the future.[29]

The Civil Service required Walcott to take another oath of office before he could retransfer.

Small scientific papers move fast and large ones move quite slowly, though the rate at which *Monograph* 51 moved makes one believe it was accursed. The tome still had not been published two years later when Walcott submitted his geologist resignation to Director Smith

> to take effect June 30, 1909. This date closes 30 years of active service in the Survey.
>
> The reason for tendering my resignation at this time is that I do not see that it will be practicable for me to take an active part to any extent, in geological work in direct connection with the Survey.
>
> It will give me great pleasure to be of such service to the organization as is practicable or acceptable to it.[30]

Charles Doolittle Walcott, Paleontologist

Smith wrote to Richard A. Ballinger, who had replaced Garfield as secretary of the interior:

> Mr. Walcott's contribution to this branch of the public service is appreciated by all who served under him as director. His administration included the years of greatest expansion of the Survey, and since giving up the Directorship he has continued his scientific work as a Survey author. His most important memoir will be published by the Survey this summer, as Monograph LI—The Cambrian Brachiopoda.[31]

Smith was too optimistic about the *Monograph,* which has a date of 1912 on the title page. Smith went on to request permission to employ Walcott as a Consulting Geologist; that status was given to Chamberlin and Van Hise. Ballinger approved, Walcott to be paid at the prevailing per diem rate.

It is appropriate to sum up what Walcott accomplished during his USGS years. First, he built a solid reputation as a world-class scientist with his investigations of Cambrian rocks and fossils, and made omniscient contributions to understanding of that time period. Second, as unofficial director, he rescued the Geological Survey when the shattered Powell was unable to act. Third, in thirteen years as director, he built "the best geological survey in all Christendom" (Rabbitt 1980). Fourth, he saved the 1897 forest reserves and helped study and protect the national forests for eight years thereafter. Fifth, for five years he adroitly and successfully steered the Reclamation Service. Sixth, he laid the basis for the Bureau of Mines.

When one adds his time as acting assistant secretary of the Smithsonian Institution in charge of the National Museum, it forms a remarkable record of public service. The old tired phrase of comparing apples and oranges is never much use, but his later efforts for the Carnegie Institution of Washington were significantly more important in development of big science in America than his aid to the National Museum.

Walcott could have rested on his laurels, but as one who did not rest, he could have concentrated on fossils when he assumed the responsibility of following in the footsteps of Henry, Baird, and Langley. Becoming secretary of the Smithsonian Institution rejuvenated him, yet over his remaining two decades, renowned scientist Walcott was in conflict with duty-bound administrator Walcott. That, however, constitutes another story.

Notes to Unpublished Sources

1. The Beginning

1. *Washington Post*, 23 July 1973.
2. *Utica Daily Press*, 10 February 1927.
3. Ibid.
4. H. S. Randall to James Hall, 9 June 1849. (Received in a letter from John W. Wells; original may be in the New York State Archives [NYSA]). Walcott Collection, Ellis L. Yochelson Papers, Smithsonian Institution Archives (hereafter cited as SIA), Washington, D.C. (hereafter cited as Yochelson Papers).

A few of Hall's letters cited are in the New York State Library, series B, 0561, New York State Museum Director's, State Geologist's, and State Paleontologist's Correspondence Files, 1824–1944, but the abbreviation NYSA has been used for convenience in designation of all Hall material.

The material included in the Walcott Collection in the Yochelson Papers includes copies of all letters cited from the various institutions listed herein, plus other items not cited from the same institutions and material from additional institutions and from individuals, including the late Sidney S. Walcott, Walcott's second son.

5. C. D. Walcott to O. C. Marsh, 30 March 1868, Othneil Charles Marsh Papers, Manuscripts and Archives Division, Stirling Library, Yale University (hereafter cited as Marsh Papers).
6. Walcott to Marsh, 6 April 1868, Marsh Papers.

2. Rust Farm

1. H. S. Bickmore to H. F. Osborn, 18 February 1910, H. F. Osborn Papers, American Museum of Natural History Library, New York, N.Y. (hereafter cited as Osborn Papers).
2. C. D. Walcott to Joseph Henry, 18 January 1872, Joseph Henry Papers, Record Unit 16, vol. 121, p. 7, SIA.
3. Walcott to Marsh, 19 January 1872, Marsh Papers.
4. Walcott to Marsh, 11 February 1872, ibid.
5. Walcott to Marsh, 21 July 1872, ibid.

6. C. D. Walcott to James Hall, 23 February 1873, James Hall Papers, NYSA, Albany, N.Y. (hereafter cited as James Hall Papers).

7. C. D. Walcott to Louis Agassiz, 2 October 1873, Louis Agassiz Letters, Museum of Comparative Zoology, Mayr Library, Harvard University (hereafter cited as L. Agassiz Letters).

8. Walcott to L. Agassiz, 12 October 1873, L. Agassiz Letters.

9. Ibid.

10. Walcott to Mrs. L. Agassiz, 22 December 1873, ibid.

11. *Utica Herald,* 4 December 1873.

3. Onward to Albany

1. Memorandum section, Walcott pocket diary, 1877, Record Unit 7004, C. D. Walcott Papers, SIA (hereafter cited as C. D. Walcott Papers).

2. James Hall to Hamilton Harris, 12 November 1877, Hall Papers.

3. James Hall to J. W. Husted, 22 August 1877, ibid.

4. C. D. Walcott to W. H. Dall, 17 April 1887, box 17, folder 28, Record Unit 7073, W. H. Dall Papers, Smithsonian Institution, Washington, D.C. (hereafter cited as Dall Papers).

5. C. D. Walcott to J. A. Lintner, 3 August 1877, box 1, J. A. Lintner Papers, Manuscript and Special Collections, New York State Library, Albany (hereafter cited as Lintner Papers).

6. Lintner to James Hall, 18 August 1877, ibid.

7. C. B. Dyer to James Hall, 1 February 1877, Hall Papers.

8. James Hall to G. W. Clinton, draft, 1 January 1879, ibid.

9. Ibid.

10. C. D. Walcott to J. W. Dawson, 14 March 1878, J. W. Dawson Papers, McGill University Archives, Montreal, Quebec, Canada (hereafter cited as Dawson Papers).

11. Walcott to Dawson, 31 March 1878, ibid.

12. *Genesse Courier,* 15 July 1878, Yochelson Papers.

13. Walcott to Lintner, 25 July 1878, box 1, Lintner Papers.

14. Walcott to Lintner, 8 August 1878, ibid.

15. Newspaper clipping, source unknown, from Watertown, N.Y.

16. Walcott to Lintner, 22 September 1878, box 1, Lintner Papers.

17. Walcott to Lintner, 9 October 1878, ibid.

18. James Hall to G. W. Clinton, draft, 1 January 1879, Hall Papers.

19. S. A. Miller to James Hall, 8 December 1878, Hall Papers.

20. Charles Barrois, translation from French of memorial presented to Academy of Sciences, Paris, 28 February 1927, box 102, folder 7, C. D. Walcott Papers.

21. *The* (Albany, New York) *Argus,* 15 April 1879, Yochelson Papers.

22. A. H. Bickmore to C. D. Walcott, 26 April 1879, A. S. Bickmore Papers, American Museum of Natural History Library, New York, N.Y.

23. James Hall to Erastus Brooks, 2 May 1879, Hall Papers.

24. C. D. Walcott to Clarence King, 2 June 1879, Yochelson Papers.

25. Clarence King to R. P. Whitfield, 16 June 1879 (original lost, xerographic copy), ibid.

4. A Grand Beginning

1. Walcott to Lintner, 17 September 1879, box 1, Lintner Papers.

2. T. W. Stanton, field notes, 1892, p. 23, U.S. Geological Survey, Field Records, Denver Federal Center, Denver.

3. Clarence King to Sumner Bodfish, 18 September 1879, Letterbook C-1, Clarence King Letterbooks, Huntington Library and Art Gallery, Pasadena, Calif.

4. Deed dated 13 December 1879 and recorded 13 January 1880, Herkimer County, New York.

5. Walcott to Lintner, 11 January 1880, box 1, Lintner Papers.

6. G. K. Gilbert to W. H. Holmes, 12 February 1880, W. H. Holmes, W. H. Holmes Random Records, vol. 2, p. 78, National Museum of American Art/National Portrait Gallery, Library, Washington, D.C. (hereafter cited as W. H. Holmes Random Records).

7. King to A. S. Bickmore, 10 April 1880, Letterbook C-1, King Papers, Huntington Library, Pasadena, Calif. (hereafter cited as King Papers).

8. King to J. J. Stevenson, 13 September 1879, ibid.

9. C. D. Walcott to Alexander Agassiz, 4 April 1880, Alexander Agassiz Letters, Museum of Comparative Zoology, Mayr Library, Harvard University (hereafter cited as A. Agassiz Letters).

10. Walcott to A. Agassiz, 1 May 1880, A. Agassiz Letters.

11. Walcott to A. Agassiz, 5 May 1880, ibid.

12. Walcott to A. Agassiz, 28 May 1880, ibid.

13. Walcott to A. Agassiz, 10 June 1880, ibid.

14. Walcott to A. Agassiz, 16 June 1880, ibid.

15. Walcott to A. Agassiz, 18 June 1880, ibid.

16. Walcott to Lintner, 27 June 1880, box 1, Lintner Papers.

17. Walcott to Lintner, 4 July 1880, ibid.

18. G. P. Howell to Walcott, 31 October 1879, box 2, C. D. Walcott Papers.

19. King to T. C. Chamberlin, 20 July 1880, Letterbook C-1, King Papers.

20. Arnold Hague to S. F. Emmons, 12 June 1880, Letters Received of S. F. Emmons, U.S. Geological Survey, RG 57, Archives II, National Archives and Records Administration, College Park, Md.

5. Eureka!

1. Edwin Kirk, 1937, six-page statement on Walcott as a geologist, Yochelson Papers.

2. King to Arnold Hague, 2 October 1880, Letterbook C-1, King Papers.

3. King to C. D. Walcott, 12 October 1880, ibid.

4. Hague to Emmons, 7 February 1881, Emmons Papers, Manuscript Division, Library of Congress, Washington, D.C.

5. Arnold Hague to G. F. Becker, 18 November 1880, G. F. Becker Papers, Manuscript Division, Library of Congress, Washington, D.C. (hereafter cited as Becker Papers).

6. S. F. Emmons to Becker, 26 October 1880, ibid.

7. C. D. Walcott to W. H. Dall, 20 March 1881, box 17, folder 28, Dall Papers.

8. C. D. Walcott to W. H. Dall, 25 January 1882, ibid.

9. C. D. Walcott to W. H. Dall, 30 January 1882, ibid.

10. C. D. Walcott to Joachim Barrande, 19 March 1882, Joachim Barrande Papers, Narodni Museum, Prague, Czech Republic.

11. Walcott to Agassiz, 8 March 1882, A. Agassiz Letters.

12. C.D. Walcott, field note book IV, 1880, 18 November 1880, Yochelson Papers.

13. S. F. Baird to C. D. Walcott, 20 May 1882, ibid.

14. Walcott to A. Agassiz, 25 May 1882, A. Agassiz Letters.

15. Walcott to A. Agassiz, 14 June 1882, ibid.

16. Helen Walcott Younger to E. L. Yochelson, 20 February 1961, Yochelson Papers.

17. W. W. Holmes, marginal note, n.d., vol. 2, p. 113, W. H. Holmes Random Records.

18. Walcott to A. Agassiz, 24 November 1882, A. Agassiz Letters.

19. Charles Haskell to C. D. Walcott, n.d., box 1, folder 8, C. D. Walcott Papers.

20. Walcott to A. Agassiz, 25 December 1882, A. Agassiz Letters.

21. C. D. Walcott to G. F. Becker, 6 June 1883, G. P. Merrill Papers, Manuscript Division, Library of Congress, Washington, D.C.

22. C. E. Dutton to Archibald Geike, 5 May 1883, Archibald Geike Papers, University of Edinburgh Library, Edinburgh, Scotland.

23. C. D. Walcott to Charles Wachsmuth, 16 November 1883, Yochelson Papers.

24. J. S. Billings, memorandum re J. C. McConnell, 16 October 1893, National Library of Medicine, Bethesda, Md.

25. *Utica Morning Herald,* 11 May 1885.

6. Potsdam

1. U.S. Geological Survey Monthly Report, C. D. Walcott, 31 August 1883, U.S. Geological Survey, RG 57, Archives II, National Archives and Records Administration, College Park, Md. (hereafter cited as Monthly Report).

2. C. D. Walcott, memorandum, 25 June 1902, Cooper Curtice Papers, Manuscript Division, Library of Congress, Washington, D.C. (hereafter cited as Curtice Papers).

3. Ibid.

4. Walcott to Curtice, 20 February 1926, Curtice Papers.

5. G. P. Merrill, incomplete manuscript history of U.S. National Museum, Library, Department of Mineral Sciences, National Museum of Natural History, Washington, D.C.

6. C. D. Walcott to H. S. Williams, 15 October 1883, Unit 1148, Williams Family Papers, Kroch Library, Division of Rare Manuscript Collections, Cornell University.

7. Walcott to A. Agassiz, 5 December 1883, A. Agassiz Letters.

8. C. D. Walcott to G. F. Matthew, 29 March 1884, G. F. Matthew Papers, New Brunswick Museum of Natural History, Library, St. John, New Brunswick, Canada (hereafter cited as Matthew Papers).

9. Walcott to Matthew, 19 June 1884, Matthew Papers.

10. Walcott to Matthew, 17 July 1884, ibid.

11. Cooper Curtice to C. D. Walcott, 27 July 1884, Yochelson Papers.

12. Curtice to Walcott, 16 August 1884, ibid.

13. Curtice to Walcott, 25 August 1884, ibid.

14. Walcott to Curtice, 10 August 1884, Curtice Papers.

15. J. W. Gentry to Curtice, 20 August 1884, ibid.

16. Walcott, 1 November 1884, Monthly Report.

17. J. W. Gentry to Curtice, 7 October 1884, Curtice Papers.

18. Gentry to Curtice, 22 October 1884, ibid.

19. Walcott to Williams, 18 December 1884, Williams Papers.

20. Walcott to Curtice, 13 May 1885, Curtice Papers.

21. C. D. Walcott to L. W. Bailey, 22 June 1885, Hall Papers.

22. C. D. Walcott to Arnold Hague, 25 April 1887, letters received, 1880–1914, Arnold Hague Papers, U.S. Geological Survey, RG 57, Archives II, National Archives and Records Administration, College Park, Md.

23. Newspaper clipping, 9 July 1886, source unknown, in Walcott 1886 pocket diary, SIA.

24. Walcott, 1 December 1886, Monthly Report.

7. Domestic and International Relations

1. Walcott, 1 February 1887, Monthly Report.
2. Walcott, 4 May 1887, ibid.
3. Walcott, 4 July 1887, ibid.
4. Walcott, 1 December 1887, ibid.
5. Walcott, 7 February 1888, ibid.
6. N. H. Winchell to A. Winchell, 29 January 1888, box 6, Alexander Winchell Papers, Bently Historical Library, Michigan Historical Collections, University of Michigan, Ann Arbor (hereafter cited as A. Winchell Papers).
7. N. H. Winchell to A. Winchell, 21 February 1888, box 6, A. Winchell Papers.
8. N. H. Winchell to A. Winchell, 22 March 1888, ibid.
9. G. K. Gilbert to C. D. Walcott, 8 April 1889, box 1, folder 6, C. D. Walcott Papers.
10. H. W. Seely to A. N. Adams, 8 June 1888, Yochelson Papers.
11. C. H. Hitchcock to Persifor Frazer, 1 June 1888, Frazer Family Papers, University Archives and Records Center, University of Pennsylvania, Philadelphia (hereafter cited as Frazer Family Papers).
12. Walcott, 2 July 1888, Monthly Report.
13. Ibid.
14. C. D. Walcott to G. F. Matthew, 24 December 1886, Matthew Papers.
15. Walcott to Matthew, 17 April 1888, ibid.
16. J. T. Howley to C. D. Walcott, [spring 1888?], and incomplete, J. T. Howley Papers, MG 105, box 3, Provincial Archives of Newfoundland and Labrador, St. John's, Newfoundland, Canada.
17. C. D. Walcott to B. F. Howell, 23 December 1925, B. F. Howell Papers, Department of Geological and Geophysical Sciences, Archives, Princeton University.
18. *Dominion Illustrated*, 6 October 1888, p. 215.
19. *Times*, 19 September 1888.
20. C. D. Walcott to W. C. Brøgger, 15 June 1889, W. Brøgger Letters, Paleontological Museum, Oslo, Norway.

8. Settling In

1. *Washington Post*, 15 June 1989.
2. C. D. Walcott to Charles Lapworth, 10 January 1890, Charles Lapworth Papers, Lapworth Museum, Lapworth Archives, University of Birmingham, Birmingham, England.

3. C. D. Walcott to C. E. Beecher, 9 March 1889, box 1, C. D. Walcott Papers.

4. C. D. Walcott to C. W. Van Horn, 9 September 1889, C. W. Van Horn Papers, Canadian Pacific Railway, Archives, Montreal, Quebec, Canada.

5. C. D. Walcott to J. M. Clarke, 15 October 1889, A4028, J. M. Clarke Papers, Manuscript and Special Collections, New York State Library, Albany.

6. Walcott to A. Winchell, 17 January 1890, box 10, A. Winchell Papers.

7. J. J. Stevenson to A. Winchell, 20 April 1890, ibid.

8. Stevenson to A. Winchell, 11 June 1890, ibid.

9. C. D. Walcott to H. B. Walcott, 20 May [1891], Yochelson Papers.

10. *Washington Star*, 16 August 1891.

11. Ibid., 31 August 1891.

12. C. D. Walcott to Alexander Agassiz, 5 June 1892, A. Agassiz Papers.

13. Arnold Hague to Becker, 3 September [1888?], Becker Papers.

14. T. C. Chamberlin to R. T. Salisbury, 28 July 1890, Letter Book I, T. C. Chamberlin Papers, Joseph Regenstein Library, Department of Special Collections, University of Chicago (hereafter cited as Chamberlin Papers).

15. C. D. Walcott to T. C. Chamberlin, 1 August 1892, C. D. Walcott Papers.

16. Walcott to Chamberlin, 7 August 1892, ibid.

17. N. W. Winchell to Persifor Frazer, 7 January 1893, P. F. correspondence, box 7, ff 8, Frazer Family Papers.

18. C. D. Walcott to Alpheus Hyatt, 12 August 1892, Alpheus Hyatt Papers, Syracuse University Library, Department of Special Collections, Syracuse University, Syracuse, N.Y.

19. Walcott to Chamberlin, 1 September 1892, C. D. Walcott Papers.

20. C. D. Walcott to J. C. Branner, 3 September 1892, J. C. Branner Papers, Stanford University Libraries, Archives, Stanford University, Stanford, Calif.

21. Walcott to Chamberlin, 21 September 1892, C. D. Walcott Papers.

22. Walcott to Chamberlin, 23 September 1892, ibid.

23. C. D. Walcott to J. C. Branner, 29 September 1892, Branner Papers.

24. Walcott to Matthew, 24 September 1892, Matthew Papers.

25. Walcott to Marsh, 12 October 1892, Marsh Papers.

26. Walcott to Chamberlin, 13 October 1892, C. D. Walcott Papers.

27. C. D. Walcott to J. C. Branner, 12 November 1892, Branner Papers.

28. C. D. Walcott to C. R. Van Hise, 10 December 1892, C. R. Van Hise Papers, U.S. Geological Survey, Great Lakes Division Papers (hereafter cited as Van Hise Papers).

9. The Director

1. Bailey Willis to Mrs. Willis, 29 January 1893, Bailey Willis Papers, Huntington Library and Art Gallery, Pasadena, Calif. (hereafter cited as Willis Papers).

2. "Survey publications," box 26, Emmons Papers.

3. Mrs. W. J. McGee to C. D. Walcott, 16 January 1893, W. J. McGee Papers, Manuscript Division, Library of Congress, Washington, D.C.

4. Walcott to Chamberlin, 5 March 1893, box 1, C. D. Walcott Papers.

5. Willis to Mrs. Willis, 7 March 1893, Willis Papers.

6. Willis to Mrs. Willis, 12 March 1893, ibid.

7. Willis to Mrs. Willis, 31 March 1893, ibid.

8. C. D. Walcott to F. J. H. Merrill, 12 October 1892, B-0561, Merrill Papers, NYSA.

9. James Hall to C. D. Walcott, 29 January 1894, NYSA.

10. *Wisconsin State Journal,* 14 August 1893.

11. Chamberlin to W. R. Harper, 9 December 1893, Letter Book III, Chamberlin Papers.

12. Chamberlin to Walcott, 27 January 1894, ibid.

13. Chamberlin to Walcott, 8 February 1894, ibid.

14. Chamberlin to Walcott, 15 March 1894, Letter Book IV, ibid.

15. Chamberlin to Walcott, 20 March 1894, ibid.

16. Chamberlin to Walcott, 7 April 1894, ibid.

17. G. K. Gilbert to C. E. Dutton, 9 May 1894, G. K. Gilbert Letterbooks, U.S. Geological Survey Library, Reston, Va.

18. Chamberlin to Walcott, 12 May 1894, Letter Book IV, Chamberlin Papers.

19. Gilbert to F. H. Newell, 23 May 1894, Gilbert Letterbook, Library, U.S. Geological Survey, Reston, Va.

20. Emmons to G. F. Becker, 11 May 1894, box 26, Emmons Papers.

21. J. P. Iddings to W. Cross, 12 May 1894, Iddings Papers, Folder 3, Number 7879, Field Records, U.S. Geological Survey, Denver, Colo.

22. Walcott to Chamberlin, 9 July 1894, box 1, C. D. Walcott Papers.

23. *The* (Boise, Idaho) *Statesman,* 26 October 1894.

24. Chamberlin to Walcott, 27 February 1895, Letter Book IV, Chamberlin Papers.

10. Following a Goode Man

1. Chamberlin to Walcott, 9 March 1895, Letter Book VI, Chamberlin Papers.

2. Chamberlin to Walcott, 21 March 1895, ibid.

3. Walcott locality description number 167, Walcott Fossil Locality Lists, Department of Paleobiology, Department of Paleobiology, National Museum of Natural History, Washington, D.C. (hereafter cited as Locality List).

4. Walcott locality description number 168, Locality List.

5. C. D. Walcott to James Hall, 11 September 1895, NYSA.

6. James Hall to C. D. Walcott, 20 September 1895, ibid.

7. *Denver Republican*, 23 March 1896.

8. Van Hise to Walcott, 26 April 1899, Van Hise Papers.

9. Chamberlin to Walcott, 7 May 1897, Letter Book IX, Chamberlin Papers.

10. Van Hise to Walcott, 17 January 1897, Van Hise Papers.

11. Walcott to S. P. Langley, 21 January 1897, box 2, C. D. Walcott Papers.

12. W. H. Phillips to W. H. Holmes, 23 March 1897, vol. 7, W. H. Holmes Random Records.

13. Walcott to Holmes, 26 March 1897, ibid.

14. Walcott to Holmes, 7 April 1897, ibid.

15. Walcott to Holmes, 11 May 1897, ibid.

16. Walcott to Holmes, 11 June 1897, ibid.

17. Walcott locality description 193, Locality List.

18. Langley to Walcott, 18 October 1897, Record 7004, box 2, folder 4, C. D. Walcott Papers.

19. Walcott to A. Agassiz, 12 March 1898, box 1, ibid.

11. Big Sky

1. C. D. Walcott to the Honorable Secretary of the Interior, 16 September 1898, box 1, C. D. Walcott Papers.

2. Walcott to Dawson, 31 December 1894, Dawson Papers.

3. Dawson to Walcott, 9 March 1885, ibid.

4. Walcott to Dawson, 2 February 1899, ibid.

5. Clipping with photograph, source unknown, but almost certainly a St. John's Newfoundland newspaper for 1899.

6. Walcott to Williams, 14 August 1900, Williams Papers.

7. C. D. Walcott to C. W. Hayes, 6 September 1900, E-81, box 25, General Correspondence, Geological Survey, RG 57, Archives II, National Archives and Records Administration, College Park, Md.

8. Walcott locality description 240, July 1900, Locality List.

9. Walcott to Williams, 17 October 1900, Williams Papers.

10. C. D. Walcott, 22 April 1901, Treasurer's letter book, p. 126, National Academy of Sciences, Washington, D.C. (hereafter cited as Treasurer's Book).

11. C. D. Walcott to E. W. Hilgard, 22 January 1900, Hilgard Family Papers, Bancroft Library, University of California, Berkeley.

12. C. D. Walcott to Simon Newcomb, 27 February 1901, p. 110, Treasurer's Book.

13. Walcott to D. C. Gilman, 15 May 1901, Daniel Coit Gilman Papers, Milton S. Eisenhower Library, Special Collections, John Hopkins University, Baltimore, Md.

14. *Washington Post,* 4 June 1901.

15. Chamberlin to Walcott, 25 May 1901, Letter Book XIII, Chamberlin Papers.

16. Walcott to Williams, 29 June 1901, Williams Papers.

17. *Los Angeles Herald,* 3 November 1901.

18. *Los Angeles Daily Times,* 8 November 1901.

19. Ibid.

12. Big Money

1. C. D. Walcott, seven-page memorandum, undated and earlier drafts, box 33, C. D. Walcott Papers.

2. Nicholas Murray Butler to C. D. Walcott, 11 December 1901, Nicholas Murray Butler Papers, Butler Library, Rare Book and Manuscript Library, Columbia University (hereafter cited as Butler Papers).

3. Butler to Walcott, 14 December 1901, Butler Papers.

4. C. D. Walcott, seven-page memorandum, undated and earlier drafts, box 33, C. D. Walcott Papers.

5. "Citation," 22 February 1902, Gilman Papers.

6. F. D. Adams to C. D. Walcott, 31 January 1902, box 1, fig. 25 (b), F. D. Adams Papers, McGill University, Archives, Montreal, Quebec, Canada.

7. C. D. Walcott to Andrew Carnegie, 1 October 1902, box 32, C. D. Walcott Papers.

8. Butler to Walcott, 26 November 1902, Butler Papers.

9. Walcott to Butler, 28 November 1902, ibid.

10. Andrew Carnegie, n.d., box 32, folder 1, SIA.

11. Chamberlin to Walcott, 24 March 1903, Letter Book XVII, Chamberlin Papers.

12. C. D. Walcott to Marcus Baker, 17 April 1903, Walcott Trustee File, Carnegie Institution of Washington Archives, Washington, D.C.

13. C. D. Walcott to H. L. Fairchild, 29 February 1904, H. L. Fairchild Papers, Rush-Rhees Library, Department of Rare Books and Special Collections, University of Rochester, Rochester, N.Y. (hereafter cited as Fairchild Papers).

14. 20 July 1903 [committee report], Yochelson Papers.

15. Baker to Walcott, 13 August 1903, Trustee Papers.

16. Walcott to Baker, 17 August 1903, ibid.

17. Baker to Walcott, 24 September 1903, ibid.

18. C. D. Walcott to W. H. Dall, 6 November 1903, box 17, folder 28, Dall Papers.

19. Eduard Suess to C. D. Walcott, 4 December 1903, Yochelson Papers.

20. Walcott to Williams, 29 December 1903, Williams Papers.

21. Chamberlin to Walcott, 12 July 1902, Letter Book XVI, Chamberlin Papers.

22. *Washington Post,* 3 April 1904.

23. Ibid.

13. Big Change

1. C. D. Walcott to R. A. Johnson, 8 September 1908, C-B 385, box 6, R. U. Johnson Papers, Bancroft Library, University of California, Berkeley (hereafter cited as Johnson Papers).

2. Walcott to Johnson, 6 October 1908, C-B 385, box 6, Johnson Papers.

3. C. D. Walcott to J. S. Billings, 26 May 1905 (reel 20), John Shaw Billings Papers (microfilm edition), Astor, Lenox, and Tilden Foundation, Rare Books and Manuscript Division, New York Public Library, New York, N.Y. (hereafter cited as Billings Papers).

4. F. B. Weeks to C. D. Walcott, 26 July 1905, Yochelson Papers.

5. Ibid.

6. M. Collen to C. D. Walcott, 30 May 1906, ibid.

7. Walcott to Billings, 20 November 1905 (reel 21), Billings Papers.

8. Walcott to Billings, 28 November 1905, ibid.

9. Board of Trustees Minutes, 12 December 1905, Carnegie Institution of Washington Archives, Washington, D.C.

10. C. D. Walcott to Andrew Carnegie, 16 December 1905, Andrew Carnegie Papers, Book 123, Manuscript Division, Library of Congress, Washington, D.C. (hereafter cited as Carnegie Papers).

11. Carnegie to Walcott, 19 December 1905, Book 123, Carnegie Papers.

12. Walcott to Carnegie, 21 December 1905, ibid.

13. J. Bertram to Walcott, 23 December 1905, ibid.

14. C. D. Walcott to W. A. Parks, 31 May 1905, W. A. Parks Papers, Royal Ontario Museum, Toronto, Canada.

15. C. D. Walcott to E. A. Hitchcock, 11 September 1906, box 1, folder 8, SIA.

16. C. D. Walcott to C. W. Hayes, 19 October 1906, E-81, box 26, General Correspondence.

17. Walcott to Fairchild, 10 December 1906, Fairchild Papers.

18. Richard Rathbun to Osborn, 4 December 1906, file 12a, Osborn Papers.

19. Walcott to Osborn, 6 December 1906, file 12b, ibid.

20. Walcott to E. A. Hitchcock, 18 December 1906, box 1, C. D. Walcott Papers.

21. W. H. Osgood to E. W. Nelson, 11 January 1907, E. W. Nelson Papers and E. A. Goodman Collection, box 7, Record Unit 7364, SIA.

22. Board of Regents, Minutes, 24 January 1906, ibid. (hereafter cited as Minutes).

23. Board of Regents, Minutes, 23 January 1907.

24. *Washington Star,* 23 January 1907.

25. Walcott to Theodore Roosevelt, 28 January 1907, C. D. Walcott, Civil Service Records.

26. J. R. Garfield to Walcott, 6 March 1907, ibid.

27. S. F. Emmons to A. Ordonez, 26 April 1907, box 28, Emmons Papers.

28. S. F. Emmons to Becker, 8 July 1907, box 18, Becker Papers.

29. Walcott to J. A. Garfield, 28 June 1907, Civil Service Records.

30. Walcott to G. O. Smith, 25 May 1909, ibid.

31. Smith to R. A. Ballinger, 14 June 1909, ibid.

References

Unpublished Papers

Adams, F. D. Papers. McGill University Archives, Montreal, Canada.

Agassiz, Alexander. Letters. Museum of Comparative Zoology, Mayr Library, Harvard University.

Agassiz, Louis. Letters. Museum of Comparative Zoology, Mayr Library, Harvard University.

Barrande, Joachim. Papers. Narodni Muzeum, Prague, Czech Republic.

Becker, G. F. Papers. Manuscript Division, Library of Congress, Washington, D.C.

Bickmore, A. S. Papers. American Museum of Natural History Library, New York, N.Y.

Billings, John Shaw. Papers. National Library of Medicine, Bethesda, Md.

Billings, John Shaw. Papers. Microfilm edition. Astor, Lenox, and Tilden Foundation, Rare Books and Manuscripts Division, New York Public Library, New York, N.Y.

Board of Regents. Minutes. Record Unit 1. Smithsonian Institution Archives, Washington, DC.

Board of Trustees. Minutes. Carnegie Institution of Washington Archives, Washington, D.C.

Branner, J. C. Papers. Stanford University Libraries, Archives, Stanford University, Stanford, Calif.

Brøgger, W. Letters. Paleontological Museum, Oslo, Norway.

Butler, Nicholas Murray. Papers. Butler Library, Rare Book and Manuscript Library, Columbia University.

Carnegie, Andrew. Papers. Manuscript Division, Library of Congress.

Chamberlin, T. C. Joseph Regenstein Library, Department of Special Collections, University of Chicago.

Clarke, J. M. Papers. Manuscript and Special Collections, New York State Library, Albany.

Curtice, Cooper. Papers. Manuscript Division, Library of Congress.

Dall, W. H. Papers. Record Unit 7073. Smithsonian Institution Archives.

Dawson, J. W. Papers. McGill University.

Emmons, S. F. Letters Received. U.S. Geological Survey, RG 57, Archives II, National Archives and Records Adminstration, College Park, Md.

References

Emmons, S. F. Papers. Manuscript Division, Library of Congress.

Fairchild, H. L. Papers. Rush-Rhees Library, Department of Rare Books and Special Collections, University of Rochester, Rochester, N.Y.

Frazer Family. Papers. University Archives and Records Center, University of Pennsylvania, Philadelphia.

Geike, Archibald. Papers. University of Edinburgh Library, Edinburgh, Scotland.

General Correspondence. U.S. Geological Survey, RG 57, Archives II, National Archives and Records Adminstration, College Park, Md.

Gilbert, G. K. Letterbooks. United States Geological Survey Library, Reston, Va.

Gilman, Daniel Coit. Papers (MS 1). Milton S. Eisenhower Library, Special Collections, John Hopkins University, Baltimore.

Hague, Arnold. Letters Received. RG 57, Archives II, National Archives and Records Adminstration, U.S. Geological Survey, College Park, Md.

Henry, Joseph. Papers. Record Unit 16. Smithsonian Institution Archives.

Hilgard Family. Papers. Bancroft Library, University of California, Berkeley.

Holmes, W. H. "Random Records." National Museum of American Art/National Portrait Gallery Library, Washington, D.C.

Howell, B. F. Papers. Department of Geological and Geophysical Sciences, Archives, Princeton University.

Howley, J. T. Papers. Provincal Archives of Newfoundland and Labrador, St. John's, Newfoundland, Canada.

Hyatt, Alpheus. Papers. Department of Special Collections, Library, Syracuse University, Syracuse, N.Y.

Iddings, Joseph Paxton. Papers. Field Records, United States Geological Survey, Denver, Colo.

International Congress of Geologists. Papers. University Archives and Records Center, University of Pennsylvania, Philadelphia.

Johnson, R. U. Papers. Bancroft Library, University of California, Berkeley.

King, Clarence. Letterbooks. Huntington Library and Art Gallery, Pasadena, Calif.

Lapworth, Charles. Papers. Lapworth Museum, Lapworth Archives, University of Birmingham, Birmingham, England.

Lintner, J. A. Papers. Manuscript and Special Collections, New York State Library, Albany.

Marsh, Othniel Charles. Papers. (Transferred from Yale Peabody Museum). Stirling Library, Manuscripts and Archives Division, Yale University.

Matthew, G. F. Papers. New Brunswick Museum of Natural History, Library, St. John, New Brunswick, Canada.

McGee, W. J. Papers. Manuscript Division, Library of Congress.

Merrill, G. P. Papers. Manuscript Division, Library of Congress.

Nelson, E. W. Papers and E. A. Goodman Collection. Record Unit 7364. Smithsonian Institution Archives.

Newell, F. J. Papers. Manuscript and Special Collections, New York State Library, Albany.

Osborn, H. F. Papers. American Museum of Natural History Library.

Parks, W. A. Papers. Royal Ontario Museum, Toronto, Canada.

Treasurer's Letter Book. National Academy of Sciences Archives, Washington, D.C.

U.S. Geological Survey, Great Lakes Division (C. R. Van Hise). Papers. State Historical Society of Wisconsin Archives, Madison.

U.S. Geological Survey. Monthly Reports. U.S. Geological Survey, RG 57, Archives II, National Archives and Records Adminstration, College Park, Md.

Van Horn, C. W. Papers. Canadian Pacific Railway Archives, Montreal, Canada.

Walcott, C. D. Civil Service Records. National Archives and Records Administration, St. Louis, Mo.

Walcott, C. D. Fossil Locality Lists. Department of Paleobiology, National Museum of Natural History, Washington, D.C.

Walcott, C. D. Papers. Record Unit 7004. Smithsonian Institution Archives.

Walcott Trustee File. Carnegie Institution of Washington Archives, Washington, D.C.

Williams Family Papers (Unit 1148). Kroch Library, Division of Rare Manuscript Collections, Cornell University.

Willis, Bailey. Papers. Huntington Library and Art Gallery, Pasadena, Calif.

Winchell, Alexander. Papers. Bently Historical Library, Michigan Historical Collections, University of Michigan, Ann Arbor.

Yochelson, Ellis L. Papers. Smithsonian Institution Archives.

Published Material by Charles Doolittle Walcott

Some of Walcott's earlier publications were released as advanced prints prior to completion of the entire volume in which they appeared. The date of the publication is important for both priority of names and to provide a more accurate chronology of Walcott's activities. However, these advanced prints are rare and do not differ from the text in the cited volume. To aid the reader who might wish to consult the article, the date of the completed volume is given in brackets at the end of the citation.

1875. Description of a new species of trilobite. *Cincinnati Quarterly Journal of Science* 22:273–74.

1875a. New species of trilobites from the Trenton Limestone at Trenton Falls, New York. *Cincinnati Quarterly Journal of Science* 2:347–49.

1875b. Notes on *Ceraurus pleurexanthemus,* Green. *Annals of the Lyceum of Natural History of New York* 11:155–59.

1875c. Description of the interior surface of the dorsal shell of *Ceraurus pleurexanthemus,* Green. *Annals of the Lyceum of Natural History of New York* 11:159–62.

References

1876. Preliminary notice of the discovery of the remains of the natatory and branchial appendages of trilobites. Advanced print. *28th Annual Report of the New York State Museum of Natural History* [1879]: 89–92.

1877. Description of new species of fossils from the Trenton Limestone. Advanced print. *28th Annual Report of the New York State Museum of Natural History* [1879]: 93–97.

1877a. Description of new species of fossils from the Chazy and Trenton Limestones. Advanced print. *31st Annual Report of the New York State Museum of Natural History* [1879]: 68–71.

1877b. Notes on some sections of trilobites, from the Trenton Limestone. Advanced print. *31st Annual Report of the New York State Museum of Natural History* [1879]: 61–63.

1879. Note on the legs of trilobites. *31st Annual Report of the New York State Museum of Natural History* [1879]: 66–67.

1879a. Descriptions of new species of fossils from the Calciferous Formation. Advanced print. *32nd Annual Report of the New York State Museum of Natural History* [1880]: 129–31.

1879b. The Utica Slate and related formations of the same geological horizon. Advanced print. *Transactions of the Albany Institute* 10 [1888]: 1–17.

1879c. Fossils of the Utica Slate and metamorphoses of *Triarthrus becki.* Advanced print. *Transactions of the Albany Institute* 10 [1888]: 13–38.

1880. The Permian and other Paleozoic groups of the Kanab Valley, Arizona. *American Journal of Science* 10:221–25.

1881. The trilobite: New and old evidence relating to its organization. *Museum of Comparative Zoology, Bulletin* 8:191–224.

1881a. On the nature of *Cyathophycus. American Journal of Science* 22:394–95.

1882. Notice of the discovery of a Poecilopod in the Utica Slate formation. *American Journal of Science* 23:151–52.

1882a. Description of a new genus of the order Eurypterida from the Utica Slate. *American Journal of Science* 23:213–16.

1883. Description of new species of fossils from the Trenton Group of New York. Advanced print. *35th Annual Report of the New York State Museum of Natural History* [1884]: 207–14.

1883a. Fresh-water shells from the Paleozoic rocks of Nevada. *Science,* n.s., 2:808.

1883b. Injury sustained by the eye of a Trilobite at the time of moulting of the shell. *American Journal of Science* 24:302.

1883c. Pre-Carboniferous strata in the Grand Cañon of the Colorado, Arizona. *American Journal of Science* 26:437–42.

1883d. The Cambrian System in the United States and Canada. Advanced print. *Philosophical Society of Washington, Bulletin* 6 [1884]: 97–102.

1884. Report of Mr. Charles D. Walcott. *Fourth Annual Report of the United States Geological Survey to the Secretary of the Interior 1882–'83 by J. W. Powell 1882–'83 Director*, 44–48.

1884b. Appendages of the trilobite. *Science*, n.s., 3:279–281.

1884c. On the Cambrian faunas of North America: Preliminary studies. *U.S. Geological Survey, Bulletin* 10.

1884d. Paleontology of the Eureka District. *U.S. Geological Survey, Monograph* 8.

1885. Report of Mr. Charles D. Walcott. *Fifth Annual Report of the United States Geological Survey to the Secretary of the Interior 1883–'84, by J. W. Powell Director*, 52–55.

1885a. Report of Mr. Charles D. Walcott. *Sixth Annual Report of the United States Geological Survey to the Secretary of Interior 1884–'85 by J. W. Powell Director*, 74–78.

1885b. Deer Creek coal-field, White Mountain Indian Reservation, Arizona, report and appendix. 48th Cong., 2d sess. S. Doc. 20, pp. 2–7.

1885c. Paleontologic notes. *American Journal of Science* 29:114–17.

1885d. Paleozoic notes: New genera of Cambrian trilobites, *Mesonascis. American Journal of Science* 29:329–31.

1885e. Notes on Paleozoic pteropods. *American Journal of Science* 30:17–21.

1886. Cambrian age of the roofing slates of Granville, Washington County, New York. Advanced print. *American Association for the Advancement of Science, Proceedings* 35 [1887]:220–21.

1886a. Second contribution to the studies on the Cambrian faunas of North America. *U.S. Geological Survey, Bulletin* 30.

1886b. Classification of the Cambrian System of North America. *American Journal of Science* 32:138–57.

1887. The Taconic System. *American Journal of Science* 33:153–54.

1887a. Note on the genus *Archaeocyathus* of Billings. *American Journal of Science* 34:145–46.

1887b. Fauna of the "Upper Taconic" of Emmons, in Washington County, New York. *American Journal of Science* 34:187–99.

1887c. Section of Lower Silurian (Ordovician) and Cambrian strata in central New York, as shown by a deep well near Utica. Advanced print. *American Association for the Advancement of Science, Proceedings* 36 [1888]: 211–12.

1887d. Discovery of fossils in the Lower Taconic of Emmons. Advanced print. *American Association for the Advancement of Science, Proceedings* 36:[1888]: 212–13.

1888. Report of Mr. C. D. Walcott. *Seventh Annual Report of the United States Geological Survey to the Secretary of Interior 1885–'86 by J. W. Powell Director*, 113–17.

1888a. The Taconic System of Emmons, and use of the name Taconic in geologic nomenclature. *American Journal of Science* 35:229–42, 307–27, 394–401.

References

1888b. Cambrian fossils from Mount Stephens, Northwest Territory of Canada. *American Journal of Science* 36:161–66.

1888c. The stratigraphical succession of the Cambrian faunas in North America. *Nature* 38:551.

1889. Report of Mr. C. D. Walcott. *Eighth Annual Report of the United States Geological Survey to the Secretary of the Interior 1886–'87 by J. W. Powell Director*, pt. 1:174–78.

1889a. Stratigraphic position of the *Olenellus* fauna in North America and Europe. *American Journal of Science* 37:374–92, 38:29–42.

1889b. Description of new genera and species of fossils from the Middle Cambrian. *United States National Museum, Proceedings for 1888* 11:441–46.

1889c. A simple method of measuring the thickness of inclined strata. *United States National Museum, Proceedings for 1888* 11:447–48.

1889d. Description of a new genus and species of inarticulate brachiopod from the Trenton Limestone. Advanced print. *United States National Museum, Proceedings for 1889* 12 [1890]: 365–66.

1890. Report of Mr. Charles D. Walcott. *Tenth Annual Report of the United States Geological Survey to the Secretary of Interior 1888–'89 by J. W. Powell Director*, 160–62.

1890a. The fauna of the Lower Cambrian or *Olenellus* zone. *Tenth Annual Report of the United States Geological Survey to the Secretary of the Interior 1888–'89 by J. W. Powell Director*, pt. 1:509–774.

1890b. Study of a line of displacement in the Grand Cañon of the Colorado, in northern Arizona. *Geological Society of America, Bulletin* 1:49–64.

1890c. A review of Dr. R. W. Ells' second report on the geology of the province of Quebec, with additional notes on the "Quebec Group." *American Journal of Science* 39:101–15.

1890d. Review of *Report of State Geologist of New York, for 1888; Forty-second Annual Report of the New York State Museum of Natural History, 1889. American Journal of Science* 39:155–56.

1890e. The value of the term "Hudson River Group" in geologic nomenclature. *Geological Society of America, Bulletin* 1:335–55.

1890f. Description of new forms of Upper Cambrian fossils. *United States National Museum, Proceedings for 1890* 13:267–79.

1891. La succession stratigraphique des faunes cambriennes dans l'Amérique du Nord. *Congrès Géologique International, Compte Rendue 4me session, Londres, 1888*, 223–25.

1891a. Auffindung von Fischresten im Untersilur. *Neues Jahrsbuch für Mineralogie, Geologie, und Paläontologie 1891* 1:284–85.

1891b. Correlation papers—Cambrian. *U.S. Geological Survey, Bulletin* 81.

1891c. The North American continent during Cambrian time. *Twelfth Annual Report of the United States Geological Survey to the Secretary of the Interior 1890–'91 by J. W. Powell Director,* pt. 1:526–68.

1892. Preliminary notes on the discovery of a vertebrate fauna in Silurian (Ordovician) strata. *Geological Society of America, Bulletin* 3:153–72.

1892a. Notes on the Cambrian rocks of Pennsylvania and Maryland, from the Susquehanna to the Potomac. *American Journal of Science* 44:469–82.

1892b. Notes on the Cambrian rocks of Virginia and the southern Appalachians. *American Journal of Science* 44:52–57.

1892c. Report of Mr. C. D. Walcott. *Thirteenth Annual Report of the United States Geological Survey to the Secretary of the Interior 1891–'92 by J. W. Powell Director,* pt. 1:135–40.

1893. Classification of clastic rocks, with particular reference to the Cambrian. *Congrès Géologique International, Compte Rendu 5me session Washington, 1891,* 168–70.

1893a. Report of Mr. C. D. Walcott. *Fourteenth Annual Report of the United States Geological Survey to the Secretary of the Interior 1891–'92 by J. W. Powell Director,* pt. 1:252–55.

1893b. The natural bridge of Virginia. *National Geographic Magazine* 5:59–62.

1893c. The geologist at Blue Mountains, Maryland. *National Geographic Magazine* 5:84–88.

1893d. Geologic time, as indicated by the sedimentary rocks of North America. *Journal of Geology* 1:639–76; *American Geologist* 12:343–68; *American Association for the Advancement of Science, Proceedings* 42 [1894]: 129–69; *Annual Report of the Smithsonian Institution for 1893* [1894]: 301–34.

1894. On the occurrence of *Olenellus* in the Green Pond Mountain series of northern New Jersey, with a note on the conglomerates. *American Journal of Science* 47:309–11.

1894a. Note on the Cambrian rocks of Pennsylvania from the Susquehana to the Delaware. *American Journal of Science* 47:37–41.

1894b. Paleozoic intraformational conglomerates. *Geological Society of America, Bulletin* 5:191–98.

1894c. Notes on some appendages of the trilobites. *Biological Society of Washington, Proceedings* 9:89–97.

1894d. Discovery of the genus *Oldhamia* in America. Advanced print. *United States National Museum, Proceedings for 1894* 17 [1895]: 313–15.

1894e. Pre-Cambrian igneous rocks of the Unkar terrane, Grand Canyon of the Colorado, Arizona; with notes on the petrographic character of the lavas by J. P. Iddings. *Fourteenth Annual Report of the United States Geological Survey to the Secretary of the Interior 1892–'93 by J. W. Powell Director,* pt. 2:497–519.

1895. Lower Cambrian rocks in eastern California. *American Journal of Science* 49:141–44.

References

1895a. The Appalachian type of folding in the White Mountain Range of Inyo County, California. *American Journal of Science* 49:169–74.

1895b. The United States Geological Survey. *Popular Science Monthly* 46:479–98.

1895c. The United States Geological Survey and its methods of work. *Engineers' Club of Philadelphia, Proceedings* 12:44–61.

1895d. Algonkian rocks of the Grand Canyon of the Colorado. *Journal of Geology* 3:312–20.

1896. *Sixteenth Annual Report of the United States Geological Survey to the Secretary of the Interior 1894–'96 by Charles D. Walcott Director,* pt. 1:1–200.

1896a. The Cambrian rocks of Pennsylvania. *U.S. Geological Survey, Bulletin* 134.

1896b. Fossil jelly fishes from the Middle Cambrian terrane. *United States National Museum, Proceedings for 1896* 18:611–14.

1896c. U.S. House. Committee on Appropriations. *Statement of Mr. Charles D. Walcott, Director of the Geological Survey.* HAp 54-J-1. 16 March 1896, 114–17.

1897. The post-Pleistocene elevation of the Inyo Range, and the lake beds of the Waucobi embayment, Inyo County, California. *Journal of Geology* 5:340–48.

1897a. Note on the genus *Lingulepis. American Journal of Science,* 4th ser., 3:404–5.

1897b. Cambrian brachiopoda: Genera *Iphidea* and *Yorkia,* with descriptions of new species of each, and of the genus *Acrothele. United States National Museum, Proceedings for 1897* 19:707–18.

1898. U.S. Senate. *Report on a Proposed Division of Mines and Mining in the United States Geological Survey.* 55th Cong., 3d sess. S. Doc. 40, pp. 2–12.

1898a. The United States forest reserves. *Appleton's Scientific Monthly* 52:1–18.

1898b. U.S. Senate. *Report on the Region South of and Adjoining Yellowstone National Park, with Especial Reference to the Preservation and Protection of the Forest and the Game Therein.* 55th Cong., 3d sess. S. Doc. 39, 3–6.

1898c. Work of the geological survey in the south. *Tradesman Annual* 19:117–20.

1898d. Fossil Medusae. *U.S. Geological Survey, Monograph* 30.

1898e. Cambrian brachiopoda *Obolus* and *Lingulella,* with descriptions of new species. Advanced print. *United States National Museum, Proceedings for 1899* 21:385–20.

1898f. Notes on the brachiopod fauna of the quartzitic pebbles of the Carboniferous conglomerates of the Narragansett basin, Rhode Island. *American Journal of Science,* 3d ser., 6:327–28.

1899. U.S. House. *Statement of Mr. Charles D. Walcott, Director of the Geological Survey. House Hearings* 599 (1): 110–15. 15 January 1899.

1899a. Report upon the condition and progress of the U.S. National Museum during the year ending June 30, 1897. *Smithsonian Institution Annual Report for 1897, Report of the United States National Museum,* 1–245.

1899b. Pre-Cambrian fossiliferous formations. *Geological Society of America, Bulletin* 10:199–214.

1899c. The United States National Museum. *Appleton's Popular Science Monthly* 55:491–501.

1899d. Cambrian fossils [of the Yellowstone Park]. *U.S. Geological Survey, Monograph* 32, pt. 2:440–78.

1900. Report upon the condition and progress of the U.S. National Museum during the year end June 30, 1898. *Smithsonian Institution Annual Report for 1898, Report of the United States National Museum*, 1–149.

1900a. Correspondence relating to collections of vertebrate fossils made by the late professor O. C. Marsh. *Science*, n.s., 11:21–24.

1900b. Random, a pre-Cambrian Upper Algonkian terrane. *Geological Society of America, Bulletin* 11:3–5.

1900c. Lower Cambrian terrane in the Atlantic province. *Washington Academy of Sciences, Proceedings* 1:301–39.

1900d. Washington as an explorer and surveyor. *Popular Science Monthly* 57:323–24.

1900e. U.S. House. *Statement of Mr. Charles D. Walcott, Director of the Geological Survey. House Hearings* 599 (2): 240–54. 3 April 1900.

1900f. U.S. House. Committee on Appropriations. *Statement of Mr. Charles D. Walcott, Director of the Geological Survey.* HAp 56N. [13 December], 75–76.

1901. The work of the United States Geological Survey in relation to the mineral resources of the United States. *American Institute of Mining Engineers, Transactions* 30:3–26.

1901a. The geographic work of the U.S. Geological Survey. *Verhandlungen des 7th International Geographen-Kongresses in Berlin, 1899* 2:707–13.

1901b. Relations of the national government to higher education and research. *Science*, n.s., 13:1001–15.

1901c. Cambrian Brachiopoda: *Obolella*, subgenus *Glypias; Bicia; Obolus*, subgenus *Westonia;* with descriptions of new species. *United States National Museum, Proccedings for 1901* 13:669–95.

1902. Cambrian Brachiopoda; *Acrotreta; Linnarssonella; Obolus;* with descriptions of new species. *United States National Museum, Proceedings for 1902* 25:577–612.

1902a. Outlook of the geologist in America. *Geological Society of America, Bulletin* 15:99–118.

1902b. *Twenty-third Annual Report of the Director of the United States Geological Survey to the Secretary of the Interior, 1901–2*, 9–217.

1902c. Vast extent of arid lands. *National Magazine* 15:571–72.

1903. *Twenty-fourth Annual Report of the Director of the United States Geological Survey to the Secretary of the Interior, 1902–3*, 1–302.

1904. U.S. House. Committee on Appropriations. *Statement of Mr. Charles D. Walcott, Director of the Geological Survey.* HAp 58-L, 95–100.

References

1904a. U.S. House. Committee on Appropriations. *Statement of Mr. Charles D. Walcott, Director of the Geological Survey, Accompanied by Mr. Joseph A. Holmes, an Expert in His Office*. HAp 58-O, 17–84.

1905. Work of the Geological Survey in mapping the reserves. *Proceedings of the American Forest Congress*. 2–6 January 1905, 364–80. Washington, D.C.

1905a. U.S. House. *Statement of Mr. Charles D. Walcott, Director. House Hearings* 601 (2): 144–64. 27 January 1905.

1905b. The Cambrian faunas of India. *Washington Academy of Sciences, Proceedings* 7:251–56.

1905c. *Twenty-sixth Annual Report of the Director of the United States Geological Survey to the Secretary of the Interior, 1904–5*, 1–322.

1905d. Cambrian brachiopods with descriptions of new genera and species. *United States National Museum, Proceedings for 1905* 28:227–337.

1906. Algonkian formations of northwestern Montana. *Geological Society of America, Bulletin* 17:1–28.

1906a. Cambrian faunas of China. *United States National Museum, Proceedings for 1906* 30:563–95.

1906b. U.S. House. *Statement of Charles D. Walcott, Director, April 13, 1906. House Hearings* 602 (2): 444–571.

1906c. Relation of government reclamation work to private enterprise. *Official Proceedings of the 14th National Irrigation Congress, Held at Boise, Idaho, September 3–8*, 50–54.

1906d. Principles which govern the United States Geological Survey in it relations with other geological surveys and working geologists. *Science*, n.s., 24:692–93.

1907. Geological work in Arkansas by Professor Purdue. *Science*, n.s., 25:109–10.

1907a. Louis Agassiz. *Smithsonian Miscellaneous Collections* 50:216–18.

1908. Cambrian sections of the Cordilleran area. *Smithsonian Miscellaneous Collections* 53:167–230.

1912. New York Potsdam-Hoyt fauna. *Smithsonian Miscellaneous Collections* 57:251–304.

1914. *Dikelocephalus* and other genera of the Dikelocephalidae. *Smithsonian Miscellaneous Collections* 57:345–412.

1916. Evidences of primitive life. *Smithsonian Institution Annual Report for 1915*, 235–55.

1917. National Parks as a scientific asset. *Proceedings of the National Parks Conference*, 113–17.

Other Published Sources

Adams, Henry. 1946. *The education of Henry Adams: An autobiography*. 1907. Reprint. Boston: Houghton Mifflin.

Agassiz, L. 1873. Discovery of the basal joint of legs of trilobites. *American Naturalist* 7:741–42.

Albritton, C. C., Jr. 1980. *The abyss of time: Changing conceptions of the earth's antiquity after the sixteenth century.* San Francisco: Freeman, Cooper, 251.

Aldrich, J. W. 1980. The Biological Society of Washington: A centennial history 1880–1980. *Biological Society of Washington, Bulletin* 4:40.

Allison, W. B. [chairman]. 1904. *Medals commemorative of the two hundredth birthday of the birth of Benjamin Franklin.* U.S. Senate. Appropriations Committee for Fiscal Year 1904. SAp 58F. 8 April 1904, 19–22.

Anonymous. 1884. Intelligence from American scientific stations. *Science*, n.s., 3:136–37.

———. 1884a. Intelligence from American scientific stations. *Science*, n.s., 3:582.

———. 1887. Review of *U.S. Geological Survey, Bulletin* 30. *Science*, n.s., 9:545–46.

———. 1887a. Review of *U.S. Geological Survey, Bulletin* 30. *American Journal of Science* 33:158–59.

———. 1891. Review of "The fauna of the Olenellus zone." *Geological Magazine* 9:32–36.

———. 1892. Review of "Correlation papers—Cambrian." *American Geologist* 9:203–5.

———. 1893. Review of "The North American continent during Cambrian time." *American Journal of Science* 45:164.

———. 1897. Scientific notes and news. *Science*, n.s., 5:222–23.

———. 1898. The Washington Academy of Sciences. *Science*, n.s., 7:253–55.

———. 1904. *The twenty-fifth anniversary of the Cosmos Club of Washington D.C., with a documentary history of the club from its organization, to November 16, 1903.* Washington, D.C.: Cosmos Club.

———. 1919. *The U.S. Reclamation Service: Its history, activities, and organization.* New York: Institute for Government Research, D. Appleton.

Arvin, Newton, ed. 1951. *The selected letters of Henry Adams.* New York: Farrar, Straus and Young.

Bartlett, R. A. 1962. *Great surveys of the American west.* Norman: University of Oklahoma Press.

———. 1985. *Yellowstone: A wilderness besieged.* Tucson: University of Arizona Press.

Bassler, R. S. 1936. *Department of Geology: Report on the progress and condition of the United States National Museum for the year ended June 30, 1935,* 45–56. Washington, D.C.: Government Printing Office.

Batten, R. L. 1987. Robert Parr Whitfield: Hall's assistant who stayed too long. *Earth Sciences History* 6:61–71.

Benson, K. R. 1987. H. Newell Martin, W. K. Brooks, and the reformation of American biology. *American Zoologist* 27:759–71.

Blum, A. S. 1987. "A better style of art": The illustrations of the *Palaeontology* of New York. *Earth Sciences History* 6:72–85.

Bradley, W. H. 1963. Geologic Laws. In *The fabric of geology.* Edited by C. C. Albritton. Reading, Mass.: Addison-Wesley.

References

Branner, J. C. 1906. Correspondence relating to the survey of the coal fields of Arkansas. *Science*, n.s., 24:532–37.

———. 1906a. The policy of the U.S. Geological Survey and its bearing upon science and education. *Science*, n.s., 24:722–28.

Brett, C. E., T. E. Whitesley, P. A. Allison, and E. Yochelson. 1997. The Walcott-Rust quarry: a Middle Ordovician trilobite Konservat-Lagerstatte. Second International Trilobite Conference, Brock University, St. Catharines, Ontario, August 22–25, 1997. Abstracts with program.

Brigham, A. P. 1888. The geology of Oneida County. *Oneida Historical Society, Transactions, 1887–88.*

Brøgger, W. C. 1886. Om alderene af Olenelluszonen i Nordamerica. *Geologiska Föreningen i Stockholm Förhandlinger* 8 (3): 183–213. [English translation prepared for C. D. Walcott].

———. 1896. Über die Vertreitung der Euloma-Niobe-Fauna. (der Ceratopygen kalk fauna) in Europa. *Nyt Magazine for Naturvidensk* 35:184–240. [English translation prepare for C. D. Walcott.]

Brooks, W. K. 1894. The origin of the oldest fossils and discovery of the bottom of the ocean. *Journal of Geology* 2:455–79.

Burchfield, J. D. 1975. *Lord Kelvin and the age of the earth.* New York: Scientific History Publications.

Butts, Lee. 1953. Cooper Curtice, "Doctor Ticks," American agricultural scientist (1856–1939). Mimeograph copy. Beltsville, Md.: National Library of Agriculture.

Calvin, Samuel, E. W. Claypool, P. Frazer, E. O. Ulrich, N. H. Winchell. 1888. Introductory. *American Geologist* 1:1–3.

Cameron, Frank. 1952. *Cottrell: Samaritan of science.* Garden City, N.Y.: Doubleday. Reprint, Tucson, Ariz.: Research Corporation, 1993.

Carmichael, Leonard, and J. C. Long. 1965. James Smithson and the Smithsonian story. New York: G. P. Putnam's Sons.

Carnegie Institution of Washington. 1903. *Year Book No. 1.* Washington, D.C.: Carnegie Institution of Washington, D.C.

Clarke, J. M. 1921. *James Hall, of Albany, geologist and palaeontologist, 1811–1898.* Albany, N.Y.

Cloud, Preston. 1987. Luminaries of the Albany era: Beecher, Schuchert, and Hall. *Earth Sciences History* 6:109–13.

———. 1988. *Oasis in space: Earth history from the beginning.* New York: W. W. Norton.

Colbert, E. H. 1992. *William Diller Matthew, paleontologist: The splendid drama observed.* New York: Columbia University Press.

Cooper, G. A. 1931. Concerning the authorship of the "Preliminary notice of the lamellibranch shells of the Upper Helderberg, Hamilton and Chemung groups, etc. Part 2." *Washington Academy of Sciences Journal* 21:439–67.

Crouch, T. D. 1980. *A dream of wings: Americans and the airplane 1875–1905.* Washington, D.C.: Smithsonian Institution Press.

Dale, T. N. 1893. The Rensselaer grit plateau of New York. *Thirteenth annual report of the United States Geological Survey to the Secretary of the Interior 1891–'92 by J. W. Powell Director,* pt. 2:293–340.

Dana, J. D. 1872. Supposed legs of trilobites. *American Journal of Science,* 3d ser., 3:221–22.

———. 1881. [Review of "The trilobite"]. *American Journal of Science,* 3d ser., 22:79.

———. 1895. *Manual of Geology, treating of the principles of the science with special reference to American geological history.* 4th ed. New York: American Book Company.

Darrah, W. C. 1951. *Powell of the Colorado.* Princeton, N.J.: Princeton University Press.

Davis, W. M. 1926. Grove Karl Gilbert, 1843–1918. *National Academy of Sciences, Memoir* 21(2):303.

Dunbar, C. O. 1943. Memorial to Charles Schuchert. *Geological Society of America, Proceedings, Annual Report for 1942,* 217–40.

Dupree, A. H. 1957. *Science in the federal government.* Cambridge: Belknap Press, Harvard University.

Dutton, C. E. 1880. United States Geological Survey, Division of the Colorado. *First Annual Report of the United States Geological Survey to the Hon. Carl Schurz Secretary of the Interior by Clarence King, Director,* 28–31.

———. 1882. Tertiary history of the Grand Cañon. *U.S. Geological Survey, Monograph 2.*

———. 1882a. The physical geology of the Grand Cañon. *Second Annual Report of the United States Geological Survey to the Secretary of the Interior 1880–'81 by J. W. Powell, Director,* 49–166.

Eagan, W. E. 1987. "I would have sworn my life upon your interpretation"; James Hall, Sir William Logan, and the "Quebec Group." *Earth Sciences History* 6:47–60.

———. 1989. The debate over the Canadian Shield. *Isis* 80:232–53.

Emmons, S. F. 1893. [Report of the Secrétaire-Général]. *Congrès Géologique International, Compte Rendu de al 5me session, Washington, 1891.* Washington, D.C.: Government Printing Office.

Fairchild, H. L. 1887. *A history of the New York Academy of Sciences, formerly the Lyceum of Natural History.* Published privately by the author.

———. 1932. *The Geological Society of America: A chapter in earth science history.* New York: Geological Society of America.

Fakundiny, R. H. 1987. The New York State Museum: Child of the geological survey that grew to be its guardian. *Earth Sciences History* 6:125–33.

Fakundiny, R. H., and J. R. Albanese. 1988. *The state geological surveys: A history,* edited by A. A. Soklow. New York: Association of American State Geologists.

Fenneman, N. H. 1931. *Physiography of the western United States.* New York: McGraw-Hill.

References

Fisher, D. 1977. Correlation of the Hadrynian, Cambrian, and Ordovician rocks in New York state. New York State Museum, map and chart series no. 25. Albany, N.Y.

Fisher, D. J. 1963. The seventy years of the Department of Geology University of Chicago, 1892–1961. Chicago: University of Chicago Press.

Flack, J. K. 1975. *Desideratum in Washington: The intellectual community in the capital city 1870–1900.* Cambridge, Mass.: Schenkman.

Follansbee, Robert. 1938. A history of the Water Resources Branch of the United States Geological Survey to June 30, 1919. U.S. Geological Survey, unpublished mimeograph. U.S. Geological Survey Library, Reston, Va.

Ford, T. D., and W. J. Breed. 1972. The Chuar Group of the Proterozoic, Grand Canyon, Arizona. *Twenty-fourth International Geological Congress, Proceedings,* sec. 1, pp. 3–18.

Foster, Mike. 1994. Strange genius: The life of Ferdinand Vandeveer Hayden. Niwot, Colo.: Roberts Rinehart Publishers.

Fowler, D. C., and C. S. Fowler. 1968, John Wesley Powell's journal: Colorado River exploration, 1871–1872. *Smithsonian Journal of History* 3:1–44.

Frazer, Persifor, Jr. 1888. A short history of the origin and acts of the international congress of geologists, and of the American committee delegates to it. *American Geologist* 1:3–11.

———. 1891. Report of the sub-committee on the Archean: A-15—A-86. *Congrès Géologique International, Compte Rendu de a 4me session, Londres, 1888.*

Geike, Archibald. 1924. *A long life's work: An autobiography.* London: Macmillan.

Gilman, D. C. 1899. *The life of James Dwight Dana—scientific explorer, mineralogist, zoologist, professor in Yale University.* New York: Harper Brothers.

Goode, G. B. [1880?]. Circular 1, Organization and administration of the United States National Museum. Copy in the Smithsonian Institution Archives, Washington, D.C.

———. 1891. The museums of the future. *Smithsonian Institution Annual Report, Report of the National Museum,* 445.

Goode, G. B., ed. 1897. *The Smithsonian Institution, 1846–1896: The history of the first half century.* Washington, D.C.: Smithsonian Institution.

Goode, J. B. 1988. *Best Addresses.* Washington, D.C.: Smithsonian Institution Press.

Gould, S. J. 1989. *Wonderful Life: The Burgess Shale and the nature of history.* W. W. Norton, New York.

Hague, Arnold. 1880. [Untitled letter report.] *First Annual Report of the United States Geological Survey to Hon. Carl Schurtz Secretary of the Interior by Clarence King, Director,* 32–35.

———. 1882. Report of Mr. Arnold Hague. *Second Annual Report of the United States Geological Survey to the Secretary of the Interior 1880–'81, by J. W. Powell, Director,* 21–35.

———. 1883. Report of Mr. Arnold Hague. *Third Annual Report of the United States Geological Survey to the Secretary of the Interior 1881–'82, by J. W. Powell, Director*, 10–14.

———. 1884. Report of Mr. Arnold Hague. *Fourth Annual Report of the United States Geological Survey to the Secretary of the Interior 1882–'83, by J. W. Powell, Director*, 16–19.

Hall, James. 1872. Reply to "Note on a question of priority." *American Journal of Science* 154:105–9.

———. 1879. Report of the director. *Thirty-first Annual Report of the New York State Museum of Natural History by the Regents of the University of the State of New York*, 5–9.

———. 1879a. Report of the director. *Thirty-second Annual Report of the New York State Museum of Natural History by the Regents of the University of the State of New York*, 5–14.

———. 1881. Report of the director. *Thirty-fourth Annual Report of the New York State Museum of Natural History by the Regents of the University of the State of New York*, ex officio trustees of the museum, 5–12.

Hall, J. W. 1884. Notice of the machinery and methods of cutting specimens of rocks and fossil specimens at the New York State Museum. *Thirty-fifth Annual Report of the New York State Museum of Natural History by the Regents of the University of the State of New York*, 121–24.

Hafertepe, Kenneth. 1984. *America's Castle: The evolution of the Smithsonian building and its institution, 1840–1878*. Washington, D.C.: Smithsonian Institution Press.

Hamilton, B. M. 1989. British geologists changing perceptions of Precambrian time in the nineteenth century. *Earth Sciences History* 8:141–49.

Hayford, J. H., and C. D. Wead. 1902. Report of the meeting of December 6, 1902. *Philosophical Society of Washington, Bulletin* 24:2.

Hellman, G. 1969. *Bankers, bones & beetles: The first century of the American Museum of Natural History*. Garden City, N.Y.: Natural History Press.

Hoffman, H. J. 1971. Precambrian fossils, pseudofossils, and problematica in Canada. *Geological Survey of Canada*, bulletin 189.

Howell, B. F. 1925. The fauna of the Paradoxides beds at Manuels, Newfoundland. *Bulletins of American Paleontology* 43:1–140.

Huntoon, P. W., G. H. Billingsly, Jr., W. J. Breed, T. D. Ford, M. D. Clark, R. S. Babcock, and E. H. Brown. 1986. *Geologic map of the Grand Canyon: Scale 1:62,500*. 3rd ed. Museum of Northern Arizona and Grand Canyon Natural History Association.

Iddings, J. P. 1893. Editorial. *Journal of Geology* 1:296–98.

———. 1919. Arnold Hague 1840–1917. *National Academy of Sciences, Biographical Memoirs* 9:21–38.

Ise, John. 1920. *The United States forest policy*. New Haven: Yale University Press.

References

James, J. F. 1891. [Review of "The fauna of the *Olenellus* zone"]. *American Geologist* 8:82–86.

Kay, G. M. 1943. Mowhawkian Series on West Canada Creek, New York. *American Journal of Science* 241:597–606.

Kevlas, Daniel, J. L. Sturchi, and P. T. Carroll. 1980. The sciences in America, circa 1880. *Science*, n.s., 209:27–32.

King, Clarence. 1875. Geological explorations of the fortieth parallel, from the Sierra Nevada to the eastern slope of the Rocky Mountains. *Report of the Secretary of War, Report of the Chief of Engineers.* 44th Cong., 1st sess., H.E. Doc. 1, vol. 2, pt. 2, app. KK, pp. 919–20.

———. 1880. *First Annual Report of the United States Geological Survey to the Hon. Carl Schurtz Secretary of the Interior by Clarence King, Director.*

King, P. B. 1949. The base of the Cambrian in the southern Appalachians. *American Journal of Science* 247:514.

Kirk, R. E. 1852. *A discourse, delivered at the funeral of Mr. Charles D. Walcott.* Utica, N.Y.: Privately printed.

Kohlstadt, S. G. 1976. *The formation of the American scientific community.* Urbana: University of Illinois Press.

Kriz, Jiri, and John Pojeta Jr. 1974. Barrande's colonies concept and a comparison of his stratigraphy with the modern stratigraphy of the middle Bohemian Lower Paleozoic rocks (Barrandium) of Czechoslovakia. *Journal of Paleontology* 48:489–94.

Laudan, Rachael. 1987. *From mineralogy to geology: The foundations of a science 1650–1830.* Chicago: University of Chicago Press.

Levenson, J. C., E. Samuels, C. Vanderser, and V. H. Winner, eds. 1988. *Letters of Henry Adams: Volume 5, 1899–1905.* Cambridge: Belknap Press, Harvard University.

Logue, J. M. 1995. *Beyond the Germ Theory: The Story of Dr. Cooper Curtice.* College Station: Texas A&M University Press.

Lurie, Edward. 1960. *Louis Agassiz, a life in science.* Chicago: University of Chicago Press.

McKee, E. D. 1928. A reconnaissance of the northeastern part of Grand Canyon National Park. *Nature Notes of Grand Canyon* 6 (3).

MacNeil, F. S. 1939. Fresh-water invertebrates and land plants of Cretaceous age from Eureka, Nevada. *Journal of Paleontology* 36:355–60.

Madsen, D. A. 1969. Daniel Coit Gilman at the Carnegie Institution of Washington. *History of Education Quarterly* 9:154–86.

Manning, T. G. 1967. *Government in science: The U.S. Geological Survey 1867–1894.* Lexington: University of Kentucky Press.

———. 1988. *U.S. Coast Survey vs. Naval Hydrology Office: 19th century rivalry in science and politics.* Tuscaloosa: University of Alabama Press.

Marcou, Jules. 1887. On the use of the name Taconic. *Boston Society of Natural History, Proceedings* 22:343–55.

———. 1888. Palaeontologic and stratigraphic "principles" of the adversaries of the Taconic. *American Geologist* 1:10–23, 67–86.

———. 1888a. *American geological classification and nomenclature.* Salem, Mass.: Privately printed.

Merriam, C. W. 1968. Paleozoic rocks of the Antelope Valley, Eureka and Nye Counties, Nevada. *U.S. Geological Survey, Professional Paper* 423.

———. 1973. Middle Devonian rugose corals of the central Great Basin. *U.S. Geological Survey, Professional Paper* 799.

———. 1974. Lower and lower Middle Devonian rugose corals from the central Great Basin. *U.S. Geological Survey, Professional Paper* 805.

Merrill, G. P. 1920. Contributions to a history of American state geological and natural history surveys. *United States National Museum, Bulletin* 109.

———. 1924. *The first one hundred years of American geology.* New Haven: Yale University Press.

Merton, R. K. 1968. The Matthew effect in science. *Science,* n.s., 159:556–63.

Meunier, Fernand. 1899. Les méduses fossils. *Sociéte Géologique de Belgique, Annales 26, Bibliographie* 2:7–19.

Miller, H. S. 1970. *Dollars for research.* Seattle: University of Washington Press.

Miller, R. F. 1988. George Frederic Matthew (1837–1923). In Trace fossils, small shelly fossils and the Precambrian-Cambrian boundary. Edited by Ed Landing, G. M. Narbonne, and Paul Myrow. In *New York State Museum, Bulletin* 463:4–7.

Miller, R. F., and D. N. Buhay. 1990. Life and letters of George Frederic Matthew: Geologist and paleontologist. *New Brunswick Museum, Publications in Natural Science* 8:89.

Milne Edwards, H. M. 1892. Des nouvelles recherches de M. Walcott relatives a la structure des trilobites seuvi de quelques considérations sur l'intérpretation des faits constatés. *Annales des Sciences Naturales 6, Zoologie* 12:19–33.

Morrison, E. E., ed. 1951. *The letters of Theodore Roosevelt.* Volume 3, *The square deal (1901–1903).*

———. 1952. *The letters of Theodore Roosevelt.* Volume 5, *The big stick (1905–1907).*

Nelson, C. M. 1987. Meek at Albany, 1852–1858. *Earth Sciences History* 6:40–46.

Noble, L. F. 1910. Contributions to the geology of the Grand Canyon area, Arizona—the geology of the Shinumo area. *American Journal of Science* 29:369–86; 497–528.

Nolan, T. E., C. W. Merriam, and J. S. Williams. 1956. The stratigraphic section in the vicinity of Eureka, Nevada. *U.S. Geological Survey, Professional Paper* 276.

O'Brien, C. J. 1970. *Eozoon canadense,* the dawn animal of Canada. *Isis* 61:206–31.

Oehser, P. H. 1949. *Sons of Science: The story of the Smithsonian Institution and its leaders.* New York: Henry Schuman.

Oliver, W. A., Jr. 1987. James Hall and fossil corals. *Earth Sciences History* 6:99–105.

Osborn, H. F. 1931. *Cope: Master naturalist.* Princeton, N.J.: Princeton University Press.

References

O'Toole, Patricia. 1990. *The five of hearts: An intimate portrait of Henry Adams and his friends 1880–1918*. New York: Clarkson Potter Publishers.

[Packard, A. S., Jr.]. 1877. Discovery of jointed limbs in trilobites. *American Naturalist* 11:692–94.

Packard, A. S., Jr. 1882. On the homologies of the crustacean limb. *American Naturalist* 16:785–99.

Pettijohn, F. J. 1988. *A century of geology 1885–1985 at the Johns Hopkins University*. Baltimore: Gateway Press.

Pinchot, Gifford. 1947. *Breaking new ground*. New York: Harcourt, Brace. Reprint, Seattle: University of Washington Press, 1972.

Powell, J. W. 1884. The cañons of the Colorado. *Chautauquan* 4 (10): 105–6.

Pyne, S. J. 1979. From the Grand Canyon to the Mariana Trench: The earth sciences after Darwin. In *The Sciences in the American context: New perspectives*. Edited by N. Reingold, 165–92. Washington, D.C.: Smithsonian Institution Press.

———. 1980. *Grove Karl Gilbert; a great engine for research*. Austin: University of Texas Press.

———. 1983. Dutton's Point: An intellectual history of the Grand Canyon. *Grand Canyon Natural History Association, Monograph* 5.

Rabbitt, M. C. 1979. *Minerals, lands, and geology for the common defence and general welfare*. Volume 1, *Before 1879*. Washington, D.C.: Government Printing Office.

———. 1980. *Minerals, lands, and geology for the common defence and general welfare*. Volume 2, *1879–1904*. Washington, D.C.: Government Printing Office.

———. 1986. *Minerals, lands and geology for the common defence and general welfare*. Volume 3, *1904–1939*. Washington, D.C.: Government Printing Office.

Rabbitt, M. C., E. D. McKee, C. B. Hunt, and Luna Leopold. 1969. The Colorado region and John Wesley Powell. *U.S. Geological Survey, Professional Paper* 669.

Rainger, Ronald. 1991. *An agenda for antiquity: Henry Fairfield Osborn and vertebrate paleontology at the American Museum of Natural History, 1890–1935*. Tuscaloosa: University of Alabama Press.

Rathbun, Richard. 1906. Report of the Assistant Secretary. *Annual Report of the Board of Regents of the Smithsonian Institution Showing the Operations, Expenditures, and Condition of the Institution for the Year Ending June 30, 1905*, 7–20.

Rees, M. N., and R. A. Robison. 1989. Days 5 and 6: Cambrian stratigraphy and paleontology of the Central House Range and Drum Mountains, Utah. [a section of] Cambrian and Early Ordovician Stratigraphy and Paleontology of the Basin and Range Province, western United States. In *28th International Geological Congress, Field trip guidebook T-125*. Edited by M. E. Taylor, 59–86. Washington, D.C.: American Geophysical Union.

Reiger, J. F. 1992. Wildlife, conservation, and the first forest reserve. In *The origins of the national forests*. Edited by H. K. Steen, 106–12. Durham, N.C.: Forest History Society.

Reingold, Nathan. 1979. National science policy in a private foundation: The Carnegie Institution of Washington. In *The organization of knowledge in Modern America 1860–1920*. Edited by A. Oleson and J. Voss J., 313–41. Baltimore: Johns Hopkins University Press.

Resser, C. E. 1939. The Spence Shale and its fauna. *Smithsonian Miscellaneous Collections* 97 (12): 1–28.

Ringwalt, J. L., ed. 1981. *American Encyclopaedia of Printing*. 1871. Reprint. New York: Garland Publishing.

Rivinus, E. F., and E. E. Youseff. 1992. *Spencer Baird of the Smithsonian*. Washington, D.C.: Smithsonian Institution Press.

Robertson, E. C., ed. 1993. *Centennial history of the Geological Society of Washington 1893–1993*. Washington, D.C.: Geological Society of Washington.

Robinson, Lucius. 1879. *Public papers of Governor Lucius Robinson: 1878–1879*. Albany: State of New York.

Rodgers, John. 1937. Stratigraphy and structure in the Upper Champlain Valley. *Geological Society of America, Bulletin* 48:1573–88.

———. 1968. The eastern edge of the North American continent during the Cambrian and early Ordovician. In *Studies of Appalachian geology: Northern and maritime*. Edited by E-an Zen, W. S. White, J. B. Hadley, and J. B. Thompson. New York: Interscience Publishers. 141–50.

Roseberry, C. R. 1964. *Capitol story*. Albany: State of New York.

———. 1982. *From Niagara to Montauk: The scenic pleasures of New York state*. Albany: State University of New York Press.

Rudwick, R. J. S. 1985. *The great Devonian controversy*. Chicago: University of Chicago Press.

Ruedemann, Rudolph. 1901. Hudson River beds near Albany and their taxonomic equivalents. *New York State Museum, Bulletin* 42 (8): 489–596.

Rust, A. D. 1891. *Record of the Rust family, embracing the descendants of Henry Rust who came from England and settled in Hingham, Massachusetts, 1634–1635*. Waco, Tex.: Privately printed.

Schneer, C. J. 1978. The great Taconic controversy. *Isis* 69:173–91.

Schuchert, Charles. 1927. Charles Doolittle Walcott paleontologist—1850–1927. *Science*, n.s., 65:486–88.

Schuchert, Charles, and C. M. LeVene. 1940. *O. C. Marsh: Pioneer in paleontology*. New Haven: Yale University Press.

Schweizer, P. C. 1989. *The art of Trenton Falls: 1825–1900*. Syracuse, N.Y.: Syracuse University Press.

Secord, J. A. 1985. John W. Salter: The rise and fall of a Victorian palaeontological career. In *From Linnaeus to Darwin*. Edited by A. Wheeler and J. Price, 61–75. London: Society for History of Natural History.

References

———. 1986. *Controversy in Victorian geology*. Princeton, N.J.: Princeton University Press.

Servos, J. W. 1983. To explore the borderland: The foundation of the Geophysical Laboratory of the Carnegie Institution of Washington. *Historical Studies in the Physical Sciences* 14:147–85.

Shaw, A. B. 1958. Stratigraphy and structure of the St. Albans area, northwestern Vermont. *Geological Society of America, Bulletin* 69:519–68.

Shor, E. N. 1974. *The fossil feud between E. D. Cope and O. C. Marsh*. N.p.: Exposition Press, 340.

Six, Achille. 1884. Les Appendices des trilobites, d'après M Ch. D. Walcott. *Société Géologique de Nord, Annales* 11:228–36.

Smith, G. O. 1922. Plain geology. *Economic Geology* 17:34–37.

———. 1927. Charles Doolittle Walcott. *American Journal of Science* 214:1–6.

Spjeldnaes, Nils. 1967. The palaeoecology of the Ordovician vertebrates of the Harding Formation. Problêmes actuels de Palêontologie (Évolution des Vertébrés), *Colloques Internationaux du Centre National de la Recherche Scientifique* 163:11–20.

Stanton, T. W. 1893. The Colorado formation and its invertebrate fauna. *U.S. Geological Survey, Bulletin* 106.

Stanton, William. 1975. *The great United States exploring expedition of 1838–1842*. Berkeley and Los Angeles: University of California Press.

Stegner, W. B. 1954. *Beyond the 100th meridian: John Wesley Powell and the second opening of the west*. Boston: Houghton Mifflin.

Stern, W. T. 1981. *The Natural History Museum at South Kensington*. London: Heinemann.

Theokritoff, George. 1964. Taconic stratigraphy in northern Washington County, New York. *Geological Society of America, Bulletin* 75:171–90.

Thomas, Howard. 1951. *Trenton Falls: Yesterday & today*. Prospect, N.Y.: Prospect Books.

Thompson, M. M. 1979. *Maps for America*. Washington, D.C.: Government Printing Office.

True, F. W. 1913. *A history of the first half-century of the National Academy of Sciences, 1863–1913*. Baltimore: Lord Baltimore Press.

Ulrich, E. O., and H. P. Cushing. 1910. Age and relations of the Little Falls dolomite (Calciferous) of the Mohawk Valley. *New York State Museum, Bulletin* 140:97–140.

Van Gundy, C. E. 1946. Faulting in east part of Grand Canyon of Arizona. *American Association of Petroleum Geologists, Bulletin* 30:1890–1909.

———. 1951. Nankoweap Group of the Grand Canyon of Arizona. *Geological Society of America, Bulletin* 73:953–59.

Van Hise, C. R. 1892. Correlation Papers—Pre-Cambrian. *U.S. Geological Survey, Bulletin* 86.

Wager, D. E., ed. 1896. *Our country and its people, a descriptive work on Oneida County, New York.* Boston: Boston History Company.

Walcott, A. S. 1923. *The Walcott Book: History and genealogy of the American family of Walcott and notes of English Walcotts.* Salem, Mass.: Sidney Perley.

Wallace, Robert. 1972. *The Grand Canyon.* New York: Time/Life Books.

Weir, Bill. 1988. *Utah Handbook.* Chico, Calif.: Moon Publications.

Weston, T. C. 1899. *Reminiscences among the rocks in connection with the Geological Survey of Canada.* Toronto: Privately printed by Warwick Bro's & Rutter.

White, C. A. 1880. Progress of invertebrate paleontology in the United States for the year 1879. *American Naturalist* 14:250–60.

Wilbur, R. L., and W. A. Du Puy. 1931. *Conservation in the Department of Interior.* Washington, D.C.: Government Printing Office.

Wilkens, Thurlow. 1988. *Clarence King: A biography.* Albuquerque: University of New Mexico Press.

Wilkinson, C. J. 1954. *The University Club of Washington, the first fifty years.* Privately printed.

Williams, G. H. 1889. Some modern aspects of geology. *Popular Science Monthly* 35:640–48.

Williams, H. S. 1896. [Review of *Bulletin* 134]. *American Journal of Science,* 4th ser., 2:84–85.

———. 1899. [Review of "Pre-Cambrian fossiliferous formations"]. *American Journal of Science* 8:78.

———. 1899a. [Review of "A Paleozoic terrane beneath the Cambrian"]. *American Journal of Science* 8:77.

Williams, Talcott, et al. 1896. *George Huntington Williams, a memorial for friends by friends—1856–1894.* Privately printed.

Willis, Bailey. 1907. Research in China, volume 1. *Carnegie Institution of Washington, Publication* 54.

———. 1947. *A yanqui in Patagonia.* Palo Alto, Calif.: Stanford University Press.

———. 1949. *Friendly China: Two thousand miles afoot among the Chinese.* Palo Alto, Calif.: Stanford University Press.

Willis, Bailey, and Robin Willis. 1934. *Geologic structures.* 3d ed. New York: McGraw-Hill.

Winchell, Alexander. 1888. The Taconic question. *American Geologist* 1:347–63.

Winchell, N. H. 1888. Report of the Sub-Committee on the Lower Paleozoic. *American Geologist* 2:193–224.

Winsor, M. P. 1991. *Reading the shape of nature.* Chicago: University of Chicago Press.

Winston, Don. 1986. Belt Supergroup Stratigraphic Correlation Section, western Montana and adjacent areas. *Montana Bureau of Mines and Geology, Geologic Map* 40.

References

Woodward, H. B. 1907. *The history of the Geological Society of London.* London: Geological Society of London.

Worster, Donald. 1985. *Rivers of empire; water, aridity, and growth of the American west.* New York: Pantheon.

Yochelson, E. L. 1967. Charles Doolittle Walcott, 1850–1927. *National Academy of Sciences, Biographical Memoirs* 39:471–540.

———. 1979. Charles D. Walcott—America's pioneer in Precambrian paleontology and stratigraphy. In *History of Concepts in Precambrian Geology.* Edited by W. O. Kupsch and W. A. S. Sarjeant, 262–92. *Geological Association of Canada, Special Paper* 19:262–92.

———. 1983. Walcott's discovery of Middle Ordovician vertebrates. *Earth Sciences History* 2:66–75.

———. 1985. *The National Museum of Natural History: 75 years in the Natural History Building.* Washington, D.C.: Smithsonian Institution Press.

———. 1987. Walcott in Albany, New York: James Hall's "Special Assistant." *Earth Sciences History* 6:86–94.

———. 1988. The *Bulletin of the Geological Society of America* and Charles Doolittle Walcott. *Geological Society of America, Bulletin* 100:3–11.

———. 1989. "Geologic time" as calculated by C. D. Walcott. *Earth Sciences History* 8:150–58.

———. 1993. The question of Primordial and Cambrian/Taconic: Barrande and Logan/Marcou. *Earth Sciences History* 12:111–20.

———. 1994. Andrew Carnegie and Charles Doolittle Walcott: The origin and early years of the Carnegie Institution of Washington. In *The Earth, the Heavens, and the Carnegie Institution of Washington.* Edited by G. Good. *American Geophysical Union, History of Geophysics* 5:1–19.

Yochelson, E. L., and M. A. Fedonkin. 1993. Paleobiology of *Climactichnites,* an enigmatic Late Cambrian fossil. *Smithsonian Contributions to Paleobiology* 74.

Yochelson, E. L., and C. A. Nelson. 1994. Walcott and Early Cambrian of eastern California: Geology in the White-Inyo area, 1894–1897. In *The Crooked Creek Guidebook.* Edited by C. A. Hall Jr. and B. Widawski. Los Angeles: White Mountain Research Station, Regents of the University of California.

Yochelson, E. L., and H. S. Yoder, Jr. 1994. Founding the Geophysical Laboratory, 1901–1905: A scientific bonanza from perception and persistence. *Geological Society of America, Bulletin* 106:336–50.

Yoder, H. S., Jr. 1994. Development and promotion of the initial scientific program for the Geophysical Laboratory. In *The earth, the heavens, and the Carnegie Institution of Washington.* Edited by G. Good. *American Geophysical Union, History of Geophysics* 5:21–28.

Index

Abiquiu, N.Mex., 126
Acadian, 170, 183, 191. *See also* Cambrian:
  Lower
Adams, F. D., 301, 401
Adams, Henry, 96, 129, 248, 327, 393, 402, 405,
  446
Adirondack Mountains, 6, 7, 15, 51; graphite
  mine in, 204
Agassiz, Alexander, 102, 105, 134, 137, 181, 255,
  323, 342
Agassiz, Louis, 20, 30, 33, 52
Albany Institute, 66, 81
Albany, N.Y., 50
Alden, N.Y., 71
Algonkian, 304, 305, 436, 441, 437
Allison Commission, 181, 200
Alpine System, 161
American Academy of Arts and Sciences, 366
American Association for the Advancement
  of Science (AAAS), 188, 201, 229, 230, 247,
  281; Section D, 236
American Association of Foresters, 429
American Committee, 200, 201, 203, 205, 209,
  221, 240
American Geologist, 207, 230, 241, 250, 283
American Journal of Science, 101, 197, 206, 232,
  268, 329
American Museum of Natural History, 66,
  136, 357, 389
American Philosophical Society, 366, 396, 448
American Society of Naturalists, 189, 232, 407
Anthropological Society of Washington, 226,
  228
Archean, 147, 304
Army Medical Museum, 389
Artesian wells, 241, 258, 296
Arthropods, 290, 292
Ast, Phillip, 53, 81, 83
Aubrey Group, 95

Bailey, L. W., 172
Baird, S. F., 94, 136, 168, 227, 341
Baker, Marcus, 341, 385, 390, 416
Barometric survey, 147
Barrande, Joachim, 22, 85, 96, 134, 197, 214
Barrois, Charles, 79
Barus, Carl, 266, 279, 401
Base line, 313
Beauharnois, Quebec, 187
Beaver, Utah, 87, 90
Becker, G. F., 120, 257, 273, 288, 310, 355, 390,
  466
Bedford, Ind., 65
Beecher, Charles, 292, 364
Bell, A. G., 343, 356, 363, 376, 378, 393, 423, 461
Belt rocks, 313, 349, 350, 462
Beltina, 355, 366, 440
Bennington, Vt., 202
Bickmore, A. S., 19, 41, 44, 56, 75, 99, 311
Big Belt Mountains, 348, 371
Billings, J. S., 388, 392, 398, 418, 431, 441, 445
Billings, Elkanah, 15, 17, 116, 162, 181, 214, 291
Biological Society of Washington, 170, 179,
  196, 227, 254
Biostratigraphy, 111
Blackwelderia, 440
Bodfish, Sumner, 87
Boise, Idaho, 299
Boone and Crockett Club, 331, 419, 446
Brachiopods, 111, 153, 247, 450; Cambrian,
  308, 320, 342, 352, 361, 400, 433, 448, 455,
  457, 461; *Conotreta rusti*, 239; *Curticia*, 435;
  genus *Acrothele*, 448, 451; genus *Acrotreta*,
  381, 385; *Jamesella*, 435; *Loperia*, 435;
  Rustella, 435; *Schuchertina*, 435
Braintree, Mass., 136
Branner, J. C., 269, 455, 467
Brøgger, Waldemar, 216, 222, 224, 370
Brooklyn Insitute of Art, 315, 325, 340, 367, 375

Index

Index

Index

Index